Major Problems in the
Early Republic, 1787–1848

MAJOR PROBLEMS IN AMERICAN HISTORY SERIES

GENERAL EDITOR
THOMAS G. PATERSON

Major Problems in the Early Republic, 1787–1848

DOCUMENTS AND ESSAYS

EDITED BY
SEAN WILENTZ
PRINCETON UNIVERSITY

D. C. HEATH AND COMPANY
Lexington, Massachusetts Toronto

Address editorial correspondence to:

D. C. Heath
125 Spring Street
Lexington, MA 02173

Cover: *Launching of the Ship* Fame by George Ropes, 1802 (detail). Essex Institute, Salem, Massachusetts.

Published simultaneously in Canada.

Printed in the United States of America.

International Standard Book Number: 0-669-24332-9

Library of Congress Catalog Number: 91-75383

N O-MP-07 06

In memory of
SUZANNE HUFFMAN
1968–1991

Preface

This book introduces major issues in the history of the United States from the nation's founding to the era of sectionalism that led to the Civil War. Its publication comes at a moment of uncertainty about the teaching of all phases of American history. For three decades a distinguished, still-growing body of scholarship, especially in social history, has been challenging older approaches that emphasized statecraft, presidential politics, and diplomacy. The effects of this turnabout have been exhilarating, not least because it has challenged certain durable myths and biases and forced historians vastly to enlarge their intellectual vistas. Even a quick glance at the table of contents will show how deeply this volume is indebted to new departures in the field.

Yet scholars now recognize that the revisionist work, with its enormous merits, has tended to fragment and thereby diminish our comprehension of the early republic—and American history as a whole. This book tries to avoid the problem by combining the newer and older approaches while helping students to steer clear of either uncritical celebration or tendentious debunking. The essays present most of the key debates that divide today's scholars, as well as classic areas of dispute about the period. In selecting these historians' interpretations, along with a rich variety of documents, my aim was to encourage students to reason through the debates and the historical evidence and generate their own lines of interpretation. The chapter introductions, as well as the headnotes to the essays and the documents, help set the questions in historical and interpretive perspective. The point, again, is to elicit neither celebration nor denigration but rather to stimulate critical thinking about how and why the United States developed as it did.

To convey the era's complexity and excitement, the book departs from most of the standard periodizations, which begin study of the early republic in 1783 or 1787 and end in 1815 or 1828. As the essays in Chapter 1 suggest, historians have grown uneasy with these dates because they interrupt in midstream the chronicle of several important social, economic, and political developments. The 1787–1848 periodization of this book allows students to explore issues that arose out of the American Revolution and extend them through the travails and achievements of the post-Revolutionary decades to the point where a more or less direct path led to the Civil War. About 1787 a generation of young Americans—among them Thomas Jefferson, James Madison, and Alexander Hamilton—began fully to supplant the older revolutionaries who had helped initiate the struggle for independence. After about 1815 another new generation, including Andrew Jackson, Henry Clay, and John C. Calhoun, took command, with ideas and concerns that at first closely paralleled those of the previous quarter-century. About 1848 still another new generation—that of Frederick Douglass, Elizabeth Cady Stanton, Abraham Lincoln, and Jefferson Davis—emerged to guide the nation toward a second American Revolution in the 1860s. The first and last of these generational transitions frame this book.

Although the chapter topics, essays, and documents reflect current scholarly trends, they also pay considerable attention to what some readers might view as very traditional, if not outmoded, subjects. Several of my most sympathetic and helpful reviewers questioned the decision to include so much about what they called the history of elite white men. I found this criticism wanting. Social history and political history are intimately connected. Social issues in the early republic acquired powerful meanings as they entered into national politics. Some issues, such as the slavery controversy, were consciously *excluded* from national politics. Politics, in turn, helped define the limits of social conflicts and accommodations. And to study politics seriously requires a close look at the nation's political leadership, which for the most part consisted of elite white men (although many of them were not *born* to wealth and privilege).

There are unavoidably a few gaps and imbalances in coverage. Partly these reflect the shape of current research on the period, particularly in social history, where there is more work on the years after 1815. Partly they reflect the state of the primary sources. (I am nearly convinced that the market revolution and the early spread of print technology brought a general rise in longwindedness.) In addition, considerations of space forced me to make difficult decisions about which of the many dimensions of the period to feature. It is inevitable that I have omitted topics that others would find of critical importance. That said, I would greatly appreciate receiving comments from students and teachers about how I can improve this collection.

My friend and occasional Maine neighbor Tom Paterson first proposed my participation in this enterprise, and for that and much else I am deeply grateful. At D. C. Heath, James Miller provided continuing encouragement, Tina Beazer and Kaydee McCann guided a messy typescript through production, and Peggy Roll arranged for a long list of permissions. Sylvia Mallory has been a model editor—enthusiastic, precise, tactful, and patient beyond the call of craft.

Several outside reviewers, then anonymous to me, offered excellent criticisms of some early blueprints and shaped the book's development. My thanks to Michael Bellesiles, Emory University; Bill Cecil-Fronsman, Washburn University; Lawrence Cress, University of Tulsa; Robert Jones, Fordham University; Sarah McMahon, Bowdoin College; Jerome Mushkat, University of Akron; Lewis Perry, Vanderbilt University; Glenda Riley, Ball State University; Joel Silbey, Cornell University; and J. Russell Snapp, Davidson College. Much of the thinking behind the book evolved in a seminar that I taught with James M. McPherson, for which I am indebted both to Jim and to a wonderfully contentious group of students. I am also deeply grateful to my other colleagues who looked over early drafts and made vital suggestions: John M. Murrin, Albert J. Raboteau, Daniel T. Rodgers, and Christine Stansell. John Catanzariti, Eugene Sheridan, and the staff of the

Thomas Jefferson Papers at Princeton were an unending source of ideas, documents, and camaraderie.

I benefited enormously from the advice of several other historians of the period, who did not let friendship stand in the way of tough criticism and who identified important sources. My thanks to Ira Berlin, Gregory Dowd, John Mack Faragher, Eric Foner, Steven Hahn, Linda K. Kerber, John Kneebone, Allan Kulikoff, Stephanie McCurry, Harry L. Watson, and Alfred F. Young. A special note is due Eugene D. Genovese, who weighed in with an especially lengthy, sharp, and witty challenge to an earlier plan. As always, the remarks and the example of David Brion Davis guided me from start to finish.

Numerous librarians around the country led me through their holdings and assisted me in identifying pertinent materials. I especially wish to thank the staffs at the Bucks County Historical Society, the Forbes Library in Northampton, Massachusetts, the Library of Congress, the Special Collections division of the Louisiana State University Library, the Massachusetts Historical Society, the New-York Historical Society, the Firestone Library at Princeton University, and the Speer Library at the Princeton Theological Seminary.

Jonathan Earle worked on this book as a research assistant with care, intelligence, and stamina. I am also grateful to Eric Lowery, who tied up some of the last loose ends. Once again Steven Jaffe helped me out of some tight situations. Christine Stansell and Jamie Wilentz have been my sweet companions from the start; Hannah Wilentz enlivened the correcting of galleys more than she will ever remember.

In her four years at Princeton, Suzanne Huffman blessed her friends, her teachers, and everyone else she met. A shrewd reader and a gifted writer, she remains even now a joyful, courageous presence. I dedicate this book to her memory.

S. W.

Contents

CHAPTER 3
The Political Crises of the 1790s
Page 62

CHAPTER 4
The Republican Jefferson and the Jeffersonian Republic
Page 90

C H A P T E R 5
Gender, Race, and Ideology in the Early Republic
Page 116

C H A P T E R 6
The War of 1812
Page 152

C H A P T E R   9
Struggles for the West
Page 288

C H A P T E R   10
The Era of Bad Feelings
Page 333

CHAPTER 11
Jacksonians, Whigs, and the Politics of the 1830s
Page 372

CHAPTER 12
Reforms in Conflict
Page 423

CHAPTER 13
Abolitionism, Antiabolitionism, and Proslavery
Page 471

CHAPTER 14
The Bitter Fruits of Manifest Destiny
Page 523

E P I L O G U E

A P P E N D I X

Major Events, 1787–1848

1787 Constitutional Convention in Philadelphia; Constitution adopted
1787–88 States ratify Constitution
1789 George Washington inaugurated first president
   Judiciary Act of 1789
1790 Alexander Hamilton's report on credit
   Samuel Slater builds first modern American factory, in
    Rhode Island
1791 Bank of the United States chartered
1792 Washington reelected
1793 Eli Whitney invents cotton gin
1794 Whiskey Rebellion
   Jay's Treaty signed
   Democratic-Republican Societies spread
1795 Pinckncy's Treaty signed
1796 John Adams elected president
1798 XYZ Affair
   Alien and Sedition Acts
   Virginia and Kentucky Resolutions
1800 Thomas Jefferson and Aaron Burr tie in electoral college vote
    for president
   Gabriel Prosser's rebellion thwarted in Virginia
1801 Jefferson elected president
   Judiciary Act of 1801
   Conflict with Tripoli begins
1802 Abolition of all federal internal taxes
1803 Louisiana Purchase
   Marbury v. *Madison*
1804 Jefferson reelected
1806 Burr conspiracy revealed
1807 Embargo Act
1808 Abolition of overseas slave trade
   James Madison elected president
1809 Repeal of Embargo Act
   Non-Intercourse Act
1810 Macon's Bill Number 2
   Annexation of West Florida
   Fletcher v. *Peck*
1811 Battle of Tippecanoe
   Bank of the United States charter runs out
1812 United States declares war on Britain
1813 Battle of the Thames
   Francis Cabot Lowell establishes cotton factory at Waltham,
    Massachusetts

1814   Hartford Convention
        Treaty of Ghent
1815   Battle of New Orleans
1816   Second Bank of the United States chartered
        James Monroe elected president
1819   Panic of 1819
        Debates over Missouri
        Dartmouth College v. *Woodward*
        McCulloch v. *Maryland*
1820   Missouri Compromise
        Monroe reelected
1822   Denmark Vesey plot thwarted
1823   Monroe Doctrine
1824   *Gibbons* v. *Ogden*
1824–25 "Corrupt Bargain" and election of John Quincy Adams to the
           presidency
1827   Philadelphia workingmen organize
1828   Tariff of Abominations
        South Carolina *Exposition and Protest*
        Andrew Jackson elected president
1829   David Walker's *Appeal*
1830   Maysville Road veto
        Indian Removal Act
1831   William Lloyd Garrison establishes *The Liberator*
        Nat Turner rebellion
        Charles G. Finney revival in Rochester
1831–32 Virginia slavery debates
1832   Jackson vetos recharter of Second Bank of the United States
        Nullification crisis begins
        Black Hawk War
        Jackson reelected president
1833   Nullification crisis resolved
        American Anti-Slavery Society formed
1834   Indian Intercourse Act
        Jackson removes federal deposits from the Second Bank of the
           United States
1835–42 Seminole War
1836   Specie Circular
        Martin Van Buren elected president
1837–43 Panic of 1837 and ensuing depression
1838   Trail of Tears
1840   Independent Treasury Act
        Split in American Anti-Slavery Society
        Formation of Liberty party
        William Henry Harrison elected president
1841   Harrison dies and John Tyler succeeds to the presidency
1842   Dorr War in Rhode Island
        Webster-Ashburton Treaty signed

1844   James K. Polk elected president
1845   Texas annexed and admitted to the Union
1846   Oregon boundary dispute resolved
        United States declares war on Mexico
        Wilmot Proviso
1848   Treaty of Guadalupe Hidalgo
        Gold discovered in California
        Seneca Falls Convention
        Free-Soil party campaign
        Zachary Taylor elected president

Interpreting the Early Republic

Succeeding generations have gravitated toward very different interpretations of the early republic. Eighty years ago, most historians believed that the decades after the Revolution brought profound battles that pitted aristocrats and merchants against planters, small farmers, and artisans. Then, forty years ago, it became academically fashionable to emphasize continuity and consensus instead of change and conflict. The early republic, historians argued, saw no great transformation; instead, a preexisting American competitive capitalism blossomed with only minimal, superficial social strife. Today's scholarship has returned to the idea that the period brought what one historian has described as "deep change." But there is no agreement at all about the origins and nature of that change and the degree of conflict it generated. Some see the developments as nothing less than the beginning of a transition to capitalism; others, as a shift from one form of capitalism to another. Still others characterize the change in different ways, using a proliferation of historical models.

At issue are not simply matters of empirical dispute but fundamental differences over how to approach the past. The more that historians have moved outside history's traditional concerns, the less they have established common ground. Research on groups once marginalized has had a particularly unsettling effect. It is not enough, some historians contend, merely to annex the history of African-Americans, women, native Americans, wage earners, and others to the familiar story line—a story line that, despite interpretive differences, has usually emphasized the expansion of American freedom and democracy. That narrative, they insist, is so flawed that it needs to be scrapped. In its place, they have substituted more pessimistic, tragic renderings of the early republic, revealing how the nation's most cherished democratic ideals and institutions were entwined, from the start, with injustice and exploitation.

These newer accounts have successfully challenged some durable collective myths. Yet they have also tended to be fragmented, telling parts of the larger story without providing a clear sense of how these parts connect. Rescuing the history of neglected groups has run the risk of ignoring or caricaturing everything that used to be considered part of the mainstream. At times, correcting past biases has led to bleak and accusatory depictions of the early republic, with only limited capacity to explain how and why things did change.

Overcoming these difficulties and writing a true, more comprehensive history of the period requires an exacting, critical look at the approaches taken by con-

temporary scholars. It also requires a thorough, open examination of older approaches that considers how these earlier ideas and interpretations might be joined with recent concerns.

⌗ E S S A Y S

The first two essays look at the historiography of the early republic and reflect on the state of current research. Gordon S. Wood, professor of history at Brown University, in the first essay discusses the main cycles of interpretive revision over the past eighty years and evaluates the larger implications of recent work. Wood's survey stops in the 1820s, but many of the same themes appear in studies about the 1830s and 1840s, as suggested in the second contribution, by the historian Sean Wilentz of Princeton University. Although both essays agree on the importance of rapid commercial expansion, Wilentz's focuses more on the social conflicts generated by that expansion. Finally, the third essay, by the late Clinton L. Rossiter, for many years a political scientist at Cornell University, assesses the growth of American nationalism from the Revolution to the Civil War. Long before what Wood describes as a virtual revolution in historical periodization, Rossiter devoted himself to writing a sweeping review of the period from the 1780s to 1860. Alert to the pluses and minuses of American development, he remained impressed by what he called a national quest for self-identity and unity. His approach and his conclusions provide a stimulating counterpoint to those found in the more recent studies examined by Wood and Wilentz.

The Significance of the Early Republic

GORDON S. WOOD

Until very recently the period from the American Revolution to the election of Andrew Jackson was the most neglected if not the most despised period of American history. This is a curious situation, and it is not easily explained. The period after all seems to have an immediate and palpable importance for all Americans. During the half century following the Revolution our political institutions were established, political parties were developed, and a political economy was worked out. It is the period when American nationalism is generally thought to have been created. All in all, so much of significance occurred in this period of the early republic that its neglect is puzzling. . . .

　　American historians have not always neglected the early republic; indeed, it has been only historians writing in the past forty years or so who have found the period unappealing and boring. The Progressive generation of historians—those professional historians whose assumptions about reality came out of the Progressive era at the beginning of the twentieth century—not only had an overarching scheme for understanding the early republic,

Excerpts from "The Significance of the Early Republic" by Gordon S. Wood, from *Journal of the Early Republic* 8 (1988): pp. 1–20. Copyright 1988 by Society for Historians of the Early Republic. Reprinted by permission.

but also had a special fascination for this period. Although the Progressive historians offered a framework for understanding all of American history, it was the period of the early republic—from the Revolution to the Age of Jackson—that particularly interested them. . . .

These historians . . . tended to see American history as a conflict between a populist majority, usually agrarian, against a narrow aristocratic or business minority. The Revolution and early republic was essentially a seesawing struggle between these two groups. The aristocratic and merchant interests of the 1760s lost control of the resistance movement to more popular and radical elements who moved Americans into revolution. By the 1780s, however, conservative aristocratic and mercantile interests had reasserted themselves to the point where they were able to write the new federal Constitution of 1787. The following decade saw a continuation of the struggle between these commercial interests led by Hamilton and popular agrarian and artisanal forces led by Jefferson. . . .

This Progressive paradigm dominated historical writing during the first half of the twentieth century. But in the years following World War II this interpretative framework was assaulted from a hundred different directions and dismantled by a thousand different monographs. . . .

[This] assault . . . took the form of denying the extent of change that took place in the period. Colonial America, it appeared from a number of studies, was not an *ancien régime* after all. Since sixty to eighty percent of adult white males could legally vote in the colonial period, the high suffrage barriers that the Progressive historians had posited turned out to be not so high after all. The churches in the eighteenth century were already weak and did not much need disestablishment. The aristocracy that existed was hardly an aristocracy by European standards and scarcely needed elimination. All in all, colonial Americans did not have much to revolt against; their revolution seemed to be essentially a mental shift. The Americans were born free and equal, and thus, as Tocqueville said, they did not have to become so. Their revolution therefore became a peculiarly conservative affair, an endorsement and realization, not a transformation of their previous history.

At the same time as historians were reinterpreting the colonial period, others were reevaluating the Jacksonian era. Not only did it now appear that the Jacksonians had less unfinished business to deal with than historians used to think, but Jacksonian society seemed less egalitarian and democratic than earlier historians had believed. Thanks to the work of Edward Pessen we found out that the distribution of wealth in the 1820s and 1830s was more unequal than earlier in the century. Indeed, other studies showed that the distribution of wealth after the Revolution was more unequal than in the colonial period. Some historians even suggested that the Jacksonian era ought to be called "the era of the uncommon man." No democratic Jacksonian Revolution had occurred after all, it seemed. It was hard to see much difference between the Democratic and Whig parties. Both were composed of men-on-the-make; certainly they did not stand for coherent social classes in conflict. Nearly everyone in the North at least seemed to belong to the middle class. America was liberal to its toes and had been so, according to Louis Hartz, from the very beginning of its history. . . .

The breakup of the Progressive framework was so complete, and the insignificance into which the early republic sank was so deep that only in the past few years has a reversal begun. The revisionist excitement that has touched other eras of American history has at last reached the early republic. . . .

Society and culture, rather than prominent men, have become the subjects of these new histories. Thus the new studies of law in this period are less interested in the decisions of Chief Justice John Marshall and more interested in the relation between law and society. No subject has been more important in forcing a new kind of history of this period—as well as others—than that of women. But it was not just that women in the early republic were doing something other than making headlines; it was also that women's roles in this period in particular appear to have dramatically changed. It was a period, Mary P. Ryan has said, of "patriarchy in disarray." New ideals of womanhood arose and new divisions of labor in the household were worked out. Such transformations have made recent studies of women's history in the early republic especially imaginative and extensive. . . .

With these histories of women and the family leading the way, we have had in the past decade or so an increasing number of other broad social histories . . . The dates covered by these new studies are significant. At last the new histories are transcending the traditional division of the historical profession between colonial and national history and are creating new periodizations. Now we have more and more books that cover the period from 1763 or 1780 to 1830, or from 1740 or 1750 to 1840. Within these new perspectives the Revolution, when it is mentioned at all, becomes merely a political event expressive of broader social and cultural changes that take longer than a decade to work themselves out. This new periodization constitutes a virtual revolution in American historiography; its implications for our understanding of our past have yet to be felt.

Perhaps equal in importance to the history of women and the family in compelling this new periodization is the attempt by historians to understand the origins of liberal capitalism. Much of the recent work in eighteenth-century history suggests that Americans were not born liberal after all. In studies of New England towns farmers now emerge as pre-modern people, almost medieval in their outlooks. They were members of patriarchal communities concerned with patrimony and kin and everything but capitalist aggrandizement. . . . Liberal capitalism and modernity were not ascribed, it seems; they had to be achieved.

Colonial society thus appears now to be more of an *ancien régime* than we used to think. It is certainly not the *ancien régime* that the Progressive historians once conjured up, of rigid classes, legally restricted voting, and rich exploitative merchants. But it is not the liberal, egalitarian, democratic society of Tocqueville's America either. It now seems to have been a hierarchical, patriarchal, society vertically, not horizontally, organized and tied together by kinship and patron-client relations. Some of this old, hierarchical, small-scale eighteenth-century world survived the Revolution and lingered on into the nineteenth century, but not much. Recent studies stress more and more the fundamental difference between the old aristocratic pre-revolutionary society and the new popular commercial society that emerged in the nineteenth century.

This sense of the differentness of the eighteenth century from what followed has been reinforced by studies of republicanism in the revolutionary era. It now seems clear that the central ideology, the central language, of the Revolution was not Lockean liberalism concerned only with private rights and popular democracy. Instead, most American revolutionary leaders ad-hered to and spoke the language of what we have called civic humanism or classical republicanism. However much this republican ideology contributed to America's future culture, it was essentially backward-looking. It was rooted in a traditional aristocratic aversion to commerce and remained com-mitted to communal goals at the expense of private desires. Thus J.G.A. Pocock has concluded that the American Revolution, far from intending to move America into a liberal, capitalistic, and democratic world, was in fact "the last great act of the Renaissance."

But if this was true, if classical republicanism was indeed elitist, hier-archical, and nostalgic, then where did the liberal, commercial, democratic, money-loving America of the early nineteenth century come from? Some historians such as Isaac Kramnick and Joyce Appleby have argued that liberalism and capitalism were there all along. Much of what they say is undoubtedly true, for the dynamic reality of American culture cannot be easily sorted out into neat ideological boxes that historians have invented. Certainly by the last half of the eighteenth century the classical republican tradition was much attenuated and domesticated, tamed and transformed by modern financial and commercial forces. But as commercial and as liberal as eighteenth-century colonial society may already have been, it was nothing compared to the scrambling, acquisitive individualistic society that emerged in the aftermath of the Revolution.

The decades following the Revolution now constitute a period of im-mense change, "deep change," as David Hackett Fischer has called it. . . . [In the 1820s,] America may have been still largely rural, still largely ag-ricultural, but now it was also largely commercial, perhaps the most thor-oughly commercialized nation in the world. Hundreds of thousands of very ordinary people were very busy buying and selling in order to realize what *Niles' Weekly Register* in 1815 said was "the almost *universal ambition to get forward.*" Every European like Frances Wright who saw firsthand this society "teeming with business" was excited, awed, or frightened. There was nothing quite like it on such a scale anywhere in the world. And it seemed to have emerged out of nowhere.

If the early republic was indeed a period of deep change, then the Progressive historians were correct after all. The changes may have been more complicated, more subtle, more confused, and more unintended than they assumed, but the changes were no less momentous. Thus however crude, class-obsessed, and anachronistic the Progressive historians were in explaining the transformation America experienced during the early republic, they were certainly right to see the period as one of great significance. . . .

The explosion of entrepreneurial energy in the early republic cannot be exaggerated. There had been only about a half-dozen business corporations in the colonial period. But in a few short decades following the Revolution they multiplied into the hundreds. . . .

Stimulating all this business bustle was a consumer revolution of immense importance. More and more people were buying luxury goods—from feather mattresses to china tea sets—that had once been the preserve of an aristocratic minority. Traditional genteel standards of ownership and display reached deeper and deeper into the population, and created in the early decades of the nineteenth century a genteel middle-class world that was already recognizably similar to our own. Now a piano in every parlor did not seem beyond ordinary people's newly awakened aspirations.

An equally important source of change was the growth and movement of people. Although the birth rate after 1800 began to decline as people became more conscious of controlling the prosperity of themselves and their children, the population as a whole continued to grow, as it had in the past, by leaps and bounds; and it was on the move as never before. In the decades following the Revolution Americans spread themselves over half a continent at speeds that astonished everyone. Between 1790 and 1820 New York's population quadrupled, Kentucky's multiplied nearly eight times. In a single decade Ohio grew from a virtual wilderness to become larger than most of the hundred-year-old colonies had been at the time of the Revolution. In a single generation, Americans occupied more territory than they had occupied during the entire 150 years of the colonial period.

Such changes, so basic and pervasive, could not help affecting every aspect of American life. In politics, the arena that drew the attention of most of the Progressive historians, the changes were most manifest. The legal qualifications for political participation were democratized. By 1825 every state but Rhode Island had achieved white manhood suffrage. But this legal change scarcely did justice to the extent of transformation. We have always known that the world of the Founding Fathers, where politics was regarded by gentlemen of leisure as an obligation of their rank and where such gentlemen were supposed only to stand for election, was supplanted in the early republic by a very different, recognizably modern world, a democratic world where competing professional politicians ran for office under the banners of modern political parties. The transformation was so sudden, so stark that people at the time could hardly miss seeing it. The newly emerging generation of the early nineteenth century, like every subsequent generation in American history, already looked back to the generation of Founding Fathers with a wistful sense that they were men the likes of whom they would never again see in America. By 1823 *Niles' Weekly Register* was already defining modern politicians as "persons who have little, if any regard for the welfare of the republic unless immediately connected with . . . their own private pursuits." But it was not just the character of politics that changed. The very nature and purpose of government was transformed. . . .

In religion the changes in the early republic were equally momentous and palpable. In a single generation the entire religious landscape of America was transformed. In this period not only were the remains of traditional religious establishments finally destroyed, but modern Christian denominationalism was created. Older religious groups, the Congregationalists, Presbyterians, and Anglicans which had dominated eighteenth-century colonial society, were now supplanted by energetic evangelical churches, Baptists, Methodists, and entirely new groups unknown to the Old World such as the Disciples of Christ. Christendom had probably not witnessed anything like the religious ferment of the Second Great Awakening on such a scale since the Reformation. The Second Great Awakening made America the most evangelically Christian nation in the world. . . .

In all aspects of life in the early republic there were changes—so many and so diverse as to be ultimately incalculable. But beneath all of them lay a basic social revolution, a fundamental shift in the way people related to one another. The republican Revolution had assaulted the sinews of family, patronage, and dependency that had held the old eighteenth-century society together and had attempted to substitute new enlightened bonds of respect and affection to tie people together. But the old society came apart faster than anyone expected, and the new enlightened bonds could not hold. The society of the early republic became atomized—with "every Man standing single," as Philadelphia gentleman George Clymer complained—to an extent the revolutionary leaders had never anticipated. By the 1820s America had become the most egalitarian, individualistic, and money-making society in western history. That it was at the same time the most evangelically Christian society in the world only accentuated the awesomeness of the change. In many respects the America of the 1820s was the exact opposite of the kind of society the Founding Fathers had wanted to create. Never before or since has American society been so unsettled and the lines of authority so confused. Everything seemed up for grabs, and no ties that did not come from volitional allegiance seemed tolerable.

It was a society dominated by ordinary people—to a degree never duplicated by any nation in modern history. We historians have trouble appreciating what this emergence of common ordinary people into consciousness really meant. Even the new social historians have often been concerned only with people kept out of the mainstream of the society or with those who did not participate fully in this democratic revolution—with Indians, blacks, women, or perhaps displaced craftsmen. Ordinary white males who made it, who constituted the sum and substance of the prosperous, scrambling, money-making society that America became are generally not the kinds of people we academics like to celebrate. Men like Mathew Lyon, who fought his way from Vermont to Kentucky scrounging votes and dollars any way he could, or Talmadge Edwards, who emerged out of nowhere to become a wealthy glove and mitten king, did not much resemble the Founding Fathers. Their nineteenth-century motto was:

On others inspiration flash,
Give them eternal fame—
But give me cash!

Many were awed and frightened by this new emerging society. It seemed
to be exploding in all directions, growing helter skelter, and moving relentlessly westward. And no one seemed in control of it. People now felt
themselves carried along in a stream, caught up in a process that was larger
and more significant than any of the individuals involved in it. This new
social experience affected everything from people's conception of the historical process—how events occurred—to their understanding of the competitive marketplace. . . . By the 1820s classical Rome was thought too stolid
and imitative to express the excitement and originality of this dynamic new
democratic society. Ancient Greece, said Edward Everett, was a better
model for America; ancient Greece was tumultuous, wild, and free, said
Everett, "free to licentiousness, free to madness." . . .

The Market Revolution, 1815–1848

SEAN WILENTZ

For many years, historians had little difficulty finding labels to describe the
period from 1815 to 1848. To some it was the age of Jackson, dominated
by Old Hickory and the Democratic party; to others, the era of the common
man, a time of sweeping democratic ferment and reform. Today such phrases
sound quaint. Two decades' worth of outstanding revisionist work has made
political historians wary of the old presidential synthesis of American history;
less attention is now paid to the specific details of Jacksonian electioneering
and policy-making, and more to such broad themes as the changing structure
of party organizations and the rise of new political ideologies. Likewise, an
outpouring of work by social historians—much of it on groups previously
slighted—has dramatically changed basic assumptions about the period and
raised new, often disturbing questions: How can the years that brought the
rise of the Cotton Kingdom and the spread of slavery reasonably be called
the era of the common man? What was the role of women in this phase of
American history? Were not at least some of the democratic advances of
the time won at the murderous expense of Native Americans?

By exploring these and other issues, recent studies have moved well
beyond the familiar chronicles of political and social elites. Unfortunately,
recent work has fragmented our understanding into a host of academic
subspecialties. It has also led, in some instances, to a denigration of formal
politics and policy, as if such "traditional" matters as the Bank War or
debates over the tariff were unimportant. The job of connecting the pieces—
and especially of recombining social and political history—has only just
begun. Still, one theme does seem to unite Jacksonian historians of various

Excerpt from "Society, Politics, and the Market Revolution" by Sean Wilentz, in Eric Foner,
ed., *The New American History*, pp. 52–59. Copyright © 1990 by Temple University. Reprinted
by permission of Temple University Press.

persuasions and suggest a way of once again viewing the period as a whole: the central importance of the market revolution, which, in one way or another, touched the lives of all Americans. . . .

The extraordinary economic changes of the early nineteenth century have never failed to impress historians. Between 1815 and 1850 Americans constructed elaborate networks of roads, canals, and early railroad lines; opened up wide areas of newly acquired land for settlement and trade; and began to industrialize manufacturing. What had been in Thomas Jefferson's day a backward rural nation on the fringes of world economic development had by midcentury established many of the preconditions necessary to its becoming a major economic power.

In the 1950s George Rogers Taylor wrote what remains the authoritative account of these changes and dubbed them, collectively, America's "transportation revolution." Since then, historians have done less to challenge Taylor's interpretation than to reexamine some of its implications. Social historians in particular have stressed that economic change radically disrupted existing systems of production and old social hierarchies, replacing them with entirely new opportunities and dependencies. Behind the technological and institutional innovations Taylor discussed was a deeper revolution in human relations, linked to the emergence of new markets in land, labor, and produce.

Much of the scholarly work on this market revolution has concentrated on northeastern cities as key sites of economic development. Intense mercantile activity there, of course, long antedated 1815. Yet between 1815 and 1848 eastern urban capitalists dramatically accelerated the pace of economic change. Often working hand in hand with state and local governments, these merchant capitalists were at the forefront of transportation improvements; they made great strides in expanding credit and financing resources and in imposing some order on currency and banking; above all, they hastened the erosion of the old artisan handicraft system and the rise of new manufacturing enterprises.

Compared to later periods in U.S. history, industrial growth between 1815 and 1848 was modest; by 1850, the majority of the nation's population still lived in rural areas and worked in agriculture, while only about 14 percent of the labor force worked in manufacturing. Nevertheless, the rate of industrial growth was impressive, especially in the Northeast. The most spectacular examples of early industrialization were the new textile mills of New England, financed by leading established seaboard merchants. Yet as labor historians have shown, mechanization and factory construction constituted only one of several strategies used to revamp manufacturing. In once bucolic single-industry towns . . . merchant capitalists altered production by dividing up craft skills and putting out as much work as possible to country girls living in outlying rural communities. Entrepreneurs in the major seaboard cities and in newer inland settlements such as Cincinnati likewise divided up artisan crafts and relied on underpaid outworkers—women, children, poor immigrants—to produce work for low piece rates. The deployment of these different methods of production brought a rapid increase in the output of raw materials and finished goods, at lower prices and of a higher quality than Americans had ever enjoyed. Simultaneously, however, the new order disrupted the customary artisan regime of masters, journeymen, and apprentices and left thousands of workers dependent on the caprices of the wage-labor market.

Changes in northeastern manufacturing were closely related to a deepening crisis in northeastern rural life. Traditionally, historians slighted the extent of social change in the American countryside before the Civil War. Although improvements in transportation and increased commercialization obviously enlarged the productive capacity of American agriculture, historians tended to assume that most family farms were small capitalist enterprises from at least the mid-eighteenth century on. Recent scholarship, however, has focused on the variety of social pressures, beginning in the 1750s and continuing through the 1840s, that undermined a distinct way of life, one geared more to barter exchange and quasi-self-sufficiency than to the production of cash crops for market. [One] major impetus for change was demographic, as the mounting population of the settled rural Northeast began to outstrip the available supply of land, leaving rural patriarchs unable to pass on sufficient acreage to their sons. By 1815 these straitened circumstances had led to a steady decline in family size and to an increase in westward migration; it had also heightened farmers' need for cash to buy additional land, thus encouraging them to shift into cash-crop production. The transportation improvements of the next thirty years facilitated that shift and brought to the countryside (at steadily decreasing prices) manufactured articles previously unavailable in the hinterland. By 1850 the vast majority of northeastern farmers had reorganized their production toward cash crops and were depending on country merchants for household items and farm implements once produced at home.

Few historians would dispute that the market revolution brought substantial material benefits to many if not most northeasterners, urban and rural. But the new abundance was hardly distributed equally. Studies of property holding have confirmed that in small country towns and in large cities alike, a tiny proportion of the northeastern population came to command the bulk of the newly created wealth. Those who benefited most from the market revolution—merchants and manufacturers, lawyers and other professionals, and successful commercial farmers, along with their families— faced life situations very different from those known to earlier generations. The decline of the household as the locus of production led directly to a growing impersonality in the economic realm; household heads, instead of directing family enterprises or small shops, often had to find ways to recruit and discipline a wage-labor force; in all cases, they had to stay abreast of or even surpass their competitors.

Perhaps the most profound set of social changes confronting this new middle class involved the internal dynamics of family life. As Nancy Cott, Mary Ryan, and others have explained, the commercialization of both city and countryside removed women from the production of goods, including goods for strictly household use. The world of the propertied began to separate into two spheres: a male public sphere of politics, business, and the market, and a female private sphere of domestic duties and child rearing. By 1850 a new romantic standard of rights and responsibilities within middle-class families had replaced the more severe patriarchal regime of the eighteenth century—a "cult of domesticity" that vaunted women's supposed moral superiority while it restricted women's place to the home, as wives, mothers, and domestic guardians.

Less fortunate northeasterners faced a very different reality, dominated by the new dependencies created by the market revolution. For those at the bottom—immigrant and black day laborers, outwork seamstresses, the casual poor—a combination of overstocked labor markets and intense competition among employers kept wages and earnings near or below subsistence levels. Even in New England, farm girls who went off to work in factories expecting decent situations and high wages found that mill conditions had deteriorated by the mid-1830s. Those small independent artisans and well-paid craft workers who survived faced the real possibility of falling into similar distress, victimized as they were by an increasingly volatile business cycle and by the downward pressures on earnings and real wages in various important trades. By the 1830s a new working class was beginning to carve out its own identity in a variety of trade unions and in political efforts aimed at redirecting the course and consequences of American economic expansion. Marginal small farmers saw their livelihoods threatened by competition from western areas opened by canal development and by the middlemen's downward pressure on prices; in addition, legal reinterpretations of property rights further shifted the balance of power against them. To all these people, middle-class respectability and the cult of domesticity meant little when measured against the struggle to achieve or preserve their economic independence—or barring that, simply to make ends meet.

Far less is known about the market revolution's social impact in the Old Northwest and the western territories, although some fine recent work has started to redirect the field. Studies of migration suggest that rural northeasterners who could not make a go of it tried to avoid entering the urban wage-labor market; the largest single supply of urban workers (at least by 1850) consisted of immigrants and their children, among them hundreds of thousands of new arrivals escaping hard times in Ireland and Germany. Native-born rural northeasterners, joined by migrants from the South, headed west instead, most of them hoping to reconstruct the independent yeoman communities that had crumbled back home. Accordingly, they bought up as much cheap western land as they could to ensure that they would be able to provide for their families and their descendants.

This new yeomanry faced numerous obstacles. First, the removal of Native Americans from the land had to be completed; federal and state authorities willingly complied, using fraud and violence as necessary. Once the lands were open, settlers found themselves pitted against capitalist farmers and speculators eager to convert the virgin land to capitalist development. As the proportion of public land sold to speculators dramatically increased, would-be settlers and squatters had to battle hard to get the land they wanted.

Once settled, farmers usually had to enter into some sort of economic relations with land speculators or bankers, either taking out mortgages or
borrowing money to pay for farm improvements.

Despite these hardships, the vast majority of settlers eventually owned
their farms outright. Most of them managed, for a time, to set up a facsimile
of the yeoman regime. But it was not to last. Hoping to develop markets
for their surplus crops, the western yeomen for the most part supported the
extension of new east-west transport routes after 1820; the impact of their
innovations quickly surpassed early expectations. By 1850 northwestern farm
operators were almost fully integrated into commercial markets; specialized
production of grain, livestock, or dairy products became the norm for successful commercial farmers. Under the pressure of reorganization, attempts
to recreate the old order of yeoman independence collapsed. Although still
dominated by small farmers, the Old Northwest emerged as one of the
leading areas of cash-crop agriculture in the world, displacing New England
and the mid-Atlantic seaboard as the supplier of eastern and overseas
markets.

The opening of the market brought prosperity and rising profits to those
farmers who secured sufficient acreage and learned to handle the new rules
of credit and competition. Like eastern businessmen (and western businessmen in the new cities along the transport routes), western commercial
farmers reordered their public and private lives in accord with the standards
of eastern middle-class domesticity. Yet like the Northeast, the Northwest
had its dispossessed and those who faced imminent dispossession. Not only
were the Native Americans removed from their lands, but so too a substantial
number of white settlers suffered from the revolution in marketing. Those
unable to get sufficient credit to improve their operations or unwilling to
learn capitalist agriculture methods wandered on the periphery of the most
concentrated settlement, squatting on unimproved land or purchasing new
land—often only to lose it. Those who could not sustain themselves and
could not travel farther on fell into tenancy and the ranks of agricultural
wage labor. In all, the rise of capitalist agriculture in the Northwest, as in
the Northeast, produced new classes of independent and dependent
Americans.

The South experienced the market revolution quite differently, though
just *how* differently has been the subject of continuing debate. The outstanding feature of southern economic and social history after 1815 was, of
course, the rise of the Cotton Kingdom and the westward expansion of
plantation slavery. Since the mid-1950s an outstanding literature on slavery
has completely overturned the old sentimentalized, racist interpretation of
the plantation as a benevolent institution, supposedly designed as much to
civilize "inferior" blacks as to reap profits for the planters. Such recent
historians as Eugene D. Genovese, Herbert G. Gutman, Lawrence Levine,
and Albert Raboteau have paid especially close attention to the slaves' own
experiences and discovered that a distinctive Afro-American culture took
shape under slavery, a culture based on religious values and family ties that
gave the slaves the power to endure and in certain ways resist the harshness

of bondage. Far from a benign world of social harmony, the plantation South was an arena of intense day-to-day struggles between masters and slaves.

Far more controversial has been the argument, advanced most forcefully by Genovese, that the expansion of slavery led to the creation of a distinctive, noncapitalist southern civilization. As Genovese sees it, the southern slaveholders' attachment to land and slaves as their chief forms of investment guaranteed that the South would remain economically and socially distinct. To be sure, the slaveholders were linked to the wider world of capitalist markets and benefited from the improvement of American commerce and finance; like all men of business, they were acquisitive and at times greedy. But, Genovese contends, the master-slave relationship—so unlike labor relations in the North—created a unique mode of social organization and understanding. At the heart of these arrangements was what Genovese calls paternalism, a system of subordination that bound masters and slaves in an elaborate network of familial rights and duties. Plantation paternalism was fraught with conflict between master and slaves, although (Genovese insists) it did help contain the slaves' rebelliousness. Above all, the slaveholders as a class—and the South as a region—did not share in the possessive individualism and atomistic liberalism that were coming to dominate northern life.

Genovese's interpretation has been extremely influential, though it has also been challenged on various fronts. In particular, historians have questioned Genovese's contention that slavery precluded southern economic development, and that the planters exercised ideological hegemony over their slaves. Generally, however, scholars today agree that the market revolution had the effect of widening the differences between northern and southern society and culture. As historians examine the worlds of southerners who were neither masters nor slaves, southern distinctiveness seems all the more apparent; at the same time, these studies have heightened our appreciation of the complexities of the slave South.

Perhaps the most interesting work of the last few years concerns the nonslaveholders who constituted the majority of the southern white population before the Civil War. Far removed from the old settlements of the Tidewater and the rich soils of the Black Belt, there lived relatively isolated communities of white householders and their families who produced mainly for their own needs and had only occasional contact with the market economy. While their way of life distinguished these southern yeomen from the commercial farmers of the North, it also set them apart from the wealthier, less egalitarian planters of their own region; jealous of their personal independence and local autonomy, the southern yeomen resented any perceived intrusion on their political rights. Cries of "white supremacy" and the yeomen's acquiescence in slavery softened these class differences, but throughout the 1830s and 1840s the southern yeomen remained deeply suspicious of the planters' wealth and power, and the possibility that the planter elite might pursue local development policies to the detriment of the backcountry.

The rediscovery of the persistent southern yeomen—in contrast to the declining northern yeomen—has reinforced the argument for growing social divergence between North and South before 1850. But in a different sense the southern yeomen's dilemmas also point out certain commonalities in the history of commercialization throughout the country, which in turn help us understand the market revolution as a national process. At one level, commercialization—as overseen by the nation's merchant capitalists, manufacturers, commercial farmers, and planters—created a hybrid political economy by introducing capitalist forms of labor and market agriculture in the North, and by fostering a different slave-based order in the South. Viewed more closely, the market revolution can also be seen to have produced new and potentially troublesome social conflicts within each major section of the country. Entrepreneurs and wage earners, middlemen and petty producers, masters and slaves, planters and yeomen all found themselves placed in unfamiliar positions, arrayed against each other in fresh struggles for power and legitimacy. In the long run the divergences between free labor and slavery would dominate other differences. Before then, however, new social relations and conflicts *within* the various sections generated social tensions that came to the fore in politics—as new parties, the Democrats and the Whigs, emerged to battle over the shape of the market revolution.

Nationalism and American Identity in the Early Republic

CLINTON L. ROSSITER

Through all the years from Washington to Lincoln the American people were engaged in an industrious search for *self-identity*. The search, we know to our sorrow, led in the end to a shattering crisis [yet] the record was one of unusual achievement, and we must not let the events of the 1850's and 1860's blind us to this truth. If this had not been so, if there had been no solid sense of continental nationhood both inclusive and exclusive, the North would never have gone to war to preserve the Union, and both victorious North and conquered South would not have moved on together toward a new, more solid sense of such nationhood. The foundations of American nationalism, as they were to prove in the hour of reckoning, had been well and truly laid by the middle of the nineteenth century, and by all odds the most important of these foundations was the nation itself. . . .

Long before the coming of the Revolution, preachers, poets, and pamphleteers were telling fellow colonists that they were "a new Jerusalem sent down from heav'n," a different and better race of men with a special destiny to cherish. The winning of independence transformed this kind of prophetic exhortation into a settled article of American faith. Yet while Americans saw and identified themselves as a new people on the face of the earth, two fateful questions remained to be answered:

From: Clinton Rossiter, *The American Quest: An Emerging Nation in Search of Identity, Unity, and Modernity* (Harcourt, Brace Jovanovich, 1971), pp. 123–135 (excerpts). © 1971, Mary Crane Rossiter.

First, were they different and better enough to rejoice confidently in the fact—and, if they were, in what ways?

Second, was the fate of America to be a country, that is, one sovereign nation like Britain and France, or a "country," that is, a parcel of related yet basically sovereign half-nations, city-states, and provinces like Germany and Italy?

In the process of answering the first question "yes" with the aid of words like "republicanism," "liberty," "opportunity," "morality," "improvement," and, finally, "democracy," and the second also "yes" with the portentous qualification expressed in the word "federal," the people of the United States found an identity that permitted the Union to develop and expand in unprecedented ways. Perhaps more important, this sense of identity then encouraged it to stand up successfully to the most severe test a nation can ever meet.

If the legacy of remembrances at the service of orators and schoolteachers was skimpy compared with that of Britain or France, the young Republic drew enough sustenance from the memory of the founding generation alone to make *history* a nourishing support of the sense of an American nationalism. Then as now the Hampdens, and also the Village Hampdens, of America liked to "look back with reverence" as keenly as forward with anticipation; as a result, the apparatus of myth, symbol, slogan and ceremony designed to emphasize the uniqueness and unity of the American people grew more impressive with each passing year. The invocations of a heroic past and visions of a glorious future indulged in by men as different in style as David Ramsay, Jedidiah Morse, Parson Weems, Jared Sparks, John Quincy Adams, William Holmes McGuffey, Rembrandt Peale, John Trumbull, Daniel Webster, John Marshall, and, pre-eminent among historians who felt the hand of God laid upon America, George Bancroft kept the apparatus working at full blast. It is interesting and highly pertinent to note that the first major public oration of an ambitious young lawyer named Abraham Lincoln—the date was January 27, 1838, the audience the Young Men's Lyceum of Springfield—referred reverently to the Founding Fathers (a few of whom were still walking around unburied) as if they were heroes who had sailed with Jason and sketched plans with Solon. In describing his own generation as the "legal inheritors" of the "fundamental blessings" of an unexampled system of personal liberty, he paid homage to a "*once* hardy, brave, and patriotic, but now lamented and departed race of ancestors," and the young men of Springfield doubtless nodded solemn approval of the description. Here was one new nation, it would seem, that had a special talent for creating and exploiting instant history, and also for believing in it. Twenty-three years later, in his Inaugural Address as President of a temporarily disunited United States, Lincoln summoned history once again to support the cause of American nationalism. "The mystic chords of memory, stretching from every battle-field, and patriot grave, will yet swell the chorus of the Union," he insisted doggedly—and how right he was to insist upon the power of common memory to reunite the nation.

While some scholars have written sadly of the poverty of the American legacy and crudeness of the techniques used to exploit it, their collective judgment strikes the mind as either precious or irrelevant. The kind of nation most Americans hoped for in the future demanded a legacy that would liberate energy without paralyzing will; at the same time, the techniques of national devotion needed to express the American character as something simple, sincere, zestful, and democratic. As to the legacy, one may well ask: Did a new nation ever have heroes quite so satisfying as the Pilgrim Fathers, the men of Jamestown, the Signers, the Framers, Benjamin Franklin, Daniel Boone, and the semidivine Cincinnatus of the West, George Washington? And as to the techniques, one may go on to ask: Are our hearts ever stirred today, as were those of our ancestors, with feelings of joyful patriotism by the oratory of thousands of ordinary men on the Fourth of July and of scores of larger-than-life men like Daniel Webster on occasions like the celebration at Plymouth in 1820 and the laying of the cornerstone at Bunker Hill in 1825? Such feelings have gone out of fashion; yet in the days of our youth they were the intellectual fertilizer of the flowering of American nationalism.

Interest also played a part, as northern men like Gouverneur Morris and southern men like John C. Calhoun proved rather forcefully in a left-handed way. Unblushing nationalists in their early years when the Union was a source of emotional nourishment to them and practical benefits to friends and neighbors, they lost their faith in later years when the waters from the source began to have a brackish taste. For most Americans between 1815 and 1850, however, the more perfect Union was a new kind of nation in which membership bestowed a range of rights, privileges, immunities, opportunities, and protections that no sensible man would wish to surrender. Those Americans who set off bravely for territory that was not yet American—Florida, Texas, California, Oregon—and expected the flag to follow in the fullness of time proved this point about the services of interest to nationhood even more forcefully than did the disillusioned Morris and the disgruntled Calhoun. They knew, as those also knew who stayed at home, that everybody would be a loser if the Union were to divide or dissolve, or if it were to permit other sovereign nations of Americans to spring up on its southwestern, Pacific, and northwestern flanks.

Although it is sometimes hard to glimpse through the dust stirred up by the fury of political debate, the violent acts committed by persons and crowds, and the unceasing tussle of North and South, a notable *consensus* of political, economic, and social principle added greatly to the vitality of American nationalism in this period. The collapse of Federalism and the rejection of English and European Radicalism left a fair field for American-style Liberalism. By 1850 the principles of bourgeois democracy had become a national tradition with no serious competition from the right, the left, the past, the future, or even from the South. Dissenters hung on, to be sure, in stately mansions in Philadelphia and Charleston, immigrant hovels in New York and Boston, socialist studies in Milwaukee and Cincinnati, and utopian communities all over the land. Most Americans, however, were dedicated in common to the beauties of personal liberty, the security of constitutionalism, the rightness of democracy, the wrongness of class distinctions, the virtue of private property, the moral necessity of hard work, the certainty of progress, and above all the uniqueness, superiority, and high destiny of the United States of America. Detractors of democracy and prophets of doom were unpopular in a land whose national character expressed itself in disbelieving laughter at the dismal proclamation of Fisher Ames in 1803 that the United States was "too big for union, too sordid for patriotism, too democratic for liberty." When it did, in the end, prove almost too big for union, the men of the south demonstrated a peculiar allegiance to the political consensus by adopting a constitution copied, with only a sprinkle of generally sensible changes, from the Constitution of 1787.

Few young nations have been more lavishly blessed, if that is the right word, by the existence of an enemy than the United States in the early years of independence; few have made more effective use of the techniques of *comparison* in the search for identity. Whether this enemy was Europe as a whole, as it was symbolically in much writing and orating of the time, or that special corner of Europe called Britain or England, as it was literally in 1812 and prospectively in 1845, its mere presence in the world helped speed up the course of self-identification in the United States. I agree with Cushing Strout that "for much of their history Americans have defined themselves through a deeply felt conflict with Europe," and would add only that in no period has this conflict been carried on more energetically, self-righteously, and, all things considered, fruitfully than [these] decades. . . . Reactive nationalism was an unusually powerful sentiment in the days of Monroe, Adams, and Jackson. Indeed, one sometimes gets the impression that men were content to define America simply as *anti-Europe* or, on certain anniversaries, *anti-England*. Washington Irving spoke for most Americans in 1832 when, after seventeen years of working at literature and playing at diplomacy in Europe, he told an audience of distinguished citizens who had assembled to welcome him home to native soil and native themes:

> I come from gloomier climates to one of brilliant sunshine and inspiring purity. I come from countries lowering with doubt and danger, where the rich man trembles and the poor man frowns—where all repine at the present and dread the future. I come from these to a country where all is life and animation; where I hear on every side the sound of exultation; where every one speaks of the past with triumph, the present with delight, the future with glowing and confident anticipation.

For all but a few fastidious or supremely self-confident Americans the comparison between the New World and the Old ranged from the invidious to the odious. America was free, fresh, democratic, virtuous, and progressive; Europe, in particular that "disolute old whore England," was oppressive, tired, crippled by class distinction, corrupt, and decaying. . . .

Finally, the dedication to *individualism* of an entire people worked in ways mysterious in nature yet plain in result to encourage America to recognize itself as a nation. The fact of American individualism antedated the use of the word by several generations; it was, by any name, one of a half-dozen distinctive characteristics of the young civilization. There could be no more dramatic testimony to the width of the gulf between Europe and America than the transformation in meaning that took place when the word was finally imported for popular use around 1840. In the school of Saint-Simon, Yehoshua Arieli has pointed out, individualism was "almost synonymous with selfishness, social anarchy, and individual self-assertion"; in the pages of John O'Sullivan's *Democratic Review* it "connoted self-determination, moral freedom, the rule of liberty, and the dignity of man."

American individualism in the time of O'Sullivan was not, of course, as simple a concept and gentle an influence as all that, for it covered a span of personal principle and conduct ranging from the kindly self-reliance of a philosopher like Emerson to the ruthless self-advancement of an entrepreneur like Commodore Vanderbilt by way of the doughty self-removal of a mountain man like Bill Williams. In later years it was to be twisted into strange and often ugly forms; in recent years it has been transformed into an ideology of self-deception with which to mask the decline of both the privacy and the independence of the person. Yet in those early, simpler years individualism was a governing principle of American life, and as such it made a rich if still neither measurable nor quite comprehensible contribution to the progress and unity of the nation. By freeing a race of ambitious men from the institutional shackles of the European past it set them to digging, tinkering, migrating, playing politics, generating visions, and taking risks at a pace that surprised, even if it often dismayed, those who came from Europe to see for themselves what the fuss was all about. By stripping these men of membership in most groups and orders of traditional society it focused a large portion of their loyalties on the most exciting object in sight: the nation. And since the nation itself seemed so permissive in practice and liberty-oriented in doctrine, those groups and orders that endured or sprang up—families, neighborhoods, churches, schools, colleges, associations, professional groups—could command the loyalties of individuals for their own purposes and then, as it were, reinforce and pass them on upward to serve the great Republic. Whether as an individual going it alone or cooperating freely with others, the American of the first half of the nineteenth century found much of his own identity precisely in being a free American.

One other loyalty-commanding order existed between the individual and the nation; and, however necessary to the growth of a continental republic, it posed a persistent, occasionally passion-provoking threat to unity. That order was the state or, in a larger sense, the region. Men pledged their allegiance, I repeat, to a *federal* nation; the allegiance was therefore of a kind that had never been known before. Although it had been tested severely in 1798–1799, 1814–1815, and 1828–1833 (and, in the judgment of many Americans, found weaker than they had expected), the allegiance gathered strength as the years passed and history, interest, consensus, comparison, and individualism all did their good work along with more tangible or visible forces such as the English language, the Constitution, and a party system seemingly designed to suppress passions and resolve crises.

By 1850 most men were convinced that to be a loyal American one had to emulate Washington, Jefferson, and John Adams, and thus also be a loyal son of state and region. Two giants of the earliest years had been undiluted nationalists, Benjamin Franklin and Alexander Hamilton, but they were obviously special cases. In the middle of the nineteenth century only an immigrant with the principles of a Francis Lieber (and with no political ambitions) could emulate them. Every important American nationalist stood with feet planted firmly in some part of the country in which he had been raised or to which he had migrated; to that part he directed a sizable portion of his public fealty. Henry Clay, John Quincy Adams, Daniel Webster, Andrew Jackson, Stephen A. Douglas, Thomas Hart Benton, Abraham Lincoln—all had love for the Union, all had love for their states and regions, all saw no conflict, rather, a mutually nourishing connection, between the two loves. These famous men and the millions of followers for whom they spoke were patriots who had met every test set by Rousseau—inclination, passion, necessity—and had attached their ultimate patriotism to a nation so huge and loose-jointed that the sight of it would have sent Rousseau, not to forget Montesquieu, into a state of shock.

The pursuit of an American identity led many citizens, not at all surprisingly, to think and speak of a "nation singled out by the searching eye and sustained by the protecting arm of a kind and beneficent Providence" for the purpose of changing "the whole aspect of human affairs on this globe." The idea of *an American mission* had taken root in the colonies as far back as 1630 when John Winthrop proclaimed Massachusetts a "city upon a hill," and in the forcing bed of the Revolution it burst into full flower. The belief in a high destiny encouraged resistance, rationalized rebellion, legitimized independence, and justified an often apparently senseless war in which Americans shed the blood of Americans as well as of Englishmen, Irishmen, Scots, and Hessians. Then, when all these astonishing events had come to pass, it moved a few choice spirits to take the lead in reconstituting the political system on the basis of a new unity forged out of the realities of an old diversity. Thereupon an entire people took up the theme of the United States as both guardian and beneficiary of a cosmic trust.

While several variations on the theme of a national mission won popular acceptance during and after the Revolution—America as asylum, America as redeemer, America as exporter of the spirit of liberty, America as the "seat of another golden age," even America as an "all powerful commonwealth" in which the countries of Europe would find their place as "colonies"—the primary destiny of these settlements-turned-republic remained constant throughout the early decades of independence, and thereby gave the United States a penetrating sense of self-identity and an exhilarating sense of self-confidence that were to support the Union nobly in its hour of trial. If the concept of mission was useful both to the incipient nation that fought the Revolution and to the fledgling nation that went in search of unity and modernity, it was indispensable to the uncertain nation that found its unity denied and modernity challenged in 1861.

Stripped of all excrescences and elaborations, the true American mission commanded the United States to stand before the world, neither boastfully nor meekly, as a model republic. It was a simple belief; and, by reason of this simplicity, it was comprehensible, viable, and endlessly serviceable. At a desperate stage in the march of history, Americans believed, God had called forth certain hardy, liberty-loving souls from the privilege-ridden nations of the Old World; He had carried these precious few to a fresh scene, thus presenting them and their descendants with the best of all possible environments for the development of a free and progressive nation; and in bestowing this special grace He had also bestowed a special obligation for the success of the special nation. Were the Americans to fail in their experiment in republican self-government, they would fail not only themselves and their posterity but also all men everywhere who deserved to be free. If such government could work here, it might also work in other parts of the world; if it could not work here, it would never work anywhere.

The final and perhaps fundamental point about this concept of mission was that *a successful America would serve literally as an experiment or model:* It would invite men of other nations to admire and imitate; it would not go into the business of exporting ideas and institutions with the sword and the dollar. The principal force for carrying the American message to a doubting world was, quite simply, the force of good example.

These pages could be filled with thousands of heartfelt declarations of faith in the mission of the independent United States as it was framed in this first, unspoiled version. Let us be content with a scatter in which remembered men declaimed in behalf of forgotten compatriots:

John Adams to himself and a few friends (1765):

> I always consider the settlement of America with reverence and wonder, as the opening of a grand scene and design in Providence for the illumination of the ignorant, and the emancipation of the slavish part of mankind all over the earth.

James Madison to his fellow delegates at Philadelphia (1787):

> It is more than probable we are now digesting a plan which in its operation will decide forever the fate of republican government.

Alexander Hamilton to the same gentlemen a few minutes later:

> I concur with Mr. Madison in thinking we are now to decide forever the fate of republican government. If we do not give to that form due stability and wisdom, it will be disgraced and lost among ourselves, disgraced and lost to mankind forever.

George Washington to the dignitaries assembled to hear his first inaugural address (1789):

> The preservation of the sacred fire of liberty and the destiny of the republican model of government are justly considered, perhaps, as *deeply,* as *finally,* staked on the experiment intrusted to the hands of the American people.

Thomas Jefferson to Dr. Priestley (1802):

We feel that we are acting under obligations not confined to the limits
of our society. It is impossible not to be sensible that we are acting for all
mankind; that circumstances denied to others, but indulged to us, have
imposed on us the duty of proving what is the degree of freedom and self-
government in which society may venture to leave its individual members.

Joseph Story to an assembly at Cambridge celebrating the fiftieth anniversary, not of independence, but of Phi Beta Kappa (1826):

We stand, the latest, and if we fail, probably the last experiment of
self-government by the people.

Andrew Jackson, no friend of Story's, to the nation in his Farewell
Address (1837):

Providence has showered on this favored land blessings without number,
and has chosen you as the guardians of freedom, to preserve it for the
benefit of the human race.

A famous poet, Henry Wadsworth Longfellow, to his extensive audience
(1849), which included the even more extensive audience of William H.
McGuffey:

> *Thou, too, sail on, O Ship of State!*
> *Sail on, O UNION, strong and great!*
> *Humanity with all its fears,*
> *With all the hopes of future years,*
> *Is hanging breathless on thy fate!*

And last, a famous historian and public servant, George Bancroft, to a
joint session of Congress gathered to pay tribute to Abraham Lincoln (1866):

In the fullness of time a Republic rose up in the wilderness of America.
Thousands of years had passed away before this child of the ages could be
born. From whatever there was good in the systems of former centuries she
drew her nourishment; the wrecks of the past were her warnings. . . .
The fame of this only daughter of freedom went out into all the lands
of the earth; from her the human race drew hope.

Since these words speak eloquently for themselves, let me limit myself
to three brief concluding observations:

First, the eloquence seems to have been entirely sincere. I have never
found, despite a severe if admittedly remote probing of psyches and motives,
any evidence to suggest that these men and those who echoed them throughout the land did not mean exactly what they said.

Second, Washington, Adams, Jefferson, and the rest were not indulging
in flights of fancy. They were, rather, expressing a solid belief that almost
all Americans carried in their minds and hearts.

And third, the belief seems to have been about as benevolent in influence
inside the United States and mild in impact outside as any concept of national
mission in modern history. It taught more Americans to be thankful, dutiful,
and moderately self-confident than to be arrogant, undisciplined, and blindly

self-willed; it pressed upon America's neighbors in every direction without furnishing a license to conquer them. In sum, the American mission stimulated a healthy nationalism that fell short of unthinking chauvinism and an exuberant expansionism that fell short of imperial conquest. [I]t performed, through the perception and eloquence of Lincoln, its last and greatest service: It gave moral justification, which was needed desperately, to the terrible war for the Union.

There were times, to be sure, when the orators of the muscular, combative version of Manifest Destiny came close to converting the American mission from the Republic-as-experiment to the Republic-as-conqueror, but a more restrained if hardly self-denying version managed to prevail. If it was the destiny of the American people to expand until neighbors as well as nature called a halt, it was not their destiny to engulf Canada, Mexico, Central America, and the islands of the Caribbean or to leap over the Pacific (ah, those more simple days!) in search of empire. The concept of mission encouraged expansion into the unsettled or only thinly settled lands of the West, for thus they could be won outright and, in American minds, altogether properly for the cause of republican liberty; it did not give the government of the United States an excuse to lord it over half the world and exact tribute from the rest. In short, the American mission helped to make *a nation with the dimensions but not the trappings of empire*. For that service, if for no other, later generations of Americans should study thoughtfully the purest version of their nation's mission, and perhaps even go to it from time to time for spiritual refreshment.

✤ *F U R T H E R   R E A D I N G*

Sidney Ahlstrom, *A Religious History of the American People* (1972)
Charles A. Beard and Mary R. Beard, *The Rise of American Civilization* (1927)
Daniel J. Boorstin, *The Americans: The National Experience* (1965)
Marcus Cunliffe, *The Nation Takes Shape, 1789–1837* (1959)
David Brion Davis, *Antebellum American Culture: An Interpretive Anthology* (1979)
Barbara J. Fields, "Ideology and Race in American History," in J. Morgan Kousser
    and James P. McPherson, eds., *Region, Race, and Reconstruction* (1982)
David Hackett Fischer, *Albion's Seed: Four British Folkways in America* (1989)
Frances FitzGerald, *America Revised: History Schoolbooks in the Twentieth Century*
    (1979)
Eric Foner, ed., *The New American History* (1990)
Louis Hartz, *The Liberal Tradition in America: An Interpretation of American Political
    Thought Since the Revolution* (1955)
James A. Henretta and Gregory H. Nobles, *Evolution and Revolution: American
    Society, 1600–1820* (1987)
Nancy A. Hewitt, "Beyond the Search for Sisterhood: Women's History in the
    1980's," *Social History* 10 (1985), pp. 249–321.
John Higham, *History* (1965)
Stanley N. Katz and Stanley Kutler, eds., *The Promise of American History* (1982)
Robert Kelley, *The Cultural Pattern in American Politics: The First Century* (1978)
Bruce Levine et al., *Who Built America? Working People and the Nation's Economy,
    Politics, Culture, and Society* (1989)

R. R. Palmer, *The Age of the Democratic Revolution: A Political History of Europe and America, 1760–1800,* 2 vols. (1959, 1964)

Edward Pessen, "We Are All Jeffersonians, We Are All Jacksonians; Or, A Pox on Stultifying Periodizations," *Journal of the Early Republic* 1 (1981): 1–20

Alexander Saxton, *The Rise and Fall of the White Republic: Class Politics and Mass Culture in Nineteenth Century America* (1990)

Charles Sellers, *The Market Revolution* (1991)

Ronald Takaki, *Iron Cages: Race and Culture in Nineteenth Century America* (1979)

Frederick Jackson Turner, *The United States, 1830–1850* (1935)

Robert Wiebe, *The Opening of American Society: From the Framing of the Constitution to the Eve of Disunion* (1984)

William Appleman Williams, *The Contours of American History* (1966)

Nancy Woloch, *Women and the American Experience* (1984)

The U.S. Constitution and the
Federalist Ascendency

The American Revolution, like all great revolutions, fractured old social relations and stimulated new forms of political talk. Through the 1770s, rival elements from the top to the bottom of the patriot coalition debated fiercely over the kind of political order they hoped to build—and especially over how democratic that order ought to be. The debates continued after the British defeat at Yorktown, amid bitter turmoil in the states capped by Shays' Rebellion in Massachusetts in 1786–1787. Leading conservative nationalists, shocked by what they saw as the democratic leveling tendencies of the state governments, began to call for a thorough revamping of the national union. Meeting in secret session in Philadelphia in 1787, delegates from twelve of the states hammered out a new federal constitution, greatly enlarging the national government's powers. But these efforts proceeded with difficulty. The Philadelphia convention reached agreement only after prolonged haggling over basic issues—and even then, some delegates refused to sign the new constitution. Thereafter, it took frantic organizing efforts and additional concessions—including promises of amendments—to beat back the objections of the so-called Anti-Federalists and win the assent of the separate states.

The ratification of the Constitution, along with the eventual addition of a federal bill of rights, set American politics on a new institutional footing. The inauguration of the revolutionary hero George Washington as the nation's first president in 1789 lent the infant government additional prestige. Yet within two years, fresh divisions appeared at the national level, separating such former allies as Alexander Hamilton and James Madison. These conflicts, stemming mainly from clashes over financial policy and political economy, showed that despite widespread acceptance of the national government, there was no agreement at all about its legitimate powers. At stake, beyond the details of constitutional interpretation, were different social visions of the new republic's future.

Interpreting these events strongly colors any understanding of the early republic, for their significance would reverberate over the decades to come and touch the lives of all Americans. What lay behind the movement for a new national constitution? Was the Constitution, as many Anti-Federalists believed, an undemocratic, even aristocratic document? Or did its adoption ultimately prove a victory for more moderate, even democratic forces? Why, so soon after ratification, did fights break out within the Washington administration? And what difference did these conflicts make to the American majority—women, slaves, and native Americans—who were excluded from the polity?

⧉ D O C U M E N T S

In the first selection, a famous speech to the Philadelphia convention, the conservative nationalist Alexander Hamilton proposes his own outline for the new federal constitution. His remarks bear comparison to the Constitution itself—and to the next document, from James Madison's celebrated *Federalist Number 10,* a defense of the new plan, written to sway a wary citizenry. Patrick Henry of Virginia refused to attend the Philadelphia convention because (he said) he "smelt a rat." In the third, two-part selection, his subsequent denunciation of the Constitution at the Virginia ratification convention provides a catalogue of the Anti-Federalists' fears and aspirations; the speech by Amos Singletary, a Massachusetts farmer and a delegate at his own state's convention, captures a more plebeian sensibility. Note how both Henry and Singletary touch on the original document's lack of a bill of rights. In the fourth document, Charles Cotesworth Pinckney relates to his fellow South Carolinians the compromises he and the other delegates reached at Philadelphia over slavery—and his satisfaction with them.

Chapter 2's remaining documents trace the growing divisions at the political top after the establishment of the federal government in 1789. Hamilton's impressive report on the public credit and assumption of the states' war debts, reprinted as the fifth document, called for full compensation to the holders of government notes, many of whom were speculators who had bought the notes well under value from hard-pressed middling citizens. The logic behind Hamilton's scheme—along with his calls for a national bank and federal excise taxes—stirred fears that the new secretary of the treasury was trying to elevate an American monied aristocracy, consisting largely of his friends and benefactors. The sixth selection, featuring the debate between Hamilton and Secretary of State Thomas Jefferson over the bank's constitutionality, suggests something about their larger philosophical conflicts and also about the limits of their stated differences as of 1791. A year later, Jefferson's friend Madison surveyed the state of political affairs, finding portents of things to come, as the final document reveals.

Alexander Hamilton Addresses the Constitutional Convention, 1787

Monday, June 18th, 1787

Mr. Hamilton—. . . What is federal? An association of several independent states into one. How or in what manner this association is formed, is not so clearly distinguishable. . . .

I hold it, that different societies have all different views and interests to pursue, and always prefer local to general concerns. . . . Men always love power, and states will prefer their particular concerns to the general welfare;

and as the states become large and important, will they not be less attentive to the general government? What in process of time will Virginia be? She contains now half a million of inhabitants—in twenty-five years she will double the number. Feeling her own weight and importance, must she not become indifferent to the concerns of the union? And where, in such a situation, will be found national attachment to the general government? . . .

To avoid the evils deducible from these observations, we must establish a general and national government, completely sovereign, and annihilate the state distinctions and state operations; and unless we do this, no good purpose can be answered. . . .

Examine the present confederation, and it is evident they can raise no troops nor equip vessels before war is actually declared. They cannot therefore take any preparatory measure before an enemy is at your door. How unwise and inadequate their powers! . . .

I believe the British government forms the best model the world ever produced, and such has been its progress in the minds of the many, that this truth gradually gains ground. This government has for its object *public strength* and *individual security*. It is said with us to be unattainable. If it was once formed it would maintain itself. All communities divide themselves into the few and the many. The first are the rich and well born, the other the mass of the people. The voice of the people has been said to be the voice of God; and however generally this maxim has been quoted and believed, it is not true in fact. The people are turbulent and changing; they seldom judge or determine right. Give therefore to the first class a distinct, permanent share in the government. They will check the unsteadiness of the second, and as they cannot receive any advantage by a change, they therefore will ever maintain good government. Can a democratic assembly, who annually revolve in the mass of the people, be supposed steadily to pursue the public good? Nothing but a permanent body can check the imprudence of democracy. Their turbulent and uncontrolling disposition requires checks. . . . I am therefore for a general government, yet would wish to go the full length of republican principles.

Let one body of the legislature be constituted during good behavior or life.

Let one executive be appointed who dares execute his powers.

It may be asked is this a republican system? It is strictly so, as long as they remain elective.

And let me observe, that an executive is less dangerous to the liberties of the people when in office during life, than for seven years.

It may be said this constitutes an elective monarchy? Pray what is a monarchy? May not the governors of the respective states be considered in that light? But by making the executive subject to impeachment, the term monarchy cannot apply. . . . Let electors be appointed in each of the states to elect the executive . . . to consist of two branches—and I would give them the unlimited power of passing *all laws* without exception. The assembly to be elected for three years by the people in districts—the senate to be elected by electors to be chosen for that purpose by the people, and to remain in office during life. The executive to have the power of negativing all laws—to make war or peace, with the advice of the senate—to make treaties with their advice, but to have the sole direction of all military operations, and to send ambassadors and appoint all military officers, and to pardon all offenders, treason excepted, unless by advice of the senate. On his death or removal, the president of the senate to officiate, with the same powers, until another is elected. Supreme judicial officers to be appointed by the executive and the senate. The legislature to appoint courts in each state, so as to make the state governments unnecessary to it.

All state laws to be absolutely void which contravene the general laws. An officer to be appointed in each state to have a negative on all state laws. All the militia and the appointment of officers to be under the national government. . . .

James Madison Defends
the New Federal Constitution, 1788

Among the numerous advantages promised by a well-constructed Union, none deserves to be more accurately developed than its tendency to break and control the violence of faction. The friend of popular governments never finds himself so much alarmed for their character and fate, as when he contemplates their propensity to this dangerous vice. He will not fail, therefore, to set a due value on any plan which, without violating the principles to which he is attached, provides a proper cure for it. The instability, injustice, and confusion introduced into the public councils, have, in truth, been the mortal diseases under which popular governments have everywhere perished; as they continue to be the favorite and fruitful topics from which the adversaries to liberty derive their most specious declamations. . . . Complaints are everywhere heard from our most considerate and virtuous citizens, equally the friends of public and private faith, and of public and personal liberty, that our governments are too unstable, that the public good is disregarded in the conflicts of rival parties, and that measures are too often decided, not according to the rules of justice and the rights of the minor party, but by the superior force of an interested and overbearing majority. . . .

By a faction, I understand a number of citizens, whether amounting to a majority or a minority of the whole, who are united and actuated by some common impulse of passion, or of interest, adversed to the rights of other citizens, or to the permanent and aggregate interests of the community.

There are two methods of curing the mischiefs of faction: the one, by removing its causes; the other, by controlling its effects.

There are again two methods of removing the causes of faction: the one, by destroying the liberty which is essential to its existence; the other, by giving to every citizen the same opinions, the same passions, and the same interests.

It could never be more truly said than of the first remedy, that it was worse than the disease. Liberty is to faction what air is to fire, an aliment without which it instantly expires. But it could not be less folly to abolish liberty, which is essential to political life, because it nourishes faction, than it would be to wish the annihilation of air, which is essential to animal life, because it imparts to fire its destructive agency.

The second expedient is as impracticable as the first would be unwise. As long as the reason of man continues fallible, and he is at liberty to exercise it, different opinions will be formed. As long as the connection subsists between his reason and his self-love, his opinions and his passions will have a reciprocal influence on each other; and the former will be objects to which the latter will attach themselves. The diversity in the faculties of men, from which the rights of property originate, is not less an insuperable obstacle to a uniformity of interests. The protection of these faculties is the first object of government. . . .

The latent causes of faction are sown in the nature of man; and we see them everywhere brought into different degrees of activity, according to the different circumstances of civil society. . . . So strong is this propensity of mankind to fall into mutual animosities, that where no substantial occasion presents itself, the most frivolous and fanciful distinctions have been sufficient to kindle their unfriendly passions and excite their most violent conflicts. But the most common and durable source of factions has been the various and unequal distribution of property. Those who hold and those who are without property have ever formed distinct interests in society. Those who are creditors, and those who are debtors, fall under a like discrimination. A landed interest, a manufacturing interest, a mercantile interest, a moneyed interest, with many lesser interests, grow up of necessity in civilized nations, and divide them into different classes, actuated by different sentiments and views. The regulation of these various and interfering interests forms the principal task of modern legislation, and involves the spirit of party and faction in the necessary and ordinary operations of the government.

No man is allowed to be a judge in his own cause, because his interest would certainly bias his judgment, and, not improbably, corrupt his integrity. With equal, nay with greater reason, a body of men are unfit to be both judges and parties at the same time; yet what are many of the most important acts of legislation, but so many judicial determinations, not indeed concerning the rights of single persons, but concerning the rights of large bodies of citizens? And what are the different classes of legislators but advocates and parties to the causes which they determine? . . .

It is in vain to say that enlightened statesmen will be able to adjust these clashing interests, and render them all subservient to the public good. Enlightened statesmen will not always be at the helm. . . .

The inference to which we are brought is, that the CAUSES of faction cannot be removed, and that relief is only to be sought in means of controlling its EFFECTS.

If a faction consists of less than a majority, relief is supplied by the republican principle, which enables the majority to defeat its sinister views by regular vote. . . . When a majority is included in a faction, the form of popular government, on the other hand, enables it to sacrifice to its ruling passion or interest both the public good and the rights of other citizens. To secure the public good and private rights against the danger of such a faction, and at the same time to preserve the spirit and the form of popular government, is then the great object to which our inquiries are directed. . . .

By what means is this object attainable? Evidently by one of two only. Either the existence of the same passion or interest in a majority at the same time must be prevented, or the majority, having such coexistent passion or interest, must be rendered, by their number and local situation, unable to concert and carry into effect schemes of oppression. . . .

From this view of the subject it may be concluded that a pure democracy, by which I mean a society consisting of a small number of citizens, who assemble and administer the government in person, can admit of no cure for the mischiefs of faction. A common passion or interest will, in almost every case, be felt by a majority of the whole; a communication and concert result from the form of government itself; and there is nothing to check the inducements to sacrifice the weaker party or an obnoxious individual. . . .

A republic, by which I mean a government in which the scheme of representation takes place, opens a different prospect, and promises the cure for which we are seeking. . . .

The two great points of difference between a democracy and a republic are: first, the delegation of the government, in the latter, to a small number of citizens elected by the rest; secondly, the greater number of citizens, and greater sphere of country, over which the latter may be extended.

The effect of the first difference is, on the one hand, to refine and enlarge the public views, by passing them through the medium of a chosen body of citizens, whose wisdom may best discern the true interest of their country, and whose patriotism and love of justice will be least likely to sacrifice it to temporary or partial considerations. . . . The question resulting is, whether small or extensive republics are more favorable to the election of proper guardians of the public weal; and it is clearly decided in favor of the latter . . .

[I]t is to be remarked that, however small the republic may be, the representatives must be raised to a certain number, in order to guard against the cabals of a few; and that, however large it may be, they must be limited to a certain number, in order to guard against the confusion of a multitude. Hence, the number of representatives in the two cases not being in proportion to that of the two constituents, and being proportionally greater in the small republic, it follows that, if the proportion of fit characters be not less in the large than in the small republic, the former will present a greater option, and consequently a greater probability of a fit choice. . . .

[A]s each representative will be chosen by a greater number of citizens in the large than in the small republic, it will be more difficult for unworthy candidates to practice with success the vicious arts by which elections are too often carried; and the suffrages of the people being more free, will be more likely to centre in men who possess the most attractive merit and the most diffusive and established characters. . . .

The smaller the society, the fewer probably will be the distinct parties and interests composing it; the fewer the distinct parties and interests, the more frequently will a majority be found of the same party; and the smaller the number of individuals composing a majority, and the smaller the compass within which they are placed, the more easily will they concert and execute their plans of oppression. Extend the sphere, and you take in a greater variety of parties and interests; you make it less probable that a majority of the whole will have a common motive to invade the rights of other citizens; or if such a common motive exists, it will be more difficult for all who feel it to discover their own strength, and to act in unison with each other. . . .

A rage for paper money, for an abolition of debts, for an equal division of property, or for any other improper or wicked project, will be less apt to pervade the whole body of the Union than a particular member of it; in the same proportion as such a malady is more likely to taint a particular county or district, than an entire State.

In the extent and proper structure of the Union, therefore, we behold a republican remedy for the diseases most incident to republican government.

Two Anti-Federalists Attack the Constitution, 1788

Patrick Henry, 1788

. . . I need not take much pains to show, that the principles of this system, are extremely pernicious, impolitic, and dangerous. Is this a Monarchy, like England—a compact between Prince and people; with checks on the former, to secure the liberty of the latter? Is this a Confederacy, like Holland—an association of a number of independent States, each of which retain its individual sovereignty? It is not a democracy, wherein the people retain all their rights securely. Had these principles been adhered to, we should not have been brought to this alarming transition, from a Confederacy to a consolidated Government. We have no detail of those great considerations which, in my opinion, ought to have abounded before we should recur to a government of this kind. Here is a revolution as radical as that which separated us from Great Britain. It is as radical, if in this transition our rights and privileges are endangered, and the sovereignty of the States be relinquished: And cannot we plainly see, that this is actually the case? The rights of conscience, trial by jury, liberty of the press, all your immunities and franchises, all pretensions to human rights and privileges, are rendered insecure, if not lost, by this change so loudly talked of by some, and inconsiderately by others. Is this same relinquishment of rights worthy of freemen? . . .

Gentlemen have told us within these walls, that the Union is gone— or, that the Union will be gone: Is not this trifling with the judgment of their fellow-citizens? Till they tell us the ground of their fears, I will consider them as imaginary: I rose to make inquiry where those dangers were; they could make no answer: I believe I never shall have that answer: Is there a disposition in the people of this country to revolt against the dominion of laws? Has there been a single tumult in Virginia? Have not the people of

Virginia, when laboring under the severest pressure of accumulated distresses, manifested the most cordial acquiescence in the execution of the laws? What could be more awful than their unanimous acquiescence under general distresses? Is there any revolution in Virginia? Whither is the spirit of America gone? Whither is the genius of America fled? It was but yesterday, when our enemies marched in triumph through our country: Yet the people of this country could not be appalled by their pompous armaments: They stopped their career, and victoriously captured them: Where is the peril now compared to that? Some minds are agitated by foreign alarms: Happily for us, there is no real danger from Europe: that country is engaged in more arduous business; from that quarter there is no cause of fear: You may sleep in safety forever for them. Where is the danger? If, Sir, there was any, I would recur to the American spirit to defend us;—that spirit which has enabled us to surmount the greatest difficulties: To that illustrious spirit I address my most fervent prayer, to prevent our adopting a system destructive to liberty. . . .

This Constitution is said to have beautiful features; but when I come to examine these features, Sir, they appear to me horridly frightful: Among other deformities, it has an awful squinting; it squints towards monarchy: And does not this raise indignation in the breast of every American? Your President may easily become King: Your Senate is so imperfectly constructed that your dearest rights may be sacrificed by what may be a small minority; and a very small minority may continue forever unchangeably this Government, although horridly defective: Where are your checks in this Government? Your strong holds will be in the hands of your enemies: It is on a supposition that our American Governors shall be honest, that all the good qualities of this Government are founded: But its defective, and imperfect construction, puts it in their power to perpetrate the worst of mischiefs, should they be bad men: And, Sir, would not all the world, from the Eastern to the Western hemisphere, blame our distracted folly in resting our rights upon the contingency of our rulers being good or bad.

Amos Singletary, 1788

Mr. Singletary said, that all gentlemen had said about a bill of rights to the Constitution, was, that what is written is written; but he thought we were giving up all power, and that the states will be like towns in this state. . . .

I should not have troubled the Convention again, if some gentlemen had not called on them that were on the stage in the beginning of our troubles, in the year 1775. I was one of them. . . . We contended with Great Britain, some said for a threepenny duty on tea; but it was not that; it was because they claimed a right to tax us and bind us in all cases whatever. And does not this Constitution do the same? Does it not take away all we have—all our property? Does it not lay *all* taxes, duties, imposts, and excises? And what more have we to give? They tell us Congress won't lay dry taxes upon us, but collect all the money they want by impost. I say, there has always been a difficulty about impost. Whenever the General Court was going to lay an impost, they would tell us it was more than trade could bear, that it hurt the fair trader, and encouraged smuggling; and there will always be the same objection: they won't be able to raise money enough by impost, and then they will lay it on the land, and take all we have got. These lawyers, and men of learning, and moneyed men, that talk so finely, and gloss over matters so smoothly, to make us poor illiterate people swallow down the pill, expect to get into Congress themselves; they expect to be the managers of this Constitution, and get all the power and all the money into their own hands, and then they will swallow up all us little folks, like the great *Leviathan,* Mr. President; yes, just as the whale swallowed up *Jonah.*

Charles Cotesworth Pinckney
Defends the Constitution, 1788

. . . As we found it necessary to give very extensive powers to the federal government both over the persons and estates of the citizens, we thought it right to draw one branch of the legislature immediately from the people, and that both wealth and numbers should be considered in the representation. We were at a loss, for some time, for a rule to ascertain the proportionate wealth of the states. At last we thought that the productive labor of the inhabitants was the best rule for ascertaining their wealth. In conformity to this rule, joined to a spirit of concession, we determined that representatives should be apportioned among the several states, by adding to the whole number of free persons three fifths of the slaves. We thus obtained a representation for our property; and I confess I did not expect that we had conceded too much to the Eastern States, when they allowed us a representation for a species of property which they have not among them.

. . . [Pinckney] then said he would make a few observations on the objections which the gentleman had thrown out on the restrictions that might be laid on the African trade after the year 1808. On this point your delegates had to contend with the religious and political prejudices of the Eastern and Middle States, and with the interested and inconsistent opinion of Virginia, who was warmly opposed to our importing more slaves. I am of the same opinion now as I was two years ago, when I used the expressions the gentleman has quoted—that, while there remained one acre of swampland uncleared of South Carolina, I would raise my voice against restricting the importation of negroes. I am as thoroughly convinced as that gentleman is, that the nature of our climate, and the flat, swampy situation of our country, obliges us to cultivate our lands with negroes, and that without them South Carolina would soon be a desert waste. . . .

By this settlement we have secured an unlimited importation of negroes for twenty years. Nor is it declared that the importation shall be then stopped; it may be continued. We have a security that the general government can never emancipate them, for no such authority is granted; and it is admitted, on all hands, that the general government has no powers but what are expressly granted by the Constitution, and that all rights not expressed were reserved by the several states. We have obtained a right to recover our slaves in whatever part of America they may take refuge, which is a right we had not before. In short, considering all circumstances, we have made the best terms for the security of this species of property it was in our power to make. We would have made better if we could; but, on the whole, I do not think them bad.

Hamilton on the Public Credit, 1790

. . . States, like individuals, who observe their engagements, are respected and trusted; while the reverse is the fate of those, who pursue an opposite conduct.

Every breach of the public engagements, whether from choice or necessity, is in different degrees hurtful to public credit. When such a necessity does truly exist, the evils of it are only to be palliated by a scrupulous attention, on the part of the government, to carry the violation no farther than the necessity absolutely requires, and to manifest, if the nature of the case admits of it, a sincere disposition to make reparation, whenever circumstances shall permit. But with every possible mitigation, credit must suffer, and numerous mischiefs ensue. It is therefore highly important, when an appearance of necessity seems to press upon the public councils, that they should examine well its reality, and be perfectly assured, that there is no method of escaping from it, before they yield to its suggestions. . . . Those who are most commonly creditors of a nation, are, generally speaking, enlightened men; and there are signal examples to warrant a conclusion, that when a candid and fair appeal is made to them, they will understand their true interest too well to refuse their concurrence in such modifications of their claims, as any real necessity may demand.

While the observance of that good faith, which is the basis of public credit, is recommended by the strongest inducements of political expediency, it is enforced by considerations of still greater authority. There are arguments for it, which rest on the immutable principles of moral obligation. And in proportion as the mind is disposed to contemplate, in the order of Providence, an intimate connection between public virtue and public happiness, will be its repugnancy to a violation of those principles.

This reflection derives additional strength from the nature of the debt of the United States. It was the price of liberty. The faith of America has been repeatedly pledged for it, and with solemnities, that give peculiar force to the obligation. . . .

To justify and preserve their confidence; to promote the encreasing respectability of the American name; to answer the calls of justice; to restore landed property to its due value; to furnish new resources both to agriculture and commerce; to cement more closely the union of the states; to add to their security against foreign attack; to establish public order on the basis of an upright and liberal policy. These are the great and invaluable ends to be secured, by a proper and adequate provision, at the present period, for the support of public credit. . . .

It will procure to every class of the community some important advantages, and remove some no less important disadvantages.

The advantage to the public creditors from the increased value of that part of their property which constitutes the public debt, needs no explanation.

But there is a consequence of this, less obvious, though not less true, in which every other citizen is interested. It is a well known fact, that in countries in which the national debt is properly funded, and an object of established confidence, it answers most of the purposes of money. Transfers of stock or public debt are there equivalent to payments in specie; or in other words, stock, in the principal transactions of business, passes current as specie. The same thing would, in all probability happen here, under the like circumstances.

The benefits of this are various and obvious.

Trade is extended by it; because there is a larger capital to carry it on. . . .

The proprietors of lands would not only feel the benefit of this increase in the value of their property, and of a more prompt and better sale, when they had occasion to sell; but the necessity of selling would be, itself, greatly diminished. . . .

It is agreed on all hands, that that part of the debt which has been contracted abroad, and is denominated the foreign debt, ought to be provided for, according to the precise terms of the contracts relating to it. The discussions, which can arise, therefore, will have reference essentially to the domestic part of it, or to that which has been contracted at home. It is to be regretted, that there is not the same unanimity of sentiment on this part, as on the other.

The Secretary has too much deference for the opinions of every part of the community, not to have observed one, which has, more than once, made its appearance in the public prints, and which is occasionally to be met with in conversation. It involves this question, whether a discrimination ought not to be made between original holders of the public securities, and present possessors, by purchase. Those who advocate a discrimination are for making a full provision for the securities of the former, at their nominal value; but contend, that the latter ought to receive no more than the cost to them, and the interest: And the idea is sometimes suggested of making good the difference to the primitive possessor. . . .

The Secretary, after the most mature reflection on the force of this argument, is induced to reject the doctrine it contains, as equally unjust and impolitic, as highly injurious, even to the original holders of public securities; as ruinous to public credit.

It is inconsistent with justice, because in the first place, it is a breach of contract; in violation of the rights of a fair purchaser.

The nature of the contract in its origin, is, that the public will pay the sum expressed in the security, to the first holder, or his *assignee.* The *intent,* in making the security assignable, is, that the proprietor may be able to make use of his property, by selling it for as much as it *may be worth in the market,* and that the buyer may be *safe* in the purchase.

Every buyer therefore stands exactly in the place of the seller, has the same right with him to the identical sum expressed in the security, and having acquired that right, by fair purchase, and in conformity to the original *agreement* and *intention* of the government, his claim cannot be disputed, without manifest injustice.

That he is to be considered as a fair purchaser, results from this: Whatever necessity the seller may have been under, was occasioned by the government, in not making a proper provision for its debts. The buyer had no agency in it, and therefore ought not to suffer. He is not even chargeable with having taken an undue advantage. He paid what the commodity was worth in the market, and took the risks of reimbursement upon himself. He of course gave a fair equivalent, and ought to reap the benefit of his hazard; a hazard which was far from inconsiderable, and which, perhaps, turned on little less than a revolution in government.

The National Bank and the Constitution: Two Views, 1791

Thomas Jefferson, 1791

I consider the foundation of the Constitution as laid on this ground: That "all powers not delegated to the United States, by the Constitution, nor prohibited by it to the States, are reserved to the States or to the people." [Xth amendment.] . . .

The incorporation of a bank, and the powers assumed by this bill, have not, in my opinion, been delegated to the United States, by the Constitution.

I. They are not among the powers specially enumerated . . .

II. Nor are they within either of the general phrases, which are the two following:—

1. To lay taxes to provide for the general welfare of the United States . . . [T]hey are not *to do anything they please* to provide for the general welfare, but only to *lay taxes* for that purpose. . . .

It was intended to lace them up straitly within the enumerated powers, and those without which, as means, these powers could not be carried into effect. . . .

2. The second general phrase is, "to make all laws *necessary* and proper for carrying into execution the enumerated powers." But they can all be carried into execution without a bank. A bank therefore is not *necessary*, and consequently not authorized by this phrase.

It has been urged that a bank will give great facility or convenience in the collection of taxes. Suppose this were true: yet the Constitution allows only the means which are "*necessary*," not those which are merely "convenient" for effecting the enumerated powers. . . .

It may be said that a bank whose bills would have a currency all over the States, would be more convenient than one whose currency is limited to a single State. So it would be still more convenient that there should be a bank, whose bills should have a currency all over the world. But it does not follow from this superior conveniency, that there exists anywhere a power to establish such a bank; or that the world may not go on very well without it. . . .

It must be added, however, that unless the President's mind on a view of everything which is urged for and against this bill, is tolerably clear that it is unauthorized by the Constitution; if the pro and the con hang so even as to balance his judgment, a just respect for the wisdom of the legislature would naturally decide the balance in favor of their opinion. It is chiefly for cases where they are clearly misled by error, ambition, or interest, that the Constitution has placed a check in the negative of the President.

Alexander Hamilton, 1791

In entering upon the argument it ought to be premised, that the objections of the Secretary of State . . . are founded on a general denial of the authority of the United States to erect corporations. . . .

Now it appears to the Secretary of the Treasury, that this *general principle* is *inherent* in the very *definition* of *Government* and *essential* to every step of the progress to be made by that of the United States; namely—that every power vested in a Government is in its nature *sovereign,* and includes by *force* of the *term,* a right to employ all the *means* requisite, and fairly *applicable* to the attainment of the *ends* of such power; and which are not precluded by restrictions and exceptions specified in the constitution; or not immoral, or not contrary to the essential ends of political society. . . .

The circumstances that the powers of sovereignty are in this country divided between the National and State Governments, does not afford the distinction required. It does not follow from this, that each of the *portions* of powers delegated to the one or to the other is not sovereign *with regard to its proper objects.* It will only *follow* from it, that each has sovereign power as to *certain things,* and not as to *other things.* To deny that the Government of the United States has sovereign power as to its declared purposes and trusts, because its power does not extend to all cases, would be equally to deny, that the State Governments have sovereign power in any case; because their power does not extend to every case. The tenth section of the first article of the constitution exhibits a long list of very important things which they may not do. And thus the United States would furnish the singular spectacle of a *political society* without *sovereignty,* or of a people *governed* without *government.* . . .

This general and indisputable principle puts at once an end to the *abstract* question—Whether the United States have power to *erect a corporation?* That is to say, to give a *legal* or *artificial capacity* to one or more persons, distinct from the natural. For it is unquestionably incident to *sovereign power* to erect corporations, and consequently to *that* of the United States, in *relation to the objects* intrusted to the management of the government. The difference is this—where the authority of the government is general, it can create corporations in *all cases;* where it is confined to certain branches of legislation, it can create corporations only in those cases. . . .

It is not denied, that there are *implied,* as well as *express* powers, and that the former are as effectually delegated as the latter. . . .

Then it follows, that as a power of erecting a corporation may as well *be implied* as any other thing; it may as well be employed as an *instrument* or *mean* of carrying into execution any of the specified powers, as any other instrument or mean whatever. The only question must be, in this as in every other case, whether the mean to be employed, or in this instance the corporation to be erected, has a natural relation to any of the acknowledged objects or lawful ends of the government. . . .

A strange fallacy seems to have crept into the manner of thinking and reasoning upon the subject. Imagination appears to have been unusually busy concerning it. An incorporation seems to have been regarded as some great, independent, substantive thing—as a political end of peculiar magnitude and moment; whereas it is truly to be considered as a *quality, capacity,* or *mean* to an end. . . .

To this mode of reasoning respecting the right of employing all the means requisite to the execution of the specified powers of the Government, it is objected that none but *necessary* and proper means are to be employed, and the Secretary of State maintains, that no means are to be considered as *necessary,* but those without which the grant of the power would be *nugatory.* Nay so far does he go in his restrictive interpretation of the word, as even to make the case of *necessity* which shall warrant the constitutional exercise of the power to depend on casual and temporary circumstances, an idea which alone refutes the construction. . . .

It is essential to the being of the National government, that so erroneous a conception of the meaning of the word *necessary,* should be exploded.

It is certain, that neither the grammatical, nor popular sense of the term requires that construction. According to both, *necessary* often means no more than *needful, requisite, incidental, useful,* or *conducive to.* It is a common mode of expression to say, that it is *necessary* for a government or a person to do this or that thing, when nothing more is intended or understood, than that the interests of the government or person require, or will be promoted, by the doing of this or that thing. The imagination can be at no loss for exemplifications of the use of the word in this sense.

And it is the true one in which it is to be understood as used in the constitution. The whole turn of the clause containing it, indicates, that it was the intent of the convention, by that clause to give a liberal latitude to the exercise of the specified powers. The expressions have peculiar comprehensiveness. They are—"to make *all laws,* necessary and proper for *carrying into execution* the foregoing powers and *all other powers* vested by the constitution in the *government* of the United States, or in any *department* or *officer* thereof." To understand the word as the Secretary of State does, would be to depart from its obvious and popular sense, and to give it a *restrictive* operation; an idea never before entertained. It would be to give it the same force as if the word *absolutely* or *indispensibly* had been prefixed to it.

James Madison Gives "A Candid State of Parties," 1792

As it is the business of the contemplative statesman to trace the history of parties in a free country, so it is the duty of the citizen at all times to understand the actual state of them. Whenever this duty is omitted, an opportunity is given to designing men, by the use of artificial or nominal distinctions, to oppose and balance against each other those who never differed as to the end to be pursued, and may no longer differ as to the means of attaining it. The most interesting state of parties in the United States may be referred to three periods: Those who espoused the cause of independence and those who adhered to the British claims, formed the parties of the first period; if, indeed, the disaffected class were considerable enough to deserve the name of a party. This state of things was superseded by the treaty of peace in 1783. From 1783 to 1787 there were parties in abundance, but being rather local than general, they are not within the present review.

The Federal Constitution, proposed in the latter year, gave birth to a second and most interesting division of the people. Every one remembers it, because every one was involved in it.

Among those who embraced the constitution, the great body were unquestionably friends to republican liberty; though there were, no doubt, some who were openly or secretly attached to monarchy and aristocracy; and hoped to make the constitution a cradle for these hereditary establishments.

Among those who opposed the constitution, the great body were certainly well affected to the union and to good government, though there might be a few who had a leaning unfavorable to both. This state of parties was terminated by the regular and effectual establishment of the federal government in 1788; out of the administration of which, however, has arisen a third division, which being natural to most political societies, is likely to be of some duration in ours.

One of the divisions consists of those, who from particular interest, from natural temper, or from the habits of life, are more partial to the opulent than to the other classes of society; and having debauched themselves into a persuasion that mankind are incapable of governing themselves, it follows with them, of course, that government can be carried on only by the pageantry of rank, the influence of money and emoluments, and the terror of military force. Men of those sentiments must naturally wish to point the measures of government less to the interest of the many than of a few, and less to the reason of the many than to their weaknesses; hoping perhaps in proportion to the ardor of their zeal, that by giving such a turn to the administration, the government itself may by degrees be narrowed into fewer hands, and approximated to an hereditary form.

The other division consists of those who believing in the doctrine that mankind are capable of governing themselves, and hating hereditary power as an insult to the reason and an outrage to the rights of man, are naturally offended at every public measure that does not appeal to the understanding and to the general interest of the community, or that is not strictly conformable to the principles, and conducive to the preservation of republican government.

This being the real state of parties among us, an experienced and dispassionate observer will be at no loss to decide on the probable conduct of each.

The anti republican party, as it may be called, being the weaker in point of numbers, will be induced by the most obvious motives to strengthen themselves with the men of influence, particularly of moneyed, which is the most active and insinuating influence. It will be equally their true policy to weaken their opponents by reviving exploded parties, and taking advantage of all prejudices, local, political, and occupational, that may prevent or disturb a general coalition of sentiments.

The republican party, as it may be termed, conscious that the mass of people in every part of the union, in every state, and of every occupation must at bottom be with them, both in interest and sentiment, will naturally find their account in burying all antecedent questions, in banishing every other distinction than that between enemies and friends to republican government, and in promoting a general harmony among the latter, wherever residing, or however employed.

Whether the republican or the rival party will ultimately establish its ascendance, is a problem which may be contemplated now; but which time alone can solve. On one hand experience shows that in politics as in war, stratagem is often an overmatch for numbers; and among more happy characteristics of our political situation, it is now well understood that there are peculiarities, some temporary, others more durable, which may favor that side in the contest. On the republican side, again, the superiority of numbers is so great, their sentiments are so decided, and the practice of making a common cause, where there is a common sentiment and common interest, in spite of circumstantial and artificial distinctions, is so well understood, that no temperate observer of human affairs will be surprised if the issue in the present instance should be reversed, and the government be administered in the spirit and form approved by the great body of the people.

⌗ *E S S A Y S*

The following essays offer very different perspectives on the framing and ratification of the U.S. Constitution. Much recent writing on the subject has concerned the ideological burdens of the framers and their opponents, as well as the relative importance of republican and liberal ideas at the nation's founding. In the first essay, Isaac Kramnick, who teaches government at Cornell University, confronts this literature and discovers several distinct (although overlapping) political vocabularies at play in 1787–1788. Donald G. Nieman, a historian at Clemson University, shifts the terms of discussion to the weight of interest in his reflections in the second essay on the Constitution's compromises with slavery. In the final selection, the historian Alfred F. Young of Northern Illinois University, an expert in the history of popular politics, assesses the democratic forces that shaped the constitutional settlement. We are left to ask whether the discussions of the republicanism and liberalism of major spokesmen adequately convey the intellectual and political landscape of the 1780s. Given these essays, how useful is it to see the Constitution simply as a conservative instrument? Was it (as some of the abolitionists put it) "a covenant with death?" Does Young's essay overestimate the influence exerted by "the genius of the people"?

The Discourse of Politics in 1787

ISAAC KRAMNICK

. . . In the "great national discussion" of the Constitution Federalists and Antifederalists . . . tapped several languages of politics, the terms of which they could easily verbalize. This article examines four such "distinguishable idioms," which coexisted in the discourse of politics in 1787–1788. None dominated the field, and the use of one was compatible with the use of another by the very same writer or speaker. There was a profusion and confusion of political tongues among the founders. They lived easily with that clatter; it is we two hundred years later who chafe at their inconsistency. Reading the framers and the critics of the Constitution, one discerns the languages of republicanism, of Lockean liberalism, of work-ethic Protestantism, and of state-centered theories of power and sovereignty.

. . . Dominating eighteenth-century political thought in Britain and America, [much recent scholarship insists], was the language of republican virtue. Man was a political being who realized his telos only when living in a *vivere civile* with other propertied, arms-bearing citizens, in a republic where they ruled and were ruled in turn. Behind this republican discourse is a tradition of political philosophy with roots in Aristotle's *Politics,* Cicero's *Res Publica,* Machiavelli, Harrington, Bolingbroke, and the nostalgic country's virtuous opposition to Walpole and the commercialization of English life. The pursuit of good is privileged over private interests, and freedom means participation in civic life rather than the protection of individual rights from interference. . . .

In response to these republican imperial claims, a group whom Gordon S. Wood has labeled "neo-Lockeans" has insisted that Locke and liberalism were alive and well in Anglo-American thought in the period of the founding. Individualism, the moral legitimacy of private interest, and market society are privileged in this reading over community, public good, and the virtuous pursuit of civic fulfillment. . . .

Can we have it both ways? We certainly can if we take Federalist and Antifederalist views as representing a single text of political discourse at the founding. A persuasive case can be made for the Federalists as liberal modernists and the Antifederalists as nostalgic republican communitarians seeking desperately to hold on to a virtuous moral order threatened by commerce and market society. The Federalist tendency was to depict America in amoral

Excerpts from "The Great National Discussion: The Discourse of Politics in 1787" by Isaac Kramnick, in *William and Mary Quarterly,* 3d ser., 45, 1 (1988), pp. 3–31.

terms as an enlarged nation that transcended local community and moral conviction as the focus of politics. The Federalists seemed to glory in an individualistic and competitive America, which was preoccupied with private rights and personal autonomy. This reading of America is associated with James Madison more than with anyone else, and with his writings in the *Federalist*.

Madison's adulation of heterogeneous factions and interests in an enlarged America . . . assumed that the only way to protect the rights of minorities was to enlarge the political sphere and thereby divide the community into so great a number of interests and parties, that

> in the first place a majority will not be likely at the same moment to have a common interest separate from that of the whole or of the minority; and in the second place, that in case they should have such an interest, they may not be apt to unite in the pursuit of it. It was incumbent on us then to try this remedy, and with that view to frame a republican system on such a scale and in such a form as will control all the evils which have been experienced.

In *Federalist* No. 10 Madison described the multiplication of regional, religious, and economic interests, factions, and parties as the guarantor of American freedom and justice. . . . Pride of place among "these clashing interests," so essential for a just order, went to the economic interests inevitable in a complex market society. They were described in the often-quoted passage from *Federalist* No. 10:

> The most common and durable source of factions has been the various and unequal distribution of property. Those who hold and those who are without property have ever formed distinct interests in society . . . creditors . . . debtors. . . . A landed interest, a manufacturing interest, a mercantile interest, a moneyed interest. . . . The regulation of these various and interfering interests forms the principal task of modern legislation.

Government for Madison . . . was a neutral arbiter among competing interests. Indeed, in *Federalist* No. 43 Madison described the legislative task as providing "umpires"; and in a letter to George Washington he described government's role as a "disinterested and dispassionate umpire in disputes." . . .

The acceptance of modern liberal society in the Federalist camp went beyond a legitimization of the politics of interest and a conviction that government's purpose was to protect the fruits of honest industry. There was also an unabashed appreciation of modern commercial society. Secretary of Education William Bennett is quite right in his recent reminder that "commerce had a central place in the ideas of the Founders." Hamilton, for example, in *Federalist* No. 12, insisted that

> the prosperity of commerce is now perceived and acknowledged by all enlightened statesmen to be the most useful as well as the most productive source of national wealth, and has accordingly become a primary object of their political cares. By multiplying the means of gratification, by promoting the introduction and circulation of the precious metals, those darling objects

of human avarice and enterprise, it serves to vivify and invigorate the channels of industry and to make them flow with greater activity and copiousness.

Hamilton was perfectly aware that his praise of private gratification, avarice, and gain flew in the face of older ideals of civic virtue and public duty that emphasized the subordination of private interest to the public good. . . .

Many of the Antifederalists, on the other hand, were still wedded to a republican civic ideal, to the making of America into what Samuel Adams called "a Christian Sparta." The very feature of pluralist diversity in the new constitutional order that Madison saw as its great virtue, the Antifederalists saw as its major defect. For the Antifederalist "Brutus" it was absurd that the legislature "would be composed of such heterogeneous and discordant principles, as would constantly be contending with each other." A chorus of Antifederalists insisted that virtuous republican government required a small area and a homogeneous population. Patrick Henry noted that a republican form of government extending across the continent "contradicts all the experience of the world." Richard Henry Lee argued that "a free elective government cannot be extended over large territories." Robert Yates of New York saw liberty "swallowed up" because the new republic was too large. . . .

Antifederalists' fears over the absence of homogeneity in the enlarged republic were as important as the issue of size. . . .

Most Antifederalists held that a republican system required similarity of religion, manners, sentiments, and interests. They were convinced that no such sense of community could exist in an enlarged republic, that no one set of laws could work within such diversity. "We see plainly that men who come from New England are different from us," wrote Joseph Taylor, a southern Antifederalist. "Agrippa," on the other hand, declared that "the inhabitants of warmer climates are more dissolute in their manners, and less industrious, than in colder countries. . . .

A just society, for many Antifederalists, involved more than simply protecting property rights. Government had more responsibilities than merely to regulate "various and interfering interests." It was expected to promote morality, virtue, and religion. Many Antifederalists, for example, were shocked at the Constitution's totally secular tone and its general disregard of religion and morality. Equally upsetting was the lack of any religious content in Federalist arguments for the Constitution. . . .

There was, not surprisingly, also a tendency in some Antifederalist circles to see the exchange principles of commercial society, so praised by the Federalists, as threats to civic and moral virtue. Would not the self-seeking activities "of a commercial society beget luxury, the parent of inequality, the foe to virtue, and the enemy to restraint"? The spread of commerce would undermine republican simplicity, for the more a people succumbed to luxury, the more incapable they became of governing themselves. As one Antifederalist put it, speaking critically of the silence of the Constitution on questions of morality, "whatever the refinement of modern politics may inculcate, it still is certain that some degree of virtue must exist, or freedom cannot live." . . .

The problem with the Federalist position for many Antifederalists was the inadequacy of its vision of community based on mere interests and their protection. The Antifederalists suspected that such a community could not persist through what Madison called in *Federalist* No. 51 "the policy of supplying, by opposite and rival interests, the defect of better motives." A proper republican community, for these Antifederalists, required a moral consensus, which, in turn, required similarity, familiarity, and fraternity. . . .

An equally strong case can be made for the Federalists as republican theorists, and here we see full-blown the confusion of idioms, the overlapping of political languages, in 1787. There is, of course, Madison's redefinition of and identification with a republicanism that involved "the delegation of the government . . . to a small number of citizens elected by the rest" as opposed to a democracy "consisting of a small number of citizens who assemble and administer the government in person." But the crucial move in No. 10 that sets Madison firmly within the republican paradigm is his assumption that the representative function in an enlarged republic would produce officeholders who would sacrifice personal, private, and parochial interest to the public good and the public interest. What made the layers of filtration prescribed by the new constitutional order so welcome was their ultimate purpose—producing enlightened public-spirited men who found fulfillment in the quest for public good. . . . Republican government over a large country would, according to Madison,

> refine and enlarge the public views by passing them through the medium of a chosen body of citizens whose wisdom may best discern the true interest of their country, and whose patriotism and love of justice will be least likely to sacrifice it to temporary or partial considerations. Under such a regulation it may well happen that the public voice pronounced by the representatives of the people will be more consonant to the public good than if pronounced by the people themselves, convened for the purpose.

The greater number of citizens choosing representatives in a larger republic would reject "unworthy candidates" and select "men who possess the most attractive merit." A large republic and a national government would lead to "the substitution of representatives whose enlightened views and virtuous sentiments render them superior to local prejudices and to schemes of injustice." We know, given Madison's candor, what this meant.

Working out the mechanisms by which this filtration process would "refine" and "enlarge" public views and enhance the quality of the men chosen to express them preoccupied the delegates at Philadelphia. This explains their lengthy deliberations over how governing officials such as the president and senators should be selected. Indirect processes of selection would, Madison wrote in his notes, "extract from the mass of the Society the purest and noblest characters which it contains." The people involved in choosing the president or senators would be, according to Jay in *Federalist* No. 64, "the most enlightened and respectable." The Senate, Madison wrote in *Federalist* No. 63, would then be made up of "temperate and respectable" men standing for "reason, justice and truth" in the face of the people's "errors and delusions." . . .

The class focus of the Federalists' republicanism is self-evident. Their vision was of an elite corps of men in whom civic spirit and love of the general good overcame particular and narrow interest. Such men were men of substance, independence, and fame who had the leisure to devote their time to public life and the wisdom to seek the true interests of the country as opposed to the wicked projects of local and particular interests. This republicanism of Madison and the Federalists was, of course, quite consistent with the general aristocratic orientation of classical republicanism, which was, after all, the ideal of the independent, propertied, and therefore leisured citizen with time and reason to find fulfillment as *homo civicus.*

. . . Many Antifederalists, for their part, saw legislatures as most representative when their membership mirrored the complexity and diversity of society—when, in fact, each geographical unit and social rank was represented. In offering the mirror, not the filter, as the model for representation, Antifederalists seemed to be calling for the representation of every particular interest and thus appear to resemble interest-centered liberals. It was they, as well as Madison in his nonrepublican passages, who, it can be claimed, articulated the politics of interest, to be sure in a language much more democratic and participatory. The classic expression of this Antifederalist interest theory of representation came from Melancton Smith, the great antagonist of Hamilton at the New York ratification convention. He told the delegates that "the idea that naturally suggests itself to our minds, when we speak of representatives, is, that they resemble those they represent. They should be a true picture of the people, possess a knowledge of their circumstances and their wants, sympathize in all their distresses, and be disposed to seek their true interests." Directly refuting the filtration model, Smith insisted that a representative system ought not to seek "brilliant talents," but "a sameness, as to residence and interests, between the representative and his constituents." . . .

The meaning of virtue in the language of civic humanism is clear. It is the privileging of the public over the private. . . . For John Adams, "public Virtue is the only Foundation of Republics." Republican government required "a positive Passion for the public good, the public Interest . . . Superior to all private Passions."

This is not all that virtue meant. Subtle changes were taking place during the founding of the American republic in the notion of virtue, and at their core was a transvaluation of public and private. Dramatic witness is given to these changes by Madison's *Federalist* No. 44 where he depicted paper money as a threat to the republican character and spirit of the American people. That spirit, however, was neither civic nor public in nature. The values at risk were apolitical and personal. Madison feared for the sobriety, the prudence, and the industry of Americans. His concern was "the industry and morals of the people." . . .

The Antifederalists, ostensible communitarian and public-oriented foils to Madisonian interest-based liberalism, could also use this more personal idiomatic notion of virtue. . . . For the Antifederalist pamphleteer "Candidus," it was not a new constitution that America needed but a return to the virtues of "industry and frugality."

The republican tradition had, to be sure, always privileged economy over luxury. From Aristotle and Cicero through Harrington and the eighteenth-century opposition to Walpole, republican rhetoric linked a virtuous republican order to the frugal abstention from extravagance and luxury. But there is more than the all-pervasive paradigm of republicanism at work here. The inclusion of industry in the litany of virtue directs us to another inheritance, to another language in which Americans in the late eighteenth century conceptualized their personal and political universe. Americans also spoke the language of work-ethic Protestantism. . . .

Central in work-ethic Protestantism was the vision of a cosmic struggle between the forces of industry and idleness. Its texts vibrated less with the dialectic of civic virtue and self-centered commerce than with the dialectic of productive hardworking energy, on the one hand, and idle unproductive sloth, on the other. Its idiom was more personal and individualistic than public and communal. Work was a test of self-sufficiency and self-reliance, a battleground for personal salvation. All men were "called" to serve God by busying themselves in useful productive work that served both society and the individual. Daily labor was sanctified and thus was both a specific obligation and a positive moral value. The doctrine of the calling gave each man a sense of his unique self; work appropriate to each individual was imposed by God. After being called to a particular occupation, it was a man's duty to labor diligently and to avoid idleness and sloth.

The fruits of his labor were justly man's. . . . Not only was working hard and seeking to prosper the mark of a just and virtuous man and idleness a sign of spiritual corruption, but work was also the anodyne for physical corruption. Hard work disciplined the wayward and sinful impulses that lay like Satan's traces within all men. . . . Contemporary scholars such as Edmund S. Morgan, J. E. Crowley, Joyce Appleby, and John Patrick Diggins have described this alternative paradigm of Protestantism and the Protestant ethic in eighteenth-century America and with it a language quite congenial to individualistic liberalism and the capitalist spirit. . . . In this vocabulary, industry, simplicity, and frugality were the signs not only of a virtuous people but also of a free people. As one Rhode Island writer put it [in 1774], "the industrious and the frugal only will be free." . . .

Communitarian critics of an individualistic interest-based politics could also speak the Protestant language of sobriety, frugality, and industry and also locate these virtues in the particularly virtuous middle ranks of life. The Antifederalists were in good company . . . when they enlisted that language to condemn what they saw as the aristocratic character of the new constitutional order. The Federal Farmer saw the new Constitution resulting from the conflict between leveling debtors "who want a share of the property of others" and men "called aristocrats" who "grasp at all power and property." Uninvolved and victimized were the larger number of "men of middling property" who worked hard and made up the "solid, free, and independent part of the community." It was Melancton Smith, the bearer of a proud Protestant name, who best made the Protestant case for the virtuous middle against Hamilton's aristocratic Constitution at the New York ratifying convention. It was an evil Constitution, Smith claimed, because it restricted representation to the idle few, excluding those who were morally superior. What is crucial to note is that virtue here is apolitical and noncivic:

> Those in middling circumstances, have less temptation—they are inclined by habit and the company with whom they associate, to set bounds to their passions and appetites—if this is not sufficient, the want of means to gratify them will be a restraint—they are obliged to employ their time in their respective callings—hence the substantial yeomanry of the country are more temperate, of better morals and less ambitious than the great.

In the political discourse of 1787 there was . . . a fourth paradigm at work, the state-centered language of power. It, too, reached back into the classical world, to the great lawgivers and founders Solon and Lycurgus, and to the imperial ideal of Alexander and Julius Caesar. Not republican city states but empire and, much later, the nation-state were its institutional units. . . .

In *Federalist* No. 1 Hamilton proclaimed his "enlightened zeal" for "the energy" and "vigor of government." His achievement, and that of the other young men at Philadelphia, was the creation of the American state. Some decades later, Hegel could find nothing in America that he recognized as the "state." But that was in comparison with established European states, and in that sense he was quite right. What little there was of an American state, however, was crafted by Hamilton, Madison, and the framers of the Constitution, who began their work *de nouveau,* from nothing. There was no royal household whose offices would become state bureaus, no royal army from a feudal past to be transformed into an expression of the state's reality.

It was the experience of war that shaped the vision of America's state-builders. The war against Britain provided them with a continental and national experience that replaced the states-centered focus of the pre-1776 generation. A remarkable number of framers of the Constitution either served in the Continental army or were diplomats or administrative officials for the Confederation or members of the Continental Congress. Indeed, thirty-nine of the fifty-five delegates to the Constitutional Convention had sat in the Congress. . . . Most of the principal Federalists had forged their identity in service to the war and the national cause and in dealing with the individual states' reluctance to assist that continental effort. . . . While most of the Antifederalists were states-centered politicians whose heroics took place before 1776, most of the Federalists were shaped by the need to realize the national interest in an international war. Their common bond was an experience that transcended and dissolved state boundaries. . . .

The lack of such an American state was profoundly dispiriting to Hamilton. In *Federalist* No. 85 he declared that "a nation without a national government is, in my view, a sad spectacle." In No. 15 he was even more distraught: "We have neither troops, nor treasury, nor government for the

Union . . . our ambassadors abroad are the mere pageants of mimic sovereignty." . . .

All of the power-centered paradigm's euphemisms for power— "strength," "vigor," "energy"—come together in Hamilton's conception of the presidential office. The presidency was the heart of the new American state for Hamilton, just as the monarch or chief magistrate was for older European nation-states. . . . Had he not argued at Philadelphia for a life term for presidents? Short of that, in *Federalist* No. 72 he supported the president's eligibility for indefinite reelection. How else, he asked, would a president be able to "plan and undertake extensive and arduous enterprises for the public benefit?" The president was the energetic builder of an energetic state.

Hamilton was preoccupied with the interrelationship between commerce, state power, and international politics. A powerful state in his vision was a commercial state. In the competitive international system, nation-states sought to improve or protect their commercial strength, which led inevitably to wars. Powerful states therefore needed standing armies and strong navies. . . .

But Hamilton did not want to build an American state with all that statehood required—a financial and commercial infrastructure, energetic leadership, and powerful military forces—merely to allow America to hold its own in a world system characterized by conflict, competition, and clashing power. He had a grander vision for the American state, a call to greatness. In *Federalist* No. 11 Hamilton wrote of "what this country is capable of becoming," of a future glory for America of "striking and animating kind." Under a properly "vigorous national government, the natural strength and resources of the country, directed to a common interest, would baffle all the combinations of European jealousy to restrain our growth." If Americans would only "concur in erecting one great American system," the American state would be "superior to the control of all transatlantic force or influence, and able to dictate the terms of the connection between the old and the new world." In the face of a vigorous American state Europe would cease to be "mistress of the world." America would become ascendant in the Western Hemisphere. . . .

We must not lose sight of the other side in the "great national discussion," however. Hamilton's discourse of power with its vision of an imperial American state attracted the fire of Antifederalists like one of Franklin's lightning rods. It was Patrick Henry who most angrily and most movingly repudiated the Federalist state. Henry's American spirit was Tom Paine's. With the Federalist state America would lose its innocence, and "splendid government" would become its badge, its dress. On the ruins of paradise would be built, if not the palaces of kings, then armies and navies and mighty empires. At the Virginia ratifying convention Henry evoked a different language of politics.

> The American spirit has fled from hence; it has gone to regions where it has never been expected; it has gone to the people of France, in search of a splendid government, a strong, energetic government. Shall we imitate

the example of those nations who have gone from a simple to a splendid government? Are those nations more worthy of our imitation? What can make an adequate satisfaction to them for the loss they have suffered in attaining such a government, for the loss of their liberty? If we admit this consolidated government, it will be because we like a great, splendid one. Some way or other we must be a great and mighty empire; we must have an army, and a navy, and a number of things. When the American spirit was in its youth, the language of America was different; liberty, sir, was then the primary object.

What was Madison's relationship to the discourse of power and the Hamiltonian state? Madison was a state-builder, too, but his state was quite different from Hamilton's, and upon these differences a good deal of American politics in the next two decades, as well as to this day, would turn. Madison and Hamilton were in agreement on many things. They agreed on the need to establish an effective unified national government. They agreed on the serious threats to personal property rights posed by the state legislatures and on the role that a central government would play in protecting these rights. They agreed on the need to have the central government run by worthy, enlightened, and deliberative men. They agreed on the Constitution as necessary to provide the essential framework for commercial development through the creation of a national market, public credit, uniform currency, and the protection of contract. To be sure, Madison's vision tilted toward agrarian capitalism and Hamilton's toward manufactures and commerce. Where they markedly disagreed, however, was in giving positive, assertive power, "energy," and "vigor" to the state. . . .

Madison saw the nation-state as necessary only to protect private rights and thus ensure justice. . . . Madison saw the central government providing an arena for competitive power, where the private bargaining of free men, groups, and interests would take place, and the state would define no goals of its own other than ensuring the framework for orderly economic life. All the state would do was regulate "the various and interfering interests" or, as Madison put it to Washington in straightforward Lockean terms, be an impartial umpire in disputes. Energy in politics for Madison would come from individuals and groups seeking their own immediate goals, not from an energetic state seeking its own heroic ends. . . .

Madison's limited Federalist state might well appear meek and tame set next to Hamilton's energetic and vigorous state, but it was a matter of perspective. To the Antifederalists, even Madison's state, limited as it was by checks and balances and its cool men resisting the temptations of lawmaking, seemed a monstrous betrayal of the Revolution and its spirit. The Constitution could be seen, then, as the last, albeit Thermidorean, act of the American Revolution. Like most revolutions, the American began as a repudiation of the state, of power, and of authority in the name of liberty. Like most revolutions, it ended with a stronger state, the revival of authority, and the taming of liberty's excesses.

Slavery and the Constitution

DONALD G. NIEMAN

During the decades following the Revolution, ideals of liberty and equality came squarely into conflict with the realities of slavery and racial subordination, systems supported by powerful economic interests and entrenched social mores. When the Revolution began, slavery existed in all of the American colonies. Slaves were most numerous in the South, where they were substantial minorities (thirty to forty-two percent) in Virginia, North Carolina, and Maryland and a majority (sixty percent) in South Carolina. Slave agricultural laborers and craftsmen were essential to the plantation economies of these states. Even in the North, where they ranged from less than two percent of the population in Massachusetts to more than ten percent in New York, slaves played an important economic role because of the general shortage of labor. Moreover, white attitudes toward blacks, which had taken root during the previous century, reinforced slavery and the system of racial hierarchy which it created. . . .

Although they faced formidable obstacles, antislavery advocates made great strides toward implementing the truths proclaimed self-evident by the Declaration of Independence. They achieved their greatest success in the North where there were few slaveholders and blacks were not numerous. Vermont, with a slave population of fifty, quickly abolished slavery in its 1777 Constitution In Massachusetts, the Supreme Court of Judicature used the equalitarian language of the state's 1780 constitution ("all men are born free and equal") to undermine the institution in the early 1780s. Northern opposition to abolition was not always so completely or quickly overcome, however. Most northern states passed post-nati abolition laws that stipulated that slaves born prior to enactment of the legislation would remain in slavery while those born thereafter would be freed when they reached adulthood. Pennsylvania (1780), Connecticut (1784), and Rhode Island (1784) quickly passed post-nati bills, but New York (1799) and New Jersey (1804) acted only after twenty years of pressure from well-organized antislavery groups. The hard-earned victory over slavery in the North was significant because it transformed slavery from a national to a sectional institution.

Southerners also subjected slavery to criticism. Baptists, Methodists, and Quakers, groups which drew members primarily from nonslaveholders, led the way. Although slaveholders refrained from calling for abolition, some acknowledged that slavery violated the ideals of the Revolution, supported legislation permitting individual owners to free their slaves, and manumitted some or all of their own slaves. In Virginia, where private manumission was widespread, the free black population grew from 2,000 in 1782 to 20,000 in 1800. Nevertheless, the private acts of well-intentioned slaveholders did not

Abridged from *Promises to Keep: African-Americans and the Constitutional Order, 1776 to the Present* by Donald G. Nieman, pp. 8–14. Copyright © 1991 by Oxford University Press, Inc. Reprinted by permission.

imperil the institution; 345,000 Virginia blacks remained in bondage in 1800. Indeed, slavery was the social and economic foundation of the planter class, the most influential group in Virginia and the rest of the South, and it was economically important to tens of thousands of farmers who owned one or two slaves. Moreover, because blacks constituted between thirty and sixty percent of the population of the southern states, even nonslaveholders— conditioned by racism to believe that blacks were incapable of freedom— equated abolition with social chaos. As a result, no southern legislature seriously considered even a gradual emancipation law during the late eighteenth century. . . .

[Still,] revolutionary principles did occasionally prevail over racial prejudice and class interest. The Constitutional Convention, however, was not one of those occasions. The delegates who met in Philadelphia during the summer of 1787 believed that the weakness of the existing national government had created an economic and political crisis that threatened America's republican experiment. Most agreed that the Articles of Confederation was the root of the problem. A new Constitution creating a strong national government was imperative in order to achieve economic recovery, promote prosperity, cope with threats from abroad, reestablish the public credit, and restrain the states from interfering with property rights. Although many delegates expressed reservations about slavery and a few passionately denounced it, there was little likelihood that the convention would take meaningful antislavery action. Constitutional reform and continued union were impossible without the support of southerners, and southern delegates were unwilling to accept constitutional provisions that threatened the economic well-being of the South and the existence of its powerful planter class. Consequently, the price of constitutional reform was northern concessions on the slavery issue.

Southerners won a significant victory in debates on representation in Congress. Although they failed to have slaves counted fully for purposes of determining representation, southern delegates did win acceptance of a provision that apportioned representatives among the states "according to their respective Numbers, which shall be determined by adding the whole Number of free Persons . . . and . . . three fifths of all other Persons." Because these "other persons" were slaves, northerners objected to the three-fifths clause, charging that it allowed southerners to use property to increase their clout in the national government. Southerners, however, insisted on the extra political security that the three-fifths clause conferred. North Carolina's William Davie, for example, explained that he "was sure that N. Carolina would never confederate on any terms that did not rate them [slaves] at least 3/5. If the Eastern [i.e., northern] States meant . . . to exclude them altogether the business was at an end." In the end, northern delegates accepted the three-fifths clause as the price of a strengthened national government that they deemed vital to their interests.

Inclusion of the three-fifths clause rested solely on considerations of sectional power and had nothing to do with whether slaves—who could not vote—would be represented in the national government or whether they were considered persons in the eyes of the law. The South's share of population and therefore seats in the House of Representatives increased from forty-one percent when only free persons were counted to more than forty-six percent under the three-fifths formula. This increased the region's strength in the House and also in presidential politics because a state's presidential electors were equal to the number of its senators and representatives. Consequently, it became an important tool that southerners would use during the next seventy years to bend national policy to their will and make the Constitution a proslavery document.

The convention also bowed to the South on the infamous slave trade. In early August, after the convention had been in session for more than two months, delegates considered a controversial proposal denying Congress authority to enact "prohibitions on ye Importations of such inhabitants or people as the sevl. States think proper to admit" or "duties by way of such prohibition." Representatives from South Carolina and Georgia, eager to protect the flow of slaves from Africa, were the principal supporters of this measure. A number of northern delegates, however, objected because it protected the most brutal aspects of slavery: tearing Africans away from their homeland; crowding them into the hot, foul holds of ships where they suffered unspeakably and many died; and selling them like cattle at auctions in America. Gouverneur Morris, the voluble Pennsylvania delegate, charged that it protected "the inhabitant of Georgia and S.C. who goes to the Coast of Africa, and in defiance of the most sacred laws of humanity tears away his fellow creatures from their dearest connections and damns them to the most cruel bondages." These northerners were joined by delegates from Maryland and Virginia who not only regarded the slave trade as immoral, but represented states that had a surplus of slaves and stood to benefit from the higher prices that would result from closing the African trade.

Although debate became acrimonious, delegates accepted a compromise. New Englanders agreed to support an obliquely worded provision prohibiting congressional interference with the slave trade for twenty years: "The Migration or Importation of such Persons as any of the States now existing shall think proper to admit, shall not be prohibited by the Congress" prior to 1808. In return, the South Carolinians supported deletion of a provision requiring two-thirds majorities for Congress to pass commercial regulations. The New Englanders thus abandoned their scruples against the slave trade in order to win a concession vital to northern commercial interests. Connecticut's Oliver Ellsworth captured the spirit of pragmatism that paved the way for the compromise: "let every State import what it pleases. The morality or wisdom of slavery are considerations belonging to the States themselves— What enriches a part enriches the whole, and the States are the best judges of their particular interest."

On the heels of the slave trade compromise, the convention quickly agreed to another southern demand. Slaveholding delegates in the convention knew that their slaves, far from being docile, frequently ran away, and they sought a constitutional remedy. Pierce Butler and Charles Cotesworth Pinckney of South Carolina moved adoption of a clause requiring "fugitive slaves and servants to be delivered up like criminals." The following day, delegates adopted the Constitution's fugitive slave clause with little debate. As finally approved, it was an indirect and obscurely worded guarantee: "No Person held to Service or Labour in one State, under the Laws thereof, escaping to another, shall, in consequence of any Law or Regulation therein, be discharged from such Service or Labor, but shall be delivered up on Claim of the Party to whom such Service or Labor may be due."

Delegates conferred perhaps the greatest Constitutional protection on slavery when they granted Congress enumerated powers rather than giving it plenary legislative authority. They did not intend to limit Congress to exercise of those powers expressly listed in the Constitution. Indeed, the framers gave it authority "to make all laws which shall be necessary and proper" for carrying out any of the enumerated powers. This broadened national authority and gave Congress considerable flexibility without threatening slavery. The nature of Congress's enumerated powers precluded it from outlawing slavery or from interfering with its day-to-day operation in any state that chose to make it lawful. The framers, concerned more with union than with liberty, thus made freedom a matter of local option.

When the final gavel fell at Philadelphia, delegates had created a framework of government that tacitly recognized slavery, offered protection to it, and, most important, strengthened the hand of its advocates in the national government. Yet it would be wrong to view the Constitution of 1787 as uniformly and consistently proslavery; the framers created an open-ended document that, while favorable to slavery in many respects, contained a reservoir of antislavery potential. Because many of the framers believed, with James Madison, that it would be "wrong to admit in the Constitution the idea that there could be property in men," they refrained from including the words "slave" or "slavery" and thus refused to give explicit recognition to the institution. Moreover, the Constitution did not require the national government to promote slavery or, as southerners would subsequently argue, refrain from any action hostile to it. For example, the slave trade clause prohibited Congress from interfering with the importation of slaves into the original states until 1808. This suggested that after that date Congress could use its power to regulate commerce (a power denied it in the Articles) to end the trade. Indeed, it did so at the earliest possible moment. Moreover, the fugitive slave clause did not require or explicitly authorize Congress to help slaveowners recapture runaways. The wording of the clause and its placement in Article IV, Section 2 (which deals with interstate relations) suggested merely that states ought not prevent slaveowners from reclaiming fugitives.

Several other features of the Constitution mitigated the concessions to slaveholders. Because Americans had begun by the late eighteenth century to migrate to the Trans-Appalachian West, the future of slavery depended on whether it moved with the settlers. The Northwest Ordinance of 1787, passed by the Confederation Congress as the Constitutional Convention met, prohibited slavery in the territories north of the Ohio River. This, coupled with the postrevolutionary emancipation acts of the northern state legislatures, was an important stride toward making slavery a local—a peculiar—institution rather than the national institution it had been in 1776. The Constitution gave Congress authority to carry out the spirit of the Northwest Ordinance and further circumscribe slavery. It empowered Congress "to make all needful Rules and Regulations respecting the Territories," thus conferring authority to exclude slavery from the western territories, thereby containing it in the southeast. Moreover, the Bill of Rights, the ten amendments which became part of the Constitution in 1791, proclaimed a host of fundamental liberties—freedom of speech, the right to jury trial, protection against unreasonable search and seizure, the guarantee of due process of law—which were hostile to the arbitrary power essential to maintain slavery.

This is not to suggest . . . that the framers were closet abolitionists who created a thoroughly antislavery Constitution. They made important concessions to slavery that proslavery advocates later effectively exploited. Nevertheless, the antislavery sensibilities of many delegates placed limits on how far they would go to protect slavery. Northern delegates made concessions to slaveholders' demands, but they did not seek to create a document that would promote slavery. Moreover, the framers did not carve the Constitution in stone. They wrote it in general language that was susceptible to a variety of interpretations. And they created a document that was inherently political because it defined governmental authority. Of necessity, such a document would evolve as rival political forces mustered their strength to shape the general language of the Constitution to their ends, whether proslavery or antislavery.

The Constitution and the "Genius" of the People

ALFRED F. YOUNG

On June 18, 1787, about three weeks into the Constitutional Convention at Philadelphia, Alexander Hamilton delivered a six-hour address that was easily the longest and most conservative the Convention would hear. Gouverneur Morris, a delegate from Pennsylvania, thought it was "the most able and impressive he had ever heard."

Beginning with the premise that "all communities divide themselves into the few and the many," "the wealthy well born" and "the people," Hamilton added the corollary that the "people are turbulent and changing; they seldom judge or determine right." Moving through history, the delegate from New York developed his ideal for a national government that would protect the few from "the imprudence of democracy" and guarantee "stability and permanence": a president and senate indirectly elected for life ("to serve during good behavior") to balance a house directly elected by a popular vote every three years. This "elective monarch" would have an absolute veto over laws passed by Congress. And the national government would appoint the gov-

Excerpts from "The Framers of the Constitution and the 'Genius' of the People" by Alfred F. Young, in *Radical History Review* 42 (1988), pp. 8–18.

ernors of the states, who in turn would have the power to veto any laws by the state legislatures.

If others quickly saw a resemblance in all of this to the King, House of Lords and House of Commons of Great Britain, with the states reduced to colonies ruled by royal governors, they were not mistaken. The British constitution, in Hamilton's view, remained "the best model the world has ever produced."

Three days later a delegate reported that Hamilton's proposals "had been praised by everybody," but "he has been supported by none." Acknowledging that his plan "went beyond the ideas of most members," Hamilton said he had brought it forward not "as a thing attainable by us, but as a model which we ought to approach as near as possible." When he signed the Constitution the framers finally agreed to on September 17, 1787, Hamilton could accurately say, "no plan was more remote from his own."

Why did the framers reject a plan so many admired? To ask this question is to go down a dark path into the heart of the Constitution few of its celebrants care to take. We have heard so much in our elementary and high school civics books about the "great compromises" within the Convention— between the large states and the small states, between the slaveholders and non-slaveholders, between North and South—that we have missed the much larger accommodation that was taking place between the delegates as a whole at the Convention and what they called "the people out of doors."

The Convention was unmistakably an elite body, . . . weighted with merchants, slaveholding planters and "monied men" who loaned money at interest. Among them were numerous lawyers and college graduates in a country where most men and only a few women had the rudiments of a formal education. They were far from a cross section of the four million or so Americans of that day, most of whom were farmers or artisans, fishermen or seamen, indentured servants or laborers, half of whom were women and about 600,000 of whom were African-American slaves.

Why did this elite reject Hamilton's plan that many of them praised? James Madison, the Constitution's chief architect, had the nub of the matter. The Constitution was "intended for the ages." To last it had to conform to the "genius" of the American people. "Genius" was a word eighteenth-century political thinkers used to mean spirit: we might say character or underlying values.

James Wilson, second only to Madison in his influence at Philadelphia, elaborated on the idea. "The British government cannot be our model. We have no materials for a similar one. Our manners, our law, the abolition of entail and primogeniture," which made for a more equal distribution of property among sons, "the whole genius of the people, are opposed to it."

This was long-range political philosophy. There was a short-range political problem that moved other realistic delegates in the same direction. Called together to revise the old Articles of Confederation, the delegates instead decided to scrap it and frame an entirely new constitution. It would have to be submitted to the people for ratification, most likely to conventions elected especially for the purpose. Repeatedly, conservatives recoiled from extreme proposals for which they knew they could not win popular support.

In response to a proposal to extend the federal judiciary into the states, Pierce Butler, a South Carolina planter, argued, "the people will not bear such innovations. The states will revolt at such encroachments." His assumption was "we must follow the example of Solomon, who gave the Athenians not the best government he could devise but the best they would receive."

The suffrage debate epitomized this line of thinking. Gouverneur Morris, Hamilton's admirer, proposed that the national government limit voting for the House to men who owned a freehold, i.e. a substantial farm, or its equivalent. "Give the vote to people who have no property and they will sell them to the rich who will be able to buy them," he said with some prescience. George Mason, author of Virginia's Bill of Rights, was aghast. "Eight or nine states have extended the right of suffrage beyond the freeholders. What will people there say if they should be disfranchised?"

Benjamin Franklin, the patriarch, speaking for one of the few times in the convention, paid tribute to "the lower class of freemen" who should not be disfranchised. James Wilson explained, "it would be very hard and disagreeable for the same person" who could vote for representatives for the state legislatures "to be excluded from a vote for this in the national legislature." Nathaniel Gorham, a Boston merchant, returned to the guiding principle: "the people will never allow" existing rights to suffrage to be abridged. "We must consult their rooted prejudices if we expect their concurrence in our propositions."

The result? Morris' proposal was defeated and the convention decided that whoever each state allowed to vote for its own assembly could vote for the House. It was a compromise that left the door open and in a matter of decades allowed states to introduce universal white male suffrage.

Clearly there was a process of accommodation at work here. The popular movements of the Revolutionary Era were a presence at the Philadelphia Convention even if they were not present. The delegates, one might say, were haunted by ghosts, symbols of the broadly based movements elites had confronted in the making of the Revolution from 1765 to 1775, in waging the war from 1775 to 1781 and in the years since 1781 within their own states.

The first was the ghost of Thomas Paine, the most influential radical democrat of the Revolutionary Era. In 1776 Paine's pamphlet *Common Sense* (which sold at least 150,000 copies), in arguing for independence, rejected not only King George III but the principle of monarchy and the so-called checks and balances of the unwritten English constitution. In its place he offered a vision of a democratic government in which a single legislature would be supreme, the executive minimal, and representatives would be elected from small districts by a broad electorate for short terms so they could "return and mix again with the voters." John Adams considered *Common Sense* too "democratical," without even an attempt at "mixed government" that would balance "democracy" with "aristocracy."

The second ghost was that of Abraham Yates, a member of the state senate of New York typical of the new men who had risen to power in the 1780s in the state legislatures. We have forgotten him; Hamilton, who was very conscious of him, called him "an old Booby." He had begun as a shoemaker and was a self-taught lawyer and warm foe of the landlord aristocracy of the Hudson Valley which Hamilton had married into. As James Madison identified the "vices of the political system of the United States" in a memorandum in 1787, the Abraham Yateses were the number-one problem. The state legislatures had "an itch for paper money" laws, laws that prevented foreclosure on farm mortgages, and tax laws that soaked the rich. As Madison saw it, this meant that "debtors defrauded their creditors" and "the landed interest has borne hard on the mercantile interest." This, too, is what Hamilton had in mind when he spoke of the "depredations which the democratic spirit is apt to make on property" and what others meant by the "excess of democracy" in the states.

The third ghost was a very fresh one—Daniel Shays. In 1786 Shays, a captain in the Revolution, led a rebellion of debtor farmers in western Massachusetts which the state quelled with its own somewhat unreliable militia. There were "combustibles in every state," as George Washington put it, raising the specter of "Shaysism." This Madison enumerated among the "vices" of the system as "a want of guaranty to the states against internal violence." Worse still, Shaysites in many states were turning to the political system to elect their own kind. If they succeeded they would produce legal Shaysism, a danger for which the elites had no remedy.

The fourth ghost we can name was the ghost of Thomas Peters, although he had a thousand other names. In 1775, Peters, a Virginia slave, responded to a plea by the British to fight in their army and win their freedom. He served in an "Ethiopian Regiment," some of whose members bore the emblem "Liberty to Slaves" on their uniforms. After the war the British transported Peters and several thousand escaped slaves to Nova Scotia from whence Peters eventually led a group to return to Africa and the colony of Sierra Leone, a long odyssey to freedom. Eighteenth-century slaveholders, with no illusions about happy or contented slaves, were haunted by the specter of slaves in arms.

During the Revolutionary Era elites divided in response to these varied threats from below. One group, out of fear of "the mob" and then "the rabble in arms," embraced the British and became active Loyalists. After the war most of them went into exile. Another group who became patriots never lost their obsession with coercing popular movements. . . .

Far more important, however, were those patriot leaders who adopted a strategy of "swimming with a stream which it is impossible to stem." This was the metaphor of Robert R. Livingston, Jr., . . . a gentleman with a large tenanted estate in New York. Men of his class had to learn to "yield to the torrent if they hoped to direct its course."

Livingston and his group were able to shape New York's constitution, which some called a perfect blend of "aristocracy" and "democracy." John Hancock, the richest merchant in New England, had mastered this kind of politics and emerged as the most popular politician in Massachusetts. In Maryland Charles Carroll, a wealthy planter, instructed his anxious father about the need to "submit to partial losses" because "no great revolution can happen in a state without revolutions or mutations of private property. If we can save a third of our personal estate and all of our lands and Negroes, I shall think ourselves well off."

The major leaders at the Constitutional Convention in 1787 were heirs to both traditions: coercion and accommodation—Hamilton and Gouverneur Morris to the former, James Madison and James Wilson much more to the latter.

They all agreed on coercion to slay the ghosts of Daniel Shays and Thomas Peters. The Constitution gave the national goverment the power to "suppress insurrections" and protect the states from "domestic violence." There would be a national army under the command of the president, and authority to nationalize the state militias and suspend the right of habeas corpus in "cases of rebellion or invasion." In 1794 Hamilton, as secretary of the treasury, would exercise such powers fully (and needlessly) to suppress the Whiskey Rebellion in western Pennsylvania.

Southern slaveholders correctly interpreted the same powers as available to shackle the ghost of Thomas Peters. As it turned out, Virginia would not need a federal army to deal with Gabriel Prosser's insurrection in 1800 or Nat Turner's rebellion in 1830, but a federal army would capture John Brown after his raid at Harpers Ferry in 1859.

But how to deal with the ghosts of Thomas Paine and Abraham Yates? Here Madison and Wilson blended coercion with accommodation. They had three solutions to the threat of democratic majorities in the states.

Their first was clearly coercive. Like Hamilton, Madison wanted some kind of national veto over the state legislatures. He got several very specific curbs on the states written into fundamental law: no state could "emit" paper money or pass "laws impairing the obligation of contracts." Wilson was so overjoyed with these two clauses that he argued that if they alone "were inserted in the Constitution I think they would be worth our adoption."

But Madison considered the overall mechanism adopted to curb the states "short of the mark." The Constitution, laws and treaties were the "supreme law of the land" and ultimately a federal court could declare state laws unconstitutional. But this, Madison lamented, would only catch "mischiefs" after the fact. Thus they had clipped the wings of Abraham Yates but he could still fly.

The second solution to the problem of the states was decidedly democratic. They wanted to do an end-run around the state legislatures. The Articles of Confederation, said Madison, rested on "the pillars" of the state legislatures who elected delegates to Congress. The "great fabric to be raised would be more stable and durable if it should rest on the solid grounds of the people themselves"; hence, there would be popular elections to the House.

Wilson altered only the metaphor. He was for "raising the federal pyramid to a considerable altitude and for that reason wanted to give it as broad a base as possible." They would slay the ghost of Abraham Yates with the ghost of Thomas Paine.

This was risky business. They would reduce the risk by keeping the House of Representatives small. Under a ratio of one representative for every 30,000 people, the first house would have only 65 members; in 1776 Thomas Paine had suggested 390. But still, the House would be elected every two years, and with each state allowed to determine its own qualifications for voting, there was no telling who might end up in Congress.

There was also a risk in Madison's third solution to the problem of protecting propertied interests from democratic majorities: "extending the sphere" of government. Prevailing wisdom held that a republic could only succeed in a small geographic area; to rule an "extensive" country, some kind of despotism was considered inevitable.

Madison turned this idea on its head in his since famous *Federalist* essay No. 10. In a small republic, he argued, it was relatively easy for a majority to gang up on a particular "interest." "Extend the sphere," he wrote, and "you take in a greater variety of parties and interests." Then it would be more difficult for a majority "to discover their own strength and to act in unison with each other."

This was a prescription for a non-colonial empire that would expand across the continent, taking in new states as it dispossessed the Indians. The risk was there was no telling how far the "democratic" or "leveling" spirit might go in such likely would-be states as frontier Vermont, Kentucky and Tennessee.

In the spectrum of state constitutions adopted in the Revolutionary era, the federal Constitution of 1787 was, like New York's, somewhere between "aristocracy" and "democracy." It therefore should not surprise us—although it has eluded many modern critics of the Constitution—that in the contest over ratification in 1787–1788, the democratic minded were divided.

Among agrarian democrats there was a gut feeling that the Constitution was the work of an old class enemy. "These lawyers and men of learning and monied men," argued Amos Singletary, a working farmer at the Massachusetts ratifying convention, "expect to be managers of this Constitution and get all the power and all the money into their own hands and then will swallow up all of us little folks . . . just as the whale swallowed up Jonah."

Democratic leaders like Melancton Smith of New York focused on the small size of the proposed House. Arguing from Paine's premise that the members of the legislature should "resemble those they represent," Smith feared that "a substantial yeoman of sense and discernment will hardly ever be chosen" and the government "will fall into the hands of the few and the great." Urban democrats, on the other hand, including a majority of the mechanics and tradesmen of the major cities who in the Revolution had been a bulwark of Paineite radicalism, were generally enthusiastic about the Constitution. They were impelled by their urgent stake in a stronger national government that would advance ocean-going commerce and protect American manufacturers from competition. But they would not have been as ardent about the new frame of government without its saving graces. It clearly preserved their rights to suffrage. And the process of ratification, like the Constitution itself, guaranteed them a voice. As early as 1776 the

New York Committee of Mechanics held it as "a right which God has given them in common with all men to judge whether it be consistent with their interest to accept or reject a constitution."

Mechanics turned out en masse in the parades celebrating ratification, marching trade by trade. The slogans and symbols they carried expressed their political ideals. In New York the upholsterers had a float with an elegant "Federal Chair of State" flanked by the symbols of Liberty and Justice that they identified with the Constitution. In Philadelphia the brick-layers put on their banner "Both buildings and rulers are the work of our hands."

Democrats who were skeptical found it easier to come over because of the Constitution's redeeming features. Thomas Paine, off in Paris, considered the Constitution "a copy, though not quite as base as the original, of the form of the British government." He had always opposed a single executive and he objected to the "long duration of the Senate." But he was so convinced of "the absolute necessity" of a stronger federal government that "I would have voted for it myself had I been in America or even for a worse, rather than have none." It was crucial to Paine that there was an amending process, the means of "remedying its defects by the same appeal to the people by which it was to be established."

In drafting the Constitution in 1787 the framers, self-styled Federalists, made their first accommodation with the "genius" of the people. In campaigning for its ratification in 1788 they made their second. At the outset, the conventions in the key states—Massachusetts, New York and Virginia—either had an anti-Federalist majority or were closely divided. To swing over a small group of "antis" in each state, Federalists had to promise that they would consider amendments. This was enough to secure ratification by narrow margins in Massachusetts, 187 to 168; in New York, 30 to 27; and in Virginia, 89 to 79.

What the anti-Federalists wanted were dozens of changes in the structure of the government that would cut back national power over the states, curb the powers of the presidency as well as protect individual liberties. What they got was far less. But in the first Congress in 1789, James Madison, true to his pledge, considered all the amendments and shepherded 12 amendments through both houses. The first two of these failed in the states; one would have enlarged the House. The 10 that were ratified by December 1791 were what we have since called the Bill of Rights, protecting freedom of expression and the rights of the accused before the law. Abraham Yates considered them "trivial and unimportant." But other democrats looked on them much more favorably. In time the limited meaning of freedom of speech in the First Amendment was broadened far beyond the framers' original intent. Later popular movements thought of the Bill of Rights as an essential part of the "constitutional" and "republican" rights that belonged to the people.

There is a cautionary tale here that surely goes beyond the process of framing and adopting the Constitution and Bill of Rights from 1787 to 1791. The Constitution was as democratic as it was because of the influence of popular movements that were a presence, even if not present. The losers helped shape the results. We owe the Bill of Rights to the opponents of the Constitution, as we do many other features in the Constitution put in to anticipate opposition.

In American history popular movements often shaped elites, especially in times of crisis when elites were concerned with the "system." Elites have often divided in response to such threats and according to their perception of the "genius" of the people. Some have turned to coercion, others to accommodation. We run serious risk if we ignore this distinction.

⌗ *F U R T H E R   R E A D I N G*

Lance Banning, "Republican Ideology and the Triumph of the Constitution, 1789–1793," *William & Mary Quarterly,* 3rd ser., 21 (1974): 167–188

Charles A. Beard, *An Economic Interpretation of the Constitution of the United States* (1913, 1935)

Richard Beeman et al., eds., *Beyond Confederation: Origins of the Constitution and American National Identity* (1987)

Lee Benson, *Turner and Beard: American Historical Writing Reconsidered* (1960)

Kenneth R. Bowling, " 'A Tub to a Whale': The Founding Fathers and the Adoption of the Federal Bill of Rights," *Journal of the Early Republic* 8 (1988): 233–252

Robert Brown, *Charles Beard and the Constitution: A Critical Analysis of "An Economic Interpretation of the Constitution"* (1956)

Richard Buel, *Securing the Revolution: Ideology in American Politics, 1789–1815* (1972)

Saul Cornell, "Aristocracy Assailed: The Ideology of Backcountry Anti-Federalism," *Journal of American History* 76 (1990): 1148–1172

Martin Diamond, "Democracy and *The Federalist:* A Reevaluation of the Framers' Intent," *American Political Science Review* 53 (1959):52–68

Stanley Elkins and Eric McKitrick, "The Founding Fathers: Young Men of the Revolution," *Political Science Quarterly* 76 (1961): 181–216

E. James Ferguson, *The Power of the Purse: A History of American Public Finance, 1776–1790* (1961)

William W. Freehling, "The Founding Fathers and Slavery," *American Historical Review* 77 (1972): 81–93

Michael Allen Gillespie and Michael Lienesch, *Ratifying the Constitution* (1989)

Robert A. Goldwin and William A. Schambra, eds., *How Democratic Is the Constitution?* (1980)

Merrill Jensen, *The Making of the American Constitution* (1964)

John Kaminski and Richard Leffler, *Federalists and Antifederalists: The Debate on the Ratification of the Constitution* (1989)

Michael G. Kammen, *A Machine That Would Go of Itself: The Constitution in American Culture* (1986)

——, *The Origins of the American Constitution: A Documentary History* (1986)

Cecilia Kenyon, "Men of Litle Faith: The Antifederalists on the Nature of Republican Government," *William & Mary Quarterly,* 3rd ser., 12 (1955): 3–43

Leonard Levy, ed., *Essays on the Making of the Constitution* (1969, 1987)

——, *Legacy of Suppression: Freedom of Speech and Press in Early American History* (1960)

Staughton Lynd, *Class Conflict, Slavery, and the U.S. Constitution: Ten Essays* (1968)

Forrest McDonald, *Novus Ordo Seclorum: The Intellectual Origins of the Constitution* (1985)

——, *E Pluribus Unum: The Formation of the American Republic, 1776–1790* (1965)

————, *We the People: The Economic Origins of the Constitution* (1958)

Jackson Turner Main, *The Antifederalists: Critics of the Constitution, 1781–1788* (1961)

John C. Miller, *The Federalist Era, 1789–1801* (1960)

David E. Narrett and Joyce S. Goldberg, eds., *Essays on Liberty and Federalism: The Shaping of the U.S. Constitution* (1988)

Thomas Pangle, *The Origins of Modern Republicanism: The Moral Vision of the American Founders and the Philosophy of Locke* (1988)

J. G. A. Pocock, ed., *Three British Revolutions: 1641, 1688, 1776* (1980)

J. R. Pole, *Political Representation in England and the Origins of the American Republic* (1966)

John P. Roche, "The Founding Fathers: A Reform Caucus in Action," *American Political Science Review* 55 (1961): 799–816

Clinton Rossiter, *1787: The Grand Convention* (1965)

Robert A. Rutland, *The Ordeal of the Constitution: The Antifederalists and the Ratification Struggle of 1787–1788* (1966)

————, *The Birth of the Bill of Rights, 1776–1791* (1955)

Bernard Schwartz, *The Bill of Rights: A Documentary History* (1971)

Robert Shalhope, "Republicanism and Early American Historiography," *William & Mary Quarterly,* 3rd ser., 39 (1982): 334–356

Herbert Storing, ed., *The Complete Anti-Federalist* (1981)

William & Mary Quarterly, 3rd ser., 44 (July 1987), special issue on the U.S. Constitution

Garry Wills, *Explaining America: The Federalist* (1981)

Gordon S. Wood, *The Creation of the American Republic, 1776–1787* (1969)

CHAPTER
3

The Political Crises
of the 1790s

⊕

Events at home and abroad deepened the cleavage in American politics after 1792. The continuing French Revolution, initially welcomed by most Americans as an extension of their own struggle, divided the population into those who were horrified by the execution of Louis XVI in January 1793, and those who remained steadfast supporters. Jay's Treaty of 1794—widely viewed as a diplomatic surrender to Great Britain and an attack on France—fanned political discontent. In towns and cities across the country, popular clubs, known collectively as Democratic Republican societies, organized to oppose the direction of Washington's administration. Popular resentment toward Secretary of the Treasury Alexander Hamilton's fiscal program led to the Whiskey Rebellion in Pennsylvania, an immense show of military force, and additional disaffection. Events reached a crisis when President Washington branded the "self-created" democratic societies as improper organizations, and blamed them for fomenting the Pennsylvania uprising.

Washington's successor, John Adams, did nothing to still the controversies. Although being a man of moderation himself, Adams found his administration increasingly entangled with hardline Federalists led by Hamilton. Relations with revolutionary France degenerated into a quasi-war. Federalist reaction to public criticism prompted passage of the repressive Alien and Sedition Acts in 1798. By the end of that year, the citizenry was edging perilously close to a civil war—or so some observers believed, as they listened to the vitriolic tone of public debate. Yet in the end, the turbulence led not to warfare but to the narrow election of Thomas Jefferson to the presidency.

Did the Federalists represent a "monocratic," regressive force in American politics, as their adversaries claimed? Were the emerging Republicans anything like the French "Jacobin" revolutionaries so feared by the Federalists? What ultimately were the major differences between the Federalists and the Republicans in the 1790s, at every level of political life? How did these differences speak to broader social conflicts?

⌗ D O C U M E N T S

In the first selected reading, pronouncements and minutes of the Democratic Society of Pennsylvania, the most important of the opposition groups of mid-decade, illustrate the members' wide-ranging concerns. Two years after the Whiskey Rebellion of 1794, the country democrat William Findley of western Pennsylvania, a prominent Anti-Federalist in 1787–1788 and later a Republican, critically but sympathetically rehearsed the rebels' grievances. President George Washington's proclamation on the rebellion, the third document, was unambiguous and carried with it his suspicion that the opposition societies were behind the lawlessness. Thomas Jefferson's letter to his Italian friend Phillip Mazzei, the fourth selection, stirred immediate controversy when it was released and printed in the newspapers. In the fifth document, Washington's famous farewell address of 1796, the outgoing president discloses his own growing sense of foreboding about the nation's future. In 1798 a grateful President John Adams sent a message (the sixth document) to some of his political supporters, indicative of his mounting political difficulties. That same year, passage of the Alien and Sedition Acts ignited a political explosion, as the next two documents reveal. The Kentucky Resolutions, authored anonymously by Jefferson, showed the depth of concern at the state level; a Federalist newspaper report on the trial under the Sedition Act, of the Massachusetts radical democrat David Brown, detailed both the mechanisms of Federalist repression and the sorts of ideas circulating in plebeian political circles. John Adams's bitter reaction to his defeat in 1801, relayed in a private letter reprinted here as the final document, contains a suggestive even-handed explanation for the changing course of American politics.

The Democratic Society of Pennsylvania Opposes Federal Policy, 1793, 1794

Principles, Articles, and Regulations, Agreed upon, Drawn, and Adopted, May 30, 1793

The rights of man, the genuine objects of Society, and the legitimate principles of Government, have been clearly developed by the successive Revolutions of America and France. Those events have withdrawn the veil which concealed the dignity and the happiness of the human race, and have taught us, no longer dazzled with adventitious splendor, or awed by antiquated usurpation, to erect the Temple of LIBERTY on the ruins of *Palaces* and *Thrones*.

At this propitious period, when the nature of Freedom and Equality is thus practically displayed, and when their value, (best understood by those, who have paid the price of acquiring them) is universally acknowledged, the patriotic mind will naturally be solicitius [sic], by every proper precaution, to preserve and perpetuate the Blessings which Providence hath bestowed upon our Country: For, in reviewing the history of Nations, we find occasion

---

Excerpts from Democratic Society of Pennsylvania minutes, Civic Festival, May 1, 1794. Reprinted by permission of Historical Society of Pennsylvania.

to lament, that the vigilance of the People has been too easily absorbed in victory; and that the prize which has been achieved by the wisdom and valor of one generation, has too often been lost by the ignorance and supineness of another.

With a view, therefore, to cultivate the just knowledge of rational Liberty, to facilitate the enjoyment and exercise of our civil Rights, and to transmit, unimpaired, to posterity, the glorious inheritance of a *free Republican Government,* the DEMOCRATIC SOCIETY of Pennsylvania is constituted and established. Unfettered by *religious* or *national* distinctions, unbiassed by party and unmoved by ambition, this Institution embraces the interest and invites the support of every virtuous citizen. The public good is indeed its sole object, . . .

Civic Festival
on ye 1st of May 1794

The Democratic Society of Pennsylvania, at their meeting in the city of Philadelphia on the 24th of April, 1794, Resolved unanimously That they would commemorate the successes of their Republican French Brethern in a Civic Festival on the first day of May 1794; and that to this Festival they would invite their Sister Society the German Republican, and all other citizens who harmonized with them in sentiment . . .

On the first day of May, agreeably to the aforesaid Resolution of the Democratic Society, about Eight hundred citizens assembled at the Country Seat of cit^n Israel Israel, now called Democratic Hall, on the Passyunk Road . . .

The Flags of the Sister Republics marked and ornamented the seat of festivity.

[The following toasts were drunk.]

A Revolutionary Tribunal in Great Britain:—May it give lessons of liberty to her King, examples of Justice to her Ministry, and honesty to her corrupt Legislature . . .

The Fair Daughters of America & France:—May they ever possess virtue to attrack merit, and sense to reward it.

The Democratic and Republic Societies of the United States:—May they preserve and dessiminate their principles, undaunted by the frowns of powers, uncontaminated by the luxury of aristocracy, till the Rights of Man shall become the Supreme Law of every land, and their separate Fraternities be absorbed, in One Great Democratic Society, comprehending the Human Race . . .

May every Free Nation consider a public debt as a public curse; and may the man who would assert a contrary opinion be considered as an enemy to his Country. . . .

Thursday, July 31st 1794

The Society met in Special Meeting, at the University, pursuant to a public notification for that purpose. . . .

Cit^n Leib offered a set of Resolutions against such opposition to the Excise or any other law of the land, as is not warranted by the Constitution of the U.S. . . .

Resolved, as the opinion of this Society, that in a Democracy, a majority ought in all cases to govern; and that where a Constitution exists, which emanated from the People, the remedies pointed out by it against unjust and oppressive laws and bad measures, ought to be resorted to; and that every other appeal but to the Constitution itself, except in cases of extremity, is improper & dangerous.

Resolved, as the opinion of this Society, that altho' we conceive Excise systems to be oppressive, hostile to the liberties of this Country, and a nursery of vice and sycophancy; we, notwithstanding, highly disapprove of every opposition to them, not warranted by that frame of Government, which has received the sanction of the People of the United States.

Resolved, that we will use our utmost efforts to effect a repeal of the Excise-laws by Constitutional means; that we will, at all times, make legal opposition to every measure which shall endanger the freedom of our Country; but that we will bear testimony against every unconstitutional attempt to prevent the execution of any law sanctioned by the majority of the people.

A Country Democrat on the Whiskey Rebellion, 1796

If the numerous difficulties encountered and hardships sustained, by the people inhabiting the western counties of Pennsylvania, were to be minutely related, and their behavior under them fairly stated, their conduct generally would be entitled to a much greater proportion of approbation than blame, and their sufferings would have a powerful claim on the sympathy of their fellow citizens. . . .

The people in the western counties anticipated their experiencing peculiar hardships from the excise. Without money, or the means of procuring it, and consuming their whiskey only in their families or using it as an article of barter, which, though it in some respects answered the place of money, yet would not be received in pay for the excise tax, they thought it hard to pay as much tax on what sold with them but at from two shillings, to two shillings and six pence, as they did where it brought double that price. These, and such like arguments, were not new. I found them in use against the state excise when I went to reside in that country. They arose from their situation, and the simplest person feeling their force, knew how to use them.

Some talked of laying aside their still altogether, till they would have time to observe the effects of the law on other places, and have time to reflect on the subject; and this method was advised, in preference to a more violent mode of opposition, by some who were apprehensive of outrages being committed. But though several peaceable men laid aside their stills or sold them, yet there never was any association or resolutions among the inhabitants to that purpose. . . .

The great error among the people was an opinion, that an immoral law might be opposed and yet the government respected, and all the other laws obeyed, and they firmly believed that the excise law was an immoral one. This theory became with many a religious principle, in defence of which they reasoned with considerable address. In endeavoring to restore order, and submission to the laws, the most arduous talk with people otherwise of good morals was to convince them of the error of this principle. As no riots that I knew of were attempted in the county where I reside, or by the people of it previous to the insurrection, and as I had never heard any person threaten any other kind of opposition than laying aside their stills, I consequently knew nothing of this principle being entertained till the insurrection took place; but I then found it to be one of the greatest obstacles to people even of good understanding signing such assurances as might imply an approbation of the law. Indeed I despair that people, residing in situations where excises, applying directly to agriculture, demand two or three times the quantum of tax in proportion to the price in the market for the produce of their farm, that the farmers in more favorable situations have to pay, can ever be brought to approve of such a law by any methods in the power of government. Their objections are obvious and easily comprehended, and address themselves powerfully to their interests; whereas the arguments arising from the unequal pressure of imposts on the inhabitants of towns, and people generally who manufacture little themselves, and consequently consume much of foreign manufactures or luxuries, not coming under their observation, are not understood nor admitted in abatement of their own complaints; consequently the citizens in situations remote from market are advocates for direct taxes, proportioned to the value of property, and always pay them without complaint. To explain the operation of other taxes, which tended to an abatement of the pressure of the excise tax, and the inequality which would arise from apportioning direct taxes according to the constitutional rule, was the great object of those who endeavored to reconcile the people to the excise law. There were circumstances however which could not be accomodated to the principles of justice. These were balanced with political considerations.

President George Washington Suppresses the Whiskey Rebellion, 1794

By the President of the United States of America, a proclamation

Whereas combinations to defeat the execution of the laws laying duties upon spirits distilled within the United States and upon stills have from the time of the commencement of those laws existed in some of the western parts of Pennsylvania; and

Whereas the said combinations, proceeding in a manner subversive equally of the just authority of government and of the rights of individuals, have hitherto effected their dangerous and criminal purpose by the influence of certain irregular meetings whose proceedings have tended to encourage and uphold the spirit of opposition by misrepresentations of the laws calculated to render them odious; by endeavors to deter those who might be so disposed from accepting offices under them through fear of public resentment and of injury to person and property, and to compel those who had accepted such offices by actual violence to surrender or forbear the execution of them; by circulating vindictive menaces against all those who should otherwise, directly or indirectly, aid in the execution of the said laws, or who, yielding to the dictates of conscience and to a sense of obligation, should themselves comply therewith; by actually injuring and destroying the property of persons who were understood to have so complied; by inflicting cruel and humiliating punishments upon private citizens for no other cause than that of appearing to be the friends of the laws; by intercepting the public officers on the highways, abusing, assaulting, and otherwise ill treating them; by going to their houses in the night, gaining admittance by force, taking away their papers, and committing other outrages, employing for these unwarrantable purposes the agency of armed banditti disguised in such manner as for the most part to escape discovery; and

Whereas the endeavors of the Legislature to obviate objections to the said laws by lowering the duties and by other alterations conducive to the convenience of those whom they immediately affect (though they have given satisfaction in other quarters), and the endeavors of the executive officers to conciliate a compliance with the laws by explanations, by forbearance, and even by particular accommodations founded on the suggestion of local considerations, have been disappointed of their effect by the machinations of persons whose industry to excite resistance has increased with every appearance of a disposition among the people to relax in their opposition and to acquiesce in the laws, insomuch that many persons in the said western parts of Pennsylvania have at length been hardy enough to perpetrate acts which I am advised amount to treason, being overt acts of levying war against the United States. . . .

Whereas by a law of the United States entitled "An act to provide for calling forth the militia to execute the laws of the Union, suppress insurrections, and repel invasions," it is enacted "that whenever the laws of the United States shall be opposed or the execution thereof obstructed in any State by combinations too powerful to be suppressed by the ordinary course of judicial proceedings or by the powers vested in the marshals by that act, the same being notified by an associate justice or the district judge, it shall be lawful for the President of the United States to call forth the militia of such State to suppress such combinations and to cause the laws to be duly executed. And if the militia of a State where such combinations may happen shall refuse or be insufficient to suppress the same, it shall be lawful for the President, if the Legislature of the United States shall not be in session, to call forth and employ such numbers of the militia of any other State or

States most convenient thereto as may be necessary; and the use of the militia so to be called forth may be continued, if necessary, until the expiration of thirty days after the commencement of the ensuing session. . . .

Whereas it is in my judgment necessary under the circumstances of the case to take measures for calling forth the militia in order to suppress the combinations aforesaid, and to cause the laws to be duly executed; and I have accordingly determined so to do, feeling the deepest regret for the occasion, but withal the most solemn conviction that the essential interests of the Union demand it. . . .

Wherefore, and in pursuance of the proviso above recited, I, George Washington, President of the United States, do hereby command all persons being insurgents as aforesaid, and all others whom it may concern, on or before the 1st day of September next to disperse and retire peaceably to their respective abodes. And I do moreover warn all persons whomsoever against aiding, abetting, or comforting the perpetrators of the aforesaid treasonable acts, and do require all officers and other citizens, according to their respective duties and the laws of the land, to exert their utmost endeavors to prevent and suppress such dangerous proceedings.

Thomas Jefferson on the "Aristocratical Party," 1796

Letter to Phillip Mazzei, April 24, 1796

. . . The aspect of our politics has wonderfully changed since you left us. In place of that noble love of liberty and republican government which carried us triumphantly through the war, an Anglican monarchical aristocratical party has sprung up, whose avowed object is to draw over us the substance, as they have already done the forms, of the British government. The main body of our citizens, however, remain true to their republican principles; the whole landed interest is republican, and so is a great mass of talents. Against us are the Executive, the Judiciary, two out of three branches of the Legislature, all the officers of the government, all who want to be officers, all timid men who prefer the calm of depotism to the boisterous sea of liberty, British merchants and Americans trading on British capital, speculators and holders in the banks and public funds, a contrivance invented for the purposes of corruption, and for assimilating us in all things to the rotten as well as the sound parts of the English model. It would give you a fever were I to name to you the apostates who have gone over to these heresies, men who were Samsons in the field and Solomons in the council, but who have had their heads shorn by the harlot England. In short, we are likely to preserve the liberty we have obtained only by unremitting labors and perils. But we shall preserve it; and our mass of weight and wealth on the good side is so great, as to leave no danger that force will ever be attempted against us. We have only to awake and snap the Lilliputian cords with which they have been entangling us during the first sleep which succeeded our labors. . . .

President Washington's Farewell Address, 1796

The unity of government which constitutes you one people is also now dear to you. It is justly so, for it is a main pillar in the edifice of your real independence, the support of your tranquility at home, your peace abroad, of your safety, of your prosperity, of that very liberty which you so highly prize. But as it is easy to foresee that from different causes and from different quarters much pains will be taken, many artifices employed, to weaken in your minds the conviction of this truth . . .

In contemplating the causes which may disturb our union it occurs as matter of serious concern that any ground should have been furnished for characterizing parties by *geographical* discriminations—*Northern* and *Southern, Atlantic* and *Western*—whence designing men may endeavor to excite a belief that there is a real difference of local interests and views. One of the expedients of party to acquire influence within particular districts is to misrepresent the opinions and aims of other districts. You can not shield yourselves too much against the jealousies and heartburnings which spring from these misrepresentations; they tend to render alien to each other those who ought to be bound together by fraternal affection. . . .

All obstructions to the execution of the laws, all combinations and associations, under whatever plausible character, with the real design to direct, control, counteract, or awe the regular deliberation and action of the constituted authorities, are destructive of this fundamental principle and of fatal tendency. They serve to organize faction; to give it an artificial and extraordinary force; to put in the place of the delegated will of the nation the will of a party, often a small but artful and enterprising minority of the community, and, according to the alternate triumphs of different parties, to make the public administration the mirror of the ill-concerted and incongruous projects of faction rather than the organ of consistent and wholesome plans, digested by common counsels and modified by mutual interests.

However combinations or associations of the above description may now and then answer popular ends, they are likely in the course of time and things to become potent engines by which cunning, ambitious, and unprincipled men will be enabled to subvert the power of the people, and to usurp for themselves the reins of government, destroying afterwards the very engines which have lifted them to unjust dominion.

As a very important source of strength and security, cherish public credit. One method of preserving it is to use it as sparingly as possible, avoiding occasions of expense by cultivating peace, but remembering also that timely disbursements to prepare for danger frequently prevent much greater disbursements to repel it; avoiding likewise the accumulation of debt, not only by shunning occasions of expense, but by vigorous exertions in time of peace to discharge the debts which unavoidable wars have occasioned, not ungenerously throwing upon posterity the burthen which we ourselves ought to bear. . . .

Observe good faith and justice toward all nations. Cultivate peace and harmony with all. Religion and morality enjoin this conduct. . . .

In the execution of such a plan nothing is more essential than that permanent, inveterate antipathies against particular nations and passionate attachments for others should be excluded, and that in place of them just and amicable feelings toward all should be cultivated. . . .

The great rule of conduct for us in regard to foreign nations is, in extending our commercial relations to have with them as little *political* connection as possible. So far as we have already formed engagements let them be fulfilled with perfect good faith. Here let us stop.

Europe has a set of primary interests which to us have none or a very remote relation. Hence she must be engaged in frequent controversies, the causes of which are essentially foreign to our concerns. Hence, therefore, it must be unwise in us to implicate ourselves by artificial ties in the ordinary vicissitudes of her politics or the ordinary combinations and collisions of her friendships or enmities. . . .

It is our true policy to steer clear of permanent alliances with any portion of the foreign world, so far, I mean, as we are now at liberty to do it; for let me not be understood as capable of patronizing infidelity to existing engagements. I hold the maxim no less applicable to public than to private affairs that honesty is always the best policy. I repeat, therefore, let those engagements be observed in their genuine sense. But in my opinion it is unnecessary and would be unwise to extend them.

John Adams Thanks His Supporters, 1798

To the inhabitants of Harrison County, Virginia

Gentlemen,

I have received with great pleasure your address from your committee. The attachment you profess to our government, calculated as it is to insure liberty and happiness to its citizens, is commendable. Your declaration, in plain and undisguised language, that the measures which have been taken to promote a good understanding, peace, and harmony between this country and France, are becoming my character and deserving your confidence, is a great encouragement to me. With you I see with infinite satisfaction, that the alarming prospect of a war, which is seen to be just and necessary, has silenced all essential differences of opinions, and that a union of sentiment appears to prevail very generally throughout our land. I believe, however, that the distinction of *aristocrat* and *democrat,* however odious and pernicious it may be rendered by political artifice at particular conjunctures, will never be done away, as long as some men are taller and others shorter, some wiser and others sillier, some more virtuous and others more vicious, some richer and others poorer. The distinction is grounded on unalterable nature, and human wisdom can do no more than reconcile the parties by equitable establishments and equal laws, securing, as far as possible, to every one his own. The distinction was intended by nature for the order of society, and the benefit of mankind. The parties ought to be like the sexes, mutually beneficial to each other. And woe will be to that country, which supinely suffers malicious demagogues to excite jealousies, foment prejudices, and stimulate animosities between them!

The Kentucky Resolutions, 1798

. . . 3. *Resolved,* That it is true as a general principle, and is also expressly declared by one of the amendments to the Constitution, that "the powers not delegated to the United States by the Constitution, nor prohibited by it to the States, are reserved to the States respectively, or to the people;" and that no power over the freedom of religion, freedom of speech, or freedom of the press being delegated to the United States by the Constitution, nor prohibited by it to the States, all lawful powers respecting the same did of right remain, and were reserved to the States or the people: that thus was manifested their determination to retain to themselves the right of judging how far the licentiousness of speech and of the press may be abridged without lessening their useful freedom, and how far those abuses which cannot be separated from their use should be tolerated, rather than the use be destroyed. And thus also they guarded against all abridgment by the United States of the freedom of religious opinions and exercises, and retained to themselves the right of protecting the same, as this State, by a law passed on the general demand of its citizens, had already protected them from all human restraint or interference. And that in addition to this general principle and express declaration, another and more special provision has been made by one of the amendments to the Constitution, which expressly declares, that "Congress shall make no law respecting an establishment of religion, or prohibiting the free exercise thereof, or abridging the freedom of speech or of the press:" thereby guarding in the same sentence, and under the same words, the freedom of religion, of speech, and of the press: insomuch, that whatever violated either, throws down the sanctuary which covers the others, and that libels, falsehood, and defamation, equally with heresy and false religion, are withheld from the cognizance of federal tribunals. That, therefore, the act of Congress of the United States, passed on the 14th day of July, 1798, intituled "An Act in addition to the act intituled An Act for the punishment of certain crimes against the United States," which does abridge the freedom of the press, is not law, but is altogether void, and of no force.

4. *Resolved,* That the lands are under the jurisdiction and protection of the laws of the State within which they are: that no power over them has been delegated to the United States, nor prohibited to the individual States, distinct from their power over citizens. And it being true as a general principle, and one of the amendments to the Constitution having also declared, that "the powers not delegated to the United States by the Constitution, nor prohibited by it to the States, are reserved to the States respectively,

or to the people," the act of the Congress of the United States, passed on the —— day of July, 1798, intituled "An Act concerning aliens," which assumes powers over alien friends, not delegated by the Constitution, is not law, but is altogether void, and of no force. . . . [W]here powers are assumed which have not been delegated, a nullification of the act is the rightful remedy: that every State has a natural right in cases not within the compact, (casus non fœderis,) to nullify of their own authority all assumptions of power by others within their limits: that without this right, they would be under the dominion, absolute and unlimited, of whosoever might exercise this right of judgment for them: that nevertheless, this commonwealth, from motives of regard and respect for its co-States, has wished to communicate with them on the subject: that with them alone it is proper to communicate, they alone being parties to the compact, and solely authorized to judge in the last resort of the powers exercised under it, Congress being not a party, but merely the creature of the compact, and subject as to its assumptions of power to the final judgment of those by whom, and for whose use itself and its powers were all created and modified: that if the acts before specified should stand, these conclusions would flow from them; that the General Government may place any act they think proper on the list of crimes, and punish it themselves whether enumerated or not enumerated by the Constitution as cognizable by them: that they may transfer its cognizance to the President, or any other person, who may himself be the accuser, counsel, judge and jury, whose *suspicions* may be the evidence, his *order* the sentence, his *officer* the executioner, and his breast the sole record of the transaction: that a very numerous and valuable description of the inhabitants of these States being, by this precedent, reduced, as outlaws, to the absolute dominion of one man, and the barrier of the Constitution thus swept away from us all, no rampart now remains against the passions and the powers of a majority in Congress to protect from a like exportation, or other more grievous punishment, the minority of the same body, the legislatures, judges, governors, and counsellors of the States, nor their other peaceable inhabitants, who may venture to reclaim the constitutional rights and liberties of the States and people, or who for other causes, good or bad, may be obnoxious to the views, or marked by the suspicions of the President, or be thought dangerous to his or their election, or other interests, public or personal: that the friendless alien has indeed been selected as the safest subject of a first experiment; but the citizen will soon follow, or rather, has already followed, for already has a sedition act marked him as its prey: that these and successive acts of the same character, unless arrested at the threshold, necessarily drive these States into revolution and blood, and will furnish new calumnies against republican government, and new pretexts for those who wish it to be believed that man cannot be governed but by a rod of iron: that it would be a dangerous delusion were a confidence in the men of our choice to silence our fears for the safety of our rights: that confidence is everywhere the parent of despotism—free government is founded in jealousy, and not in confidence. . . .

A Federalist Newspaper Describes
the Trial of David Brown, 1799

Boston, June 17

Circuit Court.

On Monday the 10th inst., David Brown, who had pleaded *guilty* to an indictment for seditious writings and practices, was sentenced by the court to pay a fine of 400 dollars, and to eighteen months imprisonment.

The indictment was lengthy. The two first counts consisted of numerous extracts from two manuscripts, written by the defendant: the contents of which he has industriously inculcated, in different parts of the commonwealth. These writings are replete with the most malignant and perverse misrepresentations of the views and measures of the government of the United States. The government is represented as 'a tyrannic

'association of about five hundred out of
'five millions, to *engross* to themselves all
'the benefit of public property, and live
'upon the ruins of the rest of the community.'

All the means which a vicious ingenuity could suggest, appear to have been used by him to create discontent, and to excite among the people hatred and opposition to their government. The last count in the indictment was for producing a label to be painted and affixed to a pole erected at Dedham, in October last, the following words recited in the indictment, made part of the inscription, 'No stamp act, no sedition, no alien bill, no land tax, Downfall to the tyrants of America, peace and retirement to the President; long live the vice president and the minority.' . . .

After the inquiry, his honor judge Chase observed to Brown that having pleaded guilty to the indictment, and thrown himself on the mercy of the court, it became him to conduct frankly and sincerely; and to evidence his sincerity and contrition by disclosing to the government those who had prompted and aided him in his mischievous and dangerous pursuits and by delivering up the list of subscribers to his pernicious writings.

He replied, that on the Monday following he would deliver to the court, in writing, some observations relative to his situation and conduct. When called to the bar to receive sentence, he delivered in a paper in which he expresses his sorrow for uttering his *political sentiments* 'more especially,' he adds, 'in the way and manner I did utter them.' By '*giving up the names*,' to which the court referred, 'I shall lose,' say he, 'all my friends.' He promises to conduct as a peaceable citizen in future, and requests that his punishment may be wholly by *imprisonment* and not by *fine*.

Judge Chase, previous to declaring the sentence of the court, made some very impressive observations to Brown, on the nature, malignity, and magnitude of his offenses and on the vicious industry with which he had circulated and inculcated his disorganizing doctrines, and imputent falsehoods; and the very alarming and dangerous excesses to which he attempted to incite the uninformed part of the community. The court, he observed, saw no satisfactory indication of a change of disposition, or ameliorations of temper; and found nothing disclosed in the paper delivered them to justify the mitigation of that punishment which his very pernicious and dangerous practices demanded. . . .

John Adams on His Defeat, 1801

Letter to Benjamin Stoddert, March 31, 1801

. . . We federalists are . . . completely and totally routed and defeated. We are not yet attainted by act of Congress, and, I hope, shall not fly out into rebellion. No party, that ever existed, knew itself so little, or so vainly overrated its own influence and popularity, as ours. None ever understood so ill the causes of its own power, or so wantonly destroyed them. If we had been blessed with common sense, we should not have been overthrown by Philip Freneau, Duane, Callender, Cooper, and Lyon, or their great patron and protector. A group of foreign liars, encouraged by a few ambitious native gentlemen, have discomfited the education, the talents, the virtues, and the property of the country. The reason is, we have no Americans in America. The federalists have been no more Americans than the anties.

E S S A Y S

How can we explain the intense political conflicts of the 1790s? The Progressive historians understood them as part of a perennial clash between agrarian democracy and urban capitalism. Subsequent historians have modified that interpretation by connecting the politics of the 1790s to earlier battles between groups they describe as rural localists and urban cosmopolitans. Beginning in the 1970s, a different line of argument emerged, casting the Federalists as commercially oriented centralizers and the opposition as the upholders of a distinctive world-view derived from classical republican thought—a republicanism that was suspicious of the corrupting influence of commerce and dedicated to the cultivation of political virtue and independence. Such scholars as Lance Banning, Drew McCoy, and John Murrin, although differing on numerous particulars, have linked the decade's crises to a deeper social and intellectual debate over the fundamental terms of republican politics in post-Revolutionary America.

In the first essay, Joyce Appleby, a professor of history at the University of California at Los Angeles, departs from the conclusions of both the Progressives and the proponents of the so-called republican synthesis. In her view, the emerging opposition championed a new kind of optimistic, individualist, egalitarian capitalist order that stood in direct contrast to hierarchical Federalism. The Federalists, she argues, and not their political enemies, were the true classical republicans. In the second selection, a direct reply to Appleby, John Ashworth, a historian at the University of East Anglia, questions Appleby's assumptions about commerce and capitalism, and insists upon the importance of slavery to any understanding of early U.S. history. We might also ask how well these interpretations account for plebeian insurgents like the whiskey rebels and David Brown.

How closely did these people conform to the schematic labels of localist vs. cosmopolitan, friends of liberty vs. friends of order, and republican vs. liberal, which historians have imposed upon them? Did capitalism necessarily disclose itself, as Appleby states, "in a benign and visionary way" to these people as well?

Capitalism and the Rise of the Republican Opposition

JOYCE O. APPLEBY

Louis Hacker noted thirty years ago that there had always been an anti-capitalist bias in the writing of American history. The reason for this is not hard to find. Historians began discussing capitalism as a specific economic system in the early twentieth century, when the ugliness of American industrialization obtruded everywhere. Capitalists themselves appeared as plutocrats grinding the faces of the poor with one hand while subverting the democratic institutions of the nation with the other. The great concentrations of wealth lodged in the "dark satanic mills" of industry made a mockery of equality of opportunity and the older justification for limiting government interference lost its liberal rationale. Capitalist apologists drew instead upon the grim determinism of the Social Darwinian doctrine of the survival of the fittest.

When historians in the early twentieth century began to examine seriously the influence of economic factors in the American past, they appeared as independent developments, the characteristics of which were established with free enterprise. Capitalism figured in historical texts then as an entity—an organic object—like an oak whose form was determined with the planting of the first acorn. Rather than imagine different groups of people in the eighteenth century responding selectively to the possibilities afforded by the market, scholars wrote about capitalism as an external force bending men and nations to its needs. Both the anticapitalist bias that Hacker commented upon and this concept of capitalism as an independent system have obscured the role that the expectation of commercial growth played in the social thought of the Jeffersonian Republicans. Instead the hard-fisted, mean-spirited drive for profits of early industrialization seemed so totally incompatible with Jeffersonian ideals that historians construed the Jeffersonians themselves as anticapitalistic. Similarly, the tendency to see industrial capitalism as the end toward which all prior economies were moving has contributed to the notion that those in the past who promoted agriculture were out of touch with the progressive developments of their day.

A number of findings of the past generation have made it possible to look anew at capitalism as it appeared to men and women at the end of the eighteenth century. It is now generally recognized that the first capitalists were farmers and landlords—the men who revolutionized English agriculture in the seventeenth and eighteenth centuries. Far from being the stronghold of conservatism, the countryside witnessed dramatic changes in the working and holding of land. The breakthrough in agricultural productivity not only freed the English from famine; it liberated their imagination as well. With old assumptions undermined, radical theories about individual freedom acquired plausibility. In England and America commercial farming was a progressive economic force suggesting to some that the future would be far different from the past. . . .

In recent work on late eighteenth-century America scholars have begun to explore the connection between the economy and the cultural milieu in which commercial engagements took place. . . .

[These analyses] can also be used to shed light on the striking regional concentrations of Federalists and Jeffersonians . . . when the promise of prosperity superseded the depressed outlook of the post-revolutionary period. The upturn in trade that coincided with the adoption of the Constitution and the rising demand for the foods and fibers grown by ordinary farmers in the wheat belt greatly increased the commercial penetration of the market throughout the 1790s. The Northern centers for growing and marketing grains then increased at twice the rate of the rest of the nation and the number of . . . cosmopolitan towns grew apace. Even Massachusetts counties that had no cosmopolitan towns in the 1780s acquired several in the 1790s. The spectacular growth in the middle states was accompanied by true prosperity. The real value of wages, profits, and land all rose substantially. The strength of the Jeffersonian movement was precisely in the fast-growing areas. As individuals, the Jeffersonians were socially and geographically mobile, particularly in the North. They were the mushroom candidates that the established political leaders scorned. In studies discriminating between new and old wealth, Jeffersonian towns are distinguished by the recentness of their money. Republicans succeeded where entrenched elites were challenged by new men, but they flourished as well without opposition in young cities like Baltimore.

In the 1790s the newness of profitable enterprise in many places and the rapidity of growth elsewhere created a division between the mobile and the established. . . . Again it is the kinds of experiences that mobility and stability promoted that counted, but the content of Republican ideology cannot be derived solely from a social category. Federalists and Republicans alike responded to the economic opportunities opening before America. Where Republicans differed from Federalists was in the moral character they gave to economic development. The promise in prosperity encouraged them to vault over the cumulative wisdom of the ages and imagine a future far different from the dreary past known to man. In taking this imaginative leap they were greatly aided by the line of economic analysis that began with English writers in the seventeenth century and culminated in Adam Smith's *Wealth of Nations*. The uniformity of economic responses from market participants, which had encouraged a succession of observers to think of social relations as a complex of exchanges between similarly rational and self-interested bargainers, pushed the Jeffersonians even further toward nineteenth-century liberalism. In England conspicuous social distinctions worked against acceptance of the economists' model as a depiction of reality, whereas the more equal social conditions that prevailed in America made it possible to think of the economists' description of the market as a template for society. What in England served as a device for understanding how nations grow wealthy through trade became in America the blueprint for a society of economically progressive, socially equal, and politically competent citizens. Capitalism thus disclosed itself in a benign and visionary way to Republicans who drew from its dynamic operation the promise of a new age for ordinary men. . . .

[I]n the very first session of Congress, . . . disputes . . . were prompted largely by the boldness with which Alexander Hamilton had asserted the new federal government's financial leadership[.] [O]pponents and proponents of the various measures came from the ranks of elected officials, which meant that national politics were largely confined to the activities of office holders. The genteel arena of conflict and the general agreement on the processes of law-making ensured decorum. Policy debates did not undermine the consensus among leaders on the proper relationship between government and governed people. Indeed, through the first four years under the new constitution the style, the procedures, and the personnel of Washington's administration largely fulfilled the hopes of those conservatives who had wanted to remove politics from popular influence and restore the august majesty of government.

The execution of Louis XVI in January of 1793 and the outbreak of war between France and England changed all this. Crowds all over America gathered to celebrate the early victories of the French Revolutionary army. Parades and bonfires spread the word that France had joined the United States in the world's ranks of republics. Foreign policy, that most arcane of all government responsibilities, became the major topic of public debate. Citizen Genêt's triumphal journey from Charleston to Philadelphia in April, a month after Washington's second inauguration, only advertised what had already become apparent—large portions of the American people had claimed the cause of France as their own. Washington adopted a neutrality policy designed to keep the United States from being drawn into the war, even at the cost of violating the spirit of the Franco-American treaty that had brought France into the war of American Independence. Jefferson and other administration critics within Congress recognized the wisdom of remaining neutral, but outside of government circles, neutrality was treated as a betrayal not just of France but of republican government as well. Orators at civic feasts held in honor of French victories reminded audiences that the enemies of France were "Royalists and Aristocrats associated for the express purpose of expelling the rights of Man from the world." These demonstrations of support for the French Revolution were often accompanied by angry denunciations of administration policies, which were now interpreted as unwarrantedly pro-English.

This public criticism in turn precipitated a much more divisive controversy about the legality of popular participation in politics. The issue came to a head with the spontaneous formation of political organizations. Variously called democratic or republican societies, these voluntary associations sprang up in forty different locations, at least one in each state of the union. Critics blamed their appearance upon the notorious Jacobin clubs currently radicalizing French politics, but this proved to be a bite without sting in a season of revolutionary enthusiasm. Having something of a private character in Philadelphia and New York City, they became the vehicles for more turbulent, public activities elsewhere. Even in the cities they provided the nucleus for organizing ad hoc meetings. There was in this mobilization of ordinary voters the menace of numbers. Ominously from the conservatives' point of view, the democratic clubs openly attacked the forms of polite society by electing to drop conventional honorifics like "sir" and "humble servant" in favor of "fellow citizen." In further imitation of the Jacobins across the Atlantic the Democratic Society of Philadelphia resolved to measure time from the era of the Revolution. Thus their secretary dated letters "in the eighteenth year of American Independence."

Clearly reckoning the general public as their own political resource, active club members reached out to one another and established correspondence across state lines. They saw to it that their resolutions and proceedings were published in each other's local newspaper, this at a time when newspapers were penetrating rural areas as never before. With several dozen voluntary clubs scrutinizing official actions and putting into circulation their invariably hostile reactions, it seemed as though the nation had acquired a second political structure competing with its government. Like kites without strings or ships without ballast, the democratic societies appeared to be alarmingly weightless to those for whom government was a heavy affair. Out of the democratic societies came the political mobilization of mere voters. The deferential quality of elections geared to choosing among virtuous candidates gave way to ones explicitly connecting men with issues instead of personal character. Newspapers in most cities became openly partisan and many towns in the middle states acquired their first journal as an outgrowth of popular interest in politics. . . .

In this supercharged atmosphere, France and England became symbols of two alternative futures or fates for the United States: England, as the model of sober, ordered constitutional government committed to securing the maximum personal freedom consonant with the flawed nature of man, and France, presenting a vision of what a society of free men might be if the chains of customs and outworn creeds were cast off. . . .

The symbolic importance of France and England heightened the significance of every policy decision American officials made between 1793 and 1801. But the symbolic overtones were not inappropriate. The French Revolution had succeeded in bringing to the surface of public life opposing conceptions of society. Republicans and Federalists did not misperceive each other. Aside from flamboyant charges of secretly conspiring to deliver the nation to a foreign power—hurled from both camps—the polemics of the 1790s clarified assumptions that had previously gone unexamined. . . .

At two critical junctures in 1794 the Washington administration adopted policies that enraged large segments of the American public. . . . When word reached Philadelphia that the British had seized over 399 ships in the West

Indies, Washington called for a build-up of American defenses. The Federalists in Congress moved to raise the excise on distilled spirits to meet the cost. The tax fell on manufactured goods as well as whiskey, but farmers west of the Alleghenies felt particularly aggrieved, because they distilled a large part of their surplus grain. Republicans, particularly political activists outside of Congress, insisted that enforcement of the excise tax was to be undertaken as a demonstration of the federal government's power. Sending revenue officers throughout the back country was, in their view, actually a vehicle for exerting authority. Already formed into democratic societies, men in western Pennsylvania offered resistance to the collection of the tax. Convinced that it was repression, not revenue, that the Federalist had in mind, they construed opposition to the whiskey tax as a republican's duty. Thoroughly alarmed when the resistance appeared to be spreading, the Federalists called for a vigorous response. Each side played into the other's fears.

When Washington led a combined state militia force of 13,000 across the mountains, the event seemed to confirm the Republicans' suspicions. The resistance to the tax actually collapsed without bloodshed, but the issue of popular participation in politics flared up with renewed heat. Many a moderate Republican repudiated the western Pennsylvanian's menacing opposition, but the Whiskey Rebellion, nonetheless, entered the pantheon of liberty's good fights. The Philadelphia Democratic Society wrangled over its inevitable resolutions for a month and the Tammany Society in New York acquired its partisan identification when moderates were outvoted by those who supported the resisters' rights. Washington himself created the occasion for further dissension when he suggested in his Congressional Address in the fall that "certain self-created societies" had been guilty of fomenting the Whiskey Rebellion.

The Senate responded approvingly to Washington's speech; the House passed a watered-down censure of the resisters by one vote. But outside of Congress, Washington's effort to stigmatize popular politics clearly missed the mark as newspapers and democratic societies took up the question of what was called "the true principles of government." Members of the clubs refused to be intimidated. Advertised meetings were held first in Baltimore, then Newark, Philadelphia, and New York. The 31 moderate members of the Tammany Society who had rushed through a resolution supporting Washington defended themselves by an appeal to what had once been a widely shared opinion: "The public's right to associate, speak and publish sentiments are only excellent as revolutionary means, when a government is to be overturned. An exercise of this right in a free and happy country like this," they wrote, "resembles the sport of firebrands; it is phrenzy, and this phrenzy is in proportion to the party zeal of the self-created associations."

Firebrands obviously had the upper hand, for their resolution was repealed at the next general meeting. New York newspaper columnists attacked the pusillanimity of Washington's defenders. "Political associations have been threatened by the arm of power," one declared. Another claimed that duplicity or terror had induced former members to yield to Washington's condemnation. "We have erred, we have strayed like lost sheep—this is the language which your folly has suggested." When apologists for the President affirmed the right of free association, but cautioned against its use, their position was ridiculed. "What good purposes can it answer," a Republican queried, "to claim the existence of a right which you deem it criminal to exercise, and then menacingly concluded "the government that is inimical to investigation is ripe for Revolution."

In this manner administration criticism of the democratic societies was turned into evidence of the government's bad intentions. The Philadelphia society stoked this particular fire, charging that the aristocratic faction in America was indefatigable in disseminating principles unfriendly to the rights of man. "It has ever been a favorite and important pursuit with aristocracy to stifle free inquiry, to envelop its proceedings in mystery, and as much as possible, to impede the progress of political knowledge. No wonder," the resolution continued, "they were afraid of societies whose objects were to cultivate a just knowledge of rational liberty." . . .

The Federalists called upon classical republican ideas to explain how the abuse of power should be checked within government by the different branches of elected officers rather than outside among a turbulent populace. But this theory now appeared as part of elitist rhetoric. Rejecting New Jersey Federalist Jonathan Dayton's traditional description of the parts of government as "the constituent centinels over the liberties of the people," a Republican writer insisted that this was not "an American conception," but rather a notion that "favored too much the poignant principles of aristocracy." In a similar vein two rural publishers attacked Federalist John Shippen, who had written that freedom of the press was a blessing only "while the People are virtuous and independent enough to check its degeneracy." Noting the condescension in Shippen's judgment, they sarcastically disqualified themselves from being able to understand "such sublime conceptions."

William Findley, a Republican congressman from western Pennsylvania, readily conceded that popular meetings led to indiscretion and promoted licentiousness. "But it does not therefore follow," he maintained, "that such meetings should be prohibited by law or denounced by the government." Doing so would be reducing the people to mere machines, he wrote, and subvert the very existence of liberty. "It is the duty of the legislature not only to accommodate the laws to the people's interests, but even as far as possible, to their preconceptions." It was not the people's wisdom that the Republicans were arguing for, but their freedom to err as their elected officials, they assumed, would also err.

Where classical republican theory had held up government as the noblest activity for men of civic virtue, the Jeffersonian Republicans celebrated the informal, voluntary political life open to all. Washington's proscription of "certain self-created societies" seemed to belittle this life. "Is our being self-created reckoned among the charges of the President?" a New Yorker asked, going on to inquire rhetorically, "Are not all private associations established on the foundation of their own authority, an authority sanctioned by the first principles of social life and guaranteed by the spirit of the laws?" The logical conclusion of the Federalists' position was finally reached by a writer in the Republican *Independent Gazetteer:* "Whatever the United States might have been previous to the American Revolution, it is pretty evident that since their emancipation from British rapacity, they are a great self-created society." Indeed, he continued, "had the British succeeded in impressing our minds with a firm belief in the infamy of self creation, we should never have been free and independent to all eternity."

During the months that this debate raged, the terms of the treaty Jay was negotiating in England were leaked to the fiery Republican editor Benjamin Franklin Bache, aptly nicknamed Lightning Rod Jr. in reference to his grandfather. The generous concessions to Britain in the treaty represented nothing less than a sell-out to the Republicans. Again raucous public meetings became the order—or the disorder—of the day. Jay's effigy stoked the flames of many a public bonfire across the land. As one of the Philadelphia Democratic Society's resolutions explained, these events had shaken Americans from their lethargy and given new impulse and new warmth to democratic institutions. They also created opportunities to explore the Federalists' pretensions of social superiority. Apparently thinking that the best offense was a good defense, Republicans enthusiastically repeated the terms of opprobrium used by Federalists. Thus one Fourth of July orator advertised that "the high prerogative set claim that the common people in this country are a set of restless, discontented, tumultuous disorganizers." Theodore Sedgwick's reference to the "ignorant herd" was linked to Edmund Burke's more notorious labeling of French commoners as the "swinish multitude." An election broadside circulated in New Jersey took the form of a deposition from a witness to a Federalist's ranting about the offense to government when common people bestir themselves in politics. "How long must government be insulted by a set of damned cut-throat Democrats?" the offender was alleged to have asked. A piece in the Republican *Farmer's Register* described those enlisted under the banner of democracy as "enthusiastic men, lovers of liberty, of warm passions and benevolent hearts"—hardly the qualities that commended themselves to Federalists. "If they are ignorant or dishonest, let their opponents prove it," the writer challenged. . . .

The rejection of the past that figured prominently in the Republican writings of the 1790s . . . represented a faith in the future that was altogether novel, a future that embraced the entire human race.

Basic to this new faith was a reconceptualization of human nature. The postlapsarian view—"in Adam's fall did sin we all"—was stigmatized, as it had not been before, as a class doctrine. "Whence is it that the doctrine of the equality of man has so long been hidden from the human race?" Phineas Hedges asked an Ulster County July 4th crowd, and proceeded to answer his rhetorical question with a history of repression starting with the Egyptians and ending with Great Britain. Typical of this new approach was Tunis Wortman's "Oration on the Influence of Social Institutions Upon Human Morals and Happiness" given before the Tammany Society in 1796. In one of the most ambitious efforts to reconcile the abilities of ordinary men with the historic proof of their debased condition, the author, a young New York lawyer, grounded his optimism about the future on the malleable nature of the human mind. Wortman developed the familiar enlightenment argument about the baleful influence of autocratic governments and pointed out the conundrum that they condemn people to ignorance and superstition and hence produce the evils that are used to justify their repressiveness. Debasing human character in this way, he said, was "the constant and uniform theme of tyrants." The subversive aspects of these statements were not lost on audiences brought up on the Calvinist doctrine of original sin. By connecting the idea of the depravity of man with the venerable rationales for authoritarian institutions, Wortman was clearly flinging down the gauntlet to those Federalist magistrates and ministers who endorsed energetic government. According to him, "excessive energy in government" accounted for "all those rigid codes of law that have subverted the natural liberties of mankind." He concluded his oration by saying that "those who think that men are naturally vicious and degraded will of consequence become attached to that form of government which embraces the greatest proportion of coercion and restraint." For other, enlightened men, the popular belief that human vices and virtues "are part of man's original constitution" had been shown up as false, Wortman said, because reason had demonstrated that ugly human qualities should be traced instead to "the errors and abuses that have at every period existed in political establishments."

These assertions about the newly discovered capacity of human beings to develop constructively under conditions of freedom undermined traditional notions about authority in several ways. By denying natural inequality they undercut the old argument that God had created the talented few for some purpose. Making authoritarian institutions the cause rather than the consequence of human waywardness turned the traditional justification for them on its head, while at the same time the new claims that human beings could take care of themselves removed the rationale for vigorous government. . . .

What clearly animated the Republicans was the principle of hope. . . . Republican hopes . . . were fed from many sources. The successful Revolution against England was one such. The foes of religious uniformity took heart from the disestablishment of the Church of England in Virginia. A tribute to the combined efforts of the dissenting Presbyterian and Baptist sects and religious rationalists like Madison and Jefferson, the decade-long struggle involved the mobilization of thousands of ordinary voters. Another lively expression of hope in the 1790s bubbled up from millenarian springs. Jedidiah Peck, for instance, mingled quotations from Thomas Paine and predictions of the global spread of representative democracy with references to monarchies as the anti-Christ, the beast, and the literal kingdom of Satan. Imagery from the Book of Revelations was frequently evoked to describe the social order aborning, and evangelical Protestants found nothing incompatible between their piety and the affirmation of the natural and imprescriptible rights of man. Another strong source of hope issued from the fact of scientific achievement. Writers spoke of the recent attainment of "the true principles of political science." One Republican announced that "comparatively society is in political science what infants are respecting knowledge." Another suggested that progressive improvement would enable men "to penetrate into the mysteries of animate and inanimate matter."

The economy nurtured hopes in two complementary ways. The sense of a new commercial age fed into expectations of fundamental change, and the conception of the economy as a natural system with lawlike regularities provided specific answers to the reservations expressed by conservatives. Hardly a Republican gathering disbanded without hearing toasts and resolutions extolling agriculture and trade. "In a free government," as one typical orator explained, "commerce expands her sails; Prompted by a spirit of enterprize and a desire of gain, men venture the dangers of a boisterous ocean in pursuit of new commodities. With wider acquaintance of man the elements of the monk and the barbarian dissolve into the sympathizing heart of a citizen of civilized life." "Legislators of the people," an anonymous writer said, "should never neglect any means of promoting agriculture. It is the basis of the happiness of the people, the strength of empires, the aliment of commerce, and the foundation of manufacturers." In a similar manner, Republican Congressman Edward Livingston toasted "The Colossus of American freedom—may it bestride the commerce of the world."

As even these celebratory remarks suggest, Republican claims for future economic development were tied to the belief in economic freedom. Alexander Hamilton labeled the idea that commerce might regulate itself a "wild speculative paradox," but Adam Smith's invisible hand was warmly clasped by the Republicans. . . .

At the most general level, the Republicans' expectation of a sustained prosperity based upon an ever-expanding global exchange of goods undercut the Federalists rationale for energetic government. It was no longer needed to protect the weak from the strong, the hungry from the hoarders, the survival of the whole from the selfish acts of the few. An increased level of productivity had solved that ancient problem. Nor in Republican thinking was government needed to direct economic activities to secure a larger share of a finite pie in an age of commercial expansion. This was what the English example offered and the Republicans feared. As one newspaper writer noted, Great Britain had enjoyed a long period of economic growth, but "the body of the British nation live in a state of abject dependence upon the potent few. The hard earned wages are wrung from the hands of the laboring part of the community" to support the government and pay the interest on a national debt that only grows larger. Here is a critique of the British funded debt that owes nothing to the classical republican obsession with political corruption. The Republicans interpret the mercantilist goals of national wealth and power as parts of another scheme of the few to wrest natural and equal rights from the many. . . .

The passionate party warfare of the 1790s did not determine whether or not America's economy would be capitalistic. That had already been decided long ago with the integration of the colonies into the great Atlantic trade. Nor did the contest between the Federalists and Republicans resemble a replay of the earlier colonial division between conservatives and innovators over such things as paper money and regulated markets, for both the Republican and Federalist parties were dominated by modernists—men committed to economic change. Rather, the fight was over the social and political context in which this change was to take place. Would the traditional division between the few and the many persist? Would the nation's economic development be directed from the center through the government's fiscal and banking policies? Would those in authority continue to be protected through laws and public usages promoting deference? The natural harmony of autonomous individuals freely exerting themselves to take care of their own interests while expanding the range of free exchange and free inquiry was the liberating alternative Republicans juxtaposed to the Federalists' expectations of orderly growth within venerable social limits. They celebrated work not for its glorification of God but rather for its contribution to human productivity and knowledge. In place of virtue, they extolled the independence of individuals and the voluntary cooperation of private persons.

Republicanism, Capitalism, and Slavery in the 1790s

JOHN ASHWORTH

. . . Professor Appleby . . . insists that it is their "rejection of the past as a respository of wisdom that constitutes the most important element in the ideology of the Jeffersonian Republicans." The Republicans, she claims, expected a different future and they displayed a new optimism about human nature. What distinguished them from their opponents was their single-minded effort to refashion the political institutions of the United States; theirs was "the first truly American political movement" and it shifted the trajectory of American political development decisively and inexorably away from the path of the mother country. In Professor Appleby's opinion it was not the Jeffersonians but the Federalists who "in all essentials . . . remained classical republicans." Both parties were capitalist but while the Federalists expected "orderly growth within venerable social limits," the Republicans were archetypal liberals who looked forward to "capitalism and a new social order."

[A] need for qualification is apparent when we consider the extent to which the Republicans espoused what Appleby terms "the principle of hope." In her view the Jeffersonians were hopeful and optimistic about the future; the Federalists, as befitted classical republicans, were not. But this is problematic. . . .

When we turn to the partisans of the 1790s, simple generalizations are . . . difficult. . . . [A]s John Zvesper points out in his excellent study of Federalist and Republican ideology, the Federalists in the late 1780s and early 1790s were both confident and optimistic. It is true that this confidence

From "The Jeffersonians: Classical Republicans or Liberal Capitalists?" by John Ashworth from *Journal of American Studies*, 18 (1984), pp. 425–435. Reprinted with the permission of Cambridge University Press.

was swiftly dissipated when the Republican challenge was mounted but this is still enough to place a question mark against Appleby's assertion. When we consider the Republicans the problem is still more complex. Undoubtedly Appleby's interpretation fits Thomas Jefferson himself, and fits him well. Jefferson's optimism does differentiate him from many classical republicans and Appleby has justly re-emphasized this. But as far as Madison is concerned her conclusions are far less satisfactory. . . . Madison expected the United States to develop, as Britain had done, a surplus population of landless poor. This was a prospect which was most unwelcome and disturbing to him. . . .

Similar problems are apparent when the concept of equality is considered. For Appleby classical republicanism seems a highly inegalitarian set of doctrines; she emphasizes its "assertion that society is divided between the few and the many—the elite and the common people." This was "an assertion of human inequality presumed to be rooted in nature and therefore unavoidable in social practice." Clearly on this definition the Federalists are more thoroughly classical than the Republicans. It was John Adams who argued most persistently for a separate chamber for the natural aristocracy and one can certainly find precedents for this in English republican thought of the seventeenth century. But there was another side to classical republicanism and it is this which other scholars . . . have stressed. It is possible to trace from Aristotle through Harrington to Trenchard and Gordon an insistence that republicanism could be subverted by a distribution of wealth that was too uneven. Indeed . . . Trenchard and Gordon had to concede that England in their day was not yet ready for a pure republic because Englishmen were too unequal in their property holdings. . . . [T]he Jeffersonians retained this suspicion of inequality but the Federalists did not—at least not to the same extent. Who then were the classical republicans? Clearly the answer depends upon the definitions being used. If classical republicanism is inegalitarian in its thrust then it is plainly the Federalists, if egalitarian then of course the Republicans would more easily qualify. In fact it is Jefferson himself who emerges as the archetypal classical republican in this respect. . . . Jefferson wished to have the natural aristocracy in government. Yet he placed a heavy reliance upon social and economic equality as a necessary foundation for republicanism. Perhaps this combination of egalitarian and inegalitarian assumptions was unusual in the United States at this time; nevertheless this aspect of the Republican leader's thought places a large question mark over Professor Appleby's thesis.

It does not, however, entirely vitiate her argument. At the very center of her interpretation is her understanding of the relationship between Republicanism and capitalism and this clearly requires close scrutiny. Now for Professor Appleby, capitalism means little more than commerce, or, more specifically, production for the market and for monetary gain as well as for subsistence needs. Undoubtedly, Republicans were in this sense capitalists since few if any of them ever condemned commerce or advocated individual self-sufficiency. Few scholars, however, have, in recent years at any rate, suggested otherwise. It is more important, though more difficult, to gauge the extent of Republican commitment to commerce and to determine how large a price the Republicans would pay for commercial development. . . .

[I]t is surely a mistake to reduce capitalism to commerce. To do so is to overlook what is specific to capitalism, namely the relation between the capitalist who owns the means of production and the labourer who has little alternative but to work for him. It is, one may suggest, the dynamic of this relationship, rather than the mere fact of production for the market, which is responsible for the extraordinary increase in productive power which the modern era has witnessed. At any rate the Republicans of the 1790s were acutely aware of the importance of this relationship: they certainly did not miss the distinction between commerce and capitalism. There is no doubt that they were deeply suspicious of the dependence which capitalism (as I have defined it) entailed. For the whole classical tradition insisted upon the need for independence. Virtue and liberty required that the individual be free to exercise his own judgment; the wage labourer lacked this freedom. Similarly a capitalist economy would necessarily contain large inequalities and these too would subvert a republic. Hence the almost universal hostility of Republicans to manufacturers. Their arguments can be traced back through the centuries to antiquity.

The Republicans then welcomed commerce in that they associated it with progress and the advancement of humanity. But it is inappropriate to argue, as does Professor Appleby, that because the United States in the 1790s was undergoing rapid commercial expansion and because the Republicans did well in commercial states like Pennsylvania and New York they were quintessentially commercial in outlook. The relationship between economy and ideology is generally more complex than this deterministic model would suggest, and many Republicans were ambivalent about commerce. [Drew] McCoy sums it up well: "American republicanism must be understood as an ideology in transition, for it reflected an attempt to cling to the traditional republican spirit of classical antiquity without disregarding the new imperatives of a more modern commercial society." It is true that the social ideal which they envisioned would prove fleeting and transitory; it is none the less one whose distinctiveness historians should recognize.

In another sense too it is misleading to label the Republicans "capitalist." It is surely clear in retrospect that the United States in the 1790s had many of the characteristics of an underdeveloped economy. One of its chief problems was a chronic shortage of capital. It was against this that many of Hamilton's policies were directed. But the laisser-faire approach of the Republicans was one which would leave this central problem unresolved. The Republicans were more concerned with acquiring land in order to preserve individual autonomy than with facilitating capital accumulation which they feared would ultimately subvert that autonomy.

One must not push this argument too far. As we have seen, it would be a mistake to argue that men like Thomas Jefferson believed that a golden age lay somewhere in the past; as Professor Appleby has shown, Republicans sought a new future. It would be a new, commercialized and as we can now term it, pre-capitalist future. And it would never arrive.

. . . Is it possible to suggest an alternative [argument]?

Clearly any such hypothesis must be highly tentative; the present state of knowledge simply will not support any firm generalizations. Yet it is surely of interest that the Republicans drew a disproportionate amount of support from the South. In the words of Richard Buel "the essential division" in politics was "between a Republican South and a Federalist New England," with the middle Atlantic states divided. There were of course exceptions but the South undoubtedly provided the Republicans with disproportionate electoral support and with the great majority of their national leaders and spokesmen. In addition to the three Presidents of the Virginia dynasty, men like John Taylor, John Randolph and Nathaniel Macon were all Southerners. In this connection it is instructive to consider what would have happened to American politics from the 1790s if there had been no states south of the Mason-Dixon line. Historians would then doubtless have recorded the successful attempt of the Federalist elite to impose a republican but avowedly anti-democratic political system upon the nation. After the turbulence which often accompanies war a regime more akin to that of the British would have emerged. But in actuality the Republican party upset all this. Nothing is more striking in retrospect than the willingness of Republican leaders to take their case to the people. Jefferson himself always insisted that the Republicans "cherished" the people while the Federalists feared or despised them. In 1787, at a time when the Federalists (as they would become) were fearful of social unrest and political upheaval, Jefferson asserted that "a little rebellion now and then is a good thing, and as necessary in the political world as storms in the natural." Buel attributes this populism to the greater security which the Southerners enjoyed in their leadership roles. Ironically, "aristocratic" Southern leaders, perhaps because of the greater economic homogeneity of the South, could embrace democracy in the confident belief that their own positions would be safe.

Buel's explanation is a perceptive one. Did Southern leadership give encouragement and organizational support to the northern Republicans? Did it make their views more popular and more respectable? As yet our knowledge is not sufficient to allow a firm answer to these questions. If they can be answered in the affirmative, however, it is difficult not to be reminded of Edmund Morgan's brilliant argument in his book *American Slavery, American Freedom.* Here Morgan claimed that it was in large part slavery which enabled Americans to embrace republicanism. Slavery created a "sense of common identity" among whites and altered the relationship between elites and masses. Because the slaveholders lived off the sweated labour of blacks the poorer whites were their allies rather than their antagonists. Similarly the main threat to republicanism, the fear of levelling if the poorer classes could vote, was much diminished if not entirely removed. As Morgan puts it: "Aristocrats could more safely preach equality in a slave society than in a free one" since slaves would never be permitted to form levelling mobs. The labour force in Virginia "was composed mainly of slaves"; this was a major structural influence upon Virginian society and it paved the way for Jefferson's celebrated eulogy of the yeoman farmer.

Morgan argues that slavery propelled Virginians and perhaps other

Americans towards republicanism. His book is concerned primarily with the period up to and including the Declaration of Independence. Critics may reply that other nations before and since have embraced republicanism without slavery and that not all slave societies have generated republican sentiment. It is thus difficult to argue that slavery is either a necessary or a sufficient condition for republicanism. But is it not possible that Morgan's insights apply with greater force to the *democratization* of the republic in the half century or so after the adoption of the Federal constitution? For at this time the United States managed this remarkable transformation without any major political or social upheaval. The importance of Jeffersonian ideology, the role of Southern leaders and the importance of Southern voters in the Republican and Jacksonian Democratic parties are all so evident as to require little comment. In the 1790s the Republicans began to popularize American politics; historians need to ask what the precise function of American slavery was in this process.

Recent studies of republican ideology have paid little attention to slavery. In one sense this is unsurprising; the ideologues themselves did not discuss the relationship between their ideas and the society which generated them. The hypothesis which connects democracy (or republicanism) with slavery cannot be tested by simple reference to partisan pronouncements since it need not assert that partisans were themselves aware of the connection. In another sense, however, the omission is rather startling. For classical societies were, of course, slave societies. Can it be a coincidence that the ideal of the autonomous and equal republican citizen should be generated in the slave societies of antiquity, and then rise to ideological dominance in the (partially) slave society of late eighteenth-century America?

The suggestion is then that the relationship between classical republicanism and Jeffersonianism is a real and important one despite Professor Appleby's criticisms. It is clearly the case that some Jeffersonians did reject some of the ideals and assumptions of classical and country thinkers and Joyce Appleby has rightly drawn attention to this. But it seems to me that she fails in her attempt to depict the Republican as a liberal capitalist. Optimistic though Jefferson may have been and commercially-minded as Madison undoubtedly was, it is surely unwise to exaggerate the similarity between their thought and that of modern Americans.

⊞ *F U R T H E R   R E A D I N G*

Harry Ammon, *The Genêt Mission* (1973)

Joyce O. Appleby, "Republicanism in Old and New Contexts," *William & Mary Quarterly,* 3rd ser., 43 (1986): 20–34

Lance Banning, "Jeffersonian Ideology Revisited: Liberal and Classical Ideas in the New American Republic," *William & Mary Quarterly,* 3rd ser., 43 (1986): 3–19

——, *The Jeffersonian Persuasion: The Evolution of a Party Ideology* (1978)

Samuel Flagg Bemis, *Pinckney's Treaty: America's Advantage from Europe's Distress, 1783–1800* (1961)

Ruth Bloch, *Visionary Republic: Millennial Themes in American Thought, 1756–1800* (1986)

Ruth Bogin, "Petitioning and the New Moral Economy of Post-Revolutionary America," *William & Mary Quarterly,* 3rd ser., 45 (1988): 391–426

Jerald A. Combs, *The Jay Treaty: Political Battleground of the Founding Fathers* (1970)

Alexander De Conde, *The Quasi-War: The Politics and Diplomacy of the Undeclared War with France, 1791–1801* (1966)

———, *Entangling Alliance: Politics and Diplomacy Under George Washington* (1958)

Michael Durey, "Thomas Paine's Apostles: Radical Emigrés and the Triumph of Jeffersonian Republicanism," *William & Mary Quarterly,* 3rd ser., 44 (1987): 661–668

Eric Foner, *Tom Paine and Revolutionary America* (1976)

Philip S. Foner, *The Democratic Republican Societies, 1790–1800* (1976)

Felix Gilbert, *To the Farewell Address: Ideas of Early American Foreign Policy* (1961)

John R. Howe, "Republican Thought and the Political Violence of the 1790s," *American Quarterly* 19 (1967): 147–165

———, *The Changing Political Thought of John Adams* (1966)

Ralph Ketchum, *Presidents Above Party: The First American Presidency, 1789–1829* (1984)

Richard Kohn, *Eagle and Sword: The Federalists and the Creation of the Military Establishment in America, 1783–1802* (1975)

Stephen G. Kurtz, *The Presidency of John Adams: The Collapse of Federalism, 1795–1800* (1957)

Walter LaFeber, "Foreign Policies of a New Nation," in William Appleman Williams, ed., *From Colony to Empire* (1972)

Eugene P. Link, *Democratic Republican Societies, 1790–1800* (1942)

Drew McCoy, *The Elusive Republic: Political Economy in Jeffersonian America* (1980)

Forrest McDonald, *The Presidency of George Washington* (1979)

Michael Merrill and Sean Wilentz, eds., *The Key of Liberty: William Manning and Plebeian Democracy, 1741–1814* (1992)

John C. Miller, *The Federalist Era, 1789–1801* (1960)

———, *Crises in Freedom: The Alien and Sedition Acts* (1951)

Edmund S. Morgan, *The Genius of George Washington* (1980)

John R. Nelson, *Liberty and Property: Political Economy and Policymaking in the New Nation, 1789–1812* (1987)

Thomas Pangle, *The Origins of Modern Republicanism: The Moral Vision of the American Founders and the Philosophy of Locke* (1983)

Daniel Sisson, *The Revolution of 1800* (1974)

Thomas P. Slaughter, *The Whiskey Rebellion: Frontier Epilogue to the American Revolution* (1986)

Marshall Smelser, "The Federalist Period as an Age of Passion," *American Quarterly,* 10 (1958): 391–419

James Morton Smith, *Freedom's Fetters: The Alien and Sedition Laws and American Civil Liberties* (1956)

William Stinchcombe, *The XYZ Affair* (1981)

Gerald Stourzh, *Alexander Hamilton and the Idea of Republican Government* (1970)

Garry Wills, *Cincinnatus: George Washington and the Enlightenment* (1984)

Alfred F. Young, ed., *Beyond the American Revolution* (1992)

———, *The Democratic Republicans of New York: The Origins, 1763–1797* (1966)

John Zvesper, *Political Philosophy and Rhetoric: A Study of the Origins of American Political Parties* (1977)

CHAPTER
4

The Republican Jefferson
and the Jeffersonian Republic

⌖

Thomas Jefferson rose to the presidency believing that his election had vindicated the ideals of the American Revolution. He returned to his beloved Virginia estate eight years later, exhausted and frustrated by his term in office, leaving the nation embroiled in diplomatic disputes with the great European powers. Over the interim he had endured the difficulties of trying to square policy and statecraft with his basic political views. Historians still argue over how well he succeeded and what his views really were.

Assessing Jefferson is difficult because of his legendary status in the nation's collective political memory as St. Thomas of Monticello—a status which has led later generations to read their own ideas into Jefferson's writings. His most famous passage, the opening section of the Declaration of Independence, remains the most inspiring statement ever written about American equality. (As we shall see, its words would resound loudly during the first half of the nineteenth century.) In other writings, including Notes on the State of Virginia *(1787), Jefferson appeared to endorse a particular vision of American freedom, based on the virtues he ascribed to independent farmers. In fact, the meanings behind these remarks are far from self-evident, especially in light of Jefferson's own subsequent conduct as president. Nor was Jefferson a saint, as his political enemies (since joined by some revisionist historians) hastened to point out. Nevertheless, his was the most important individual presence in American political life at the opening of the nineteenth century. By coming to terms with him and his travails, we may better understand the tensions that shaped the new republic, in a world beset by revolution, war, and reaction.*

Every major event of Jefferson's presidency raises questions, beginning with his inaugural address. What lay behind Jefferson's conciliatory tone, in contrast to his pronouncements of the 1790s? How can the Louisiana Purchase of 1803—a costly enterprise undertaken by an energetic executive—be reconciled with Jefferson's professed devotion to frugality, strict construction of the Constitution, and limited executive powers? What was at stake in Jefferson's battles over the judiciary? Why, in the face of harassment on the high seas, did Jefferson implement his embargo policy, yet another act of federal coercion? In effect, was

President Jefferson truly a Jeffersonian? If so, what do we mean by ''Jeffersonian''? And what implications did his beliefs and actions have for the nation at large?

✢ D O C U M E N T S

Jefferson's first inaugural address, reprinted here as the first document, outlined a set of shared principles that supposedly united Republicans and Federalists. In the second document, comprising excerpts from two letters—one from Alexander Hamilton, the other from John Randolph, a young Republican congressman from Virginia—the correspondence suggests how Jefferson looked to opponents inside and outside his own party at the start of his presidency. The Louisiana Purchase usually counts as one of Jefferson's great triumphs. Yet it never would have happened if a Haitian black revolution had not spoiled Napoleon's dream of a New World empire. In the third document Robert R. Livingston, the U.S. minister to France, betrays the accidental and improvised circumstances surrounding the purchase negotiations. And Jefferson's exchange in the fourth document with his friend and adviser Wilson Cary Nicholas about the purchase raises further questions about the president's constitutional views. The celebrated Supreme Court decision in the case of *Marbury* v. *Madison,* written by Chief Justice John Marshall and excerpted as the fifth document, illuminates the continuing battle over the central government's powers and internal structure. Although the *Marbury* decision favored the administration on the specific matters at issue, Marshall's reasoning led in directions that were at odds with ideas associated with Jefferson since the 1790s. By 1804 early divisions had unleashed some passionate political hatreds, as the sixth selection illustrates. The Federalist Timothy Pickering commented on the Senate debate over the Republican removal of a federal justice; two years later, the Old Republican John Taylor of Caroline offered a very different judgment of Jefferson and his followers. In the final selection, four brief excerpts—a private letter and a public defense from Jefferson and protest petitions from two New England towns—reveal different sides of the debate over the embargo.

President Thomas Jefferson
on Political Reconciliation, 1801

During the contest of opinion through which we have passed, the animation of discussion and of exertions has sometimes worn an aspect which might impose on strangers unused to think freely and to speak and to write what they think; but this being now decided by the voice of the nation, announced according to the rules of the constitution, all will, of course, arrange themselves under the will of the law, and unite in common efforts for the common good. All, too, will bear in mind this sacred principle, that though the will of the majority is in all cases to prevail, that will, to be rightful, must be reasonable; that the minority possess their equal rights, which equal laws must protect, and to violate which would be oppression. Let us, then, fellow citizens, unite with one heart and one mind. Let us restore to social intercourse that harmony and affection without which liberty and even life itself are but dreary things. And let us reflect that having banished from our land that religious intolerance under which mankind so long bled and suffered, we have yet gained little if we countenance a political intolerance as despotic, as wicked, and capable of as bitter and bloody persecutions. During the throes and convulsions of the ancient world, during the agonizing spasms of infuriated man, seeking through blood and slaughter his long-lost liberty, it was not wonderful that the agitation of the billows should reach even this distant and peaceful shore; that this should be more felt and feared by some and less by others; that this should divide opinions as to measures of safety. But every difference of opinion is not a difference of principle. We have called by different names brethren of the same principle. We are all republicans—we are all federalists. If there be any among us who would wish to dissolve this Union or to change its republican form, let them stand undisturbed as monuments of the safety with which error of opinion may be tolerated where reason is left free to combat it. I know, indeed, that some honest men fear that a republican government cannot be strong; that this government is not strong enough. But would the honest patriot, in the full tide of successful experiment, abandon a government which has so far kept us free and firm, on the theoretic and visionary fear that this government, the world's best hope, may by possibility want energy to preserve itself? I trust not. I believe this, on the contrary, the strongest government on earth. I believe it is the only one where every man, at the call of the laws, would fly to the standard of the law, and would meet invasions of the public order as his own personal concern. Sometimes it is said that man cannot be trusted with the government of himself. Can he, then, be trusted with the government of others? Or have we found angels in the forms of kings to govern him? Let history answer this question.

Let us, then, with courage and confidence pursue our own federal and republican principles, our attachment to our union and representative government. Kindly separated by nature and a wide ocean from the exterminating havoc of one quarter of the globe; too high-minded to endure the degradations of the others; possessing a chosen country, with room enough for our descendants to the thousandth and thousandth generation; entertaining a due sense of our equal right to the use of our own faculties, to the acquisitions of our industry, to honor and confidence from our fellow citizens, resulting not from birth but from our actions and their sense of them; enlightened by a benign religion, professed, indeed, and practiced in various forms, yet all of them including honesty, truth, temperance, gratitude, and the love of man; acknowledging and adoring an overruling Providence, which by all its dispensations proves that it delights in the happiness of man here and his greater happiness hereafter; with all these blessings, what more is necessary to make us a happy and prosperous people? Still one thing more, fellow citizens—a wise and frugal government, which shall restrain men from injuring one another, which shall leave them otherwise free to regulate their own pursuits of industry and improvement, and shall not take from the mouth of labor the bread it has earned. This is the sum of good government, and this is necessary to close the circle of our felicities.

. . . [I]t is proper that you should understand what I deem the essential principles of our government, and consequently those which ought to shape its administration. I will compress them within the narrowest compass they will bear, stating the general principle, but not all its limitations. Equal and exact justice to all men, of whatever state or persuasion, religious or political; peace, commerce, and honest friendship, with all nations—entangling alliances with none; the support of the state governments in all their rights, as the most competent administrations for our domestic concerns and the surest bulwarks against anti-republican tendencies; the preservation of the general government in its whole constitutional vigor, as the sheet anchor of our peace at home and safety abroad; a jealous care of the right of election by the people—a mild and safe corrective of abuses which are lopped by the sword of the revolution where peaceable remedies are unprovided; absolute acquiescence in the decisions of the majority—the vital principle of republics, from which there is no appeal but to force, the vital principle and immediate parent of despotism; a well-disciplined militia—our best reliance in peace and for the first moments of war, till regulars may relieve them; the supremacy of the civil over the military authority; economy in the public expense, that labor may be lightly burdened; the honest payment of our debts and sacred preservation of the public faith; encouragement of agriculture, and of commerce as its handmaid; the diffusion of information and the arraignment of all abuses at the bar of public reason; freedom of religion; freedom of the press; freedom of person under the protection of the *habeas corpus;* and trial by juries impartially selected—these principles form the bright constellation which has gone before us, and guided our steps through an age of revolution and reformation. The wisdom of our sages and the blood of our heroes have been devoted to their attainment. They should be the creed of our political faith—the text of civil instruction—the touchstone by which to try the services of those we trust; and should we wander from them in moments of error or alarm, let us hasten to retrace our steps and to regain the road which alone leads to peace, liberty, and safety. . . .

Two Politicians on Jefferson, 1801

Alexander Hamilton to James Bayard, January 16, 1801

[I]t is too late for me to become [Jefferson's] apologist. Nor can I have any disposition to do it. I admit that his politics are tinctured with fanaticism, that he is too much in earnest in his democracy, that he has been a mischevous enemy to the principal measures of our past administration, that he is crafty and persevering in his objects, that he is not scrupulous about the means of success, nor very mindful of truth, and that he is a contemptible hypocrite. But it is not true as is alleged that he is an enemy to the power of the Executive, or that he is for confounding all the powers in the House of Rs. It is a fact which I have frequently mentioned that while we were in the administration together he was generally for a large construction of the Executive authority, and not backward to act upon it in cases which coincided with his views. Let it be added, that in his theoretic Ideas he has considered as improper the participations of the Senate in the Executive Authority. I have more than once made the reflection that viewing himself as the reversioner, he was solicitous to come into possession of a Good Estate. Nor is it true that Jefferson is zealot enough to do anything in pursuance of his principles which will contravene his popularity, or his interest. He is as likely as any man I know to temporize—to calculate what will be likely to promote his own reputation and advantage; and the probable result of such a temper is the preservation of systems, though originally opposed, which being once established, could not be overturned without danger to the person who did it. To my mind a true estimate of Mr J.'s character warrants the expectation of a temporizing rather than a violent system. That Jefferson has manifested a culpable predilection for France is certainly true; but I think it a question whether it did not proceed quite as much from her *popularity* among us, as from sentiment, and in proportion as that popularity is diminished his zeal will cool. Add to this that there is no fair reason to suppose him capable of being corrupted, which is a security that he will not go beyond certain limits. It is not at all improbable that under the change of circumstances Jefferson's Gallicism has considerably abated. . . .

John Randolph to Joseph H. Nicholson, January 1, 1801

'Tis true that I have observed, with a disgust, which I have been at no pains to conceal, a spirit of *personal* attachment evinced by some of the supporters of Mr. J[efferson] whose republicanism has not been the most unequivocal. . . . There are those men who support republicanism from *monarchical* principles—and if the head of that very great and truly good and wise man can be turned with adulatory nonsense, they will endeavor to persuade him that our salvation depends on an individual. This is the essence of monarchy—and with this doctrine I have been, am, and ever will be at issue.

Robert R. Livingston on the Louisiana Purchase Negotiations, 1803

I have just come from the Minister of the Treasury. Our conversation was so important, that I think it necessary to write it, while the impressions are strong upon my mind; and the rather, as I fear I shall not have time to copy and send this letter, if I defer it till morning.

By my letter of yesterday, you learned that the Minister had asked me whether I would agree to purchase Louisiana, & c. On the 12th, I called upon him to press this matter further. He then thought proper to declare that his proposition was only personal, but still requested me to make an offer; and, upon declining to do so, as I expected Mr. Monroe the next day, he shrugged up his shoulders, and changed the conversation. Not willing, however, to lose sight of it, I told him I had been long endeavoring to bring him to some point; but, unfortunately, without effect: that I wished merely to have the negotiation opened by any proposition on his part; and, with that view, had written him a note which contained that request. . . . He told me he would answer my note, but that he must do it evasively, because Louisiana was not theirs. I smiled at this assertion, and told him I had seen the treaty recognizing it. . . . I told him I should receive with pleasure any communication from him, but that we were not disposed to trifle; that the times were critical, and though I did not know what instructions Mr. Monroe might bring, I was perfectly satisfied that they would require a precise and prompt notice; that I was very fearful, from the little progress I had made, that my Government would consider me as a very indolent negotiator. He laughed, and told me that he would give me a certificate that I was the most importunate he had met with. . . .

I told him that the United States were anxious to preserve peace with France; that, for that reason, they wished to remove them to the west side of the Mississippi; that we would be perfectly satisfied with New Orleans and the Floridas, and had no disposition to extend across the river; that, of course, we would not give any great sum for the purchase; that he was right in his idea of the extreme exorbitancy of the demand, which would not fall short of one hundred and twenty-five millions; that, however, we would be ready to purchase, provided the sum was reduced to reasonable limits. He then pressed me to name the sum. I told him that this was not worth while, because, as he only treated the inquiry as a matter of curiosity, any declaration of mine would have no effect. If a negotiation was to be opened, we should (Mr. Monroe and myself) make the offer after mature reflection. This compelled him to declare, that, though he was not authorized expressly to make the inquiry from me, yet, that, if I could mention any sum that came near the mark, that could be accepted, he would communicate it to the First Consul [Napoleon Bonaparte]. I told him that we had no sort of authority to go to a sum that bore any proportion to what he mentioned; but that, as he himself considered the demand as too high, he would oblige me by telling me what he thought would be reasonable. He replied that, if we would name sixty millions, and take upon us the American claims, to the amount of twenty more, he would try how far this would be accepted. I told him that it was vain to ask anything that was so greatly beyond our means; that true policy would dictate to the First Consul not to press such a demand; that he must know that it would render the present Government unpopular, and have a tendency, at the next election, to throw the power into the hands of men who were most hostile to a connection with France; and that this would probably happen in the midst of a war. I asked him whether the few millions acquired at this expense would not be too dearly bought?

He frankly confessed that he was of my sentiments; but that he feared the Consul would not relax. I asked him to press this argument upon him, together with the danger of seeing the country pass into the hands of Britain. I told him that he had seen the ardor of the Americans to take it by force, and the difficulty with which they were restrained by the prudence of the President; that he must easily see how much the hands of the war party would be strengthened, when they learned that France was upon the eve of a rupture with England. He admitted the weight of all this: "But," says he, "you know the temper of a youthful conqueror; everything he does is rapid as lightning; we have only to speak to him as an opportunity presents itself, perhaps in a crowd, when he bears no contradiction. When I am alone with him, I can speak more freely, and he attends; but this opportunity seldom happens, and is always accidental. Try, then, if you can not come up to my mark. Consider the extent of the country, the exclusive navigation of the river, and the importance of having no neighbors to dispute you, no war to dread." I told him that I considered all these as important considerations, but there was a point beyond which we could not go, and that fell far short of the sum he mentioned. . . .

I speak now without reflection, and without having seen Mr. Monroe, as it was midnight when I left the Treasury Office, and is now near 3 o'clock. It is so very important that you should be apprized that a negotiation is actually opened, even before Mr. Monroe has been presented, in order to calm the tumult which the news of war will renew, that I have lost no time in communicating it. We shall do all we can to cheapen the purchase; but my present sentiment is that we shall buy. . . .

Jeffersonian Constitutionalism and the Louisiana Purchase, 1803

Wilson Cary Nicholas to Thomas Jefferson, September 3, 1803

I have reflected much upon the conversation that I had with you, when I had last the pleasure of seeing you, about the power of the government of the U.S. to acquire territory, and to admit new States into the union. Upon an examination of the constitution, I find the power as broad as it could well be made, 3d. art. 4th., except that new states cannot be formed out of the old ones without the consent of the *state* to be dismembered; and the exception is a proof, to my mind, that it was not intended to confine the congress in the admission of new states to what was then the territory of the U.S. Nor do I see any thing in the constitution that limits the treaty making power, except the general limitations of the powers given to the government, and the evident objects for which the government was instituted. . . .

Thomas Jefferson to Wilson Cary Nicholas, September 7, 1803

I am aware of the force of the observations you make on the power given by the Constitution to Congress to admit new states into the Union, without restraining the subject to the territory then constituting the United States. But when I consider that the limits of the United States are precisely fixed by the treaty of 1783, that the constitution expressly declares itself to be made for the United States, I cannot help believing the intention was to permit Congress to admit into the union new states which should be formed out of the territory for which and under whose authority alone they were then acting. I do not believe it was meant that they might receive England, Ireland, Holland & c. into it, which would be the case on your construction. When an instrument admits two constructions, the one safe, the other dangerous, the one precise the other indefinite, I prefer that which is safe and precise. I had rather ask an enlargement of power from the nation where it is found necessary, than to assume it by a construction which would make our powers boundless. Our peculiar security is in the possession of a written constitution. Let us not make it a blank paper by construction. I say the same as to the opinion of those who consider the grant of the treaty making power as boundless. If it is, then we have no constitution. If it has bounds, they can be no others than the definitions of the powers which that instrument gives. It specifies and delineates the operations permitted to the federal government, and gives all the powers necessary to carry these into execution. Whatever of these enumerated objects is proper for a law, Congress may make the law. Whatever is proper to be executed by way of a treaty, the President and Senate may enter into the treaty; whatever is to be done by a judicial sentence, the judges may pass the sentence. Nothing is more likely than that their enumeration of powers is defective. This is the ordinary case of all human works. Let us go on then perfecting it, by adding by way of amendment to the constitution, those powers which time and trial show are still wanting. But it has been taken too much for granted that by this rigorous construction the treaty power would be reduced to nothing. . . . I confess then I think it important in the present case to set an example against broad construction by appealing for new power to the people. If however our friends shall think differently, certainly I shall acquiesce with satisfaction, confiding that the good sense of our country will correct the evil of construction when it shall produce ill effects. . . .

Chief Justice John Marshall on the Powers of the Judiciary, 1803

The constitution vests the whole judicial power of the United States in one Supreme Court, and such inferior courts as congress shall, from time to time, ordain and establish. . . .

In the distribution of this power it is declared that "the Supreme Court shall have original jurisdiction in all cases affecting ambassadors, other public ministers and consuls, and those in which a state shall be a party. In all other cases, the Supreme Court shall have appellate jurisdiction."

It has been insisted, at the bar, that as the original grant of jurisdiction, to the Supreme and inferior courts, is general, and the clause, assigning original jurisdiction to the Supreme Court, contains no negative or restrictive words, the power remains to the legislature, to assign original jurisdiction to that court in other cases than those specified in the article which has been recited; provided those cases belong to the judicial power of the United States.

If it had been intended to leave it in the discretion of the legislature to apportion the judicial power between the supreme and inferior courts according to the will of that body, it would certainly have been useless to have proceeded further than to have defined the judicial power, and the tribunals in which it should be vested. The subsequent part of the section is mere surplusage, is entirely without meaning, if such is to be the construction. If congress remains at liberty to give this court appellate jurisdiction, where the constitution has declared their jurisdiction shall be original; and original jurisdiction where the constitution has declared it shall be appellate; the distribution of jurisdiction, made in the constitution, is form without substance. . . .

The question, whether an act, repugnant to the constitution, can become the law of the land, is a question deeply interesting to the United States; but, happily, not of an intricacy proportioned to its interest. It seems only necessary to recognize certain principles, supposed to have been long and well established, to decide it.

That the people have an original right to establish, for their future government, such principles, as, in their opinion, shall most conduce to their own happiness is the basis on which the whole American fabric has been erected. The exercise of this original right is a very great exertion; nor can it, nor ought it, to be frequently repeated. The principles, therefore, so established, are deemed fundamental. And as the authority from which they proceed is supreme, and can seldom act, they are designed to be permanent.

This original and supreme will organizes the government, and assigns to different departments their respective powers. It may either stop here, or establish certain limits not to be transcended by those departments.

The government of the United States is of the latter description. The powers of the legislature are defined and limited; and that those limits may not be mistaken, or forgotten, the constitution is written. To what purpose are powers limited, and to what purpose is that limitation committed to writing, if these limits may, at any time, be passed by those intended to be restrained? The distinction between a government with limited and unlimited powers is abolished, if those limits do not confine the persons on whom they are imposed, and if acts prohibited and acts allowed, are of equal obligation. It is a proposition too plain to be contested, that the constitution controls any legislative act repugnant to it; or, that the legislature may alter the constitution by an ordinary act.

Between these alternatives there is no middle ground. The constitution is either a superior paramount law, unchangeable by ordinary means, or it is on a level with ordinary legislative acts, and, like other acts, is alterable when the legislature shall please to alter it.

If the former part of the alternative be true, then a legislative act contrary to the constitution is not law: if the latter part be true, then written constitutions are absurd attempts, on the part of the people, to limit a power in its own nature illimitable.

Certainly all those who have framed written constitutions contemplate them as forming the fundamental and paramount law of the nation, and, consequently, the theory of every such government must be, that an act of the legislature, repugnant to the constitution, is void. . . .

If an act of the legislature, repugnant to the constitution, is void, does it, notwithstanding its invalidity, bind the courts, and oblige them to give it effect? Or, in other words, though it be not law, does it constitute a rule as operative as if it was a law? This would be to overthrow in fact what was established in theory; and would seem, at first view, an absurdity too gross to be insisted on. It shall, however, receive a more attentive consideration.

It is emphatically the province and duty of the judicial department to say what the law is. Those who apply the rule to particular cases, must of necessity expound and interpret that rule. If two laws conflict with each other, the courts must decide on the operation of each.

So if a law be in opposition to the constitution; if both the law and the constitution apply to a particular case, so that the court must either decide that case conformably to the law, disregarding the constitution; or conformably to the constitution, disregarding the law; the court must determine which of these conflicting rules governs the case. This is of the very essence of judicial duty.

If, then, the courts are to regard the constitution, and the constitution is superior to any ordinary act of the legislature, the constitution, and not such ordinary act, must govern the case to which they both apply.

Those, then, who controvert the principle that the constitution is to be considered, in court, as a paramount law, are reduced to the necessity of maintaining that courts must close their eyes on the constitution, and see only the law.

This doctrine would subvert the very foundation of all written constitutions. It would declare that an act which, according to the principles and theory of our government, is entirely void, is yet, in practice, completely obligatory. It would declare that if the legislature shall do what is expressly forbidden, such act, notwithstanding the express prohibition, is in reality effectual. It would be giving to the legislature a practical and real omnipotence, with the same breath which professes to restrict their powers within narrow limits. It is prescribing limits, and declaring that those limits may be passed at pleasure. . . .

The judicial power of the United States is extended to all cases arising under the constitution. . . .

Federalists and Old Republicans Engage in Political Warfare, 1804, 1806

Timothy Pickering to Rufus King, March 3, 1804

In this debate (I am sorry it was not public) there were manifested a virulence and rancour which shocked every man who had any feelings of justice or humanity. Let this party progress in the course they have rapidly travelled two years past, and before Mr. Jefferson's second presidency expires, I shall not be surprised, if I live so long, to see bloody victims of their ambition,

"Timothy Pickering to Rufus King," Pickering papers, 14 (1804). Reprinted by permission of the Massachusetts Historical Society.

inexorable malice and revenge. One or two Marats or Robespierres, with half a dozen congenial spirits would carry along enough [. . .] to make a majority in the Senate, to concur in any measures: and by similar means they would be forced through the House of Representatives. [. . .]

John Taylor to Wilson Cary Nicholas, April 14, 1806

. . . Had the present administration done something for principle, by over-turning the sedition law construction of the constitution—or by shortening the Senate's tenure—or diminishing the president's patronage—or making that office rotatory, it would have invigorated principle to struggle for honest government, far beyond the exploits of diminishing the public debt, and coextensively increasing it by purchasing Louisiana;—for brilliant as they are, the counting-house duskishness of the subjects will rapidly consign them to oblivion; whilst the fame of ingrafting some principle into our policy, capable of redeeming and preserving its purity, would live forever. [. . .]

Contemporary Views of the Pros and Cons of Jefferson's Embargo, 1808, 1809

Thomas Jefferson, Letter to Dr. Thomas Leib, June 23, 1808

. . . With respect to the federalists, I believe we think alike; for when speaking of them, we never mean to include a worthy portion of our fellow citizens, who consider themselves as in duty bound to support the constituted authorities of every branch, and to reserve their opposition to the period of election. These having acquired the appellation of federalists, while a federal administration was in place, have not cared about throwing off their name, but adhering to their principle, are the supporters of the present order of things. The other branch of the federalists, those who are so in principle as well as in name, disapprove of the republican principles & features of our Constitution, and would, I believe, welcome any public calamity (war with England excepted) which might lessen the confidence of our country in those principles & forms. I have generally considered them rather as subjects for a mad-house. But they are now playing a game of the most mischevious tendency, without perhaps being themselves aware of it. They are endeavoring to convince England that we suffer more by the embargo than they do, & that if they will but hold out awhile, we must abandon it. It is true, the time will come when we must abandon it. But if this is before the repeal of the orders of council, we must abandon it only for a state of war. The day is not distant, when that will be preferable to a longer con-tinuance of the embargo. But we can never remove that, & let our vessels go out & be taken under these orders, without making reprisal. Yet this is the very state of things which these federal monarchists are endeavoring to bring about; and in this it is but too possible they may succeed. But the

---

Edgehill-Randolph papers, no. 1397. Reprinted by permission of University of Virginia Library.

fact is, that if we have war with England, it will be solely produced by their manœuvres. I think that in two or three months we shall know what will be the issue.

Thomas Jefferson, Annual Message, 1808

[The embargo] necessarily remains in the extent originally given to it. We have the satisfaction, however, to reflect that in return for the privations imposed by the measure, and which our fellow-citizens in general have borne with patriotism, it has had the important effects of saving our mariners and our vast mercantile property, as well as of affording time for prosecuting the defensive and provisional measures called for by the occasion. It has demonstrated to foreign nations the moderation and firmness which govern our councils, and to our citizens the necessity of uniting in support of the laws and the rights of their country, and has thus long frustrated those usurpations and spoliations which, if resisted, involved war; if submitted to, sacrificed a vital principle of our national independence. . . .

Resolutions of the town of Beverly, Massachusetts, 1809

The [citizens of Beverly] have witnessed with regret too strong a propensity to palliate and overlook the unjust aggressions of one foreign nation, and to exaggerate and misrepresent the conduct of another; that the measures pursued are calculated and designed to force us into a war with Great Britain,—a war which would be extremely detrimental to our agriculture, fatal to our commerce, and which would probably deprive us forever of the Bank fishery,—and to unite us in alliance with France, whose embrace is death.

Legislative Petition, town of Alfred, Maine, 1809

We are poor inhabitants of a small town, rendered poorer by the wayward, inconsistent policy of the general government; but life and liberty are as dear to us as to our opulent brethren of the South, and we flatter ourselves that we have as much love of liberty and abhorrence of slavery as those who oppress us in the name of Republicanism. We love liberty in principle but better in practice. We cling to a union of the States as the rock of our salvation; and nothing but a fearful looking for of despotism would induce us to wish for a severance of the band that unites us. But oppression did sever us from the British empire; and what a long and continued repetition of similar acts of the government of the United States would effect, God only knows!

⌗ E S S A Y S

The late historian Richard Hofstadter of Columbia University, the author of the first selection, disputes Jefferson's reputation as a radical visionary and portrays him as a man of caution. In the second essay, Forrest McDonald of the University of Alabama also rejects the Jefferson of legend but sees him as a consistent anti-modern ideologue. Drew McCoy, a professor of history at Clark University, in the final essay agrees with McDonald about some of the origins of Jefferson's thinking but stresses the dynamic element in Jefferson republicanism—and the ironies that flowed from it. All three essays might be fruitfully compared with those in the previous two chapters for their differing interpretations of ideology and interest in the early republic.

Jefferson as Cautious Pragmatic

RICHARD HOFSTADTER

It was characteristic of Jefferson that he perceived the keen political conflict of the years just preceding his election not as an opportunity but as a difficulty. Thanks to the efforts both of his detractors and his admirers, his historical reputation has caused us to misread him. In the Federalist tradition, later taken up by so many historians, he was a theorist, a visionary, a radical; and American liberals have praised him for the same qualities the Federalists abhorred. The modern liberal mind has been bemused by his remarks about the value of a little rebellion now and then, or watering the tree of liberty with the blood of tyrants, or having a complete constitutional revision every twenty or thirty years. But Jefferson's more provocative utterances, it has been too little noticed, were in his private correspondence. His public statements and actions were colored by a relative caution and timidity that reveal a circumspect and calculating mind—or, as so many of his contemporary foes believed, a guileful one. He was not enraptured by the drama of unrestrained political conflict; and with the very important exception of some of his views on foreign policy and war, his approach to public policy was far from utopian. He did not look forward to a vigorously innovative administration—he had seen enough of that. The most stunning achievement of his presidential years, the Louisiana Purchase, was an accident, the outcome of the collapse of Napoleon's ambitions for a Caribbean empire—the inadvertent gift of Toussaint L'Ouverture and the blacks of Haiti to this slaveholding country. Its most stunning disaster was the embargo, and the embargo itself came from Jefferson's penchant, here misapplied, for avoiding conflict. His was, as Hamilton put it in his tardy burst of pragmatic insight, a temporizing and not a violent disposition.

This disposition dictated an initial strategy of conciliation toward the Federalists, which led to a basic acceptance of the Hamiltonian fiscal system, including even the bank, to a patronage policy which Jefferson considered to be fair and compromising and hoped would appease moderate Federalists, and to an early attempt to pursue neutrality and to eschew aggravating signs of that Francophilia and Anglophobia with which the Federalists so obsessively and hyperbolically charged him. But for our concern, it is particularly important to understand that in Jefferson's mind conciliation was not a way

Richard Hofstadter, *The Idea of a Party System: The Rise of Legitimate Opposition in the United States, 1780–1840*, pp. 150–161. Copyright © 1969 by the Regents of the University of California.

of arriving at coexistence or of accommodating a two-party system, but a technique of absorption: he proposed to win over the major part of the amenable Federalists, leaving the intractables an impotent minority faction rather than a full-fledged opposition party. . . .

"The symptoms of a coalition of parties give me infinite pleasure," wrote Jefferson less than three weeks after delivering his inaugural address. "Setting aside a few only, I have been ever persuaded that the great bulk of both parties had the same principles fundamentally, and that it was only as to our foreign relations there was any division. These I hope can be so managed as to cease to be a subject of division for us. Nothing shall be spared on my part to obliterate the traces of party and consolidate the nation, if it can be done without abandonment of principle." His inaugural address itself had been designed to strike the first conciliatory note, and on the key question of party conflict it was a masterpiece of statesmanlike equivocation. It had a number of grace notes that might be calculated to appease opposition sensibilities: a prideful reference to American commerce, a strong hint about sustaining the public credit, an injunction to "pursue our own Federal and Republican principles," the memorable promise of "peace, commerce, and honest friendship with all nations, entangling alliances with none," obeisance to the memory of Washington as "our first and greatest revolutionary character," modest remarks about the fallibility of his own judgment, a promise not only to try to hold the good opinion of his supporters but also "to conciliate that of others by doing them all the good in my power," and finally, that *sine qua non* of inaugural addresses, especially necessary from one widely deemed "an atheist in religion"—an invocation of divine aid.

But it was in speaking of American conflicts that Jefferson achieved his finest subtlety. The acerbity of American political conflict, he suggested, would deceive "strangers unused to think freely and to speak and to write what they think." But now that the issue had been decided, Americans would unite for the common good. "All, too, will bear in mind this sacred principle, that though the will of the majority is in all cases to prevail, that will to be rightful must be reasonable; that the minority possess their equal rights, to violate which could be oppression." Let us restore harmony and affection to our society, he pleaded, and banish political intolerance as we have banished religious intolerance. That the agonies and agitations of Europe should have reached our shores and divided our opinions over proper measures of national safety is hardly surprising, but "every difference of opinion is not a difference of principle. We have called by different names brethren of the same principle. We are all republicans; we are all federalists."

In expressing these healing sentiments, which set a fine precedent for other chief executives taking office after acrimonious campaigns, Jefferson succeeded at a focal moment in reassuring many Federalists. Hamilton thought the address "virtually a candid retraction of past misapprehensions, and a pledge to the community that the new President will not lend himself to dangerous innovations, but in essential points tread in the steps of his predecessors." It contained some foolish but also many good ideas, George Cabot judged. "It is so conciliatory that much hope is derived from it by the Federalists," and he thought it "better liked by our party than his own." . . .

Yet the Federalists would have been much deceived if they had imagined that the striking sentence, "We are all republicans; we are all federalists," implied that Jefferson would put the principles of the two *parties,* and hence the parties themselves, on a nearly equal footing of legitimacy. The context, as well as various private utterances, showed that he meant only that almost all Americans believed both in the federal union and in the general principles of republican government, and that therefore the two parties stood close enough to be not so much reconciled as *merged,* and merged under his own standard. One can only concur here with Henry Adams's remark that Jefferson "wished to soothe the great body of his opponents, and if possible to win them over; but he had no idea of harmony or affection other than that which was to spring from his own further triumph." . . .

Chance plays its part in history. Jefferson's plan of conciliation was favored by a fortunate lull in the European wars, since peace negotiations between France and Great Britain, begun in the month of his inauguration, were concluded a year later in March 1802 when the Treaty of Amiens was at last ratified. For a few years, before war broke out again in May 1803, issues of foreign policy were less exacerbating than they had been at any time since the unwelcome arrival of Citizen Genêt. The field was thus left briefly clear for Jefferson's conciliatory strategy on domestic matters to register its effect. The essence of the strategy consisted not in what he did during these first twenty-four months of his administration—for the little he and his party did was provocative enough—but in what he did not do. One could write an alternative scenario for the Jeffersonians, which would call for an all-out attack on the bank charter, a wholesale removal of Federalist officeholders, an inundation of the judiciary with new Republican appointees, an intimate orientation toward France and increasing hostility to England—all things which the most fearful Federalists had reason, by their own lights, to expect. And here some examination of Jefferson's restraint on patronage and the Hamiltonian system is in order.

From the very earliest moment of his administration, Jefferson made it clear to some of his intimates that, however strong the Republican clamor for jobs, restraint in removals was a necessary part of his conciliatory plan. In effect, at an early and vital moment in national development, his patronage policy set the principle that to have been a political opponent of an incoming administration did not necessarily mean the loss of one's job in the civil service. That he found an efficient and respectable body of civil servants when he entered office was a tribute to the administrative practices of his predecessors; that he refused to sweep them out wholesale in response to pressure from office-hungry Republicans was a tribute to him. Rather than clean out Federalist officeholders like a petty chieftain in a partisan vendetta, he tried to arrive at a formula for what might be called civil-service coexistence—a formula that would consider both the needs of his partisans for rewards and the sensibilities of the main body of Federalist officeholders. . . .

The Hamiltonian system was a less formidable problem. As issues, funding, and assumption were dead, killed by the very success of Hamilton's system, and it would have been quixotic in Jefferson to revive them, or to try to reanimate an issue with which William Branch Giles had long before failed to rally Republican forces in Congress. "Some things," Jefferson wrote to Dupont de Nemours in January 1802, "may perhaps be left undone from motives of compromise for a time, and not to alarm by too sudden a reformation." As for Hamilton's system, though it might have been avoided in the beginning, it could now no longer be thrown off. "We can pay his debts in 15 years: but we can never get rid of his financial system. It mortifies me to be strengthening principles which I deem radically vicious, but this vice is entailed on us by the first error. In other parts of our government, I hope we shall be able by degrees to introduce sound principles and make them habitual." There follows the characteristic sentence: "What is practicable must often control what is pure theory."

Even the Bank, always more objectionable than funding or assumption, would be accepted and retained. Not only was there no attempt to repeal or impair its charter, but under Secretary of the Treasury Gallatin's urgings, its operations were actually extended. To the five banks already existing, the Republicans added three branches, in Washington (1802), Savannah (1802), and New Orleans (1805), the first and last of these on Gallatin's initiative. Jefferson, of course, never gave up his hostility to banks, and he saw in the Bank of the United States, which he still believed to be unconstitutional, a rival political force of great potentiality, one which, "penetrating by its branches every part of the Union, acting by command and in phalanx, may, in a critical moment, upset the government." For the safety of the Constitution, he wrote Gallatin, he was solicitous to "bring this powerful enemy to a perfect subordination under its authorities." And yet he was willing to accept its existence, even its expansion, so long as he could go on grumbling and denouncing it. Gallatin kept assuring him that it was useful, and here again what was practicable was allowed to control pure theory, and Jefferson's relatively sophisticated sense of politics overruled his agrarian economics. Madison was to follow him in approving the Bank's continuance—a matter, he said, of "expediency and almost necessity," a thing confirmed by "deliberate and reiterated precedents." In 1811, when the Bank was permitted to die with the expiration of its twenty-year charter, and at a moment when the country was about to need it most, it had many friends among the agrarian Republicans, who were reluctant to see it go.

It was, of course, the state banks, chartered by Republican legislatures, that multiplied and flourished during the first decade of Republican rule, and toward these Jefferson, without relinquishing his anti-bank prejudices, adopted a most politic attitude. "I am decidedly in favor," he wrote Gallatin in July 1803, "of making all the banks Republican by sharing deposits among them in proportion to the dispositions they show; if the law now forbids it, we should not let another session of Congress to pass without amending it. It is material to the safety of Republicanism to detach the mercantile interest from its enemies and incorporate them into the body of its friends." Instead of trying to keep his party purely and dogmatically agrarian—a utopian and surely defeatist course—he was prepared to see it linked to the capitalistic growth of the country, to encourage the development within its ranks of a mercantile-financial entrepreneurial segment, and thus to have it develop into a heterogeneous coalition, based not only upon geographical but upon economic diversity as well. In this he and his associates succeeded; but in encouraging the further politicization of the banking of the country, and in committing themselves as much as they did to the state banks, they laid the groundwork for the destructive attack on central banking that came with the Jacksonian era.

Jefferson as Reactionary Ideologue

FORREST McDONALD

Even in his own time, Jefferson was regarded by friends and foes alike as a champion of liberty—whatever that elusive word may mean. Jefferson himself never wrote a systematic treatise on the subject, and he never thought it through as a concept. Its meaning to him can scarcely have been a conventional one, since Jefferson owned several hundred human beings during his lifetime and theirs, never made any serious effort to liberate them, purchased at least eight more while he was president, and once asked his friend Madison to acquire a black person for a visiting French lady who sought to be amused by breeding them—a request which the libertarian Madison cheerfully honored. Nor can liberty as Jefferson conceived of it have had much to do with such legal and constitutional rights—enshrined in English and American law from the seventeenth to the twentieth century— as the writ of habeas corpus, freedom of the press, freedom from unlawful search and seizures, and judicial review of the acts of legislatures and law enforcers. Regarding some of these, Jefferson wrote strong words of support; but equally often he denounced the abuse of these "rights," and when he exercised executive authority he was capable of running roughshod over them in what he regarded as a higher interest.

All of which is to say that to regard Jefferson as an apostle of abstract liberty, with the connotations that later generations would impart to it, is a distortion of history and a perversion of his vision for mankind. He saw broadly, but only from where he stood. . . .

Jeffersonian Republicanism was an ideology and an idea, a system of values and a way of looking at things; and as the aphorism goes, ideas and ideals have consequences. But it was also a program of action, carefully crafted and methodically executed; and as we are sometimes wont to forget, actions have consequences, too. To appraise Jefferson's presidency, it is therefore necessary to take both sets of criteria into account.

In the realm of ideas and ideology, Jeffersonian Republicanism was a body of thought that had been taken largely from the Oppositionist tradition of eighteenth-century England, principally as incorporated in the writings of Charles Davenant, John Trenchard, Thomas Gordon, James Burgh, and most particularly Henry St. John, Viscount Bolingbroke. . . . [W]e are speaking of *oppositionist* thought: Bolingbroke and his predecessors and followers (whether calling themselves Tories or Commonwealthmen or Real Whigs) were condemning and seeking to undo the Financial Revolution and its attendant political corruption, as epitomized by the ministry of Sir Robert Walpole. In its stead, they proposed to restore a pristine and largely imaginary past in which life was rural, relationships were personal, the gentry ruled as a natural aristocracy, the main corpus of the citizenry was an honest yeomanry, commerce and craft-manufacturing existed only as handmaidens to agriculture, standing armies and privileged monopolies and fictitious paper wealth were all unknown, and government was limited—limited to an essentially passive function as impartial arbiter and defender of the existing social order, and limited by the unwritten but inviolable Constitution, dividing power among three separate, distinct, and coequal branches. In other words, the Jeffersonians' ideological forebears were reactionaries, swimming against the tide of history, for the world aborning was the depersonalized world of money, machines, cities, and big government.

The Jeffersonians, though castigated by their enemies as dangerous innovators and radicals, were likewise resisting the emergence of the modern world. They had seen the Hamiltonian Federalists attempting to transform and corrupt America, even as the Oppositionists had seen Walpole and the new monied classes transform and corrupt England, and they swallowed the Oppositionists' ideas and ideology whole. The Jeffersonians republicanized Bolingbroke, to be sure, developing the doctrine that absolute separation of powers, with a strictly limited presidency, was guaranteed by the written Constitution. In their hearts, however, they did not trust paper constitutions, and their view of Jefferson's mission as president did not differ substantively and significantly from Bolingbroke's idea of a Patriot King: a head of state who would rally the entire nation to his banner, and then, in an act of supreme wisdom and virtue, voluntarily restrain himself and thus give vitality and meaning to the constitutional system. The Republicans also added the doctrine of states' rights, but that was mainly a tactical position which most of them abandoned—except rhetorically—once they came into control of the national government. The only genuine changes they brought to the ideology were two. One was to relocate its social base, from that of an Anglican gentry to that of southern slaveholders, Celtic-American back-country men, and evangelical Protestants. The other was to put the ideology into practice.

If who they were and what they were seeking are thus understood, it is evident that they remained remarkably true to their principles throughout Jefferson's presidency—despite charges to the contrary by a host of critics. . . . Moreover, they were remarkably successful in accomplishing what they set out to do. They set out to destroy the complex financial mechanism that Hamilton had built around the public debt, and they went a long way toward that goal—so close that if war could have been avoided for another eight years, their success might have been total. They also set out to secure the frontiers of the United States by expanding the country's territorial domain into the vast wilderness, and they succeeded so well that it became possible to dream that the United States could remain a nation of uncorrupted farmers for a thousand years to come.

And yet on the broader scale they failed, and failed calamitously—not because of their own shortcomings, but because their system was incompatible with the immediate current of events, with the broad sweep of history, and with the nature of man and society. As an abstract idea, Bolingbrokism *cum* Jeffersonian Republicanism may have been flawless, and it was certainly appealing. In the real world, it contradicted and destroyed itself.

At the core of the Republicans' thinking lay the assumption, almost Marxian in its naïveté, that only two things must be done to remake America as an ideal society and a beacon unto mankind. First, the public debt must be extinguished, for with it would die stockjobbing, paper-shuffling, "monopoly" banking, excisemen, placemen, and all the other instrumentalities of corruption that the Walpole/Hamilton system "artificially" created. Second, governmental power must be confined to its constitutional limits, which implied reduction of the functions of government but also, and more importantly, meant adherence to the rules of the separation of powers—that being the only legitimate method, in their view, whereby a free government could exercise its authority. If ancient ways were thus restored, the Jeffersonians believed, liberty and independence would inevitably follow. In turn, liberty and independence—by which they meant the absence of governmental restraint or favor and the absence of effective interference from foreign powers—would make it possible for every man, equal in rights but not in talents, to pursue happiness in his own way and to find his own "natural" level in the natural order.

Things did not work out that way, especially in regard to relations with foreign powers: far from freeing the country from foreign interference, Republican policy sorely impaired the nation's ability to determine its own destiny. In their eagerness to retire the public debt, the Jeffersonians tried diligently to economize. Toward that end they slashed military and naval appropriations so much as to render the United States incapable of defending itself—at a time when the entire Western world was at war. Simultaneously, in their haste to destroy all vestiges of the Hamiltonian system, the Jeffersonians abolished virtually all internal taxes. This relieved the farmers and planters of an onerous tax burden and arrested the proliferation of hated excisemen, but it also made national revenues almost totally dependent upon duties on imports—which meant dependent upon the uninterrupted flow of international commerce, which in turn depended upon the will of Napoleon Bonaparte and the ministers of King George III.

For two or three years the Jeffersonians were extremely lucky. That is to say, during that period the kaleidoscope of events in Europe turned briefly and flukishly in their favor. They obtained Louisiana as a result of a concatenation of circumstances that was wildly improbable and was never to be repeated. They were able to pay off much of the public debt and to accumulate sizable treasury surpluses because Great Britain, out of consideration for its own interests, allowed the Americans to engage in a trade of debatable legality, thus swelling the volume of American imports and, concomitantly, the revenues flowing into the United States Treasury.

From 1803 onward, however, each turn of the international wheel was less favorable to the United States. By 1805 it was apparent that West Florida—for which the Jeffersonians hungered almost obsessively, since its strategic and economic value was considerably greater than that of all Louisiana excepting New Orleans—would not become American in the way that Louisiana had. In the same year it began to be clear that the British would not long continue to allow the United States to grow wealthy by trading with Britain's mortal enemies.

But for their ideology, the Jeffersonians could have reversed their earlier policy stance, embraced Britain, and become hostile toward France and Spain, thus enabling the nation to continue to prosper and expand. Given their ideological commitment, they could not do so. Moreover, given the consequences of their actions so far, they lacked the strength to make even a token show of force against Great Britain. Thus in 1807, when both Britain and France forbade the United States to engage in international commerce except as tributaries to themselves, the embargo—a policy of pusillanimity and bungling, billed as a noble experiment in peaceful coercion—was the only course open to them.

At home, as they became ever more deeply impaled upon the horns of their self-created international dilemma, the Jeffersonians became progressively less tolerant of opposition or criticism. From the beginning they had shown considerable disdain for the federal courts; as Jefferson's second term wore on, this disdain degenerated into contempt for due process of law and for law itself. Thus the embargo became a program of domestic tyranny in inverse ratio to its ineffectiveness as an instrument of international policy: the more the policy was found wanting, the more rigorously was it enforced.

The embargo, then, both as a bankrupt foreign policy and as a reign of domestic oppression, was not a sudden aberration but the logical and virtually certain outcome of the Jeffersonian ideology put into practice: the ideology's yield was dependence rather than independence, oppression rather than liberty. . . .

Jefferson and the Empire of Liberty

DREW McCOY

Many years after his first election to the presidency, Thomas Jefferson commented that "the revolution of 1800" was "as real a revolution in the principles of our government as that of 1776 was in its form." Jefferson was undoubtedly using the term "revolution" not in the modern sense of a radical

Drew McCoy, *The Elusive Republic: Political Economy in Jeffersonian America* (University of North Carolina Press, 1980), pp. 185–189, 196–199, and 202–208. Reprinted by permission of the University of North Carolina Press.

creation of a new order, but in the traditional sense of a return to first principles, of a restoration of original values and ideals that had been over-turned or repudiated. For him, the election of 1800 was a revolution because it marked a turning back to the true republican spirit of 1776. Jefferson was excited by the prospect of the first implementation of the principles of America's republican revolution in the national government created by the Constitution of 1787, since in his eyes a minority faction consisting of an American Walpole and his corrupt minions had captured control of that government almost immediately after its establishment. . . . Jefferson's fun-damental goal in 1801 was to end this threatened "Anglicization" of both American government and society. In so doing he would restore the basis for the development of a truly republican political economy. . . .

Within the Jeffersonian framework of assumptions and beliefs, three essential conditions were necessary to create and sustain such a republican political economy: a national government free from any taint of corruption, an unobstructed access to an ample supply of open land, and a relatively liberal international commercial order that would offer adequate foreign markets for America's flourishing agricultural surplus. The history of the 1790s had demonstrated all too well to the Jeffersonians the predominant danger to a republican political economy of corruption emanating from the federal government. They were especially troubled by the deleterious po-litical, social, and moral repercussions of the Federalists' financial system, which they regarded as the primary vehicle of corruption both in the political system and in the country at large. . . .

In itself, the electoral revolution of 1800 promised to remove the primary threat to a republican economy posed by the machinations of a corrupt administration. But the Jeffersonians also had to secure the other necessary guarantors of republicanism: landed and commercial expansion. Although the pressure of population growth on the supply of land in the United States had never been a problem of the same immediate magnitude as political corruption, the social and economic dislocations of the 1780s had prompted some concern with this matter. Through the Louisiana Purchase of 1803, undoubtedly the greatest achievement of his presidency, Jefferson appeared to eliminate this problem for generations, if not for centuries, to come. But the third and thorniest problem, in the form of long-standing restrictions on American commerce, proved far more frustrating and intractable. Through an embargo and finally a war the Jeffersonians consistently tried but failed to remove this nagging impediment to the fulfillment of their republican vision.

The presidential administrations from 1801 to 1817 appear more con-sistent when viewed from this perspective—that is, as a sustained Jeffer-sonian attempt to secure the requisite conditions for a republican political economy. Securing such a political economy, as the Jeffersonians conceived of it, required more than merely capturing control of the government from a corrupt minority faction; it also required the elimination of specific dangers and the maintenance of certain conditions, and these concerns largely shaped the Jeffersonian approach to both domestic and foreign policy. There was never any question that positive, concrete measures would have to be taken to forestall the development of social conditions that were considered antithetical to republicanism. Hamilton and the Federalists had threatened to make American society old and corrupt long before its time. Now the Jeffersonians set out to reverse the direction of Federalist policy in order to maintain the country at a relatively youthful stage of development. Hoping to avoid the social evils both of barbarous simplicity and of overrefined, decadent maturity, the Jeffersonians proposed to escape the burden of an economically sophisticated society without sacrificing a necessary degree of republican civilization. Their aspiration to evade social corruption and the ravages of time was a fragile and demanding dream, and the quest to fulfill it was not without its ironies.

On the one hand, the Republican party attracted political support from scores of Americans whose outlook can properly be termed entrepreneurial. Opposition to the Federalist system was never limited to agrarian-minded ideologues who unequivocally opposed a dynamic commercial economy. Many Jeffersonians were anxious to participate in the creation of an expansive economy and to reap its many rewards. Frustrated by the failure of Federalist policies to serve their immediate needs, ambitious men-on-the-make, engaged in a variety of economic pursuits, enlisted under the banner of Jeffersonianism in a crusade to secure the advantages and opportunities they desired. Perhaps some of them saw no contradiction between their personal material ambitions and the traditional vision of a simple, bucolic republic articulated by the leader of their party. Assessing the economic psychology of many of these enterprising Jeffersonians, one scholar has suggested the complex paradox "of capitalists of all occupations denying the spirit of their occupations," adding that "it appears that many Republicans wanted what the Federalists were offering, but they wanted it faster, and they did not want to admit that they wanted it at all." Such a characterization cannot be applied, however, to Jefferson and Madison, and in their case we observe a more poignant irony. As their experience as policymakers soon demonstrated, the Jeffersonian endeavor to secure a peaceful, predominantly agricultural republic demanded a tenaciously expansive foreign policy—a foreign policy that ultimately endangered both the peace and the agricultural character of the young republic. . . .

The Mississippi crisis of 1801–1803, which culminated in the Louisiana Purchase, affected crucial and long-standing American concerns. Since the 1780s most Americans had regarded free navigation of the Mississippi River and the right of deposit at New Orleans as essential to the national interest. Without the access to market that these conditions permitted, westward expansion would be stalled, because settlers in the trans-Appalachian regions necessarily depended on the Mississippi and its tributaries to sustain them as active and prosperous republican farmers. The Pinckney Treaty of 1795 temporarily resolved this nagging problem, since the Spanish agreed in the treaty to grant the United States free navigation of the Mississippi with a three-year right of deposit at New Orleans. This treaty, along with the Jay

Treaty of the same year, cleared the way for a burst of western settlement. By 1801 the Mississippi River provided the primary access to market for the produce of more than half a million Americans living in the trans-Appalachian West, especially in Kentucky and Tennessee. When Spain made a secret agreement in 1800 to transfer possession of Louisiana back to France, however, the old problem took on a new and more ominous dimension. As Jefferson and most Americans immediately recognized, Napoleonic ambitions in the Mississippi valley posed a far more serious threat to the westward course of American empire than Spain ever had.

To add insult to injury, before formally transferring Louisiana to Napoleon, the Spanish intendant at New Orleans revoked the American right of deposit in violation of the Pinckney Treaty. Many Americans, including eastern Federalists as well as westerners, responded with outraged belligerence and threats of war. Jefferson shrewdly contained this war fever and proceeded cautiously, employing a strategy that ultimately contributed to the convergence of circumstances that made the Louisiana Purchase possible. The Purchase solved once and for all the Mississippi problem that had festered for twenty years—the United States gained formal control of the river, both its eastern and western banks, and of New Orleans.

In the minds of many Americans, the question of the Mississippi River involved much more than a narrow concern with the prosperity or profits of western farmers. What they saw to be at stake in the Mississippi crisis of 1801–1803 was the very character of western society itself. This concern with social character, especially with the interdependence of economic life and the moral integrity of the individual personality, was part of a fundamentally republican world view. To Americans committed to the construction of a republican political economy, it was imperative that public policy be directed toward the creation of social conditions that would permit and even foster the maintenance of a virtuous people. . . . What the Louisiana Purchase made possible, according to many commentators, was the existence of a republican civilization in the American West.

Most important, control of the Mississippi permitted westerners to engage in a secure and dynamically expanding foreign commerce and, as always, Americans saw the significance of commerce in very broad social and moral terms. It was repeatedly asserted that an active commerce that provided a secure and dependable access to foreign markets was absolutely necessary to establish and maintain the republican character of western society. A primary concern here was the familiar emphasis on "industry" as the cornerstone of the republican personality. Obstructions to foreign commerce, it was argued, always "palsied" the labor of American farmers and discouraged their industry by destroying incentives to production. Eventually, such obstructions led to indolence, lethargy, dissipation, and barbarous decadence—characteristics hardly befitting a republican people. . . .

By rectifying the chronic problem of an uncertain, rapidly fluctuating demand for western agricultural surpluses, the Purchase thus served an important social and moral purpose. "No ruinous fluctuations in commerce need now be apprehended," noted another western commentator, for "agriculture may depend upon those steady markets which trade shall open to industry." There could be no doubt that a "want of markets for the produce of the soil" always had disastrous consequences, for "it saps the foundations of our prosperity; subverts the end of society, and literally tends to keep us in that rude, uncultivated state, which has excited the derision and contempt of other communities." "As long as this is the state of our country," the same observer queried in familiar fashion, "what encouragement is there for the mind to throw off its native ferocity?" By permanently securing control of the Mississippi River and the promise of boundless foreign markets beyond, the Louisiana Purchase did more than pave the way for economic prosperity. By providing the incentive to industry that shaped a republican people, it laid the necessary basis for the westward expansion of republican civilization itself. . . .

If the American republic was in a race against time, as many Republicans believed, the Louisiana Purchase indeed offered a boost to the republican cause. "The history of the world," noted Abraham Bishop, a prominent Connecticut Republican, "teaches that nations, like men, must decay. Ours will not forever escape the fate of others. Wealth, luxury, vice, aristocracies will attack us in our decline: these are evils of society, never to be courted, but to be put to as distant a day as possible." Viewed in this light, the acquisition of Louisiana was of crucial importance to all Americans, not just to southerners and westerners, for it pushed far into the future that dreaded day when America would become a densely populated society characterized by inequality, luxury, and dependence. "We see in Louisiana an assurance of long life to our cause," Bishop exulted. "The Atlantic states, as they advance to that condition of society, where wealth and luxury tend to vice and aristocracies, will yield to that country accessions of enterprising men. The spirit of faction, which tends to concentrate, will be destroyed by this diffusion." Expansion across space was the only effective antidote to population growth, development through time, and the corruption that accompanied them. "What territory can be too large," David Ramsay asked rhetorically in 1804, "for a people, who multiply with such unequalled rapidity?" "By enlarging the empire of liberty," noted President Jefferson in 1805, "we multiply its auxiliaries, and provide new sources of renovation, should its principles, at any time, degenerate, in those portions of our country which gave them birth."

Jefferson's notion of a continuously expanding "empire of liberty" in the Western Hemisphere was a bold intellectual stroke, because it flew in the face of the traditional republican association of expansion and empire with luxury, corruption, and especially despotism. The familiar bugbear of the Roman Empire and its decline through imperial expansion was the most common source of this association. According to Jefferson and most American republicans, expansion would preserve, rather than undermine, the republican character of America. In addition to forestalling development through time and diffusing the spirit of faction, expansion was crucial to American security in its broadest sense. Removing the French from Louisiana also removed the need for a dangerous military establishment in the face of a contiguous foreign threat. It greatly reduced, too, the likelihood of American involvement in a ruinous war that would impose on the young republic the vicious Old World system of national debts, armies, navies, taxation, and the like. For a plethora of reasons, in short, peaceful expansion was sustaining the Jeffersonian republic.

But if the Louisiana Purchase removed some serious obstacles to the realization of Jefferson's republican empire, it also exposed some of the tensions and contradictions within that vision. Since the proper functioning of the empire required both westward and commercial expansion, an assertive, even aggressive, foreign policy would often be necessary to secure the republic. The Jeffersonians frequently boasted of the isolation and independence of the United States; curiously, this claim obscured the fact that American republicanism demanded both an open international commercial order and the absence of any competing presence on the North American continent. The United States could isolate itself from foreign affairs and the potential for conflict only if it was willing to resign its tenacious commitment to westward expansion and free trade. To do this, however, would be to abandon the two most important pillars of the Jeffersonian vision of a republican political economy. Indeed, given the commitment to that vision, the national independence and isolated self-sufficiency boasted of by the Jeffersonians were illusory. . . .

The Jeffersonian vision of an expanding republican civilization demanded this unimpeded access to foreign markets—for economic, social, and moral reasons—and to this extent the republic was something less than the fully autonomous and self-sufficient entity the Jeffersonians usually portrayed it to be. If the necessary guarantors of the Republican vision included an interventionist foreign policy, territorial aggression, Indian removal or management, and even war, might not the means of achieving an escape from time subvert their fundamental purpose? Ultimately, as the events of Jefferson's second administration and Madison's presidency demonstrated, the struggle to secure the Jeffersonian republic culminated in the need to wage a second war for American independence.

✠ *F U R T H E R   R E A D I N G*

Henry Adams, *History of the United States During the Administrations of Thomas Jefferson and James Madison,* 9 vols. (1889–1891)

Joyce O. Appleby, "What Is Still American in the Political Philosophy of Thomas Jefferson?" *William and Mary Quarterly,* 3rd ser., 39 (1982): 287–309

Lance Banning, *The Jeffersonian Persuasion: The Evolution of a Party Ideology* (1978)

Daniel J. Boorstin, *The Lost World of Thomas Jefferson* (1948)

Irving Brant, *James Madison,* 6 vols. (1941–1961)

James Broussard, *The Southern Federalists, 1800–1816* (1978)

Noble E. Cunningham, *In Pursuit of Reason: The Life of Thomas Jefferson* (1987)

———, *The Jeffersonian Republicans in Power: Party Operations 1801–1809* (1963)

———, *The Jeffersonian Republicans* (1957)

Alexander De Conde, *This Affair of Louisiana* (1976)

Richard E. Ellis, *The Jeffersonian Crisis: Courts and Politics in the Young Republic* (1971)

David Hackett Fischer, *The Revolution in American Conservativism: The Federalist Party in the Era of Jeffersonian Democracy* (1970)

Richard Hofstadter, "Thomas Jefferson: The Aristocrat as Democrat," in Hofstadter, *The American Political Tradition and the Men Who Made It* (1948)

Lawrence S. Kaplan, *Entangling Alliance With None: American Foreign Policy in the Age of Jefferson* (1987)

Linda K. Kerber, *Federalists in Dissent: Imagery and Ideology in Jeffersonian America* (1970)

Ralph Ketchum, *Presidents Above Party: The First American Presidency 1789–1828* (1984)

Russell Kirk, *Randolph of Roanoke: A Study of Conservative Thought* (1961)

Leonard Levy, *Jefferson and Civil Liberties: The Darker Side* (1963)

Drew McCoy, *The Last of the Fathers: James Madison and the Republican Legacy* (1989)

———, *The Elusive Republic: Political Economy in Jeffersonian America* (1980)

Dumas Malone, *Jefferson,* 6 vols. (1948–1971)

Richard K. Matthews, *The Radical Politics of Thomas Jefferson: A Revisionist View* (1983)

R. Kent Newmyer, *The Supreme Court Under Marshall and Taney* (1968, 1986)

Bradford Perkins, *Prologue to War: England and the United States, 1805–1812* (1968)

Merrill Peterson, *Thomas Jefferson and the New Nation: A Biography* (1970)

———, *The Jefferson Image in the American Mind* (1960)

Norman K. Risjord, *The Old Republicans: Southern Conservativism in the Age of Jefferson* (1965)

Robert Shalhope, *John Taylor of Caroline: Pastoral Republican* (1980)

Marshall Smelser, *The Democratic Republic, 1801–1815* (1968)

Francis N. Stites, *John Marshall: Defender of the Constitution* (1981)

Robert W. Tucker, *Empire of Liberty: The Statecraft of Thomas Jefferson* (1990)

Gore Vidal, *Burr: A Novel* (1973)

James Sterling Young, *The Washington Community, 1800–1828* (1966)

CHAPTER
5

Gender, Race, and Ideology

in the Early Republic

⌗

Power flowed through many channels in the early republic. Much of the formal political debate from 1787 through 1815 concentrated on finance, constitutional interpretation, and diplomacy—with direct consequences for various aspects of the new nation's political economy. As we have already seen, these specific conflicts necessarily involved general questions about American slavery and its future. Territorial expansion—the great promise of the Louisiana Purchase— raised the inevitable prospect of negotiations and conflict with native American tribes. Both of these matters, in turn, exposed deep, sometimes unexamined assumptions about an artificial concept—race. Nor was that all. Inscribed on the customs, the laws, the very iconography of the early republic were codes of gender, linked to idealized notions of womanhood and domestic order.

Recent historians have spent a great deal of time and imagination in reconstructing the heretofore hidden worlds of women, slaves, free blacks, and Indians. Their discoveries refute any simple line of reasoning, especially one that would dwell on the victimization of selected portions of the population. Women, blacks, and Indians, subject to inequality and worse, were neither ciphers nor passive, pitiable objects. Their actions and beliefs decisively affected their own situations and those of more powerful Americans. Nor were the histories of gender and race things apart, wholly distinct from what used to be thought of as the main currents of U.S. history. Virtually nothing about the early republic—including seemingly straightforward political questions—looks quite the same once we consider these broader definitions of power.

What, then, were the prevailing ideologies of gender and race in post-Revolutionary America? Were they monolithic and static, or did they vary at different times and in different classes and regions? How are we to judge the rationales offered by different sorts of Americans? How was it that some of the stauncher champions of American democracy took various forms of subordination for granted? How did women, blacks, and Indians act and react? What are we to make of the palpable differences within each of these groups? And how did the conflicts and accommodations over ideas about race and gender affect formal politics and diplomacy—and vice versa—if not at all.

116

⌗ *D O C U M E N T S*

The first selection features three short documents—an engraving, a painting, and excerpts from the letters of an educated daughter of wealth from Maine—that capture a few of the contradictory impulses shaping early republican notions of womanhood. How might these images and sentiments have struck a slave family or a small farmer's family in the backcountry? Thomas Jefferson's opinion on Indians and blacks appeared in his *Notes on the State of Virginia,* written in the mid-1780s and excerpted in the second selection here. In 1800 Jefferson's Virginia was shaken by an abortive uprising in and around Richmond, undertaken by the slave Gabriel Prosser; in the third document, Benjamin Woolfolk, one of the co-conspirators, provides details of the plot, redolent with biblical imagery. What does the conspirators' understanding of religion say about cultural interactions in the early republic? A different Christian frame of mind is revealed in the fourth document, an address "to the people of colour" by Richard Allen and Absalom Jones, both ex-slaves living in Philadelphia and leaders of the city's emerging African Methodist Episcopal church. Another Philadelphian, the white Methodist John Watson, in the fifth selection, betrays a sense of cultural and religious anxiety about black worship—and its effects on white believers. Timothy Dwight, the president of Yale University, commemorated the Puritans' bloody war with the Pequot Indians from 1634 to 1637, as part of his epic poem, "Greenfield Hill," excerpted as the sixth document. The seventh and eighth documents, respectively a letter from Thomas Jefferson to the governor of Indiana Territory, William Henry Harrison, and a treaty struck by Harrison with the Delaware Indians, provide us insight into the theory and practice of Jeffersonian Indian policy. The final document is a contemporaneous parable delivered by a Shawnee chief, and conveys one of several native American responses to U.S. expansion.

Contemporary Views of Republican Womanhood
Woman Constricted

"Keep Within the Compass," sepia engraving, c. 1785–1805, Henry Francis Dupont Winterthur Museum

Woman as Republican Emblem

Liberty and Washington, unknown artist (*ca.* 1800–1810). Courtesy New York State Historical Association, Cooperstown.

Letters from Eliza Southgate to Her Cousin
Moses Porter, 1800–1801

September, 1800

. . . As I look around me I am surprised at the happiness which is so generally enjoyed in families, and that marriages which have not love for a foundation on more than one side at most, should produce so much apparent harmony. I may be censured for declaring it as my opinion that not one woman in a hundred marries for love. A woman of taste and sentiment will surely see but a very few whom she could love, and it is altogether uncertain whether either of them will particularly distinguish her. If they should, surely she is very fortunate, but it would be one of fortune's random favors and such as we have no right to expect. The female mind I believe is of a very pliable texture; if it were not we should be wretched indeed. Admitting as a known truth that few women marry those whom they would prefer to all the world if they could be viewed by them with equal affection, or rather that there are often others whom they could have preferred if they had felt that affection for them which would have induced them to offer themselves,—admitting this as a truth not to be disputed,—is it not a subject of astonishment that happiness is not almost banished from this connexion? Gratitude is undoubtedly the foundation of the esteem we commonly feel for a husband. . . . I do not esteem marriage absolutely essential to happiness, and that it does not always bring happiness we must every day witness in our acquaintance. A single life is considered too generally as a reproach; but let me ask you, which is the most despicable—she who marries a man she scarcely thinks *well* of—to avoid the reputation of an old maid—or she, who with more delicacy, [rather] than marry one she could not highly esteem, preferred to live single all her life, and had wisdom enough to despise so mean a sacrifice, to the opinion of the rabble, as the woman who marries a man she has not much love for—must make. I wish not to alter the laws of nature—neither will I quarrel with the rules which custom has established and rendered indispensably necessary to the harmony of society. But every being who has contemplated human nature on a large scale will certainly justify me when I declare that the inequality of privilege between the sexes is very sensibly felt by us females, and in no instance is it greater than in the liberty of choosing a partner in marriage; true, we have the liberty of refusing those we don't like, but not of selecting those we do. This is undoubtedly as it should be. But let me ask you, what must be that love which is altogether voluntary, which we can withhold or give, which sleeps in dullness and apathy till it is requested to brighten into life? Is it not a cold, lifeless dictate of the head,—do we not weigh all the conveniences and inconveniences which will attend it? And after a long calculation, in which the heart never was consulted, we determine whether it is most prudent to love or not. . . .

May, 1801

. . . I believe I possess decent talents and should have been quite another being had they been properly cultivated. But as it is, I can never get over some little prejudices which I have imbibed long since, and which warp all the faculties of my mind. I was pushed on to the stage of action without one principle to guide my actions,—the impulse of the moment was the only incitement. I have never committed any grossly imprudent action, yet I have been folly's darling child. I trust they were rather errors of the head than the heart, for we have all a kind of inherent power to distinguish between right and wrong, and if before the heart becomes contaminated by the maxims of society it is left to act from impulse though it have no fixed principle, yet it will not materially err. Possessing a gay lively disposition, I pursued pleasure with ardor. I wished for admiration, and took the means which would be most likely to obtain it. I found the mind of a female, if such a thing existed, was thought not worth cultivating. I disliked the trouble of thinking for myself and therefore adopted the sentiments of others—fully convinced to adorn my person and acquire a few little accomplishments was sufficient to secure me the admiration of the society I frequented. I cared but little about the mind. I learned to flutter about with a thoughtless gaiety— a mere feather which every breath had power to move. I left school with a head full of something, tumbled in without order or connection. I returned home with a determination to put it in more order; I set about the great work of culling the best part to make a few sentiments out of—to serve as a little ready change in my commerce with the world. But I soon lost all patience (a virtue I do not possess in an eminent degree), for the greater part of my ideas I was obliged to throw away without knowing where I got them or what I should do with them; what remained I pieced as ingeniously as I could into a few patchwork opinions,—they are now almost worn threadbare, and as I am about quilting a few more, I beg you will send me any spare ideas you may chance to have that will answer my turn. . . .

June, 1801
As to the qualities of mind peculiar to each sex, I agree with you that sprightliness is in favor of females and profundity of males. Their education, their pursuits would create such a quality even though nature had not implanted it. The business and pursuits of men require deep thinking, judgment, and moderation, while, on the other hand, females are under no necessity of dipping deep, but merely "skim the surface," and we too commonly spare ourselves the exertion which deep researches require, unless they are absolutely necessary to our pursuits in life. We rarely find one giving themselves up to profound investigation for amusement merely. Necessity is the nurse of all the great qualities of the mind; it explores all the hidden treasures and by its stimulating power they are "polished into brightness." Women who have no such incentives to action suffer all the strong energetic qualities of the mind to sleep in obscurity; sometimes a ray of genius gleams through the thick clouds with which it is enveloped, and irradiates for a moment the darkness of mental night; yet, like a comet that shoots wildly from its sphere, it excites our wonder, and we place it among the phenomenons of nature, without searching for a natural cause. Thus it is the qualities with which nature has endowed us, as a support amid the

misfortunes of life and a shield from the allurements of vice, are left to moulder in ruin. . . .

Women have more imagination, more sprightliness, because they have less discernment. I never was of opinion that the pursuits of the sexes ought to be the same; on the contrary, I believe it would be destructive to happiness, there would be a degree of rivalry exist, incompatible with the harmony we wish to establish. I have ever thought it necessary that each should have a separate sphere of action,—in such a case there could be no clashing unless one or the other should leap their respective bounds. Yet to cultivate the qualities with which we are endowed can never be called infringing the prerogatives of man. Why, my dear Cousin, were we furnished with such powers, unless the improvement of them would conduce to the happiness of society? Do you suppose the mind of woman the only work of God that was "made in vain." The cultivation of the powers we possess, I have ever thought a privilege (or I may say duty) that belonged to the human species, and not man's exclusive prerogative. Far from destroying the harmony that ought to subsist, it would fix it on a foundation that would not totter at every jar. Women would be under the same degree of subordination that they now are; enlighten and expand their minds, and they would perceive the necessity of such a regulation to preserve the order and happiness of society. . . . I had rather be the meanest reptile that creeps the earth, or cast upon the wide world to suffer all the ills "that flesh is heir to," than live a slave to the despotic will of another.

I am aware of the censure that will ever await the female that attempts vindication of her sex, yet I dare to brave that censure that I know to be undeserved. It does not follow (O what a pen!) that every female who vindicates the capacity of the sex is a disciple of Mary Wolstoncraft. Though I allow her to have said many things which I cannot but approve, yet the very foundation on which she builds her work will be apt to prejudice us so against her that we will not allow her the merit she really deserves,— yet, prejudice set aside, I confess I admire many of her sentiments. . . .

Thomas Jefferson on Indians and Blacks, 1787

The Indian of North America being within our reach, I can speak of him somewhat from my own knowledge, but more from the information of others better acquainted with him, and on whose truth and judgment I can rely. From these sources I am able to say, . . . that he is neither more defective in ardor, nor more impotent with his female, than the white reduced to the same diet and exercise: that he is brave, when an enterprize depends on bravery; education with him making the point of honor consist in the destruction of an enemy by stratagem, and in the preservation of his own person free from injury; or perhaps this is nature; while it is education which teaches us to honor force more than finesse: that he will defend himself against a host of enemies, always choosing to be killed, rather than to surrender, though it be to the whites, who he knows will treat him well: that in other situations also he meets death with more deliberation, and endures tortures with a firmness unknown almost to religious enthusiasm with us: that he is affectionate to his children, careful of them, and indulgent in the extreme: that his affections comprehend his other connections, weakening, as with us, from circle to circle, as they recede from the center: that his friendships are strong and faithful to the uttermost extremity: that his sensibility is keen, even the warriors weeping most bitterly on the loss of their children, though in general they endeavor to appear superior to human events: that his vivacity and activity of mind is equal to ours in the same situation; hence his eagerness for hunting, and for games of chance. The women are submitted to unjust drudgery. This I believe is the case with every barbarous people. With such, force is law. The stronger sex therefore imposes on the weaker. It is civilization alone which replaces women in the enjoyment of their natural equality. . . An inhuman practice once prevailed in this country of making slaves of the Indians. It is a fact well known with us, that the Indian women so enslaved produced and raised as numerous families as either the whites or blacks among whom they lived. —It has been said, that Indians have less hair that the whites, except on the head. But this is a fact of which fair proof can scarcely be had. With them it is disgraceful to be hairy on the body. They say it likens them to hogs. They therefore pluck the hair as fast as it appears. But the traders who marry their women, and prevail on them to discontinue this practice, say, that nature is the same with them as with the whites. Nor, if the fact be true, is the consequence necessary which has been drawn from it. Negroes have notoriously less hair than the whites; yet they are more ardent. . . . The principles of [Indian] society forbidding all compulsion, they are to be led to duty and to enterprize by personal influence and persuasion. Hence eloquence in council, bravery and address in war, become the foundations of all consequence with them. To these acquirements all their faculties are directed. Of their bravery and address in war we have multiplied proofs, because we have been the subjects on which they were exercised. Of their eminence in oratory we have fewer examples, because it is displayed chiefly in their own councils. Some, however, we have of very superior lustre. . . .

Before we condemn the Indians of this continent as wanting genius, we must consider that letters have not yet been introduced among them. Were we to compare them in their present state with the Europeans North of the Alps, when the Roman arms and arts first crossed those mountains, the comparison would be unequal, because, at that time, those parts of Europe were swarming with numbers; because numbers produce emulation, and multiply the chances of improvement, and one improvement begets another. Yet I may safely ask, How many good poets, how many able mathematicians, how many great inventors in arts or sciences, had Europe North of the Alps then produced? And it was sixteen centuries after this before a Newton could be formed. I do not mean to deny, that there are varieties in the race of man, distinguished by their powers both of body and mind. I believe there are, as I see to be the case in the races of other animals. I only mean to suggest a doubt, whether the bulk and faculties of animals depend on the side of the Atlantic on which their food happens to grow, or which furnishes the elements of which they are compounded? Whether nature has enlisted herself as a Cis or Trans-Atlantic partisan? . . .

The first difference [between blacks and whites] which strikes us is that of color. Whether the black of the negro resides in the reticular membrane between the skin and scarf-skin, or in the scarf-skin itself; whether it proceeds from the color of the blood, the color of the bile, or from that of some other secretion, the difference is fixed in nature, and is as real as if its seat and cause were better known to us. And is this difference of no importance? Is it not the foundation of a greater or less share of beauty in the two races? Are not the fine mixtures of red and white, the expressions of every passion by greater or less suffusions of color in the one, preferable to that eternal monotony, which reigns in the countenances, that immoveable veil of black which covers all the emotions of the other race? Add to these, flowing hair, a more elegant symmetry of form, their own judgment in favor of the whites, declared by their preference of them, as uniformly as is the preference of the Oranootan for the black women over those of his own species. The circumstance of superior beauty, is thought worthy attention in the propagation of our horses, dogs, and other domestic animals; why not in that of man? Besides those of color, figure, and hair, there are other physical distinctions proving a difference of race. They have less hair on the face and body. They secrete less by the kidnies, and more by the glands of the skin, which gives them a very strong and disagreeable odor. . . . They seem to require less sleep. A black, after hard labor through the day, will be induced by the slightest amusements to sit up till midnight, or later, though knowing he must be out with the first dawn of the morning. They are at least as brave, and more adventuresome. But this may perhaps proceed from a want of forethought, which prevents their seeing a danger till it be present. When present, they do not go through it with more coolness or steadiness than the whites. They are more ardent after their female: but love seems with them to be more an eager desire, than a tender delicate mixture of sentiment and sensation. Their griefs are transient. Those numberless afflictions, which render it doubtful whether heaven has given life to us in mercy or in wrath, are less felt, and sooner forgotten with them. In general, their existence appears to participate more of sensation than reflection. To this must be ascribed their disposition to sleep when abstracted from their diversions, and unemployed in labor. An animal whose body is at rest, and who does not reflect, must be disposed to sleep of course. Comparing them by their faculties of memory, reason, and imagination, it appears to me, that in memory they are equal to the whites; in reason much inferior . . . and that in imagination they are dull, tasteless, and anomalous. It would be unfair to follow them to Africa for this investigation. We will consider them here, on the same stage with the whites, and where the facts are not apocryphal on which a judgment is to be formed. It will be right to make great allowances for the difference of condition, of education, of conversation, of the sphere in which they move. Many millions of them have been brought to, and born in America. Most of them indeed have been confined to tillage, to their own homes, and their own society: yet many have been so situated, that they might have availed themselves of the conversation of their masters; many have been brought up to the handicraft arts, and from that circumstance have always been associated with the whites. Some have been liberally educated, and all have lived in countries where the arts and sciences are cultivated to a considerable degree, and have had before their eyes samples of the best works from abroad. The Indians, with no advantages of this kind, will often carve figures on their pipes not destitute of design and merit. They will crayon out an animal, a plant, or a country, so as to prove the existence of a germ in their minds which only wants cultivation. They astonish you with strokes of the most sublime oratory; such as prove their reason and sentiment strong, their imagination glowing and elevated. But never yet could I find that a black had uttered a thought above the level of plain narration; never see even an elementary trait of painting or sculpture. In music they are more generally gifted than the whites with accurate ears for tune and time, and they have been found capable of imagining a small catch. Whether they will be equal to the composition of a more extensive run of melody, or of complicated harmony, is yet to be proved. Misery is often the parent of the most affecting touches in poetry.—Among the blacks is misery enough, God knows, but no poetry. Love is the peculiar œstrum of the poet. Their love is ardent, but it kindles the senses only, not the imagination. Religion indeed has produced a Phyllis Whately; but it could not produce a poet. The compositions published under her name are below the dignity of criticism. . . . The improvement of the blacks in body and mind, in the first instance of their mixture with the whites, has been observed by every one, and proves that their inferiority is not the effect merely of their condition of life. . . . I advance it therefore as a suspicion only, that the blacks, whether originally a distinct race, or made distinct by time and circumstances, are inferior to the whites in the endowments both of body and mind. . . .

There must doubtless be an unhappy influence on the manners of our people produced by the existence of slavery among us. The whole commerce between master and slave is a perpetual exercise of the most boisterous passions, the most unremitting despotism on the one part, and degrading submissions on the other. Our children see this, and learn to imitate it; for man is an imitative animal. This quality is the germ of all education in him. From his cradle to his grave he is learning to do what he sees others do. If a parent could find no motive either in his philanthropy or his self-love, for restraining the intemperance of passion towards his slave, it should always be a sufficient one that his child is present. But generally it is not sufficient. . . . The man must be a prodigy who can retain his manners and morals undepraved by such circumstances. . . . With the morals of the people, their industry also is destroyed. For in a warm climate, no man will labour for himself who can make another labour for him. This is so true, that of the proprietors of slaves a very small proportion indeed are ever seen to labour. And can the liberties of a nation be thought secure when we have removed their only firm basis, a conviction in the minds of the people that these liberties are of the gift of God? That they are not to be violated but with his wrath? Indeed I tremble for my country when I reflect that God is just: that his justice cannot sleep for ever . . . I hope . . . under the auspices of heaven, for a total emancipation, and that this is disposed, in the order of events, to be with the consent of the masters, rather than by their extirpation.

The Confessions of "Ben," a Co-Conspirator in Gabriel Prosser's Rebellion, 1800

. . . Mr. Prosser's Gabriel wished to bring on the business as soon as possible. Gilbert said the summer was almost over, and he wished them to enter upon the business before the weather got too cold. Gabriel proposed that the subject should be referred to his brother Martin to decide upon. Martin said there was this expression in the Bible, delays breed danger; at this time, he said, the country was at peace, the soldiers were discharged, and the arms all put away; there was no patroling in the country, and that before he would any longer bear what he had borne, he would turn out and fight with his stick. Gilbert said he was ready with his pistol, but it was in need of repair; he gave it to Gabriel, who was [to] put it in order for him. I then spoke to the company and informed them I wished to have something to say. I told them that I had heard in the days of old, when the Israelites were in service to King Pharoah, they were taken from him by the power of God, and were carried away by Moses. God had blessed him with an angel to go with him, but that I could see nothing of that kind in these days. Martin said in reply: I read in my Bible where God says if we will worship Him we should have peace in all our land; five of you shall conquer a hundred, and a hundred a thousand of our enemies. After this they went on consultation upon the time they should execute the plan. Martin spoke and appointed for them to meet in three weeks, which was to be of a Saturday night. Gabriel said he had 500 bullets made. Smith's George said he was done the corn and would then go on to make as many crossbows as he could. Bowler's Jack said he had got 50 spiers [sic] or bayonets fixed at the end of sticks. The plan was to be as follows: We were all to meet at the briery spot on the Brook; 100 men were to stand at the Brook bridge; Gabriel was to take 100 more and go to Gregory's tavern and take the arms which were there; 50 more were to be sent to Rocketts to set that on fire, in order to alarm the upper part of the town and induce the people to go down there; while they were employed in extinguishing the fire Gabriel and the other officers and soldiers were to take the Capitol and all the arms they could find and be ready to slaughter the people on their return from Rocketts. Sam Bird was to have a pass as a free man and was to go to the nation of Indians called Catawbas to persuade them to join the negroes to fight the white people. As far as I understood all the whites were to be massacred, except the Quakers, the Methodists, and the Frenchmen, and they were to be spared on account as they conceived of their being friendly to liberty, and also they had understood that the French were at war with this country for the money that was due them, and that an army was landed at South Key, which they hoped would assist them. They intended also to spare all the poor white women who had no slaves.

The above communications are put down precisely as delivered to us by Ben, alias Ben Woolfolk. Given under our hands this 17th day of September, 1800.

GERVAS STORRES,
JOSEPH SELDEN

Ben, alias Ben Woolfolk, sentenced to death for conspiracy and insurrection Sept. 16th, pardoned Sept. 18th.

Free Blacks Appeal for Freedom and Christian Forbearance, 1794

To the People of Colour

Feeling an engagement of mind for your welfare, we address you with an affectionate sympathy, and as desirous of freedom as any of you; yet the bands of bondage were so strong, that no way appeared for our release, yet at times a hope arose in our hearts that a way would be open for it, and when our minds were mercifully visited with the feeling of the love of God, then these hopes increased, and a confidence arose that he would make way for our enlargement, and as a patient waiting was necessary, we were sometimes favoured with it, at other times we were very impatient, then the prospect of liberty almost vanished away, and we were in darkness and perplexity.

We mention our experience to you, that your hearts may not sink at the discouraging prospects you may have, and that you must put your trust in God, who sees your condition, and as a merciful father pitieth his children, so doth God pity them that love him; and as your hearts are inclined to serve God, you will feel an affectionate regard towards your masters and mistresses, and the whole family where you live, this will be seen by them, and tend to promote your liberty, especially with such as have feeling masters, and if they are otherwise you will have the favour and love of God dwelling in your hearts, which you will value more than any thing else, which will be a consolation in the worst condition you can be in, and no master can deprive you of it; and as life is short and uncertain, and the chief end of our having a being in this world, is to be prepared for a better, we wish you to think of this more than any thing else; then will you have a view of that freedom which the sons of God enjoy; and if the troubles of your condition end with your lives, you will be admitted to the freedom which God hath prepared for those of all colours that love him; here the power of the most cruel master ends, and all sorrow and tears are wiped away.

To you who are favoured with freedom, let your conduct manifest your gratitude toward the compassionate masters who have set you free, and let no rancour or ill-will lodge in your breasts for any bad treatment you may

Absalom Jones and Richard Allen, *A Narrative of the Proceedings of the Black People During the Late Awful Calamity in Philadelphia in the Year 1793* (Philadelphia, 1794), pp. 26–27.

have received from any; if you do, you transgress against God, who will not hold you guiltless, he would not suffer it even in his beloved people Israel, and can you think he will allow it unto us?

There is much gratitude due from our colour towards the white people, very many of them are instruments in the hand of God for our good, even such as have held us in captivity, are now pleading our cause with earnestness and zeal; and we are sorry to say, that too many think more of the evil than of the good they have received, and instead of taking the advice of their friends, turn from it with indifference; much depends upon us for the help of our colour more than we are aware; if we are lazy and idle, the enemies of freedom plead it as a cause why we ought not to be free, and say we are better in a state of servitude, and that giving us our liberty would by an injury to us, and by such conduct we strengthen the bands of oppression, and keep many in bondage who are more worthy than ourselves; we intreat you to consider the obligations we lay under to help forward the cause of freedom, we who know how bitter the cup is of what the slave hath to drink, O how ought we to feel for those who yet remain in bondage? Will even our friends excuse, will God pardon us, for the part we act in making strong the hands of the enemies of our colour?

John Watson on Black Methodism, 1819

We have, too, a growing evil, in the practice of singing in our places of public and society worship, *merry* airs, adapted from old *songs,* to hymns of our composing: often miserable as poetry, and senseless as matter, and most frequently composed and first sung by the illiterate *blacks* of the society. Thus instead of inculcating sober Christianity in them who have the least wisdom to govern themselves; lifting them into spiritual pride and to an undue estimation of their usefulness. . . .

Such singing has been described, has we know, been ordinarily sung in most of our prayer and camp meetings: sometimes two or three are heard at a time or in succession. In the meantime, one and another of musical feelings, and consonant animal spirits, has been heard stepping the merry strains with all the precision of an avowed *dancer*. Here ought to be considered too, a most exceptionable error, which has the tolerance at least of the rulers of our camp meetings. In the *blacks'* quarter, the coloured people get together and sing for hours together, short scraps of disjointed affirmations, pledges, or prayers, lengthened out with long repetition *choruses*. These are all sung in the merry chorus-manner of the Southern harvest field, or husking-frolic method of the slave blacks; and also very greatly like the Indian dances. With every word sung, they have a sinking of one or other leg of the body alternately; producing an audible sound of the feet at every step, and as manifest as the steps of actual negro dancing in Virginia, & c. If some, in the meantime, sit, they strike the sounds alternately on each

John Watson, *Methodist Error: or, Friendly, Christian Advice, to those Methodists, Who Indulge in Extravagant Emotions and Bodily Exercise* (Trenton, 1819), pp. 28–30.

thigh. What in the name of religion, can countenance or tolerate such gross perversions of our true religion! but the evil is only occasionally condemned, and the example has already visibly affected the religious manners of some whites. From this cause, I have known in some camp meetings, from 50 to 60 people crowd into one tent, after the public devotions had closed, and there continue the whole night, singing tune after tune (though with occasional episodes of prayer) scarce one of which were in our hymn books. . . .

Timothy Dwight Describes "The Destruction of the Pequods," 1794

When o'er th' Atlantic wild, by Angels borne,
Thy pilgrim barque explor'd it's western way,
With spring and beauty bloom'd the waste forlorn,
And night and chaos shrunk from new-born day.
Dumb was the savage howl; th' instinctive lay
Wav'd, with strange warblings, thro' the woodland's bound;
The village smil'd; the temple's golden ray
Shot high to heaven; fair culture clothed the ground;
Art blosom'd; cities sprang; and sails the ocean crown'd.

As on heaven's sacred hill, of hills the queen,
At thy command, contention foul shall cease,
Thy solar aspect, every storm serene,
And smooth the rugged wild of man to peace;
So here thy voice (fair earnest of the bliss!)
Transform'd the savage to the meekly child.
Hell saw, with pangs, her hideous realm decrease;
Wolves play'd with lambs; the tyger's heart grew mild;
And on his own bright work the GODHEAD, look'd and smil'd. . . .

Oh had the same bright spirit ever reign'd;
Nor trader villains foul'd the Savage mind;
Nor Avarice pin'd for boundless breadth of land;
Nor, with slow death, the wretches been consign'd
To India's curse, that poisons half mankind!
Then, O divine Religion! torture's blaze
Less frequent round thy tender heart had twin'd;
On the wild wigwam peace had cast it's rays,
And the tremendous whoop had chang'd to hymns of praise.

Fierce, dark, and jealous, is the exotic soul,
That, cell'd in secret, rules the savage breast.
There treacherous thoughts of gloomy vengeance roll,
And deadly deeds of malice unconfess'd;
The viper's poison rankling in it's nest.
Behind his tree, each Indian aims unseen:
No sweet oblivion soothes the hate impress'd:

Years fleet in vain: in vain realms intervene:
The victim's blood alone can quench the flames within.

Their knives the tawny tribes in slaughter sleep,
When men, mistrustless, think them distant far;
And, when blank midnight shrouds the world in sleep,
The murderous yell announces first the war.
In vain sweet smiles compel the fiends to spare;
Th' unpitied victim screams, in tortures dire;
The life-blood stains the virgin's bosom bare;
Cherubic infants, limb by limb expire;
And silver'd Age sinks down in slowly-curling fire.

Yet savages are men. With glowing heat,
Fix'd as their hatred, friendship fills their mind;
By acts with justice, and with truth, replete,
Their iron breasts to softness are inclin'd.
But when could War of converts boast refin'd?
Or when Revenge to peace and sweetness move?
His heart, man yields alone to actions kind;
His faith, to creeds, whose soundness virtues prove,
Thawn in the April fun, and opening still to love.

Senate august! that sway'st Columbian climes,
Form'd of the wife, the noble, and humane,
Cast back the glance through long-ascending times,
And think what nations fill'd the western plain.
Where are they now? What thoughts the bosom pain,
From mild Religion's eye how streams the tear,
To see so far outspread the waste of man,
And ask "How fell the myriads, HEAVEN plac'd here!"
Reflect, be just, and feel for Indian woes severe.

But cease, foul Calumny! with sooty tongue,
No more the glory of our fires belie.
They felt, and they redress'd, each nation's wrong;
Even Pequod foes they view'd with generous eye,
And, pierc'd with injuries keen, that Virtue try,
The savage faith, and friendship, strove to gain:
And, had no base Canadian fiends been nigh,
Even now soft Peace had smil'd on every plain,
And tawny nations liv'd, and own'd MESSIAH's reign.

President Jefferson Displays Machiavellian Benevolence Toward the Indians, 1803

Thomas Jefferson to William Henry Harrison

. . . You will receive herewith an answer to your letter as President of the Convention; and from the Secretary of War you receive from time to time information and instructions as to our Indian affairs. These communications being for the public records, are restrained always to particular objects and occasions; but this letter being unofficial and private, I may with safety give you a more extensive view of our policy respecting the Indians, that you may the better comprehend the parts dealt out to you in detail through the official channel, and observing the system of which they make a part, conduct yourself in unison with it in cases where you are obliged to act without instruction. Our system is to live in perpetual peace with the Indians, to cultivate an affectionate attachment from them, by everything just and liberal which we can do for them within the bounds of reason, and by giving them effectual protection against wrongs from our own people. The decrease of game rendering their subsistence by hunting insufficient, we wish to draw them to agriculture, to spinning and weaving. The latter branches they take up with great readiness, because they fall to the women, who gain by quitting the labors of the field for those which are exercised within doors. When they withdraw themselves to the culture of a small piece of land, they will perceive how useless to them are their extensive forests, and will be willing to pare them off from time to time in exchange for necessaries for their farms and families. To promote this disposition to exchange lands, which they have to spare and we want, for necessaries, which we have to spare and they want, we shall push our trading uses, and be glad to see the good and influential individuals among them run in debt, because we observe that when these debts get beyond what the individuals can pay, they become willing to lop them off by a cession of lands. At our trading houses, too, we mean to sell so low as merely to repay us cost and charges, so as neither to lessen or enlarge our capital. This is what private traders cannot do, for they must gain; they will consequently retire from the competition, and we shall thus get clear of this pest without giving offence or umbrage to the Indians. In this way our settlements will gradually circumscribe and approach the Indians, and they will in time either incorporate with us as citizens of the United States, or remove beyond the Mississippi. The former is certainly the termination of their history most happy for themselves; but, in the whole course of this, it is essential to cultivate their love. As to their fear, we presume that our strength and their weakness is now so visible that they must see we have only to shut our hand to crush them, and that all our liberalities to them proceed from motives of pure humanity only. Should any tribe be fool-hardy enough to take up the hatchet at any time, the seizing the whole country of that tribe, and driving them across the Mississippi, as the only condition of peace, would be an example to others, and a furtherance of our final consolidation. . . .

The Practice of Jeffersonian Benevolence: William Henry Harrison's Treaty with the Delaware Indians, 1804

The Delaware tribe of Indians finding that the annuity which they receive from the United States, is not sufficient to supply them with the articles which are necessary for their comfort and convenience, and afford the means of introducing amongst them the arts of civilized life, and being convinced that the extensiveness of the country they possess, by giving an opportunity to their hunting parties to ramble to a great distance from their towns, is the principal means of retarding this desirable event; and the United States being desirous to connect their settlements on the Wabash with the state of Kentucky: therefore the said United States, by William Henry Harrison, governor of the Indiana territory, superintendent of Indian affairs, and their commissioner plenipotentiary for treating with the Indian tribes northwest of the Ohio river; and the said tribe of Indians, by their sachems, chiefs, and head warriors, have agreed to the following articles, which when ratified by the President of the United States, by and with the advice and consent of the Senate, shall be binding on the said parties.

ARTICLE 1. The said Delaware tribe, for the considerations hereinafter mentioned, relinquishes to the United States forever, all their right and title to the tract of country which lies between the Ohio and Wabash rivers, and below the tract ceded by the treaty of Fort Wayne, and the road leading from Vincennes to the falls of Ohio.

ARTICLE 2. The said tribe shall receive from the United States for ten years, an additional annuity of three hundred dollars, which is to be exclusively appropriated to the purpose of ameliorating their condition and promoting their civilization. Suitable persons shall be employed at the expense of the United States to teach them to make fences, cultivate the earth, and such of the domestic arts as are adapted to their situation; and a further sum of three hundred dollars shall be appropriated annually for five years to this object. The United States will cause to be delivered to them in the course of the next spring, horses fit for draft, cattle, hogs and implements of husbandry to the amount of four hundred dollars. The preceding stipulations together with goods to the amount of eight hundred dollars which is now delivered to the said tribe, (a part of which is to be appropriated to the satisfying certain individuals of the said tribe, whose horses have been taken by white people) is to be considered as full compensation for the relinquishment made in the first article. . . .

A Shawnee Parable of Resistance, 1803

[T]he representation of an old Shawanee Chief, who, in 1803, harangued a council at Fort Wayne[:] . . .

"The Master of Life," said he, very proudly, "who was himself an Indian, made the Shawaneese before any others of the human race, and *they* sprang from his brain." He added, that the Master of Life "gave them all the knowledge which he himself possessed; that he placed them upon the great island; and that all the other red people were descended from the Shawaneese:—that after he had made the Shawaneese, he made the French and English out of his breast, and the Dutch out of his feet; and for your Long-Knives kind," said he, addressing himself to the Governor, "he made them out of his hands. All these inferior races of men he made white, and placed them beyond the great lake,"—meaning the Atlantic Ocean.

"The Shawaneese for many ages continued to be masters of the continent, using the knowledge which they had received from the Great Spirit, in such a manner as to be pleasing to him, and to secure their own happiness. In a great length of time, however, they became corrupt, and the Master of Life told them he would take away from them the knowledge they possessed, and give it to the white people, to be restored when, by a return to good principles, they would deserve it. Many years after that, they saw something white approaching their shores; at first they took it for a great bird, but they soon found it to be a monstrous canoe, filled with the very people who had got the knowledge which belonged to the Shawaneese. After these white people landed, they were not content with having the knowledge which belonged to the Shawaneese, but they usurped their lands also. They pretended, indeed, to have purchased these lands; but the very goods which they gave for them was more the property of the Indians than the white people, because the knowledge which enabled them to manufacture these goods actually belonged to the Shawaneese. But these things will soon have an end. The Master of Life is about to restore to the Shawaneese both their knowledge and their rights, and he will trample the Long-Knives under his feet."

✳ *E S S A Y S*

The following essays raise theoretical as well as substantive questions about gender and race in the early republic. In the first essay, Jan Lewis, a historian teaching at Rutgers University, explores what she calls the early republic's "Edenic" image of womanhood and marriage—a paradox, based partly on the story of Adam and Eve, in which women were supposed to seduce men into virtue. Lewis draws her conclusions from a wide range of moral fables, advice literature, and belles-lettres, stressing their connection to broader political themes. How widely did these conceptions spread in the early republic? What are the advantages—and limits—of analyzing this kind of source material?

Lewis's contribution points out some of the potential connections to be drawn between "traditional" historians' concerns and the history of women and gender. Similar links can be found in the next two essays, which examine white-Indian relations from very different perspectives. Bernard Sheehan, a professor of history at Indiana University, explores Jeffersonian Indian policies and the motives he thinks lay behind them. In contrast, James H. Merrell, a professor of history at Vassar College, evaluates how the Indians themselves shaped their troubled encounters with white settlers, government officials, and the military. What insights do these essays provide on the documents earlier in this chapter on whites and African-Americans?

The Republican Wife

JAN LEWIS

To the extent that the success of the republican endeavor rested upon the character of citizens, republicanism demanded virtue of women, not because

Excerpts from "The Republican Wife: Virtue and Seduction in the Early Republic" by Jan Lewis from *William and Mary Quarterly,* 3rd ser., XLIV (1987), pp. 699–703, 706–710. Reprinted by permission of the author.

it numbered them as citizens but because it recognized how intimately women, in consensual unions, were connected to men. A virtuous man required a virtuous mate. Moreover, republicanism called upon every means at its disposal to assure male virtue. That obsession with virtue, deriving its force from the fusion of Protestant and republican notions of character, persisted long after the Revolution had been won and the Constitution ratified. Well into the nineteenth century, Americans linked the fate of their nation to the virtues of its people. Even if, as several historians have suggested, certain thinkers, before the end of the eighteenth century, had embraced liberalism and its premise of the self-interested individual, popular writers and, presumably, their audience had not. One writer put it emphatically: "Private vices are *not* public benefits." . . . [T]hat conceptualization of society—which continued to see the family as the microcosm of the wider world and to insist that "public good must grow out of private virtue"—held out a significant role for women.

"A woman of virtue and prudence is a public good—a public benefactor." She has the power to make "public decency . . . a fashion—and public virtue the only example." And how is woman to accomplish that great end? By her influence over the manners of men. Indeed, "nothing short of a general reformation of manners would take place, were the ladies to use their power in discouraging our licentious manners." Such a role might seem trivial did Americans not consider "the general reformation of manners" one of the young nation's most important goals, and did they not think women fully capable of contributing to it. Women might begin by reforming themselves, for "there is not a more certain test of national depravity, than that which presents itself in the degeneracy of female manners."

Male manners, however, were of more concern, and in changing them women were to play their most important role. So argued men, such as the essayist who held that women who were the beneficiaries of a "virtuous and refined education" might contribute "no less to public good than to private happiness. A gentleman, who at present must degrade himself into a fop or a coxcomb in order to please the ladies, would soon find that their favor could not be gained but by exerting every manly talent in public and private life." That same view could be expressed by a woman—for example, Miss C. Hutchings, who assured her fellow boarding-school graduates of the influence of "female manners on society in general": "were all women rational, unaffected and virtuous, coxcombs, flatterers and libertines would no longer exist." Such arguments rested on several important new assumptions. First, although the concern with "manners" betokened an upper-class emphasis upon gentility, the insistence that women are—or can be—a moral force transforms manners into mores, into the moral foundation of the society. Thus "it is . . . to the virtues of the fair . . . that society must be indebted for its moral, as well as its natural preservation." Second, women play their moral role not by denying their sexuality, by becoming "passionless," but by using it to tempt men to be good.

This conceptualization of female influence seems to have intrigued men and women in the decades just after the Revolution. Magazines printed and reprinted numbers of articles with similar titles and sentiments: "Female Influence," "Scheme for Increasing the Power of the Fair Sex," "The Influence of the Female Sex on the Enjoyments of Social Life," "The Power of Beauty, and the Influence the Fair Sex might have in Reforming the Manners of the World." These, with a host of similar articles, argued that the potential for beneficial female influence was almost unlimited.

The height of a woman's influence was reached during the period of "love and courtship," which, "it is universally allowed, invest a lady with more authority than in any other situation that falls to the lot of human beings." A young man who addressed his classmates at Columbia College's commencement elaborated: "She can mold the taste, the manners, and the conduct of her admirers, according to her pleasure." Moreover, "she can, even to a great degree, change their tempers and dispositions, and super-induce habits entirely new." Thus it was not in childhood that a man was most malleable; rather, it was when, grown to maturity, he sought the favors of a young lady that he was most susceptible to influence. "By the judicious management of this noble passion [love], a passion with which the truly accomplished of the fair sex never fail of inspiring men, what almost miraculous reformations may be brought about?"

Once she had seduced him into virtue, the married woman's task was to preserve her husband in the exalted state to which her influence had raised him. "It rests with her, not only to confirm those virtuous habits which he has already acquired, but also to excite his perseverance in the paths of rectitude." The boldness of this formulation is stunning. What earlier Americans perceived as Eve's most dangerous characteristic, her seductiveness, is here transformed into her capacity for virtue. Woman was to lead man into rectitude, to lure him to the exercise of manly virtue. What miraculous reformations became possible when the attraction between the sexes, which for millennia had been considered the cause of the fall of mankind, could be transformed into the bedrock of the nation! Women indeed had great power—nothing less than the ability, as one magazine implored, "to make our young men, not in empty words, but in deed and in truth, republicans.". . .

The Edenic vision of marriage served to bridge the antipatriarchalism of the eighteenth century and the domesticity of the nineteenth. If the patriarchal model of familial relationships was suited to a hierarchically organized society, and if, as Nancy F. Cott has suggested, domesticity went hand in hand with mid-nineteenth-century democratic liberalism, the Edenic vision fit just as nicely with the canons of republicanism. Like republicanism itself, Edenic republican marriage presented itself as egalitarian. Republican characterizations of marriage echoed with the words *equal, mutual,* and *reciprocal,* and marriage was described as a friendship between equals. An essay "Addressed to the Ladies," for example, urged "every young married woman to seek the friend of her heart in the husband of her affection. There, and there only, is that true equality, both of rank and fortune, and cemented by mutual interests, and mutual . . . pledges to be found. . . . There and there only will she be sure to meet with reciprocal confidence, unfeigned attachment and tender solicitude to soothe every care." Indeed, no word better summarizes republican notions of marriage than *friendship*. "Marriage is, or should be, the most perfect state of friendship. Mutual interest produces mutual assistance." Another writer defined the good marriage in almost the same words as "the highest instance of human friendship." In fact, "love" was nothing more than "friendship raised to its highest pitch."

Marriage, quite simply, was friendship exalted. Its pleasures derived from "mutual return of *conjugal love*. . . . When two minds are . . . engaged by the ties of reciprocal sincerity, each alternately receives and communicates a transport that is inconceivable to all, but those that are in this situation." Marriage was intended, another writer concluded, "to be the basis and the cement of those numberless tender sympathies, mutual endearments and interchanges of love between the mutual parties themselves, which make up not the morality only, but even the chief happiness of conjugal life." Marriage was moral because it fused "virtuous love and friendship; the one supplying it with a constant rapture, the other regulating it by the rules of reason." True marriage was quite unlike "those unnatural and disproportionate matches that are daily made upon worldly views, where interest or lust are the only motives." True marriage was proportionate; put another way, it was symmetrical. Indeed, the mutuality and reciprocity that republicans so prized were inconceivable in an asymmetrical union—the "slavery" of so-called barbaric cultures, in which women were thoroughly subordinated to men.

That republican marriage was symmetrical does not mean that it was fully egalitarian; rather, men and women were opposite sides of the same coin or, as a popular fable had it, two halves of a being that had once been sundered. Neither could be whole until it found its other half. Nor could the halves be fully moral when separate, for Eve's love and Adam's reason were equally necessary to the prelapsarian vision. As heirs to the Enlightenment, American republicans sought the happy medium between—or, more precisely, a fusion of—passion and intellect, head and heart. Eighteenth-century moral philosophy, as it was popularized in American magazines, taught both that passion must be regulated by reason and that "no real felicity can exist independent of susceptibility and affection, and the heart of him who is cold to the soothing voice of friendship, dead to the melting strains of love, and senseless to the plaintive pleadings of distress, is a mansion only calculated for demoniac spirits, or a cheerless dwelling for disgust and spleen." Adam and Eve, reason and love, are each indispensable, and the symmetrical marriage brings them together.

For this reason—that in checking passion and socializing reason the conjugal union made mankind truly virtuous—marriage was the model for society. The single life, according to John Witherspoon, writing as "Epaminondas" in the *Pennsylvania Magazine* on the eve of the Revolution, "narrows the mind and closes the heart." He asserted unequivocally the "absolute necessity of marriage for the service of the state." The pure love of marriage formed the basis for "social virtue," for "while other passions concentrate man on himself, love makes him live in another, subdues selfishness, and reveals to him the pleasure of ministering to the object of his love. . . . The lover becomes a husband, a parent, a citizen." The "marriage institution," then, "is the first to produce moral order." For that reason, "marriage has ever been considered by every wise state the sinew of its strength and the foundation of its true greatness." Marriage formed the basis of all other relationships, both in the family, because it led to parenthood, and in the society, because it schooled men in the disinterested benevolence that was supposed by republican ideologues to constitute virtue. In sum, as an essayist in the *Key* put it, "nothing is so honorable as MARRIAGE, nothing so comfortable both to body and mind. . . . It is marriage alone that knits and binds all the sinews of society together and makes the life of man honorable to himself, useful to others, and grateful to the God of nature. . . . Is there anything on earth nearer heaven?" Lest that promise of heaven-on-earth be insufficient to persuade his readers, the writer continued: "That MAN who resolves to live without WOMAN, or that WOMAN who resolves to live without MAN, are [sic] ENEMIES TO THE COMMUNITY in which they dwell, INJURIOUS TO THEMSELVES, DE-STRUCTIVE TO THE WORLD, APOSTATES TO NATURE, and REB-ELS AGAINST HEAVEN AND EARTH." The man or woman who proposed to live alone, then, was heretic and traitor both.

Like republicanism, the doctrine of symmetrical marriage subordinated individual interest to the greater good of the whole. Accordingly, marriages based upon interest were to be loathed; true marriage was the model for disinterested benevolence. Unlike the canon of domesticity, in which "women's self-renunciation was called upon to remedy men's self-alienation," idealized republican marriage required men and women both to display virtue. Male and female were two halves of one whole whose name was concord; the ideal marriage was a scene of prelapsarian harmony. As the author of "On the Necessity of Domestic Concord" noted, "peace" was more important even than "plenty." In order for "harmony" and "concord" to prevail, husband and wife were to be of one mind; they could not disagree. To prevent a conflict-filled marriage, one must choose one's mate wisely; probably no consideration was more important than "a similarity of sentiments and dispositions," for where there is "a union of souls, and a consistent harmony of mental ideas . . . discord will keep at an awful distance, and a universal sympathy, productive of an ineffable bliss, will ever attend them. . . . O happiness divine! source of concordant minds!" An essayist in *New York Magazine* expressed the same idea more matter-of-factly: "There cannot be too near an equality, too exact a harmony, betwixt a married couple." Indeed, "the idea of power on either side should be totally banished."

Conjugal affection, then, was not coercive. Nor did it admit of any "selfish or sensual alloy." Marriage was the republic in miniature; it was chaste, disinterested, and free from the exercise of arbitrary power. And, like republican citizens, husband and wife were most likely to find happiness when, as Witherspoon suggested, they shared the same rank, the same education, and the same habits of life. . . .

Jeffersonian Philanthropy and the American Indian

BERNARD SHEEHAN

. . . Determined to make the continent a civilized domain, the new nation was forced to deal with the problem of the Indian. From the first formulation of policy in the Washington administration until the decision in the 1820s to move the tribes beyond the Mississippi, a basic consistency informed the white man's attitude toward the Indian. He generally believed that savagery would recede, while civilization spread its influence over the entire continent. In the actual relations between the two societies, this meant that the government, with the steady application of pressure, obtained new lands from the Indians by treaty. Usually, the acquisition merely ratified what had already taken place: the movement of frontier population into the Indian territory. Often enough, when the event proved that more strength than the unorganized frontier could bring to bear would be required to dislodge the tribes, the government contributed its military power. The Indian always retreated, the white man always advanced.

Yet governmental policy, and a substantial portion of civilized opinion, appraised the situation with more subtle ends in mind than simply forcing the Indian aside. The elimination of savagery, many reasoned, could be accomplished in more refined and humanitarian ways. The Indian need not be destroyed; in fact, most men involved in government Indian affairs, and all those privately interested in the native's welfare, agreed that the white man had a moral obligation to himself and to his posterity to see that the tribesman survived. If the Indian were transformed, if he adopted civilization and lived like a white man, his savage ways would disappear, and he would endure to become a useful member of the white man's world. Every administration from Washington to John Quincy Adams and a variety of private philanthropic organizations supported this policy. When the process of civilizing the native proved slow of accomplishment, when some foolhardy Indians stubbornly retained their savage habits, or, more important, when the frontier moved faster than the federal authorities could impress on the tribes the need to adopt civilization, the government more than willingly employed force and manipulation to achieve its ends. Ultimately, however, governmental policy could best be fulfilled by civilizing the Indian and incorporating him into the white man's society.

Indian-white relations approached a climax in the decades after the Revolution. The Indians now had few options. Retreat in the Northwest meant conflict with other, more hostile tribes. Retreat in the South meant that more sedentary peoples faced the prospect of abandoning lands long held and changing the very basis of their social life. Moreover, the influence of civilization had taken effect. Many Indians, particularly the mixed bloods among the tribes, understood the white man's aims. Determined to stand their ground, they used knowledge acquired from civilization to resist him.

Bernard W. Sheehan, *Seeds of Extinction: Jeffersonian Philanthropy and the American Indian* (University of North Carolina Press, 1973), pp. 3–12. Reprinted by permission of the publisher.

Some Indians reacted differently; with their social order under severe strain—in places on the verge of disintegration—they showed signs of desperation and malaise. But whether the effect of civilized contact served to strengthen the Indian's capacity to survive or to push him to the point of social collapse, the problem demanded a solution.

From the other side of the dilemma of cultural conflict, American society in the late eighteenth and early nineteenth centuries seemed likely to overwhelm any obstruction to its advance, particularly the comparatively feeble opposition offered by the Indian tribes. Little had changed in the white man's attitude since the first meeting between the two societies. From the beginning, the eventual disappearance of savagery had been accepted, and there had also been a strong missionary impulse to save the Indian from himself by making him a Christian. But by the latter part of the eighteenth century, that long-held mission to subdue the continent and obliterate the last vestiges of the savage world became more than a definition of how things ought to be or even how they would eventually become. Instead it became an immediate imperative that seemed entirely within reach. The generation that threw off British rule and created a new government had few thoughts that its wishes could be denied by some roving bands of savage Indians. On the contrary, the self-esteem and confidence of the Revolutionary and early national generations made it difficult for them to believe that the Indians would not also see the desirability of an end to savagery and their acceptance of civilization.

The essential unity of the period from the Revolution to the late 1820s, when the government decided on the removal of the eastern tribes, can be seen in both the character of Indian-white relations and in the content of the white man's thinking. The process that began with Independence and the expansion of the nation reached a fitting denouement in removal. Similarly, the ideas around which white men constructed their understanding of the relationship between the two societies persisted throughout the period.

In his *Notes on the State of Virginia,* published in the 1780s, Jefferson made the most perceptive summary statement about the nature of Indian society. His interpretation was not so much original or even profound, but it reflected accurately—it summed up in a way that only Jefferson could— the basic thinking of his age on the subject of Indian-white relations. Furthermore, Jefferson held political power for eight crucial years at the heart of the period. After the 1790s, when the last major conflicts (aside from the War of 1812) took place between the eastern tribes and the white man, he had an opportunity to put into effect the policy of incorporating the Indian into the white man's society. In the years following his retirement from office, those who directed the government's relations with the tribes acted under the aegis of Jeffersonian theory and policy. Although the years from the Revolution to removal produced ample diversity in politics and ideology, on the question of the Indian and his relationship to civilization they were substantially Jeffersonian. . . .

Jefferson led the age, not because his ideas were original, but because they represented a consensus. His prominence as a political leader enhanced the importance of his activities in favor of the Indians. Also, his position of influence in scientific affairs gave his opinions on the Indian's future a special stature. In his *Notes on Virginia,* his presidency of the American Philosophical Society, his extensive correspondence with the important minds of the period, and finally in his determination, while he held political power, to change the character of tribal society, Jefferson held a central position in the late eighteenth and early nineteenth centuries. Judged in the light of a widely held body of opinion on the nature of Indian-white relations, the age can be called Jeffersonian. . . .

The Indian became a victim of the white man's proclivity for conceptualization and idealization. Though at any given time ideas only partially coerced events, few areas of public interest were as immediately susceptible to the influence of big ideas as the relations between primitive man and civilization. Typically, Jeffersonian thinking stressed the improving aspects of the human situation. In the manner of the eighteenth-century rationalist mind, Jefferson and his generation viewed the future optimistically. Indeed, nature itself provided the means for its own improvement. Human will became less important than the unfolding development of nature's self-realization. And this process was inclusive: nature produced no sports, no extraneous energies, no incongruous elements. The same cosmic verities, easily discernible, reassuring, and intrinsically progressive, characterized all of creation. An extension of this principle of inclusion brought the human being into close relationship with his physical surroundings and opened him to environmental influence. Tightly bound within the ever-changing and beneficent order of nature, men became in great measure what the world made them. Differences among men, variety in nature, could be explained by environmentalism, as could any changes induced by a reaction to nature or by positive human decision.

Moreover, the ends of human development came within the broad conceptions of paradise and the noble savage. These stereotypes explained the differences between civilization and primitive existence, and they also presented the white man with an ideal his whole society might strive to reach. Most writers employed the concepts for rhetorical convenience or sometimes to relieve the frustrations of civilized life. But paradise and the noble savage also drew on powerful motive forces in Western thought—forces that, together with environmentalism, the Jeffersonian age set to work for the purpose of civilizing the Indian.

A deep-seated benevolence, intending for the Indian the best that civilization could offer, translated this theoretical statement into a design for action. Furthermore, the conviction that the Indian had only a short period in which to complete the work of incorporation added an element of realism. The force of frontier extension pressed heavily against the successful completion of the philanthropic plan. And when the native did not make the progress expected of him, doubts that had been only fleeting before became profound fears that he would be destroyed. Philanthropy, as a consequence, though still reflecting the optimism of the age, became anxious and itself seemingly aggressive. The full import of Jeffersonian theory and the intensity of philanthropic anticipation imposed the necessity of success. When nature did not yield immediate results, when the actualities of acculturation stretched the process beyond the time afforded by the advancing frontier, Jeffersonian optimism turned to compulsion, mostly covert but sometimes frankly espoused, to complete its task.

Still, the aggressiveness of philanthropy arose from deeper sources than the tension between Jeffersonian hope and the historical obstacles to its realization. The philanthropic mind was at base obtrusive and compulsive in its determination to have its way. Though it praised the Indian for his many abilities, it conceded native society nothing in the way of permanence. Philanthropy treated the tribes as objects of commiseration whose sole purpose after the arrival of the white man should have been the speedy adoption of civilization. It demanded a total transformation in full confidence that what was to come would in all ways be superior to what had been. If philanthropy seemed supercilious, it betrayed no false voice to the Indian. Self-satisfied, righteous, morally aggressive, and paternal, it tended to infantilize the Indian and to destroy the integrity of his culture. But the strength of its moral drive only reflected the consistency of its principles and the profoundest goodwill. Because it believed itself in league with the cosmos, philanthropy imposed a terrible burden on the Jeffersonian conscience, and it asked of the Indian an impossible achievement.

Specifically, the philanthropic plan required that the Indian abandon the hunter-warrior culture, the tribal order, and the communal ownership of land. It commanded him to become civilized by adopting a variety of manners and artifacts and, most important, by choosing to live according to the white man's individualist ideology. Had such a change been possible, it would have meant a total upheaval in the native's social order. But for the white man, the step did not seem so great. Americans had always conceived of their version of civilization as distinct from Europe's, a peculiar growth of the new continent. The Indian should have found no difficulty in adjusting his primitive but distinctly New World manner of life to the similarly distinct middling conception of society familiar to the Jeffersonian age. Envisioning only a minor transition from the wilderness to the garden, philanthropy could afford to be confident.

What the philanthropists intended for the Indian bore little resemblance to the reality. The relations between white and Indian, both the formal efforts at conversion and the informal contacts between the two societies, profoundly affected the tribal order. Civilization introduced new artifacts, redirected the economic and social life of the tribes, and severely damaged substantial portions of tribal culture. Indian life changed as a consequence of meeting the white man; many Indians took significant steps in the direction of becoming civilized. But the tribal order remained intact. Despite much disintegration and malaise, and also a noticeable degree of acculturation among the native peoples, they remained recognizable as Indians. Philanthropic ideology, with scarcely any recognition of the tendency of culture to persist or of the inherent tentativeness in the acculturative process, had asked the Indian to abandon totally his ancient manner of life. The simplicity of Jeffersonian theory, which supposed such cultural obliteration possible, left the philanthropic mind unprepared for the failure of its program.

This hiatus between what the Jeffersonian age expected would occur as a consequence of its plans for the native tribes and what actually did happen raises a problem of interpretation. In effect, the philanthropic mind formulated its conception of Indian society and its proposal for how that society ought to evolve in relation to civilization with little attention to the actualities of the Indian experience. Jeffersonian theory operated with considerable coherence in one sphere and provided those who believed in it with a rationale for profoundly influencing the native way of life, but it offered no explanation for what really happened to the Indian. It could account for none of the negative consequences of Indian-white relations: the breakdown of tribal society, the failure of the civilizing program to lead to the incorporation of the Indians into the white man's world, and the steadfast refusal of many Indians to take the final step into civilization. While the Indians grappled with the disorientation of their societies and the acquisition of new ways of living, philanthropic thinking remained static. No major changes occurred in Jeffersonian theory between the Revolution and 1830. The decision to support removal in the 1820s had as its purpose the preservation of the theoretical structure rather than any fundamental revision. It in no way affected the philanthropic commitment to the eventual incorporation of the natives. As a consequence, the philanthropic mind can best be explained by a logical but static exposition of its internal content. The description of policy and its effects on native society, however, must be seen developing in time as the Indians reacted to the application of the white man's power.

Furthermore, since Jeffersonian theory had so utterly misconstrued the nature of tribal culture and the possibilities for its reform, the historical guilt so often imputed to the white man could scarcely be applied to the philanthropist. True enough, philanthropy played its part in the overall attack on the native society; it intended to destroy the Indian's world. But it made no such frontal assault on the tribes as did the Indian-hating frontier. Its crime, if it committed one, could be ascribed to naïveté, perhaps even an excess of goodwill, but not the intentional inflicting of pain on a less powerful people. More to the point, the Jeffersonian brand of philanthropy could be justly accused of treating the native more like a precious abstraction than a living human being. For the Indian it wanted only the best, but that meant ultimately the elimination of the tribal order, for which the Jeffersonian age must bear its share of responsibility. Its crime was a willful failure of the intellect but not of the will.

Indian-White Relations in the New Nation

JAMES H. MERRELL

The Revolutionary generation's plans for the Indian were succinctly expressed by a band of intoxicated soldiers in 1779. At a Fourth of July banquet held during General John Sullivan's march into Iroquois territory, the of-

James H. Merrell, "Declarations of Independence: Indian-White Relations in the New Nation," in Jack P. Greene, ed., *The American Revolution: Its Character and Limits.* Copyright © 1987 by New York University. Reprinted by permission of the publisher.

ficers' tenth toast was to "Civilization or death to all American Savages." After the war the phrase would become common among those interested in Indian affairs. "[C]ivilized or extinct," "moralized or exterminated," "Civilization or extinction," "war or civilization"—the refrain runs through private correspondence, public speeches, and official records well into the nineteenth century. If Indians did not become white they soon would be extinct, wiped out either by force of arms or in a less violent war of attrition . . .

[After the Revolution,] American arrogance—whether expressed in an "informal war" by settlers, forced land cessions to a state, or the federal conquest theory—rested upon more than hatred of Indians and a desire for revenge. There was reason to believe that the United States could indeed subdue the native nations on its borders. The patriots had just defeated the most powerful country on earth; if necessary, could they not turn around and score a similar success against Indians? Arrayed against approximately 2.4 million inhabitants of the new nation were perhaps 150,000 natives, and it was unlikely that these scattered peoples could ever coordinate an effective defense, divided as they were into some eighty-five different tribes. . . .

Had the United States been successful, there would have been a real revolution in Indian-white relations. As it turned out, however, Indian resistance made the Americans eat their words. Government commissioners or land companies generally found natives to listen to a harangue or sign a treaty. Someone was always willing to do that much, from fear or greed or a genuine hope that peace would last. A few might even tell an agent what he wanted to hear, agreeing that "you have every thing in your power— you are great, and we see you own all the country." But most refused to sit still for the verbal or physical pounding. Great Britain had lost to the Americans; her allies most certainly had not, for despite rebel invasions of Cherokee and Iroquois territories, Indians more than held their own against American forces, especially in the Ohio region. Moreover, they had never signed a peace treaty, and without that consent the King "had no right Whatever to grant away to the States of America, their Rights or properties. . . ."

Indians had a number of weapons at their disposal to back up their words. In Florida Spanish officials stood ready to do whatever they could to discomfit the new nation, including aiding its native neighbors. The British in Canada had an even bigger score to settle, and to stir up trouble they kept a string of forts on the American frontier in violation of the Treaty of Paris. Among the natives, leaders such as Alexander McGillivray of the Creeks and the Mohawk Joseph Brant emerged who were ideally suited to make the most of the situation. Both had been educated in colonial schools and could slip easily across the cultural divide to bargain with Europeans. In 1784 McGillivray struck deals with the Spanish that made him Commissary among the Creeks and guaranteed the nation, among other things, the goods needed to defend itself "from the Bears and other fierce Animals." Meanwhile Brant led the Iroquois exodus to Canada, received a commission as Captain of the Northern Confederate Indians, and worked hand in hand with the British to stiffen native resistance.

Fancy titles and fluent English would have gotten the two leaders nowhere without native support. Both were as well-connected among their own people as they were well-versed in European ways. McGillivray threaded his way cautiously through the intricate web of Creek politics, never claiming a higher title than was due him by custom, manipulating the traditional forum of the National Council to forge an unprecedented unity in Creek society. Brant set his sights even higher, aiming at nothing less than a pan-Indian confederacy to resist the Americans. . . .

Hopes for national or international unity ultimately foundered on the rocks of traditional localism and cultural diversity. Nonetheless, even temporary alliances and partial confederacies that were encouraged by Britain or Spain proved more than a match for the Americans. In 1786 and again in 1787, Creek and Cherokee war parties armed by Spaniards and assisted by Shawnees drove settlers out of disputed territories in Tennessee and Georgia. In 1790 and 1791 Ohio Indians with help from southern nations destroyed American armies marching to subdue them. A delegation sent by President Washington a year later to warn that "[t]he warriors of the United States number like the Trees in the woods" was unable to get the message across before Indians killed or captured most of the party.

These were only the more embarrassing in a long series of reverses that gave the talk of conquest, compensation, and extermination a rather hollow ring. Americans could lay claim to the entire continent if they wished; it was theirs only on paper. . . . It was time to try another approach. . . .

The idea of rescuing the Indians from themselves had preoccupied Englishmen and their American cousins since the days of the Hakluyts. Despite repeated failures, the dream endured, even during the darkest days of the Revolution. In the early stages of the conflict . . . Congress considered spreading the gospel and "the civil arts" among the natives. . . . Thereafter some treaties promised certain Indian nations statehood, and at least one state legislature debated the wisdom of offering bounties to citizens who would marry natives. . . .

Such sentiments might well have remained submerged had the United States managed to prove its theory of conquest. When Indians made a mockery of American claims, the ideology of conversion and coexistence was available to justify, even sanctify, a different approach. The plan made sense for several reasons. First, the new nation was acutely sensitive to its image, both among contemporaries and in the eyes of generations yet unborn. "Indians have their rights and our Justice is called on to support them," Virginia governor Benjamin Harrison argued in 1782. "Whilst we are nobly contending for liberty will it not be an eternal blot on our National character if we deprive others of it who ought to be as free as ourselves." . . .

Quite apart from a concern with appearances, there was good reason to believe that the scheme would work. In the heady days of the postwar era, when America had thrown off the yoke of tyranny and France appeared to be following suit, anything seemed possible, even success in an enterprise that had known little but failure. Moreover, the design seemed to rest on sound philosophical foundations. From the Revolution to the Jacksonian era, thoughtful Americans agreed that societies progressed along the same path (a path which reached "its present state of perfection" with Euro-American culture), that differences among peoples could be attributed to environmental influences, and that therefore native Americans could be guided along the path toward "civilization." When Jefferson argued that the "proofs of genius given by the Indians of N. America, place them on a level with Whites in the same uncultivated state," others were quick to concur and make plans to cultivate them. . . .

Success seemed all the more likely because deep fissures appeared to be opening in the . . . traditional native culture. During the 1780s armed resistance to American pretensions had forced the United States to back down, but Indians paid a terrible price. By 1794, when Anthony Wayne shattered the Ohio Indian confederacy at Fallen Timbers and the last of the Cherokee opposition crumbled, the cost was becoming painfully clear. For twenty years Cherokees, Iroquois, and other Indians had endured invasions of their homelands and the destruction of towns, crops, and orchards. To purchase peace Cherokees had given up more than half of their 40,000 square miles of territory between 1776 and 1794, the Iroquois even more. Every cession entailed painful uprooting from ancient homes and resettlement in an ever-smaller circle. Worse still, dislocation had combined with warfare and disease to reduce native population. In the last quarter of the eighteenth century the Six Nations lost half of its eight to ten thousand people, and Cherokee numbers fell from sixteen thousand to ten thousand.

Cultural disorientation followed close on the heels of physical devastation. As hunting lands vanished under the plow, game disappeared from the forests that remained, and warfare became less common, the customary avenues that native men had followed to acquire social status and vital merchandise began to close. They compensated in various ways—hiring themselves out to whites, displaying their skills in early versions of a wild west show, stealing horses in search of the risks and rewards once provided by the hunt—but nothing was a satisfactory substitute for more traditional endeavors. At the same time, the tribal elder began to feel as obsolete as the hunter and warrior, for the changes in native existence threatened to make his vast knowledge of ancient lore irrelevant to future generations. . . .

As if the signs of demoralization were not promising enough, American hopes of changing Indians received another boost from vocal natives who wanted to avoid destruction and combat despair by embracing white ways. During the Revolution Delawares had made instruction in American customs part of the price of their support for the rebels. Thereafter some Indians from virtually every nation pestered the government for education and urged their people to take advantage of it. Cornplanter of the Senecas, the Shawnee chief Black Hoof, Cherokees like James Vann and Charles Hicks, a Catawba named John Nettles, Hendrick Aupaumut of the Stockbridge—these and many more believed that the only chance of survival lay in abandoning the old ways, and they complained about "people who have hardly any holes in their heads" to let in new ideas.

Thus the time seemed ripe to erase the dismal record of frustration and failure that had marked efforts to win Indians over in the past, and during

Washington's administration the federal government set to work with its chisels. Its first move was to pry Indian affairs from the clutches of the states, where much of the initiative had lain during the Confederation period. Next it charted the course the nation should follow, passing laws to recognize native sovereignty, forbid trespassers on Indian land, regulate trade, and provide technology along with lessons in its proper use. . . .

In retrospect it seems surprising that the dream of assimilating Indians did not die sooner than it did, for it met opposition from every corner of American society. As usual, distance made the heart grow fonder: men far removed from daily contact with another world . . . could talk all they wished about justice, Americanization, and assimilation. People on the frontier still spoke a radically different language, a language learned in childhood from the gruesome tales of savage exploits popular at the time. . . . Frontier hatred of Indians was so common, so intense, so deep-seated that no policy or proclamation could root it out, and it fueled the indifference to Indian lives and Indian lands against which the federal government struggled.

Controlling western officials proved as difficult as taming settlers. Most governors of the states bordering on Indian nations stood closer to the frontiersman than to the national government, for these men were themselves heavily involved in western expansion. . . .

Natives with few friends nearby looked to the nation's capital for protection. But even there, where the policies originated, there was deep ambivalence about the native American. If talk of "blood Hounds" and "beasts of prey" had died down, it could readily be adopted again if circumstances warranted. Nor could the clamor for making Indians white drown out the whispers of doubt. If anything, the whispers grew louder, for Americans were gradually coming to adopt a color scheme that made assimilation all but impossible. The old belief that beneath the layer of bear grease, dirt, or sunburn was a white person yearning to be cleaned up was slowly being replaced by the notion that Indians were "redskins." . . .

The limits of America's commitment to federal policy were clear in the failure of the government to practice what it preached. . . .

[I]f implementation of national policy was a thorny problem, federal officials made it all the more difficult by giving it low priority. Fulfilling promises to Indians invariably took second place to western expansion. The Revolutionary generation fervently believed that it was America's destiny to people the continent, and nothing could be permitted to stand in the way. Thus the government promised that Indians could keep their lands, yet quickly stopped returning territory fraudulently acquired and sent delegations to bring "to reason" those who refused to sell more—approaching Choctaws, for example, no less than forty times in thirty years. Thus the government established public factories to eliminate trade abuses, yet proposed that the debts accumulated at these trading posts be used to coerce recalcitrant leaders. Thus the government promised to supply the personnel and funds necessary to teach Indians white ways, yet appropriated little money, sent few teachers, and often abandoned the projects it did undertake. It was a sorry record by any standard of measurement.

Last but by no means least, a federal government busy battling its own doubts and stiff opposition from the states and the frontier also confronted native peoples even less enthusiastic about the program than their white neighbors. . . .

Some natives blunted the white man's offensive with indifference. Catawbas, for example, proved enormously frustrating to their would-be saviors. . . . Many spoke English, answered to names like Brown, Harris, or Ayers, lived in log cabins, and dressed much like everyone else in the Carolina uplands. It seemed almost too easy to finish the job already begun: shortly after 1800 a series of missionaries set up shop near the Nation, built a school, and preached God's word. Their message fell on barren ground. The Indians listened politely enough (some children even trooped into the schoolroom), but after a while they "Became unattentive" and drifted off. Whites were baffled and angry. . . .

While some peoples met the vanguard of European culture with indifference, others counterattacked. Between 1800 and 1812 many natives developed a world view that served as an antidote to the poisons injected by close encounters with whites. The excitement began when certain individuals among Creeks, Cherokees, Shawnees, Iroquois, and other tribes experienced a dramatic vision of a better way. Virtually all of these holy men were from obscure, even corrupt, backgrounds. The Creek Josiah Francis (Hilis Hadjo, or "Crazy Medicine") was exceptional only in his deeply superstitious nature. The Shawnee Prophet (Tenskwatawa) was a poor hunter and worse warrior, a corpulent, quarrelsome man whose forte seemed to be drinking. Handsome Lake of the Senecas was a more prominent member of his nation, but he, too, was a notorious drunkard whose alcoholic excesses shattered the peace of his village. Each emerged from these depths a changed man, bearing a message of hope that had enormous appeal in native America and sparked a series of revitalization movements. It was, as one observer among the Creeks later recalled, "the age and time of prophecy."

The Indians who flocked to hear the new messiahs were responding to a deeply felt need for answers to the confusion of their times. Men like Handsome Lake or Tenskwatawa commonly rise to prominence when people feel that they have lost their way, when the accepted theories of how the world should be can no longer account for the world as it actually is. While the movement may be considered a sign of desperation, it can also be construed as a creative response to rapid change, an attempt to bring theory and reality into line again. Indians in the new nation accomplished this by stressing certain themes, themes that focused upon a return to traditional ways. Prophets uniformly condemned the consumption of alcohol, the outbreaks of violence in the village, and the accumulation of private property, urging their listeners to restore communal harmony, familiar ceremonies, and customary respect for tribal elders. No prophet's message was blindly devoted to tradition or entirely devoid of European influence. Both Handsome Lake and Tenskwatawa condemned the ancient medicine societies and customary marriage practices while incorporating Christian notions of sin and confession. Nonetheless, the thrust of the movement ran directly counter to American culture.

If the visions and visionaries had common origins and stressed common themes, they assumed very different shapes. Those who visited Prophetstown in present Indiana after 1805 to hear the gospel according to Tenskwatawa, and the Creeks who later listened with approval to the Prophet's brother, Tecumseh, imbibed a powerfully nativistic, explicitly anti-American doctrine. Indians were to have nothing to do with the Americans, "the children of the Evil Spirit," "the scum of the great Water," who were like a great ugly crab that had crawled from the sea. Hunters were to pay only half of their debts to the traders, women were not to marry whites, anyone meeting an American in the forest was to greet him from a distance but never shake hands. Avoidance would prevent further pollution. To root out the contamination that had already occurred, natives must forsake the plow and the loom, kill the cattle, hogs, and fowl, shed the clothing and weapons, and stop eating the white man's bread.

The Prophet's potent message became explosive when Tecumseh translated it from the spiritual to the political realm. Disgusted by the seemingly endless series of land cessions extracted from Indians, Tecumseh grafted onto Tenskwatawa's words the old talk of a pan-Indian confederacy that would halt American encroachment and prevent—by force if need be— further land deals. Before 1810 he had eclipsed his brother and attracted followers from Ohio to the Mississippi River. To add to this core of support he ventured to Canada to receive assurance of British aid and south of the Ohio River to enlist the backing of the Southern nations. Choctaws and Chickasaws proved unreceptive, but among the Creeks, where he had kinfolk and where the rift between traditional and "progressive" factions was widening, Tecumseh received a more enthusiastic welcome. He taught people there the new war songs, instructed them in the "Dance of the Lakes," and returned north in the fall of 1811 with high hopes of making his dream a reality. In only three years, however, war with the Americans would destroy both dream and dreamer, and the Prophet, who survived the conflict, sank back into the obscurity from which he had come.

By then the Creek movement Tecumseh had helped nurture had also met a violent death. What started out as a civil war between traditionalists (termed Red Sticks) and those under the influence of the United States became a general conflict when Creek prophets led the Red Sticks in an attack on Americans holed up in Fort Mims in August 1813. Armies from Tennessee, Georgia, and the Mississippi Territory allied with Choctaws, Cherokees, and non-nativist Creeks and headed into the nation. The Red Stick prophets met them with an arsenal that included dyed cow tails, medicine bags, magic rods, a "Holy Ground Town" protected by an invisible barrier no white person could cross, and a belief that the enemy's bullets could be rendered harmless by native medicine. It was not enough; within a year three thousand Creeks lay dead and Andrew Jackson was dictating a harsh peace. . . .

Whether they responded with quiet indifference, open violence, or something in between, it was increasingly clear that most of these native groups were never going to be a showcase for government policies. Hopes came to focus more and more on the Cherokees, who, despite their short-lived revival, were generally considered "the most civilized tribe in America." Here, if anywhere, the seeds of white culture would take root and flourish. A visitor to the nation in the early decades of the nineteenth century found it easy to agree with missionary claims that "Cherokees are rapidly adopting the laws and manners of the whites." Family farms replaced communal holdings, and on those farms were cattle and hogs, plows and spinning wheels, slaves and wagons, the whole supported by a large and growing network of roads, mills, and blacksmith shops. The political achievement was no less impressive. After 1800 the nation's leaders had developed a representative government and a judicial system modeled closely on American practices. . . .

Confident claims by satisfied missionary boards could not disguise the fact that something was going terribly wrong in the Cherokee mountains. It was not so much that many remained outside the circle of Christianity and civilization, sniping at missionaries and complaining about the web of alien laws spun by the nation's leaders; these skeptics would be won over in time. It was not so much that people who did avidly embrace white ways saw nothing wrong with consulting conjurors as well as clergymen or pulling their children out of school to attend ballplays or dances; that, too, would pass. The real problem was that even those most willing to follow the missionaries' lead in everything still did not care to follow their mentors into white society. Instead, Cherokees used the skills taught them to develop a powerful national spirit along new lines and beat the white man at his own game in the courts, the Congress, and the forum of public opinion. The limits of Cherokee enthusiasm were clear in 1817 when the United States offered each of them citizenship and 640 acres. Only 311 of 3,200 heads of household took the government up on its offer, and before long many of these had repented and returned to the Cherokee fold.

The most obvious expression of this reluctance to change came in 1827 when leading Cherokees met to draft a national constitution akin to state and federal versions. In one sense they were doing nothing more than codifying the laws passed over the previous two decades. Yet their deliberations also represented an emphatic rejection of the campaign to assimilate them into American society. The constitution was an assertion of sovereignty, a claim that Cherokees were an independent people and chose to remain so. It was, in short, a declaration of independence. Lest anyone miss the point, the nation's leaders scheduled the constitutional convention to convene on July 4.

By then the tide against federal policy was running so strong that neither assimilation nor national sovereignty was likely. The frontiersman's opinions were the same. What had changed was the stance of the states, the view of the federal government, and the climate of opinion. Southern governors had never liked the Indian policies drafted in Washington; after the War of 1812 they went a step further, declaring that even if those policies were successful and the Indian thoroughly Americanized, under no circumstances would he be accepted as a citizen. A free person of color, perhaps, but equal to whites, never. . . .

Washington went along now because the number of people committed to the old policies dwindled rapidly after 1815. In 1818 John C. Calhoun, one of Henry Knox's successors as Secretary of War, announced that "[t]he time seems to have arrived when our policy towards them should undergo an important change. . . . Our views of their interest, and not their own, ought to govern them." A year later he told a Cherokee delegation to become white or "become extinct as a people. You see that the Great Spirit has made our form of society stronger than yours, and you must submit to adopt ours." . . .

The notion that Indians were by nature equal to whites and could be improved was out of fashion. In its place was a growing sense that the two peoples were fundamentally different, that an impenetrable racial barrier divided them and doomed every reform effort. This, of course, was precisely what inhabitants of the frontier—both white and Indian—had been saying all along. But now authorities on both sides of the Atlantic were taking anatomical measurements and offering "scientific" theories that gave innate racial differences an aura of respectability. . . .

⌗ *F U R T H E R   R E A D I N G*

Ira Berlin, "Time, Space, and the Evolution of Afro-American Society in British North America," *American Historical Review* 85 (1980), 44–78

Robert F. Berkhofer, *The White Man's Indian: Images of the American Indian from Columbus to the Present* (1978)

Ruth Bloch, "The Gendered Meanings of Virtue in Revolutionary America," *Signs* 13 (1987), 37–58

Nancy F. Cott, *The Bonds of Womanhood: "Woman's Sphere" in New England, 1780–1835* (1977)

Margaret Washington Creel, *"A Peculiar People": Slave Religion and Community Culture Among the Gullahs* (1988)

Philip Curtin, *The Atlantic Slave Trade: A Census* (1969)

David Brion Davis, *Slavery and Human Progress* (1986)

———, *The Problem of Slavery in the Age of Revolution, 1770–1823* (1975)

———, *The Problem of Slavery in Western Culture* (1967)

Angie Debo, *The Rise and Fall of the Choctaw Republic* (1961)

Richard Drinnon, *Facing West: The Metaphysics of Indian Hating and Empire Building* (1980)

R. David Edmunds, *Tecumseh and the Quest for Indian Leadership* (1984)

———, *The Shawnee Prophet* (1983)

Reginald Horsman, *Expansion and American Indian Policy, 1783–1812* (1967)

———, "The Dimensions of an 'Empire for Liberty': Expansionism and Republicanism," *Journal of the Early Republic* 9 (1989), 1–20

Joan M. Jensen, *Loosening the Bonds: Mid-Atlantic Farm Women, 1750–1850* (1986)

Winthrop Jordan, *White over Black: American Attitudes Toward the Negro, 1550–1812* (1968)

Linda K. Kerber, *Women of the Republic: Intellect and Ideology in Revolutionary America* (1980)

Allan Kulikoff, *Tobacco and Slaves: The Development of Southern Cultures in the Chespeake, 1680–1800* (1986)

Jan Lewis, *The Pursuit of Happiness: Family Values in Jefferson's Virginia* (1983)

William G. McLoughlin, *Cherokees and Missionaries, 1789–1839* (1984)

————, *Cherokee Renascence in the New Republic* (1980)

James Merrell, *The Indians' New World: Catawbas and Their Neighbors from European Contact Through the Era of Removal* (1989)

Edmund S. Morgan, "Slavery and Freedom: The American Paradox," *Journal of American History* 59 (1972), 5–29

Gerald Mullin, *Flight and Rebellion: Slave Resistance in Eighteenth-Century Virginia* (1972)

Gary Nash, *Forging Freedom: The Formation of Philadelphia's Black Community, 1720–1840* (1988)

————, *Red, White, and Black: The Peoples of Early America* (1982)

Mary Beth Norton, *Liberty's Daughters: The Revolutionary Experience of American Women, 1750–1800* (1980)

Orlando Patterson, *Slavery and Social Death: A Comparative Study* (1982)

Francis Paul Prucha, *American Indian Policy in the Formative Years: The Indian Trade and Intercourse Acts, 1780–1834* (1962, 1970)

Albert J. Raboteau, *Slave Religion: The "Invisible Institution" in the Antebellum South* (1980)

Carroll Smith Rosenberg, *Disorderly Conduct: Visions of Gender in Victorian America* (1985)

Laurel Thatcher Ulrich, *Midwife's Tale: The Life of Martha Ballard, Based on Her Diary, 1785–1812* (1990)

Anthony F. C. Wallace, *The Death and Rebirth of the Seneca* (1969)

CHAPTER
6

The War of 1812

⊞

The War of 1812 may be the least remembered major military conflict in U.S. history—and for good reason. It began after years of diplomatic wrangling and mishaps generated by the Napoleonic Wars in Europe. At the outset, the United States was badly unprepared for a war with Great Britain. There was dissension among the citizenry as well as among the troops. In New England, the center of antiwar sentiment, early misgivings turned into talk of resistance and secession. Although the Americans won significant victories over the British (notably on the Great Lakes), the United States also suffered some grave and embarrassing setbacks—above all, the burning of Washington, D.C. and the temporary flight of the federal government in August 1814. The Treaty of Ghent that finally ended the hostilities did little to achieve the nation's war aims, despite public crowing about the republic's vindication.

Yet notwithstanding its uncertainties and ignominies, the War of 1812 was an important passage in the early republic's history. The events leading to its outbreak marked the arrival of a new element in national politics, a coalition of aggressive young Republicans known as the War Hawks. These men, most conspicuously Henry Clay and John C. Calhoun, added a more expansive view of nationalist development to their party and would play crucial roles in Washington over the next thirty years. At the other end of the spectrum, antiwar criticism from New England Federalists, culminating in the Hartford Convention of 1814, spelled the ultimate doom of the Federalist party.

Nor was the war's impact limited to party politics. Much of the fiercest fighting engaged U.S. forces and their Indian allies against other Indian tribes, allied with the British, along the country's northwestern and southwestern boundaries. Here, the United States won some crushing victories of enduring significance, not least for the expansion of slavery. Economically, the interruption of trade with Britain stimulated the infant northeastern manufacturing economy. The financial pressures of mobilization and support convinced many Americans of the need to revive the Bank of the United States and to rationalize the credit system. And the war's final act, the Battle of New Orleans, brought a new hero to national attention—the plebeian-born planter, Indian fighter, and scourge of the British Empire, Major General Andrew Jackson of Tennessee.

In short, the War of 1812, like all U.S. wars, dramatized some of the most powerful trends and tensions in American life. In their postwar euphoria, citizens cheered the preservation of their fragile republican experiment. On closer, retrospective examination, the war also seems to have accelerated changes in that experiment. What those changes were, how deeply they ran, and how they affected different groups of Americans remain matters of historical dispute.

✤ D O C U M E N T S

One of the more inflammatory issues behind the war was the British practice of impressment—the seizure of men suspected of being British citizens (among them, as it turned out, thousands of Americans) for service in the Royal Navy. Some captives went to horrible lengths, including self-mutilation, to avoid this fate. By 1811 Republican editors were up in arms, as the first document, excerpted from a Massachusetts editorial blast at French-fearing Federalists, loudly indicates. The second selection turns to the abiding tensions in the West, in an account of a meeting in 1810 between the militant Shawnee leader Tecumseh and the governor of Indiana Territory, William Henry Harrison. Harrison's defeat of Tecumseh at the Battle of Tippecanoe the following year at least temporarily lent credence to those tribal leaders (notably the Choctaw, Pushmataha) who thought that Tecumseh's stance was desperate and suicidal. But the militants were not yet finished.

The remaining documents trace the coming of the war and its impact. In the third document, dating from 1811, representative Felix Grundy of Tennessee outlines the growing concerns and aspirations of the outspoken western War Hawks. Grundy and John C. Calhoun of South Carolina authored the Congressional War Report, backing a formal declaration of hostilities; included as the fourth selection is a brief excerpt from the report's conclusion. The young Massachusetts Federalist Daniel Webster prepared one of his first important public statements in 1812, replying to the prowar party point by point; the passages excerpted here in selection five concern impressment.

The sixth document recounts the events leading to and following the Battle of the Thames. The final defeat of Tecumseh in the battle proved of lasting significance, partly because it eventually boosted the political careers of Richard Mentor Johnson (who boastfully and dubiously claimed credit for killing the chief) and William Henry Harrison. The seventh document, a brief memoir by the New England textile magnate Nathan Appleton, discusses one of the war's major economic effects. The next selection features the Republican Nathaniel Boileau's impassioned Independence Day speech of 1814, delivered at his father's farm, the site of a British atrocity during the Revolution. Boileau cast the continuing war as a life-or-death struggle over the future of republicanism itself. (In his remarks on the yeomanry, Boileau quotes directly from Jefferson's *Notes on the State of Virginia*.) How might he have reacted to the newspaper dispatches (document nine) describing the burning of Washington several weeks later?

The Hartford Convention's resolutions, reprinted as the next document, offer a synopsis of the New England Federalists' discontent. Unfortunately for the dissenters, two events followed closely on their proceedings—the signing of the Ghent Treaty and the American victory at New Orleans (which actually occurred *after* the treaty had been signed). The Federalists never recovered from their political disgrace. And as the final document, a broadside of a popular song, reveals, a patriotic upsurge ensued, self-deluding though it may have been. It centered on a man with whom Americans would be reckoning for many years to come—Andrew Jackson.

A Republican Newspaper Protests Against British Impressment, 1811

The British were the first aggressors upon our neutral rights, and their outrages gave rise to those of France. Notwithstanding this, our government, by the measure of the Embargo, and Nonintercourse act which repealed the Embargo, placed them both upon the same footing. . . .

In examining the conduct of England and France toward this country for five years past, the question is not which nation alone is culpable, as they are both so: The only question is, which is the *greatest* and most *iniquitous aggressor?* That G. Britain stands convicted is evident from the fact, that the first order violating our neutral rights came from her—that order being also the root of all the rest.

But, independent of this, there is another atrocity incident solely to Great Britain, of the blackest and most savage complexion, which would alone convict her of being beyond all comparison the *greatest aggressor.* We refer to her barbarous THEFTS OF AMERICAN CITIZENS! Which have of late increased in an astonishing degree. Not only vessels on the high seas bound on foreign voyages have been stopped by these outlaws, and American sailors impressed, but even *coasting vessels* have been arrested, and persons in the characters of PASSENGERS stolen from them! . . . Yet we have men among us, who notwithstanding these repeated villainies of the British are calling upon us to *unfurl the American banner against France,* and to form an alliance with the British nation! In the very face of the wanton attack on the Chesapeake, and these thefts of American citizens, such men have the hardihood to insult the people of the U. States, by saying that G. Britain has done us no particular injury!

What is the state of our Foreign Relations? . . .

Our rights are absolute, not contingent—and we cannot allow Great Britain, any more than France, to justify her injuries on the ground that her enemy is equally culpable.

In defense of their rights, the United States have taken a stand; they must maintain it—they seek only for a respect of their rights; they may by perseverence obtain it. It is to be hoped that our government will not, by any hasty or indecisive conduct, weaken the effects of the measures they have taken. . . . Let both do us justice; we will be the friend of both.

Tecumseh Confronts Governor William Henry Harrison, 1810

In the year 1809, Governor Harrison purchased from the Delawares, Miamis, and Pottawatomies, a large tract of land on both sides of the Wabash river, and extending up the said river about sixty miles above Vincennes. Tecumseh was absent at the time, and his brother, the Prophet, made no objections to the treaty, but when Tecumseh returned, he manifested great dissatis-

The Independent Chronicle [Boston], May 27, 1811.

faction, and threatened some of the chiefs with death, who had made this treaty. Harrison hearing of his dissatisfaction, sent an invitation to him to repair to Vincennes to see him, and assured him, that any claims he might have to the lands ceded by that treaty, were not affected by the treaty at all—that he might come on and present his claims, and if they were found to be valid, the lands would be given up, or an ample compensation made for it.

Accordingly, on the 12th of August [1810], Tecumseh arrived at Vincennes, accompanied by a large number of his warriors. When the council convened, Tecumseh arose and said, "Brothers, I have made myself what I am; I would that I could make the red people as great as the conceptions of my own mind. When I think of the Great Spirit that rules over all, I would not then come to Governor Harrison, to beg of him to tear this treaty in pieces, but I would say to him, brothers, you have liberty to return to your own country. Once, there was not a white man in all this country. Then, it all belonged to the redmen; children of the same parents—placed on it by the Great Spirit, to keep it, to travel over it, to eat its fruits, and fill it with the same race. Once a happy people, but now made miserable by the white people, who are never satisfied, but always encroaching on our land. They have driven us from the great salt water, forced us over the mountains, and would shortly push us into the lakes, but we are determined to go no further. The only way to stop this evil, is for all the red-men to unite in claiming a common right in the soil, as it was at first, and should be now, for it never was divided, but belonged to all. No one tribe has a right to sell even to each other, much less to strangers, who demand all, and will take no less.

"The white people have no right to take the land from the Indians who had it first—it is ours—it belongs to us. *We* may sell, but all must agree; any sale made by a part is not good. The last sale is bad. It was made by a part only; a part do not know how to sell; it requires all to make a bargain for all; a part cannot do it."

Harrison in reply, declared to Tecumseh, that he and his band had no right to interfere or say one word in this matter, as he said the Shawnees had been driven from Georgia by the Creek Indians, and therefore, had no claim to land in this country. This exasperated the chief, and he pronounced the declaration of Harrison, a falsehood. Harrison told him he was a bad man, and for some time it was apprehended that a serious conflict would ensue. Harrison ordered Tecumseh from the house immediately, which order was obeyed.

However, the council was resumed the next day. On again assembling in the morning, the Indians were invited by the governor into the house, where seats were provided for the governor, his attendants, and the Indian chiefs.

Tecumseh declined going into the house, but proposed that the council be held outside, under the shade of some trees near-by, to which, Harrison objected, telling him, that it would be troublesome to remove the seats from the house. Tecumseh replied, "that it would be unnecessary to remove more than what would accommodate the white people; that, as for him and his friends, they would sit on the ground; that red-men were accustomed to sitting on the ground; that the earth was their mother, and they loved to recline on her bosom."

Nothing was effected at that council, but on the next day, the parties again met, but nothing like a reconciliation was effected. Harrison informed Tecumseh, before they separated, that he would lay the case before the President of the United States, and await his decision on the subject. Tecumseh replied, "Well, as the great chief is to decide the matter, I hope the Great Spirit will put sense enough in his head to cause him to order you to give up those lands. It is true, that he may sit in his fine house and drink his wine, while you and I shall have to fight it out."

Felix Grundy Gives the War Hawks' Battle Cry, 1811

. . . What, Mr. Speaker, are we now called on to decide? It is, whether we will resist by force the attempt, made by [the British] Government, to subject our maritime rights to the arbitrary and capricious rule of her will; for my part I am not prepared to say that this country shall submit to have her commerce interdicted or regulated, by any foreign nation. Sir, I prefer war to submission.

Over and above these unjust pretensions of the British Government, for many years past they have been in the practice of impressing our seamen, from merchant vessels; this unjust and lawless invasion of personal liberty, calls loudly for the interposition of this Government. To those better acquainted with the facts in relation to it, I leave it to fill up the picture. My mind is irresistibly drawn to the West.

. . . It cannot be believed by any man who will reflect, that the savage tribes, uninfluenced by other Powers, would think of making war on the United States. They understand too well their own weakness, and our strength. They have already felt the weight of our arms; they know they hold the very soil on which they live as tenants at sufferance. How, then, sir, are we to account for their late conduct? In one way only; some powerful nation must have intrigued with them, and turned their peaceful disposition towards us into hostilities. Great Britain alone has intercourse with those Northern tribes; I therefore infer, that if British gold has not been employed, their baubles and trinkets, and the promise of support and a place of refuge if necessary, have had their effect. . . .

This war, if carried on successfully, will have its advantages. We shall drive the British from our Continent—they will no longer have an opportunity of intriguing with our Indian neighbors, and setting on the ruthless savage to tomahawk our women and children. That nation will lose her Canadian trade, and, by having no resting place in this country, her means of annoying us will be diminished. . . . I am willing to receive the Canadians as adopted brethren; it will have beneficial political effects; it will preserve the equilibrium of the Government. When Louisiana shall be fully peopled, the Northern States will lose their power; they will be at the discretion of others; they can be depressed at pleasure, and then this Union might be endangered—I therefore feel anxious not only to add the Floridas to the South, but the Canadas to the North of this empire. . . .

The Congressional War Report, 1812

From this review of the multiplied wrongs of the British Government . . . it must be evident to the impartial world, that the contest which is now forced on the United States, is radically a contest for their sovereignty and independence. Your committee will not enlarge on any of the injuries, however great, which have had a transitory effect. They wish to call the attention of the House to those of a permanent nature only, which intrench so deeply on our most important rights, and wound so extensively and vitally our best interests, as could not fail to deprive the United States of the principal advantages of their Revolution, if submitted to. The control of our commerce by Great Britain, in regulating, at pleasure, and expelling it almost from the ocean; the oppressive manner in which these regulations have been carried into effect, by seizing and confiscating such of our vessels, with their cargoes, as were said to have violated her edicts, often without previous warning of their danger; the impressment of our citizens from on board our own vessels on the high seas, and elsewhere, and holding them in bondage till it suited the convenience of their oppressors to deliver them up; are encroachments of that high and dangerous tendency, which could not fail to produce that pernicious effect; nor would these be the only consequences that would result from it. The British Government might, for a while, be satisfied with the ascendency thus gained over us, but its pretensions would soon increase. The proof which so complete and disgraceful a submission to its authority would afford of our degeneracy, could not fail to inspire confidence, that there was no limit to which its usurpations, and our degradation, might not be carried.

Your committee, believing that the free-born sons of America are worthy to enjoy the liberty which their fathers purchased at the price of so much blood and treasure, and seeing in the measures adopted by Great Britain, a course commenced and persisted in, which must lead to a loss of national character and independence, feel no hesitation in advising resistance by force; in which the Americans of the present day will prove to the enemy and to the world, that we have not only inherited that liberty which our fathers gave us, but also the will and power to maintain it. Relying on the patriotism of the nation, and confidently trusting that the Lord of Hosts will go with us to battle in a righteous cause, and crown our efforts with success, your committee recommend an immediate appeal to arms. . . .

Federalist Daniel Webster Criticizes the War, 1812

We are not, sir, among those who feel an unmanly reluctance to the privations, or a nervous sensibility to the dangers of war. Many of us had the

Charles A. Wiltse, ed., *The Papers of Daniel Webster: Speeches and Formal Writings* (Hanover; New Hampshire University Press, 1986), I, pp. 3–17 excerpted.

honor of aiding, by our humble efforts, in the establishment of our independence, and of exposing our lives, in more than one field of danger and
blood, in our country's service. We are ready to meet those scenes again,
whenever it can be shown that the vindication of our national honor, or the
preservation of our essential rights, demands it. . . .

If we could perceive that the present war was just; if we could perceive
that our rights and liberties required it; if we could perceive that no Administration, however wise, honest, or impartial, could have carried us clear
of it; if we could perceive its expediency, and a reasonable hope of obtaining
its professed objects; if we could perceive those things, the war would, in
some measure, cease to be horrible. It would grow tolerable, in idea, as its
expediency should be made manifest. Its iron and bloody features would
soften, as its justice grew apparent. Give us but to see, that this war hath
clear justice, necessity, and expediency on its side, and we are ready to pour
out our treasure, and our blood in its prosecution.

But we are constrained to say, that we cannot, in conscience, ascribe
the foregoing characteristics, to the present war. We are not, sir, the apologists of other nations, nor will our voice ever be heard, to varnish wrongs,
inflicted either on the interest or honor of our native land. But we deem it
necessary, to every justifiable war, not only that its justice be as plain and
visible as the light of Heaven, but that its objects be distinct and clear, in
order that every man may see them; that they be great, in order that every
man perceive their importance; that they be probably attainable, in order
that every citizen may be encouraged to contend for them. We are wholly
mistaken, if the causes assigned for the present war against England will
bear the test of these principles.

The impressment of our seamen, which forms the most plausible and
popular of the alleged causes of war, we believe to have been the subject
of great misrepresentation. We have as much sympathy as others, for those
who suffer under this abuse of power. We know there are instances of this
abuse. We know that native American citizens have been, in some cases,
in too many cases, impressed from American merchant ships, and compelled
to serve on board British ships of war. But the number of these cases has
been extravagantly exaggerated. Every inquiry on the subject strengthens
our conviction, that the reputed number bears little relation to the true
number. . . .

It is impossible, under these circumstances, for us to believe, that the
evil of impressment does exist, in the degree of enormity pretended. If so
many of our seafaring fellow-citizens were actually in bondage, they must
have been taken from among the inhabitants of the Atlantic coast. They
would be from among our brethren, sons, relations and friends. We should
be acquainted with them, and their misfortunes. We should hear the cries
of their wives and children, their parents and relatives, quite as soon as our
fellow-citizens of the South and the West.

It is well worthy of notice, that the greatest apparent feeling on this
subject of impressments, and the greatest disposition to wage war on that
account, are entertained by the representatives of those states, which have

no seamen at all of their own; while those sections of the community, in which more than three-fourths of the mariners of the United States have their homes, are, by great majorities, against that war, among the professed objects of which, the release of impressed seamen forms so principal a figure.

It is well known that England pretends to no right of impressing our seamen. She insists, only, that she has a right to the service of her own subjects, in time of war, even though found serving on board the merchant ships of other nations. This claim we suppose to be neither unfounded, nor novel. It is recognized by the public law of Europe, and of the civilized world. Writers of the highest authority maintain, that the right belongs to all nations. For the same reason, say they, that the father of a family may demand the aid of his children to defend himself and his house, a nation may call home her subjects to her defence and protection, in time of war.

But if this were not so, is our nation to plunge into a ruinous war, in order to settle a question of relative right, between the government of a foreign nation and the subjects of that government? Are we to fight the battles of British seamen? . . .

Fatal, indeed, would it be to important interests of the navigating states, if the consequence of this war should be that the American flag shall give the American character to all who sail under it, and thus invite thousands of foreign seamen to enter into our service, and thrust aside our own native citizens.

But this evil of impressment, however great it may be, is at least not greater now, than it was in the time of Washington. That great man did not, however, deem it an evil to be remedied by war. Neither did it occur to President Adams, nor even to President Jefferson, that it would be wise or politic, for the purpose of attempting to rescue a very small portion of our seamen from captivity, to commence a war, which must inevitably, as this war will, consign ten times as many to a captivity as bad.

England has always professed a willingness to adjust this subject by amicable arrangement. She has repeatedly called on us to do our part, towards affecting such adjustment. She has reminded us of the facility—we may say the falsity, with which American protections are obtained; of the frequent instances, in which Irishmen and others, that cannot speak a word of our language, are found with American protections in their pockets. She has, expressly, and officially, offered to prohibit, by severe laws, all impressments from American vessels, if the American Government would enact laws prohibiting American officers from granting protections, of certificates of citizenship to British subjects. She has also, through her Ministers, offered to restore every native seaman, that our Government could name, as being under impressment. For years preceding the Declaration of War, our Government has been, in a manner, silent on this subject. . . .

What is it, then, that hath since given to this subject a sudden and unusual importance? What is it, that hath so completely stifled the voice of the friends of the seamen, and at the same time called into action such powerful sympathies in the bosom of strangers? What is it, that hath raised the voice, beyond the western mountains, so loud and clamorous for their protection by war, while the fathers and brethren, the friends and relatives, the wives and children of these very seamen—nay even the seamen themselves, deprecate this war, as the greatest calamity that could fall upon them?

The blockade, and Orders in Council, the other causes of war, bear no better examination than the subject of impressment. The blockade, now so grievous to be endured, we know was regarded, at the time it was laid, as a measure favorable to our interests. We know this, upon the express declaration of Mr. Monroe, then our Minister in England. We have his own words, that it should be regarded "in a favorable light," and that it "promised to be highly satisfactory to our commercial interests."

By what train of reasoning this favor is now turned into an injury, and an injury of such magnitude as to justify war, we are utterly at a loss to comprehend. . . .

Three Documents on the Battle of the Thames, 1813

Richard Mentor Johnson to William Henry Harrison, September 20, 1813

. . . A party of the M. volunteers under my command this morning returned from the River Raisin on an expedition to Brownstown with a principal warrior of the Shawnee Profit, a Shawnee named Masalamata well known to . . . others of the Indians with me . . . & whom they took as Prisoner. I have had much conversation with him & send you what has been the result & what I conclude [?] may be relyed on as his statement corroborates that of two Frenchman who came to this place a few days ago. He says Tecumseh & most of his party including warriors, women, &c. are on Gross il Island near Maldin, that the other hostile Tribes are variously encamped on this side of the lake waters. That the Miamis & Wyandots since the *death of Roundhead* have manifested a disposition to yield upon your approach. The others are determined to fight & if the forces march on this side of the crossing of Huron[,] Battle will be given. . . .

William Henry Harrison to the Secretary of War, October 5, 1813

I have the honor to inform you that by the blessing of Providence the army under my command has this morning obtained a complete victory over the combined Indians & British forces under the command of Genl. Procter. I believe that nearly the whole of the enemy's Regulars are taken or killed. Amongst the former are all the superior officers excepting Genl. Procter— my mounted men are now in pursuit of him—our loss is very trifling. The brave Colo. R. M. Johnston is the only officer whom I have heard of that is wounded—he badly but I hope not dangerously.

The Killing of Tecumseh

The Battle of the Thames, October 5, 1813, as rendered after the fact by an American primitive artist. The work is a stylized and inaccurate vignette of Tecumseh's death at the hands of Colonel Richard M. Johnson. The Granger Collection.

Nathan Appleton on the Coming of the Power Loom, 1858

My connection with the Cotton Manufacture takes date from the year 1811, when I met my friend Mr. Francis C. Lowell, at Edinburgh, where he had been passing some time with his family. We had frequent conversations on the subject of the Cotton Manufacture, and he informed me that he had determined, before his return to America, to visit Manchester, for the purpose of obtaining all possible information on the subject, with a view to the introduction of the improved manufacture in the United States. I urged him to do so, and promised him my co-operation. He returned in 1813. He and Mr. Patrick T. Jackson, came to me one day on the Boston exchange, and stated that they had determined to establish a Cotton manufactory, that they had purchased a water power in Waltham, (Bemis's paper mill,) and that they had obtained an act of incorporation, and Mr. Jackson had agreed to give up all other business and take the management of the concern.

The capital authorized by the charter was four hundred thousand dollars, but it was only intended to raise one hundred thousand, until the experiment should be fairly tried. Of this sum Mr. Lowell and Mr. Jackson, with his brothers, subscribed the greater part. They proposed to me that I should take ten thousand of this subscription. I told them, that theoretically I thought the business ought to succeed, but all which I had seen of its practical operation was unfavorable; I however was willing to take five thousand dollars of the stock, in order to see the experiment fairly tried, as I knew it would be under the management of Mr. Jackson; and I should make no complaint under these circumstances, if it proved a total loss. My proposition was agreed to, and this was the commencement of my interest in the cotton manufacture. . . .

The first measure was to secure the services of Paul Moody, of Ames- bury, whose skill as a mechanic was well known, and whose success fully justified the choice.

The power loom was at this time being introduced in England, but its construction was kept very secret, and after many failures, public opinion was not favorable to its success. Mr. Lowell had obtained all the information which was practicable about it, and was determined to perfect it himself. He was for some months experimenting at a store in Broad street, employing a man to turn a crank. It was not until the new building at Waltham was completed, and other machinery was running, that the first loom was ready for trial. Many little matters were to be overcome or adjusted, before it would work perfectly. Mr. Lowell said to me that he did not wish me to see it until it was complete, of which he would give me notice. At length the time arrived. He invited me to go out with him and see the loom operate. I well recollect the state of admiration and satisfaction with which we sat by the hour, watching the beautiful movement of this new and wonderful machine, destined as it evidently was, to change the character of all textile industry. This was in the autumn of 1814. . . .

From the first starting of the first power loom, there was no hesitation or doubt about the success of this manufacture. The full capital of four hundred thousand dollars was soon filled up and expended. An addition of two hundred thousand was afterwards made, by the purchase of the place below in Watertown. . . .

Nathaniel Boileau on the British Juggernaut, 1814

[A]t the commencement of the French revolution, every true American, every friend to liberty and the equal rights of man, felt a deep solicitude in their success. We exulted in the pleasing prospect, that while the French had been fighting with us in the cause of liberty and mingling their blood with ours in our contest for independence, they had caught the sacred spark of liberty which would kindle an unextinguishable fire to illuminate, and ultimately emancipate the world from the thraldom of slavery. We fondly fancied we saw the millenium approaching, when nations should learn war no more, and universal peace and good will among men should pervade the world. For, if all the governments were republican, and acted upon its true genuine principles, war would be banished from the earth; the conflicting interests of nations would be amicably negociated and adjusted; there would be no aggressions, and war and its causes must vanish. But the powers of hell and the government of Britain, equally hostile to the happiness of man, combined to blast our pleasing anticipations. The era was not yet arrived when Satan was to be bound a thousand years, and these *allied* powers are loosed for a little season to torment the world. Had it not been for the interference of England, I am persuaded the French people would have established a government as similar to ours as their habits, their manners, and their information would have permitted. To the British government may be fairly attributed the principal part of that wide scene of desolation spread over the greater part of Europe, and the shedding of oceans of blood more than sufficient to float their thousand ships. Will justice sleep forever—will the day of retribution not come, when it shall be made to drink of the cup of wrath and indignation of the Almighty, whom it has insulted by the wanton destruction of millions of his creatures? . . .

The British, their agents and their emissaries in this country, curse the day of American independence, fain would they blot it from among the days of the year, and at all events if possible blot it from your memories, well aware that to accomplish that object it would prepare the way to slip the halter unawares about your necks. . . . Our government, after having exhausted every possible means to obtain justice by negociation, to preserve our citizens from insult and robbery on the high seas, appeal to the interest of the British, who could not be influenced by a sense of justice, by laying an embargo. Instantly British agents, partisans and mercenary traders raise the hue and cry, the measure is denounced as unconstitutional and ruinous, as terrapin policy, pusillanimous and weak and wicked. They shout war—war, assert our rights by the sword rather than by restrictive measures. A separation of the states is threatened, and an imbecile congress is alarmed and the embargo is repealed. Thus avarice, that mammoth passion, which swallows up every other feeling, and annihilates every noble generous sentiment of the soul that can elevate human nature, triumphs over principle and sound policy. With mortification I utter it—there are thousands calling themselves Americans, who are prepared to sell the liberty and independence of their country for gold. But do those men who were for war direct, and on whose account principally it originated, do they, when once declared, support it either with their persons or their purses? No! with a few honorable exceptions, they not only refuse personal and pecuniary assistance, but use every effort to prevent others from doing it. I am fully persuaded, that had the embargo been persevered in and rigidly enforced, and had it not been for the factions in and out of congress, who encouraged the British to persevere in their injustice towards us, reiterating that we could not be kicked into a war—war never would have been necessary; and I firmly believe that all the blood that has and will be shed in the contest, will stick to the skirts of these enemies to our government and to the equal rights of man and nations.

The embargo being repealed, the enemy were encouraged to heap insult upon insult, injury upon injury, injustice upon injustice, till there was no alternative left but war or unconditional submission, an abandonment of our independence. Our government, bound by the most solemn obligations of duty, as well as honor, adopted the latter alternative. And if ever there was a just war on earth, or could be conceived, the present war on our part is of that description. If it is unjust, what will you say of the war of the revolution? At that time we were colonies of England, and acknowledged George III as our legitimate sovercign. He imposed a light duty of a few cents upon a pound of tea which was the principal actual pressure of which we complained, for the abstract principle, whether we should be taxed without our consent, had not been carried into oppressive operation. But the present war is not about an abstract principle, it is about positive absolute rights, inseparable from a free and independent nation. We have not only been taxed to an enormous, incalculable extent: we have been robbed, insulted, many of our citizens murdered and many dragged into the most degrading slavery. In fine, the cause of the war, as to principle, liberty, and independence, is the same as that of the revolution, with the additional cause of aggravated insult and wrong. . . .

The United States presents an interesting spectacle to the world. The crisis is the most important that ever has occurred in the history of man. You stand alone, the only free people on the globe. Your liberty is assailed by one of the most mighty nations on earth, which has, by force and fraud, enslaved the greatest portion of Europe. Single-handed you must fight her. Where will you look for an ally? where for an intercessor? Will you look to France, that nation who gallantly stepped forward to assist you with her blood and her treasure in gaining your liberty and independence? Alas! an independent monarch no longer sits upon the throne. Louis the 18th holds his crown as a fief from England. Can you look for an intercessor in the affections and gratitude of the French people? Alas, that has been forfeited by the acts of a former government. . . .

Our situation indeed is perilous, but by no means desperate. It is true, the success of the war has not been so great as our sanguine hopes anticipated, but perhaps equal to what rational expectations would justify. In the lapse of more than thirty years of peace, our hands had forgot to war, and our fingers to fight: our officers wanted experience, and our soldiers discipline. This evil is every day lessening. In the commencement of the revolutionary war, we met with many disasters; we had Arnolds then, we have Hulls now; we finally conquered then, we shall now—let us persevere and our motto be "Liberty or Death." Notwithstanding the many disasters on land, there have not been wanting feats of valor and heroism never surpassed by the best discipline, and most veteran troops. And on the waters, the American navy has acquired laurels which will not fade by a comparison with the most brilliant achievements recorded in the naval history of any nation. It is one of the characteristics of a republican government, inaptness for war. This is urged by some as an objection to its form; but perhaps it is one of its greatest blessings. It tends to preserve peace, it is not in the power of any individual to plunge the nation into a war, to gratify his resentment, or to feed his ambition, contrary to the interest and wishes of the nation; the impulse must be given by the people, and the enthusiasm of liberty and the energy of patriotism will more than compensate for want of a standing army, always dangerous to the liberties of any country. . . .

Ye heroes of the revolution, patriots in the days of trial, although your heads are bleached with years, and the day of vigorous action and exertion be past, your country demands much from you; your experience and your counsel are put in requisition—tell your sons that more than thirty years of experience have taught you, that liberty is an inestimable gem, worth preserving, worth purchasing at the expense of all they have—tell them of the labors, the toils, the dangers, the privations you underwent to procure it—shew them your honorable scars, and tell them it was not for yourselves alone that you spent your wealth, your strength and your blood, but to purchase a rich inheritance for them, to whom you commit the invaluable prize for safe-keeping. . . . tell them, that patriotism, which is the love of our country, a sincere devotion to its interest, and fixed determination to promote, by all honorable means and consistently with universal benevo-lence, the happiness of the society with which we are connected, is one of the noblest passions that can warm and animate the human breast; that it is the characteristic of a man of honor and a gentleman, and must take place of pleasure, profit and all other private gratifications; and whoever wants this virtue is an *open* enemy, or an *inglorious* neuter, to mankind in pro-portion to the misapplied advantages with which nature or fortune has blessed him . . .

And my worthy countrywomen, who are wives and mothers, your coun-try asks much from you. Patriotism is limited to no sex, you owe important duties to society. We ask you not to turn Amazons, to wield the sword or to push the bayonet; the sensibility of your hearts and the delicacy of your frames unfit you for martial deeds. It has already been intimated that virtue is the only firm and lasting basis on which the temple of liberty can be erected, a republican government rest. Be yours then the task "to teach the young idea how to shoot" and mould the tender mind to virtue; as your infants draw the balmy nourishment from your bosoms, instil into their souls the principles of virtue, morality and religion; as you dandle them on your knee, teach their infant tongues to lisp the praises of patriots and heroes, and long live the republic . . .

And you, fair rising daughters of Columbia, your country also has claims on you. Permit me to inform you, if you have not already discovered it, that your influence is almost irresistible over the youthful heart. Fain would I enlist your charms and your influence in the cause of liberty and your country—tell the youth who would address you, that you have no smiles for him who refuses to step forward in the cause of freedom and inde-pendence, that your arms shall never enfold him who declines to use his arms in defence of you and liberty from violence and insult; that your bosoms shall never be *pillows* on which a *traitor* or an *enemy* to his country shall recline, that the *brave* only deserve the fair. . . .

It is my pride and my pleasure that I address the yeomanry of my country, the "cultivators of the earth, the chosen people of God, if ever he had a chosen people on earth, whose breasts he has made the peculiar deposit for genuine and substantial virtue; it is the focus where he keeps alive the sacred fire which otherwise might escape from the face of the earth. Corruption of manners in the mass of cultivators is a phenomenon of which no age or nation has furnished an example." Be careful then to preserve the purity of your manners. Governments and people have a reciprocal influence on the morals of each other. Your government is now pure, but if you become corrupt, so will your government; and thus will you mutually aid in accelerating each other into moral depravity, which must issue in the loss of civil and religious liberty. I would avail myself of every opportunity to impress deeply upon the yeomanry of the country, the importance of their situation in a moral as well as a political point of view—they are the principal bones and sinews of the nation. At this time more especially would I wish to impress upon you the importance and responsibility of your situation; you are the main stay and prop and sheet anchor of liberty—the eyes of the United States, the eyes of the world, the eyes of the oppressed of all nations are upon you, deeply solicitous that this their last asylum should be preserved. If you fail in the present conflict, liberty will be banished from the earth, there will not be a spot on the globe on which she can rest the sole of her foot; it is her last retreat. . . .

Newspaper Accounts of the Burning of Washington, D.C., 1814

I arrived at Washington on Sunday, the 21st. . . . At that time, the officers of government and the citizens were very apprehensive of an attack from the British, who had landed a force on the Patuxent. Their numbers had not been ascertained, but reports were various, stating them from 4000 to 16,000. . . . [T]he public officers were all engaged in packing and sending off their books and the citizens their furniture. On Monday, this business was continued with great industry, and many families left the city. The specie was removed from all the Banks in the district. . . .

[T]he battle commenced, and was contested . . . with great spirit and gallantry, until it appeared useless for so small a force, very badly supported, to stand against *six thousand regulars*. . . . [R]etreat was ordered, when the President, who had been on horseback with the army the whole day, retired from the mortifying scene and left the city on horseback. . . .

When we remarked, in our paper of yesterday, that private property had in general been scrupulously respected by the enemy during his late incursion, we spoke what we believed, from a hasty survey, and perhaps without sufficient inquiry. Greater respect was certainly paid to private prop-

National Intelligencer [Washington, D.C.], August 31, 1814.

erty than has usually been exhibited by the enemy in his marauding parties. No houses were half as much *plundered* by the enemy as by the knavish wretches about the town who profited from the general distress. There were, however, several private buildings wantonly destroyed, and some of those persons who remained in the city were scandalously maltreated. . . .

The enemy was conducted through the city by a former resident, who, with other detected traitors, is now in confinement.

[The British commanding officer] Cockburn was quite a mountebank in the city, exhibiting in the streets a gross levity of manner, displaying sundry articles of trifling value of which he had robbed the President's house, and repeating . . . coarse jests and vulgar slang . . . respecting the chief magistrate and others. . . .

Resolutions of the Hartford Convention, 1814

Therefore resolved,

That it be and hereby is recommended to the legislatures of the several states represented in this Convention, to adopt all such measures as may be necessary effectually to protect the citizens of said states from the operation and effects of all acts which have been or may be passed by the Congress of the United States, which shall contain provisions, subjecting the militia or other citizens to forcible drafts, conscriptions, or impressments, not authorised by the constitution of the United States.

Resolved, That it be and hereby is recommended to the said Legislatures, to authorize an immediate and earnest application to be made to the government of the United States, requesting their consent to some arrangement, whereby the said states may, separately or in concert, be empowered to assume upon themselves the defense of their territory against the enemy. . . .

Resolved, That the following amendments of the constitution of the United States be recommended to the states represented as aforesaid. . . .

First. Representatives and direct taxes shall be apportioned among the several states which may be included within this Union, according to their respective numbers of free persons, including those bound to serve for a term of years, and excluding Indians not taxed, and all other persons.

Second. No new state shall be admitted into the Union by Congress, in virtue of the power granted by the constitution, without the concurrence of two thirds of both houses.

Third. Congress shall not have power to lay any embargo on the ships or vessels of the citizens of the United States, in the ports or harbors thereof, for more than sixty days.

Fourth. Congress shall not have power, without the concurrence of two thirds of both houses, to interdict the commercial intercourse between the United States and any foreign nation, or the dependencies thereof.

Fifth. Congress shall not make or declare war, or authorize acts of hostility against any foreign nation, without the concurrence of two thirds of both houses, except such acts of hostility be in defense of the territories of the United States when actually invaded.

Sixth. No person who shall hereafter be naturalized, shall be eligible as a member of the senate or house of representatives of the United States, nor capable of holding any civil office under the authority of the United States.

Seventh. The same person shall not be elected president of the United States a second time; nor shall the president be elected from the same state two terms in succession.

Resolved, That if the application of these states to the government of the United States, recommended in a foregoing resolution, should be unsuccessful, and peace should not be concluded, and the defense of these states should be neglected, as it has been since the commencement of the war, it will, in the opinion of this convention, be expedient for the legislatures of the several states to appoint delegates to another convention, to meet at Boston in the state of Massachusetts, on the third Thursday of June next, with such powers and instructions as the exigency of a crisis so momentous may require. . . .

The Birth of a Hero: Andrew Jackson, (Undated)

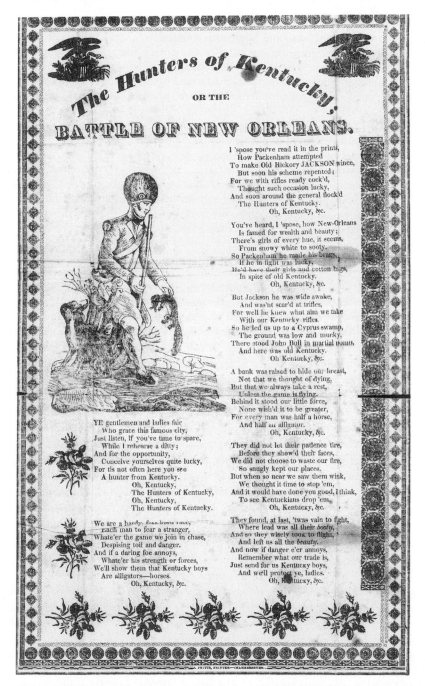

"The Hunters of Kentucky, or the Battle of New Orleans," a broadside of a widely popular song celebrating the victory of "Old Hickory Jackson." Library of Congress.

ⵌ E S S A Y S

Why did the U.S. government go to war in 1812? One strong and venerable interpretation claims that national honor was genuinely at stake. Another sees the territorial desires of western expansionists as the driving force behind prowar sentiment, a conclusion that at least partially accounts for the wartime sectional divisions. Still another view holds that diplomatic and political incompetence, and especially the bungling of President James Madison, plunged the nation into a war that it was ill prepared to undertake.

The essays below advance differing political and ideological understandings of the war's origins, focusing on domestic factors. In the first essay, Roger H. Brown, a professor of history at American University, places the conflict in the context of the previous quarter-century of American political strife, emphasizing both the Republicans' partisan motives and the larger impulse to prove, once and for all, that the republican experiment could succeed. Brown acknowledges the depth of internal conflicts but highlights what he considers the partisan irrationalities, born of inexperience with party competition, that helped shape public debate. In the second essay, Steven Watts, a professor of history at the University of Missouri, does not discount psychological factors but roots the war in what he sees as a continuing struggle between republican and liberal outlooks. His close reading of the Congressional War Report forms part of his larger contention that the war helped consolidate a liberal predominance over American political life. In considering the merits of these essays, it is important to ask how far any essentially ideological interpretation of domestic politics goes toward explaining the war's origins.

The War of 1812 and the Struggle for Political Permanency

ROGER H. BROWN

Deeply and bitterly divided we went to war in 1812. Public demonstrations across the nation showed the split in opinion. Illuminations, parades, and cannon-firing welcomed the decision; tolling church bells, flags at half-mast, and empty shops and counting houses bore witness to condemnation. Federalists in the city of Providence, Rhode Island, set church bells slowly ringing, and Republicans countered with cannon and recruiting drums. Sailors in Boston harbor fought off a Federalist boarding party after their Republican captain refused demands to lower his flag to half-mast. Republican "huzzas and acclamations" at a Philadelphia coffee house greeted a public reading of the war resolution; Federalist "hissers" were told to take their business elsewhere, "that they must not *now* consider this as a *British* Coffeehouse; henceforth it must be and shall be, an *American* Coffee-house." Editorial opinion was also divided along party lines. Federalist journals denounced the "dreadful tidings," and reported: "Dissatisfaction, disgust, and apprehensions of the most alarming nature have seized on every mind." This "overwhelming calamity—so much dreaded by many—so little expected by the community at large" had at last taken place. Republican editors

Roger H. Brown, *The Republic in Peril: 1812* (New York: Columbia University Press, 1964), 177–191 excerpted.

were exultant. "*War,* long expected, long demanded by an indignant nation, comes now, gloriously, in place of *base, infamous, abject* submission." No "true American" could read the President's summons to war "without feeling an honest and implicit confidence in the truth and justice of the great cause in which his country is engaged." Were these fellow citizens of a common country?

Experienced observers would not have been surprised at such responses. Ever since the early 1790s when Republicans first organized against the Hamiltonian program the two parties had clashed on practically every measure brought forward. The constant conflict evoked gloomy predictions from contemporaries. "The prejudices and self will of parties and party men to support principles and measures right or wrong if it is brought forward by their political friends has appeared to me for some time very dangerous," warned the New York Republican, Thomas Sammons. Federalists and Republicans "have each in turn supported and opposed the same acts and measures with but few exceptions—no reformation appears to take place, every one is just, all parties are right at Least in their own opinion." Would this not lead to ultimate disaster? The "internal heat of parties may raise to burn—as by a continual rubbing of two pieces of timber the heat encreases till fire proceeds and often consumes the timber." . . .

Party suspicion and animosity cut deep into local affairs. Federalists and Republicans in Newburyport, Massachusetts, libeled each other in party newspapers, organized separate marine insurance companies, and avoided all possible social contact; their ladies even refused to call on the wives of rival partisans. Federalist and Republican householders in nearby Salem had homes in different neighborhoods, and their rival news sheets and banking corporations reflected deep-grained suspicions that barred men from common enterprises. Feeling in this town ran so high that in 1799 the Republican Crowninshields boycotted the funeral of a relative who had married the famous Federalist merchant, Elias Hasket Derby. In 1802 Federalists officially excluded leading Republican families from the dancing assembly, that "crowning glory of the social season." Time had not played tricks on the memory of New Hampshire's William Plumer when he recalled in 1818 how in the former era the "spirit of party ran high, divided families, neighborhoods, towns & states; and, blind to public interest, embittered the sweets of social life, and hazarded the rights of the nation." . . .

Was there any truth in these conceptions, or were they wholly mistaken? Some Federalists remained skeptical of republicanism. Alexander Hamilton, as we have seen, harbored life-long doubts on this score: "It is yet to be determined by experience whether [republicanism] be consistent with that stability and order in government which are essential to public strength and private security and happiness." George Cabot of Massachusetts deemed it impossible to have good government in America because any "government *altogether popular* in form tends irresistibly to place in power the levellers of public authority, order, and law." But this does not necessarily prove that these men plotted to subvert the state. It has never been established that Hamilton conspired at any time to destroy the government. As late as

1802 he could write to Gouverneur Morris of his continuing efforts "to prop the frail and worthless fabric." Charles Carroll of Carrollton, a Maryland Federalist leader, in 1800 denied that anyone in his party plotted monarchy and declared that these Republican "declaimers in favor of freedom & equality act in such a questionable shape I cannot help suspecting their sincerity."

True, after 1800 a few Federalists conspired to bring about secession and establishment of a northern confederacy. But they had a scant following. . . . Not until 1814 did Federalist leaders convene at Hartford to air grievances and formally draft a program for reform. It is difficult to determine just what kind of government Federalist secessionists would have established had they been able to have their way—suffrage limited to substantial property holders, possibly a senate and executive for life. No one ever actually sought to establish hereditary forms, much less the Hanoverian restoration that Governor Elbridge Gerry of Massachusetts feared. . . .

What of the Republican leaders whom the Federalists believed to be irresponsible, ambitious demagogues? No important leader, except for Aaron Burr, comes close to this stereotype. If either Jefferson or Madison were cynical self-servers, then an entire generation of historians and biographers have totally misread the record. The Clintons, Samuel Smith, William Branch Giles, and Michael Leib have traditionally worn the label, but much evidence points to their integrity of motive. William Plumer, a candidate for governor of New Hampshire in 1812, probably spoke for most Republican leaders when he claimed a higher commitment than mere personal ambition: "The result of the election, to me, appears doubtful and uncertain—and if I could separate myself from the *cause* I should feel little anxiety on the subject." The New Hampshire politician had ambition, but it was to serve an interest larger than himself. Wilson Cary Nicholas in 1808 put the matter in a nutshell: "Our sole object is the public good, the greater the pressure the more merit in saving the republic, let us my friend do our duty and I have no doubt all will be right. At all events we shall have the satisfaction of knowing that any disaster that may befall our Country cannot be ascribed to us or our measures."

Republican and Federalist views of party opposites are largely false. Both parties grossly distorted rival intentions and motives into wild parodies of the truth. Why? How does one explain this blindness and misunderstanding? . . . Part of the answer lies in irrational motives of fear. Federalists harbored deep fears of mass disorders led by unscrupulous demagogues. Republicans feared the propensity of men in office to grasp greater and more permanent power for themselves. . . . As late as 1840 survivors of these party struggles remained convinced of the correctness of their suspicions. "We still know aged men," wrote an historian in that year, "who firmly believe that all the federal party were identical with the Tories of the revolution, and others who associate their democratic opponents with the Jacobins of France." . . .

More fundamental was a personal inexperience with political parties that encouraged men to identify opponents with their fears. There was no personal knowledge of parties such as we know them today—organizations that seek to gain political power but also remain firmly committed to the national welfare and institutions. Eighteenth-century political thought extolled the blessings of the harmonious commonwealth and condemned sustained, organized party activity. A generation reared in this tradition instinctively presumed prolonged opposition to rest on selfish, even traitorous, motives. Furthermore, as the history of former republics revealed, parties in their pursuit of power had characteristically ignored the common good. Their paralyzing squabbles and treasonable intrigues had led to the downfall of these republics. It was against the evil of party activity that Washington, in the famous Farewell Address, had warned his countrymen against "the spirit of party." In governments "of the popular character, in Governments purely elective, it is a spirit not to be encouraged." Distrust of parties explained Jefferson's remark that it would be the "bitterest" day of his life when he became convinced of the permanence of political parties. If Republicans and Federalists had lived through and witnessed an epoch in which parties had proven themselves equally devoted to the national welfare and institutions, they would have been far less susceptible to such wild distortions. But their experience, derived as it was from history and the factional contests of the colonial period, gave them no reason to believe in the highmindedness of opponents; if anything, it gave them positive reason to believe the contrary.

Republicans in 1812 feared that submission would gravely weaken public confidence in republicanism. Repeated negotiation and commercial restrictions caused, as Calhoun put it, "distrust at home and contempt abroad." Was it true that Americans had actually begun to mistrust their republican government? . . . Hamilton remained consistently skeptical, and, by the end of the 1790s when Federalists found themselves challenged by the Republican mob, others joined him. In the Jeffersonian period Republicans began to have doubts. William Jarvis, a Boston leader, admitted in 1808 that if the American people did not support the administration and obey the embargo, then "we must with reluctance admit a doubt of the stability of republican institutions." John McKim, Jr., the Baltimore leader, wrote Henry Clay in 1812 that if the government now gave way to the Orders in Council "we may as well give up our Republican Government and have a Despot to rule over us." . . .

True, one can also find brave avowals of confidence in the future destiny of republicanism. . . . John C. Calhoun was optimistic on the subject of the strength of the government and in 1813 affirmed his resolve to advance the war effort, despite Federalist menaces and threats of disunion. "I speak personally. I by no means dispair of the destiny of our nation or government. National greatness and perfection are of slow growth, often checked often to appearance destroyed. The intelligence, the virtue and the tone of public sentiment are too great in this country to permit its freedom to be destroyed by either domestic or foreign foes."

Calhoun's faith, however, had not always been so high. After all, he had worried in the spring of 1812 that the war might fail and that failure would cause "the greatest injury to the character of the government." Edward Fox, the Philadelphia Republican, took a very gloomy view of the future of republicanism. Continued factional strife would surely lead men to agree to "any change" that "will promise quiet and tranquillity." Still, he knew that others were less pessimistic. "I know it is a maxim with you," he wrote to Jonathan Roberts, the Pennsylvania congressman, "not to dispair of the Commonwealth." Confidence obviously varied among individuals and rose and fell with passing events.

It is difficult to estimate the extent to which the public at large had come to doubt the efficacy of their government. There are occasional letters from citizens which suggest the beginning of a trend. An obscure Virginian told James Monroe that "the Predictions of the Tories, seems as Though they were now coming to Pass, to wit, that our republic could endure, for a short time only; for want of Internal stability, or virtue amongst our Rulers." . . . The Philadelphia *Aurora,* an outspoken critic of Republican pusillanimity since 1809, in 1812 warned that "the national reputation has been sinking ever since, and the people are daily losing confidence in the justice and fidelity of their government." Had effective measures been taken three years ago "the nation would have obtained the respect of the world, and the government the confidence of the people." . . .

The Jefferson administration took office in 1801 determined to check a presumed swing towards monarchy and preserve the government from Federalist control. Facing the problem of commercial depredation and impressment brought on by the Napoleonic wars, Jefferson and his advisers determined they must protect commerce if reputation was to be preserved abroad and public confidence upheld at home. Commercial restriction and negotiation afforded the means by which he and his successor sought to attain these ends. By mid-1811 it became clear that these weapons were useless in the contest with Great Britain. The inducements of nonimportation, embargo, nonintercourse, the Macon law, and possible conflict with France had failed; the presumed repeal of the French Decrees as they affected American neutral rights had produced no comparable British action; Britain continued her seizures and not only refused to repeal her Orders as they affected American neutral commerce, but made demands that revealed determination to make them codeterminate with her struggle with France. The Madison administration saw that no course remained but war or submission. Madison, Monroe, and their party associates in Congress and in the country at large believed submission would gravely imperil the very objects they had long sought. Aside from economic privation, infringement of national sovereignty, and the loss of national honor and morale, submission would work grave injury to the party and to the prestige of republicanism. Republicans rejected submission and reluctantly took the other alternative. Preparing for war they endeavored to use the threat of military force in a final effort to induce repeal. When this too failed the President recommended war—a war that now would put an end to impressment as well.

Sentiment in Congress on the question of war divided closely along party lines, Republican and Federalist. The great majority of Republicans supported war because they, like the President, saw no other option. They concurred with the reasoning which led the President and secretary of state to this conclusion. They were able to agree because they trusted the good faith and integrity of all past efforts to achieve settlement. They could agree to Henry Clay's avowal that: "Not a man in the nation could really doubt the sincerity with which those in power have sought, by all honorable pacific means, to protect the interests of the country." Had these policies and negotiations been the work of Federalists they would doubtless have opposed them. But they were not; they were the work of fellow Republicans, men who could be trusted.

Within the limits set by this consensus there developed sharp disagreements among Republicans as to when and how hostilities should begin. Should not war delay until the country was better prepared? Should it not begin in a limited way, confined to the sea? The safety of the persons and property of constituents in northern and eastern localities made strong cases for an affirmative to both these propositions. In the final days of peace, men already at odds with administration leadership openly challenged the agreed-upon strategy in an unsuccessful bid for limited belligerency against one or both belligerents. Opposing these efforts were a hard core of southern and western members championing a strategy that would better satisfy the needs of the country and their own constituents as they conceived them to be.

Not all Republicans could support the declaration of war. A few from northern and eastern constituencies, after defeat of the limited war strategy, voted against war because they feared ruinous effects from a war inadequately prepared for on the lives and property of constituents and on the party. Clintonians joined them out of conviction that they and their leaders held an unused key to accommodation with Great Britain and fearing Federalist resurgence from a premature war. Economic interest and distorted views of the evil character of the war and fear of its results account for other scattered opposition.

The Federalists furnished the greatest number of votes against the war. A united and determined band, they could not agree to the reasoning which led to the position that war was just and unavoidably necessary. The Republicans had never tried seriously to negotiate with Great Britain; they had deliberately created and protracted the embroilment for their own nefarious purposes. Federalists at the outset had scoffed at Republican war pronouncements and military legislation as more political maneuvering. When the Republicans took the nation into war, the Federalists attributed this unexpected move to such apparent causes as French partialities, the disgrace of retreat, a corrupt presidential bargain, and base territorial ambitions. It was an unnecessary and immoral war, clearly avoidable and fully justifying righteous and determined opposition—an opposition which many expected would eventually return them to power.

President Madison in the years 1811–12 faced the difficult task of arousing the country and warning Great Britain that war would take place if she did not repeal her Orders. Striving to give his adversary an avenue of retreat and to prevent possible preemptive attack before the country was adequately prepared, he failed on both these counts. Owing to his ambiguous pronouncements, their discrepancy with those of congressional colleagues, and Federalist propaganda, much of the country and the British government remained throughout most of the session unaware of administration intentions. The complexity of the issue and the presence of men who doubted the willingness of the administration to make war made it vital for the President to make clear, bold policy statements in order to arouse the country and convey warning to the adversary. There was some sense to the effort to respect British pride. There was less logic in the effort to convey a determination to fight and yet give no motive at all for prior attack. Madison had few illusions that Britain would yield without actual war, and his main task should have been to prepare the country as quickly and effectively as possible for military action against this formidable adversary. In the face of the consequent unpreparedness, Republicans from different areas of the country divided among themselves as to when and how force should be applied. Sectional and interest-group pressures are natural to our form of government: all the more reason for efforts to remove the conditions that generated these forces. Americans adequately warned of impending hostilities would have had sufficient opportunity to prepare for conflict. Madison was an able, astute negotiator, highly accomplished in the ways of traditional eighteenth-century European diplomacy. He was beyond his depth, however, in managing the affairs of an unruly, fractious nineteenth-century republic as it moved towards war.

The year 1812 for the student of our early history bears an heretofore unperceived meaning. The waning prestige of republicanism in 1787 had given deep urgency to the movement that produced a new blueprint of republican government—the Constitution. By 1812 republicanism seemed again in peril. Contemporaries perceived the parallel between the two periods. The present moment, exclaimed Calhoun of South Carolina, "is a period of the greatest moment to our country. No period since the formation of our constitution has been equally important." Once again men felt that a momentous outcome hung in balance. We must consider our actions with great care, urged William King of North Carolina, "when the destinies of the country are about to be launched on an untried ocean, and when the doubt is about to be solved, whether our Republican Government is alike calculated to support us through the trials and difficulties of war, and guide us in safety down the gentle current of peace."

Nor did the sense of urgency concerning republicanism and the party dissipate after war began. The nation had shown it could declare war. It must now show that it could wage war. A letter from Secretary Monroe to Senator William H. Crawford reveals a continuing concern. Would the Senator call to discuss candidates to head a confused and leaderless War Department, asked the Secretary, at a particularly low point in American fortunes? "This is the time when the arrangements that are to insure success to the republican party and to free government for our country, are to be made, or which will lay the foundation for their overthrow." From the Virginia son-in-law of the Secretary of State, George Hay, a state party leader, came this warning. "According to my limited views of the state of things in the UStates, this is the crisis of the republican cause. If it sustains the present shock, it will prevail and flourish for many years. The undivided strength of its friends ought therefore to be exerted with the utmost vigilance and circumspection." A speedy recruitment of an efficient military force, wrote William W. Bibb of Georgia in 1814, involved "the safety, if not the very existence of this free government." Only with news of the Peace of Ghent did there come relief from the sense of crisis. There had been disasters in this war, but also triumphs. Jonathan Roberts spoke for many when in 1815 in a letter to his brother he appraised the war. It had not been a defeat or even a stalemate but a victory—for the party and for republicanism.

> We have not got a stipulation about impressments and orders in council nor about indemnity—But victory perches on our banner & the talisman of invincibility no longer pertains to the tyrants of the Ocean—But the triumph over the Aristocrats and Monarchists is equally glorious with that over the enemy—It is the triumph of virtue over vice of republican men & republican principles over the advocates and doctrines of Tyranny.

There would be future crises which would call into doubt the energy and staying power of the American Republic. But to many Americans like Roberts the War of 1812 was one long stride in the march towards permanency.

The Liberal Impulse to War

STEVEN WATTS

The vast, multifaceted changes in post-Revolutionary America subtly transformed its republican society. In the process, . . . citizens of the early republic experienced and participated in a reshaping of familiar notions of society, culture, economy, and personality. By 1810 these liberalizing tendencies were converging on and reshaping American political ideology. The subterranean agitation of such influences in the political world of the young nation—along with the overt pressures in foreign affairs—gradually forced to the surface a new breed of political men, especially within the Republican majority.

These insurgent Republicans—men like Henry Clay, Charles J. Ingersoll, Spencer H. Cone, Hezekiah Niles, and Felix Grundy—did not remain insurgent very long. Eloquent and forceful, they resolved to overcome the early-nineteenth-century "crisis of republicanism" by political innovation. These Liberal Republicans, as they accurately might be called, found political sustenance in the emerging values of a growing market society: self-made success, moral free-agency, decision of character and self-control, entrepreneurial production, the home market, an ethos of energy and assertion. Melding these values with traditional republican commitments, they surged to the forefront of American political discourse as opinion-shapers. They also pulled in their wake older, often more traditional, but ultimately receptive Republicans. . . .

Steven Watts, *The Republic Reborn: War and the Making of Liberal America, 1790–1820* (Baltimore: Johns Hopkins University Press, 1987), pp. 250–274 excerpted.

In the hands of these Jeffersonians, eighteenth-century American republicanism thus shifted noticeably toward what would become nineteenth-century liberalism. This new ideological orientation took shape around several intellectual and moral convictions: that pursuit of many self-interests would result in the public good; that politics was the arena for sorting and settling the interests of self-controlled individuals; that energy in foreign affairs and a productive home market in political economy best promoted the expansive young republic; and finally, that progress and growth rather than decay and decline promised to color the future of the United States. And by 1812, war with Great Britain had become the catalyst for the formulation of a politics of the marketplace. . . .

With his election in 1810, Henry Clay became the youngest Speaker of the House of Representatives in American history. The dynamic Kentuckian, only thirty-three years old, defeated the venerable Jeffersonian stalwart from North Carolina, Nathaniel Macon. The election proved to be far-reaching. Symbolically, it marked the passing of a political baton between generations, because like a host of other fledgling congressmen, many of whom first came to Washington in 1810, Clay was an energetic Liberal Republican. While respectful of Jeffersonian maxims and contemptuous of Federalist social elitism and economic mercantilism, this youthful and talented group nonetheless displayed a new ideological sensibility. They were determined to rewrite the Republican agenda in accordance with imperatives of liberalizing change in the post-Revolutionary republic. In a practical sense, Clay's selection also made an immediate impact. "Harry of the West" wasted little time in packing key House committees with able and assertive Liberal Republicans.

The most important of those committees was that dealing with foreign affairs. Thanks to Clay's skillful manipulations, it emerged as a showcase for Liberal Republican talent. Peter B. Porter of New York became chairman, and he was supported by two freshman congressman soon to be noted for their oratory and legislative leadership: John C. Calhoun of South Carolina and Felix Grundy of Tennessee. The Foreign Relations Committee became the center around which the deliberations of the Twelfth Congress revolved. From the late fall of 1811 to the early summer of 1812, the reports and recommendations emanating from this small assemblage dominated the flow of Congressional discourse. The committee acted as the lever by which the Jeffersonian Republican machinery was inched slowly toward confrontation with Great Britain. . . .

Questions of finance, taxes, commercial policy, strengthening of military forces, the degree of popular mobilization—all in the context of impending war—riveted the attention of most congressmen.

Exhaustive and exhausting discussions of these issues revealed an emerging pattern. Most Federalists gradually backed away from initial support of war preparation and began to emphasize the great dangers of conflict with the powerful Great Britain. A handful of traditional Republicans joined in this dissent, fearing that war would fatally undermine republican institutions. On the other hand, moderate administration Republicans steadily deserted the time-honored strategy of peaceful coercion to endorse a vigorous defense of American rights. From the smoke of this political battlefield the Liberal Republicans emerged in a strong position of leadership. Having pushed hard and steady for a military solution to the crisis, they succeeded in shaping a Republican consensus for war. By late spring, all the war preparations recommended by the Foreign Relations committee had passed through Congress, although some survived only in diluted form.

On April 1, 1812, decisive action began. On that day President Madison asked Congress for a sixty-day embargo on American shipping—the measure was understood as clearing the commercial decks for war—and it was passed and signed on April 6. Although more vigorous than many other of his Presidential messages, it still appeared to be a workmanlike document. It methodically listed those British affronts to America's position as "an independent and neutral nation": the plundering of American neutral commerce, impressment of American sailors, harassment of the American coastline, encouragement of Indian raids, and the "sweeping system of Blockades" by the British on the European continent. The failure of the embargo and diplomatic protest, Madison admitted, had exhausted the patience of the young republic. "We behold, in fine, on the side of Great Britain, a state of war against the United States, and on the side of the United States, a state of peace towards Great Britain." Perhaps as a reminder of his characteristic republican reluctance to take the nation into war, Madison made a point of ultimately placing this "solemn question" in the hands of Congress. "I am happy in the assurance," the President concluded warily, "that the decision will be worthy of the enlightened and patriotic councils of a virtuous, a free, and a powerful nation."

Congressional Liberal Republicans displayed none of Madison's hesitance. In the absence of Peter Porter—who had already left Washington for military service—acting Chairman John C. Calhoun presented to the House on June 3 a bill to declare war on Great Britain. Before submitting the war measure, however, the brilliant young South Carolinian gave to Congress on behalf of the Foreign Relations Committee one of the most fascinating and suggestive documents in the history of the early republic. Largely the work of Calhoun—with Felix Grundy likely adding several rhetorical touches—the "Report on the Causes and Reasons for War" revealed more than its authors probably intended or even knew. Although cast as a review of British-American relations since 1805, the passionate eloquence of the War Report overflowed its form. Superficially, it summed up the ideological impulses that fired the war demands of the Liberal Republicans. But at a deeper level it indicated how an emerging liberal ideology drew together the social, cultural, and psychological hopes and frustrations of a people experiencing massive changes in their lives and focused them in a national crusade. Pulsating with the nervous energy of a liberalizing society, the War Report exhibited the whole complex pattern of the Jeffersonian motivation to war in 1812. A close examination of its language reveals several layers of meaning—conscious beliefs, half-conscious fears, unconscious drives—amid the flashing rhetoric.

"No people ever had stronger motives to cherish peace. . . . But the period has now arrived, when the United States must support their character and station among the nations of the earth, or submit to the most shameful degradation." With this ringing declaration, the War Report launched its appeal for military confrontation with Great Britain from an ideological base. Calhoun and his Liberal Republican associates here clearly conveyed their belief that the peaceful instincts of republicanism had grown weary and that the time had come for an infusion of energy. They developed this point further in the text, cautiously referring to "the commercial restrictions to which the United States resorted as an evidence of their sensibility, and a mild retaliation of their wrongs." Although carefully avoiding direct attack on this policy of their Jeffersonian elders, the Liberal Republicans stressed that "the motive was mistaken, if their [Americans'] forbearance was imputed either to the want of a just sensibility to their wrongs, or a determination . . . to resent them." The point could not have been clearer: regarding traditional republican antiwar sentiment, "the time has now arrived when this system of reasoning must cease."

The War Report further pressed the case for an energized political vision by asserting, first, the great need for a show of American vigor and strength in war. "The United States must act as an independent nation, and assert their rights, and avenge their wrongs, according to their own estimate of them," read the document. Second, the Liberal Republicans insisted that the republic be capable of meeting this challenge. Scornful of those who feared for the fragility of republican institutions and themselves bolstered by an appreciation of America's liberalizing growth since the Revolution, they showed little fear. The United States "have suffered no wrong, they have received no insults, however great, for which they cannot obtain redress," noted the text confidently.

This spirit of ideological innovation was sustained by similar sentiments rising outside the halls of Congress. By mid-1812 most Republicans were convinced of the need to overcome republican prejudices against war-making. Scoffing at traditional republican qualms about "a standing army," the *Western Intelligencer* rejoiced in June 1812, "It will be a moving, fighting conquering army—and as soon as its duty is done, it will be disbanded." The *National Intelligencer,* seeing in 1812 the commencement of a "new era" for the United States, went so far as to suggest that only war could save "our present system of government." Lack of success would likely "diminish our confidence in republican principles." The *Richmond Enquirer* expressed even better this regenerative ideological impulse. Announcing the declaration of war in an editorial entitled "The New Era," the editors proclaimed, "The energies of the Republic are fast disclosing themselves; and may God desert those who now desert their country!"

"The hostility of the British Government to these States has . . . made manifest that the United States are considered by it as the commercial rival

of Great Britain, and that their prosperity and growth are incompatible with her welfare." With these phrases the War Report disclosed a related, overt motivation to war. Unlike traditional republicans fearful of luxury and decay, young Jeffersonians like Calhoun and Grundy had observed and drawn confidence from America's economic "prosperity and growth" since the Revolution. However, the entrepreneurial energy of the liberalizing young republic demanded free market access. As the War Report explained elsewhere of overseas trade, Americans "with their usual industry and enterprise, had embarked in it, a vast proportion of their shipping, and of their capital." But the British had initiated "a system of hostility on the commerce of the United States." To the Liberal Republicans, this explicit denial of markets and implicit denial of entrepreneurialism could not be tolerated.

Explicating the war's economic motivation in more detail, the Foreign Relations Committee unfolded an important additional argument. On the first page of the text, the War Report indicted British aggression against "an important branch of the American commerce, which affected every part of the United States, and involved many of their citizens in ruin." Here the authors referred not to the carrying or reexport trade, but to the sale of commodities actually produced in the American Republic. So while certain maritime groups opposed war to keep open the lanes of trade for commercial carriers, Liberal Republicans sympathetic to productive farming and manufacturing interests endorsed war to protect the American-produced commodities that filled many of those lanes. This distinction—and the 1812 conflict—put a line of demarcation between two stages in the economic development of the young republic: an older commercial capitalism and an expansive, entrepreneurial, producing capitalism.

Another point in the War Report suggested a final overt motive in the economic rationale for military action. Near the end of a long discussion of commercial violations by both France and England, the report's authors inserted a significant statement: "An utter inability alone, to resist could justify a quiet surrender of our rights. . . . To that condition the United States are not reduced nor do they fear it." In the context of an economic discussion, and given the nature of Liberal Republican rhetoric over the previous two-score months, the statement's meaning was clear. In the eyes of many Republicans, the rapid development of domestic manufactures and internal commerce since 1790 had bolstered the republic's capacity for war. They could endorse the conflict with confidence, believing that an expanding home market would provide economic strength for survival. Moreover, support for an Anglo-American war would likely quicken the shift toward a reliable home trade and wean America from a decadent dependence on foreign commerce.

The War Report's assurances of American economic vitality was once more but the crest of a large public wave. By June 1812 Republican popular discourse was bursting with indignant claims from American producers eager for war. For more than two years the *Richmond Enquirer* had been insisting that it was "unwise to plunge this country into war, to enrich a few merchants" engaged in "the carrying trade." However, as the editors insisted just as often, "when G.B. declares to us; 'you shall not export your *own* productions . . . you shall not send your own articles to their natural markets'; we ask, whether we are to submit to his proud pretension." Congressman Jonathan Roberts of Pennsylvania agreed. Productive Americans would not fight for "a speculative right or an empty name" of the carrying trade, he argued, but they would defend "our fair export trade." General Andrew Jackson utilized a similar appeal in March 1812, calling for militia volunteers to help protect "free trade" and "open a market for the productions of our soil." A July 4, 1812, resolution from two Virginia counties stated this argument for war most succinctly: "The right . . . to seek unmolested a market for the products of the labor of our hands forms another of those imprescriptible rights, appertaining to our national sovereignty, and most essential interests." . . .

Thus, by declaring war in 1812 many Jeffersonians hoped that America's republican government would draw badly needed energy from her dynamically growing society and economy. Instead of merely guarding the commonweal or nurturing public and private virtue, the revitalized republic would assert itself in war to demonstrate productive prowess, social vitality, and civic strength. By this process, the Liberal Republicans accelerated the departure of ideology and political economy from traditional republican moorings.

"But one sentiment pervaded the whole American Nation. No local interests were regarded, no sordid motives felt. Without looking to the parts which suffered most, the invasion of our rights was considered a common cause, and from one extremity of our union to the other, was heard the voice of a united People." With this rhetorical flourish the War Report brought to light another layer of war impulses lying just beneath the evident rationalizations of political economy and ideology. In this submerged realm of social relations and cultural values, desires and compulsions of doubt and guilt over rapidly liberalizing social change found partial resolution in war. As this passage indicated, the workings of "civism" comprised one such impulse. As we have seen, countless observers noted that the post-Revolutionary decades witnessed an unprecedented fragmentation of American society as a rapidly growing population, geographical mobility, and social aspiration created a society of people on the make. By the early nineteenth century, deference had declined. Moral restraints on wealth-making had withered. The traditional community context for individual action had faded. In this fragmenting context, Americans confronted problems of commitment beyond pure self-interest. In what form was loyalty to the commonweal possible? How could private and public virtue exist in a society increasingly devoted to the main chance? The War Report's clarion call indicated one attractive answer. Taking the battlefield against Great Britain would transcend mere self-regard by blending "the voice of a united people" in "one sentiment," in "common cause." By providing such a compelling opportunity for civism, the War of 1812 comprised a ritual absolution of guilt for many American possessive individuals.

"The mad ambition, the lust of power . . . of Great Britain . . . [Facing

this] degrading submission to the will of others . . . the United States have had to resist, with the firmness belonging to their character, the continued violation of their rights." The text of Calhoun and Grundy here moved half-consciously to the terrain of cultural values. By juxtaposing the unrestrained craving of Great Britain with the firm "character" of the young republic, the War Report touched a cultural nerve. In the consolidating liberal society of the early republic, popular discourse had given new meaning to the word "character." Signifying "reputation" in the eighteenth century, by 1812 the term was also coming to designate one's inner moral structure. More specifically, it connoted the self-control of the self-made man. In one sense the character ethic referred to the shaping of one's own destiny through marshaling talent and ambition, and the 1812 war gave vent to that impulse. As depicted in the War Report, an aristocratic, mercantilist Great Britain was confining American entrepreneurialism by dominating the ocean and exercising "an unbounded and lawless tyranny." War thus materialized in part as a means for citizens of a hard-working liberal society to break artificial restrictions and to assert control over their destiny. As the War Report noted, the "high character of the American people" only required a proving ground. "Forbearance has ceased to be a virtue," wrote the authors in the language of self-control. "There is an alternative only, between the base surrender of their rights and a manly vindication of them."

This affirmation of character, however, carried still another meaning: not just control over one's own destiny, but repression of one's instinctual and emotional appetites. The directives of an emerging capitalist culture—hard work, individual opportunity-seeking, calculating judgments—necessitated self-discipline as well as self-assertion, and that meant avoiding the temptations of avarice, immorality, and self-indulgence. War in 1812 provided a singular opportunity in the cultural struggle for repression. For years critics had railed against the manipulative, voluptuous materialism of the commercializing young republic, and now Great Britain became the target for the projection of such fears, and war a means of opposing them. As the War Report described, the "lust," "mad ambition," "commercial avarice," and "unbounded tyranny" of England demanded that Americans resist "with the firmness belonging to their character." Embodying "no sordid motives" but only moral purpose, and exploding the manipulative masks endemic to "Teagomania," war appeared in 1812 as a compelling exercise for repression of base instinct and elevation of self-disciplined character.

"Happily for the United States, their destiny, under the aid of Heaven, is in their own hands." As this War Report sentence related, many Republicans found but a short distance between self-control and a belief in divine assistance in their movement toward conflict in 1812. In other words, the war of 1812 served as a clarion call for American "civil religion." Heirs of a Protestant millennial tradition, Americans tended to see their society as an exemplary gathering of godly, industrious communities counterpoised between the heathen Indian and the decadent popery of Europe. As good republicans, they also envisioned the United States as a virtuous, enlightened, vigorous New World polity arrayed against the hoary, tyrannical oli-

garchies of the Old World. These two strands of national hubris first had intertwined during the American Revolution, and the nation's post-1790 socioeconomic growth only reinforced this sense of the republic's special mission. In 1812 war seemed to offer a rich historical moment for the fulfillment of America's divine destiny. With commingled Protestant hopes and republican dreams, the War Report assured Americans that they could join battle with Great Britain "confidently trusting the Lord of Hosts will go with us to Battle in a righteous cause."

"We wish to call attention of the House to those injuries . . . as could not fail to deprive the United States of the principal advantages of their Revolution, if submitted to. . . . The proof which so complete and disgraceful a submission . . . would afford of our degeneracy, could not fail to inspire confidence, that there was no limit to which, our degradation, might not be carried." With these curiously emotional sentiments, the War Report finally brought close to the surface a cluster of deeply submerged impulses to war. Bowing to the legacy of the Revolution and the Founding Fathers, the authors followed with familiar warnings about their own generation's "degeneracy." Like many other citizens of the young nation, these Liberal Republicans betrayed acute anxiety over their position and status in a congealing liberal society. Burdened with an image of the heroic and self-sacrificing Fathers, and guilty over the growing materialism and grasping competitiveness of the post-Revolutionary generation, these Sons had inflicted on themselves a crisis of authority. By sacrificing material pursuits and joining together in heroic enterprise against a threatening enemy, in 1812 they could prove themselves worthy heirs to the Founders. In war the Sons could authenticate the emerging spirit of capitalism and show liberal man to be as morally purposeful as republican man. In war they could uphold and guarantee for Americans "the principal advantages of their Revolution."

"Our flag has given no protection . . . ; it has been unceasingly violated, and our vessels exposed to dangers by the loss of men taken from them. . . . An exemption of the citizens of the United States from this degrading oppression, and their flag from violation, is all that they have sought. . . . The United States must act, and avenge their wrongs." If violent conflict in 1812 promised to resolve these Republican Sons' crisis of authority, the War Report revealed that war also addressed another psychological difficulty. Through this oblique use of imagery—ostensibly a discussion of impressment's horrors—Calhoun and Grundy half-consciously pictured war as a "return of the repressed." As Richard Sennett has argued, for the modern personality continually beset by repressions, conformities, and commercial banalities it is often the case that "to be aggressive is to be alive." The War Report suggested that in 1812 the Liberal Republicans had indeed tapped a hidden desire among their countrymen for cathartic, violent escape from repressive demands for self-control. The document angrily denounced—in highly sensual language—the "violation" of "exposed" Americans. It also bitterly complained of Great Britain's disregard for "obligations which have heretofore been held sacred by civilized nations." It indignantly denounced England's Indian allies for

commencing "that system of savage warfare on our frontiers which has been at all times indiscriminate in its effects, on all ages, sexes, and conditions and so revolting to humanity." Sensing an acute libidinous appeal to repressed character-types, the Liberal Republican authors emotionally denounced such forbidden outrages. Yet they quickly turned to offer their *own* acceptable, organized, and civilized mode of violent release: war. By entering on an aggressive crusade to quash "savagery"—by mustering violence in the name of resisting violence—Americans could escape momentarily and legitimately the iron cage of repression. As the Liberal Republicans described in the War Report, in a psychologically explosive atmosphere struggling Americans were "calling on their Government to avenge their wrongs."

"The attempts to dismember our Union, and overthrow our excellent constitution, by a secret mission [we denounce]. . . . It must be evident to the impartial world, that the contest which is now forced . . . is radically a contest for their sovereignty and independence." With this rhetorical lightning flash, the Liberal Republicans fleetingly disclosed the visage of the "personae" as it anxiously moved toward war in 1812. Complaining here of a furtive British political mission in 1811 designed to foment division in the American republic, the authors of the War Report also unconsciously portrayed a hidden, knotty identity function of the conflict. They lashed out emotionally at an external enemy seeking by "a secret mission" to "dismember our Union, and overthrow our excellent constitution." This highly symbolic language objectified the pressures descending on the individual psyche in this era of liberalizing change, and suggested its subsequent tendency toward fragmentation. This imagery also indicated that the early-nineteenth-century "personae"—a diffuse personality structure lacking identity beneath the manipulative masks of liberal social relations—was drawn to the cohesive dynamic of war. As other phrases from the War Report suggested, the conflict offered a "total" pseudo-identity by paranoid definition. The authors extravagantly condemned the evil enemy for assailing American individuals: "Our citizens are wantonly snatched from their country, and their families; deprived of their liberty and doomed to an ignominious and slavish bondage." The Liberal Republicans darkly discerned a "system of hostile aggression, by the British government." What was even more outlandish was their perception of "full proof that there is no bound to the hostility of the British government . . . no act, however unjustifiable, which it would not commit." Thus Americans, by creating and fighting an evil foe bent on their destruction, could find psychological cohesion themselves. As Calhoun and Grundy wrote—probably with more significance than they realized for the "personae" of liberalizing Americans—the war was "radically a contest for their sovereignty and independence."

The War Report of the Liberal Republicans, in the complexity and symbolism of its language, thus displayed the various threads of motivation leading to the war declaration in the summer of 1812. Its final paragraph, designed as a stirring call to arms by the young members of the Foreign Relations Committee, emotionally wove these threads into whole cloth:

Your committee, believing that the freeborn sons of America are worthy to enjoy the liberty which their Fathers purchased at the price of so much blood and treasure, and seeing in the measures adopted by Great Britain, a course commenced and persisted in, which must lead to a loss of National character and Independence, feel no hesitation in advising resistance by force—In which Americans of the present day will prove to the enemy and to the World, that we have not only inherited the liberty which our Fathers gave us, but also the will and power to maintain it. Relying on the patriotism of the Nation, and confidently trusting that the Lord of Hosts will go with us to Battle in a righteous cause, and crown our efforts with success, your Committee recommend an immediate appeal to Arms.

Certain historians have suggested that in many ways the War Report resembled nothing so much as a second American "Declaration of Independence." Its serial condemnation of a depraved Great Britain, its appeals for American resistance and assertion, and its defiant cadences of barely restrained emotion suggested an almost self-conscious duplication of the brave polemic of 1776. There is a germ of truth here, and it is easy to see the 1812 conflict as merely a second, pale "War for Independence," with Calhoun, Clay, and Grundy attempting to play the heroic roles of Jefferson, Adams, and Washington. However, a close, penetrating reading of the War Report reveals much more. Rather than simply a bellicose expression of growing nationalist sentiment, the demands in the document for a vigorous "independence" carried myriad deeper meanings. Its authors actually painted a miniature portrait of the liberal impulse to war in 1812 and its complex characteristics—an expansive entrepreneurial economy, an energized republican ideology, the desire for civism and self-control, reverence for American civil religion, and the personae's frantic search for authority, emotional release, and identity. Thus the War Report ultimately tells us much about the transforming forces at work in the early republic. It illustrates how the young Liberal Republicans captured politically many of the aspirations and deeper confusions accruing to consolidating liberal capitalism and projected them into a conflict with Great Britain. . . .

⧉ *F U R T H E R   R E A D I N G*

Henry Adams, *History of the United States During the Administrations of Jefferson and Madison* (1889–1891)

James M. Banner, Jr., *To the Hartford Convention: The Federalists and the Origins of Party Politics in Massachusetts, 1789–1815* (1970)

Irving Brant, *James Madison* (1941–1961)

Kate Coffey, *The Twilight's Last Gleaming: Britain vs. America, 1812–1815* (1977)

Harry L. Coles, *The War of 1812* (1965)

Lawrence D. Cress, *Citizens in Arms: The Army and the Militia in American Society to the War of 1812* (1982)

Clifford L. Egan, *Neither Peace Nor War: Franco-American Relations, 1803–1812* (1983)

———, "The Origins of the War of 1812: Three Decades of Historical Writing," *Military Affairs* 38 (1974): 72–75

Warren H. Goodman, "The Origins of the War of 1812: A Survey of Changing Interpretations," *Mississippi Valley Historical Review* 28 (1941), 171–186

William James Gribben, *The Churches Militant: The War of 1812 and American Religion* (1973)

Ronald L. Hatzenbuehler and Robert L. Ivie, *Congress Declares War: Rhetoric, Leadership, and Partisanship in the Early Republic* (1983)

Donald R. Hickey, *The War of 1812: A Forgotten Conflict* (1989)

Reginald Horsman, *The War of 1812* (1969)

Ralph Ketchum, *James Madison* (1971)

John K. Mahon, *The War of 1812* (1972)

Frank L. Owsley, *Struggle for the Gulf Borderlands: The Creek War and the Battle of New Orleans* (1981)

Bradford Perkins, *Prologue to War: England and the United States, 1805–1812* (1963)

Julius M. Pratt, *The Expansionists of 1812* (1925)

Robert A. Rutland, *The Presidency of James Madison* (1990)

Marshall Smelser, *The Democratic Republic, 1800–1815* (1968)

J. C. A. Stagg, *Mr. Madison's War: Politics, Diplomacy, and Warfare in the Early Republic* (1983)

John Sugden, *Tecumseh's Last Stand* (1985)

J. Leitch White, Jr., *Britain and the American Frontier, 1783–1815* (1975)

The Rise of Northern Capitalism

Through the War of 1812, the conventional wisdom held that the United States would long be primarily a rural nation of small-scale producers. The Jeffersonians, in particular, foresaw an expansive democratic republic populated mainly by independent farmers, craftsmen, and their households. By the end of the nineteenth century, however, such prophecies would prove false; in fact, as early as the 1840s, interlocking developments in the North presaged the rise of a very different social order than the Jeffersonians had predicted.

After 1815, for example, the construction of numerous internal improvement projects shortened what had once seemed vast distances, and facilitated commerce. In the countryside, a combination of demographic pressures and revamped opportunities hastened the regional shift toward commercial production and reliance on merchant middlemen that had begun in the eighteenth century. Manufacturing enterprises ranging from steam-powered factories to tiny sweatshop garrets proliferated in the established seaboard cities and in new urban centers carved out of the wilderness. These cities, in turn, became a prominent feature of the northern landscape. Especially after 1840, a rising proportion of the new urban working class consisted of recent immigrants who brought customs and religious views to Yankee America that seemed exotic and (to some) threatening. Along with these changes came disorienting transformations in social relations, affecting everything from the most intimate aspects of domestic life to the most conspicuous displays of wealth and status.

Some historians have stressed the material benefits that accrued from this economic development, and have left a picture of spectacular progress and invention. Others have pointed to the social injuries that accompanied economic growth—the miseries of urban poverty, the widening of social and economic inequality, and the growing sense of dependence and powerlessness associated with wage labor. Today these disputes show up in arguments over the sources of what some scholars have called the market revolution. Did these changes arise from the unleashing of a preexisting American capitalism? Or did they mark a new departure, undertaken by some Americans at the direct expense of others? In a sense, scholars have returned to the same issues that divided the people whom they have studied. Did the rise of northern capitalism represent a triumph for basic American principles, a modification of those principles, or perhaps an outright denial?

⌗ D O C U M E N T S

The economic and social transformation of the northern countryside involved an uneven but ultimately irresistible shift away from established forms of general farming and local exchange (with only limited involvement in commercial markets) toward commercial production. What were the sources of this shift, and what were its consequences with regard to household and family life, rural class relations, and the wider regional economy? Certain clues appear in the first document, including excerpts from the letters of Mary Graham, the wife of a farmer and petty craftsman in western Massachusetts, and a brief statement from a didactic magazine for farmers. In the second selection, a biography of the New York merchant and political leader Gideon Lee maps a different road out of the countryside and couples it with a real-life celebration of a self-made man; Aléxis de Tocqueville's reflections on the American pursuit of wealth, from his *Democracy in America,* are more somber. Closely related to the rise of the new northern businessman was the elaboration of a distinctive code of female domestic duties, which quickly spread to northern middle-class families generally. In the third selection, two samplings illustrate some of the tensions between ideals and realities—one from a popular advice book, the other from the family correspondence of Abigail May Alcott, the reformer, wife of Bronson Alcott, and mother of Louisa May Alcott.

Women, many of them daughters of the countryside, also formed the bulk of the early labor force in some of the leading manufacturing sectors, especially the New England textile industry. The fourth selection includes a series of impressions of Lowell, Massachusetts, the most famous of the new factory towns. A different pattern of industrial growth, based on labor-intensive methods, unfolded in the major seaports, including New York. In the fifth document, a British immigrant cabinetmaker recalls his own New York experiences from a decade earlier; and a short report from the reform-minded *New York Tribune* provides another angle on conditions in the trade.

Two starkly opposed views of capitalist growth complete this documentary section. Thomas Skidmore, a Connecticut-born machinist, emerged as the leading spokesman of New York's Working Men's movement in 1829. His book of that same year, *The Rights of Man to Property!,* angrily indicted some of the fundamentals of the emerging order and offered a new social blueprint—one based on a peaceful, democratic, electoral revolution, a general division of property holdings, and an end to inheritance. A decade later, Alonzo Potter, an Episcopalian clergyman, delivered a stalwart defense of capitalist justice and wage labor.

Views on the Commercialization of the Countryside

Mary Graham Describes Life on a Massachusetts Farm, 1835–1844

Buckland, April 6th 1835

Near and very dear friends,

I believe I shant wait in silence any longer for a letter. We have traveled too and from the Post Office for weeks, in vain. I now sit down to inquire the cause—is it sickness of death, or have you removed to the far west, to seek the goodly land, or did you during the extreme cold weather last winter freeze up and have not yet thawed out. If this be the cause do write and let us know and we will try to render you some assistance. . . . Will tell you somthing about our own family. Here we are all in comfortable health. L and myself have had to work as hard as we have been able, and a good deal harder than we wanted to. We are very much confined at home. I have not visited an afternoon in the town of B[uckland] for more than a year except at N's twice or three times. I have shoes a plenty to bind, from six to eight and twelve pairs in a week—and with all the rest have got four as dirty, noisy, ragged children to take care of as any other woman, they look as though they would do to put out in the cornfields in about six or eight weeks to keep away the crows. . . .

Buckland Feb. 5, 1837

Dear Friends at Northamption . . .

Hardly know what to say about ourselves, but will say this we have plenty of hard work and poor keeping and money at interest, and are always like to have. I can hardly feel reconciled to not visiting you this winter, but so much to do and so much money at interest that we cant get enough to bear our expences down there back again. Of course we must stay at home. . . .

Buckland Feb. 12, 1839

Dear Brother and Sister . . .

I now seat myself to acknowledge the reception of a few lines from you some weeks since. Probably you have expected an answer before this, which I allow to be reasonable, but by way of apology will just say that I work in the shop most of the time. We have been unusually [crowded?] with work, have been obliged to be in the shop early and late. Of course not much time to write. . . . We received a letter from Clark and Caroline a few weeks since, they were in Indianna, New Albany, Floyd County. She has had a son and lost it. They were in comfortable health when they wrote. . . . We have had a terrible freshet and from accounts think it did considerable damage in your region. The bridge at the Falls barely escaped, one shop was washed away and several dwelling houses were in danger. Cousin G's was among the number. . . .
PS Perhaps you may wonder what I do in the shop so much. I do the pegging, hammer the leather and considerable of the fitting. . . .

Buckland March 3, 1844

Dear Brother and Sister,

I suppose I must answer your letter whether I want to or not. To tell the truth, I don't want to, for I don't feel like writing to anyone. You wanted all the news. I have some that is not very pleasant to me. In the first place, Lucius has sold us out of house and home with the [privilege] of staying here until the first of June. If he can rake and scrape enough after paying his debts to set his family down in Wisconsin he is determined to go. So you wonder that I feel sad. Nothing but poor health and poverty to begin with in a new country looks dark to me. But I can't help it, go we must I suppose if the means can be raised. Don't know as I shall be permitted to visit you, expect he will think that every dollar must be saved to go to the far West. Do come and see us *once more* for I can't endure that I shall never see you again. . . .

The New England Farmer *on the Rules of Commercial Production, 1849*

Industry, well directed, will give a man a competency in a few years. The greatest industry misapplied is useless . . .

[T]here is my friend, Nat Notional, the busiest and most industrious mortal in existence; as the old saying goes "he has too many irons in the fire," and with all his industry, he goes behindhand.

A few years ago, he concluded to give up the dairy business, in consequence of the low price of butter and cheese; sold his cows at a low figure, and purchased sheep at a high rate, for wool then demanded a high price. By the time he got fairly into the raising of wool, down went the price of wool, and up went the price of butter and cheese. He then sold his sheep, and purchased cows again, for cheese was up and wool was down. And finally, he changed his business so often, because he wasn't contented to thrive, little by little, as Seth Steady did, that he got completely used up, and is now only fit for California, or some other wool-gathering project. . . .

Perspectives on the Self-Made Man

A Sketch of the Life of Gideon Lee, 1843

Among the many distinguished sons of New England, she has none worthier to present to the rising generation, as a model of imitation, than he whose name furnishes the subject of this biographical notice—. . . .

GIDEON LEE was born in the town of Amherst, in the state of Massachusetts, on the 27th of April, 1778. He lost his father when quite a child, and was left to the care of his mother, of whom he always spoke in terms of the warmest affection. While yet in infancy, he went to reside with an uncle, a farmer, in whose service he discharged the humble duties of looking after the cattle, and was employed in such other occupations as were suitable to his strength and age. . . .

After remaining some time under the care, and in the employment of his uncle, he was apprenticed to the tanning and shoemaking—it being the practice then to conduct both branches by the same person—. . . . His genius, however, seemed better adapted to the tanning, for which department of the business he always retained a strong partiality. Up to this period his opportunities for acquiring knowledge were extremely limited: a few weeks schooling during the winter, and such books as accidentally fell in his way, were all the means vouchsafed to him. After learning his trade, or trades, he commenced business on his own account, in the town of Worthington, Mass., and by his industry and strict attention to it, soon won the regard and confidence of his neighbors. He was enabled to obtain credit for the purchase of leather, which he manufactured into shoes, always paying promptly for it at the period he had agreed. The first hundred dollars he earned, and that could honestly be called his own, he appropriated to educating himself at the *Westfield Academy;* and when that sum was exhausted, he again betook himself to his labor. His diligence and application were remarkable, usually working sixteen hours out of the twenty four. . . .

The great points in Mr. Lee's character developed themselves early. They were a strong love for, and veneration of, *truth*—a high sense of honor, an independent and laborious mind as well as body, a heart that embraced in its charities the physical and moral welfare of his fellows, punctuality in the discharge of *all* his duties, a love of order and of system, and an indomitable perseverence in accomplishing whatever measure he undertook. . . .

After prosecuting his business for some time in the manner detailed, he formed a partnership with a Mr. Hubbard; subsequently they were burned out, and he lost what little property he had accumulated. He then dissolved with his partner, and removed to the city of New York. But before establishing himself there, he made a voyage to St. Marys, Georgia, taking with him some small ventures of leather, and accompanying a party who went out for the purpose of cutting live-oak timber for the United States navy. . . .

He suffered much on this . . . journey; and before reaching New York, his money, the little that he had, was exhausted. . . .

In the year 1807, Mr. Lee married the daughter of Major Samuel Buffington, of Worthington, Mass., a distinguished soldier of the Revolution, and shortly after established himself in the city of New York, in the business in which he ultimately became so successful and eminent. He commenced in a little wooden shantee, in Ferry st., still standing, which he called "Fort Lee;" where, as he expressed it, he "entrenched himself." The custom among leather dealers at that day was, to sell on book account, and have annual settlements; he adopted a different plan, and instead of selling on account, he sold at lower prices, and took notes payable in bank. This was an innovation on an ancient custom, that was looked on with disfavor by his neighbors—a revolution that they stoutly resisted. But, aided by being appointed agent for an extensive tanning establishment, styled the "Hampshire Leather Manufactory," he overcame all opposition, and laid the foundation, in the city of New York, for a branch of domestic industry which speedily rivalled the other Atlantic cities. His punctuality in his payments, and the industry and fidelity with which he discharged the duties of the agency, won the confidence of the gentlemen who were the managers of the company, and contributed to give him a credit and standing which otherwise might have taken years to obtain. His prudence and economy enabled him to accumulate means for enlarging his business; and, but for feeble health, the future to him was a bright path of success. . . . [His business secure, Lee entered politics in the 1820s and eventually was elected mayor of the city of New York.]

In his dying charge to his sons, he enjoined them always to "fill up the measure of time." "Be," said he, "always employed profitably in doing good, in building up; aim to promote the good of yourselves and of society; no one can do much good without doing some harm, but you will do less harm by striving to do good; be industrious, be honest." These were the last intelligible words he uttered, and were as characteristic as they were worthy of him. . . .

Aléxis de Tocqueville on the Pursuit of Wealth, 1835

In America I saw the freest and most enlightened men, placed in the happiest circumstances which the world affords; it seemed to me as if a cloud habitually hung upon their brow, and I thought them serious and almost sad even in their pleasures.

It is strange to see with what feverish ardor the Americans pursue their own welfare; and to watch the vague dread that constantly torments them lest they should not have chosen the shortest path which may lead to it.

A native of the United States clings to this world's goods as if he were certain never to die; and he is so hasty in grasping at all within his reach, that one would suppose he was constantly afraid of not living long enough to enjoy them. He clutches everything, he holds nothing fast, but soon loosens his grasp to pursue fresh gratifications.

In the United States a man builds a house to spend his latter years in it, and he sells it before the roof is on; he plants a garden, and lets it [rents] just as the trees are coming into bearing; he brings a field into tillage, and leaves other men to gather the crops; he embraces a profession, and gives it up; he settles in a place, which he soon afterward leaves, to carry his changeable longings elsewhere. If his private affairs leave him any leisure, he instantly plunges into the vortex of politics; and if at the end of a year of unremitting labor he finds he has a few days' vacation, his eager curiosity whirls him over the vast extent of the United States, and he will travel fifteen hundred miles in a few days, to shake off his happiness. Death at length overtakes him, but it is before he is weary of his bootless chase of that complete felicity which is for ever on the wing.

At first sight there is something surprising in this strange unrest of so many happy men, restless in the midst of abundance. The spectacle itself is however as old as the world; the novelty is to see a whole people furnish an exemplification of it.

. . . He who has set his heart exclusively upon the pursuit of worldly welfare is always in a hurry, for he has but a limited time at his disposal to reach it, to grasp it, and to enjoy. The recollection of the brevity of life is a constant spur to him. Besides the good things which he possesses, he every instant fancies a thousand others which death will prevent him from trying if he does not try them soon. This thought fills him with anxiety, fear, and regret, and keeps his mind in ceaseless trepidation, which leads him perpetually to change his plans and his abode.

If in addition to the taste for physical well-being a social condition be superadded, in which the laws and customs make no condition permanent, here is a great additional stimulant to this restlessness of temper. Men will then be seen continually to change their track, for fear of missing the shortest cut to happiness.

It may readily be conceived, that if men, passionately bent upon physical gratifications, desire eagerly, they are also easily discouraged: as their ultimate object is to enjoy, the means to reach that object must be prompt and easy, or the trouble of acquiring the gratification would be greater than the gratification itself. Their prevailing frame of mind then is at once ardent and relaxed, violent and enervated. Death is often less dreaded than perseverance in continuous efforts to one end.

The equality of conditions leads by a still straighter road to several of the effects which I have here described. When all the privileges of birth and fortune are abolished, when all professions are accessible to all, and a man's own energies may place him at the top of any one of them, an easy and unbounded career seems open to his ambition, and he will readily persuade himself that he is born to no vulgar destinies. But this is an erroneous notion, which is corrected by daily experience. The same equality which allows every citizen to conceive these lofty hopes, renders all the citizens less able to realize them; it circumscribes their powers on every side, while it gives freer scope to their desires. Not only are they themselves powerless, but they are met at every step by immense obstacles, which they did not at first perceive. They have swept away the privileges of some of their fellow-creatures which stood in their way; but they have opened the door to universal competition: the barrier has changed its shape rather than its position. When men are nearly alike, and all follow the same track, it is very difficult for any one individual to walk quick and cleave a way through the dense throng which surrounds and presses him. This constant strife between the propensities springing from the equality of conditions and the means it supplies to satisfy them, harasses and wearies the mind.

It is possible to conceive men arrived at a degree of freedom which should completely content them; they would then enjoy their independence without anxiety and without impatience. But men will never establish any equality with which they can be contented. . . . When inequality of conditions is the common law of society, the most marked inequalities do not strike the eye; when everything is nearly on the same level, the slightest are marked enough to hurt it. Hence the desire of equality always becomes more insatiable in proportion as equality is more complete.

Among democratic nations men easily attain a certain equality of conditions; they can never attain the equality they desire. It perpetually retires from before them, yet without hiding itself from their sight, and in retiring draws them on. At every moment they think they are about to grasp it; it escapes at every moment from their hold. They are near enough to see its charms, but too far off to enjoy them; and before they have fully tasted its delights, they die. . . .

In democratic ages enjoyments are more intense than in the ages of aristocracy, and especially the number of those who partake in them is larger. But, on the other hand, it must be admitted that man's hopes and his desires are often blasted, the soul is more stricken and perturbed, and care itself more keen.

Contemporary Statements on the Cult of Domesticity

Mrs. A. J. Graves's Advice to American Women, 1843

To woman it belongs . . . to elevate the intellectual character of her household, to kindle the fires of mental activity in childhood, and to keep these steadily burning with advancing years . . . The men of our country, as things are constituted among us, find but little time for the cultivation of science and general literature—studies so eminently calculated to refine the mind and purify the taste, and which furnish so exhaustless a fund of elevated enjoyment to the heart. And this is the case even with those who have acquired a fondness for intellectual pursuits in early life. The absorbing passion for gain, and the pressing demands of business, engross their whole attention. Thus the merchant becomes a merchant, and nothing more; and the mind of the lawyer is little else than a library of cases and precedents, of legal records and commentaries. The physician loses sight of the scientific studies to which his profession so naturally directs him, contents himself with the same beaten track, and becomes a mere practitioner or operator. And the mechanic and agriculturist too often settle down into mere manual laborers, by suffering practical details wholly to occupy their minds as well as their bodies. The only relief to this absorbing devotion to "material interests" is found in the excitement of party politics.

These two engross the whole moral, intellectual, and physical man; and, to be convinced of this, we need not follow the American to his place of business or to political meetings—we have only to listen to his fireside conversation. It might be supposed that the few waking hours he spends at home in the bosom of his family, he would delight to employ upon such subjects as would interest and improve his wife and children, and that he would avail himself of these opportunities to refresh his wearied mind with new matters of thought. But in place of this, what is the perpetual theme of his conversation? Business and politics, six per cent bank discounts, stock-jobbing, insolvencies, assets, liabilities—cases at court, legal opinions and decisions—neuralgia, gastric irritation, fevers, etc.—Clay, Webster, the Bank bill, and other political topics of the day: these are the subjects incessantly talked about by the male members of the family when at home, and which the females, of course, are neither expected to take any special interest in nor to understand. Or perhaps the wife may take her turn in relating the history of the daily vexations she experiences in her household arrangements, while the husband's eye is gazing on vacancy, or his mind is occupied by his business cares. Woman should be made to take an intelligent interest in her husband's affairs, and may be benefited by a knowledge of the value of money, its best mode of investment; or by being instructed in the laws of physiology and of hygiene; but she can receive neither pleasure nor profit from hearing the cabalistic terms familiar only to the initiated in the mysteries of financiering, or the occult words and phrases which the professional man employs to communicate his knowledge or the results of his observations. The husband should doubtless sympathize with the wife in her domestic trials; but he cannot, nor ought he to, become interested in every trivial vexation she may meet with. There should, then, be some common ground on which both may meet with equal pleasure and advantage to themselves and to their offspring; and what is there so appropriate to this end as *intellectual pursuits?*

What a certain writer has said of sons, may also be said, with equal truth, of many husbands: "they seem to consider their homes as mere places of boarding and lodging"; and, we may add, forget that it is the dwelling-place of their wives and children. So long as they provide for the physical wants of their families, they think their duty is fulfilled; as though shelter, food, and clothing could satisfy the necessities of immortal minds. They are liberal, perhaps, even to profusion, in surrounding their families with all that can minister to physical comfort, and the indulgence of vanity and pride, but they neglect to excite or to satisfy the more exalted desire for intellectual adorning and spiritual improvement. It is here our men are wanting; and female influence must supply the defect. A mother should sedulously cultivate the intellectual tastes of her children, and surround them with objects calculated to stimulate and gratify their ambition for knowledge. Her own mind should not only be richly stored with the wisdom of the past, but she should keep herself familiar with the current literature of the day, with the progress of science, and the new and useful truths it is constantly bringing to light. Out of all this fullness of knowledge she should communicate freely to her children, and labor by her conversation gently to draw her husband away from his contracted sphere of thought, to enter with her upon a more extended field of observation and reflection. She should entice him to forget his business and his politics, and to devote the few hours he spends at home to those higher pleasures of the mind, which will not only yield a delightful refreshment at the time, but enable him to return with renewed vigor to the routine of his daily labors.

Letter of Abigail May Alcott to Lucretia and Samuel May, 1833

Philadelphia, June 22[d]. 1833—

Dear Sam and Lu,

It is a good while since I wrote to you. I write but seldom to any one, excepting father; I frequently have an opportunity to send him a line and I always improve it . . . it costs me but little effort—but a full connected letter seems to me now a formidable undertaking—my eyes are very uncertain—and my time is abundantly occupied with my babies—It seems to me at times as if the weight of responsibility connected with these little immortal beings would prove too much for me—am I doing what is right? Am I doing enough? Am I not doing too much, is my earnest inquiry. I am almost at times discouraged if I find the result prove unfavorable—My Anna is just at that critical period when the diseases incident to her age makes her irritable and engrossing; and yet so intelligent as to her making inferences about everything which is done for her, or that I may mistake the motive which instigates many of her actions. Mr. A. aids me in general principles but nobody can aid me in the detail—credit is a theme of constant thought— an object of momentary solicitude—if I may neglect every thing else, I must be forgiven—I know—you laugh at me and think me a slave to my children and think me foolishly *anxious*—I can hear it all, better than one reproach of conscience, or one thoughtless word or look given to my Anna's inquiry. —

Well dear Lu. How do you like the fair sex—An't they dear little creatures? What's her name? How I should love to take my Louisa (who is all smiles and love) and stand the day with you, and tend baby. I hope dear you get sympathy and care and kindness and tender love from all about you—. These are moments when tenderness and love are our best instrument and support. I hear that John is a "noble boy" and has made a visit to Boston—can't he make a visit to Phil^d with father—I'll take the best care of him—If I talk long about you I shall cry and then good bye letter . . . Am just as tearful as ever when I think of the few dear ones left me on earth—but when I stick to my little family and my round of little duties I am brave and invincible as a lion. . . .
Abba

Impressions of the Lowell Mills, 1833, 1844, 1845

Regulations of the Appleton Company, 1833

REGULATIONS

TO BE OBSERVED BY ALL PERSONS EMPLOYED IN THE FACTORIES OF THE

APPLETON COMPANY.

The Overseers are to be punctually in their rooms at the starting of the mill, and not to be absent unnecessarily during working hours. They are to see that all those employed in their rooms are in their places in due season. They may grant leave of absence to those employed under them, when there are spare hands in the room to supply their places ; otherwise they are not to grant leave of absence, except in cases of absolute necessity.

All persons in the employ of the Appleton Company are required to observe the regulations of the overseer of the room where they are employed. They are not to be absent from their work, without his consent, except in case of sickness, and then they are to send him word of the cause of their absence.

They are to board in one of the boarding houses belonging to the Company, and conform to the regulations of the house where they board.

A regular attendance on public worship on the Sabbath is necessary for the preservation of good order. The Company will not employ any person who is habitually absent.

All persons entering into the employment of the Company are considered as engaging to work twelve months, and those who leave sooner will not receive a discharge unless they had sufficient experience when they commenced, to enable them to do full work.

All persons intending to leave the employment of the Company, are to give two weeks' notice of their intention to their overseer ; and their engagement with the Company is not considered as fulfilled, unless they comply with this regulation.

Payments will be made monthly, including board and wages, which will be made up to the last Saturday in every month, and paid in the course of the following week.

These regulations are considered part of the contract with all persons entering into the employment of the Appleton Company.

G. W. LYMAN, *Agent.*

Tompe & Press, Gorham-Street.

Museum of American Textile History.

Letters from "Susan," a Mill Worker, 1844

I went into the mill to work a few days after I wrote to you. It looked very pleasant at first, the rooms were so light, spacious, and clean, the girls so pretty and neatly dressed, and the machinery so brightly polished or nicely painted. The plants in the windows, or on the overseer's bench or desk, gave a pleasant aspect to things. You will wish to know what work I am doing. I will tell you of the different kinds of work.

There is, first, the carding-room, where the cotton flies most, and the girls get the dirtiest. But this is easy, and the females are allowed time to go out at night before the bell rings—on Saturday night at least, if not on all other nights. Then there is the spinning-room, which is very neat and pretty. In this room are the spinners and doffers. The spinners watch the frames; keep them clean, and the threads mended if they break. The doffers take off the full bobbins, and put on the empty ones. They have nothing to do in the long intervals when the frames are in motion, and can go out to their boardinghouses, or do any thing else that they like. In some of the factories the spinners do their own doffing, and when this is the case they work no harder than the weavers. These last have the hardest time of all— or can have, if they choose to take charge of three or four looms, instead of the one pair which is the allotment. And they are the most constantly confined. The spinners and dressers have but the weavers to keep supplied, and then their work can stop. The dressers never work before breakfast, and they stay out a great deal in the afternoons. The drawers-in, or girls who draw the threads through the harnesses, also work in the dressing-room, and they all have very good wages—better than the weavers who have but the usual work. The dressing-rooms are very neat, and the frames move with a gentle undulating motion which is really graceful. But these rooms are kept very warm, and are disagreeably scented with the "sizing," or starch, which stiffens the "beams," or unwoven webs. There are many plants in these rooms, and it is really a good green-house for them. The dressers are generally quite tall girls, and must have pretty tall minds too, as their work requires much care and attention.

I could have had work in the dressing-room, but chose to be a weaver; and I will tell you why. I disliked the closer air of the dressing-room, though I might have become accustomed to that. I could not learn to dress so quickly as I could to weave, nor have work of my own so soon, and should have had to stay with Mrs. C. two or three weeks before I could go in at all, and I did not like to be "lying upon my oars" so long. And, more than this, when I get well learned I can have extra work, and make double wages, which you know is quite an inducement with some.

Well, I went into the mill, and was put to learn with a very patient girl—a clever old maid. I should be willing to be one myself if I could be as good as she is. You cannot think how odd every thing seemed to me. I wanted to laugh at every thing, but did not know what to make sport of first. They set me to threading shuttles, and tying weaver's knots, and such things, and now I have improved so that I can take care of one loom. I could take care of two if I only had eyes in the back part of my head, but I have not got used to "looking two ways of a Sunday" yet.

At first the hours seemed very long, but I was so interested in learning that I endured it very well; and when I went out at night the sound of the mill was in my ears, as of crickets, frogs, and jewsharps, all mingled together in strange discord. After that it seemed as though cotton-wool was in my ears, but now I do not mind at all. You know that people learn to sleep with the thunder of Niagara in their ears, and a cotton mill is no worse, though you wonder that we do not have to hold our breath in such a noise.

It makes my feet ache and swell to stand so much, but I suppose I shall get accustomed to that too. . . . I never saw so many pretty looking girls as there are here. Though the number of men is small in proportion there are many marriages here, and a great deal of courting. I will tell you of this last sometime. . . .

You ask if the girls are contented here: I ask you, if you know of *any one* who is perfectly contented. Do you remember the old story of the philosopher, who offered a field to the person who was contented with his lot; and, when one claimed it, he asked him why, if he was so perfectly satisfied, he wanted his field. The girls here are not contented; and there is no disadvantage in their situation which they do not perceive as quickly, and lament as loudly, as the sternest opponents of the factory system do. They would scorn to say they were contented, if asked the question; for it would compromise their Yankee spirit—their pride, penetration, independence, and love of "freedom and equality" to say that they were *contented* with such a life as this. Yet, withal, they are cheerful. I never saw a happier set of beings. They appear blithe in the mill, and out of it. If you see one of them, with a very long face, you may be sure that it is because she has heard bad news from home, or because her beau has vexed her. But, if it is a Lowell trouble, it is because she has failed in getting off as many "sets" or "pieces" as she intended to have done; or because she had a sad "break-out," or "break-down," in her work, or something of that sort.

You ask if the work is not disagreeable. Not when one is accustomed to it. It tried my patience sadly at first, and does now when it does not run well; but, in general, I like it very much. It is easy to do, and does not require very violent exertion, as much of our farm work does.

A Lowell Woman Worker's Protest, 1845

. . . For the purpose of illustration, let us go with that light-hearted, joyous young girl who is about for the first time to leave the home of her childhood, that home around which clusters so many beautiful and holy associations, pleasant memories, and quiet joys; to leave, too, a mother's cheerful smile, a father's care and protection; and wend her way toward this far famed "city of spindles," this promised land of the imagination, in whose praise she has doubtless heard so much.

Let us trace her progress during her first year's residence, and see whether she indeed realizes those golden prospects which have been held out to her. Follow her now as she enters that large gloomy looking building—she is in search of employment, and has been told that she might here obtain an eligible situation. She is sadly wearied with her journey, and withal somewhat annoyed by the noise, confusion, and strange faces all around her. So, after a brief conversation with the overseer, she concludes to accept the first situation which offers; and reserving to herself a sufficient portion of time in which to obtain the necessary rest after her unwonted exertions, and the gratification of a stranger's curiosity regarding the place in which she is now to make her future home, she retires to her boarding house, to arrange matters as much to her mind as may be.

From "Voices from Lowell," 1845, in Philip Foner, ed., *The Factory Girls*, 1977, pp. 135–138 (Urbana: University of Illinois Press, 1977).

The intervening time passes rapidly away, and she soon finds herself once more within the confines of that close noisy apartment, and is forthwith installed in her new situation—first, however, premising that she has been sent to the Counting-room, and receives therefrom a Regulation paper, containing the rules by which she must be governed while in their employ; and lo! here is the beginning of mischief; for in addition to the tyrannous and oppressive rules which meet her astonished eyes, she finds herself compelled to remain for the space of twelve months in the very place she then occupies, however reasonable and just cause of complaint might be hers, or however strong the wish for dismission; thus, in fact, constituting herself a slave, a very slave to the caprices of him for whom she labors. Several incidents coming to the knowledge of the writer, might be somewhat interesting in this connection, as tending to show the prejudicial influence exerted upon the interests of the operative by this unjust requisition. The first is of a lady who has been engaged as an operative for a number of years, and recently entered a weaving room on the Massachusetts Corporation: the overseers having assured her previous to her entrance, that she should realize the sum of $2.25 per week, exclusive of board; which she finding it impossible to do, appealed to the Counting-room for a line enabling her to engage elsewhere but it was peremptorily refused. . . .

But to return to our toiling Maiden,—the next beautiful feature which she discovers in this *glorious* system is, the long number of hours which she is obliged to spend in the above named close, unwholesome apartment. It is not enough, that like the poor peasant of Ireland, or the Russian serf who labors from sun to sun, but during one half of the year, she must still continue to toil on, long after Nature's lamp has ceased to lend its aid—nor will even this suffice to satisfy the grasping avarice of her employer; for she is also through the winter months required to rise, partake of her morning meal, and be at her station in the mill, while the sun is yet sleeping behind the eastern hills; thus working on an average, at least twelve hours and three fourths per day, exclusive of the time allotted for her hasty meals, which is in winter simply one half hour at noon,—in the spring is allowed the same at morn, and during the summer is added 15 minutes to the half hour at noon. Then too, when she is at last released from her wearisome day's toil, still may she not depart in peace. No! her footsteps must be dogged to see that they do not stray beyond the corporation limits, and she *must,* whether she will or no, be subjected to the manifold inconveniences of a large crowded boarding-house, where too, the price paid for her accommodation is so utterly insignificant, that it will not ensure to her the common comforts of life; she is obliged to sleep in a small comfortless, half ventilated apartment containing some half a dozen occupants each; but no matter, *she is an operative*—it is all well enough for her; there is no "abuse" about it; no, indeed; so think our employers,—but do we think so? time will show. . . .

Reader will you pronounce this a mere fancy sketch, written for the sake of effect? It is not so. It is a real picture of "Factory life"; nor is it one half so bad as might truthfully and justly have been drawn. But it has been asked, and doubtless will be again, why, if these evils are so aggravating, have they been so long and so peacefully borne? Ah! and why have they? It is a question well worthy of our consideration, and we would call upon every operative in *our* city, aye, throughout the length and breadth of the land, to awake from the lethargy which has fallen upon them, and assert and maintain their rights. We call upon you for action—*united and immediate action*. But, says one, let us wait till we are stronger. In the language of one of old, we ask, when shall we be stronger? Will it be the next week, or the next year? Will it be when we are reduced to the service conditions of the poor operatives of England? for verily we shall be and that right soon, if matters be suffered to remain as they are. Says another, how shall we act? we are but one amongst a thousand, what shall we do that our influence may be felt in this vast multitude? We answer there is in this city an Association called the Female Labor Reform Association, having for its professed object, the amelioration of the condition of the operative. Enrolled upon its records are the names of five hundred members—come then, and add thereto five hundred or rather five thousand more, and in the strength of our united influence we will soon show these *drivelling* cotton lords, this mushroom aristocracy of New England, who so arrogantly aspire to lord it over God's heritage, that our rights cannot be trampled upon with impunity; that we will no longer submit to that arbitrary power which has for the last ten years been so abundantly exercised over us. . . .

On the Lives of Big-City Craftsmen, 1845

A British Cabinetmaker Describes His Life in New York City, 1845

I was a cabinet-maker by trade, and one of the many who, between the years 1825–35, expatriated themselves in countless thousands, drawn by the promise of fair wages for faithful work, and driven by the scanty remuneration offered to unceasing toil at home, and the overpowering pressure of the burthens imposed by the state, at a time when none of that sympathy which now occupies so large a portion of the public mind was shown to or felt for the working classes. Many an anxious look did poor parents at that day cast on the expectant faces of their little ones when seated round the table, on comparing the demand for bread with the small and uncertain supply, and with a shudder of horror half anticipated the piteous cry of hunger and misery. Work they did, work unceasingly; but apparently to no good; the wolf would never go away from the door, and was always heard scratching on the outside. . . . I had always read in books and letters on America, that work was ever abundant, and to be obtained without difficulty; but all my experience proves the contrary, at least as regards New York. At the first place I entered, the proprietor informed me that trade was "pretty well used up," and "no hands were wanted." Another gave as a reason for not requiring any addition to his number of workmen that "General Jackson had tinkered the constitution too successfully for business to be what it ought to be for a pretty considerable time." At a third place, a lad waiting in the store, in reply to my query, hailed a companion working at the back of the house, "Hiram, call the boss:" the boss came, and on repeating my inquiry, he observed, "My stock of furniture is going off, that's a fact; but I can't take hands on for want of the pewter."

It would be tedious to detail all the reasons given by the "bosses" on whom I called during my walks, which were continued unsuccessfully for a week. In only a single instance did I hear any thing like an expression of jealousy of strangers; one manufacturer remarked in an angry tone, that "the city was overcrowded with foreigners who took away work that by right belonged to the citizens." "Go west," was the general observation, "go west; the city's too full; any quantity of work out west." My means, however, did not admit of my undertaking another long journey; and on the eighth day I was fortunate enough to find employment from a master tradesman who had emigrated from England twenty years previously; he now lived in his own house, had a capital business, and was worth many thousand dollars. On telling him that I had been advised to go to the country, he said, "Don't do any such thing; if you can't get a living in New York, you can't in any part of the Union; I have tried both, and know it."

This was cheering. I went to work the next morning; and in the course of the same week had the good luck to meet with two rooms and a pantry to let, in a small farmhouse, which I hired for sixty-five dollar yearly rent. During my first day's work I found my shopmates were from many different countries; two were Americans, one Irish, one English, two Germans, and one Frenchman. On my first entrance, the foreman, an American, called out to the representative of the emerald isle, "Look here, Paddy; here's another Johnny Bull come over to be civilized." John Bull, however, can afford to be laughed at. After we became acquainted we went on very pleasantly together: the superior skill of the Germans and Frenchman was of the highest service to me, who had much to learn, never having worked but in a provincial town in England; and as the Frenchman could not speak a word of English, and worked at the next bench to mine, my French studies were materially benefited by the conversations I had with him, and the more so as he was a remarkably intelligent workman. . . .

The markets of New York teem with a rich supply of vegetables and fruits in the fine season: the duty of going to market is not confined exclusively to females; most of it is done by the men. I have often started for the market as early as five o'clock in the morning, in order to be ready for work at six, as well as to take advantage of the cool hours for the buying of meat, which in the hot months must be cooked soon after it is killed, to prevent putrefaction. What a tempting sight to an Englishman is the display of pine-apples, melons, peaches, and profusion of tropical fruits! I have frequently bought a large and juicy melon for three cents, and a peck of the most delicious peaches for ten cents, whose flavour, ripened by the glowing sun of an American sky, far exceeds all that I have ever tasted in this country. He only who has panted under that sultry sky can have any adequate conception of the luxury and enjoyment of cutting open a rich cool melon, and suffering its pulpy substance to dissolve in the mouth. It is then we gratefully feel how bountifully Nature compensates for all her apparent annoyances and inconveniences.

To one who has been accustomed to see meat sold, as in England, by ounces—to weigh the loaf against the appetite—the abundance and cheapness of an American market are very gratifying. Instead of buying a chop, wherewith to flavour a large mass of potatoes, he will carry home a quarter of a sheep or a lamb, or a solid rib of beef, with as many vegetables as he can well stagger under, pleased with the anticipation that the tender frames of his little growing family will receive due development under the generous nourishment. In such a case there is no stint; no uneasy thoughts about the coming day's supply; no impending dread of hungry looks or hungry stomachs among those who claim his best affections. This, I have often thought, is the chief cause of the firmer tone and manner which soon becomes apparent in the person of newly-arrived emigrants: shadowed forth in glowing colours in the letters which they write to their friends at home. Unfortunately it too often ends here:—the physical is fostered, but the moral is neglected. . . .

These prices are, however, subject to great fluctuations: the severe winters cause a general rise in all kinds of vegetable produce; at such times twelve or eighteen cents will be charged for a cabbage; from the month of January to May, the scarcity of green food is universal. The price of bread also is not less uncertain: I have often paid six cents for a loaf, which a few weeks earlier in the season would not have cost more than half that sum. For more than half of the five years that we lived in New York, the prices of provisions were, with very slender exceptions, as high as those in the large towns of [England]. . . .

On landing in New York I made up my mind to lose none of the advantages it offered by want of diligence on my part. During the first two years I took but one holiday, and that was passed in company with a French shopmate, in a glorious stroll on the wave-beaten sands, and among the breezy woods of Staten Island. In summer we began work at six; at eight took half an hour for breakfast, and then worked till twelve, when came an hour for dinner; after which we kept on till six, seven, or eight, as we pleased, deferring our third meal until the close of our daily labour. In the winter we took breakfast before daylight, so as to arrive at the workshop by the time that we could see to work, thereby gaining time, and saving ourselves a walk in unpleasant weather. On leaving at eight in the evening, I carried with me a portion of my tools, and set myself to make up such articles of furniture as we most needed; and frequently have I found myself still busy, impatient for the completion of the object that would afford us at once convenience and ornament, at the striking of the "wee short hour ayont the twal." At other times, after laying down my load of tools, I would find it difficult to resist the feeling of weariness induced by eleven hours of previous labour, and sinking instinctively into a chair, take up a book, and soon forget my mechanical duties. It will show how far I was possessed by the utilitarian feeling that, on such occasions, I thought on going to bed that I had lost an evening. I did not then know that this was one of the methods made use of by nature for restoring her balance, compensating for the tension of muscular exertion.

It took another form in the workshop: there it frequently happened about the middle of the afternoon of some sultry summer's day, or of a stormy day in winter, after several weeks of real hard work unrelieved by any change, that a simultaneous cessation from work took place, no one could tell why, though no surprise was manifested that, in the one case, we placed ourselves near an open window, or in the other that we drew round the stove. Then, as it were by tacit agreement, every hand held out its contribution of "loose change;" the apprentice was sent on his errand, and speedily returned laden with wine, brandy, biscuits, and cheese. The appropriation of these refreshments was sure to call forth songs from those who felt musical; after which came a proposition for a further supply, which provoked a more noisy vocalization, while the conversation which had been animated became excited. With a third instalment we concluded the day, and went home half in wonder at our folly, half vexed at our loss of time, feelings which the dizziness of our heads and the uneasiness of our limbs rendered more acute the next day. . . .

In the summer of 1836, when the inflated state of commerce and speculation had reached its height, when prices and rents were increasing in a like proportion, a strike took place among the cabinet-makers. They were dissatisfied with the wages then paid for their labour; and having compiled a new price-book as the basis of their claims, they held meetings; appointed committees; and on a given day, with very few exceptions, ceased working in all the shops of the city. The Americans of our workshop were among the noisiest of the strike, and naturally expected that I should join them; but to this, for several reasons, I was disinclined. First, I considered that I was receiving quite as high wages as my manual skill deserved; next, I felt disposed to attach more importance to the claims of my family than to the ill-considered demands of a body of men, of which the greater part were but the stepping-stones for a few selfish individuals; and last, my "turning out" would have been but an ill return for the kindness of my employer, who had given me work in the anxious time immediately following our arrival, and befriended me in various ways afterwards. Two or three deputations were sent to argue with me on the subject; in vain I expressed my belief that the unsatisfactory rate of wages was rather to be attributed to the unprecedented influx of workmen from abroad, than to any other circumstance; they silenced, without convincing me; and finding me firm, they resorted to threats, and promised to waylay and "hammer" me on my way home from work, and concluded their arguments with a highflown and frothy exposition of the rights of man—of the bounden duty of the minority to yield to whatever the majority may enact. Threats succeeded no better than arguments; I kept on working during the whole of the strike, and in the six weeks that it lasted earned forty-eight dollars; while the others, although in a few instances they obtained a rise, were, at the end of a month after, working at the old wages, having lost nearly half of the best season, and in many cases were supplanted by other artisans which the continued tide of emigration poured into the city. A year or two afterwards I accidentally met one of the members of the deputations, who, recognising me, stopped for a few minutes to speak of his recollections of the event, and added, with a laugh, "You were the toughest customer we had; but I guess it would have been better for us had we all done as you did."

A Newspaper Exposé of Labor in New York, 1845

THE CABINET-MAKERS

A great falling off in the earnings of Cabinet-Makers has taken place during the last ten years. In 1836 an average hand could make by the piece from $12 to $15 per week, and the pay to those who worked by the week was about the same. In 1840 wages fell to about $8 per week, and now probably a majority of the Journeymen in this Trade do not make more than $5 per week. Smart hands who work in establishments where the very best kind of work is turned out are paid $8.

The cause of the great decrease in the wages of Cabinet-Makers is in a great measure the immense amount of poor Furniture manufactured for the Auction-Stores. This is mostly made by Germans, who work rapidly, badly and for almost nothing. There are persons who are constantly on the watch for German emigrants who can work at Cabinet-Making—going on board the ships before the emigrants have landed and engaging them for *a year* at $20 or $30 and their board, or on the best terms they can make. The emigrants of course know nothing of the state of the Trade, prices, regulations, &c. &c. and become willing victims to any one who offers them immediate and permanent employment. This it is which has ruined the Cabinet-Making business, and the complaints on the part of the Journeymen are incessant. There is, however, no remedy for the evil, as we see. So pervading is the idea among the great purchasing classes, the housekeepers, that it must of course be good economy to buy *cheap* things, that good work and good prices must of necessity go a-begging.

Thomas Skidmore on the Rights of Man to Property, 1829

. . . One thing must be obvious to the plainest understanding; that as long as property is unequal; or rather, as long as it is so enormously unequal, as we see it at present, that those who possess it, *will* live on the labor of others, and themselves perform none, or if any, a very disproportionate share, of that toil which attends them as a condition of their existence, and without the performance of which, they have no *just* right to preserve or retain that existence, even for a single hour.

It is not possible to maintain a doctrine to the contrary of this position, without, at the same time, maintaining an absurdity no longer tolerated in enlightened countries; that a part, and that a very great part, of the human race, are doomed, of right, to the slavery of toil, while others are born, only to enjoy.

I, for one, disavow every such doctrine. . . .

We live near to a great epoch, in the history of our own country—the Revolution that separated us from England—we are acquainted with the distinguished men, who performed a prominent part, as well in the separation of the two countries, as in erecting the new governments that succeeded. We are able to know their minds, and to judge for ourselves, how far they were adequate to institute government, on principles of original right; for it was on such principles *as they understood them,* that they supported the Revolution and erected the political edifices that in consequence became necessary.

Of all these, no man, more than Mr. Jefferson, deserves to be considered, as possessing in his own mind, not only "the standard of the man," but the standard of the age. If there was any one capable of ascending to first principles, it was he; and if it was not to be expected of him, how was it to be expected of any one else? Yet Mr. Jefferson speaks of the rights of man, in terms, which when they come to be investigated closely, appear to be very defective and equivocal. I do not mean, that he thought or meant them so; for it is evident that the contrary was the fact. Let us quote him, however; let us weigh his expressions; let us arrive at his intentions in the most legitimate manner: and then see, if I am borne out, in my declaration. If I am, I shall be sustained. If I am not, I shall fail, and deserve to do so. He says:—

"We hold these truths to be self-evident; that all men are created equal; that they are endowed by their Creator with certain unalienable rights; that among these are life, liberty, and the *pursuit of happiness.*" These are his words in the declaration of American Independence.

Whoever looks over the face of the world, and surveys the population of all countries; our own, as well as any and every other; will see it divided into rich and poor; into the hundred who have every thing, and the million who have nothing. If, then, Mr. Jefferson, had made use of the word *property,* instead of *"the pursuit of happiness,"* I would have agreed with him. Then his language would have been clear and intelligible, and strictly conformable to natural right. For I hold, that man's natural right to *life* or *liberty,* is not more sacred or unalienable, than his right to property. But if property is to descend only to particular individuals from the previous generation, and if the many are born, having neither parents nor any one else, to give them property, equal in amount to that which the sons of the rich receive from their fathers and other testators, how is it established that they are created equal? In the pursuit of happiness, is property of no consequence? Can any one be as happy without property of any kind, as with it? Is even liberty and life to be preserved without it? Do we not every day, see multitudes, in order to acquire property in the very pursuit of that happiness which Mr. Jefferson classes among the unalienable rights of man, obliged to sacrifice both liberty and health and often ultimately life, into the bargain? If then property be so essential and indispensable in the pursuit of happiness, as it appears to be, how can it be said, that I am created with an equal right to this happiness—with another, when I must purchase property of him, with labor and suffering—and when he is under no necessity to purchase the like of me at the same costly price? If we are created equal—how has he the right to monopolize all, or even an undue share of the property of the preceding generation? If, then, even the rights of liberty and life, are so insecure and precarious, without property—how very essential to *their* preservation is it, that "the pursuit of happiness"—should be so construed, as to afford title to that, without which, the rights of life and liberty are but an empty name? . . .

Mankind have enquired *too little* after their rights, their interests, and their happiness. If it had not been so, such enormities could not have been allowed to take place, daily and forever before our eyes, without having been remedied. They could not have been plunged into such deep distress and degradation as we now see them. The high and the lofty, those who have become so, from the inevitable operation of causes, which they did not bring into being; and which neither they have had, nor could have had the power to control; would have been tumbled from their elevations, and seated on a level with their fellow-beings. Then would they have enjoyed their equal chance of acquiring property; for then, would they have had only their equal share of it, to begin with; and with this, they could have had only their proper opportunity to employ their industry and talents; others would have been in the same enviable situation; and no one would then be found, in such necessitous condition, that he must work or die; and work, too *on such terms, that a very great share of the value of his labor must go to the employer,* or to him, who, no matter how, affords the means of employment!

It is not long since a member of the Common Council of this city, I do not now recollect his name, and on some occasion of which I do not re-member exactly the nature, indulged in a strain of feeling and invective against the poor, [and] . . . launched out into some intemperate expressions against those, whose lot, as society is now modelled, it is to perform THE LABOR THAT SUPPORTS US ALL; such as this, "that he who would not work *ought* to starve." There is no occasion to question the general truth of the observation; but the barbarous *feeling* with which, it struck me, it was uttered, could not fail to raise my indignation. I could not but resent it in the name of my fellow-beings, as an insult to that class who now perform all the work that is done in our support, as well of the honorable member, as of all others, implying an unwillingness to work, which there is no kind of propriety in laying to their charge. But it implied also more. It implied, that *it is right enough* for a certain description of men, among us, to live without labor of their own; while others are called upon to labor, not only enough to support themselves, but to support also, these DRONES in the hive into the bargain. . . . Why is it, that men, at our Hall, or elsewhere, should not be called upon to perform the labor that supports them, as well as other men? If a man will not work, why should he not starve? This is a question which may well be asked, if it is intended to mean, that *all* men, shall be called upon to work alike; and to depend solely upon the labor of their own hands, and draw nothing from the labor of others, but what they are willing to pay for with an equal return in labor of their own hands, I agree to it. . . . Is it not quite as reasonable for a poor man to eat a good dinner, without having labored to earn it, as for a rich man to do it? Is there a difference in rights? Is there one sort of rights for one class of men, and another for another? May one do lawfully what the other will do criminally; have we two codes of law among us? Have we a law for the Lilliputians and another for the Brobdingnaggians? We have been told, in the Declaration of Independence, that "all men are created equal"; but if one man must work for his dinner, and another need not, and does not, how are we equal? If the gentleman shall say, the rich man has property, and the poor man has not; then the question is only changed for another; what is his *right* to such property? . . .

Under the present unequal distribution of property, where labor is the sole resource the poor have, by which to maintain their existence, degraded as it is, by the slavery in which they are plunged, it is not wonderful that they have been found to be opposed to the introduction of improvements. Fruitless and unavailing as such opposition is, it is yet less unreasonable than at first sight it may appear to be. It is true, that one consequence of such improvement, as we have already shown, is, that a poor man even, may obtain 4,800 times as much as he could obtain without it; yet, it may be asked, may he not be an ultimate loser? May not improvement extend to such a degree, that there will be no demand for his labor? Or if it does not reach this point, will it not approach so near it, as to make him an extreme sufferer? . . .

The Steam-Engine is not injurious to the poor, when they can have the benefit of it; and this, on supposition, being *always* the case, instead of being looked upon, as a curse, would be hailed as a blessing. If, then, it is seen that the Steam-Engine, for example, is likely to greatly impoverish, or destroy the poor, what *have* they to do, but TO LAY HOLD OF IT, AND MAKE IT THEIR OWN? LET THEM APPROPRIATE ALSO, in the same way, THE COTTON FACTORIES, THE WOOLEN FACTORIES, THE IRON FOUNDERIES, THE ROLLING MILLS, HOUSES, CHURCHES, SHIPS, GOODS, STEAM-BOATS, FIELDS OF AGRICULTURE, &c. &c. &c. in manner as proposed in this work, AND AS IS THEIR RIGHT; and they will never have occasion any more to consider that as an evil which never deserved that character; which, on the contrary, is all that is good among men; and of which, we cannot, under these new circumstances, have too much. It is an equal division of property that MAKES ALL RIGHT, and an equal transmission of it to posterity, KEEPS IT SO.

Reverend Alonzo Potter Defends Wage Labor, 1841

[T]he chief motive to labour, freely exercised, must be the result accruing to the labourer. This is technically called his *wages*. And, since the more productive labour is rendered by machinery, by subdivision of employments, and facilitation of exchanges, the greater must be the aggregate quantity of the good things of life produced, it seems self-evident that the share falling to the lot of each individual labourer, as his recompense or wages, *ought* to be proportionately augmented. And such doubtless would be the case were the labourer, his employer, and other joint partners in the work of production left free to apportion among themselves their respective shares, untrammelled on the one hand by unwise laws, and on the other by unfair combinations; it being supposed, of course, that each party is honest and moderately intelligent. The great principles, in short, of *free labour, and free disposal of its produce,* would seem, in such case, amply sufficient to secure an equitable distribution of property among the several classes who contribute to its creation; and the benefits they thence derive would so stimulate their exertions as to cause a continued increase, not merely in the wealth of the society, but also in the share of that wealth falling to the lot of any individual member. . . .

[U]nder a system of free and equitable exchange, the recompense (wages) of every labourer will be by no means equal, nor even exactly proportioned to the severity or duration of his employment. It must be determined by the *value* of his produce in the market. And this will increase in proportion to the talent, skill, and application of the labourer, or any other circumstances which may render his labour more *productive* than that of another. A man whose natural powers of body or mind enable him to contribute more efficiently to the general work of production than another, may equitably expect, and will, under the system of free exchange, receive a larger share of the gross general produce. The same is true of one who, by advantages of education or continued application, has acquired a superior degree of skill or knowledge in any of the arts of industry, and of one, too, whose reputation for integrity and vigilance in his employer's service secures him peculiar confidence. The increased reward thus obtained by increased productiveness is the motive and necessary stimulus to most of those efforts for rendering labour more productive, which have carried mankind forward from the savage to the civilized state, and must be depended upon for inciting him to yet farther advances. Every attempt to equalize the wages of different employments or individuals by compulsory arrangements has the certain effect of damping the ardour of industry, putting a stop to improvement, and thus checking the march of production. . . .

All this seems so obvious to the most ordinary capacity as hardly to be worth dwelling upon. And yet there are persons who still—in the present light of civilization, in the nineteenth century, and in the midst of all the evidence which is afforded, wherever we turn our eyes, of the prodigious part which capital is playing in the production of the necessaries, comforts, and luxuries of human life—declaim against capital as the poison of society, and the taking of interest on capital by its owners as an abuse, an injustice, a robbery of the class of labourers! Such blindness is to me truly unaccountable. That those who observe the prevalence of great misery among the inferior classes of workmen in some wealthy countries—who witness and deplore the fact, that, in spite of all the manifold improvements which are continually adding to the productiveness of labour, the share of the gross production which falls to the common labourer does not increase, perhaps even diminishes—that, on viewing this anomaly, they should conclude *something* to be wrong, is no source of astonishment to me, for I arrive at the same necessary conclusion from the same observation. But that any sane person should attribute the evil to *the existence of capital*—that is, to the employment of wealth in aiding the production of farther wealth, instead of being unproductively consumed, almost, if not quite, as fast as it is created, or unproductively hoarded to satisfy the lust of the miser—is indeed wonderful. Why, without capital, the Island of Great Britain would not afford subsistence to a hundredth part of its present population. Destroy the *security* for the free enjoyment or disposal of capital, deny its owner the privilege of accepting what any one may find it for his advantage to give for its use, and every individual will soon be reduced to his unaided resources. He will find nowhere any store of food on which to live while he is digging, and sowing, and protecting his immature crop; no stock of tools with which to work, or of clothes and other necessaries of existence. All trades would stop at once, for every trade is carried on by means of capital. Men would at once be reduced to the isolation and helplessness of barbarism.

But perhaps it is in the imagination of these schemers that there should not be a general destruction, but only *a general division,* of the capital now existing among the present race of labourers; so that each, it is thought, would for some time, at least, be provided with a stock of food, clothes, and tools, with which to continue the business of production. We suppose something like this is contemplated. But, putting out of sight the injustice, confusion, and attendant horrors of the frightful scramble which is here disguised under the smooth name of a general division of property (a scramble which, in the extremely complicated and artificial state of society characterizing a country like ours, must be attended with infinitely more violence, convulsion, and disturbance than any political catastrophe on record), how, we must beg to ask, is production to go on afterward? In a very short time, a large part of the population—*all the idle*—and in such a crisis there can be but little industry—will have consumed their share of the plunder in riot and excess. Admitting that others have gone to work industriously in the production of the things they require, each for himself; have ploughed and sown, and spun and wove; have stored corn in their granaries, and cattle in their homesteads, and fuel, and clothing, and comforts of various kinds in their lofts, and cellars, and warehouses, what is to become of all that large body who, having squandered away their share of the general booty, will have left no means of maintenance? It is clear that one of two things must occur. Either they will, if sufficiently numerous and strong, call for *another division of property,* that is, *once more* plunder the barns, granaries, homesteads, and warehouses of the industrious; or, if they are not strong enough to attempt this, they will humble themselves to the owners of these same barns and warehouses, and petition for food and clothing in return for all they have to offer, *their labour;* that is to say, they will apply to them for *employment and wages.* If the owners of property refuse their petition, starvation and disease must rapidly carry them off; not, however, before they have robbed, and plundered, and done all the injury to the remainder of society which their despair and destitution will prompt. If their request *is* acceded to, the old system of masters and men, *capitalists and labourers,* will recommence; and the society—at least whatever portion of it we can suppose to have survived the shock of such a convulsion—will be reconstituted on its old and natural principles, to recommence the difficult march of improvement, and with the feeble hope of regaining, after the lapse of years, perhaps of ages, the elevated position we are at present so fortunate as to occupy, as yet unscathed; to reproduce slowly and painfully the vast stock of accumulated capital which it once possessed, but which, in a fit of popular insanity, had been broken down and scattered to the winds.

The security of property, and the liberty of consuming or employing it in whatever way the owner pleases or finds most for his interest, is, as has been truly observed, the first of the *rights of industry,* and the essential condition of its progressive activity. But of all modes of employing property, the very last which it would occur to an enlightened friend of humanity to obstruct, is its employment *in aiding production*—that is, as *capital.* It is quite clear that the profit or interest to be gained by the employment of capital is the principal motive to its accumulation, and the *only* one to its employment in furthering production. It is quite clear that, if the owner of capital is not allowed to make what profit he can upon it by lending it to others, no one will accumulate more capital than he can use himself; and nearly all savings would thenceforward be hoarded in cellars and closets, instead of aiding industry and facilitating production.

⌗ *E S S A Y S*

Stuart Bruchey, an economic historian at Columbia University, has long been interested in entrepreneurship and the roots of U.S. economic growth. His survey of early industrialization in the first essay touches on the hardships that accompanied the expansion of manufacturing, but concludes that class divisions and identities did not run very far or deep. In the second essay, a study of Thomas Skidmore's New York, the historian Sean Wilentz of Princeton University reaches different conclusions, at least concerning the metropolitan working class, in part because of the conditions that arose in that city's mammoth sweated trades. Significantly, by midcentury almost all the workers in these New York trades were immigrants, and upwards of half in the clothing trades were women—the main focus of the final selection. Christine Stansell, a professor of history at Princeton University, looks at the New York scene from the sidewalks of the Bowery and identifies crucial ambiguities in the lives of the city's young women workers—complicating and enriching our understanding of class, culture, and northern capitalism.

*The Early American Industrial Revolution

STUART BRUCHEY

. . . [T]he thirty-year period 1785–1815 witnessed the first advance of the Industrial Revolution in America, but in any comparative sense it was feeble and unenduring.

The 1820s begin the telling of a different story, one whose principal theme—gradually accelerating industrialization—continues to develop in all the subsequent decades before the Civil War. Let us begin with the reminder that families almost everywhere, from early on in the colonial period, had made in their own homes, and for their own use rather than for sale, a wide variety of products, including soap and candles, leather and maple sugar, and especially wearing apparel. Indeed, as late as 1820 an estimated two-thirds of the clothing worn in the United States were products of household manufacture. Commercial sources of goods and services also existed. Particularly in the more populous East, household manufacturing was supplemented by the labors of craftsmen such as cobblers, blacksmiths, curriers, coopers, hatters, tailors, and weavers working in their little shops, often in their own homes, making hats, shoes, clothing, and other goods to order. In addition, gristmills, sawmills, and other neighborhood industries such as ironworks, paper mills, wool carding and fulling mills, potash plants, breweries, tanneries, and brickyards continued to be commonplace, especially in older, more settled communities. This "household-handicraft-mill complex" accounted for a large portion of American manufacturing at the end of the War of 1812. In frontier areas, and in communities lacking in improved transportation facilities, the complex continued to be visible deep into the nineteenth century, with mills and furnaces producing largely for local or nearby consumption. Elsewhere it began to break up, most markedly wherever canals, steamboats, or railroads made easily available the products of domestic or foreign factories. Household manufacturing appears to have reached a peak about 1815, after which decline was so rapid that the transfer from homemade to shop- and factory-made goods was generally complete before 1830.

In contrast to this decline, especially pronounced in the 1820s, a number of leading manufacturing industries grew at decade rates far exceeding the 35 percent increase in population. The cotton textile industry was one of the most important. In 1807 the fifteen or twenty mills in existence employed a total of approximately 8,000 spindles. By 1811, according to Albert Gallatin's report to Congress of the preceding year, an estimated eighty-seven firms were expected to have ten times this number of spindles in operation. By 1820 the spindle total had risen from 80,000 to 191,000. These increases pale before those of the 1820s: in 1831 spindles in use numbered nearly 1.25 million. Cotton textiles had become a very substantial industry. In New England alone the output of cotton cloth is estimated to have risen from less than 4 million yards in 1817 to 323 million in 1840. During the same years, textile prices fell substantially more than those of other commodities— that of ordinary sheeting, for example, falling to about one-fourth its former level. A combination of factors led to the price declines: better textile machinery (which cut wage costs), a fall in the price of raw cotton, and growth in the number of skilled technicians.

These developments not only go far to explain the decline of household manufacturing, the rapid substitution of store-bought fabrics for homespun, they also help to explain why daughters of farming families, deprived of their former domestic occupation, were receptive to efforts made by textile manufacturers to recruit them.

As in cotton textiles, so also in the production of woolen goods, carpets, paper, flint glass, lead, sugar and molasses, salt, iron, and steam engines. Factory consumption of wool rose from 400,000 pounds in 1810 to 15 million in 1830, with fully half the increase occurring between 1816 and 1830. Carpet production grew from an output of 9,984 yards in 1810 to 1,147,500 in 1834, with most of the increase occurring during a four- or five-year period beginning in 1827. Production of the steam engine, first manufactured in the United States in 1805, was stimulated especially after 1815 by the development of steamboats. During the 1820s, 359 engines were required for this purpose alone. In 1830 Pittsburgh produced 100 engines, and Cincinnati 150.

Had engines destined for steamboats plying the western rivers been manufactured in the East and then shipped west, shipping costs would obviously have been prohibitive. They are exceptions to the rule that most manufactured goods were made in the East, an area embracing New England and the Middle Atlantic states, extending from Maine to Maryland and west to the Appalachian Mountains. Not only did supply originate mainly in the East: so too did demand. Indeed, the region created its own demand. Precisely because it allocated increasing proportions of its resources to manufacturing, finance, and commerce—in contrast to the West and South, which devoted most of their resources to the production of agricultural goods— per capita income growth in the East was the highest in the nation, specifically, 25 percent higher in 1840. Most of the trade in the manufactured products of the East was therefore an intraregional trade. Foreign markets and those of other American regions took only limited quantities, the North-South trade, for example, being estimated at between 20 and 25 percent of northern manufacturing output in 1840.

The techniques by which these goods were produced varied in part with the kind of product involved and the locus of manufacturing, but in general three methods were employed: enlarged shop or handicraft production, the domestic or putting-out system, and the factory system. The financial resources and managerial expertise of wholesale merchants were often crucial to the first two. As in colonial years, a master craftsman continued to direct the work of journeymen and apprentices in his shop, but the numbers of those workers increased in consonance with rising demand. Instead of making goods on order for local customers, he sold his output to a wholesale merchant for distribution in more distant markets. The putting-out system was largely confined to the production of shoes, textiles, and wearing apparel, with the merchant supplying leather, for example, to men who worked in their own homes and with their own tools. As the volume of demand continued to mount, these dispersed workers were often gathered into a central shop, where tasks were carefully differentiated and production was supervised.

In the boot and shoe industry in Massachusetts, for example, workmen in central shops specialized in tasks such as the cutting of leather and the lining or stitching and binding of uppers, lasting, and soling, all manual operations in which they employed their own tools. With the introduction of mechanical devices for cutting and rolling leather, and then of pegging machines and sewing machines between 1840 and 1860, machinery displaced these tools. Power to drive the machines, however, began to be utilized only after the outbreak of the Civil War. It is the use of power, together with the performance of all tasks of production under the same roof, so to speak— rather than partially in the central shop and partially elsewhere—that defines the factory.

Factories made their first appearance in the textile industries, a development favored by the circumstance that much of the largest segment of American demand was for uniform coarse fabrics that were more dependent on machinery, and hence on centralized production, than fine goods requiring the skills of the artisan. Cotton textiles showed the way—the Boston Manufacturing Company erected the first modern factory at Waltham, Massachusetts, in 1813—and almost immediately displaced what had been the leading homespun occupation of the colonies, namely, the making of linen cloth. Unlike flax, wool met no similar rivalry from competing fibers, and although carding mills sustained homespun and household industries longer than in the case of cotton, the largest textile factories in America before 1860 made woolen goods. Except for carpet manufacturing, which grew rapidly in the 1820s, and the anthracite furnaces and rolling mills of eastern Pennsylvania and western New Jersey, which were rapidly becoming major factory operations by the later 1840s, factory organization appears to have made its way gradually into the structure of industry. . . . By 1860 the factory system was "rapidly becoming important in practically every industrial field and the stage was set for its phenomenal development in postwar years."

Factories, mills devoted (usually) to a single process, and the putting-out system together wrought an enormous increase in the volume of manufactured goods. According to a recent estimate, between the years 1809 and 1839 manufacturing output climbed an average of 59 percent per decade, soaring by 153 percent in the 1840s before settling back to a more modest 60 percent in the 1850s. By 1860 the American manufacturing sector ranked second or third among the nations of the world.

A fundamental part of any explanation of the advance of industry during these years was the relative scarcity of labor in the United States. Although both capital and labor were in shorter supply in the United States than in Great Britain—and this was especially true of unskilled labor—labor was the scarcer factor of production, particularly from about the mid-1830s. Its relative dearness gave manufacturers an economic incentive to save on that factor by investing in capital-using innovations, the more so because skilled machinery makers were more plentifully available. Although heavy machinery tools were imported from England, skilled American labor built the machinery used in most industries and adapted it to specialized needs as well.

In the textile industry, for example, the largest New England firms constructed the first machine shops in the United States in order to supply their own requirements. The more manufacturers sought to mechanize, however, the wider the market for machines. The textile machine shops responded at first by making machines for other industries as well as their own. They then split off from their parent firms and became independent, after about 1840 becoming highly specialized in response to mounting demand. By the 1850s visiting English technicians could observe that "in the adaptation of special apparatus to a single operation in almost all branches of industry, the Americans display an amount of ingenuity, combined with undaunted energy, which as a nation we should do well to imitate."

They had begun to display that ingenuity in the manufacture of textiles as early as the decade 1814–1824. By 1818 the chief mechanic of the Boston Manufacturing Company, Paul Moody, had developed warping and dressing machines and had modified the spinning frame to enable it to spin filling yarn directly onto bobbins for use in the subsequent weaving process. Other important American adaptations and inventions were the ring spindle, the Goulding automatic roving machine, the self-acting temple, and various self-stopping devices in case of breakage. The mechanization of weaving proceeded rapidly after Francis Cabot Lowell designed his power loom in 1813. The power loom was then soon adapted to the weaving of woolens and worsteds, industries in which Americans also made important advances in carding and in the finishing processes.

In sum, Americans radically improved many of the processes involved in the manufacture of textiles. But their ingenuity was by no means confined to that industry. Viewing the progress of technology throughout the economy generally, the commissioner of patents observed in 1843, "The advancement of the arts, from year to year, taxes our credulity, and seems to presage the arrival of that period when human improvement must end." Although the number of patents issued each year has many faults as a statistical series, it is not without interest that the average annual number increases from 535 between 1820 and 1830, to 646 between 1841 and 1850, and to 2,525 the following decade. . . .

The amount of urban growth during these decades is impressive. Despite a tripling of the land area between 1790 and 1860, population grew even more rapidly and increased in density from 4.5 to 10.6 per square mile. Urbanization accounts for a major part of this growth, and while the share of the population living in cities (defined by the census as consisting of 2,500 or more people) grew in every decade from 1790 save one, 1810–1820, it was not till the 1820s, the decade of rapid manufacturing development, that sustained growth commenced. All the eastern states experienced "urban take-offs" in the 1820s, reaching peak acceleration rates in the 1840s and 1850s.

Much of this growth had its source in manufacturing development. In the first place, the great eastern ports continued to expand as they attracted manufacturing because of their "large markets, ample supplies of labor, raw and semi-manufactured material inputs, access to low-cost transport whether by natural water, canal, or railroad and with their efficient commercial and financial sectors." Philadelphia, for example, had owed most of its colonial development to its shipping and commerce, but in the early nineteenth century the city's foreign trade deteriorated. Growth thereafter came "primarily from the expansion and transformation of its manufacturing sector."

Long distinguished for the variety and excellence of its handicrafts, the city once again prospered with the expansion of the textile, machinery, metal, chemical, and drug industries.

The founding of new towns served as the second way in which manufacturing contributed to urban growth. The mushroom growth of many of these towns, such as Lowell, which was transformed in a few years from a farming district to a city of 20,000 people and then went on to become the largest of the mill towns of the antebellum years and the nation's leading center of textile production, can only be called astonishing. Lawrence, Massachusetts, founded in 1845, had a population of 17,639 only fifteen years later. Manchester, New Hampshire, went from 3,235 in 1840 to 20,107 in 1860. New Bedford, Massachusetts, whose population was 4,361 in 1800 and only 12,087 forty years later, rose to 22,300 in the next twenty years as textile manufacturing there began an expansion that was destined to be sensational following the Civil War. Newburyport, Massachusetts, a seaport city in decline, possessing fewer people in 1840 than it had boasted thirty years before, doubled its population because of textile manufacturing between 1840 and 1860.

As early as 1820, two-thirds of Philadelphia's labor force was engaged in manufactures and trades. Even in the adjacent counties of the eastern hinterland one worker in five was so employed. Fortunately, the new mills and factories that undermined the primary economic activities of farmers' daughters—the spinning of yarn and weaving of cloth at home—also offered employment opportunities which many found impossible to resist. The consequence was a mass movement of women into the early mills. By 1860 the cotton textile industry in New England alone employed more than sixty thousand women.

Studies of the origins and composition of the labor force in the Lowell mills shows conclusively that sheer economic need did not drive these young women to work, at least not the needs of their families. Rather, they wished to earn wages in order to provide for a dowry, buy clothes, further their education, or achieve other personal objectives. Their earnings in the mid-1830s amounted merely to about $3.25 for a seventy-three-hour work week, but room and board in company boarding houses cost only $1.25, leaving them a surplus of about $2.00 a week. These wages compare favorably with earnings in domestic service, teaching, and sewing, three of the main alternative occupations open to women in these years. Men fared better: their daily earnings were more than twice those paid to women. Unlike males, whose wages reflected the going rate in New England for each trade or skill group, piece rates offered females were not subject to market constraint. Since no well-developed market for female industrial workers existed, at least in the earlier years, the lower limit of female wages had to be set just high enough to attract young women from farms and away from such competing female employments as household manufacturing and domestic service. All the supervisory positions in the Lowell mills, it should be added, were reserved for men.

Reductions in wage rates, lengthening of the workday, or resort to the "speed-up" and "stretch-out" (respectively, increasing the operating speed of machinery and assigning additional machines to be tended by each operative) provoked sporadic strikes by female operatives in the 1820s and 1830s before giving way in the next decade to a more coordinated and organized form of struggle—the Ten Hour movement. Occasionally the struggles resulted in some gains for women, but in the long run protests failed to halt the deterioration of earlier standards. Then, with the arrival in Boston of tens of thousands of Irish immigrants and a stepped-up inflow from Quebec, the visible protests ceased. In dire economic need as they often were, the Irish were in no position to complain about wage reductions or the increasing pace of work. And the mills offered steady and relatively well-paid jobs, certainly in comparison with domestic service or outdoor labor. In consequence, although the textile corporations took advantage of the opportunity to reduce piece rates and increase the pace of work for immigrant and native alike, the 1850s stand out as a period of industrial peace. Yet, if the great availability of immigrants was to pave the way for more onerous conditions of work, immigrant women were soon to benefit from a change in the composition of the workforce. The departure of native women in large numbers enabled the immigrants to move up to higher-paying jobs in the weaving and dressing rooms.

Female operatives in Massachusetts were by no means alone in protesting the often harsh working conditions attending industrialization. The 1830s were a decade of deep unrest in the ranks of American labor, and many labor organizations rose to protest some of the consequences of the transformation of an older system of production based on close relationships between master craftsmen, journeymen, and apprentices. Now that the urban craft shops had lost their independence and become mere links in a production and distribution chain managed by wholesale merchants, a widening gulf separated employer and worker. To defend their wages, hours, and skilled positions, skilled workers organized local trade societies within individual crafts, urban central labor groupings—or trades unions—and even national unions. Although a strike by male artisans for the ten-hour day initially failed in Boston in 1825, within a decade numerous trades in Philadelphia, New York, and elsewhere had achieved the desired reduction in the hours of labor. At times their efforts even won governmental support, as in 1835 when the Philadelphia common council agreed to a ten-hour limit on local public works. With the signing of an executive order by President Van Buren in 1840 making ten hours the legal length of the working day for federal employees, the early labor movement achieved its crowning success.

Early labor organizations at the national level expired with the coming of depression in 1837. Nor did labor organizations enjoy much success in the political arena in the form of Workingmen's parties. . . .

Early trade unionism failed partly because, although economic and class differences certainly existed, class lines fell lightly over the contours of an essentially fluid society. Even on the eve of the Civil War, individual proprietorships and partnerships rather than corporations predominated as forms of business enterprise, which suggests that for most purposes the sums required as investment capital to enter business were within the capacities of many individuals. Not until the 1850s did incorporation and the factory system take their sharp rise, and even then much machinery remained light, wooden, and inexpensive. Perhaps not surprisingly, therefore, it is only in the 1850s that the industrial worker came to regard himself as a permanent wage earner—probably because of the rising capital requirements of machinery powered by steam.

Till then, many workers were aspiring entrepreneurs hoping to use their savings to establish their own small businesses—with the aid, perhaps, of investments or loans from extended-family members or friends. In Paterson, New Jersey, for example, the typical manufacturer in the new locomotive, machinery, and tool industries had been a skilled craftsman or had served an apprenticeship and founded his business as a small proprietorship or partnership. And in Newark, New Jersey, the leading industrial city in the nation on the eve of the Civil War, it was artisans who, by amassing the necessary capital, developing new processes, utilizing the labor of male immigrants from northern Europe, and locating new markets, were the architects of growth. Such firms could expand the volume of production per worker by teaching new skills to semiskilled workers and pouring their funds into materials. Small businesses flourished—in the making of shoes, hats, saddles, jewelry, trunks, and leather—perhaps nearly a third of them representing capital investments of $1,000 or less in 1850.

If we add to this scenario of opportunity for small businessmen in manufacturing the reality of comparable openings in the nonindustrial sector (for example, in retail and wholesale storekeeping) and in the rapidly growing urban service sector (for example, for lawyers, real estate agents, employment bureaus, innkeepers, and teachers of bookkeeping), the buoyantly confident and entrepreneurial cast of the national mood of the antebellum years becomes an understandable phenomenon. Of course, other circumstances also worked to sustain that mood. The ending of the second war with England had seen independence preserved and the nation poised to begin one of the greatest economic conquests of history. Before the American people stretched an agricultural domain of imperial dimensions. Indeed, the acquisition of the Louisiana Territory from France in 1803, which more than doubled the size of the national domain, had prompted President Jefferson to remark that there was now room enough for a thousand generations. Merchant vessels, so recently caught in a crossfire of British orders-in-council and Napoleonic responses under the Continental system, to say nothing of the wartime pincers of the British fleet itself, now stood ready once again to turn their cargoes in the world's ports. Prices of American staples, responding to a series of poor crops in Europe and to a mounting English demand for cotton, were beginning to rise on world markets and to generate increases in land sales, rapid movement to the West, and demand for "internal improvements" to weld the newer sections of the country onto the older ones along the Atlantic coast. Standing on the threshold of what John Higham has aptly termed an age of boundlessness, the American people put their faith in the power of individual initiative to enrich themselves and the nation as well. Perhaps above all, they wished to root the political independence of their fledgling republic in the soil of economic growth.

Metropolitan Industrialization

SEAN WILENTZ

Between 1825 and 1850, New York became the most productive manufacturing city in the United States—the metropolitan center of a manufacturing complex that reached as far south as Delaware and that by the late 1840s was probably the fastest-growing large industrial area in the world. These extraordinary developments utterly changed the city's crafts, but in ways very different from those evoked by the usual images of early industrial growth. Huge firms absorbed thousands of craft workers—but did not eradicate the city's small producers. New, highly sophisticated steam-powered machines thundered in the factory districts—but most of New York's largest manufacturers intensified the division of labor already underway rather than invest in labor-saving machinery. Although a few, rapidly growing trades dominated the city's manufacturing economy, hundreds more remained, leaving New York with a manufacturing sector of almost baffling diversity. Then, as now, Americans looked elsewhere to interpret the coming industrial era. Nevertheless, at midcentury the most productive manufacturing center in the nation was neither a mechanized contrivance like Lowell nor a single-trade boomtown like Lynn, but a metropolitan labyrinth of factories and tiny artisan establishments, central workrooms and outworkers' cellars, luxury firms and sweatwork strapping shops.

The physical oddities of the early industrial metropolis should not deceive us: a revolution, and not just an expansion of production, took place in New York's workshops—a revolution that *Hunt's Merchants' Magazine* described in 1849 as very much "in keeping with the spirit of the age." It was a revolution already begun in 1825; although it would continue into the Gilded Age and beyond, by 1850 it had transformed the very meaning of labor and independence in the city's largest trades. . . .

In 1845, the New York *Daily Tribune* prepared a series of reports on the condition of labor in New York. What the *Tribune* reporters found shocked them, and they groped for explanations—especially to account for the outrageous underbidding and exploitation that riddled the city's largest trades. A few years later, after he had read the works of the greatest urban journalist of the age, a *Tribune* correspondent named George Foster had found the right term: it was "sweating," "the accursed system . . . so thoroughly exposed in the recent investigations of Mr. Mayhew in the 'Morning Chronicle,'" a system that had come to prevail "proportionally to as great an extent in this city as in London." One or anther variation of sweating

From *Chants Democratic: New York City & The Rise of the American Working Class, 1788–1850* by Sean Wilentz, pp. 107–108, 109–129. Copyright © 1984 by Sean Wilentz. Reprinted by permission of Oxford University Press, Inc.

emerged in almost all of New York's early industrial trades. It arose in its purest forms in the consumer finishing trades, and most notoriously in the production of clothing.

It took only ten years, from 1825 to 1835, for New York's clothing revolution to conquer the local market; by 1850, it had created and captured the lion's share of a national trade in ready-made clothes for men. The original instigators were the city's cloth wholesalers, auctioneers, and job-bers, whose command of the English import market and broadening avenues to New England invited further adaptation and expansion of the contracting schemes of the early slopshop entrepreneurs. Their success, and that of the master tailors turned manufacturers whom they supplied with cloth and credit, was neither an act of Providence nor an inevitable working-out of the growth of commerce. Of all of New York's middlemen and manufac-turers, the clothiers were the most astute at perfecting aggressive merchan-dizing methods; more important, it was the clothiers who first mastered the art of extending liberal credit to local retailers and country dealers, to expand their own contacts and squeeze their competitors in other cities (and smaller New York dealers) out of the market. By 1835, they had turned the New York trade in ready-mades into one of the nation's largest local industries, with some firms employing between three and five hundred hands each. A large portion of their output was for the "cheap" trade—in precut apparel for southern customers (as well as the "Negro cottons" for southern slaves), dungarees and hickory shirts for western farmers and miners, and shoddy clothing for the urban poor. Beginning in the early 1830s, the clothiers also entered the respectable market, introducing superior lines, fiercely promoted by the jobbers and retailers, for clerks, shopkeepers, and wealthy patrons who lacked the time or money to patronize a custom tailor. There was some initial resistance to this noncustom work among the most cosmopolitan cus-tomers—but by the late 1840s the clothiers had changed people's minds. In 1849, a breathless report in *Hunt's* noted with admiration that the clothing of one ready-made firm was "adapted to all markets and for all classes of men, from the humblest laborer to the fashionable gentleman." With this democratization of product and the continued growth of the southern market, the New York clothing trade became an antebellum manufacturing giant. By 1850, the largest New York firms hired as many as five thousand tailors and seamstresses to turn out goods "with a degree of precision that would astonish the negligent observer."

The rise of the ready-mades metamorphosed New York tailoring at every level of production. Some of the old-fashioned master craftsmen did survive, largely in the fancy trade: New York business directories from the 1850s still boasted of Broadway's rows of custom fitters and gentlemen tailors. After about 1830, however, even the finest custom masters began to feel the competitive pinch. Some large custom firms like Brooks Brothers' entered the ready-made market for themselves and divided their shops into separate departments for custom work and the cheaper lines; as early as 1835, master tailors' advertisements stressed the availability of ready-mades as much as the skills of the proprietor and his journeymen. Some small custom masters who lacked the funds to finance a ready-made operation set aside defective work and tried to sell it off as "precut." Others went to work for the manufacturers, either as foremen or as semi-independent retailers, vending a specific firm's ready-mades and doing a bit of custom tailoring on their own. A few of these men went on to become large employers themselves; they, and the clothing merchants, oversaw not enlarged craft firms but entirely new kinds of enterprises.

The focal point of the clothing outwork system was the New York version of the central shop—often an attractive structure when seen from the street, its shapely lines and graceful columns beckoning customers to inspect the stock. Once inside, a patron would see only the ample stores and the retinue of clerks; behind the scenes, the elite of the clothing work force, the in-shop cutters, prepared the predesigned patterns. The head cutters, the overseers of that elite, numbered about fifty in all in the city. With an average annual income of between $1,000 and $1,500 each, they were probably the best-paid craft workers in New York. Certainly they were the most privileged. Apart from their power to discipline workers, the head cutters (sometimes called "piece masters") were in charge of giving out all work to the journeymen, outworkers, and contractors. On the basis of their appraisal— or whims—a cutter or stitcher could earn a decent living or an excellent one. Impartiality in these matters was not among the head cutter's virtues. "Generally," the *Tribune* reported, "he has his favorites, perhaps a brother, or cousin, or a particular friend, who gets the 'cream of the shop' and is thus frequently able to make $30 or $40 per week." With their incomes, with their close control over the daily operations and the lives of their subordinates, and with the confidence of their manufacturer-employers, head cutters could reasonably expect one day to open their own businesses.

The cutters enjoyed relatively high wages (roughly $10 to $12 per week) and regular employment, but none of the foremen's powers. Rapid, regular work schedules prevailed in the cutting rooms. At the Devlin and Brothers' firm, cutters were divided into bureaus for coats, pants, vests, and trimmings, while the entire production process, one reporter observed, "was reduced to a system," in which every piece of work had its own number and a ticket with the workman's name. Emphasis fell on speed and accuracy in cutting predetermined designs; "Southern-trade cutting," a term synonymous with rapid rather than artful work, was the most common task in New York's major clothing firms at least as early as the mid-1830s. Any slip, momentary slowdown, or simple disagreement with the foreman could deprive a cutter of the best work in the shop; if he could not adjust to the pace, he was fired.

From the cutting rooms (again, out of sight of the customers), the head cutter or piece master distributed the cut cloth to the outworkers and contractors, and it was here that the worst depredations of sweating began. A variety of outwork schemes existed. While most contractors were small masters unable to maintain their own shops, or journeymen looking for the surest road to independence, some cutters and in-shop journeymen also managed to subcontract a portion of their work on the sly. Major firms dealt directly with outworkers. In all cases, the system invited brutal competition and a successive lowering of outwork piece rates. At every level of the contracting network, profits came from the difference between the rates the contractors and manufacturers received and the money they paid out for overhead and labor. Two factors turned these arrangements into a matrix of unremitting exploitation: first, the successive bidding by the contractors for manufacturers' orders (as well as the competition between manufacturers) depressed the contractors' income; second, the reliance of the entire trade on credit buying by retailers and country dealers prompted postponement of payment to all workers until finished work was done—and, hence, chronic shortages of cash. The result: employers steadily reduced the rates they paid their hands and often avoided paying them at all for as long as possible. To middle-class reformers, the great villain of the system was the contractor himself, the "sweater," the "remorseless sharper and shaver," who in league with the cruel landlord fed greedily on the labor of poor women and degraded journeymen. But the contractors and manufacturers had little choice in the matter, as they tried to underbid their competitors and survive on a wafer-thin margin of credit. "If they were all the purest of philanthropists," the *Tribune* admitted in 1845, "they could not raise the wages of their seam-stresses to anything like a living price." Hounded by their creditors, hunted by the specter of late payment and bankruptcy, the contractors and garret masters lived an existence in which concern for one's workers was a liability and in which callousness (and, in some recorded cases, outright cruelty) became a way of life. Some were not above underhanded tricks to earn the extra dollar (the most widespread complaints concerned contractors who withheld wages on the pretense that an outworker's handiwork was not of the proper quality); all maintained their independence from the only source available to them, the underpaid labor of the outworkers and garret hands.

The sufferings of the outwork and garret-shop hands—the vast majority of clothing-trade workers—taxed the imaginations of even the most senti-mental American Victorians; if the reformers' accounts sometimes reduced a complex situation to a moral fable, they in no way falsified the clothing workers' conditions. All pretensions to craft vanished in the outwork system; with the availability of so much cheap wage labor, formal apprenticing and a regular price book had disappeared by 1845. At any given moment in the 1830s and 1840s, the underbidding in the contracting network could depress outwork and garret-shop piece rates so low that stitchers had to work up to sixteen hours a day to maintain the meanest of living standards: in 1850, some of the largest southern-trade clothing firms in the Second Ward paid their *male* workers, on the average, well below subsistence wages. Housing was difficult to come by and could amount to no more than a cellar dwelling or a two-room flat, shared with two or more families; single men crammed into outwork boardinghouses. During slack seasons or a bad turn in trade, the clothing workers struggled harder to make ends meet, with a combination of odd jobs, charity relief, and the starchiest kinds of cheap food. Poor journeymen tailors had little recourse but to sweat themselves and their families or, if they were single, to strike informal arrangements with girls and widows to work beside them, while they handled the negotiations with the head cutters or contractors: as a German immigrant later recalled, one

New York adage from the 1850s ran, "A tailor is worth nothing without a wife and very often a child." The seamstresses and tailors' wives—consigned the most wearisome work (shirt sewing worst of all) and subjected to the bullying and occasional sexual abuse of the contractors—bore the most blatant exploitation; the men, working either as petty contractors or the patresfamilias of the family shops, enjoyed, by comparison, a measure of independence—but only that, as unionists noted in the 1850s. By themselves, such conditions were difficult; they were aggravated by the tendency for outwork and garret-shop wages to diminish further as workers tried to increase their earnings by intensifying their labor and by taking on larger lots of work, thus causing short-term gluts in the labor market and still lower piece rates—what Mayhew elaborated as the principle that "overwork makes for underpayment." Even more, the rise of the ready-mades accentuated the seasonal fluctuations in labor demand. In April and October, when manufacturers prepared for the spring and fall sales seasons, regular work was relatively plentiful; for the rest of the year, as much as two-thirds of the clothing work force had to string together temporary work in an already overstocked labor market.

Life for most New York shoeworkers was no better. Like clothing production, the boot-and-shoe trade changed dramatically with the expansion of the city's trade contacts and the wholesalers' pursuit of markets. By 1829, four major footwear jobbers had opened in Manhattan; by 1850, the number had increased tenfold. The most enterprising major concerns kept pace with the clothing dealers and extended their inland markets southward to Alabama and as far west as Texas. Unlike the clothiers, however, New York firms never took the national lead in the production of respectable ready-mades: most either relied on established firms in shoemaking capitals like Lynn or Haverhill or hired their own workers in outlying towns, where, the *Tribune* reported in 1845, "the workmen can live for almost half the sum it costs our city mechanics." What remained in New York, apart from a busy custom trade, was repair work, ladies' shoemaking, bootmaking and production of the cheapest lines of shoes, either for government military contractors or for wholesale exporters in the southern trade. The shoemakers were left either to what the English writer Joseph Sparkes Hall called "the cheapening system" or to an endless competition for custom orders.

The transforming effects of credit, competition, and mercantile sponsorship were dramatized in one of the trade's success stories, the rise of John Burke. Burke, an Irishman, had learned the shoemakers' craft in Dublin, where he also dabbled in radical, anti-British politics. Disgusted with famine conditions and with Ireland's inability to break British rule, he determined to try his fortune in "the Great Republic," and in 1847 he arrived in New York. Having landed jobs in the leather-cutting rooms of some of the best custom shops, Burke quickly learned that the New York trade was very different from the Irish: to earn his competence, he would have to curry favor and credit from his employers' customers. The erstwhile radical craftsman became an entrepreneur. Within two years of his arrival, he proudly reported that "all the customers were my friends"; by 1852, thanks to a timely loan from Moses Beach, the editor and chronicler of the city's mercantile fortunes, Burke opened his own shop. Over the next ten years, Burke expanded his business (eventually buying out one of his former employers, an event he noted with blustery pride) and with Beach's backing eventually began to "gain first place in the shoe trade." He readily admitted that without the help of his "good friends," his life would have remained "a fight against mishaps, disappointments, and adversity." For the thousands of journeymen who lacked Burke's combination of skills, contacts, and charm, such a life of adversity was unavoidable: those who would gain their independence had little choice but to become contractors, to be stigmatized as "the greatest tyrants in the entire trade," in a competitive shoemakers' world where, as Hall remarked, "money *bulk* and not money *worth* becomes the only standard of business."

The division of labor in boot- and shoemaking followed the same general pattern as in the clothing trade. Work in the custom shops and in the shops of the ladies' shoemakers and the bootmakers was divided into the very few skilled cutting chores (handled by men like Burke) and the simpler, more repetitive tasks of the crimpers, fitters, and bottomers. Most journeymen could expect to earn at best six dollars per week from the easier work; to supplement their incomes, they completed an array of ornamental "extras," the most time-consuming and exacting chores in the better branches of the trade. In the shops, apprenticeship, in decline even before 1825, was reported "pretty much done away with" by 1845. Outside of the shops, the demands of garret work and outwork led the *Tribune* to reckon in 1845 that no class of mechanics averaged so great an amount of work for so little money as the journeymen shoemakers. Chronic unemployment and underemployment were even more severe in shoemaking than in tailoring, leaving the journeymen to labor at a breakneck pace whenever work came their way. Family-shop arrangements . . . became ever more common:

> We have been in some fifty cellars in different parts of the city [the *Tribune* reported], each inhabited by a Shoe-maker and his family. The floor is made of rough plank laid loosely down, and the ceiling is not quite so high as a tall man. The walls are dark and damp and a wide desolate fireplace yawns at the center to the right of the entrance. There is no outlet back, and of course no yard privilges of any kind. The miserable room is lighted only by a shallow sash, partly projecting above the surface of the ground, and by the little light that struggles down from the steep and rotting stairs. In this apartment often live the man and his work bench, his wife, and five or six children of all ages; and perhaps a palsied grandfather and grandmother and often both. . . . Here they work, here they cook, they eat, they sleep, they pray. . . .

Outwork binders, almost all of them women, were placed in backstairs chambers, where they worked from before sunrise until after sundown for piece rates that brought in as little as fifty cents a day. Small masters, in a losing battle against the wholesalers and the Lynn trade, made the cheapest grade of shoes and survived, the *Tribune* claimed in 1845, on "the chance job of gentlemen's or children's mending brought in by the rich people above ground in the neighborhood who are not celebrated for paying a poor cobbler high prices."

Sweating assumed different forms and took slightly longer to develop in the furniture trades. The shift began in about 1830, when the larger master furniture makers, hoping to reduce their wage bills and circumvent the existing price books, solicited British and European artisans to emigrate to New York. Within five years, hundreds of cabinetmakers had settled in Manhattan, many of them Germans from declining craft towns, creating the oversupply of hands the masters wanted; one English cabinetmaker, upon his arrival in Manhattan in 1834, was advised to leave the overcrowded city as soon as he could, since steady furniture work was hard to find. . . . In their search for cheap labor, however, the masters also undercut their own position, as some of the Germans began entering the business for themselves and managed to undersell the established firms by hiring other Germans at low wages. Small German shops soon dotted the shores of the Hudson and East rivers, producing inexpensive goods for the wholesalers and paying piece rates well below those expected by native-born journeymen. In response, the established masters . . . turned out cheaper lines (so-called butcher furniture) and cut some of their journeymen's wages accordingly, which only led the furniture jobbers to order more goods from the small garret shops. By the early 1840s, garret contracting operations had inundated the trades; agents prowled the city's wharves looking for immigrants to steer to the cheap shops. Furniture making, though immune to the usual forms of outwork, became a sweated contract trade.

The majority of furniture workers divided into a small elite corps of custom workmen and the contract suppliers to the wholesalers and retailers. First-rate hands continued to turn and fashion elegant designs . . . and earned as much as fifteen dollars for a sixty-hour week, but by the mid-1840s such work was scarce, open to fewer than one in twenty furniture employees. Apprenticeship continued, although by one investigator's estimate in 1853, not one in fifty cabinetmakers was an apprentice; those who remained were taken on for periods of two to four years, a span the *Herald* claimed "those who have had an experience in the trade say is almost impossible to obtain a complete practical knowledge of it." The "second-class" or "botch" workers labored at restricted, repetitive tasks, either in the larger manufactories along the Hudson or in the colonies of cabinetmaking garret shops on the Lower East Side, places where, as the cabinetmaker Ernest Hagen remembered, the work was strictly divided and masters "generally made a speciality of one piece only." Their plight, as reported in the *Herald*, was quite similar to that of the tailors, as intense competition between contractors and small masters led to a system of underbidding "in which the contending parties seem to lose all sense of honor or justice." By 1850 the furniture journeymen complained that most furniture workers could not expect to earn as much as "the common standard prices paid to hod carriers and sewer-diggers, little better than starving prices."

Tailoring, shoemaking, and furniture making were the most dramatic examples of consumer finishing trades beset by similar problems. In others— hat and bonnet making, umbrella making, and many more—one form or another of piecework, outwork, and sweating arose between 1825 and 1850;

in still others, such as cigarmaking, the full force of the bastardization of craft would be felt within a generation. In all of them, we confront, in the most extreme way, the divided legacy of early-nineteenth-century capitalist growth. There can be little question that the transformation of New York consumer finishing improved material life for millions of Americans, in the form of cheaper clothes, cheaper shoes, and cheaper furniture, in greater quantities (and of higher quality) than ever before. For those at the very bottom of the outwork network—especially, after 1845, the famine-ravaged Irish—even work in the sweatshops and outwork cellars and the driven life of a petty contractor were preferable to rural disaster and, for some, starvation; for the fortunate few like John Burke, it was still possible to expect to earn, by one means or another, an independent estate. But none of this alters what was the harder truth in the sweated trades—that the cost of productivity, of salvation from agrarian calamity, and of opportunity for some was the collapse of the crafts and their replacement with a network of competition, underbidding, and undisguised exploitation—all in a city where the mercantile elite and the more successful manufacturers accumulated some of the greatest fortunes in America. These changes were invisible to most customers and chroniclers, hidden from view in the back-room cutters' bureaus and in the out-workers' cellars. To upper- and middle-class New York, the onset of metropolitan industrialization appeared mainly as a dazzling cavalcade of new commodities, "suited to every market." To the craft workers, it was the intensity of labor, the underpayment, and the subordination to the rule of another that was most apparent. Above all else, it was the very transparency of exploitation, the self-evident inequalities of power and material expectations at every level of production, that made the sweated consumer finishing trades the most degraded crafts in New York. It would also make these trades the most troubled of all during the city's labor upheavals after 1825.

Working-Class Youth: The Gals and Boys of the Bowery
CHRISTINE STANSELL

Between the founding of the republic and the Civil War, a new conception of womanhood took shape in America, preeminently in Northeastern towns and cities. Within the propertied classes, women constituted themselves the moral guardians of their families and their nation, offsetting some of the inherited liabilities of their sex. Laboring women were less fortunate: The domestic ideals from which their prosperous sisters profited did little to lighten the oppressions of sex and class they suffered. They were also more troublesome, since their actions—indeed, their very existence as impoverished female workers—violated some of the dearest held genteel precepts of "woman's nature" and "woman's place." . . .

Glancing at the history books, it is difficult at first to discern those

Excerpts from *City of Women: Sex and Class in New York, 1789–1860* by Christine Stansell (Knopf: Random House Inc. 1986), pp. xi–xiii, 77–100. From paperback ed.

problematic poor women. When laboring women do appear in scholarship about the nineteenth century, it is usually as timid and downtrodden souls, too miserable and oppressed to take much of a part in making history. Mired in terrible working conditions, they toil long hours for starvation wages, seemingly powerless in the face of employers' abuse. At moments, inexplicably, they fight back by organizing short-lived, generally ineffectual trade unions. In general, however, they seem to succumb to the timeless fatalism of the poor—archetypal victims caught in a history of bondage and determinism. In this context of silence and passivity, it is easy to imagine these women simply as pale reflections of more articulate and active historical participants, as either feminine versions of working-class men or working-class versions of middle-class women.

On closer inspection, however, more varied and lively characters materialize: shrewd little girls, truculent housewives, feckless domestic servants, astute trade unionists. All these women played a part in the thoroughgoing changes in work, family and politics in nineteenth-century New York, initiating and responding to change in ways that were often different from both men of their class and their sisters in the middle class. . . . Like other female relationships, women's involvement with men depended on practical matters of daily life and survival as well as on emotional connections. Imagination and need, passion and practicality flowed together into courtship and marriage; the need to get a living, as well as love and desire, brought lovers and spouses together. The exchange, of course, was far from equal: In a city where it was difficult for any woman to support herself and where no mother could earn a living wage, women needed men more than men needed women. The fact of female economic dependency continued to breed hostility on both sides.

As in other areas of domestic life, however, the working-class neighborhoods gave women leverage in their dealings with men. Neighbor women often challenged, if not misogynistic ideology, then at least the ways in which men turned sexual hostilities into physical abuse. Similarly, outside the tenement neighborhoods, groups of young women helped to create a working-class youth culture which, by the 1840s, offered single women some latitude of movement and play. The self-conscious feminine solidarities of the propertied classes, the "bonds of womanhood," held little meaning for tenement mothers and factory girls. Nonetheless, new female presences in the city's streets, workshops, dance halls, and even (fitfully) in the labor movement helped to shift somewhat the balance of power between the sexes. In these overlapping domains, small and cramped as they were, women found some freedom from customary modes of masculine control. . . .

New York was full of single young women. . . . These girls and young women were departing from a centuries-old pattern whereby a girl growing up moved as a dependent from one household to another—from her father's house to her employer's to her husband's. Traditionally, girls were more tightly bound into the web of domestic industry and thus less mobile than boys. Although in eighteenth-century America the numbers of single women among the strolling poor drifting into the cities increased greatly, those women seem to have either moved into servants' positions or ended up in almshouses. In Philadelphia in 1775, for example, the self-supporting woman living on her own or with other women was virtually unknown.

In antebellum New York, new patterns of female residence developed. Of course, families in the New World, insofar as they could, did stretch to incorporate solitary young immigrants. Girls who left Ireland alone often moved in with uncles, aunts or married siblings once in New York. Other young women on arrival went immediately into domestic service, where the supervision of their employers' households limited whatever independence they might have gained in migrating. Still others, however, lived outside family networks, as lodgers on their own. My survey of the residences of 600 workingwomen in New York in 1855 shows that, in fact, 224 of 400 single workingwomen were living independently of uncles, aunts, grandparents and parents. Working girls might double up with sisters or workmates, "sleeping anyhow and anywhere" in households headed by workmates' parents or fellow villagers; they supported themselves through manufacturing employment, alternating factory or outside work with spells in domestic service. By the 1850s, the community of single women also reached beyond family households. Working girls crammed together into shared rooms in previously all-male boardinghouses and in tenements. "Many of these shop girls sleep half a dozen to a garret," Virginia Penny, a self-styled New York version of the London social investigator Henry Mayhew, reported in 1863. Factory workers only slept there, but outworkers—sewing workers who labored at home—also could turn shared rooms into all-female cooperative workshops. . . .

Young women and girls on their own played an important role in the development of an urban culture of young single people, male and female. Although much of the terrain of popular culture continued to be men's up through the Civil War, sociable resorts and practices began to open up for the mingling of the sexes as early as the 1790s. . . . As girls reached puberty and beyond, street chores and outdoor games led into a landscape of sexual desire, where heterosexual machinations opened up new vistas. Sexuality was often the ticket of admission—the key to social pleasure, the coin of heterosexual exchange.

Antebellum working-class youth culture encompassed the bawdy houses and some of the traditional rowdy pastimes of what was still a rough maritime town, but as early as 1820 it also occupied new corners of the city. Holiday excursions to the country, for example, were special treats in which women included themselves. Parties of young men and women or groups of women set out on Sundays on ferry rides to Long Island, boat trips on the East River and carriage rides to the rural retreats of northern Manhattan. Rose Butler, a servant-girl on trial for arson in 1819, in detailing her descent into crime, chronicled some of these amusements. She had first used money pinched from her mistress to take some friends carriage riding; later, on the Fourth of July, she "went with some girls, on board the steam-boat, on a party of pleasure, and paid the charges," and spent the rest at a bawdy house "on a frolic." "It was in this manner," she concluded, "I squandered away the money I had stolen—in frolicking and rioting in the dance-houses and other places" at Corlears Hook, where poor girls mingled with workingmen and sailors. . . .

But sexual territory was also dangerous ground where the same mobility that gave women some degree of freedom—the continual movement of people in and around each others' lives—also rendered them more vulnerable to male entrapment and abandonment.

The mentality of early national life also enhanced that vulnerability. . . . [A]s long as the heterosexual marketplace of leisure remained closely connected to the older, male-dominated milieu of the bawdy houses, different conceptions of relations between men and women had little chance to emerge. The development of new possibilities awaited a more distinct working-class culture, where men's consciousness of how much they held in common with other wage earners—in other words, a working-class consciousness—would lead them to look more kindly on their female peers. This was a culture where the self-conscious community of class experience would to some degree encompass women, and where the slumming gentleman would prove an unwelcome guest.

. . . That milieu began to materialize in the 1830s on the Bowery, the broad avenue running up and down the east side of the island. Lined with workshops, manufactories and workers' and small masters' dwellings, the Bowery was the plebeian counterpart of element Broadway to the west. In the two decades before the Civil War, it became a byword for working-class culture. . . . All sorts of working people frequented its environs. The Bowery was the main thoroughfare for cheap goods, the heart of the butcher district, and a staging ground for public amusements—parades, horse races, and fights between the juvenile gangs for which the street became notorious. Evenings on the Bowery were the special province of young people. At the end of the working day and on Saturday night, the dance halls, oyster houses and the famed Bowery Theater, built in 1827, came alive with workingwomen, journeymen and laborers looking for marital prospects, sexual encounters and general good times. In many ways, this culture resembled that of the bawdy houses. Men set the tone, and abusiveness toward women, if no longer explicitly celebrated in jokes and songs, still entered into the proceedings. Still, Bowery culture involved changes in the relations of single, young men and women; it marginalized older forms of misogyny and celebrated instead the possibilities of gregariousness between the sexes. While the reality often fell short, the ideal still represented an opening in gender relations. . . .

Through the 1830s, the peculiar features of Bowery life—vociferous crowds at the theaters, riotous volunteer fire companies and truculent street gangs—became sufficiently well known to cohere into a cultural identity recognizable to outsiders; in the early 1840s, the Bowery produced its first metropolitan "type," the Bowery Boy. Valorous, generous and unabashedly rough-hewn in manners and speech, the Boy descended from the Bowery "fire laddie" of the famed workingmen's volunteer fire companies in the 1830s; unlike the latter, however, the Bowery Boy aspired to fashion and style. An ordinary journeyman or apprentice, "he was but little seen during the day, being engaged at his employment," but at night, he appeared as a very different person. "These 'B'hoys' had fashions of their own . . . they were the most consummate dandies of the day," Abram Dayton, born into the prestigious old Knickerbocker elite, amusedly recalled. The Bowery Boy made up his costume according to a precise code of dress.

> The hair . . . was one of his chief cares. . . . At the back of the head it was cropped as close as scissors could cut, while the front locks permitted to grow to considerable length were matted by a lavish application of *bears grease,* the ends tucked under so as to form a roll, and brushed until they shone like glass bottles . . . a black, straight, broad-brimmed hat, polished as highly as a hot iron could effect, was worn with a pitch forward . . . a large shirt collar turned down and loosely fastened, school boy fashion, so as to expose the full proportions of a thick, brawny neck; a black frock coat with skirts extending below the knee; a flashy satin or velvet vest . . . pantaloons tight to the knee. . . . A profusion of jewelry as varied and costly as the b'hoy could procure. His rolling swaggering gait on the promenade on the Bowery; his position, at rest, reclining against a lamp or awning post; the precise angle of the ever-present cigar; the tone of voice, something between a falsetto and a growl; the unwritten slang which constituted his vocabulary cannot be described.

A revivified version of the working-class dandy and the Irish "jackeen," the Bowery Boy, like the blood several decades before, depended on the backdrop of the streets to set off his self-consciously dashing presence; unlike the blood, however, he defied respectable conventions of dress. . . .

Bowery culture, for all its masculinism, its celebration of the virtues of physical prowess and pugnacity, grew out of different associations than those of traditional workingmen's leisure. Although the Bowery Boy was an aggressively working-class character, he drew his identity from an awareness of a set of cultural images rather than from a common workplace experience. His class consciousness was distinct from that of the organized labor movement. The Bowery flourished after the Panic of 1837, when New York's assertive labor organizations of the 1830s had collapsed. The Bowery Boy did not spin out his associations with his fellows on the basis of common membership in a trade union or an ethnic group or even an organized gang; rather, he defined himself through his use of his leisure time. In an after-hours world, he created commonalties through dressing, speaking and acting in certain ways, always (as one former Boy remembered) holding himself "ready for excitement." In other words, he was a member of youth culture, a milieu characterized by a symbiotic relationship to its own symbolic elaboration.

This youth culture, connected to but not contingent upon the masculine camaraderie of the workplace, offered women some part in its process of imagining itself. One of the accoutrements of the Boy's persona was "his girl hanging on his arm"—in journalistic and theatrical treatments, the "Lize" to the brave "Mose." When thus fully equipped, "it would have been injudicious to offer him any obstruction or to utter an offensive remark." "Lize" was a young workingwoman: a factory girl, shopgirl, milliner, dressmaker, book folder, map colorer, flower maker, or seamstress. Wage work and the loosening of domestic obligations that wages purchased made her presence possible. George Foster, the would-be Dickens of the New York scene, noted how such young women emerged in a crowd at the end of the workday, streaming toward the east side: "all forming a continuous procession which . . . loses itself gradually in the innumerable side-streets leading thence into the unknown regions of Proletaireism in the East End." Many of them ended up on the Bowery, sashaying up and down the avenue with crowds of girlfriends or on the arms of their young men. For women, the allure seems to have been exclusively heterosexual. Although the beginnings of a gay male subculture were just visible—Whitman, for one, was part of it—the social conditions for a lesbian milieu seem to have been absent in what was still a heavily masculine culture. Still, the young women of the Bowery, decked out in fancy clothes, beckoned to every newly arrived country girl, a collective symbol of certain pleasures of city life.

The streets offered a panoply of places for the sexes to mingle. The Bowery promenade was a main attraction, dazzling in the array of costumes paraded there; for those with a little money in their pockets, there were also more elaborate amusements. The theaters offered melodrama, burlesque and blackface minstrelsy at cut-rate admission; dime museums and eating-places served as meeting grounds for trysts and flirtation. Ice cream [a delicacy] in the 1790s . . . had become cheap enough to make the ice cream parlor a democratic resort; oyster shops also provided inexpensive fare—all the oysters you could eat for six cents a customer. Vauxhall Gardens, founded in 1798 and taken over by the virtuoso showman Phineas Barnum in 1840, featured "variety shows"—the precursors of vaudeville—skits, dancing, singing and comedy. Balls, held at nearby Tammany Hall, firehouses or dance halls, were the high festivals of Bowery life. In these "high-flyer stampedes," dancing was a matter of acrobatic strength as well as dexterity and grace, with results that moved George Foster to a characteristic moment of metropolitan pride: "New York is undoubtedly the greatest place for dancing in all Anglo Saxdom," he ventured in relation to a Bowery dance. The balls drew "the foldinggirls and seamstresses, the milliners' apprentices, the shopgirls," by the scores: "All unmarried womanhood" from the lower east side came, it seemed to Foster, dressed in their finest clothes. Indeed, sometimes young women sponsored dances of their own, clubbing together for food and liquor, while male guests provided the music. . . .

The workingwomen who took part in these pleasurable times created a striking public presence. They were distinguished by their self-conscious "airs," a style of dress and manner which was a studied departure from ladyhood, an implicit rejection of bourgeois female decorum. Genteel rules of gender dictated that "womanly" women minimize what they saw in public of others and what others saw of them. . . . Muted colors, a costume that covered the flesh except for the face (including obligatory gloves and hat), and an aloof manner were the hallmarks of a lady. Differences in the public presentation of the self became in nineteenth-century genteel culture an important means of distinguishing the "true" woman from her imitators or counterfeits. Thus popular perception identified her antithesis, the prostitute, as much by her demeanor in public as by her actual sexual behavior: A prostitute was, in common parlance, a woman "on the town," recognizable by her brightly colored dress, the comparative absence of coverings (most tellingly, the omission of a hat) and her open, searching gaze.

The young workingwomen of the Bowery developed a style different from either of these feminine modes, one that allowed them freedoms similar to those of the prostitute, but that nonetheless advertised their own singularity. Bowery girls—or "Gals"—presented themselves not as streetwalkers on the prowl but as members of a high-spirited peer group, reveling in their associations with each other. . . .

A special mentality underlay these various expressions of youthful pleasure. It was this mentality—the way that the laboring people of the Bowery understood themselves in social and aesthetic terms—that made the avenue a coherent cultural milieu rather than just a place for good times. "Boweriness," a later New Englander would label it. "Boweriness," for both men and women, signified a celebration of the possibilities of working-class life. A unique blend of high-spiritedness and decorum, Boweriness was fundamentally mannered, enforcing its own standards of courtesy and polite conduct: The "airs" that so amused upper-class observers were the Bowery's rendition of urbane deportment. To be sure, there was still plenty of rowdiness. In the Bowery Theater, pandemonium reigned. George Foster, journalist about town, observed that "compared with the performances in the audience, the ranting and bellowing and spasmodic galvanism of the actors on the stage, are quite tame and commonplace." But the theater uproar was also ritualized, a patterned response to cues from the actors and the audience and quite different from the besotted jollity of the bawdy houses. Outside the theater, pleasure seekers in the promenade, at the pleasure gardens and in the oyster shops contained their exuberance within a self-consciously dignified civility. Down by the seamier environs of the waterfront, workingmen could still spend an evening of blood sports at the terrier and rat fights at "Sportsmen's Hall," and at Five Points, they could make the rounds of the dives. The Bowery catered to different tastes. Its most successful establishments created an aura of modishness by minimizing the presence of drinking, brawling and prostitution. Harry Hill's popular concert hall and saloon, for instance, gave free admission to women dressed in fashionable street wear, but banished anyone caught soliciting.

Much of this sense of decorum was associated with a rough courtesy toward women, a mingling of a minimal respect with men's own sense of class pride. The Bowery was not egalitarian in its gender relations, but Bowery style did repudiate some kinds of antagonisms toward women, primarily those that were bound up with blatant class exploitation. While voyeuristic "aristos" had found some welcome at turn-of-the-century bawdy houses, gentlemen looking for liaisons with working girls ran into frank hostility on the Bowery. "The b'hoys are little inclined to disguise the open contempt and hatred he inspires," Foster reported of the gentleman intruder.

"Should he become at all demonstrative in his attention to any of the ladies," he was likely to come to blows with her protectors. Abram Dayton, who himself had once been a gentleman looking for a good time on the avenue, remembered how risky flirtations could be. "The Broadway exquisite who ventured 'within the pale' was compelled to be very guarded in his advances towards any fair one . . . any approach to familiarity either by word or look was certain to be visited by instant punishment." Women joined in. "The g'hals themselves despise him," Foster noted of the "aristo." If a fight developed, Dayton recalled, the women rallied to the Boys' side, cheering them on as in a faction fight in Ireland or a street fight in New York.

The Boys' antagonism to the prowling outsider was a way by which they defined exclusive rights to "their" women. The workingmen's own sense of the widening distance between rich and poor, Broadway and the Bowery, employer and employee, colored their perceptions of working-class women. The rise of the Bowery was inseparable from the growth of working-class consciousness between 1830 and 1860. In this context, the rough version of republican ideology that the Bowery Boys inherited—the celebration of the virtues of manual labor and physical prowess, the virile patriotism, the truculence toward outside authority—promoted a change in republican views of women. Like their eighteenth-century predecessors, Bowery men saw public life—in their case, working-class life—as a place where men were the main show and women the supporting cast. But in contrast to earlier attitudes, theirs was a paternalist stance that stressed the protective rather than antagonistic elements of their involvement with women. The visibility of the Bowery Gals must have contributed to this shift. As independent wage earners, women themselves cast off some symbolic associations with dependency.

The Boys' defense of their female guests was certainly not egalitarian or comradely, but neither was it overtly misogynist. For all the limitations of working-class paternalism—and we will see there were many—this paternalism still granted working-class women a greater ability to lay claim to some respect. On one level, the Boys, in delineating their turf, laid claims to territory in women. But on another, they challenged the unabashed sexual predation of the gentleman. In doing so, they acknowledged some obligations to their female companions, albeit in a fundamentally patronizing way.

The expansive heterosexuality of the Bowery, however, also competed with the rougher side of its working-class republicanism: the bellicosity, the masculinism (women on the sidelines), the localism and the insular loyalties. In the 1830s, the Boweryites' pugnacious defense of their rights against interfering outsiders erupted not only in melees with rival fire companies and gangs but in antiblack, antiabolitionist riots and the first stirrings of anti-immigrant nativism; in 1849 it led some of the Boys to a bloody showdown with the police at the elite Astor Place Theater over the appearance there of the British rival of "their" actor, the American Shakespearean Edwin Forrest of the Bowery Theatre. A culture so concerned with vaunting its male insiders—the true American boys—at the expense of everyone else (the Irish, the English, the blacks, the wealthy and genteel) must often have cast women as parasitic outsiders.

Thus while working-class consciousness undermined some features of eighteenth-century misogyny, still others persisted. Sexual hostilities may have gone underground, but they did not disappear, either from the Bowery or from the wider working-class world around it. The abuse of women, especially sexual abuse, remained a male prerogative; for some, it became a form of recreation. Group rapes, virtually unknown in the court records of the early nineteenth century, appear occasionally in court proceedings after 1830. "Getting our hide" was one perpetrator's term for a gang rape. The assailants were the same sorts of young workingmen who frequented the Bowery; their victims might have been, in other circumstances, their companions at the dance halls or oyster shops. . . . While class-conscious notions of respect and protectiveness toward workingwomen could mitigate their harshest behavior, men continued to prey upon women outside the dance halls. Forced sex in courting became, if anything, more omnipresent as courting itself became more attenuated. Women alone on the streets continued to be targets for seduction and rape. The Boweryites may have despised gentlemen rakes, but the working class itself had plenty of seducers and rapists within its own ranks.

Still, while the Bowery marginalized rather than eradicated male predation, it also encouraged greater reciprocity, sexual and social, between young men and women. As was the case elsewhere in New York life, men took more than they gave. But a commercial culture that depended on the exchange of money for amusement and pleasure at least had this effect: Its practices of heterosexual exchange implied a more contingent notion of men's rights over women. Commercial culture promoted the assumption that women owed sexual favors in return for men's generosity. From women's perspective, this was hardly egalitarian, but it was an improvement on the view that women were legitimate targets for sexual coercion simply by virtue of their sex. Young women themselves probably played an active part in promoting this sexual code. Although the evidence reveals little on this point, we can speculate that youth culture allowed *female* peer groups to exert some pressure on young men by delineating their own ideas of when it was acceptable for girls to acquiesce to male demands. If indeed this was the case, such collectivities might have replaced neighborhood sanctions on courting with their own ways of protecting young women from sexual abuse and illegitimate pregnancy.

Certainly, the Bowery and all it embodied of young working people's lives was a source of some kind of collective consciousness for working-women. The pride of the Bowery Gal was not just the reflected glow of her escort. In Bowery styles of dress and decorum, the workingwoman elaborated a presence distinct from that of the Victorian lady. It was a presence, moreover, of considerable imaginative and symbolic power. To be sure, it gave women very little of a foothold in formal institutions of working-class life—trade unions, benefit societies, party politics—but this is no surprise; women in public were, after all, still only a scant step removed from prostitution. . . . [H]owever, . . . the new sense of women as part of a working-class public presence would bring about important, if tentative, changes in trade union organizing. Most important, the possibilities of the Bowery Gal would continue, throughout the rest of the nineteenth century, to pose an alternative mode of feminine self-realization to the bourgeois ideal of true womanhood.

⌗ *F U R T H E R   R E A D I N G*

Jeremy Atack and Fred Bateman, *To Their Own Soil: Agriculture in the Antebellum North* (1987)

Mary H. Blewett, *Men, Women, and Work: Class, Gender, and Protest in the New England Shoe Industry, 1780–1910* (1988)

Stuart Blumin, *The Emergence of the Middle Class: Social Experience in the American City, 1760–1860* (1989)

Amy Bridges, *A City in the Republic: Antebellum New York and the Origins of Machine Politics* (1985)

Christopher Clark, *The Roots of Rural Capitalism: Western Massachusetts, 1780–1860* (1990)

Thomas Cochran, *Frontiers of Change: Early Industrialism in America* (1981)

Paul Conkin, *Prophets of Prosperity: America's First Political Economists* (1980)

Nancy F. Cott, *Bonds of Womanhood: "Woman's Sphere" in New England, 1780–1835* (1977)

Clarence H. Danhof, *Change in Agriculture: The Northern United States, 1820–1870* (1969)

Alan Dawley, *Class and Community: The Industrial Revolution in Lynn* (1976)

Joseph Dorfman, *The Economic Mind in American Civilization* (1946–1959)

Thomas Dublin, *Women at Work: The Transformation of Work and Community in Lowell, Massachusetts, 1826–1860* (1979)

Paul Faler, *Mechanics and Manufacturers in the Early Industrial Revolution: Lynn, Massachusetts, 1780–1860* (1981)

Paul W. Gates, *The Farmer's Age: Agriculture, 1815–1850* (1960)

Herbert G. Gutman, *Work, Culture, and Society in Industrializing America* (1974)

Steven Hahn and Jonathan Prude, eds., *The Countryside in the Age of Capitalist Transformation: Essays in the Social History of Rural America* (1985)

Bray Hammond, *Banks and Politics in America from the Revolution to the Civil War* (1957)

James A. Henretta, "Families and Farms: *Mentalité* in Pre-Industrial America," *William & Mary Quarterly*, 3rd series, 35 (1978), 3–32

Morton J. Horwitz, *The Transformation of American Law, 1780–1860* (1977)

David A. Hounshell, *From the American System to Mass Production, 1800–1932: The Development of Manufacturing Technology in the United States* (1984)

Joan M. Jensen, *Loosening the Bonds: Mid-Atlantic Farm Women 1750–1850* (1986)

Paul E. Johnson, "The Modernization of Mayo Greenleaf Patch: Land, Family, and Marginality in New England, 1766–1818," *New England Quarterly* 55 (1982), 488–516

Gary Kulik, "Pawtucket Village and the Strike of 1824: The Origins of Class Conflict in Rhode Island," *Radical History Review* 17 (1978), 5–37

Allan Kulikoff, "The Transition to Capitalism in Rural America," *William & Mary Quarterly*, 3rd series, 46 (1989), 120–144

Bruce Laurie, *Artisans Into Workers: Labor in Nineteenth-Century America* (1989)

———, *Working People of Philadelphia, 1800–1850* (1980)

James T. Lemon, *The Best Poor Man's Country: A Geographical Study of Early Southeastern Pennsylvania* (1972)

Diane Lindstrom, *Economic Development in the Philadelphia Region, 1810–1850* (1978)

David Montgomery, "The Shuttle and the Cross: Weavers and Artisans in the Kensington Riots of 1844," *Journal of Social History*, 5 (1972), 411–446

———, "The Working Classes of the Pre-Industrial City, 1780–1830," *Labor History*, 9 (1968), 3–22

Douglass North, *The Economic Growth of the United States, 1790–1860* (1966)

Glenn Porter and Harold C. Livesay, *Merchants and Manufacturers: Studies in the Changing Structure of Nineteenth-Century Marketing* (1971)

Jonathan Prude, *The Coming of Industrial Order: Town and Factory Life in Rural Massachusetts, 1810–1860* (1983)

Howard Rock, *Artisans of the New Republic: The Tradesmen of New York City in the Age of Jefferson* (1979)

Steven J. Ross, *Workers on the Edge: Work, Leisure, and Politics in Industrializing Cincinnati* (1985)

Randolph A. Roth, *The Democratic Dilemma: Religion, Reform, and the Social Order in the Connecticut River Valley of Vermont, 1791–1850* (1987)

Mary P. Ryan, *Cradle of the Middle Class: The Family in Oneida County, New York, 1790–1865* (1981)

Philip Scranton, *Proprietary Capitalism: The Textile Manufacture at Philadelphia* (1983)

Richard B. Stott, *Workers in the Metropolis: Class, Ethnicity, and Youth in Antebellum New York City* (1990)

George Rogers Taylor, *The Transportation Revolution, 1815–1860* (1951)

Anthony F. C. Wallace, *Rockdale: The Growth of an American Village in the Early Industrial Revolution* (1978)

Norman Ware, *The Industrial Worker, 1840–1860* (1924)

CHAPTER
8

The Slaveholders' Regime

⽥

Economic expansion did not halt at the Mason-Dixon line. Technological improvements like the cotton gin, along with the explosive growth of textile production in the northern states and Great Britain, brought a boom in world cotton markets, which in turn gave a tremendous boost to the southern slave economy. By 1850 southern cotton producers held a commanding share in the cultivation of the Industrial Revolution's most valuable agricultural commodity. Slavery became the basis for an economic empire that stretched as far west as Texas. The Cotton Kingdom, a cornerstone of national prosperity, was responsible for more than half the total value of U.S. exports.

Some of the most distinguished historical research of the past thirty years has centered on a thorough reevaluation of the early-nineteenth-century slave South. Much of that work has focused on the relations between masters and slaves and has exploded the old racist assumptions about slavery as an uplifting institution. But the more that scholars study the South, the more complicated the region seems. What, for example, are we to make of the majority of white southerners, small farmers on the margins of the plantation economy who owned no slaves and who sometimes voiced distrust of their rich planter neighbors? How did free blacks fare in the Old South? Did women, slave and free, experience slavery any differently than men? To what extent did the slaves create an autonomous culture, independent of the impositions of their masters? Was slavery in the cotton districts basically similar to that in the cities or in the non-cotton-growing parts of the region? And above these questions loom even larger ones. Did slavery render the South a distinctive, noncapitalist civilization, increasingly at odds with Yankee capitalism? Or was southern slavery basically a variant of American capitalism—one founded primarily as a system of racial subordination and control? Is there much that is worthy of respect, even admiration, in antebellum southern society and culture? Or did slavery poison every aspect of southern life, and by extension, of American life?

⽥ *DOCUMENTS*

The first document, an excerpt from a letter to a young Louisiana planter, St. John Richardson Liddell, from his father, elaborates some of the plantation and

238

community ideals of the planter class. The instructions in the second selection from the prominent South Carolina planter and politician James H. Hammond to his overseer detail the rules of plantation management. The third selection includes the diary entries of another South Carolinian, Thomas B. Chaplin, and two brief letters from Georgia. These documents illustrate the difficulties of putting such management rules into practice. The fourth selection presents various first-person accounts of slavery. Solomon Northup, a runaway slave, recounted life on a Louisiana plantation from a field hand's point of view, as part of his celebrated autobiography published in 1855. Other varieties of the slaves' experiences turn up in a letter from a slave overseer, George Skipwith, to his absentee owner, and in the recollections of Lizzie Williams (transcribed in the 1930s). The fourth selection closes with a broadside of 1823, announcing a Richmond slave auction.

In 1840 nearly a quarter of a million free blacks lived in the South—8 percent of the region's African-American population. Concentrated largely in the eastern upper South, and vulnerable to discrimination and economic marginality, they nevertheless forged a collective identity and built impressive community institutions. The fifth selection, a petition from a group of "free persons of color" to the Virginia legislature, illustrates the tensions of living at the boundary between freedom and slavery. (The petition was rejected.)

In the sixth document, the English actress Frances Kemble, who married the Georgia planter Pierce Butler in the 1830s, recorded her impressions of her new home. Although she was hardly a typical plantation mistress—among other things, she held strong antislavery views—Kemble's remarks offer a shrewd woman's perspective on the "peculiar institution." A wholly different point of view comes across in the seventh selection, the angry complaints of two Georgia yeoman farmers. Although these documents date from the early 1850s, they reflect long-standing divisions among southern whites.

In the last selection, documents from three very different Virginians, provoked by Nat Turner's failed insurrection in 1831, dramatize the themes of resistance and counterresistance to slavery at a critical turning point. Turner's confessions, as taken down by Thomas R. Gray, reveal something of the mental world of the militant leader. Months later, the Virginia legislature debated whether slavery should be ended, with representatives of the western and piedmont districts of the state leading the criticism of the institution. (It would be the last such debate in the Old South.) After reviewing the rebellion and its aftermath, Thomas Roderick Dew, a professor of law and political economy at the College of William and Mary, wrote one of the most forceful defenses of slavery to that time.

A Planter Instructs His Son, 1841

Elmslay, Wednesday, April 7, 1841

Dear John, . . .

. . . You are now placed in a situation that you can command a credit— you can make money (which you have never yet done) and now your views on this must be somewhat expanded—You have declined a profession, accepted the service of a poor domestic and civil life as that of a planter— you have no other means of supporting yourself & you have settled down in that way—Therefore you must work these matters to the best advantage— I do not reflect on you that you have not done better—nor you ought to

reflect on me that I have not done better for you—I have now layed down a foundation one of your own seeking and I think a pretty good one—I might have done better—others have not done so well but you now have a fine property and it now only requires your own frugal Industry, econimy, and good Management to make you comfortable the balance of your life and at the same time to send me some aid occasionally as I may need it in the decline of life. But this is a kind of responsibility placed on your shoulders that you have to fulfil. That is the relation in which you stand as to Master & Slave of which you understand as well as I can tell you—Never require of your Slaves too much—treat them with kindness, chastise them well for disobedience and refractory conduct—keep a clear conscience on these matters . . . At the stage of life you are now at—it may be expected that you will or may accumulate more property of various kinds which will still involve you in more thoughts & some trouble in the management—of this you must accustom yourself to attend to whilst in youth and that you ought to do so closely and attentively, not to depend too much on others to look after it, as by negligence you may loose much. Do learn to Watch every thing closely. in doing so you will always find a great advantage. I would wish you that in the public business of your County and Parish that you always take a deep interest. Serve your country in some capacity or other always suitable to the station you bear in society and really to do all the good you can and as little harm as possible—never flinch from the smallest office and with the highest regard to the laws & constitution of your government. You will laugh at my letters . . . I suppose—but you must recollect that I have a deep interest in all your actings I may do wrong myself but admonish others from doing so and more particularly one that carries my name immediately under me——
I would wish him perfect. . . .

J. H. Hammond's Instructions to His Overseer, 1840–1850

CROP.

1 A good crop means one that is good taking into consideration every thing—negroes, land, mules, stock, fences, ditches, farming utensils, &c., &c., all of which must be kept up & improved in value. The effort therefore must not be merely to make *so many* cotton bales or such an amount of other produce, but as much as can be made without interrupting the steady increase in value of the rest of the property.

Remarks.—There should be an increase in number, & improvement in condition & value of negroes; abundant provisions of all sorts for every thing, made on the place, carefully saved & properly housed; an improvement in the productive qualities of the land, & general condition of the plantation; mules, stock, fences & farming utensils in fine order at the close of the year; as much produce as could possibly be made under these circumstances, ready for market in good season, & of prime quality.

OVERSEER.

2 The Overseer will never be expected to work in the fields, but he must always be with the hands when not otherwise engaged in the Employer's business, & will be required to attend on occasion to any pecuniary transaction connected with the plantation.

Remarks. —The Overseer should never give away, sell or exchange, nor buy, order or contract for any thing without the full knowledge of the Employer & positive orders to do so. . . .

6 The Overseer will be expected not to degrade himself by charging any negro with carrying news to the Employer. There must be no news to carry. The Employer will not encourage tale-bearing, but will question every negro indiscriminately whenever he thinks proper about all matters connected with the plantation, & require him to tell the truth. Whenever he learns anything derogatory to the Overseer he will immediately communicate it to him.

Remarks. —The Overseer must show no favoritism among negroes. . . .

11 The negroes must be made to obey & to work, which may be done by an Overseer, who attends regularly to his business, with very little whipping. Much whipping indicates a bad tempered, or inattentive manager, & will not be allowed. The Overseer must never on any occasion—unless in self defence—kick a negro, or strike with his hand, or a stick, or the butt-end of his whip. No unusual punishment must be resorted to without the Employer's consent.

Remarks. —He must never threaten a negro, but punish offences immediately on knowing them; otherwise he will soon have run-aways. . . .

ALLOWANCES.

1 Allowances are given out once a week. No distinction is made among work-hands, whether they are fullhands or under, field hands or adjuncts about the yard, stables, &c.

Remarks. —Negroes are improvident with a longer interval between allowances many will consume, waste or barter their provisions before it closes & must commit thefts, or have insufficient & unwholesome food during a portion of the time; demoralyzing & rendering them physically incapable of doing full work, if not producing sickness. They should, also, be brought into that contact with the master, at laest [least] once a week, of receiving the means of subsistence from him.—

2 Each work-hand gets a peck of meal every Sunday morning—the measure filled & piled as long as it will stand on it, but not packed or shaken.

Remarks.—Every negro must come in person for meal allowance, & in clean clothes.—Sweet potato[e]s may be given in the winter after Christmas in part for meal, where preferred, at the rates of one bushel of potatos for a peck of meal. There must be a watch kept that they do not sell the potatos.

3 Each work hand gets 3 lbs. of bacon or pickled pork every Monday night. Fresh meat may be substituted at the rates of 3½ lbs. of fresh pork, (uncured, but salted) or 4 lbs. of beef or mutton, or 4½ of pork offal. When 1 pint of molasses is given the meat is reduced to 2½ lbs. of bacon or pickled pork, beef or mutton, or 3½ lbs. of pork offal. Mixed allowances of bacon & fresh meat are given in the same proportions. The entire amount of meat is weighed out from the smoke house & divided satisfactorily in the presence of the Overseer. Fresh beef may be given late in summer & on 'till spring— never in full allowances unless in cold weather. Fresh pork & pork offal only at hog-killing times. Each ditcher, who gives full satisfaction in his work for a week, receives an extra pound of meat on Wednesday night. The Drivers are allowed a small extra of meat whenever they may apply for it— which is rarely done. They receive also an extra pint of molasses every week.

Remarks.—If meat was given on Sunday many would consume it the same day in entertaining or eating in consequence of having nothing else to do. Frequent cases of sickness have resulted on Mondays from this cause.— Daily allowances would be better than weekly, but is troublesome. By giving it daily & cooking it there will be the advantages of regularity in the hours, quantity & quality of their meals, with the certainty of its being perfectly done. It is said to make full return to have an appointed cook for twenty hands.—All fresh meat should be well salted before given out & mutton at no time for over two days allowance. A little salt should be given out from time to time. Negroes are apt to hang fresh meat in their chimneys where the smoke preserves the outside from putrifying until the inner part is per- fectly rotten. This should be guarded against.—In the long hot days of summer an extra pound of meat should be given occasionally. . . .

SUCKLERS.

13 Sucklers are not required to leave their houses until sun-rise, when they leave their children at the children's house before going to field. The period of suckling is 12 mos. Their work lies always within ½ mile of the quarter. They are required to be cool before commencing to suckle—to wait 15 minutes, at least, in summer, after reaching the children's house before nursing. It is the duty of the nurse to see that none are heated when nursing, as well as of the Overseer & his wife occasionally to do so. They are allowed 45 minutes at each morning to be with their children. They return 3 times a day until their infants are 8 mos. old—in the middle of the forenoon, at noon, & in the middle of the afternoon: till the 12th mo. but twice a day, missing at noon: during the 12th mo. at noon only. On weaning, the child is removed entirely from its Mother for 2 weeks, & placed

in charge of some careful woman without a child, during which time the Mother is not to nurse it at all.

Remarks.—The amount of work done by a Suckler is about ⅗ of that done by a full-hand, a little increased toward the last. . . .

OLD & INFIRM.

15 Those, who from age & infirmities are unable to keep up with the prime hands, are put in the suckler's gang.

PREGNANT.

16 Pregnant women, at 5 mos. are put in the suckler's gang. No plowing or lifting must be required of them.

Sucklers, old, infirm & pregnant, receive the same allowances as full-work hands.

CONFINEMENT.

17 The regular plantation midwife shall attend all women in confinement. Some other woman learning the art is usually with her during delivery. The confined woman lies up one month, & the midwife remains in constant attendance for 7 days. Each woman on confinement has a bundle given to her containing articles of clothing for the infant, pieces of cloth & rag, & some extra nourishment, as sugar, coffee, rice & flour for the Mother.

SICKNESS.

18 No negro will be allowed to remain at his own house when sick, but must be confined to the hospital. Every reasonable complaint must be promptly attended to, & with any marked or general symptom of sickness, however trivial, a negro may lie up a day or so at laest [least]. Homoeopathy is exclusively practiced. As no physician is allowed to practice on the plantation—there being no Homoeopathist convenient—each case has to be examined carefully by the master or overseer to ascertain the disease. The remedies next are to be chosen with the utmost discrimination. The vehicles, (tumblers & aprons) for preparing & administering with, are to be thoroughly cleansed. The directions for treatment, diet, &c. most implicitly followed; the effects & changes cautiously observed, & finally the medecines securely laid away from accidents & contaminating influences. In cases, where there is the slightest uncertainty, the books must be taken to the bed-side, & a careful & thorough examination of the case, & comparison of remedies, made before administering them. The Overseer must record in the prescription book every dose of medecine administered.

HOURS.

19 The first morning horn is blown an hour before day-light. All work-hands are required to rise & prepare their cooking, &c. for the day. The second horn is blown just at good daylight, when it is the duty of the driver to visit every house & see that all have left for the field. The plow hands leave their houses for the stables, at the summons of the plow driver, 15 minutes earlier than the gang, the Overseer opening the stable doors to them. At 11 ½ M. the plow hands repair to the nearest weather house. At 12 M. the gang stop to eat dinner. At 1 P.M. through the greater part of the year, all hands return to work. In summer the intermission increases with the heat to the extent of 3 ½ hours. At 15 minutes before sun-set the plowhands, & at sun-set the rest, knock off work for the day. No work must ever be required after dark. No negro will be allowed to go hunting at night. The negroes are allowed to visit among themselves until the night horn is blown, after which no negro must be seen out of his house, & it is the duty of the driver to go around & see that he is in it. The night horn is blown at 8 ½ P.M. in winter, & at 9 P.M. in summer. The head driver has charge of & blows the horn.

DRIVER.

20 The head driver is the most important negro on the plantation, & is not required to work like the other hands. He is to be treated with more respect than any other negro by both master & overseer. He is on no occasion to be treated with any indignity calculated to lose the respect of the other negroes, without breaking him. He is required to maintain proper discipline at all times. To see that no negro idles or does bad work in the field & to punish it with discretion on the spot. The driver must never be flogged, except by the master, but in emergencies that will not admit of delay. Of this, however, he is to be kept in entire ignorance. He is permitted to visit the master at any time without being required to get a card, though, in general, he is expected to inform the Overseer when he leaves the place, & present himself on returning. He is expected to communicate freely whatever attracts his attention, or he thinks information of interest to the master. He is a confidential servant & may be a guard against any excuses or omissions of the Overseer.

MARRIAGE.

21 Marriage is to be encouraged as it adds to the comfort, happiness & health of those who enter upon it, besides insuring a greater increase. Permission must always be obtained from the master before marriage, but no marriage will be allowed with negroes not belonging to the master. When sufficient cause can be shewn on either side, a marriage may be annulled, but the offending party must be severely punished. Where both are in wrong

both must be punished, & if they insist on separating must have 100 lashes apiece. After such a separation neither can marry again for 3 years. For first marriage a bounty of $5.00 to be invested in household articles, shall be given. If either has been married before, the bounty shall be $3.50. A third marriage shall not be allowed but in extreme cases, & in such cases, or where both have been married before, no bounty will be given.

CHURCH.

22 All are privileged & encouraged to go to Church on Sundays, but no religious meeting is allowed on the plantation beyond singing & praying, & at such times as will not conflict with the plantation hours, & always with the permission of the Master or Overseer. Church members are privileged to dance on all holyday occasions, & the class leader or deacon who may report them shall be reprimanded or punished at the discretion of the master.

VISITING.

23 All visiting with strange negroes is positively forbidden. Negroes living at one plantation & having wives at the other can visit them only between Saturday night & Monday morning, & must get a pass card at each visit. The pass consists of a card with the full name of the place of destination on it & the first letter of the place of leaving below. The card must be delivered to the Overseer immediately on reaching the place named on it, & a return card asked for just before returning. The card is the recognized & required permit in all visiting & any negro leaving the plantation without it, or off the most direct route, shall be punished on detection by the Overseer, & is liable to punishment from any one meeting him. Not more than 6 ordinary at a time can leave the quarter, except for Church. Negroes are subject to the regulations of the place they are at any moment upon, & it is as much the duty of the Overseer & driver to observe them as those under their ordinary charge. . . .

NEGRO PATCHES.

Adjoining each negro house is a piece of ground convenient for a fowl-yard & garden. No fowl-yard or garden fence shall reach nearer than 60 feet to the negro houses. Negroes may have patches in various parts of the plantation (always getting permission from the master) to cultivate crops of their own. A field of suitable size shall be planted in pindars, & cultivated in the same manner as the general crop, the produce of which is to be divided equally among the work-hands. Negroes are not allowed to grow crops of corn or cotton for themselves, nor to have any cattle or stock of any kind of their own.

REWARDS.

The head driver receives on Christmas day $5.00 from the master; the plow driver $3.00; the midwife $2.00 & the nurse $1.00 for every actual increase of two on the place; the ditch driver $1.00 & the Stock Minder $1.00. Any of these rewards may be with-held where any negligence or misbehavior has occurred in the various departments, attributable to, or not promptly reported or corrected by the recipients. For every infant 13 months old & in sound health, that has been properly attended to the Mother shall receive a muslin or calico frock.

PUNISHMENTS.

The following is the order in which offences must be estimated & punished: 1st Running away.—2nd Getting drunk or having spirits.—3rd Stealing hogs.—4th Stealing.—5th Leaving plantation without permission.—6th Absence from house after horn blow at night.—7th Unclean house or person.—8th Neglect of tools.—9th Neglect of work.—The highest punishment must not exceed 100 lashes in one day & to that extent only in extreme cases. The whip lash must be one inch in width or a strap of one thickness of leather 1 ½ inches in width, & never severely administered. In general 15 to 20 lashes will be a sufficient flogging. The hands in every case must be secured by a cord. Punishment must always be given calmly & deliberately & never when angry or excited.

Southerners' Commentaries on Recalcitrant Slaves 1833–1845

Entries from Thomas B. Chaplin's Journal, 1845

May 15th. [1845] Went very early in the morning to take a cat hunt with the Major, but instead of starting a wildcat we started 2 runaways belonging to Isaac Sandiford—Charles & Peter. We got a number of fellows working in the adjacent fields & gave chase, but they were too cunning for us & gave us the slip, taking to the marsh after dropping their bag of provisions— cooking utensils &c &c. Returned and dined with the Major. Commenced thinning and hauling cotton on Carters Hill. It looks very sick and puny for its age. Returned home about ¼ past 3 p.m. & found that our folks had not yet dined. Shame to say it, we rise *later,* dine *later* & go to bed earlier than anyone on St. Helena Island.

May 16th. As soon as I was up, heard that sheep had been killed in the pen last night. Went to investigate the matter, found the meat in old Sancho's house. Rode in the field after breakfast, had Sancho tried. As soon as he found that he was found out he said that Mr. Sandiford's Charles (the fellow that we started yesterday) came and gave him the meat, but after several very doubtful tales I came to the conclusion that Sancho was leagued with the runaways. As he says that Charles was to return the same night & eat some of the meat with him & that he had retired into Toomer's woods for the day, rode over to the Major's, got the Capt. & himself to ride with me in search of the fellow. We traversed the woods & hedges in vain—saw nothing of the runaway, so returned home.

May 17th. Anthony did not catch Charles last night, but saw the other fellow that is out with Charles named Dick. Did not catch him. But I am convinced that my man Sancho harbors the pair of them, as they have both been to see him. What shall be done with this old rascal? . . .

Finished thinning and hauling the first planting of cotton & commenced hauling March corn. The only Negroes now sick are Rose since yesterday, Tony—22 days, viz. since the 27th of April. Peggy has not gone out to work yet. In fact she does not *want* to do anything. She has now been laying up for 82 or more days. . . .

May 23rd. Boat returned before I got up in the morning. They found the Negroes at Perry's & brought them over. They had no clothes but what they had on their backs. Sent the boat home. Ben & Violet went home in it, to work in my field the balance of the year.

Gained two hands

Col. Johnson & William Fickling had a falling out the other day, about the trial of a Negro woman for assault & battery. . . .

June 6th. Had fodder corn planted in the stable yard, for the benefit of the milk cow & calf. Heard that man Bidcome, down on the estate of W. S. Chaplin, had caught runaway Dick belonging to Mr. Sandiford. He & Charles, his companion, were in the sheep pen, had two sheep tied. Charles escaped by knocking down one of the men.

John B. Lamar to Mrs. Howell Cobb, April 26, 1846

Yours of the 22nd came duly to hand. With reference to the building of your negro house, I expect it would be best under all the circumstances to have it done as John proposed, let some one find all the materials & do the work at a specific price. But $250 is a high price for a negro house & unless it is to be a mighty fine negro house.

Whoever does the work ought to furnish certain specifications, such as the dimensions of the house, the number of lights &c so that you can have some means of judging if you are not paying double price.

My man Ned the carpenter is idle or nearly so at the plantation. He is fixing gates & like the idle groom in Pickwick trying to fool himself into the belief that he is doing something. But on considering his general character for intemperance & disobedience, & quarrelsomeness I have concluded it would be best to pay a little too much for the house, rather than inflict him on you at this time. While I was gone I had him in town & on returning found that he had been drunk & fighting, and misbehaving in every way, so that I have banished him to rural life. He is an eye servant. If I was with him I could have the work done soon & cheap, but I am afraid to trust him off where there is no one he fears. He is doing literally nothing at home, and sparing him would not be a cents expense as to that, but I conclude that you do not feel like being annoyed, just now, as I fear & almost know he would annoy you, by getting drunk & raising a row on the lot. I shall sell the rascal the first chance I get.

Elisha Cain, Overseer, to Alexander Telfair, Planter, November 4, 1833

I get on Prety well with all the negroes Except Darkey she is the most troublesome one on the place Making disturbances amongst the Rest of the negroes and there is hardly any of them will Even go near the yard, she is of such a cruel disposition, not Even her sisters family. she could not stay in the yard with the girls you sent up without making an interruption with them. at length she got so high I went there and give her a moderate correction and that had a Bad affect she then threatened their lives and said that she would poison them they become alarmed and ask me permission to move to the Quarter I give them leave they have Been in the Quarter about one weeke. as I have commenced the subject I will give you a full history of my Belief of Darkey. to wit I believe her disposition as to temper is as Bad as any in the whole world I believe she is as unfaithful as any I have Ever Been acquainted with in every respect I believe she has Been more injury to you in the place where she is than two such negroes would sell for. I do not believe there is any negro on the place But would do Better than she has Ever done since I have been acquainted with her. I have tryed and done all I could to get on with her hopeing that she would mend. But I have Been disappointed in Every instant. I can not hope for the better any longer.

Accounts of Slavery, 1823–c. 1930s

Solomon Northup Recalls Life Under Slavery

[I]nasmuch as some may read this book who have never seen a cotton field, a description of the manner of its culture may not be out of place.

The ground is prepared by throwing up beds or ridges, with the plough— back-furrowing, it is called. Oxen and mules, the latter almost exclusively, are used in ploughing. The women as frequently as the men perform this labor, feeding, currying, and taking care of their teams, and in all respects doing the field and stable work, precisely as do the ploughboys of the North.

The beds, or ridges, are six feet wide, that is, from water furrow to water furrow. A plough drawn by one mule is then run along the top of the ridge or center of the bed, making the drill, into which a girl usually drops the seed, which she carries in a bag hung round her neck. Behind her comes a mule and harrow, covering up the seed, so that two mules, three slaves, a plough and harrow, are employed in planting a row of cotton. This is done in the months of March and April. Corn is planted in February.

When there are no cold rains, the cotton usually makes its appearance in a week. In the course of eight or ten days afterwards the first hoeing is commenced. This is performed in part, also, by the aid of the plough and mule. The plough passes as near as possible to the cotton on both sides, throwing the furrow from it. Slaves follow with their hoes, cutting up the grass and cotton, leaving hills two feet and a half apart. This is called scraping cotton. In two weeks more commences the second hoeing. This time the furrow is thrown towards the cotton. Only one stalk, the largest, is now left standing in each hill. In another fortnight it is hoed the third time, throwing the furrow towards the cotton in the same manner as before, and killing all the grass between the rows. About the first of July, when it is a foot high or thereabouts, it is hoed the fourth and last time. Now the whole space between the rows is ploughed, leaving a deep water furrow in the center. During all these hoeings the overseer or driver follows the slaves on horseback with a whip, such as has been described. The fastest hoer takes the lead now. He is usually about a rod in advance of his companions. If one of them passes him, he is whipped. If one falls behind or is a moment idle, he is whipped. In fact, the lash is flying from morning until night, the whole day long. The hoeing season thus continues from April until July, a field having no sooner been finished once, than it is commenced again.

In the latter part of August begins the cotton picking season. At this time each slave is presented with a sack. A strap is fastened to it, which goes over the neck, holding the mouth of the sack breast high, while the bottom reaches nearly to the ground. Each one is also presented with a large basket that will hold about two barrels. This is to put the cotton in when the sack is filled. The baskets are carried to the field and placed at the beginning of the rows.

When a new hand, one unaccustomed to the business, is sent for the first time into the field, he is whipped up smartly, and made for that day to pick as fast as he can possibly. At night it is weighed, so that his capability in cotton picking is known. He must bring in the same weight each night following. If it falls short, it is considered evidence that he has been laggard, and a greater or less number of lashes is the penalty. . . .

There may be humane masters, as there certainly are inhuman ones— there may be slaves well-clothed, well-fed, and happy, as there surely are those half-clad, half-starved and miserable; nevertheless, the institution that tolerates such wrong and inhumanity as I have witnessed, is a cruel, unjust, and barbarous one. Men may write fictions portraying lowly life as it is, or as it is not—may expatiate with owlish gravity upon the bliss of ignorance— discourse flippantly from arm chairs of the pleasures of slave life; but let them toil with him in the field—sleep with him in the cabin—feed with him on husks; let them behold him scourged, hunted, trampled on, and they will come back with another story in their mouths. Let them know the *heart* of the poor slave—learn his secret thoughts—thoughts he dare not utter in the hearing of the white man; let them sit by him in the silent watches of the night—converse with him in trustful confidence, of "life, liberty, and the pursuit of happiness," and they will find that ninety-nine out of every hundred are intelligent enough to understand their situation, and to cherish in their bosoms the love of freedom, as passionately as themselves.

Overseer George Skipwith Writes His Absentee Master, 1847

hopewell July the 8 1847

Sir

on the forth day of July i reseved your letter dated may the 25. i wrote to you the 15 of June the second time giveing you a true statement of the crops, horses, hogs, and chickens. but i am sorry that I shall have to [write] you princeable about other matters. I hav a good crop on hand for you, borth of cotton and corn. this you know could not be don without hard work. i have worked the people but not out of reason. and i have whiped none without a caus   the persons whome i have correct i will tell you thir name and thir faults. Suky who I put to plant som corn and after she had been there long anuf to have been done i went there and she had hardly began it   i gave her some four or five licks over her clothes   i gave isham too licks over his clothes for coveering up cotten with the plow. I put frank, isham, Evally, Dinah, Jinny evealine and Charlott to sweeping cotten going twice in a roe. and at a Reasonable days worke they ought to hav plowed seven accers a peice. and they had been at it a half of a day. and they had not done more than one accer and a half and i gave them ten licks a peace upon their skins   i gave Evlyann eight or ten licks for misplacing her hoe. that was all the whiping I hav done from the time that I pitched the crop untell we commenced cutting oats. . . . when i come to them at twelve o clocke, they had cut some nineteen roes. and it would not take them more than ten minutes to cut one roe. Shadrack was the ruler among them, i spoke these words to him, you do not intend to cut these oats untill i whip every one of you. Shadrack did not say any thing to me. but Robert spoke these words saying that he knoed when he worked. i told him to shut his lips and if he spoke a nother worde i would whip him right of[f]   but he spoke again the second time saying that he was not afraid of being whiped by no man. i then gave him a cut with the whip. he then flong down his cradle and made a oath and said that he had as live die as to live and he said that he did not intend to stay here. he then tried to take the whip out of my hand, but i caught him fast by the collar and holed him. i then told the other boys to strip him and they don so   i then whiped untell i thought that he was pretty could   but i was deseived for as soon as i leave him and went to the hoe hands, he come up to the house to our preacher and his family becaus he knoed that they would protect him in his Rascality for he had herd that they had said that they were worked to death and that they were lowed no more chance for liveing than they were dogs or hogs. tho the preacher did not say any thing to me about whiping Robert neither to

Autograph Letter from George Skipwith, July 8, 1847, Cocke Family Papers (#2433-B), Manuscripts Division, Special Collections Department, University of Virginia Library. Reprinted with permission.

mas John but went down to the Shop and holed about an hours chat with the negroes   i do not knoe what his chat was to them but i ask Dr. Weeb. what was good for a negro that w[as] whipt albut to death and he had much to say about it. Dr. Weeb saw that his chat was calculated to incurage the people to rebel against me, and he went and told mas John about what he had herd and mas John took him and come up here to see if he was punished in the way he had herd. but as soon as the Dr put his hand upon him he told mas John that there was nothing the matter with him. mas John then ordered him to his worke and told him that he did not have what his crime was deserving him, and at some lesure time he intend to give him a good wallening and then he would knoe how to behave him self. he rode over the land and saw what they had done, and instead of finding fault of me he said i ought to have given the other three the same.

Lizzie Williams Looks Back on the Days of Slavery, Ca. 1930s

I'se born in Selma, Alabama, I can't mind how long ago, but just about ninety years. . . .

I'se born and live on old man Billy Johnson's plantation—thousands acres of ground and plenty of niggers. My pappy, he always belong to old man Billy. He not such a bad man but de Lord knows I'se seed better ones. When I'se right smart size, Missy Mixon, she was Marse Billy's wife's sister, she get Marse Billy to let her have me. She was a good woman. She took me to town to live and make a little white girl out of me. Y'all knows what I means. I got treated more like de white folks dan de rest of de niggers.

But 'twarn't long afore Missy send me to New Orleans to nurse de sick child of her sister. I never was satisfied down dere. Everybody so different. But de next year we go back to Alabama.

I went to Marse Ellis Mixon's. He terrible mean to his niggers. But I belong to de missus, she always treat me good. All de little niggers have to learn to work when dey little; get out and pull weeds. Dey never had no time to play. Most dem niggers was scared to death, just like de ones on Billy Johnson's plantation. Dey know dey get whipped just like a mule if dey act like dey don't wanna work. Dey never get much to eat, just side meat, corn bread and 'lasses. Old Billy he had overseers what was mean to de poor niggers. Sometime dey ties dem up and dey strip dem and dey whips dem with cowhide, else dey lets other niggers do it.

All de niggers have to go to church, just like de white folks. Dey have a part of de church for demselfs. After de War we have a church of our own. All de niggers love to go to church and sing. I mind a lot of de songs we used to sing in de fields. I mind my pappy used to sing in de field: "Get on Board, Little Chillen, Get on Board." Sometimes dey baptize in de river. Den dey sing:

> I wanna be ready,
> I wanna be ready,
> I wanna be ready, good Lord, to walk in Jerusalem just like John.
> John say de city was just four square,

To walk in Jerusalem just like John,
But I'll meet my mother and father dere,
To walk in Jerusalem, just like John.

I 'members about de patterollers. De niggers have to get a pass from de massa or de missus if dey go anywhere. De patterollers just like police. About dozen of dem ride along together. First thing dey say: "Where you pass?" Den if you have one dey lets you go but if you don't have one dey strips you to de waist and dey lams you good till de blood comes. Sometimes dey rolls you over a barrel and lams you while de barrel rolls.

I mind a tale my pappy tell about one time he see de patterollers comin'. He scared to death 'cause he didn't have no pass. He know if dey finds him what dey do. So Pappy he gets down in de ditch and throw sand and grunts like a hog. Sure 'nough, dey thinks he a hog and dey pass on, 'cept one who was behind de others. He say, "Dat am de gruntin'est old hog I ever hear. I think I go see him." But de others dey say: "Just let dat old hog alone and mind you own business." So dey pass on. Pappy he laugh about dat for long time.

I mind old Mose, he have monthly pass from de massa but he forget it one day and de patterollers whip him and throw him in de calaboose. In de mornin' when de massa wake and find no fresh water and no fire in de stove and de cows not milked, he say: "I know Mose in de callaboose," and he have to go after Mose.

Lots of de poor niggers run away, but 'twarn't no use. Dere weren't no place to go. Dey was always lookin' for you and den you had to work harder dan ever, besides all kinds of punishment you got. Den dey nearly starve you to death, just feed you on bread and water for long time.

De niggers never know nothin' about learning', just work all dey's fit for. De only thing I ever do with a book is just to dust it off. I mind two little niggers whose missy teach dem to read. Emily, she look like a white gal. She was treated just like she white. Her daddy was a white man. Emily was a smart gal. She belong to one of de Johnson mens. She do all de sewin' for her missy. When de missy go to buy clothes for de chillen she always take Emily along. Her pappy pay no more attention to her dan to de rest of de niggers. But de missy she was good to her. She never stay in de quarters; she stay in de house with de white folks. But Emily had de saddest look on her yaller face 'cause de other niggers whisper about her pappy. Many de poor nigger women have chillen for de massa, dat is if de massa a mean man. Dey just tell de niggers what to do and dey know better dan to fuss.

Old Missus she good to me. I mind one time I got terrible mad and say some ugly words. Marse Ellis he come up behind me and he say: "Lizabeth I gwine to wallop you good for dat." I commence cryin' and run to de missus and she say: "Look here, Ellis Mixon, y'all mind you own business and look after you own niggers. Dis one belongs to me." Just de same, when de missus went upstairs Marse Ellis take me in de smokehouse and start to hit me. I yell for de missus and when she come she plenty mad. Marse say he never meant to whip me, just scare me a little.

Messrs. Brooke and Hubbard Announce an Auction, 1823

10 LIKELY and VALUABLE
SLAVES
AT AUCTION.

On **THURSDAY** the 24th inst.
WE WILL SELL,
In front of our Office, without any kind of init or reserve for cash,
AT 11 O'CLOCK,
10 *AS LIKELY NEGROES*
As any ever offered in this market; among them is a man who is a superior Cook and House Servant, and a girl about 17 years old, a first rate House Servant, and an excellent seamstress.

BROOKE & HUBBARD,
Auctioneers.

Wednesday, July 23, 1823.   *Richmond va*

Broadside, Richmond, Virginia, 1823. Chicago Historical Society.

Free Blacks Petition the State of Virginia, 1838

To the Honorable Legislature of the State of Virginia
The undersigned humbly beg leave to represent unto your Honorable body that they are free people of color residing within the jurisdiction of the Corporation of Fredricksburg and natives of the State of Virginia—some of them descendants of soldiers of the revolution—others having been personally engaged in aiding the efforts of their country in the late War with England—That many of them are possessed of property, real as well as personal, & have therefore an abiding interest in preserving the peace and good order of the community. They beg leave further to represent that so general has become the diffusion of knowledge, that those persons who are so unfortunate as not to be in some slight degree educated, are cut off from the ordinary means of self-advancement & find the greatest difficulty in gaining an honest livelihood. In consequence of this consideration of things and of the prohibitory statutes of Virginia on this subject, the Undersigned have been heretofore compelled to send their children abroad for instruction. The expence attendant upon this course, though heavy to persons of small means, is the least important part of the evils growing out of it. The residence of their children in the North not merely deprives them of the fostering care

of their parents, but unavoidably exposes them to the risk of having their minds poisoned by doctrines alike inimical to the good order of society & destructive of their own interests.

Moved by these considerations, your petititioners humbly beg that an act be passed, authorizing a school in the Corporation of Fredricksburg, for the instruction of the free people of color resident therein—subject never-theless to such conditions & restrictions as to your honorable body may seem necessary & proper—And your petitioners will ever pray &c. &c.

The above petition having been [duly?] considered a Majority of the company [illegible] Mr. James Wilkins to be the bearer of the same to [illegible] presentation of Spotsylvania County.

Frances Kemble on Racism, Religion, and Fear in Georgia, 1838–1839

. . . [T]he Irish hate the Negroes more even than the Americans do, and there would be no bound to their murderous animosity if they were brought in contact with them on the same portion of the works of the Brunswick Canal. Doubtless there is some truth in this; the Irish laborers who might come hither would be apt enough, according to a universal moral law, to visit upon others the injuries they had received from others. They have been oppressed enough themselves to be oppressive whenever they have a chance; and the despised and degraded condition of the blacks, presenting to them a very ugly resemblance of their own home, circumstances naturally excite in them the exercise of the disgust and contempt of which they themselves are very habitually the objects; and that such circular distribution of wrongs may not only be pleasant, but have something like the air of retributive right to very ignorant folks, is not much to be wondered at. Certain is the fact, however, that the worst of all tyrants is the one who has been a slave; and, for that matter (and I wonder if the Southern slaveholders hear it with the same ear that I do, and ponder it with the same mind?), the command of one slave to another is altogether the most uncompromising utterance of insolent truculent despotism that it ever fell to my lot to witness or listen to. "You nigger—I say, you black nigger—you no hear me call you—what for you no run quick?"

All this, dear E[lizabeth], is certainly reasonably in favor of division of labor on the Brunswick Canal; but the Irish are not only quarrelers, and rioters, and fighters, and drinkers, and despisers of niggers—they are a passionate, impulsive, warmhearted, generous people, much given to pow-erful indignations, which break out suddenly when not compelled to smoulder sullenly—pestilent sympathizers too, and with a sufficient dose of American atmospheric air in their lungs, properly mixed with a right proportion of ardent spirits, there is no saying but what they might actually take to sym-

John A. Scott, ed., *Journal of a Residence on a Georgia Plantation in 1838–39 by Frances Anne Kemble* (New York: Knopf, 1961).

pathy with the slaves, and I leave you to judge of the possible consequences. You perceive, I am sure, that they can by no means be allowed to work together on the Brunswick Canal. . . .

Upon my word, E[lizabeth], I used to pity the slaves, and I do pity them with all my soul; but, oh dear! oh dear! their case is a bed of roses to that of their owners, and I would go to the slave block in Charleston tomorrow cheerfully to be purchased if my only option was to go thither as a purchaser. I was looking over this morning, with a most indescribable mixture of feelings, a pamphlet published in the South upon the subject of the religious instruction of the slaves, and the difficulty of the task undertaken by these reconcilers of God and Mammon really seems to me nothing short of piteous. "We must give our involuntary servants" (they seldom call them slaves, for it is an ugly word in an American mouth, you know) "Christian enlightenment," say they; and where shall they begin? "Whatsoever ye would that men should do unto you, do ye also unto them"? No; but "Servants, obey your masters"; and there, I think, they naturally come to a full stop. This pamphlet forcibly suggested to me the necessity for a slave Church Catechism, and also, indeed, if it were possible, a slave Bible. If these heaven-blinded Negro enlighteners persist in their pernicious plan of making Christians of their cattle, something of the sort must be done, or they will infallibly cut their own throats with this two-edged sword of truth, to which they should in no wise have laid their hand, and would not, doubtless, but that it is now thrust at them so threateningly that they have no choice. Again and again, how much I do pity them! . . .

I will tell you something curious and pleasant about my row back [from St. Simon's Island]. The wind was so high and the river so rough when I left the rice island, that just as I was about to get into the boat I thought it might not be amiss to carry my life preserver with me, and ran back to the house to fetch it. Having taken that much care for my life, I jumped into the boat, and we pushed off. The fifteen miles' row with a furious wind, and part of the time the tide against us, and the huge broad, turbid river broken into a foaming sea of angry waves, was a pretty severe task for the men. They pulled with a will, however, but I had to forego the usual accompaniment of their voices, for the labor was tremendous, especially toward the end of our voyage, where, of course, the nearness of the sea increased the roughness of the water terribly. The men were in great spirits, however (there were eight of them rowing, and one behind was steering); one of them said something which elicited an exclamation of general assent, and I asked what it was; the steerer said they were pleased because there was not another planter's lady in all Georgia who would have gone through the storm all alone with them in a boat; i.e., without the protecting presence of a white man. "Why," said I, "my good fellows, if the boat capsized, or anything happened, I am sure I should have nine chances for my life instead of one"; at this there was one shout of "So you would, missus; true for dat, missis"; and in great mutual good humor we reached the landing at Hampton Point.

As I walked home I pondered over this compliment of Mr. [Butler]'s slaves to me, and did not feel quite sure that the very absence of the fear which haunts the Southern women in their intercourse with these people, and prevents them from trusting themselves ever with them out of reach of white companionship and supervision, was not one of the circumstances which makes my intercourse with them unsafe and undesirable. The idea of apprehending any mischief from them never yet crossed my brain; and in the perfect confidence with which I go among them, they must perceive a curious difference between me and my lady neighbors in these parts; all have expressed unbounded astonishment at my doing so.

Reflections on Yeoman Egalitarianism, 1850–1851

David Moseley to Hugh A. Haralson, April 17, 1850

. . . look out for hard times and then the poor hard working democrats will be charged with it all and indeed there will be to much truth in it for if they would consider that their labour builds (or mostly) all the Great Citties furnish them with all their fine and lordly plate and fine furniture pairs of horses fine carriages and fine trappings and the fine jewelry and gay clothes which is worn . . . then they would keep more of the products of their labour out of the hands of the non producers and compel them to work starve or beg (or steel) the latter of which too many do or that which is as bad that is cheat them out of it. it is the producer that pays all the Great Government salaries builds all the navy and great harbors feeds the idle clothes the proud in short it is the producer that supports the publick and private enterprises of the whole country, and yet we readily and volunarily ape the rich buy superfluities and dainties that contaminates the mind and enfeebles the body and pay great profits on both thereby making out selves the servants of the non producers and I said the poor democrats . . . because they are genuinely the poor while the rich are the aristocrats (alias Whigs).

Letter to the Editor, Rome *[Georgia]* Weekly Courier, *September 25, 1851*

I am a plain farmer, but I hope I am nevertheless a freeman. I have to work hard for my living, and make my bread by the sweat of my brow. I was warned to appear in town last Saturday to muster. When we were dismissed, we were notified that Mr. Colquitt would speak in the afternoon. This set me to thinking and I found others were thinking too. How, thinks I to myself, does it happen that we are called out, when we are all busy gathering our little crop of cotton and hay . . . and compelled to come to Rome through the heat and dust to muster! I then recollected that our General . . . and . . . Colquitt . . . were anxious to make everyone like themselves; and if the people wouldn't come to town and hear without, they would get up a sham muster and make them come and hear anyhow. This sorter raised me that I should be compelled to have the same politics of my general . . . The next attempt, I fear . . . will be to march us poor working people up to the polls, and with their swords swinging over our heads, make us vote for who they please. As to this man they call Colquitt, I have heard of him before, with his black coffin and the flag with the nigger on it, and swords and such . . . and I have no use for him and his talk. I should like to know whether this is a free country, or whether we are to be dragged out from our business to gratify military men and political demogogues.

Contemporary Attacks and Counterattacks on Slavery, 1831–1832

The Confessions of Nat Turner, recorded 1831

And on the 12th of May, 1828, I heard a loud noise in the heavens, and the Spirit instantly appeared to me and said the Serpent was loosened, and Christ had laid down the yoke he had borne for the sins of men, and that I should take it on and fight against the Serpent, for the time was fast approaching when the first should be last and the last should be first. [Question] Do you not find yourself mistaken now? [Answer] Was not Christ crucified? And by signs in the heavens that it would be made known to me when I should commence the great work—and until the first sign appeared, I should conceal it from the knowledge of men—And on the appearance of the sign (the eclipse of the sun last February), I should arise and prepare myself, and slay my enemies with their own weapons. And immediately on the sign appearing in the heavens, the seal was removed from my lips, and I communicated the great work laid out before me to do, to four in whom I had the greatest confidence (Henry, Hark, Nelson, and Sam)—It was intended by us to have begun the work of death on the 4th of July last— Many were the plans formed and rejected by us, and it affected my mind to such a degree, that I fell sick, and the time passed without our coming to any determination how to commence—Still forming new schemes and rejecting them, when the sign appeared again, which determined me not to wait longer.

Since the commencement of 1830, I had been living with Mr. Joseph Travis, who was to me a kind master, and placed the greatest confidence in me: in fact, I had no cause to complain of his treatment of me. On Saturday evening, the 20th of August, it was agreed between Henry, Hark and myself, to prepare a dinner the next day for the men we expected, and then to concert a plan, as we had not yet determined on any. Hark, on the following morning, brought a pig, and Henry brandy, and being joined by Sam, Nelson, Will, and Jack, they prepared in the woods a dinner, where, about three o'clock, I joined them. . . .

I saluted them on coming up, and asked Will how came he there, he answered, his life was worth no more than others, and his liberty as dear to him. I asked him if he thought to obtain it? He said he would, or lose his life. This was enough to put him in full confidence. Jack, I knew, was only a tool in the hands of Hark, it was quickly agreed we should commence at home (Mr. J. Travis') on that night, and until we had armed and equipped ourselves, and gathered sufficient force, neither age nor sex was to be spared (which was invariably adhered to). We remained at the feast, until about two hours in the night, when we went to the house and found Austin; they all went to the cider press and drank, except myself. On returning to the house Hark went to the door with an axe, for the purpose of breaking it open, as we knew we were strong enough to murder the family, if they were awakened by the noise; but reflecting that it might create an alarm in the neighborhood, we determined to enter the house secretly, and murder them whilst sleeping. Hark got a ladder and set it against the chimney, on which I ascended, and hoisting a window, entered and came down stairs, unbarred the door, and removed the guns from their places. It was then observed that I must spill the first blood. On which, armed with a hatchet, and accompanied by Will, I entered my master's chamber, it being dark, I could not give a death blow, the hatchet glanced from his head, he sprang from the bed and called his wife, it was his last word, Will laid him dead, with a blow of his axe, and Mrs. Travis shared the same fate, as she lay in bed. The murder of this family, five in number, was the work of a moment, not one of them awoke; there was a little infant sleeping in a cradle, that was forgotten, until we had left the house and gone some distance, when Henry and Will returned and killed it; we got here, four guns that would shoot, and several old muskets, with a pound or two of powder. We remained some time at the barn, where we paraded; I formed them in a line as soldiers, and . . . carrying them through all the manoeuvres I was master of. . . .

The Virginia Legislature Debates Slavery's End, 1832

Mr. [Marshall] said he felt himself at liberty to say that he was opposed to slavery as a practical evil, particularly in that part of the country where he was best acquainted—exclusively a graingrowing region—and it all concurred with him, the day would ultimately come when the evil would disappear. He objected to slavery, not because it implies moral turpitude, or because it is a sin to be the owner of a slave. If it be a sin, then let the censure fall on those who introduced the evil, and have transmitted it to their offspring. We suffer the consequence of their transgression. "The fathers have eaten sour grapes, and the childrens' teeth are set on edge." It is a law of our nature, immutable as the will of Him who is the Author of Nature, that the sins of the fathers are visited upon the children. But why censure only our colonial ancestors? England, who fastened upon us the nefarious traffic, who rejected every solicitation for relief from its appalling consequences, and who now consumes, and profits by the produce of their labour—England ought first to atone for her participation in the guilt. If it be a sin, then let those who were the vile panders of the crime, who brought them to our shores for the profits of the voyage, and had not the poor excuse of requiring their labour in the cultivation of the soil—let them wash their polluted hands by some great act of national explation before they lift them in prayer to Heaven's majesty for the abolition of slavery. No, Sir; if slavery be a sin, we cannot, collectively or individually, be deemed culpable, until some wise, well digested, safe, practicable plan for its abolition, shall have been offered to our acceptance, and shall have been deliberately rejected.

Nor is it because of its demoralizing tendency that slavery should be abolished. The slaves are ignorant, it is true; and therefore it may be inferred, that much evil prevails among them; but he questioned whether they are not as exempt from the commission of gross crime as the lowest classes of any other country. With regard to the white portion of our community, the citizens of Virginia, of either sex, may lay as just a claim to purity of morals, to elevation of thought and action, to probity in all the transactions of life, as the citizens of any other State, or the people of any other country on the Globe.

Again:—The ordinary condition of the slave is not such as to make humanity weep for his lot. Compare his condition with that of the labourer in any part of Europe, and you will find him blessed with a measure of happiness nearly if not altogether equal. He could say this, with great confidence of that part of Virginia where he resided. The negro there is perfectly happy—he is treated with the most indulgent kindness—he is required to do the some work, and no more than is performed by the white man—he is clothed with the best fabric of the factories, and he is fed literally with the fat of the land.—It is not for his sake, then, nor to ameliorate his condition, that abolition is desirable. Wherefore, then, object to slavery? Because it is ruinous to the whites—retards improvement—roots out an industrious population—banishes the yeomanry of the country—deprives the spinner, the weaver, the smith, the shoe-maker, the carpenter of employment and support. This evil admits of no remedy; it is increasing, and will continue to increase, until the whole country will be inundated with one black wave covering its whole extent, with a few white faces here and there fleating on the surface. The master has no capital but what is vested in human flesh; the father, instead of being richer for his sons, is at a loss to provide for them—there is no diversity of occupations, no incentive to enterprize. Labour of every species is disreputable, because performed mostly by slaves. Our towns are stationary, our villages almost every where declining, and the general aspect of the country marks the curse of a wasteful, idle, reckless population, who have no interest in the soil, and care not how much it is impoverished. Public improvements are neglected, and the entire continent does not present a region for which nature has done so much, and art so little. If cultivated by free labour, the soil of Virginia is capable of sustaining a dense population, among whom labour would be honorable, and where "the busy hum of men" would tell that all were happy, and that all were free. . . .

But the question will be asked, what remedy do you propose for this growing evil? To this he would reply—strike at the annual increase of the colored population—endeavor to remove gradually as many of the blacks who are now free, and of those who may hereafter be emancipated for that purpose, as the resources of this great commonwealth will permit. Invoke the aid of the U. States, in the promotion of these objects and the ulterior one of purchase and deportation. Let every man retain his slave who wishes to keep him; and let the fund for transportation or for purchase and removal, be exclusively under State control.

Thomas Roderick Dew Defends Slavery, 1832

1st. It is said slavery is wrong, in the *abstract* at least, and contrary to the spirit of Christianity. To this we answer as before, that any question must be determined by its circumstances, and if, as really is the case, we cannot get rid of slavery without producing a greater injury to both the masters and slaves, there is no rule of conscience or revealed law of God which *can* condemn us. . . . With regard to the assertion, that slavery is against the spirit of Christianity, we are ready to admit the general assertion, but deny most positively that there is any thing in the Old or New Testament, which would go to show that slavery, when once introduced, ought at all events to be abrogated, or that the master commits any offence in holding slaves. The Children of Israel themselves were slave-holders, and were not condemned for it. When they conquered the land of Canaan they made one whole tribe "hewers of wood and drawers of water," and they were at that very time under the special guidance of Jehovah; they were permitted expressly to purchase slaves of the heathens, and keep them as an inheritance for their posterity—and even the Children of Israel might be enslaved for six years. When we turn to the New Testament, we find not one single passage at all calculated to disturb the conscience of an honest slave-holder. No one can read it without seeing and admiring that the meek and humble Saviour of the world in no instance meddled with the established institutions of mankind—he came to save a fallen world, and not to excite the black passions of men and array them in deadly hostility against each other. From no one did he turn away; his plan was offered alike to all—to the monarch and the subject—the rich and the poor the master and the slave. . . .

2dly. *But it is further said that the moral effects of slavery are of the most deleterious and hurtful kind;* and as Mr. Jefferson has given the sanction of his great name to this charge, we shall proceed to examine it with all that respectful deference to which every sentiment of so pure and philanthropic a heart is justly entitled.

"The whole commerce between master and slave," says he, "is a perpetual exercise of the most boisterous passions—the most unremitting despotism on the one part, and degrading submission on the other. Our children see this, and learn to imitate it, for man is an imitative animal—this quality is the germ of education in him. From his cradle to his grave, he is learning what he sees others do. If a parent had no other motive, either in his own philanthropy or self love, for restraining the intemperance of passion towards his slave, it should always be a sufficient one that his child is present. But generally it is not sufficient. The parent storms, the child looks on, catches the lineaments of wrath, puts on the same airs in the circle of smaller slaves, gives a loose to his worst of passions, and thus nursed, educated, and daily exercised in the worst of tyranny, cannot but be stamped by it with odious peculiarities." Now we boldly assert that the fact does not bear Mr. Jefferson out in his conclusions. He has supposed the master in a continual passion— in the constant exercise of the most odious tyranny, and the child, a creature of imitation, looking on and learning. But is not this master sometimes kind and indulgent to his slaves? does he not mete out to them, for faithful service, the reward of his cordial approbation? Is it not his interest to do it? and when thus acting humanely, and speaking kindly, where is the child, the creature of imitation, that he does not look on and learn? We may rest assured, in this intercourse between a good master and his servant, more good than evil *may* be taught the child, the exalted principles of morality and religion may thereby be sometimes indelibly inculcated upon his mind, and instead of being reared a selfish contracted being, with nought but self to look to—he acquires a more exalted benevolence, a greater generosity and elevation of soul, and embraces for the sphere of his generous actions a much wider field. Look to the slave-holding population of our country, and you everywhere find them characterized by noble and elevated sentiment, by humane and virtuous feelings. We do not find among them that cold, contracted, calculating *selfishness,* which withers and repels every thing around it, and lessens or destroys all the multiplied enjoyments of social intercourse. . . .

Let us now look a moment to the slave, and contemplate *his* position. Mr. Jefferson has described him as hating, rather than loving his master, and as losing, too, all that *amor patriae* which characterizes the true patriot. We assert again, that Mr. Jefferson is not borne out by the fact. We are well convinced that there is nothing but the mere relations of husband and wife, parent and child, brother and sister, which produce a closer tie, than the relation of master and servant. We have no hesitation in affirming, that throughout the whole slave-holding country, the slaves of a good master are his warmest, most constant, and most devoted friends; they have been accustomed to look up to him as their supporter, director, and defender. Every one acquainted with southern slaves, knows that the slave rejoices in the elevation and prosperity of his master; and the heart of no one is more gladdened at the successful debut of young master or miss on the great theatre of the world, than that of either the young slave who has grown up with them, and shared in all their sports, and even partaken of all their delicacies—or the aged one who has looked on and watched them from birth to manhood, with the kindest and most affectionate solicitude, and has ever met from them all, the kind treatment and generous sympathies of feeling tender hearts. . . .

3dly. *It has been contended that slavery is unfavourable to a republican spirit:* but the whole history of the world proves that this is far from being the case. In the ancient republics of Greece and Rome, where the spirit of liberty glowed with most intensity, the slaves were more numerous than the freemen. Aristotle, and the great men of antiquity, believed slavery necessary to keep alive the spirit of freedom. In Sparta, the freeman was even forbidden to perform the offices of slaves, lest he might lose the spirit of independence. In modern times, too, liberty has always been more ardently desired by slave-holding communities. "Such," says Burke, "were our Gothic ancestors; such, in our days, were the Poles; and such will be all masters of slaves who are not slaves themselves."—"These people of the southern (American) colonies are much more strongly, and with a higher and more stubborn spirit, attached to liberty, than those of the northward." And from the time of Burke down to the present day, the southern states have always borne this same honourable distinction. . . .

It seems to us, that those who insist most upon it, commit the enormous error of looking upon every slave in the whole slave-holding country as actuated by the most deadly enmity to the whites, and possessing all that reckless, fiendish temper, which would lead him to murder and assassinate the moment the opportunity occurs. This is far from being true; the slave, as we have already said, generally loves the master and his family; and few indeed there are, who can coldly plot the murder of men, women, and children; and if they do, there are fewer still who can have the villany to execute. We can sit down and imagine that all the negroes in the south have conspired to rise on a certain night, and murder all the whites in their respective families; we may suppose the secret to be kept, and that they have the physical power to exterminate; and yet, we say the whole is *morally impossible.* No insurrection of this kind can ever occur where the blacks are as much civilized as they are in the United States. . . . Any man who will attend to the history of the Southampton massacre, must at once see, that the cause of even the partial success of the insurrectionists, was the very circumstance that there was no extensive plot, and that Nat, a demented fanatic, was under the impression that heaven had enjoined him to liberate the blacks, and had made its manifestations by loud noises in the air, an eclipse, and by the greenness of the sun. It was these signs which determined *him,* and ignorance and superstition, together with implicit confidence in Nat, determined a few others, and thus the bloody work began. So fearfully and reluctantly did they proceed to the execution, that we have no doubt but that if Travis, the first attacked, could have waked whilst they were getting into his house, or could have shot down Nat or Will, the rest would have fled, and the affair would have terminated *in limine.*

We have read with great attention the history of the insurrections in St. Domingo, and have no hesitation in affirming, that to the reflecting mind, that whole history affords the most complete evidence of the difficulty and almost impossibility of succeeding in these plots, even under the most favourable circumstances. It would almost have been a *moral miracle,* if that revolution had not succeeded. The French revolution had kindled a blaze throughout the world. The society of the *Amis des Noirs* (the friends of the blacks,) in Paris, had educated and disciplined many of the mulattoes, who were almost as numerous as the whites in the island. The National Assembly, in its mad career, declared these mulattoes to be equal in all respects to the whites, and gave them the same privileges and immunities as the whites. During the ten years, too, immediately preceding the revolution, more than 200,000 negroes were imported into the island from Africa. It is a well known fact, that newly imported negroes are always greatly more dangerous than those born among us; and of those importations a very large proportion consisted of Koromantyn slaves, from the Gold Coast, who have all the savage ferocity of the North American Indian. And lastly, the whites themselves, disunited and strangely inharmonious, would nevertheless have suppressed the insurrections, although the blacks and mulattoes were nearly *fifteen-fold* their numbers, if it had not been for the constant and too fatal interference of France. The great sin of that revolution rests on the *National Assembly*, and should be an awful warning to every legislature to beware of too much tampering with so delicate and difficult a subject as an alteration of the fundamental relations of society. . . .

5thly, and lastly. *Slave labour is unproductive, and the distressed condition of Virginia and the whole South is owing to this cause.* Our limits will not allow us to investigate fully this assertion, but a very partial analysis will enable us to show that the truth of the general proposition upon which the conclusion is based, depends on circumstances, and that those circumstances do not apply to our southern country. . . .

We have already seen that the principle of idleness triumphed over the desire for accumulation among the savages of North and South America, among the African nations, among the blacks of St. Domingo, &c., and nothing but the strong arm of authority could overcome its operation. In southern countries, idleness is very apt to predominate, even under the most favourable circumstances, over the desire to accumulate, and slave labour, consequently, in such countries, is most productive. Again, staple-growing states are, *caeteris paribus,* more favourable to slave labour than manufacturing states. Slaves in such countries may be worked in bodies under the eye of a superintendent, and made to perform more labour than freemen. There is no instance of the successful cultivation of the sugar cane by free labour. St. Domingo, once the greatest sugar-growing island in the world, makes now scarcely enough for her own supply. We very much doubt even whether slave labour be not best for all southern agricultural countries. Humboldt, in his New Spain, says he doubts whether there be a plant on the globe so productive as the banana, and yet these banana districts, strange to tell, are the poorest and most miserable in all South America, because the people only labour a little to support themselves, and spend the rest of their time in idleness. There is no doubt but slave labour would be the most productive kind in these districts. We doubt whether the extreme south of the United States, and the West India islands, would ever have been cultivated to the same degree of perfection as now, by any other than slave labour.

But it is said free labour becomes cheaper than slave labour, and finally extinguishes it, as has actually happened in the West of Europe; this we are ready to admit, but think it was owing to a change in the tillage, and the rise of manufactures and commerce, to which free labour alone is adapted. . . .

⌗ *E S S A Y S*

In numerous books and essays, the historian Eugene D. Genovese of Atlanta University has offered a sustained and subtle class interpretation of the slave South, covering the worlds of both masters and slaves. In the opening selection, he explores what he considers the region's distinctive, noncapitalist form of paternalism—a web of obligations and expectations that bound masters and slaves together and ultimately fortified the masters' rule. George M. Fredrickson of Stanford University is a leading authority on the history of white racism. In the second essay, he directly challenges Genovese's writings for their alleged lack of focus on racial fears and prejudices as a foundation of planter-class ideology. In the final essay, Lawrence W. Levine, a historian at the University of California at Berkeley, concentrates on the slaves and their culture, in a sensitive reading of the meanings contained in various secular folk tales. His conclusions bear directly on the larger questions provoked by Genovese and Fredrickson about the character (and extent) of planter domination over southern life. Consider, too, how Levine's analysis might extend to the character of slave religion, mentioned in several of the preceding documents.

Paternalism and Class Relations in the Old South

EUGENE D. GENOVESE

Cruel, unjust, exploitative, oppressive, slavery bound two peoples together in bitter antagonism while creating an organic relationship so complex and ambivalent that neither could express the simplest human feelings without reference to the other. Slavery rested on the principle of property in man— of one man's appropriation of another's person as well as of the fruits of his labor. By definition and in essence it was a system of class rule, in which some people lived off the labor of others. American slavery subordinated one race to another and thereby rendered its fundamental class relationships more complex and ambiguous; but they remained class relationships. The racism that developed from racial subordination influenced every aspect of American life and remains powerful. But slavery as a system of class rule predated racism and racial subordination in world history and once existed without them. Racial subordination, as postbellum American developments and the history of modern colonialism demonstrate, need not rest on slavery. Wherever racial subordination exists, racism exists; therefore, southern slave society and its racist ideology had much in common with other systems and societies. But southern slave society was not merely one more manifestation of some abstraction called racist society. Its history was essentially determined by particular relationships of class power in racial form.

The Old South, black and white, created a historically unique kind of paternalist society. To insist upon the centrality of class relations as manifested in paternalism is not to slight the inherent racism or to deny the intolerable contradictions at the heart of paternalism itself. Imamu Amiri Baraka captures the tragic irony of paternalist social relations when he writes that slavery "was, most of all, a paternal institution" and yet refers to "the filthy paternalism and cruelty of slavery." Southern paternalism, like every other paternalism, had little to do with Ole Massa's ostensible benevolence,

Excerpts from *Roll Jordan, Roll: The World the Slaves Made* by Eugene Genovese (New York: Pantheon, 1974), pp. 3–25. Pantheon Books, Random House, Inc.

kindness, and good cheer. It grew out of the necessity to discipline and morally justify a system of exploitation. It did encourage kindness and affection, but it simultaneously encouraged cruelty and hatred. The racial distinction between master and slave heightened the tension inherent in an unjust social order.

Southern slave society grew out of the same general historical conditions that produced the other slave regimes of the modern world. The rise of a world market—the development of new tastes and of manufactures dependent upon non-European sources of raw materials—encouraged the rationalization of colonial agriculture under the ferocious domination of a few Europeans. African labor provided the human power to fuel the new system of production in all the New World slave societies, which, however, had roots in different European experiences and emerged in different geographical, economic, and cultural conditions. They had much in common, but each was unique.

The slaveholders of the South, unlike those of the Caribbean, increasingly resided on their plantations and by the end of the eighteenth century had become an entrenched regional ruling class. The paternalism encouraged by the close living of masters and slaves was enormously reinforced by the closing of the African slave trade, which compelled masters to pay greater attention to the reproduction of their labor force. Of all the slave societies in the New World, that of the Old South alone maintained a slave force that reproduced itself. Less than 400,000 imported Africans had, by 1860, become an American black population of more than 4,000,000.

A paternalism accepted by both masters and slaves—but with radically different interpretations—afforded a fragile bridge across the intolerable contradictions inherent in a society based on racism, slavery, and class exploitation that had to depend on the willing reproduction and productivity of its victims. For the slaveholders paternalism represented an attempt to overcome the fundamental contradiction in slavery: the impossibility of the slaves' ever becoming the things they were supposed to be. Paternalism defined the involuntary labor of the slaves as a legitimate return to their masters for protection and direction. But, the masters' need to see their slaves as acquiescent human beings constituted a moral victory for the slaves themselves. Paternalism's insistence upon mutual obligations—duties, responsibilities, and ultimately even rights—implicitly recognized the slaves' humanity.

Wherever paternalism exists, it undermines solidarity among the oppressed by linking them as individuals to their oppressors. A lord (master, *padrone, patron, padrón, patrão*) functions as a direct provider and protector to each individual or family, as well as to the community as a whole. The slaves of the Old South displayed impressive solidarity and collective resistance to their masters, but in a web of paternalistic relationships their action tended to become defensive and to aim at protecting the individuals against aggression and abuse; it could not readily pass into an effective weapon for liberation. Black leaders, especially the preachers, won loyalty and respect and fought heroically to defend their people. But despite their will and considerable ability, they could not lead their people over to the attack against the paternalist ideology itself.

In the Old South the tendencies inherent in all paternalistic class systems intersected with and acquired enormous reinforcement from the tendencies inherent in an analytically distinct system of racial subordination. The two appeared to be a single system. Paternalism created a tendency for the slaves to identify with a particular community through identification with its master; it reduced the possibilities for their identification with each other as a class. Racism undermined the slaves' sense of worth as black people and reinforced their dependence on white masters. But these were tendencies, not absolute laws, and the slaves forged weapons of defense, the most important of which was a religion that taught them to love and value each other, to take a critical view of their masters, and to reject the ideological rationales for their own enslavement.

The slaveholders had to establish a stable regime with which their slaves could live. Slaves remained slaves. They could be bought and sold like any other property and were subject to despotic personal power. And blacks remained rigidly subordinated to whites. But masters and slaves, whites and blacks, lived as well as worked together. The existence of the community required that all find some measure of self-interest and self-respect. Southern paternalism developed as a way of mediating irreconcilable class and racial conflicts; it was an anomaly even at the moment of its greatest apparent strength. But, for about a century, it protected both masters and slaves from the worst tendencies inherent in their respective conditions. It mediated, however unfairly and even cruelly, between masters and slaves, and it disguised, however imperfectly, the appropriation of one man's labor power by another. Paternalism in any historical setting defines relations of superordination and subordination. Its strength as a prevailing ethos increases as the members of the community accept—or feel compelled to accept—these relations as legitimate. Brutality lies inherent in this acceptance of patronage and dependence, no matter how organic the paternalistic order. But southern paternalism necessarily recognized the slaves' humanity—not only their free will but the very talent and ability without which their acceptance of a doctrine of reciprocal obligations would have made no sense. Thus, the slaves found an opportunity to translate paternalism itself into a doctrine different from that understood by their masters and to forge it into a weapon of resistance to assertions that slavery was a natural condition for blacks, that blacks were racially inferior, and that black slaves had no rights or legitimate claims of their own.

Thus, the slaves, by accepting a paternalistic ethos and legitimizing class rule, developed their most powerful defense against the dehumanization implicit in slavery. Southern paternalism may have reinforced racism as well as class exploitation, but it also unwittingly invited its victims to fashion their own interpretation of the social order it was intended to justify. And the slaves, drawing on a religion that was supposed to assure their compliance and docility, rejected the essence of slavery by projecting their own rights and value as human beings. . . .

Half the slaves in the South lived on farms, not on plantations as defined by contemporaries—that is, units of twenty slaves or more. Typically, a twenty-slave unit would embrace only four families. If a big plantation is to be defined as a unit of fifty slaves, then only one-quarter of the southern slaves lived on big plantations. The slaveholders of the Caribbean or Brazil would have been amused by this definition, for their own plantations usually had more than one hundred slaves. For the slaves in those areas dominated by farms, some degree of contact among slaves of different masters compensated for the absence of the big plantation community. But slaves on small farms within the areas dominated by large plantations risked greater isolation unless neighboring planters and slaves welcomed them as guests.

By reputation farmers treated their slaves better than planters did, but this reputation depended on a questionable belief in a major difference between practices in the predominantly small-farm Upper South and those in the plantation Lower South. Good treatment of slaves, as defined by the masters, did not necessarily constitute good treatment from the slaves' point of view. Travelers usually reported that most small farmers showed their slaves greater consideration and worked them more humanely. . . .

No clear verdict emerges from the slaves' reports. Farmers, small planters, and big planters seem to have been more or less alike in this respect. To Anna Hawkins, an ex-slave from Georgia, her alcoholic small-farm master was "the meanest man that ever lived," and the evidence of a number of ex-slaves lent credence to the charge that some small farmers bought slaves before they could profitably use them or decently feed and care for them. Others reported that they received kind treatment and said they felt like part of the family. . . . If white and black accounts are weighed, the pace of work and the material conditions seem to have differed on the small farms, but the range of treatment seems about the same as that prevailing on the big plantations.

Farms of ten slaves or less did not develop an extensive division of labor. The white farmer and his wife divided chores, but the extent of specialization among the slaves rarely went beyond the assignment of one or two women to house work; and even they had to work in the fields when needed. A common effort by master and slave at work together produced an easy familiarity, reinforced by living arrangements. The mistress or perhaps a female slave cooked for all at the same time and in the same way. Only segregation at table drew a caste line. The slaves either slept in one small house with the master's family or in a cabin that faced on the same yard. Slave and free, black and white, lived close to one another, and their relationship led to a widespread reputation for "better treatment." . . .

The argument for the greater humanity of the small slaveholders turned, to a great extent, on the fact of greater intimacy, of rough camaraderie, and of mutual sympathy born in common quarters. But, as Kenneth Stampp observes, there is no reason to believe that the slaves always welcomed this intimacy, for it meant constant scrutiny by whites and drastically reduced contact with fellow blacks. . . .

Plantation slaves did not clamor to be sold to small farmers even when they had a choice. After noting that slaves on small farms had more freedom of movement than those on the plantations, Olmsted added that they rarely wanted to be sold to the up country. When he asked a slaveholder for an explanation, he was told that blacks feared the mountains. He regarded the answer as irrational and suggested that the slaves did not want to find themselves among an overwhelming white majority. The slaveholder might have had a point, for among some West Africans highlands and mountains are regarded as the dwelling place of the gods and are indeed to be feared. But above all, slaves wanted to avoid sale to masters of scanty means, not primarily for reasons of the status attached to a rich master—an attitude much exaggerated by contemporary and subsequent commentators—but because they understood that their own family and community security depended upon their owner's solvency. . . .

A large majority of plantation slaves lived with resident owners, and a large additional minority with part-time resident owners. If the approximate half of all rural slaves who lived on units smaller than plantations are included, then the overwhelming majority of the slaves of the South lived with their masters and worked under their supervision. The correlation between cruelty and absenteeism proposed by some abolitionists and by planters with uneasy consciences has some truth, but it breaks down. The blame for too many evils falls directly upon the shoulders of resident planters, who caused them themselves or whose overseers did while working under their daily review, whereas too many other masters, with hundreds of slaves on scattered plantations, strove to guarantee humane treatment, to keep families together, and to keep their overseers on as tight a leash as circumstances permitted. If the absence of these masters exposed the slaves to their overseers' harsher side, the solidity of the masters' fortunes also minimized the risk of sale and community disruption.

The blame for much of the cruelty to slaves, as well as for much of the inefficiency in southern agriculture, nevertheless fell on the overseers. Hardly a planter could be found, except on the South Carolina and Georgia coast where a particularly respected class of overseers operated, who did not claim that they were at best a necessary evil. . . .

Contrary to legend, no more than one-third and possibly only one-fourth of the rural slaves worked under overseers, and many of these either worked under an overseer and a resident planter simultaneously or under an overseer who was a relative of the planter. Kenneth Stampp has suggested that the total number of overseers roughly equaled the number of units with thirty or more slaves, but most of these units probably had resident owners. . . .

Overseers were either the sons or close kin of the planters, who were learning to be planters in their own right; or floaters who usually lived up to the reputation of their class, the "po' white trash," and created for all overseers a particularly bad reputation; or, the largest group, a semiprofes-

sional class of men who expected to spend their lives overseeing or wanted
to earn enough money to buy a farm. However much the professionals, who
constituted the majority, may have striven to meet their responsibilities to
masters and even slaves, their chances for success rarely ran high. Outside
the aristocratic low country of the eastern seaboard and the Mississippi Delta,
overseers came and went every two or three years. When they did not fall
short in performance, they often fell victim to the slaveholders' notion that
a change of overseers was good in itself. Whatever the reasons and whoever
among the whites deserves the blame, those slaves who worked under these
rough and exploited men often suffered much harshness.

Slaveholders fired overseers for a variety of reasons. They fired those
who treated their slaves too leniently, and much more often, those who
treated them too harshly. "It is an indisputable fact," reported Solon Robinson, "that an overseer who urged the slaves beyond their strength, or that
inflicted cruel or unnecessary punishment, or failed to see them well-fed, or
kindly taken care of when sick, would be as sure to lose his place, as though
he permitted them to be idle and waste their time." . . .

The overseers who fell under the charge of indulgence did not necessarily
have a more humane or less racist attitude toward the slaves. Rather, they
knew that they would not keep their jobs without some degree of support
in the quarters, and accordingly, they tried to curry favor. No sensible
slaveholder wanted a man who could not maintain a certain level of morale
among the slaves. Thus, the slaves had an opening. They knew it, and they
seized it.

The overseers' problems included the effect that the class distance between them and their employers had on the slaves. Confronted with employers who, even when respectful and friendly, held them at arm's length,
the overseers could hardly have expected the slaves to offer them more
respect than that which fear induced. As William Kauffman Scarborough
aptly concludes, the overseers, ostracized by those above and forbidden by
edict and convention from associating with those below, lived in a social
vacuum. When they deferred to their employers, they courted disdain; when
they showed some spirit, they courted dismissal. In either case they were
branded as lacking "dignity"—no small charge in this quasi-traditional society. Since the overseer lacked status and dignity, he had for the most part
to rely on force; but since, in the diabolical workings of the world in which
he found himself, he ultimately needed the approval of the victims of his
force, he also had to win friends.

Whatever the racist pretensions, whatever the cries for white unity across
class lines, whatever the "obvious fact" that a sane master should take the
word of his overseer against that of his slaves, the masters, who were indeed
sane, did no such stupid thing. An overseer had to control the people: that
was what he got paid for. To control the people meant maintaining a certain
level of morale. How he did it was his business. If he did not do it, the
reason and the fault were of academic interest. He had to go. But beneath
this ruthless indifference lay a simple truth. The masters understood that
their slaves had brains, ability, self-discipline, and an interest, however psy-

chologically antagonistic, in the smooth running of the plantation which fed black and white alike. Therefore, it was the overseer's business to manage them, not vice versa. . . .

Any sensible master, notwithstanding all pretensions and professions, trusted his slaves against his overseer. Overseers came and went; the slaves remained. A shrewd and successful Alabama planter, who said that "an overseer is only wanted because the negroes can't be trusted," demanded that his overseers hide their faults from the slaves: "But if not possible then never in any event whatever request or require the negroes to conceal his faults from the employer—In such case the overseer is unmanned—better to retire at once from a place he can but disgrace, when afraid his hands may tell on him." . . .

In keeping overseers they neither trusted nor fully respected under surveillance, masters necessarily relied on their slaves for information. After Charles M. Manigault received a letter attributing an unexpectedly short rice crop to weather and tides, he wrote back: "You must make use of your usual prudence to ferret out *this mystery* by enquiring of the driver, trunk-minder & without shewing that you believe in the Overseer's incapacity. Then make up your mind whether he is an *imbécille* [sic]—or whether he be not in fault & all other qualities are tolerable." . . .

The overseers, smarting under these rebukes and this implicit denigration, struck back when they could. William Capers, one of Manigault's strong overseers, who had been taught his job by an uncle, asserted, as his uncle had before him, that a man who would place any confidence in a Negro was a damned fool. . . .

The slaves took advantage of these conflicts to make life easier for themselves, and even tough taskmasters among the slaveholders intervened occasionally in their behalf. In some cases the overseers adjusted well and actually won the affection of the slaves, who would praise their fairness. But usually tension prevailed. And with it, the slaves ran great risks, for whenever they succeeded in curbing an overseer's power and wringing some additional living space, they incurred his wrath and, one way or another, had to take blows.

The slaves' success in playing master and overseer against each other emerged in stark form in an article written by a slaveholder for a widely read agricultural journal. He quoted "a very shrewd old negro man" as saying, "Dese nic' yune oberseers ain't wut nuthin; one man like mas' Dick is wut more'n all uv em put together." Naturally, the writer approved the old slave's stated preference for Ole Massa, which "struck me as sensible." The old slave was much shrewder than the writer knew. He had calmly set himself up to judge the relative merits of white men and demonstrated that all he had to do to get away with it was to indulge in a little flattery.

The game had unpleasant consequences. Most obviously, it reinforced the slaves' dependence on the master. Negatively, it provided, in the overseer, a conducting rod for their dissatisfactions; the master often dropped from sight as the man responsible for their condition. Positively, the periodic intervention of the master in their defense against excesses reinforced his self-image and his image in the quarters as a protector. . . .

The hostility between slaves and overseers reflected a more general hostility between slaves and lower-class whites. Several famous runaways left biting accounts of those they perceived as "poor whites." Frederick Douglass opened his famous *Life and Times* with a reference to having been born among "a white population of the lowest order, indolent and drunken to a proverb." He provided a portrait of Edward Covey, a poor white man working his way up as a professional "nigger breaker," who obtained needed labor for his farm by renting slaves at a nominal sum from planters who wanted them cured of "impudence." Douglass added a moving account of being beaten and abused by white shipyard workers, yet he also testified to some sympathy from Irish workers on the Baltimore wharf. . . .

Ex-slaves later recalled poor white neighbors as "one of our biggest troubles." Those poor whites would encourage slaves to steal and then cheat them in trade; would steal themselves and blame slaves; would seduce impressionable young slave girls; and above all, provided the backbone of the hated slave patrols, which whipped and terrorized slaves caught without passes after curfew. And besides, the slaves regarded the poor whites as the laziest and most dissolute people on earth; it was probably the slaves who dubbed the poor whites "trash."

The slaveholders heartily concurred in their slaves' attitude toward the poor whites and tried to strengthen it. But actual relations between slaves and local poor whites were complex and included much more than mutual distaste and hatred. Many of the slaves who stole their masters' goods sold them to poor whites at drinking and gambling parties, which could promote genuine friendships and encourage a dangerous ambivalence on both sides. The same poor white who proved a brute on patrol might help a particular slave to run away or to outwit his master. Sometimes, the poor whites befriended slaves in order to spite a slaveholder they hated or envied, or conversely, out of a sudden burst of *noblesse oblige* modeled on the planters; sometimes because of a particular friendship with a slave that had developed despite racist attitudes. The slaveholders felt that no white man other than the most degraded would enter into such illicit and even leveling associations with blacks, and that nothing except trouble for the plantation community would come from these contacts.

But, the slaveholders could go only so far in encouraging their slaves' contempt for the poor whites, for it quickly became a safe vehicle for expressing contempt for all whites. When the slaves sang, "I'd rather be a nigger than a poor white man," they were attacking prevalent racist doctrine, at least in its most extreme form. Gustavus A. Ingraham of Maine, trying to build up a small business in Augusta, Georgia, wrote in 1840 that the Negroes "are however too sycophantic as a race but there are some exceptions and these are too proud to speak to a common white man like myself."

The slaveholders had other worries. Many suspected that nonslaveholders would encourage slave disobedience and even rebellion, not so much out of sympathy for the blacks as out of hatred for the rich planters and resentment of their own poverty. White men sometimes were linked to slave insurrectionary plots, and each such incident rekindled fears. By deciding that lower-class whites who associated with blacks were "degraded," the slaveholders explained away the existence of such racial contacts and avoided reflecting on the possibility that genuine sympathy might exist across racial lines. They also upheld stern police measures against whites who illicitly fraternized with blacks, and justified a widespread attempt to keep white and black laborers apart. The circumstances of lower-class white-black contact therefore encouraged racist hostilities and inhibited the maturation of relationships of mutual sympathy if not equality.

Such relationships of mutual sympathy between slaves and poor whites did exist. They remained few in number, but their existence was ominous in a society in which no sane member of the ruling class wanted to take chances. Lewis Clarke, a successful runaway, recalled a slave woman who suffered fifty lashes for slipping food to a sick old poor white neighbor. Olmsted reported a slave's stout defense of poor Cajuns as good, hard-working people. Recollections by former slaves during the twentieth century are especially compelling since their postemancipation relationships with poor whites could rarely have been such to inspire a romantic reading of the long past. Most spoke harshly of the poor whites and especially recalled their vicious behavior as members of the patrols. But some added other information and judgments. They recalled poor whites and immigrant laborers who appealed to the slaves, often successfully, for food and help in desperate circumstances. They spoke compassionately of the terrible struggle the poor whites had and of how their suffering often rivaled or exceeded that of the slaves. They spoke of kindnesses shown by poor whites to slaves of hard masters and of hired white laborers who worked side by side with the slaves ("helped us") and who shared the good times as well as the backbreaking labor.

Fanny Kemble, in an account of the hiring of Irishmen and blacks to dig a canal, captured the quality of race relations among the poor as well as the potential. The planters, she wrote, insisted on segregating the laborers ostensibly to prevent violence, for the Irish were believed anxious to take every opportunity to abuse the blacks. Mrs. Kemble reflected:

> They [the Irish] have been oppressed enough themselves to be oppressive whenever they have a chance; and the despised and degraded condition of the blacks, presenting to them a very ugly resemblance of their own home circumstances, naturally excites in them the exercise of the disgust and contempt of which they themselves are very habitually the objects; and that such circular distribution of wrongs may not only be pleasant, but have something like the air of retributive right to very ignorant folks, is not much to be wondered at. . . . But the Irish are not only quarrelers, and rioters, and fighters, and drinkers, and despisers of niggers—they are a passionate, impulsive, warm-hearted, generous people, much given to powerful indignations, which break out suddenly when not compelled to smoulder sullenly—pestilent sympathizers too, and with a sufficient dose of American

atmospheric air in their lungs, properly mixed with a right proportion of ardent spirits, there is no saying but what they might actually take to sympathy with the slaves, and I leave you to judge of the possible consequences. You perceive, I am sure, that they can by no means be allowed to work together on the Brunswick Canal.

The scattered incidents recalled by ex-slaves merely hint at the potential perceived by Mrs. Kemble and feared by the slaveholders. Whether in time changing conditions would have created a new political situation remains a matter of speculation; under the political and social conditions of the Old South, interracial solidarity could not develop into a serious threat to the regime. The hostility of the poor whites toward the blacks reinforced the regime and forced the slaves into increased reliance on the protection of their masters and other "good" and "quality" whites. The overseers thus came to symbolize not so much the class oppression of slavery as the racist hostility of all lower-class whites. The attitudes of the blacks and poor whites were not to pass away easily, and their consequences during Reconstruction and the Populist period were devastating.

The Role of Race in the Planter Ideology of South Carolina

GEORGE M. FREDRICKSON

If the legendary Old South of dashing cavaliers and their fair ladies existed anywhere outside of the imagination of romantic writers, it was in South Carolina and especially in the lowcountry. Here one could find great houses to rival the country seats of the English gentry, slave quarters large enough to be villages, and immense plantings of rice and sea island cotton worked by hordes of slaves. By the 1820s and 1830s, with the rise of short staple cotton, the piedmont above Columbia had also become a region of great plantations, and the Tidewater culture and much of its splendor had moved upcountry. Since it was in the plantation districts of South Carolina that the aristocratic life style reached its culmination, it is here also that one would expect to find the fullest development of a distinctive world-view or ideology reflecting the hopes and fears of the men who ruled the Old South and eventually led its struggle for independence. . . .

In his discussion of the emerging world-view of the Old South's ruling class, [Eugene] Genovese does not pay any special attention to South Carolina. But the Palmetto State would seem to provide an ideal testing ground for his thesis that it was the rise of a paternalistic world-view within a precapitalist ruling class that accounts for the triumph of proslavery and secessionist ideologies. [I]t was here that the trappings of aristocracy were most in evidence and here that southern cultural nationalism and the defense of slavery as a positive good were most insistently promulgated. Is it possible, then, that the rulers of South Carolina were—in aspiration if not in literal fact—a precapitalist landed aristocracy, who found that their survival in a

Excerpts from *The Arrogance of Race: Historical Perspectives on Slavery, Racism, and Social Equality* by George M. Fredrickson (Wesleyan University Press, 1988), pp. 15–25.

bourgeois world required extreme measures and ultimately an armed struggle against the hated proponents of capitalism, middle-class democracy, and so-called free labor?

Stripped to its essentials, Genovese's thesis requires us to believe that a paternalistic relationship between master and slave gave rise to a slave-holders' philosophy or world-view that was antithetical to the aggressive, bourgeois-capitalist ethos of the North. Southern planters, he contends, should not be regarded as deviant capitalists with peculiar interests. Nor were they particularly Negrophobic; for their paternalism was apparently a real barrier to the kind of race hate that could emerge in a bourgeois society. To understand them and their actions, we have to acknowledge that "theirs was an aristocratic, antibourgeois spirit with values and mores emphasizing family and status, a strong code of honor, and aspirations to luxury, ease and accomplishment. In the planter's community paternalism provided the standard of human relationships, and politics and statecraft were the re-sponsibility of gentlemen." In Genovese's view this ruling class went to war in 1861 because an emerging capitalist world order was increasingly denying its right to exist.

The apparent advantage of Genovese's class analysis is its comprehen-siveness. He does not have to deny the existence of economic concerns or racial consciousness. He can simply subsume these orientations under his broader conception of class culture and interest. To survive, a ruling class obviously needs to protect its economic base and to maintain its sense of superiority over lower or dependent classes by relying on whatever symbols of social differentiation are available. Effective hegemony over slaves and lower-class whites was achieved, he contends, primarily because the planters' paternalistic outlook and behavior made possible a pattern of mutual loyalties and responsibilities that did not eliminate class conflict but did serve to contain it. If blacks were regarded as inferior and suited only for slavery, they were also treated with condescending affection and won for themselves customary rights and privileges reminiscent of those accorded to dependent peasant communities in other precapitalist societies.

Magnificent in its theoretical complexity and sophistication, Genovese's interpretation becomes problematical when we try to apply it to the living and breathing aristocrats of antebellum South Carolina. Paternalism can be defined in various ways, but presumably it must involve some sense of quasi-kinship transcending barriers of caste or race. If so, it becomes difficult to establish that South Carolina planters were consciously and sincerely pater-nalistic. Certainly they were aristocratic. At bottom, an aristocracy is any social class that possesses a strong sense of itself as having both the right and the obligation to rule over the rest of society, and that generally succeeds in imposing its will. It need not be closed, but can incorporate new blood so long as the *arrivistes* have the right personal attributes and play the game according to the rules. But aristocracies do not have to be paternalistic. If they are particularly fearful or contemptuous of their underlings and if they have sufficient power at their disposal, they can rule almost exclusively by coercion and intimidation for long periods of time. To deny this possibility would be to take an exceedingly conservative and romantic view of the history of human inequality.

At the heart of Genovese's hypothesis is his conception of the master-slave relationship as involving intimate ties of dependency and mutual obligation. As he makes clear in *Roll, Jordan, Roll*, the relationship was not devoid of conflict and ambiguity; indeed, masters and slaves had quite different conceptions of what was due them. But the ability of the slaves to translate customary patronage into "rights" did not alter the slaveholder's belief that his dominance was a beneficent exercise of paternal responsibility over his dependents. Such an ideology did not preclude stern discipline or even cruelty, but presumably it put real limits on repression and Negrophobia. But did South Carolina slaveholders really view their connection with their bondsmen in this quasi-familial light? Often they asserted that slaves were well treated and contented with their lot. Sometimes slaves were described as "childlike"; but it does not necessarily follow that this alleged childishness made them, even in a symbolic sense, the children of their masters. Indeed, planter spokesmen in South Carolina frequently confessed that force was the real basis of their authority and that slavery was more like a repressed state of war than a peaceful patriarchy. In 1822, Edwin C. Holland, a member of the lowcountry gentry, described the slaves as "the Jacobins of the country against whom we should always be on guard." They are, he continued, "the *anarchists* and *the domestic enemy; the common enemy of civilized society,* and the barbarians who would IF THEY COULD become the destroyers of our own race." The following year, in the wake of the Denmark Vesey conspiracy, a group of Charlestonians petitioned the state legislature for a strengthening of slave discipline and concluded that "the only principle that can maintain slavery [is] the principle of fear." Such sentiments did not disappear with the subsiding of the insurrection panic of the 1820s. In 1845, James Henry Hammond, one of the most articulate and influential of South Carolina's proslavery apologists, conceded in an open letter to a British abolitionist that southern masters had been forced "to abandon our efforts to attach [the slaves] to us, and control them through their affections and pride. We have had to rely more and more on the power of fear." He attributed this state of affairs to abolitionist agitation, but we know from his biographers and personal records that Hammond ran his own plantation as a strict disciplinarian who took nothing for granted, partly because he had once found it necessary to break the spirit of an entire slave force that had grown insubordinate from lenient rule.

It is well established that the lash, or the threat of the lash, was used constantly by masters in South Carolina, as elsewhere in the slaveholding South, to make the slaves "stand in fear." Firm discipline, sustained by a dread of punishment, was deemed absolutely essential to plantation profits and efficiency. The need for a quasi-military discipline and an almost icy lack of familiarity between masters and slaves was a constant refrain in the literature of plantation management. And the lash was not the ultimate sanction of the master's authority. On the basis of what we now know about the strong family attachments of slaves, it appears that the threat of sale may have been the keystone of coercive slave control. The mere ability of a master to separate a slave irrevocably from family and friends gave him a capacity for intimidation far beyond that of any precapitalist landlord dealing with his serfs or tenants. The kind of leverage that this power provided can perhaps be illustrated by the following entry from the 1858 diary of an upcountry slaveholder: "This morning I had a difficulty with Matt. I tied him up and gave him a gentle admonition in the shape of a good whipping. I intended to put him in jail and keep him there until I sold him, but he seemed so penitent and promised so fairly and the other negroes promising to see that he behaved himself in the future that I concluded that I would try him again."

Much additional evidence could be amassed to show that force and intimidation rather than a flexible set of paternalistic understandings was often at the root of the master-slave relationship. Many planters apparently felt that their very lives depended on being able to strike terror in the hearts of their slaves when the occasion demanded. Much of the talk about loyal and contented bondsmen was probably cant or self-deception. The British journalist William Howard Russell reported from South Carolina in 1861,

> No planter hereabouts has any dread of his slaves, but I have seen within the short time I have been in this part of the world, several dreadful accounts of murder and violence, in which masters suffered at the hands of their slaves. There is something suspicious in the constant, never ending statement that "we are not afraid of our slaves." The curfew and the night patrol in the streets, the prison and watch-houses, and the police regulations, prove that strict supervision, at all events, is needed and necessary.

The lowland gentry would have had particularly strong reasons to fear and distrust their slaves, because they usually had little face-to-face contact with most of them and no reason to count on their personal loyalty. After accompanying the master of a large plantation north of Georgetown on a tour of his estate, Russell made the following observation about the demeanor of the field hands in the presence of their owner: "The men and women were apathetic, neither seeking nor shunning us, and *I found that their master knew nothing about them.* It is only the servants engaged in household duties who are at all on familiar terms with their masters." It is worth noting in this connection that the lowcountry planters usually spent their summers in their town houses in Charleston to escape the fever in the country districts and that on large South Carolina plantations it was common for the slave quarters to be a mile or more away from the big house.

The sense of mutual alienation that apparently existed between masters and field slaves, at least on the big plantations, was not simply a result of the scale of economic organization. The sense of racial difference and, on the part of the whites, of racial superiority probably constituted a formidable barrier to the growth of paternalistic intimacy. Historians have strangely neglected the role of racial attitudes and ideologies in shaping the way that planters viewed their slaves. Genovese acknowledges planter racism but de-emphasizes its significance. Other historians have suggested that planter-politicians made racist pronouncements mainly as a propaganda device to secure the support of Negrophobic nonslaveholders who might be induced to support slavery as a source of racial control or as a foundation for their own superior status as whites. It has been assumed that when planter spokesmen were addressing their peers and being true to their own world-view, they tended to defend slavery as an application of patriarchal principles of social organization and not simply as a device to ensure white supremacy. But a re-examination of the image of slaves and slavery found in the utterances of the most sophisticated and articulate spokesmen for the South Carolina gentry suggests that for them the appeal to race was not merely a device to win over the nonslaveholders but reflected their own conviction that blacks were beings so radically different from themselves that the master-slave relationship could not be adequately described in terms of kinship or even class.

Perhaps the most comprehensive and thoughtful defense of servitude offered by a South Carolinian was the famous 1838 "Memoir on Slavery" by Chancellor William Harper of the South Carolina College. While appearing at times to defend slavery in the abstract as the logical extension of a conservative philosophy of social order and hierarchy, Harper actually ended up attributing central importance to the deficiencies of the black character as a justification of the condition:

> If there are sordid, servile, and laborious offices to be performed, is it not better that there should be sordid, servile, and laborious beings to perform them? If there were infallible marks by which individuals of inferior intellect, could be selected at their birth—would not the interests of society be served, and would not some sort of fitness seem to require that they should be selected for inferior and servile offices? And if this race be generally marked by such inferiority, is it not fit they should fill them?

Harper of course went on to argue that blacks constituted just such a race. After quoting a traveler who had described Africans in their native environment as "slothful people . . . nearer to the nature of brute creation than perhaps any other people on the face of the globe," Harper concluded that such a people represented "the very material out of which slaves ought to be made"; for "in general their intellectual capacity is very limited and their feelings animal and coarse—fitting them peculiarly to discharge the lower and merely mechanical offices of society."

Hammond, who besides being a planter-intellectual, also served his state as governor and senator, struck a similar note in *his* proslavery pronouncements. In his public letters of 1845, Hammond characteristically denied that he was "an advocate of slavery in the abstract." "I might say that I am no more in favor of slavery in the abstract than I am of poverty, disease, deformity, or any other inequality in the condition of the human family." Slavery for him was something that had to be accepted, along with other so-called evils, because it was an inevitable consequence of the imperfect condition of human society. What justified the institution therefore was not moral dogma but the facts of life, such as the alleged fact that "the African, if not a distinct, is an inferior race, and never will effect, as it never has effected, as much in any other condition as in that of slavery. . . ."

On another occasion Hammond demonstrated very vividly his belief that slavery was at bottom a racial matter and not a system that could be universally applied to any laboring class. "You speak of African slavery," he wrote to the editor of the London *Spectator* in 1836, "as if it were the slavery of . . . [Anglo-Saxon or Celt] . . . But it is not, and you are wholly wrong. I would not cage an eagle or even a hawk. Shall we therefore rear no poultry?"

Probably the definitive statement of the South Carolina proslavery ideology was Hammond's famous "mudsill" speech in the United States Senate in 1858, where he told his colleagues,

> In all social systems there must be a class to do the menial duties, to perform the drudgery of life. That is a class requiring but a low order of intellect and but little skill. Its requisites are vigor, docility, fidelity. Such a class you must have. . . . It constitutes the very mud-sill of society. . . . Fortunately for the South we have found a race adapted to that purpose to her hand. . . . We do not think that whites should be slaves either by law or necessity. Our slaves are black, of another, inferior race. The *status* in which we have placed them is an elevation. They are elevated from the condition in which God first created them by being made our slaves.

Societies without a naturally servile group, he implied, would have to have their chores performed by biological equals who could *not* be enslaved and who would therefore have both the capacity and the opportunity to rebel against the leisure class. Hence the South's claim to be a superior civilization came less from slavery per se than from the fortunate accident that it had an enslavable race in its midst and would thus be immune from the kind of class conflict that was inevitable in societies such as England or the North, which had the misfortune to be populated almost exclusively by Celts and Saxons. Hammond would have agreed heartily with Alexander Stephens's famous cornerstone speech of 1861, in which the latter described the enslavement of an inferior race as the foundation of the southern Confederacy, and, at the same time, repudiated the subordination and serfdom of whites by other whites as "a violation of the laws of nature."

If any further evidence is required to show that the defense of slavery in South Carolina was essentially a racial defense, we need only look at what John C. Calhoun actually said when he first proclaimed that slavery was a positive good in 1837. It was, he made clear, a positive good only in the special circumstances that existed in the South—"where two races of different origin, and distinguished by color, and other physical differences, as well as intellectual, are brought together."

Racism, therefore, was not an incidental aspect of the slaveholder's philosophy in South Carolina but a crucial element. Certainly there was a conservative or anti-Utopian emphasis on social hierarchy as a practical necessity, but this was accompanied by a conviction that a stable system of social stratification was possible *only* when an inferior race was present to serve as a mudsill. South Carolinians combined a racist conception of the black as a natural slave with a theory of society that would make a positive good out of the presence of larger numbers of black slaves. Unlike the exclusionist racism that thrived in the North and cropped up occasionally in other parts of the South, there was no hankering among the planters of South Carolina for a homogeneous white society. They needed blacks and they knew it; but they also regarded the mass of slaves with a mixture of fear and contempt. The mudsill theory served to keep blacks in their servile station while justifying their presence.

It may have been otherwise in Virginia and the upper South generally. In the presence of a more diversified economy, relatively smaller plantations, and a higher proportion of nonslaveholding whites and free blacks, race relations seem to have been somewhat more relaxed, and there apparently was less compulsion to justify slavery by denigrating black humanity. In Virginia substantial resistance arose, first to a positive defense of slavery, later to a defense based primarily on race, and finally to secession in the name of racial slavery. It was presumably no accident that it was Virginia and not South Carolina that produced in George Fitzhugh a proslavery theorist who for a time played down the importance of race differences and defended slavery as a quasi-familial institution. But Genovese is probably wrong to see Fitzhugh's thought as "the logical outcome of the slaveholders' philosophy." The South Carolina mudsill theory, which stressed dominance rather than paternalism and radical race difference more than the human ties that might develop between masters and slaves, would seem to be a stronger candidate. South Carolina was not only the cradle of southern nationalism and proslaveryism, but also of articulate southern racism. The correlation does not seem accidental.

Spokesmen for the South Carolina planter class were probably expressing their own real perceptions, and not simply rationalizing their economic interests when they described blacks as "sordid, servile, and laborious beings," closer to brute creation than to white humanity. Since few of them had much direct contact with the mass of their slaves, they had little opportunity to develop feelings of sympathy for them or more than a purely self-interested concern for their welfare. Aristocracy might have flowered in South Carolina but paternalism in any meaningful sense did not, precisely because of the tremendous sense of social and racial distance between masters and slaves that was characteristic of the large plantations. . . .

Folk Tales and the Slaves' Culture

LAWRENCE W. LEVINE

Although the range of slave tales was narrow in neither content nor focus, it is not surprising or accidental that the tales most easily and abundantly

Excerpts from *Black Culture and Black Consciousness: Afro-American Folk Thought From Slavery to Freedom* by Lawrence W. Levine (New York: Oxford University Press, 1977), pp. 102–121, 134–135.

collected in Africa and among Afro-Americans in the New World were animal trickster tales. Because of their overwhelmingly paradigmatic character, animal tales were, of all the narratives of social protest or psychological release, among the easiest to relate both within and especially outside the group. . . . In its simplest form the slaves' animal trickster tale was a cleanly delineated story free of ambiguity. The strong assault the weak, who fight back with any weapons they have. The animals in these tales have an almost instinctive understanding of each other's habits and foibles. Knowing Rabbit's curiosity and vanity, Wolf constructs a tar-baby and leaves it by the side of the road. At first fascinated by this stranger and then progressively infuriated at its refusal to respond to his friendly salutations, Rabbit strikes at it with his hands, kicks it with his feet, butts it with his head, and becomes thoroughly enmeshed. In the end, however, it is Rabbit whose understanding of his adversary proves to be more profound. Realizing that Wolf will do exactly what he thinks his victim least desires, Rabbit convinces him that of all the ways to die the one he is most afraid of is being thrown into the briar patch, which of course is exactly what Wolf promptly does, allowing Rabbit to escape.

This situation is repeated in tale after tale: the strong attempt to trap the weak but are tricked by them instead. Fox entreats Rooster to come down from his perch, since all the animals have signed a peace treaty and there is no longer any danger: "I don' eat you, you don' boder wid me. Come down! Le's make peace!" Almost convinced by this good news, Rooster is about to descend when he thinks better of it and tests Fox by pretending to see a man and a dog coming down the road. "Don' min' fo' comin' down den," Fox calls out as he runs away. "Dawg ain't got no sense, yer know, an' de man got er gun." Spotting a goat lying on a rock, Lion is about to surprise and kill him when he notices that Goat keeps chewing and chewing although there is nothing there but bare stone. Lion reveals himself and asks Goat what he is eating. Overcoming the momentary paralysis which afflicts most of the weak animals in these tales when they realize they are trapped, Goat saves himself by saying in his most terrifying voice: "Me duh chaw dis rock, an ef you dont leff, wen me done . . . me guine eat you."

At its most elemental, then, the trickster tale consists of a confrontation in which the weak use their wits to evade the strong. Mere escape, however, does not prove to be victory enough, and in a significant number of these tales the weak learn the brutal ways of the more powerful. Fox, taking advantage of Pig's sympathetic nature, gains entrance to his house during a storm by pleading that he is freezing to death. After warming himself by the fire, he acts exactly as Pig's instincts warned him he would. Spotting a pot of peas cooking on the stove, he begins to sing:

> Fox and peas are very good,
> But Pig and peas are better.

Recovering from his initial terror, Pig pretends to hear a pack of hounds, helps Fox hide in a meal barrel, and pours the peas in, scalding Fox to death.

In one tale after another the trickster proves to be as merciless as his stronger opponent. Wolf traps Rabbit in a hollow tree and sets it on fire, but Rabbit escapes through a hole in the back and reappears, thanking Wolf for an excellent meal, explaining that the tree was filled with honey which melted from the heat. Wolf, in his eagerness to enjoy a similar feast, allows himself to be sealed into a tree which has no other opening, and is burned to death. "While eh duh bun, Buh Wolf bague an pray Buh Rabbit fuh leh um come out, but Buh Rabbit wouldnt yeddy [hear] um." The brutality of the trickster in these tales was sometimes troubling ("Buh Rabbit . . . hab er bad heart," the narrator of the last story concluded), but more often it was mitigated by the fact that the strong were the initial aggressors and the weak really had no choice. The characteristic spirit of these tales was one not of moral judgment but of vicarious triumph. Storytellers allowed their audience to share the heartening spectacle of a lion running in terror from a goat or a fox fleeing a rooster; to experience the mocking joy of Brer Rabbit as he scampers away through the briar patch calling back to Wolf, "Dis de place me mammy fotch me up,—dis de place me mammy fotch me up"; to feel the joyful relief of Pig as he turns Fox's song upside down and chants:

> Pigs and peas are very good,
> But Fox and peas are better.

Had self-preservation been the only motive driving the animals in these stories, the trickster tale need never have varied from the forms just considered. But Brer Rabbit and his fellow creatures were too humanized to be content with mere survival. Their needs included all the prizes human beings crave and strive for: wealth, success, prestige, honor, sexual prowess. Brer Rabbit himself summed it up best in the tale for which this section is named:

> De rabbit is de slickest o' all de animals de Lawd ever made. He ain't de biggest, an' he ain't de loudest but he sho' am de slickest. If he gits in trouble he gits out by gittin' somebody else in. Once he fell down a deep well an' did he holler and cry? No siree. He set up a mighty mighty whistling and a singin', an' when de wolf passes by he heard him an' he stuck his head over an' de rabbit say, "Git 'long 'way f'om here. Dere ain't room fur two. Hit's mighty hot up dere and nice an' cool down here. Don' you git in dat bucket an' come down here." Dat made de wolf all de mo' onrestless and he jumped into the bucket an' as he went down de rabbit come up, an' as dey passed de rabbit he laughed an' he say, "Dis am life; some go up and some go down."

There could be no mistaking the direction in which Rabbit was determined to head. It was in his inexorable drive upward that Rabbit emerged not only as an incomparable defender but also as a supreme manipulator, a role that complicated the simple contours of the tales already referred to.

In the ubiquitous tales of amoral manipulation, the trickster could still be pictured as much on the defensive as he was in the stories which had him battling for his very life against stronger creatures. The significant difference is that now the panoply of his victims included the weak as well as the powerful. Trapped by Mr. Man and hung from a sweet gum tree until he can be cooked, Rabbit is buffeted to and fro by the wind and left to contemplate his bleak future until Brer Squirrel happens along. "This yer my cool air swing," Rabbit informs him. "I taking a fine swing this morning." Squirrel begs a turn and finds his friend surprisingly gracious: "Certainly, Brer Squirrel, you do me proud. Come up here, Brer Squirrel, and give me a hand with this knot." Tying the grateful squirrel securely in the tree, Rabbit leaves him to his pleasure—and his fate. When Mr. Man returns, "he take Brer Squirrel home and cook him for dinner."

It was primarily advancement not preservation that led to the trickster's manipulations, however. Among a slave population whose daily rations were at best rather stark fare and quite often a barely minimal diet, it is not surprising that food proved to be the most common symbol of enhanced status and power. In his never-ending quest for food the trickster was not content with mere acquisition, which he was perfectly capable of on his own; he needed to procure the food through guile from some stronger animal. Easily the most popular tale of this type pictures Rabbit and Wolf as partners in farming a field. They have laid aside a tub of butter for winter provisions, but Rabbit proves unable to wait or to share. Pretending to hear a voice calling him, he leaves his chores and begins to eat the butter. When he returns to the field he informs his partner that his sister has just had a baby and wanted him to name it. "Well, w'at you name um?" Wolf asks innocently. "Oh, I name um Buh Start-um," Rabbit replies. Subsequent calls provide the chance for additional assaults on the butter and additional names for the nonexistent babies: "Buh Half-um," "Buh Done-um." After work, Wolf discovers the empty tub and accuses Rabbit, who indignantly denies the theft. Wolf proposes that they both lie in the sun, which will cause the butter to run out of the guilty party. Rabbit agrees readily, and when grease begins to appear on his own face he rubs it onto that of the sleeping wolf. "Look, Buh Wolf," he cries, waking his partner, "de buttah melt out on you. Dat prove you eat um." "I guess you been right," Wolf agrees docilely, "I eat um fo' trute." In some versions the animals propose a more hazardous ordeal by fire to discover the guilty party. Rabbit successfully jumps over the flames but some innocent animal—Possum, Terrapin, Bear—falls in and perishes for Rabbit's crime.

In most of these tales the aggrieved animal, realizing he has been tricked, desperately tries to avenge himself by setting careful plans to trap Rabbit, but to no avail. Unable to outwit Rabbit, his adversaries attempt to learn from him, but here too they fail. Seeing Rabbit carrying a string of fish, Fox asks him where they came from. Rabbit confesses that he stole them from Man by pretending to be ill and begging Man to take him home in his cart which was filled with fish. While riding along, Rabbit explains, he threw the load of fish into the woods and then jumped off to retrieve them. He encourages Fox to try the same tactic, and Fox is beaten to death, as Rabbit knew he would be, since Man is too shrewd to be taken in the same way twice. . . .

The many tales of which these are typical make it clear that what Rabbit craves is not possession but power, and this he acquires not simply by obtaining food but by obtaining it through the manipulation and deprivation of others. It is not often that he meets his match, and then generally at the hands of an animal as weak as himself. Refusing to allow Rabbit to cheat him out of his share of the meat they have just purchased, Partridge samples a small piece of liver and cries out, "Br'er Rabbit, de meat bitter! Oh, 'e bitter, bitter! bitter, bitter! You better not eat de meat," and tricks Rabbit into revealing where he had hidden the rest of the meat. "You is a damn sha'p feller," Partridge tells him. "But I get even wid you." Angry at Frog for inviting all the animals in the forest but him to a fish dinner, Rabbit frightens the guests away and eats all the fish himself. Frog gives another dinner, but this time he is prepared and tricks Rabbit into the water. "You is my master many a day on land, Brer Rabbit," Frog tells him just before killing and eating him, "but I is you master in the water."

It is significant that when these defeats do come, most often it is not brute force but even greater trickery that triumphs. Normally, however, the trickster has more than his share of the food. And of the women as well, for sexual prowess is the other basic sign of prestige in the slaves' tales. Although the primary trickster was occasionally depicted as a female—Ol' Molly Hare in Virginia, Aunt Nancy or Ann Nancy in the few surviving spider stories—in general women played a small role in slave tales. They were not actors in their own right so much as attractive possessions to be fought over. That the women for whom the animals compete are frequently the daughters of the most powerful creatures in the forest makes it evident that the contests are for status as well as pleasure. When Brer Bear promises his daughter to the best whistler in the forest, Rabbit offers to help his only serious competitor, Brer Dog, whistle more sweetly by slitting the corners of his mouth, which in reality makes him incapable of whistling at all. If Rabbit renders his adversaries figuratively impotent in their quest for women, they often retaliate in kind. In the story just related, Dog chases Rabbit, bites off his tail, and nothing more is said about who wins the woman.

More often than not, though, Rabbit is successful. In a Georgia tale illustrating the futility of mere hard work, Brer Wolf offers his attractive daughter to the animal that shucks the most corn. Rabbit has his heart set on winning Miss Wolf but realizes he has no chance of beating Brer Coon at shucking corn. Instead, he spends all of his time during the contest singing, dancing, and charming Miss Wolf. At the end he sits down next to Coon and claims that he has shucked the great pile of corn. Confused, Wolf leaves the decision up to his daughter:

> Now Miss Wolf she been favoring Brer Rabbit all the evening. Brer Rabbit dancing and singing plum turned Miss Wolf's head, so Miss Wolf she say, "It most surely are Brer Rabbit's pile." Miss Wolf she say she "plum 'stonished how Brer Coon can story so." Brer Rabbit he take the gal and go off home clipity, lipity. Poor old Brer Coon he take hisself off home, he so tired he can scarcely hold hisself together.

In another Georgia tale the contest for the woman seems to be symbolically equated with freedom. Fox promises his daughter to any animal who can pound dust out of a rock.

> Then Brer Rabbit, he feel might set down on, 'cause he know all the chaps can swing the stone hammer to beat hisself, and he go off sorrowful like and set on the sand bank. He set a while and look east, and then he turn and set a while and look west, but may be you don't know, sah, Brer Rabbit sense never come to hisself 'cepting when he look north.

Thus inspired, Rabbit conceives of a strategy allowing him to defeat his more powerful opponents and carry off the woman.

In the best known and most symbolically interesting courting tale, Rabbit and Wolf vie for the favors of a woman who is pictured as either equally torn between her two suitors or leaning toward Wolf. Rabbit alters the contest by professing surprise that she could be interested in Wolf, since he is merely Rabbit's riding horse. Hearing of this, Wolf confronts Rabbit, who denies ever saying it and promises to go to the woman and personally refute the libel as soon as he is well enough. Wolf insists he go at once, and the characteristic combination of Rabbit's deceit and Wolf's seemingly endless trust and gullibility allows Rabbit to convince his adversary that he is too sick to go with him unless he can ride on Wolf's back with a saddle and bridle for support. The rest of the story is inevitable. Approaching the woman's house Rabbit tightens the reins, digs a pair of spurs into Wolf, and trots him around crying, "Look here, girl! what I told you? Didn't I say I had Brother Wolf for my riding-horse?" It was in many ways the ultimate secular triumph in slave tales. The weak doesn't merely kill his enemy: he mounts him, humiliates him, reduces him to servility, steals his woman, and, in effect, takes his place.

Mastery through possessing the two paramount symbols of power—food and women—did not prove to be sufficient for Rabbit. He craved something more. Going to God himself, Rabbit begs for enhanced potency in the form of a larger tail, greater wisdom, bigger eyes. In each case God imposes a number of tasks upon Rabbit before his wishes are fulfilled. Rabbit must bring God a bag full of blackbirds, the teeth of a rattlesnake or alligator, a swarm of yellowjackets, the "eyewater" (tears) of a deer. Rabbit accomplishes each task by exploiting the animals' vanity. He tells the blackbirds that they cannot fill the bag and when they immediately prove they can, he traps them. He taunts the snake, "dis pole *swear* say you ain't long as him." When Rattlesnake insists he is, Rabbit ties him to the stick, ostensibly to measure him, kills him, and takes his teeth. Invariably Rabbit does what is asked of him but finds God less than pleased. In some tales he is chased out of Heaven. In others God counsels him, "Why Rabbit, ef I was to gi' you long tail aint you see you'd 'stroyed up de whol worl'? Nobawdy couldn' do nuttin wid you!" Most commonly God seemingly complies with Rabbit's request and gives him a bag which he is to open when he returns home. But Rabbit cannot wait, and when he opens the bag prematurely "thirty bull-dawg run out de box, an' bit off Ber Rabbit tail again. An' dis give him a short tail again."

The rabbit, like the slaves who wove tales about him, was forced to make do with what he had. His small tail, his natural portion of intellect—these would have to suffice, and to make them do he resorted to any means at his disposal—means which may have made him morally tainted but which allowed him to survive and even to conquer. In this respect there was a direct relationship between Rabbit and the slaves, a relationship which the earliest collectors and interpreters of these stories understood well. Joel Chandler Harris, as blind as he could be to some of the deeper implications of the tales he heard and retold, was always aware of their utter seriousness. "Well, I tell you dis," Harris had Uncle Remus say, "ef deze yer tales wuz des fun, fun, fun, en giggle, giggle, giggle, I let you know I'd a-done drapt um long ago." From the beginning Harris insisted that the animal fables he was collecting were "thoroughly characteristic of the negro," and commented that "it needs no scientific investigation to show why he selects as his hero the weakest and most harmless of all animals, and brings him out victorious in contests with the bear, the wolf, and the fox." . . .

This testimony—and there is a great deal of it—documents the enduring identification between black storytellers and the central trickster figure of their tales. Brer Rabbit's victories became the victories of the slave. This symbolism in slave tales allowed them to outlive slavery itself. So long as the perilous situation and psychic needs of the slave continued to characterize large numbers of freedmen as well, the imagery of the old slave tales remained both aesthetically and functionally satisfying. By ascribing actions to semi-mythical actors, Negroes were able to overcome the external and internal censorship that their hostile surroundings imposed upon them. The white master could believe that the rabbit stories his slaves told were mere figments of a childish imagination, that they were primarily humorous anecdotes depicting the "roaring comedy of animal life." Blacks knew better. The trickster's exploits, which overturned the neat hierarchy of the world in which he was forced to live, became their exploits; the justice he achieved, their justice; the strategies he employed, their strategies. From his adventures they obtained relief; from his triumphs they learned hope. . . .

It can be argued that by channelizing the bondsmen's discontent, reducing their anxieties, and siphoning off their anger, slave tales served the master as well as the slave. In a sense of course they did, and the fact that tales and songs were often encouraged by the masters may indicate a gleaning of this fact on their part as well. But in terms of the values they inculcated, the models of action they held up for emulation, the disrespect and even contempt they taught concerning the strong, the psychic barriers they created against the inculcation of many of the white world's values, it would be difficult to maintain that they should be viewed primarily as a means of control. What the tales gave to the masters with one hand they more than took back with the other. They encouraged trickery and guile; they stimulated the search for ways out of the system; they inbred a contempt for the powerful and an admiration for the perseverance and even the wisdom of the undermen, they constituted an intragroup lore which must have intensified feelings of distance from the world of the slaveholder.

✣ F U R T H E R   R E A D I N G

Herbert Aptheker, *American Negro Slave Revolts* (1941)
Ira Berlin, *Slaves Without Masters: The Free Negro in the Antebellum South* (1974)
Robin Blackburn, *The Overthrow of Colonial Slavery, 1776–1848* (1988)
John Blassingame, *The Slave Community: Plantation Life in the Antebellum South* (1972)
Jane Turner Censer, *North Carolina Planters and Their Children, 1800–1860* (1984)
Catherine Clinton, *The Plantation Mistress: Woman's World in the Old South* (1982)
Philip D. Curtin, *The Atlantic Slave Trade: A Census* (1969)
David Brion Davis, *Slavery and Human Freedom* (1985)
——, *The Problem of Slavery in the Age of Revolution, 1770–1823* (1975)
——, "Slavery and the Post–World War II Historians," *Daedalus* 103 (1974), 1–16
Carl N. Degler, *Neither Black Nor White: Slavery and Race Relations in Brazil and the United States* (1971)
Stanley M. Elkins, *Slavery: A Problem in American Institutional and Intellectual Life* (1959)
Barbara Jeanne Fields, *Slavery and Freedom on the Middle Ground: Maryland During the Nineteenth Century* (1985)
Robert W. Fogel, *Without Consent or Contract: The Rise and Fall of American Slavery* (1989)
—— and Stanley L. Engerman, *Time on the Cross: The Economics of American Negro Slavery* (1974)
Lacy K. Ford, *Origins of Southern Radicalism: The South Carolina Upcountry, 1800–1860* (1988)
Elizabeth Fox-Genovese, *Within the Plantation Household: Black and White Women in the Old South* (1988)
George Fredrickson, *White Supremacy: A Comparative Study in American and South African History* (1981)
——, *The Black Image in the White Mind: The Debate on Afro-American Character and Destiny, 1817–1914* (1971)
Eugene D. Genovese, *The Political Economy of Slavery* (1965)
—— and Elizabeth Fox-Genovese, *Fruits of Merchant Capital: Slavery and Bourgeois Property in the Rise and Expansion of Capitalism* (1983)
Kenneth Greenberg, *Masters and Statesmen: The Political Culture of American Slavery* (1985)
Herbert G. Gutman, *The Black Family in Slavery and Freedom, 1750–1925* (1975)
——, *Slavery and the Numbers Game: A Critique of "Time on the Cross"* (1975)
Michael Hindus, *Prison and Plantation: Crime, Justice, and Authority in Massachusetts and South Carolina, 1767–1878* (1986)
Nathan I. Huggins, *Black Odyssey: The Afro-American Ordeal in Slavery* (1978)
Michael P. Johnson and James L. Roark, *Black Masters: A Free Family of Color in the Old South* (1984)
Jacqueline Jones, " 'My Mother Was Much of a Woman': Black Women, Work, and the Family Under Slavery," *Feminist Studies* 8 (1982): 235–269
Charles Joyner, *Down By the Riverside: A South Carolina Slave Community* (1984)
Herbert S. Klein, *Slavery in the Americas: A Comparative Study of Virginia and Cuba* (1967)
Peter Kolchin, *Unfree Labor: American Slavery and Russian Serfdom* (1987)

Suzanne Lebsock, *The Free Women of Petersburg: Status and Culture in a Southern Town, 1784–1860* (1984)

Philip D. Morgan, "Work and Culture: The Task System and the World of Low-Country Blacks, 1700–1880," *William & Mary Quarterly*, 3rd series, 39 (1982), 564–599

James Oakes, *The Ruling Race: A History of American Slaveholders* (1982)

Orlando Patterson, *Slavery and Social Death: A Comparative Study* (1982)

Ulrich B. Phillips, *Life and Labor in the Old South* (1929)

———, *American Negro Slavery* (1918)

Albert J. Raboteau, *Slave Religion: The Invisible Institution in the Antebellum South* (1978)

George P. Rawick, ed., *The American Slave: A Composite Autobiography* (1972)

C. Duncan Rice, *The Rise and Fall of Black Slavery* (1975)

Willie Lee Rose, ed., *A Documentary History of Slavery in North America* (1976)

Larry Schweikart, *Banking in the American South from the Age of Jackson to Reconstruction* (1987)

Anne Firor Scott, *The Southern Lady, from Pedestal to Politics: 1830–1930* (1970)

Kenneth M. Stampp, *The Peculiar Institution: Slavery in the Ante-Bellum South* (1956)

Robert S. Starobin, *Industrial Slavery in the Old South* (1970)

Sterling Stuckey, *Slave Culture: Nationalist Theory and the Foundations of Black America* (1987)

Henry Irving Tragle, *The Southampton Slave Revolt of 1831* (1971)

Mark Tushnet, *The American Law of Slavery: Considerations of Humanity and Interest* (1981)

Deborah Gray White, *Ar'n't I a Woman: Female Slaves in the Plantation South* (1985)

C. Vann Woodward, *American Counterpoint: Race and Slavery in the North-South Dialogue* (1971)

Gavin Wright, *The Political Economy of the Cotton South* (1978)

Bertram Wyatt-Brown, *Southern Honor: Ethics and Behavior in the Old South* (1982)

CHAPTER
9

Struggles for the West

⌗

In 1815 the western line of white settlement reached into the Ohio River Valley and beyond the Appalachians to the banks of the Mississippi River. Over the next thirty-five years, newcomers pushed northward into Wisconsin and westward into Missouri, Arkansas, and Texas; in the 1840s the opening of overland passages and the California gold rush brought thousands more to the Far West. By 1850, when California entered the Union as the thirty-first state, the United States was well on its way to becoming a transcontinental empire of a kind that the Jeffersonian generation had only begun to imagine.

In a bygone time, scholars interpreted this western expansion as an unbroken, triumphant struggle against hostile forces of man and nature. That romantic view remains at the core of American culture, linked to a national ideal of irresistible and universal progress. Historians, however, have grown more dubious. Americans, after all, did not simply win the West. In fact, the native Americans lost *the region, in a long series of battles and treaty negotiations that could not have been more brutal and treacherous.*

Nor did the western struggles solely take place between Indians and white settlers. In Texas and the Southwest, new arrivals, speculators, and (eventually) the U.S. government fought mixed-blood Hispanics and the government of Mexico, in the process commencing relations that remain troubled to this day. Other sorts of conflicts developed among the newcomers. Social and emotional adjustments to the frontier proved demanding for men and women alike. Slaveholders tried to ensure that the new territories would be open to slavery, a prospect that appalled nonslaveholders. Although prosperity came to those who kept up with a rapidly commercializing agriculture, poorer migrants, squatters, and would-be yeomen found themselves pitted against land speculators, financiers, and other creditors. For significant numbers of families who sought a life of independence, removal to the West brought a very different existence as tenant farmers or wage laborers. By the 1830s the reverberations of all these struggles reached the halls of Congress, in debates over federal land policy and Indian removal.

None of this is to deny the fortitude and bravery of those who made the journey west, or the monumental feats they accomplished. Clearly, however, any assessment of western development before 1850 must come to terms with the conflicts and costs as well as the achievements that accrued from U.S. expansion, and with the connection of all these factors to larger national developments. In particular, how did the pursuit of Jefferson's "empire of liberty" affect American political institutions and values?

⊞ D O C U M E N T S

In the early 1830s Illinois was rocked by an alliance of the Sac and Fox tribes (both previously resettled west of the Mississippi) who defiantly returned to occupy lands that another Indian nation had earlier ceded. In the first part of Chapter 9's opening selection, white settlers petition the Illinois governor over their fears of a full-scale Indian invasion—fears that led to a mobilization of the state militia and regular troops, which proceeded to repel the tribes across the Mississippi and slaughter most of the Indians whom they caught. The surrender speech of the Indians' leader Chief Black Hawk, reprinted as the second part of document one, marked the ultimate expulsion of the northern woodland tribes.

In the Southwest, the 1830s brought the successful Texan war for independence from Mexico, which would in time provoke fresh sectional antagonisms in U.S. politics. The two documents in selection two—a settlers' call to arms, and the impressions of a Mexican lieutenant-colonel, leading to the battle of the Alamo—present different sides of the war. (Note, though, the latter's criticisms of his own leaders, as well as of their foe.) A decade later, adventurers, speculators, and would-be settlers of every description began arriving in California, enlarging the area beyond the pioneer *ranchero* population. At the decade's end, most newcomers arrived with hopes of cashing in on the gold rush; a traveler's notes and a prospector's memoirs in the third selection offer different views of what the migrants found just before and during the great gold discoveries.

The remaining documents explore some of the tensions that came in the wake of white settlement. In the fourth selection, Governor Edward Coles of Illinois, a staunch antislavery man, responds anxiously to proslavery efforts to alter the state's constitution in the aftermath of the Missouri Compromise (see Chapter 10). Although Cole's side won in Illinois, the battle over slavery in the West would long endure. The popular writer Caroline M. Kirkland's semifictional accounts of life in the Northwest, excerpts from which compose the fifth document, transcended modish sentimentalism with some tart, opinionated observations about commerce, class, gender, and community. In the final selection, two documents from the U.S. Senate debate in 1837 over a public land bill illuminate larger western disputes over the roles of settlers and speculators in the newly opened territories. Senator Walker's speech defended poorer settlers and lambasted the idea that western speculators simply spurred economic growth and public benefits. Some of Walker's colleagues countered that the speculators were indeed developing opportunities for all; Senator King, however, tried to show that the very people Walker praised were actually greedy speculators in disguise.

Documents on the Black Hawk War, 1831, 1832

Citizens of Rock River, Illinois, Petition Governor John Reynolds, 1831

April 30th 1831—

His excelency the Governor of the State of Illinois—

We the under signed being Citizens of Rock River & its Vicinity—beg leave to State to your Honor The Gravences we labor under & Pray your protection against the Sac and Fox tribe of Indians who have again taken procesion of our Lands near the mouth of Rock river & its Vicinity They Have and now are Burning our fences destroying our crops of Wheat now Growing by turning in all their Horses They Also threaten our lives if we attempt to plant corn and say they will cut it up & That we have Stole their Lands from them and they are determined to exterminate us provided we dont leave the country with out Your Honour no doubt is aware of the out ragous—that were commited by said indians Here before particularly last fall they all most destroyed all our crops & made several attempts on the owners lives when they attempted to prevent their depridations and Actually wounded one man by Stabing him in several places This spring they act in a much more out rageous and menacing maner So that we consider our selv's compeled to beg of you protection which the Agent and Garison on Rock Island refuses to give In as much as they say they have no orders from Government Therefore Should we not receive amediate aid from Your Honour we shall be compelled to aband our Setlement and the lands which we have purchased of Government Therefore we have no doubt but your Honour will better anticipate our condition than it is represented And grant us amediate relief in that manner that to you may seem most likely to produce the desired affect. The number of Indians now among us are abot six or seven Hundred they say there is more coming and that the patowatomies & some of the Winebagoes will help them in case of an uruption with the whites The Warriours now here are the Black Hawk's party with other chiefs the Names of which we are not acquainted with Therefore—looking up to you for protection we beg leave ever to remain yous &c

Black Hawk Surrenders, 1832

You have taken me prisoner with all my warriors. I am much grieved, for I expected, if I did not defeat you, to hold out much longer, and give you more trouble before I surrendered. I tried hard to bring you into ambush, but your last general understands Indian fighting. The first one was not so wise. When I saw that I could not beat you by Indian fighting, I determined to rush on you, and fight you face to face. I fought hard. But your guns were well aimed. The bullets flew like birds in the air, and whizzed by our ears like the wind through the trees in the winter. My warriors fell around me; it began to look dismal. I saw my evil day at hand. The sun rose dim on us in the morning, and at night it sunk in a dark cloud, and looked like a ball of fire. That was the last sun that shone on Black Hawk. His heart is dead, and no longer beats quick in his bosom. He is now a prisoner to the white men; they will do with him as they wish. But he can stand torture, and is not afraid of death. He is no coward. Black Hawk is an Indian.

He has done nothing for which an Indian ought to be ashamed. He has fought for his countrymen, the squaws and papooses, against white men, who came, year after year, to cheat them and take away their lands. You know the cause of our making war. It is known to all white men. They ought to be ashamed of it. The white men despise the Indians, and drive them from their homes. But the Indians are not deceitful. The white men speak bad of the Indian, and look at him spitefully. But the Indian does not tell lies; Indians do not steal.

An Indian who is as bad as the white men, could not live in our nation; he would be put to death, and eat [sic] up by the wolves. The white men are bad school-masters; they carry false looks, and deal in false actions; they smile in the face of the poor Indian to cheat him; they shake them by the hand to gain their confidence, to make them drunk, to deceive them, and ruin our wives. We told them to let us alone; but they followed on and beset our paths, and they coiled themselves among us like the snake. They poisoned us by their touch. We were not safe. We lived in danger. We were becoming like them, hypocrites and liars, adulterers, lazy drones, all talkers, and no workers.

We looked up to the Great Spirit. We went to our great father. We were encouraged. His great council gave us fair words and big promises, but we got no satisfaction. Things were growing worse. There were no deer in the forest. The oppossum and beaver were fled; the springs were drying up, and our squaws and papooses without victuals to keep them from starving; we called a great council and built a large fire. The spirit of our fathers arose and spoke to us to avenge our wrongs or die. . . . We set up the war-whoop, and dug up the tomahawk; our knives were ready, and the heart of Black Hawk swelled high in his bosom when he led his warriors to battle. He is satisfied. He will go to the world of spirits contented. He has done his duty. His father will meet him there, and commend him. . . .

Two Reports on the Texas Revolution, 1836

The Settlers' Call to Arms, 1836

Fellow Freemen,
The despot dictator, and his vassel myrmidonns [sic], are fast displaying their hostile colums on the frontier of our heretofore happy and blessed Texas. Their war cry is, "death and destruction to every Anglo-American, west of the Sabine;" their watch word, actually, "beauty and booty." Many of you met the veteran soldiers of Europe, when they dared to invade the land of our fathers, under the same sacrilegious watch word—you chartered and gloriously drove them back to the ocean; you made tyrants tremble at the name of American freemen, and taught them that the soil of an independent people is not to be polluted by the footsteps of a mercenary soldier. And will you *now,* as Texian freemen, as fathers, as husbands, as sons, and as brothers, suffer the *colored* hirelings of a cruel and faithless despot, to feast and revel, in your dearly purchased and cherished homes? Figure to yourselves, my countrymen, the horror and misery that will be entailed on you should the ruffians once obtain foothold on our soil? Your beloved wives, your mothers, you daughters, sisters, and helpless innocent children given up to the dire pollution, and massacre of a hand of barbarians!! Your farms redeemed by you from the wilderness, with so much pain and labor, laid waste! and where now flourish the rich products of the husbandman,

will be seen the briar and bramble, and our *garden of Texas* again become a dreary wild, occupied only by the savage of the desert, and the cruel animals of the forest; and the *name of Texas* will only be remembered by its fearful sufferings, and as having been once inhabited by a civilized, but unfortunate people.

As a fellow freeman, I earnestly entreat you, at once to prepare for the field and "let us on" to the scene of action. There is not a moment to lose; I shall be ready to take my place in the ranks of the defenders of "home and firesides" on the 10th of next month, and anxiously invite all who possibly can, to meet me in the town of Washington on that day, prepared for a decive [sic] and glorious campaign. *United* Texas has nothing to fear and everything to hope. Let our motto be "Victory and Independence, or an honorable grave," and our watch word "the tyrant dead or alive, or a visit to his palace."

[February, 1836?]   John W Hall

Lieutenant-Colonel José Enrique de la Peña on the Texas Uprising and the Battle of the Alamo, 1836

Public documents had analyzed the events in Texas during the last months in 1835 and the telling of them alone sufficed to prove the injustice of the colonists' aggression. The insults lavished upon the nation as represented by the customs officials and commanders of military detachments, the disregard for laws, and the attitudes with which the colonists looked upon those who had given them a country were more than sufficient causes to justify war on our part. They were the aggressors and we the attacked, they the ingrates, we the benefactors. When they were in want we had given them sustenance, yet as soon as they gained strength they used it to destroy us.

The neglect, the apathy, or, even more, the criminal indifference with which all [Mexican] governments without exception have watched over the national interests; the failure to enforce the colonization laws; the lack of sympathy with which the colonists had been regarded and the loyalty that these still had for their native country; these things led us into these circumstances. Because of all this, war was inevitable, for between war and dishonor there was no doubt as to the choice; however, it was necessary to prepare for it with mature judgment and to carry it out cautiously because the national honor was in the balance and it was less harmful to postpone the campaign than to expose the nation to ridicule by trying to carry it out contrary to the rules of the game.

It was necessary for all Mexicans of all classes and political parties to rally around the government in order to bring it forth successfully out of an undertaking that concerned everyone equally; but unfortunately this could not be. . . .

On the 3rd of March [1836] between eight and nine in the morning,

Excerpts from *With Santa Anna in Texas: A Personal Narrative of the Revolution* by José Enrique de la Peña. Translated by Carmen Perry, pp. 4–5, 40–52. Published by Texas A&M University Press and reprinted with their permission.

after the troops had put on their dress uniforms, we marched toward Béjar, entering between four and five in the afternoon within sight of the enemy, who observed us from inside their fortifications. . . . We entered Béjar just as the roar of cannon and martial music were announcing General Urrea's victory [at San Patricio]. . . .

On the 17th of February the commander in chief had proclaimed to the army: "Comrades in arms," he said, "our most sacred duties have brought us to these uninhabited lands and demand our engaging in combat against a rabble of wretched adventurers to whom our authorities have unwisely given benefits that even Mexicans did not enjoy, and who have taken possession of this vast and fertile area, convinced that our own unfortunate internal divisions have rendered us incapable of defending our soil. Wretches! Soon will they become aware of their folly! Soldiers, our comrades have been shamefully sacrificed at Anáhuac, Goliad, and Béjar, and you are those destined to punish these murderers. My friends: we will march as long as the interests of the nation that we serve demand. The claimants to the acres of Texas land will soon know to their sorrow that their reinforcements from New Orleans, Mobile, Boston, New York, and other points north, whence they should never have come, are insignificant, and that Mexicans, generous by nature, will not leave unpunished affronts resulting in injury or discredit to their country, regardless of who the aggressors may be."

This address was received enthusiastically, but the army needed no incitement; knowing that it was about to engage in the defense of the country and to avenge less fortunate comrades was enough for its ardor to become as great as the noble and just cause it was about to defend. . . . For their part, the enemy leaders had addressed their own men in terms not unlike those of our commander. They said that we were a bunch of mercenaries, blind instruments of tyranny; that without any right we were about to invade their territory; that we would bring desolation and death to their peaceful homes and would seize their possessions; that we were savage men who would rape their women, decapitate their children, destroy everything, and render into ashes the fruits of their industry and their efforts. Unfortunately they did partially foresee what would happen, but they also committed atrocities that we did not commit, and in this rivalry of evil and extermination, I do not dare to venture who had the ignominious advantage, they or we! . . .

When our commander in chief haughtily rejected the agreement that the enemy had proposed, [the Alamo's Commander, William B.] Travis became infuriated at the contemptible manner in which he had been treated and, expecting no honorable way of salvation, chose the path that strong souls choose in crisis, that of dying with honor, and selected the Alamo for his grave. . . .

Our commander became more furious when he saw that the enemy resisted the idea of surrender. He believed as others did that the fame and honor of the army were compromised the longer the enemy lived. . . . But prudent men, who know how to measure the worth of true honor, those whose tempered courage permits their venturing out only when they know beforehand that the destruction they are about to wreak will profit them and who understand that the soldier's glory is the greater, the less bloody the victory and the fewer the victims sacrificed; these men, though moved by the same sentiments as the army and its commander, were of the opinion that victory over a handful of men concentrated in the Alamo did not call for a great sacrifice. In fact, it was necessary only to await the artillery's arrival at Béjar for these to surrender; undoubtedly they could not have resisted for many hours the destruction and imposing fire from twenty cannon. The sums spent by the treasury on the artillery equipment brought to Texas are incalculable; the transportation alone amounts to thousands of pesos. Either they did not wish or did not know how to make use of such weaponry; had it been judiciously employed, it would have saved us many lives, and the success of the campaign would have been very different indeed. . . .

Travis's resistance was on the verge of being overcome; for several days his followers had been urging him to surrender, giving the lack of food and the scarcity of munitions as reasons, but he had quieted their restlessness with the hope of quick relief, something not difficult for them to believe since they had seen some reinforcements arrive. Nevertheless, they had pressed him so hard that on the 5th he promised them that if no help arrived on that day they would surrender the next day or would try to escape under cover of darkness; these facts were given to us by a lady from Béjar, a Negro who was the only male who escaped, and several women who were found inside and were rescued by Colonels Morales and Miñón. . . .

Once the order was issued, even those opposing it were ready to carry it out; no one doubted that we would triumph, but it was anticipated that the struggle would be bloody, as indeed it was. . . .

The Alamo was an irregular fortification without flank fires which a wise general would have taken with insignificant losses, but we lost more than three hundred brave men. . . .

Our commander made much of Travis's courage, for it saved him from the insulting intimation that the critical circumstances surrounding Travis would have sufficed to spare the army a great sacrifice.

Beginning at one o'clock in the morning of the 6th, the columns were set in motion, and at three they silently advanced toward the river, which they crossed marching two abreast over some narrow wooden bridges. . . .

The columns advanced with as much speed as possible; shortly after beginning the march they were ordered to open fire while they were still out of range, but there were some officers who wisely disregarded the signal. Alerted to our attack by the given signal, which all columns answered, the enemy vigorously returned our fire, which had not even touched him but had retarded our advance. Travis, to compensate for the reduced number of the defenders, had placed three or four rifles by the side of each man, so that the initial fire was very rapid and deadly. . . .

From his point of observation, General Santa Anna viewed with concern this horrible scene and, misled by the difficulties encountered in the climbing of the walls and by the maneuver executed by the third column, believed we were being repulsed; he therefore ordered Colonel Amat to move in with the rest of the reserves; the Sapper Battalion, already ordered to move their column of attack, arrived and began to climb at the same time. He then also ordered into battle his general staff and everyone at his side. This gallant reserve merely added to the noise and the victims, the more regrettable since there was no necessity for them to engage in the combat. . . .

A quarter of an hour had elapsed, during which our soldiers remained in a terrible situation, wearing themselves out as they climbed in quest of a less obscure death than that visited on them, crowded in a single mass; later and after much effort, they were able in sufficient numbers to reach the parapet, without distinction of ranks. The terrified defenders withdrew at once into quarters placed to the right and the left of the small area that constituted their second line of defense. They had bolted and reinforced the doors, but in order to form trenches they had excavated some places inside that were now a hindrance to them. Not all of them took refuge, for some remained in the open, looking at us before firing, as if dumbfounded at our daring. . . .

Among the defenders there were thirty or more colonists; the rest were pirates, used to defying danger and to disdaining death, and who for that reason fought courageously; their courage, to my way of thinking, merited them the mercy for which, toward the last, some of them pleaded; others, not knowing the language, were unable to do so. In fact, when these men noted the loss of their leader [Travis] and saw that they were being attacked by superior forces, they faltered. Some, with an accent hardly intelligible, desperately cried, *Mercy, valiant Mexicans;* others poked the points of their bayonets through a hole or a door with a white cloth, the symbol of ceasefire, and some even used their socks. Our trusting soldiers, seeing these demonstrations, would confidently enter their quarters, but those among the enemy who had not pleaded for mercy, who had no thought of surrendering, and who relied on no other recourse than selling their lives dearly, would meet them with pistol shots and bayonets. Thus betrayed, our men rekindled their anger and at every moment fresh skirmishes broke out with renewed fury. The order had been given to spare no one but the women and this was carried out, but such carnage was useless and had we prevented it, we would have saved much blood on our part. Those of the enemy who tried to escape fell victims to the sabers of the cavalry, which had been drawn up for this purpose, but even as they fled they defended themselves. An unfortunate father with a young son in his arms was seen to hurl himself from a considerable height, both perishing at the same blow.

This scene of extermination went on for an hour before the curtain of death covered and ended it: shortly after six in the morning it was all finished; the corps were beginning to reassemble and to identify themselves, their sorrowful countenances revealing the losses in the thinned ranks of their officers and comrades, when the commander in chief appeared. He could see for himself the desolation among his battalions and that devastated area littered with corpses, with scattered limbs and bullets, with weapons and torn uniforms. Some of these were burning together with the corpses, which

produced an unbearable and nauseating odor. The bodies, with their black-
ened and bloody faces disfigured by a desperate death, their hair and uniforms burning at once, presented a dreadful and truly hellish sight. What
trophies—those of the battlefield! Quite soon some of the bodies were left
naked by fire, others by disgraceful rapacity, especially among our men. The
enemy could be identified by their whiteness, by their robust and bulky
shapes. What a sad spectacle, that of the dead and dying! What a horror,
to inspect the area and find the remains of friends—!

Two Views of California, 1846, 1848

Edwin Bryant Reaches the Sacramento Valley, 1846

August 30 [1846].—The temperature this morning was pleasant, and the
atmosphere perfectly clear and calm. We commenced our march early, determined, if possible, to force our way out of the mountains and to reach
Johnson's, the nearest settlement in the valley of Sacramento, about 40
miles, above or north of Sutter's Fort, before we encamped.

After travelling some three or four miles rising and descending a number
of hills, from the summit of one more elevated than the others surrounding
it, the spacious valley of the Sacramento suddenly burst upon my view, at
an apparent distance of fifteen miles. A broad line of timber running through
the centre of the valley indicated the course of the main river, and smaller
and fainter lines on either side of this, winding through the brown and flat
plain, marked the channels of its tributaries. I contemplated this most welcome scene with such emotions of pleasure as may be imagined by those
who have ever crossed the desert plains and mountains of western America,
until Jacob, who was in advance of the remainder of the party, came within
the reach of my voice. I shouted to him that we were "out of the woods"—
to pull off his hat and give three cheers, so loud that those in the rear could
hear them. Very soon the huzzas of those behind were ringing and echoing
through the hills, valleys, and forests, and the whole party came up with an
exuberance of joy in their motions and depicted upon their countenances.
It was a moment of cordial and heartfelt congratulations.

Taking a direct course west, in order to reach the valley at the nearest
point, we soon struck a small horse-trail, which we followed over low gravelly
hills with grassy hollows between, timbered with the evergreen oak, forming
in many places a most inviting landscape. About one o'clock we discovered
at the distance of half a mile, a number of men, apparently twenty or thirty.
Some of them were dressed in white shirts and pantaloons, with the Mexican
sombrero, or broad-brim hat, others were nearly naked and resembled the
Indians we had frequently seen on the eastern side of the Sierra. They had
evidently discovered us before we saw them, for they seemed to be in great
commotion, shouting and running in various directions. Some of our party
suggested that they might be a body of Mexican soldiers stationed here for
the purpose of opposing the entrance of the emigrants into California, a
conjecture that seemed reasonable, under the probable existing relations

between Mexico and the United States. However, upon a careful examination I could not discover that they had any arms, and felt pretty well assured from their movements, that they were not an organized body of soldiers. But halting until the whole party came up, I requested them to see that all their pieces were charged and capped, which being done, we moved forward to the point (a small grove of oaks on a gentle elevation) where the most numerous body of the strange men were concentrated. We rode up to them, at the same time holding out our hands in token of friendship, a signal which they reciprocated immediately.

They were evidently very much rejoiced to find that we had no hostile designs upon them. With the exception of two half-breed Spaniards, they were Indians, and several of them conversed in Spanish, and were or had been the servants of settlers in the valley. One of the half-breeds, of a pleasing and intelligant countenance and good address, introduced us to their chief, (El Capitan,) and wished to know if we had not some tobacco to give him. I had a small quantity of tobacco, about half of which I gave to the chief, and distributed the residue among the party as far as it would go. I saw, however, that the chief divided his portion among those who received none. *El Capitan* was a man of about forty-five, of large frame and great apparent muscular power, but his countenance was heavy, dull, and melancholy, manifesting neither good humor nor intelligence. His long, coarse, and matted hair fell down upon his shoulders in a most neglected condition. A faded cotton handkerchief was tied around his head. I could see none of the ornaments of royalty upon him, but his clothing was much inferior to that of many of his party, who I presume had obtained theirs by laboring for the white settlers. Many of them were in a state of nudity.

We soon learned from them that they were a party engaged in gathering acorns, which to these poor Indians are what wheat and maize are to us. They showed us large quantities in their baskets under the trees. When dried and pulverized, the flour of the acorn is made into bread or mush, and is their "staff of life." It is their chief article of subsistence in this section of California. Their luxuries, such as bull-beef and horse-meat, they obtain by theft, or pay for in labor at exorbitant rates. . . .

We inquired the distance to the residence of Mr. Johnson. They made signs indicating that it was but a short distance. After some little delay we prevailed upon one of them who was naked, by promising him a reward, to accompany us as our guide. He conducted us safely, in about an hour and a half, to the house of Mr. Johnson, situated on Bear creek, a tributary of the Rio de los Plumas, near the edge of the valley of the Sacramento. The house of Mr. Johnson is a small building of two rooms, one-half constructed of logs, the other of adobes or sun-dried bricks. Several pens made of poles and pickets surround the house. A building of any kind, inhabited by civilized beings, was almost a curiosity to us. Some of our party, when about a mile distant, fancied from something white which they saw in the door, resembling at a distance the shape of a woman clad in light garments, that it was Mrs. Johnson, who would be there to welcome them with all the hospitality of an American lady. Great was their disappointment, however, when they came in front of the door, to find it closed. A light frame with a raw-hide nailed upon it, was the construction of the door. The central portion of the raw-hide was white, the natural color of the animal from which it had been taken, and into this melted the graceful figure, and the welcome countenance of the white woman in white. Mr. Johnson was not at home, and the house was shut up. This we learned from a little Indian, the only human object we could find about the premises; he intimated by signs, however, that Mr. Johnson would return when the sun set.

We encamped under some trees in front of the house, resolved to do as well as we could, in our half-famished condition, until Mr. J. returned. In looking around the place; we saw where a quantity of wheat had been threshed, consequently there should be flour in the house. In one of the pens there were several young calves, showing conclusively that there must be milk. There was a small attempt at gardening, but no vegetables visible. We tried to prevail upon the Indian to bring us some flour, but the little heathen shook his head, either not understanding us or signifying that he could not get at it. We then made him comprehend that we wanted milk, and after showing him a bright-colored cotton handkerchief, he demanded our bucket and started with it after the cows. They were brought to the pen where the calves were confined, and one of them being fastened by the horns with a raw-hide rope, the calf was admitted to her to keep her gentle during the process of milking. Our bucket was nearly filled with rich milk, and this, with a cup of coffee, took off the edge of our hunger.

In the mean time we performed our ablutions in the creek, and having shed our much-worn clothing, we presented most of it to the naked Indian who acted as our guide. He was soon clad in a complete suit from head to feet, and strutted about with a most dandified and self-satisfied air. A small pocket looking-glass completed his happiness. He left us with a bundle of rags under his arms, nearly overjoyed at his good luck.

At sunset the dogs about the house began to bark most vociferously, and ran off over a gentle rise of ground to the north. Two men on horseback soon made their appearance on the rising ground, and, seeing us, rode to our camp. They were two Franco-Americans, originally from Canada or St. Louis, who had wandered to California in some trapping expedition, and had remained in the country. They were arranging to build houses and settle permanently in this neighborhood. From them we learned the gratifying intelligence, that the whole of Upper California was in possession of the United States. Intelligence, they further stated, had been received, that General Taylor, after having met and defeated the Mexican forces in four pitched battles, killing an incredible number, some forty or fifty thousand, had triumphantly marched into the city of Mexico. The last part of this news, of course, judging from the situation of General Taylor when we left the United States, (war not having then been declared,) was impossible; but sifting the news and comparing one statement with another, the result to our minds was, that General T. had been eminently successful, defeating the Mexicans, whenever he had met them, with considerable slaughter. This, of course, produced much exultation and enthusiasm among us.

We informed the two gentlemen, that we had been for some time entirely destitute of provisions, and were in a state bordering on starvation. One of them immediately started off at a gallop to his cabin not far distant, and soon returned with a pan of unbolted flour and some tallow to cook it with. This, he said, was all he had, and if such had not been the case, he would have brought us something more. But we could not comprehend the use of tallow in cooking. We, however, afterwards learned that beef-tallow in California is used for culinary purposes in the same manner that hog's-lard is with us; and, on the whole, the prejudice against it being done away with by habit, I do not know that the former is not preferable to the latter—so much does habit and prejudice enter into the account and make up the sum of our likes and dislikes. We felt very grateful to this gentleman for his opportune present, for he would receive no compensation for it; and the fires were immediately blazing to render his generous donation of practical benefit.

Mr. Johnson returned home about nine o'clock. He was originally a New England sailor, and cast upon this remote coast by some vicissitudes common to those of his calling, and finally turned farmer or ranchero. He is a bachelor, with Indian servants, and stated that he had no food prepared for us, but such as was in the house was at our service. A pile of small cheeses, and numerous pans of milk with thick cream upon them, were exhibited on the table, and they disappeared with a rapidity dangerous to the health of those who consumed them.

Mr. J. gave us the first number of the first newspaper ever published in California, entitled *The Californian*, and published and edited at Monterey by Dr. Robert Semple, a native Kentuckian. It was dated about two weeks back. From the columns of this small sheet we gleaned some farther items of general intelligence from the United States, all of great interest to us. The leading paragraph, under the editorial head, was, in substance, a call upon the people of California to set about the organization of a territorial government, with a view to immediate annexation to the United States. This seemed and sounded very odd. We had been travelling in as straight a line as we could, crossing rivers, mountains, and deserts, nearly four months beyond the bounds of civilization, and for the greater distance beyond the boundaries of territory claimed by our government; but here, on the remotest confines of the world as it were, where we expected to visit and explore a foreign country, we found ourselves under American authority, and about to be "annexed" to the American Union. Events such as this are very remarkable, and are well calculated to excite the pride and vanity, if they do not always tally with the reason and judgment, of American citizens and republicans.

James H. Carson on Life in the Early Gold Mines, 1848

No roads marked the way to the traveller in California then: but, guided by the sun and well-known mountain peaks, we proceeded on our journey. No ferries were in operation for our passage across the deep and rapid streams. The site of the now beautiful and flourishing city of Stockton, was then alone in its native greatness; no steamboat's whistle was heard to startle the affrighted elk, nor had the newsboys' call been heard, or solemn bell called forth the sons of prayer. But still there was a little mud. Heedless of all difficulties, on, on I sped, until Mormon Island, on the South Fork, brought me up. Some forty or fifty men were at work with the cradle machines, and were averaging about eight ounces per day to the man. But a few moments passed before I was knee deep in water, with my wash-basin full of dirt, plunging it about endeavoring to separate the dirt from the gold. After washing some fifty pans of dirt, I found I had realised about four bits' worth of gold. Reader, do you know how an *hombre* feels when the gold fever heat has suddenly fallen to about zero? I do. Kelsey's and the old dry diggings had just been opened, and to them I next set out; a few hours' ride brought me to the Indian-trading camp of Captain Weber's famed company, where I saw sights of gold that revived the fever again. I saw Indians giving handsful of gold for a cotton handkerchief or a shirt—and so great was the income of the Captain's trading houses that he was daily sending out mules packed with gold, to the settlements. And no man in California was more deserving of this good fortune than Capt. Weber; he was one of the men of the Bear Flag. His time and fortunes had been given to the American cause, and he was ever seen in our ranks where danger threatened. Geology had not been deeply studied by our sons of the "forest wild," and many were the conjectures formed as to *whar* the gold came from; they could find it in the river any where; and at last they came to the sage conclusion that it was washed down from some place where the earth was a bed of gold, and as it continued to tumble about, became worn into the thin scales as they found it. As I have intimated, to find the source whence the gold came was the great object, and many prospecting parties were sent out with this purpose in view. The Indians who were working for Capts. Sutter and Weber gave them leading information, so that they were enabled to know the direction in which new discoveries were to be made.

A party accompanied Mr. Kelsey, and discovered the first dry diggings, which were named Kelsey's diggings, after their discoverer. The next discovered was the old dry diggings, out of which so many thousands of dollars have since been taken. . . . The old dry diggings were situated at Hangtown, in El Dorado county. In June, July and August, 1848, it was the centre of attraction for gold diggers. The population then there (exclusive of Indians) consisted of about three hundred—old pioneers, native Californians, deserters from the Army, Navy, and Colonel Stevenson's volunteers, were there mingled together, the happiest set of men on earth. Every one had plenty of dust. From three ounces to five pounds was the income per day to those who would work. The gulches and ravines were opened about two feet wide and one foot in depth along their centres, and the gold picked out from amongst the dirt with a knife. When they failed to realise two or three ounces per day by this method, the diggings were pronounced worked-out, and new ones were hunted up.

Clothing was not to be had for love or gold; and I have seen many an *hombre* with as much gold as he could carry, whose skin "peeped out through many a rent."

The first scales for weighing gold were made by taking a piece of pine wood for the beam, pieces of sardine boxes for scales, and silver dollars for weights. Gold dust could be purchased in any quantity at four and five dollars per ounce in the diggings, and for six and eight dollars in the coast towns.

Sutter's Fort was the great mart for trade. Sutter's Embarcadero, where the city of Sacramento now is, was the landing-place for goods from San Francisco, from which place they were transported to the stores at the fort, and there exposed for sale.

Honesty (of which we now know so little) was the ruling passion amongst the miners of '48. Old debts were paid up; heavy bags of gold dust were carelessly left laying in their brush homes; mining tools, though scarce, were left in their places of work for days at a time, and not one theft or robbery was committed.

In August, the old diggings were pronounced as being "dug out," and many prospecting parties had gone out. Part of Weber's trading establishments had secretly disappeared, and rumors were afloat that the place where all the gold "came from" had been discovered South, and a general rush of the miners commenced that day. . . .

The discovery of Sutter's Creek and Rio Seco was made in July, and the Moquelumne-river diggings, at which there was but little done, that season. Mr. Wood, with a prospecting party, discovered at the same time Wood's Creek, on the Stanislaus, out of which the few who were there then were realising two and three hundred dollars per day, with a pick and knife alone. . . .

In 1846 and '47, the price of the finest horses was $20; fat bullocks, $6; wild mares, 75 cents each; flour and vegetables, "we didn't had any." We lived on beef and beans—beef dried, fried, roasted, boiled and broiled, morning, noon and night: as much as every man wanted, without money or price; with a change, at times, to elk, venison and bear steak. The emigrants of 1846 did not expect to find any luxuries in California, with the exception of a balmy atmosphere and a rich soil—and they well knew that industry would soon supply the rest. The discovery of gold raised the price of stock in proportion with everything else. Horses and mules in the mines were worth from two to four hundred dollars; cattle from one to two hundred dollars per head. I have seen men give two and three hundred dollars for mules and horses—ride them from one digging to another—take their saddles off, and set the animals loose (never looking for them again), remarking that "it was easier to dig out the price of another, than to hunt up the one astray."

The morals of the miners of '48 should here be noticed. No person worked on Sunday *at digging* for gold—but that day was spent in *prospecting* in the neighborhood, by the more sedate portion of the miners; while others spent it in playing at poker, with lumps of gold for checks; others, collected in groups, might be seen under the shades of neighboring trees, singing songs, playing at "old sledge" and drinking whisky—in all of which proceedings, harmony, fun and good will to each other were the prominent features. We had ministers of the gospel amongst us, but they never preached. Religion had been forgotten, even by its ministers, and instead of their pointing out the narrow way which leads to eternal happiness, "on each returning Sabbath morn," they might have been seen with pick-axe and pan, travelling untrodden ways in search of "filthy lucre" & treasure that "fadeth away," or drinking good health and prosperity with friends.

Illinois Governor Edward Coles on the Proslavery Movement, 1823

Vandalia, Illinois, April 22, 1823.

Dear Sir:

. . . There has long existed in this State a strong party in favor of altering the constitution and making it a slave-holding State; while there is another party in favor of a convention to alter the constitution, but deny that Slavery is their object. These two parties have finally, by the most unprecedented and unwarrantable proceedings (an account of which you have no doubt seen in the newspapers), succeeded in passing a resolution requiring the sense of the people to be taken at the next general election (August, 1824,) on the propriety of calling a convention for the purpose of altering the constitution. Knowing that this measure would be strenuously urged during the late session of the Legislature, and that many who professed to be hostile to the further introduction of Slavery, would advocate it, and believing that it would have a salutary effect to furnish them an opportunity of evincing the sincerity of their professions; and being also urged by a strong sense of the obligations imposed on me, by my principles and feelings, to take notice of the subject, I called the attention of the Legislature in a speech I delivered on being sworn into office (a printed copy of which I sent you by mail) to the existence of Slavery in the State, in violation of the great fundamental principles of the ordinance, and recommended that just and equitable provision by made for its abrogation. As I anticipated, this part of my speech created a considerable excitement with those who were openly or secretly in favor of making Illinois a slaveholding, rather than making it really as well as nominally, a free State—who wished to fill it rather than empty it of slaves. Never did I see or hear in America of party spirit going to such lengths, as well officially as privately, as it did here on this question. Indeed, it seems to me that Slavery is so poisonous as to produce a kind of delirium in those minds who are excited by it. This question, and the manner of carrying it, is exciting great interest throughout the State, and has already kindled an extraordinary degree of excitement and warmth of feeling, which will no doubt continue to increase until the question is decided. I assure you, I never before felt so deep an interest in any political question. It preys upon me to such a degree, that I shall not be happy or feel at ease until it is settled. It is impossible to foresee the injurious effects resulting to this State or the unhappy consequences which may arise to the Union, from the success of the slave party in this State. Many of us who immigrated to this State under the solemn assurance that there should exist here "neither slavery nor involuntary servitude," will, if the slave faction succeeds, be compelled to sacrifice or abandon our property and seek new homes, we know not where, or remain in a community whose principles we shall disapprove of, and whose practice will be abhorrent to our feelings. And already we hear disputed the binding effect of the ordinance—the power of Congress to restrict a State, etc., etc., from which I fear, if the introduction of Slavery should be tolerated here, the discussions on the expediency and unconstitutionality of the measure will not in all probability be confined to the citizens of this State. But this is a part of the question too painful for me to dwell on. I trust the good sense and virtue of the citizens of Illinois will never sanction a measure so well calculated to disturb the harmony of the Union and so injurious to its own prosperity and happiness, as well as so directly opposite to the progress of those enlightened and liberal principles which do honor to the age. But to insure this it is necessary that the public mind should be enlightened on the moral and political effects of Slavery. . . .

Caroline M. Kirkland on Western Life, 1839, 1845

A New Home, Who'll Follow?, 1839

Whoever comes into Michigan with nothing, will be sure to better his condition; but wo to him that brings with him any thing like an appearance of abundance, whether of money or mere household conveniences. To have them, and not be willing to share them in some sort with the whole community, is an unpardonable crime. You must lend your best horse to *qui que ce soit* to go ten miles over hill and marsh, in the darkest night, for a doctor; or your team to travel twenty after a 'gal;' your wheel-barrows, your shovels, your utensils of all sorts, belong, not to yourself, but to the public, who do not think it necessary even to *ask* a loan, but take it for granted. The two saddles and bridles of [the town] spend most of their time travelling from house to house a-man-back; and I have actually known a stray martingale to be traced to four dwellings two miles apart, having been lent from one to another, without a word to the original proprietor, who sat waiting, not very patiently, to commence a journey.

Then within doors, an inventory of your plenishing of all sorts, would scarcely more than include the articles which you are solicited to lend. Not only are all kitchen utensils as much your neighbor's as your own, but bedsteads, beds, blankets, sheets, travel from house to house, a pleasant and effectual mode of securing the perpetuity of certain efflorescent peculiarities of the skin. . . .

But the cream of the joke lies in the manner of the thing. It is so straightforward and honest, none of your hypocritical civility and servile gratitude! Your true republican, when he finds that you possess any thing which would contribute to his convenience, walks in with, 'Are you going to use your horses *to-day?*' if horses happen to be the thing he needs.

'Yes, I shall probably want them.'

'O, well; if you want them——I was thinking to get 'em to go up north a piece.'

Or perhaps the desired article comes within the female department.

'Mother wants to get some butter: that 'ere butter you bought of Miss Barton this mornin.'

And away goes your golden store, to be repaid perhaps with some cheesy, greasy stuff, brought in a dirty pail, with, 'Here's your butter!'

A girl came in to borrow a 'wash-dish,' 'because we've got company.' Presently she came back: 'Mother says you've forgot to send a towel.'

'The pen and ink, and a sheet o' paper and a wafer,' is no unusual request; and when the pen is returned, you are generally informed that you sent 'an awful bad pen.'

I have been frequently reminded of one of Johnson's humorous sketches. A man returning a broken wheel-barrow to a Quaker, with, 'Here, I've broke your rotten wheel-barrow usin' on't. I wish you'd get it mended right off, 'cause I want to borrow it again this afternoon.' The Quaker is made to reply, 'Friend, it shall be done:' and I wish I possessed more of his spirit. . . .

When we first took our delighted abode in the 'framed house,' a palace of some twenty by thirty feet, flanked by a shanty kitchen, and thatched with oak shingles—a sober neighbor, who having passed most of his life in the country, is extremely philosophical on the follies of civilization, took my husband to task on the appearance of the ghost of a departed parlor carpet, which he said was 'introducing luxury.' Whether from this bad example, I cannot tell, but it is certain that our neighbors are many of them beginning to perceive that carpets 'save trouble.' Women are the most reasonable beings in the world; at least, I am sure nobody ever catches a woman without an unanswerable reason for anything she wishes to do. Mrs Micah Balwhidder only wanted a silver tea-pot, because, as all the world knows, tea tastes better out of silver; and Mrs Primrose loved her crimson paduasoy, merely because her husband had happened to say it became her.

Of the mingled mass of our country population, a goodly and handsome proportion—goodly as to numbers, and handsome as to cheeks and lips, and thews and sinews, consists of young married people just beginning the world; simple in their habits, moderate in their aspirations, and hoarding a little of old-fashioned romance, unconsciously enough, in the secret nooks of their rustic hearts. These find no fault with their bare loggeries. With a shelter and a handful of furniture they have enough. If there is the where-withal to spread a warm supper for 'th' old man' when he comes in from work, the young wife forgets the long, solitary, *wordless* day, and asks no greater happiness than preparing it by the help of such materials and such utensils as would be looked at with utter contempt in a comfortable kitchen;

and then the youthful pair sit down and enjoy it together, with a zest that the *'orgies parfaites'* of the epicure can never awaken. What lack they that this world can bestow? They have youth, and health, and love and hope, occupation and amusement, and when you have added 'meat, clothes, and fire,' what more has England's fair young queen? These people are contented, of course.

There is another class of settlers neither so numerous nor so happy; people, who have left small farms in the eastward States, and come to Michigan with the hope of acquiring property at a more rapid rate. They have sold off, perhaps at considerable pecuniary disadvantage, the home of their early married life; sacrificed the convenient furniture which had become necessary to daily comfort, and only awake when it is too late, to the fact that it kills old vines to tear them from their clinging-places. These people are much to be pitied, the women especially.

> The ladies first
> 'Gin murmur—as becomes the softer sex.

Woman's little world is overclouded for lack of the old familiar means and appliances. The husband goes to his work with the same axe or hoe which fitted his hand in his old woods and fields, he tills the same soil, or perhaps a far richer and more hopeful one—he gazes on the same book of nature which he has read from his infancy, and sees only a fresher and more glowing page; and he returns to his home with the sun, strong in heart and full of self-gratulation on the favorable change in his lot. But he finds the home-bird drooping and disconsolate. *She* has been looking in vain for the reflection of any of the cherished features of her own dear fire-side. She has found a thousand deficiencies which her rougher mate can scarce be taught to feel as evils. What cares he if the time-honored cupboard is meagerly represented by a few oakboards lying on pegs and called shelves? His tcaequipage shines as it was wont—the biscuits can hardly stay on the brightly glistening plates. Will he find fault with the clay-built oven, or even the tin 'reflector?' His bread never was better baked. What does he want with the great old cushioned rocking-chair? When he is tired he goes to bed, for he is never tired till bed-time. Women are the grumblers in Michigan, and they have some apology. Many of them have made sacrifices for which they were not at all prepared, and which detract largely from their every-day stores of comfort. The conviction of good accruing on a large scale does not prevent the wearing sense of minor deprivations.

Another large class of emigrants is composed of people of broken fortunes, or who have been unsuccessful in past undertakings. These like or dislike the country on various grounds, as their peculiar condition may vary. Those who are fortunate or industrious look at their new home with a kindly eye. Those who learn by experience that idlers are no better off in Michigan than elsewhere, can find no term too virulent in which to express their angry disappointment. The profligate and unprincipled lead stormy and uncomfortable lives any where; and Michigan, *now* at least, begins to regard such characters among her adopted children, with a stern and unfriendly eye, so that the few who may have come among us, hoping for the unwatched and unbridled license which we read of in regions nearer to the setting sun, find themselves marked and shunned as in the older world. . . .

It seemed, we afterwards learned, that the [Bank] Commissioners had seen some suspicious circumstances about the management of the Bank, and returned with a determination to examine into matters a little more scrupulously. It had been found in other cases that certain 'specie certificates' had been locomotive. It had been rumored, since the the new batch of Banks had come into operation, that

> Thirty steeds both fleet and wight
> Stood saddled in the stables day and night—

ready to effect at short notice certain transfers of assets and specie. And in the course of the Tinkerville investigation the Commissioners had ascertained by the aid of hammer and chisel, that the boxes of the 'real stuff' which had been so loudly vaunted, contained a heavy charge of broken glass and tenpenny nails, covered above and below with halfdollars, principally '*bogus.*' Alas, for Tinkerville! and alas, for poor Michigan!

The distress among the poorer classes of farmers which was the immediate consequence of this and other Bank failures, was indescribable. Those who have seen only a city panic, can form no idea of the extent and severity of the sufferings on these occasions. And how many small farmers are there in Michigan who have *not* suffered from this cause?

The only adequate punishment which I should prescribe for this class of heartless adventurers, would be to behold at one glance all the misery they have occasioned; to be gifted with an Asmodean power, and forced to use it. The hardiest among them, could scarcely, I think endure to witness the unroofing of the humble log-huts of Michigan, after the bursting of one of these Dead-sea apples. Bitter indeed were the ashes which they scattered!

How many settlers who came in from the deep woods many miles distant where no grain had yet grown, after travelling perhaps two or three days and nights, with a half-starved ox-team, and living on a few crusts by the way, were told when they offered their splendid-looking bank-notes, their hard-earned all, for the flour which was to be the sole food of wife and babes through the long winter, that these hoarded treasures were valueless as the ragged paper which wrapped them! Can we blame them if they cursed in their agony, the soulless wretches who had thus drained their best blood for the furtherance of their own schemes of low ambition? Can we wonder that the poor, feeling such wrongs as these, learn to hate the rich, and to fancy them natural enemies?

Western Clearings, 1845

To be early in the field is the farmer's maxim. He waits only for light enough to work by, before calling up his men, who are apt to be up before he calls them, so contagious is the enthusiasm of the hour. No one likes to be a laggard in harvest. And then the early morning air is so fresh and so inspiriting; the brightening hues of the pearly East so irresistibly glorious, the rising of the sun so majestic, that even the dull soul feels, and the dull eye gazes, with an admiration not unmixed with awe. Two hours' labour before the six o'clock breakfast lays bare a wide space in the field, for very numerous are the strong arms brought up to the work. This season is the test of the husbandman's capabilities, whether as master or man. The unthrifty is behindhand in his preparations. He has depended upon *luck* for his assistants, and put off looking for or engaging them until the last moment. Luck, as usual, takes care of those who take care of themselves, and so neighbour Feckless is obliged to take up with the leavings. When it is time to begin, scythes want sharpening and rifles are worn out or lost, and perhaps a ride of ten miles is necessary to repair the deficiency. Before harvest is half over, the stock of provisions proves scanty, and half a day must be spent in borrowing of the neighbours. With all these and many more drawbacks, the work goes on but slowly, and the crop is perhaps not properly secured in season. Wheat will become so dead ripe that much is lost in the gathering, or perhaps successive rains, when it ought to be under cover, will rust and ruin it entirely. Neighbour Feckless has of course no barn; (in the new country better farmers cannot always afford one;) and being obliged to put up his grain in a hurry, it is perhaps not sufficiently dried, or not well stacked; in which case every grain will sprout and grow in such a way that the entire mass becomes one body of shoots, so that it must be torn apart, and is only fit to feed the cattle with. "Bad luck!" sighs our poor friend.

Far otherwise runs the experience of the thriving farmer. All is ready betimes, and due allowance made for lee-way and "peradventures." He is not obliged to overwork himself or his people. He goes forward in his own business in order to insure its success. It is proverbial in the country that "Come, boys!" is always better than "Go, boys!" Neighbour Thrifty knows this so well that if he be not in the freshness of his strength, so that he can take the lead in mowing or reaping, he will yet engage in some part of the day's labours, which will keep him in the midst of his men, so that the influence of his eye and of his voice may be felt, without his incurring the odious suspicion of being a mere overseer or task-master. And what a various congregation is that which does his bidding! Not mere day-labourers—for the country furnishes comparatively few of these—but all men of all kinds. Do you want your wagon-wheel mended? The wheelwright, if he have no fields of his own, is busy in those of his neighbour. The carpenter will not drive a nail for love or money, for he too is "bespoke." You are unlucky if your nag need shoeing at this critical period, for the son of Vulcan will not have time to light a fire in his own smithy, perhaps for a fortnight. Peep into the village school-house; you will find none there but minors, in a very literal sense; wee things who would be only in the way at home. All boys who are old enough to rake or run on errands are sure to be in the field, and the girls are helping at home to boil and bake. The interests of learning have for the time the go-by. This is so well understood that in most places the master abdicates for the season in favour of the female sovereign, again to resume the sceptre when Winter grasps his.

Stranger than all, even law-suits are suspended, for the justice is in the field; witnesses are swinging the cradle; all possible jurymen are scattered miles apart, mowing the broad savannahs; and the contending parties themselves are too much engrossed, each with his own business, to wish matters pushed to extremities at such a crisis. Even the young lover almost forgets the flaxen ringlets of his sweetheart in the bustle of a field-day, and if he meet the damsel at evening will be apt to entertain her with an account of his achievements with the cradle or the sickle. Idleness is banished so completely that even the incurably lazy bustle about as if they too wished to do something. It is amusing to see one of this class at this juncture. In the general rush of business and consequent scarcity of strong arms, he knows that even his aid is of consequence. Feeling this to be emphatically his day, he is disposed to make the most of it. He accordingly assumes a swaggering air; don't know whether he'll come or not: but, on the whole, guesses he'll help! He braces up for the occasion, lays by his rifle and his fishing-tackle, and like a spinning-top whirls round bravely for a while, but if not now and then lashed into speed by some new motive, soon subsides into his natural state of repose. We have known a worthy of this tone promise to "help" four different farmers, and after all, take down his rifle and "guess he'd better go and try if he couldn't see a deer!"

The good woman within doors is far from being idle all this time. Hers is the pleasant though rather arduous task of keeping the harvesters in heart for the labours of the day, and for this purpose she summons all her skill and forethought, and sets forth all her good cheer. Pies and cake and all manner of rustic dainties grace her bounteous board; for her reputation is at stake, since she is supposed at this time to do her very best. To set a poor table at harvest is death to any housewifely reputation. Good humour too is very desirable, where work is to be done; and to this we all know good cheer is apt to contribute; and no mistress likes to see her table surrounded by sour faces, even if the work should go on as well as ever. The providing for a dozen or two of harvest-hands is not a matter of any especial research; since although, as we have hinted, some delicacies are always included, yet the main body of the meal, three times a day, is formed of pork and hot bread. Where these are abundant, (and no Western farmer need lack either), the adjuncts are matter of small moment. Pork and hot bread three times a day! No wonder they can work twelve hours out of the twenty-four. To labour any less on such diet would be suicide.

Speculators, Squatters, and the Senate Debate over Public Land Policy, 1837

Robert Walker, Mississippi, 1837

Mr. Walker said, the great principle contained in the bill now under consideration, was to arrest monopolies of the public lands, and limit the sale to settlers or cultivators. The adoption of this measure would have a material influence upon the revenue of the Government, and the prosperity of the country. Before investigating the details of the bill, it would be proper to examine the preliminary question: whether the great principle upon which the bill reposes, is such as to recommend it to the favorable consideration of the American Senate. So long as Congress offers for sale hundreds of millions of acres of land, with no limitation upon the extent of the purchase, vast quantities of these lands must pass into the hands of a few capitalists, thus authorized and invited by the Government to make the purchase; and when these capitalists confined their operations to the acquisition of lands unoccupied by any settler, it was clearly erroneous to denounce such speculations during the continuance of the existing system. It was the system that was wrong; and so long as it was continued, any denunciation of those who purchased large bodies of the unoccupied public lands was worse than ridiculous. Such purchases had been made, and would continue to be made, by many respectable citizens, in accordance with the invitation of the Government, and any denunciation of such purchasers would only react upon the Congress which adopted the existing system, as well as every succeeding Congress which refuses its repeal or modification. But the question recurs, does this system best promote the prosperity of the American people? and shall we continue to invite and encourage the monopoly of the public lands by a few individuals, or to amend the existing system as to sell the public lands only in limited quantities, sufficient for farms or plantations, and thus reserve for these great and useful purposes this noble public domain? Whether these lands shall thus be reserved for sale only for settlement or cultivation, or whether they shall be permitted to pass into the hands of a few individuals, by townships, counties, and even entire States, in a single year, is the true question which we must determine.

The evils of the existing system were only fully developed during the past year and that which preceded it. By the returns from the Land Office, the sales, exclusive of those at Pontotoc, Mississippi, during the first three quarters of the past year, amounted to $20,063,430, and the number of acres sold, to 15,934,430. Thus upon the same ratio, the sales of the year 1836 amounted to twenty million of acres, and upwards of twenty-five millions of dollars; and including the sales at Pontotoc to more than twenty-one million of acres, and more than twenty-seven million of dollars. In a single year thus a portion of the public domain has been sold, nearly equal in superficial extent to the great State of Ohio, and exceeding the superficies of five New England States, containing more than two millions of people. In this manner, entire States are swept in a single year into the hands of speculators, who may thus exercise a greater control over the destiny of these States for half a century to come, than the national and State legislatures combined. Can any system be devised more destructive of equal rights and republican principles? In vain shall we have struck down the feudal system, with its accompanying relation of lord and vassal, if we create and continue here this worse than feudal vassalage, this system of American landlords engrossing millions of acres, and regulating the terms of sale or settlement. In vain shall we have abolished the system of primogeniture and entailments, as calculated to create landed monopolies, if we sustain the existing policy, by which a few capitalists may engross in a single year the ownership of States, and control the destiny of millions. An extent of territory equal to five States passing in a single year into the hands of speculators! must not this create here a landed aristocracy without the title, but more wealthy and powerful than the sinking nobility of England? It will establish a fourth estate, more controlling than the Legislative, Executive, and Judicial power. It will control agriculture and its products, by regulating the price of landed property. It will certainly introduce into the new States, the system of landlord and tenant, by which the occupant will not be the owner of the soil he cultivates, but the tributary of some absentee landlord, who will, in the shape of an annual rent, reap nearly all the profits of the labor of the cultivator. It will establish a relation of abject dependance on the one hand, and tyrannical power on the other. It will impoverish the many, and enrich the few. It will create a war of capital against labor, of the producer against the non-producer, of the cultivator against the speculator; a war in which this Government will be arrayed on the side of the speculator, enlarging his dominion, increasing his power, until in a few years more, he will acquire a complete monopoly, and maintain an undisputed empire throughout the Valley of the West. . . .

There can be no greater injury to any country than the monopoly of its lands by a few individuals, thus keeping those lands out of the hands of settlers and cultivators, and condemning vast regions of fertile lands to remain for years waste and uncultivated. The West, for many years, has been endeavoring to obtain from Congress a reduction of the price of the public lands; but the continuation of the existing system is worse than a refusal to reduce the price; it is equivalent to a law raising the price to settlers and cultivators from one dollar and twenty-five cents per acre, to a price varying from five to thirty dollars per acre. It is well known that within the last few years, vast bodies of public lands have been purchased by speculators at one dollar and twenty-five cents per acre, and resold to settlers or cultivators at prices varying from five to thirty dollars per acre. And what must soon be the inevitable result of continuing the existing system? At the rate of twenty-one million of acres per annum, speculators in a very few years must own nearly every acre of good land in the present new States and organized Territories of the Union. When this monopoly shall be complete, and no good land remains the property of the Government, will not a still higher price be demanded for those lands by those who hold them? If we abolish the system of sales to speculators, these millions of acres of good land, now owned by the Government, will pass, from time to time, at the minimum price, into the hands of settlers or cultivators, which otherwise would be purchased by speculators, and resold by them at from five to thirty dollars per acre. Every Senator who votes against this bill, votes for continuing a system by which this vast enhancement to settlers and cultivators, of the price of the public lands, must soon take place. There can be no greater curse to any country, no more serious impediment to its prosperity, than the high price of its unoccupied lands. It prevents or postpones the settlement of those lands, and decreases the wealth, products, and population of a State. It is equivalent to a decree of man condemning to remain waste and uncultivated vast regions created by nature inexhaustibly fertile, and inviting the hand of improvement. What Senator, from any new State, has not seen whole townships of land remaining in the hands of speculators, waste and unoccupied, where otherwise purchases by settlers or cultivators would have been made at the minimum price of the Government, and where would now be smiling farms and prosperous villages. . . .

John P. King, Georgia, 1837

This motion had, [Senator King] said, again given rise to a great deal of eloquence on the high virtues of squatters. A happy talent that, possessed by his friend from Mississippi, of being eloquent just as well on one subject as another. A real genuine squatter was really one of the driest subjects for eloquence that ever presented itself to the mind of any orator. If he were going, he said, to work himself up into a paroxysm of eloquence, a squatter was about the last subject he should select to stir up this emotion. He would as soon go to the penitentiary to select subjects for canonization, as to go among the squatters to inspire him with eloquence. He should not know on what point of a squatter's character to become pathetic, and would, therefore, be constantly in danger of crying at the wrong place. The Senator from Mississippi [Mr. Walker] might produce impressions on some generous hearts by his imaginary pictures of the humble virtues of these law-breakers. But, if so, it must be upon those who know nothing about them. There might be some exceptions, but take the border squatters as a class, and they were certainly the most worthless set of men who have any claim to the honors of being American citizens. They were mostly an idle, profligate set of men, who hover along the frontier settlements, with their heads full of all sorts of schemes for living without profitable labor. They are, said he, men frequently who find it very convenient to be exempt from the operation of the laws, both civil and criminal; they therefore generally keep beyond the organized limits of the country. They produce not the worth of a dollar to add to the exports of the country, and they consume nothing that pays a tax to the Government. They perform no civil duties, and discharge none of the obligations of society. They penetrate beyond your borders, often in the neighborhood of Indian tribes, or among them, and, by squatting upon the land of the Government, and stealing their provisions from the Indians, they literally live by unlawful depredation. They are the very men who provoke most of your Indian wars, which cost us millions of money, and many lives better than their own. Where is their merit, to give them this heavy claim to favor over the rest of the citizens of the country? Yet, they come here asking heavy rewards for crime, and large premiums for a violation of the laws. Yes, and gentlemen, with the evidences of outrage in the very petitions they present, press their claims upon the sympathies of the Senate by fancy pictures of the humble virtues of the industrious poor. The honest, laborious cultivator of the soil appeals to you to protect him against the avarice and rapacity of the odious speculator. Why, sir, said he, such is the influence of language upon the thoughts of men, that to the mere force of names and epithets may perhaps be attributed three fourths of all the error and delusion by which the views and sentiments of men have ever been misled. Something like an excitement has been got up in the chamber, by applying epithets to men entirely inconsistent with their character. Men who violate the laws, trespass upon the public property, and treat the authority of the Government with habitual contempt, are here christened the hard-handed, honest-hearted cultivators of the soil, deserving the peculiar favor of the Government, whilst the orderly citizen, who keeps within your surveys, complies with all the formalities of your laws, and buys what the Government has to sell, at the price the Government fixes on it, is branded as an avaricious speculator, a land glutton, an odious character, who deserves some signal mark of the displeasure of the Government and country. Great merit is claimed for these hardy yeomanry who penetrate the wilderness, and select and settle upon the choice spots, before the lands are brought into market; the dangers they encounter and risks they run, in making these settlements, are supposed to entitle them to these choice selections, on which they make such enormous profits as soon as the pre-emption is secured. Why, sir, the midnight housebreaker might just as well insist that he had an honest claim to all the property in the house, to compensate him for the risk of breaking in. Did any body suppose a squatter ever "penetrated the wilderness," in advance of the surveys and settlements, from patriotic motives? Who told them to suffer these dreadful privations? We forbid them by law; and yet, to make large speculations with little or no labor, they patriotically violate the law, and then claim to be rewarded for it. These great cultivators, he said, pioneered for us without our consent, selected all the choice spots, mill seats, water powers, town sites, &c., and so soon as they secure a pre-emption, and sell out for enormous profits, they patriotically "penetrate the wilderness," endure dreadful hardships, and, for the good of their country, squat down somewhere else. The Senator from Ohio, from actual observation, had given us an idea of the farms of these cultivators, and which was shown also, to a great extent, by documents from the land offices, and notoriously true. They build a three-cornered pen, (a square pen being too onerous,) and sow it in grain, or they plant a few stalks of red pepper or tomatoes. This crop is recommended, by not requiring a close enclosure, and because it will grow in the shade; for these public benefactors, who make such sacrifices for the good of the country, are often too lazy to belt a sapling. By these picked settlements they often make enormous profits for themselves, or those capitalists who have hired them to squat. It was, he said, emphatically, not a system of settlement and cultivation, but of squatting and speculation. These selections, made in this way before the country is brought into market, frequently sell for a profit of five or ten thousand dollars; (these prices he had known given in a few instances himself;) and in one noted instance a million and a half is the estimated value. Why give to a few adventurers, whatever might be their character, such an immense advantage over the rest of their fellow-citizens? . . .

⧉ *E S S A Y S*

These two selections offer different approaches to the economic and social history of white settlement on the prairie. In the first essay, Robert Swierenga, a professor of history at Kent State University, contests the idea that territorial land speculators were greedy exploiters, and explains how they facilitated economic growth in early Iowa. John Mack Faragher of Mount Holyoke College, the author of the second essay, takes an intensive look at a single community, Sugar Creek, Illinois, and traces how it changed from the 1830s through the 1850s. Although Faragher dismisses some of the charges against "nonresident speculators," his account of the decline and fall of an older form of community, and the hardening of new class distinctions, contrasts with Swierenga's more upbeat assumptions about economic development. These interpretations clearly echo the debates of the time. They also raise larger issues about early settler society—and how and why it developed as it did.

The Speculators' Role on the Frontier

ROBERT SWIERENGA

Until the stock offerings of modern corporations became the dominant attraction for surplus capital in the later decades of the nineteenth century, real estate—particularly western—was no doubt the principal form of American investment. Men from all walks of life, including future President Abraham Lincoln, turned to frontier Iowa for sound investments. Beginning with the trade in claims in eastern Iowa in the 1830's and culminating in the land office rush of the Fifties, speculators, large and small, acquired an ever increasing quantity of raw land. Finally, at the outset of the Civil War, these land merchants probably owned more than one-half of the entire state.

In the face of such intense activity and what historians have written of it, the reader of contemporary literature expects to find a great deal of sustained criticism directed at speculators. Surprisingly, however, this is not the case. A careful survey of Iowa newspapers and periodicals reveals that speculators were excoriated only intermittently; usually in conjunction with the major depressions of the late 1830's and 1850's, with bitterly fought political campaigns, or with attempts to justify claim club activity.

During the depression years of 1838 and 1839, when President Martin Van Buren proclaimed for public sale dozens of townships in eastern Iowa, settlers immediately raised the traditional hue and cry for postponement. And almost as inevitably, they couched their appeal in the rhetoric of the poor settler who lacked funds to enter his land and was therefore in danger of falling into the clutches of "greedy" speculators "who grind the faces of the poor." . . .

Although nonresidents bore the brunt of the criticism, local farmer-speculators did not entirely escape censure, at least not from agriculturalists

Excerpts from *Pioneers and Profits: Land Speculation on the Iowa Frontier* by Robert Swierenga, pp. 210–227. Reprinted by permission of Iowa State University Press.

such as B. F. Conkey, secretary of the State Agricultural Society. There was a lesson to be learned from the adversity, Conkey admonished: "The recent hard times have given a new impulse to agriculture, by teaching the people that speculating in lands is not the best use to which they can be put or the most sure to return large profits. . . ."

Politicos also tried to capitalize on any ill will which might be engendered against speculators. One crafty Democrat pinned on his opponent the epithets "prince of speculators," "a 40 per cent man," and "a moneylender and shaver." Conversely, early in 1841 when Congress discussed a preemption bill sponsored by the Democratic administration, a Whig editor, loath to have the opposition gain any credit, denounced the proposed law as a mere gambit to get Western votes and charged that it would aid the "richest and most grasping speculator" instead of the poor settler. . . .

Claim club advocates were probably the chief critics of nonresident speculators. Although the law allowed claimants to preempt no more than a quarter section of the public domain, early residents in Iowa invariably tried to monopolize two and three times this amount and force later arrivals to pay them a premium. A pioneer Des Moines resident, H. B. Turrill, recalled how in the spring of 1848, with the first land sales scheduled for the fall of the year, residents banded together to protect their illegal claims in the fertile Des Moines River Valley. The lands, Turrill asserted, "were worth from two to twelve dollars an acre, even at that time, and the holders of them, could they obtain a good title at reasonable rates, were to be esteemed fortunate." By "reasonable rates," he added, the claimants meant "no more than the lowest government price." Understandably, these people were highly incensed at the prospect of nonresident speculators forcing them at the upcoming public auction to raise their bids and thereby lose a handsome profit. The claim club was the answer. Although these claims were illegal and often involved land other than settlers' homesteads, the club members customarily "resolved," as did the association in Des Moines, "that we will in all cases discountenance the speculator, or other person, who shall thus attempt any innovation upon the homes of the rightful settlers." Thus, the nonresident speculator became the scapegoat—a role he has occupied ever since.

Derogatory comment concerning speculators can be matched with a fair amount of charitable utterances from those recognizing the social services of large investors to the frontier community. As moneylenders, they "assisted many a good man to secure a home," declared an early county historian. True, a western editor added, the settler "may be compelled to pay 50 and possibly 100 per cent for his loan for one year; but even at the latter sum his land will cost him but $2.50 an acre, which he probably deems worth $5 to $10." . . .

The variety of opinion expressed in the above paragraphs simply illustrates the fact that western communities split in their attitude toward nonresident speculators. Bankers, lawyers, and businessmen in general realized that local capital was inadequate to meet the needs of a burgeoning economy; eastern capital must be courted. Settlers groups, on the other hand, contained many who, rightly or wrongly, were critical. Apparently the western attitude toward large investors was one of ambivalence.

Unlike the picture painted by claim club speculators and politicians, the evidence suggests that in the Middle West as in the eastern states earlier, nonresident investors and local residents usually enjoyed rather cordial relations. Common sense indeed would indicate as much. As businessmen, capitalists were careful to curry the good will of their prospective customers. Rare was the moneylender who would rouse the ire of residents by bidding on their claims at the public sales. At one of the first auctions in the state, in Burlington in December of 1838, the local editor reported that speculators "did not attempt to bid against the settlers and the latter have thus been permitted to enter a half section of the best land in the United States at $1.25 per acre." Similarly, as a speculator reported: "I have been here about two weeks but have not been able to Secure a Single acre of . . . land nor has any one Else obtained any except Settlers. . . . Big bidders" such as himself, he went on to explain, bid only on land *"not claimed by Settlers."* Necessarily, therefore, competition was fierce and few large investors obtained as much land as they desired. . . .

Settlers were equally as dependent on the willingness of businessmen to extend loans. Cyrus Sanders, assistant bidder of the claim association of Johnson County, recounted that many local settlers, although lacking funds, started for the Dubuque auction of 1840 "expectant of meeting capitalists at the sale, of whom they could borrow the money." John E. Stoner of Marengo in Iowa County was one such settler. As Stoner recounted in the third person some years later, he "went to Iowa City, when the land office was located there, to enter some land, without a cent of money, and asked in the office if there was a man there who would enter forty acres of land for him and give him a bond for a deed and one year in which to pay for it, when a Dr. Bower said he would enter eighty acres and take his [Stoner's] note, which was done. These gentlemen had never met before, and never but once afterward." Such acts of faith on the part of residents whose homesteads were likely at stake, presupposed a rather solid working relationship between lender and debtor. As one participant later declared: "It seemed opportune for both settler and capitalist to meet and arrange terms so pleasantly. It demonstrated that capital and labor were friendly elements, and could work together." . . .

A final bit of evidence which indicates a lack of animosity between land speculators and local residents is seen in the large number of prominent Iowa speculators who won elective office in local, state, or national government at some time during the ante bellum period. Presumably, if Hawkeye citizens had felt a deep antipathy to speculators they could easily have registered their displeasure at the polls. For large land dealers and investors were perennial candidates for elective public office in frontier Iowa. A comparison of lists of large speculators with elected public officials, however, reveals a considerable overlapping. Of the 648 Iowans who entered over 1,000 acres of Congress land in Royce Cession 262, 33 served in the Iowa senate from 1838 through 1860 (19 for two and three terms), while 38 secured seats in the lower house (15 for two to five terms). Two, James W. Grimes and Samuel J. Kirkwood, won the governorship and 10 held state-wide offices including treasurer, auditor, supreme court justice, superintendent of public instruction, and superintendent of the state penitentiary. On the national scene, James W. Grimes, George A. Jones, and Samuel J. Kirkwood represented the Hawkeye State in the U.S. Senate, and John P. Cook, Lincoln Clark, Henry Clay Dean, Bernhart Henn, and William Thompson won election to the House of Representatives. J. B. Grinnell began his stint in Congress in 1863. . . .

Leaving ultimate moral judgments aside, it might be well to reassess the role of the frontier land speculator. The bill of indictment levied against him charges that he created "speculator's deserts" by forcing immigrants to look elsewhere for land they could afford; he "played hob with the finances of local governments by his refusal to pay taxes"; and, most important of all, he caused a rapid increase in the un-American institution of tenancy. Speculators' deserts, it is argued, were the result of the deliberate policy of speculators to demand exorbitant prices for their land, or more simply to withhold it from market until population pressure in the vicinity brought the inevitable price rise. Settlers, unable to pay this "unearned increment" to the middlemen, looked farther afield for cheaper land they could afford, thus dispersing themselves over wider areas. The end result was to raise the cost of road construction and maintenance, necessitate the creation of many small and inefficient units of local government, and require extra facilities for schools, churches, libraries, grange halls, and other social institutions. The refusal of nonresident speculators to meet their tax obligations further increased the financial burden on local citizens, whose property was already all too easily assessed. Facing ruinous taxes and usurious interest rates on their mortgages, the farmers were virtually forced to deplete their soil, which led to erosion and lower land values. A year or two of bad crops and the independent yeoman slipped into the tenant class. Such are the major complaints against speculators, although the list is by no means exhausted.

On closer scrutiny, most of these "social costs" cannot legitimately be assessed against speculators. The charge that speculators retarded settlement rests on the unproven assumption that they demanded excessive prices for their land or held it off the market for a number of years. Since most large investors and particularly the major operators in Iowa were professional realtors, they could hardly have engaged in such practices and remained in business. Necessarily, they pressed sales at reasonable rates. Profits lay in increasing the volume of sales, thereby gaining a rapid turnover of their funds, not in withholding land from market. Senator John P. King of Georgia addressed himself specifically to this point in a congressional speech at the time. "It was a great mistake," King asserted, "to suppose that large land companies or speculators were in the habit of holding up their lands at exorbitant and forbidding prices. . . ." Operating frequently on borrowed capital and competing with low-priced government land, they generally offered their land at only a "moderate advance of the original cost." Nevertheless, he concluded, by "operating upon a large scale, a small advance affords a handsome profit. . . ."

Rather than retard settlement, speculators likely promoted it. As wholesale land buyers, they were, as one Iowa historian aptly stated, "the most potent of all agencies" in opening the West to settlement. Their nationwide advertising and their reputation for offering land of better than average quality attracted many buyers to the Hawkeye State. Most important of all, they provided the credit that so many smaller investors and settlers needed to acquire real estate. . . .

Before speculators can be charged with fostering tenancy, the extent to which they rented land or forced defaulted mortgagees into tenancy must be demonstrated. [T]he experience of James Easley, is illuminating. Over the 27 years of his career in the western land business, the Virginian rented but a few quarter sections—mostly lead-bearing land in Missouri. . . . Easley first considered renting his raw land in Iowa in the mid-1870's, when two farmers requested permission to harvest the grass in return for paying taxes. Because there were no strings attached, Easley agreed. But a third farmer, who offered to fence one of Easley's vacant tracts in exchange for its use as a pasture, met with an outright refusal, despite the fact that the land had returned no revenue to offset nearly twenty years of tax levies. In no way would he jeopardize his freedom to sell at any time, Easley explained to the disappointed rancher. The same rationale governed the Virginian's mortgage policy and ruled out the possibility of tenancy when his mortgagees defaulted on their notes. Rather than permit farmer-owners to become his tenants, Easley granted extentions of time and accepted token payments until the crises might pass. Only after owners allowed three to five years to elapse without payment did Easley foreclose, and then the property was resold to another buyer as soon as possible. Thus, owners did not become tenants, at least on Easley's land.

Although James Easley may have been atypical, there is little evidence that other large speculators in Congress land rented their property. No reference is found to tenants in any of their surviving business papers nor in the rather extensive incoming correspondence of Cook, Sargent & Downey of Iowa City. This is not to assert, of course, that no large investors rented. By the 1870's and 1880's, one can find numerous instances of absentee landlords, particularly in the western counties along the Missouri slope. These landlords, however, were not the large speculators of the ante bellum period who figured so prominently in the disposal of the public domain in Iowa.

The leading realtors throughout the state, when they advertised in the local press, similarly did not offer along with their other functions to manage rental property for nonresidents. The nearest approximation—one of only two examples found—was the proposal to "rent and lease Houses, Lots, and Farms," made in 1857 by the Iowa Central Real Estate Agency of Des Moines in the advertising section of the first published history of the capital city. For a land agency to undertake the management of rental property, however, does not prove that nonresident speculators fostered tenancy on the Iowa frontier, or even that such individuals were the major leaseholders. Retired farmers and widows frequently preferred renting rather than selling their farms. Prosperous farmers sometimes leased their excess acreage to neighbors. Mechanics, craftsmen, and local professional and businessmen often owned farms which they rented. So did farmers who entered government employ. Charles Mason of Burlington, for example, leased his farm while serving as a judge on the Iowa supreme court.

Within the framework of the social and economic assumptions of their time, nonresident investors served a useful and often beneficial function. By extending credit, paying taxes, hiring realtors to locate, enter, and sell land, buying advertising space in local newspapers, and employing residents to patrol timber tracts in their areas, speculators created many jobs and funneled large amounts of capital into frontier Iowa at a time when it was desperately needed. By increasing the rate of public land sales, especially of land not immediately optimum for farming, speculators widened the tax base of frontier communities and assisted the federal treasury to convert its vast land resources into much-needed revenue. Despite some criticism by contemporaries and almost universal disparagement in subsequent historical literature, these entrepreneurs were as essential to the economic development of the West as were their clients, the frontier farmers.

The Transformation of a Rural Community: Commonality and Class in Sugar Creek

JOHN MACK FARAGHER

The rugged, individualistic frontiersman is an *idée fixe* of American popular culture, which may suggest why historians have paid relatively little attention to community life in the American West. Over the past seventy-five years, free-market conservatives from Herbert Hoover to Ronald Reagan have praised the individualistic "spirit of the frontier," taking their cues from historian Frederick Jackson Turner, who argued that "the frontier is productive of individualism" and that the "immemorial custom of tribe or village community" fell victim to the American pioneer experience. "Complex society," Turner wrote in 1893, "is precipitated by the wilderness into a kind of primitive organization based on the family. The tendency is anti-social." For "these slashers of the forest, these self-sufficing pioneers, raising the corn and live stock for their own need, living scattered and apart," Turner wrote, "individualism was more pronounced than community life."

Many nineteenth-century observers of the "Old West" saw more evidence of community than did Turner. In the 1830s, Illinois editor James Hall, for example, emphasized the communal behavior of settlers.

From *Sugar Creek: Life on the Illinois Prairie* by John Mack Faragher (New Haven: Yale University Press, 1986), pp. 130–136, 181–190.

Exposed to common dangers and toils, they become united by the closest ties of social intercourse. Accustomed to arm in each other's defense, to aid in each other's labour, to assist in the affectionate duty of nursing the sick, and the mournful office of burying the dead, the best affections of the heart are kept in constant exercise; and there is, perhaps, no class of men in our country, who obey the calls of friendship, or the claims of benevolence, with such cheerful promptness, or with so liberal a sacrifice of personal convenience.

With Hall's views others found themselves in agreement, although dissenting, perhaps, from the rosy glow of his affect. After living in a raw Michigan backcountry community for several years in the 1830s New Yorker Caroline Kirkland grudgingly admired the "homely fellowship" among her neighbors, although she often felt oppressed by prying eyes and wagging tongues. "Any appearance of a desire to avoid this rather trying fraternization is invariably met by a fierce and indignant resistance," she complained; "the spirit in which was conceived the motto of the French revolution, 'la fraternité ou la mort,' exists in full force among us." English immigrant George Flower observed that among his Illinois neighbors any man who tried to live in isolation from others, like the stereotypical frontier individualist was considered to be committing a serious offense against civility. "You may sin and be wicked in many ways, and in the tolerant circle of American society receive a full and generous pardon," Flower explained to his English readers, "but this one sin can never be pardoned." "In no part of the world," concluded Scotsman John Bradbury, after a tour of America, "is *good neighbourship* found in greater perfection than in the western territory."

In Turner's defense, he built his argument on certain truths. As a group, American farmers were uncommonly free of the obligations that tied many of their European and Latin American counterparts to village society. And, after all, farming men and women did spent most of their time pursuing solitary tasks within the limiting circle of the family. Nevertheless, communal sinew bound together the backcountry society of Sugar Creek. By no means was the dominant tendency "anti-social," as Turner imagined. With a remarkable degree of gregariousness, farm families reached out from their log cabins to their neighbors for work and play, politics and prayer.

The foundation of American agriculture was the private ownership of the means of agrarian production by men, householders who headed a family labor system. Some of these had families with children too young to lend a hand and thus were able to convert less land to productive use, or had families without the labor benefits of nearby kin. Families who came with savings, on the other hand, could afford to hire labor to break land, split rails, or herd cattle. Families pursued but could only imperfectly achieve the goal of self-sufficiency with surplus. A stratification of wealth was inevitable but modest: in 1838, two decades after the settlement of Sugar Creek had begun, the wealthiest 10 percent of owners held a quarter of the privately owned acreage.

But when embedded in a culture that practiced traditions of common use, family proprietorship could provide a foundation for family security.

Sugar Creek farmers, like their ancestors and counterparts throughout the nation, utilized important rural productive resources in common with their neighbors. Custom allowed farmers, for example, to hunt game for their own use though they might be in woodlands owned by someone else. Hogs running wild in the timber and surviving on the mast paid no heed to property lines. And despite an 1831 prohibition against "stealing" timber from un-claimed congress land, settlers acted as if the resources of these acres be-longed to the neighborhood in common and helped themselves, "hooking" whatever timber they needed. William Oliver, an English observer of Illinois pioneer life, reported that settlers often ransacked unclaimed lands for wood, "never cutting a stick of their own for any purpose so long as there is any suitable that can be stolen from Uncle Sam, as they facetiously term the United States government."

The prairies, according to Moses Wadsworth of Sugar Creek, were con-sidered "a range, open and free" by the community. Before the 1850s, few farmers fenced their pastures but instead enclosed their fields to keep out grazing stock. "A great many cattle are reared on the prairies, which are occupied in common by the inhabitants," Patrick Shirreff noted in 1835, and Englishwoman Rebecca Burlend observed that "all unenclosed lands, whether purchased of government or otherwise are considered common pasturage." "Commons on the prairie" allowed any family to graze cattle, though they might afford only a forty-acre timber parcel, or might not have the wherewithal to file on congress land at all, so squatted. Prairie cattle grew hardy but bred randomly, so cows bore out of season, gave relatively little milk, and their calves suffered a high death rate.

Other priorities, however, outranked the confinement and control of mating necessary for systematic stock improvement. In the late 1820s, the Illinois legislature passed an act prohibiting the running of bulls on the open prairies, a measure designed to improve livestock by regulating breeding. "No one dreamed," recalled the politician Thomas Ford, "that a hurricane of popular indignation was about to be raised, but so it was: the people took sides with the little bulls. The law was denounced as being aristocratic, and intended to favor the rich, who, by their money, had become possessed of large bulls, and were to make a profit by the destruction of the small ones." Farmers opposed stock improvement because they believed it struck at the communal resource pool that supported the independence of small proprietors. Thus was common use linked to the practice of "democracy." Illinois governor John M. Palmer, who had farmed Macoupin County land south of Sugar Creek during the 1830s, admitted to an assembly of old settlers near Drennan's Prairie, in 1871, that he had been "strongly dem-ocratic in his opinions in regard to the rights of the people cutting timber where they wished and taking up hogs running at large. The people in early days considered this legitimate."

Common use extended to productive chattel property as well as land. One Sugar Creek settler, Daniel Parkinson, wrote that once an emigrant family had selected a site for their farmstead, the neighbors invariably dropped by to introduce themselves, to express "the warmest sentiments of friendship and good-will," and to assure the head of household "that every thing they possessed, in the way of tools, teams, wagons, provisions, and their own personal services, were entirely at his command." By the end of this first visit, the newcomer family found themselves "well acquainted, and upon the best terms of friendship, with the whole neighborhood." When his family first occupied their cabin, wrote John Regan, an English immigrant to central Illinois, "all the goodwives of the neighborhood" came calling, bringing milk, eggs, and needlework to worry over as they shared community gossip with his wife, and bringing him the news that if their husbands "could aid me in any way, I had only to say so and they would do all they could 'to help me get along.'" "Milk, cream, butter, and all articles for table use, as well as kitchen furniture, maintain a brisk circulation through the community; vegetables and fruits are regarded as common property," Elizabeth Ellet wrote during a tour through central Illinois in the early 1850s. "The borrowing system," she concluded, "is in full operation in these parts."

The "borrowing system" allowed scarce tools, labor, and products to circulate to the benefit of all and responded to the ongoing neighborhood need for exchange and mutual assistance. People utilized this neighborly network for most of the transactions necessary to the practice of farming. To have productive implements "and not be willing to share them in some sort with the whole community is an unpardonable crime," Caroline Kirkland warned prospective emigrants. "Your wheel-barrows, your shovels, your utensils of all sorts, belong, not to yourself, but to the public, who do not think it necessary even to *ask* a loan, but take it for granted." Outsiders, unversed in these customs, frequently misunderstood the social conventions of communal sharing. When Kirkland sent over a side of beef to a needy neighbor she anticipated grateful thanks, but received instead a merely perfunctory "Oh! your pa wants to *change*, does he? Well, you may put it down." Similarly, Frances Trollope complained that when she loaned household implements, her neighbors responded matter-of-factly, "well, I expect I shall have to do a turn of work for this; you may send for me when you want me." Trollope malevolently concluded that westerners would do almost anything "to avoid uttering that most un-American phrase, 'I thank you.'" She may have been right. But Kirkland and Trollope did not seem to understand that gifts given "unconditionally" required no "thanks" but were part of a system of exchange ("'change") that created an obligation to provide reciprocal aid in the future. Western traveler Charles Latrobe nicely summed up the "borrowing system": "a life in the woods teaches many lessons, and this among the rest, that you must both give assistance to your neighbors, and receive it in return, without either grudging or pouting."

"It was a fixed fact," wrote Sugar Creek farmer James Megredy, "that when one or more of the community would be sick with chills or jaundice, or something else, his neighbors would meet and take care of his harvest, get up wood, or repair his cabin, or plant his corn, or whatever was necessary to be done for the comfort of his family or himself." Household emergencies, however, were not the only occasion for exchanges of labor. Before wage labor became fundamental to the rural economy, 'changing labor was a regular part of day-to-day operations. In their account books, literate farmers carefully "put down" each exchange with their neighbors: "to six days work planting corn [$]3.00"; to 1/2 stack of hay .75": these entries recorded work performed or products traded. "By 3/4 day harvesting .75"; "by one day butchering hogs .50": these recorded work received in exchange. At the beginning of the farm year, in March 1849, Eddin Lewis recorded in his farm book an "old account against James Wilson" for $5.00. During that year, Lewis received from this neighbor nearly 250 pounds of bacon, valued at $4.75 per hundred-weight, in exchange for which he put in twenty days on Wilson's place hauling timber, hewing logs, and gathering corn—labor valued at fifty cents per day. At year's end, Lewis carried over to the next season a continuing credit of $2.89 to Wilson. Such ledgers often ran for years, the debt being settled only upon the death of one of the parties.

The surviving account book of a Sugar Creek blacksmith, John Smith, shows how this reciprocal system accomplished a social division of labor. From July to March of 1837–38, widow Sarah Smith ran up a bill of $10.99 at Smith's shop for shoeing, sharpening tools, and purchasing nails, hinges, and door latches. Over the next nine months she brought into his shop produce from her farm, including 15 pounds of veal, 110 pounds of beef, and over 250 pounds of flour. When he balanced the account, the blacksmith carried over a credit to Mrs. Smith of $2.84. The Sugar Creek community included not only a smith, but a wheelwright, a carpenter, a potter, and several millers, tanners, and physicians, and each conducted his operations in a similar manner. At the mills "they would not take any money," Lemira Gillet recalled, "everything was done on the halves," millers taking "toll-wheat," a share of the milled product, as their fee. In the public interest the county commissioners set rates at mills, as well as those at taverns and ferries; a miller could retain a maximum of an eighth-weight of milled wheat, a seventh-weight of corn, oats, or buckwheat.

The use of monetary values in these accounts, however, suggests that local exchanges within the borrowing system were affected by forces larger than the local community. In other regions of the United States, for example, the values in farmer's account books accurately reflected prices in market centers, so the exchange value of commodities—whether tools, produce, or labor—was clearly a material fact in the relationships between farmers. The effects of the Atlantic economy had long been felt in the valleys of central Illinois, and farmers were no more immune to them than hunters. But though the borrowing system was influenced by market forces, it remained distinct from the market itself. As the medium of marketplace exchange, specie had to be turned to use, invested. Farmers and local craftsmen who frequently extended credit, by contrast, never charged interest, for money in their exchanges functioned simply as a measure of account. "Money is so scarce and hard to be got, we must live without buying much," Lucy Maynard wrote to her sister in Ohio; "but most people get along on what they produce or trade with others for." The borrowing system and the market were separate in the eyes of the settlers. The market provided the opportunity to sell a "surplus" in order to raise the money necessary, for instance, for land purchases. The borrowing system provided access to goods, tools, and community labor that made a sufficiency possible, even for small producers.

It was not the market but the social exchange network, the borrowing system, that could bring out the whole neighborhood for collective labor at "bees," a metaphorical allusion to the social and productive character of those immigrant insects. In the backcountry of Illinois these events were more frequently called "frolics," emphasizing the prominently featured drinking and competitive sport that accompanied them. Men joined in log-rolling frolics, wolf- and snake-hunting frolics, husking and reaping frolics, while women assembled for picking, sewing, and quilting frolics. Both sexes took part in these frolics in a spirit of intense competition. "It was the custom" at log rollings, former schoolmaster Samuel Williams later reminisced, "to select two captains, and they to choose their men; then the ground was carefully divided into two parts. There was generally considerable ambition as to who was to get done first." Male frolics celebrated physical prowess, and wrestling or racing often took up as much time as working. "Trials of strength were very common among the pioneers," according to R. B. Rutledge; "lifting weights, as heavy timbers piled one upon another, was a favorite pastime." Wives were not merely in the background, preparing the "edibles" for the hungry workers, but were just as likely engaged in productive frolics of their own, with their own kinds of competition. Elizabeth McDowell Hill told of a spinning frolic where two young ladies "spun a race" to determine who could lay claim to a certain eligible farmer. "They began at six in the morning and spun until six in the evening. Two old ladies carded for them, one for each. At six o'clock Nancy was thirty rounds ahead. Forever afterward the fair Sarah had to look elsewhere for her swain."

Of all the frolics, settlers most frequently recalled the cabin "raising." By custom, the settler family made all the preparations: the farmer and his boys cut the ash, oak, or walnut; logged off eighty or so appropriate lengths and hewed them to proper thickness; prepared oak or chestnut clapboards, shingles, joists, and spans—work that took many days. Once the building materials had been hauled to the chosen spot, the householder could circulate "round among his neighbours, to request their assistance which will be cheerfully rendered without any remuneration, except good cheer, and it may be, future assistance of a similar kind." "Men an' neighbours," John Regan overheard one farmer toast his comrades at a house-raising, "w're boun' to help every feller who's honest, to make him a home." On the appointed day, men from the surrounding country arrived early, leveling the home site and laying the first logs on the ground at the direction of a local "raising master," whose only blueprints were stored in memory. As men rolled one log after another up supporting poles and into place, axmen at each corner notched intersecting ends to "nest" one within the next in the "half-dovetail" tradition of Upland South construction. The "hands" raised the basic structure in one day. It then fell to the family to chop out doors, windows, and fireplace openings, to fit frames and doors, to lay the roof, and "chink" the gaps between the logs.

Freeholds in Sugar Creek were linked through a reciprocal network.

The cabin raising inducted newcomers into the neighborhood system by creating a web of common obligations, thus demonstrating the mixture of private and communal that characterized the backcountry economy. . . .

Squatters made up over half of the one hundred and thirteen farm households along Sugar Creek in 1830. Poor farm families could build their cabins and plant their corn on unclaimed acres, graze their stock on prairie commons, and hook their timber from congress land. Old settlers later looked back on these times as a "golden age," but Sugar Creek was no Arcadia. Squatter families might subsist for much of the year on boiled pumpkins and the watery milk of a couple of mangy cows, while their better-off neighbors feasted on fried pork, corn pone, and butter. Nevertheless, the communal customs of the borrowing system provided a self-sufficing place for the poor as well as the well-to-do, and the rhetoric of this democratic age promised the conversion of squatting farmers into owner-operators.

Twenty years later, squatting had indeed disappeared from Sugar Creek life, replaced, however, not by universal republican ownership, but by tenantry and the rural proletarianization of the poor. Of the forty-six heads of squatter families of 1830, only nine succeeded in buying Sangamon County land over the next decade, and most left the county, leaving little behind to document the causes of their failure to become landowners. The experience of Robert Pulliam, the pioneer of Sugar Creek, however, illustrates some of the difficulties that settlers could experience in buying and holding land.

In November 1823, Robert Pulliam purchased 480 acres, including the sugar grove, from the federal government, paying six hundred dollars, five hundred of which he borrowed from Springfield merchant-speculators at an annual rate of 12.5 percent, putting up his property as security. During the 1820s, the one-legged pioneer and his family not only farmed and raised stock, but each year produced a thousand pounds or more of maple sugar, ground the corn of neighbors at the horse mill, and dispensed corn whiskey at the public house—income-producing activities that helped to meet the annual interest payments of over sixty dollars. The Pulliam children married into neighborhood families, two daughters eventually moving to Iowa with their husbands and children. The youngest son, George, a retarded invalid, lived at home.

The five-hundred-dollar note came due in the early 1830s, and circumstances suggest that the pioneer desperately sought ways to increase his income in order to pay off the looming principal. Pulliam borrowed some $1,150 from fifteen different lenders at usurious rates of up to 50 percent and paid off the original note; with a scheme of damming the creek and establishing a new water mill near the sugar grove, he purchased an adjacent eighty acres across the creek in 1831 and filed a request for an ad quod damnum with the county commissioners. But the projected dam did not materialize, and Pulliam soon had difficulty meeting the payments on the new series of loans. In August of 1832, two of his creditors obtained default judgments against him in local justice courts; and when Pulliam failed to pay, they placed a notice in the *Sangamo Journal* that "Pulliam had deserted from this state," and that his property would be attached and auctioned— in effect, a call for all Pulliam's creditors to join en masse in the assault on his property. Over the next few weeks, while Pulliam laid low, several justices of the peace issued judgments against the pioneer for over five hundred and fifty dollars in back debts.

Had Pulliam established a better record with the local justices of the peace, things might have gone better for him, but the feisty frontiersman had appeared before them many times during the 1820s for the default of small debts and offenses "against the peace and dignity of the people." In the most grave of these infractions, Pulliam's neighbor Henry Clark swore before Zachariah Peter in June 1830 that Pulliam "did by force and arms in a violent manner accost him the said Henry while imploid with James Clark in driving several *yoak* of cattle from said Pulliams. The said Pulliam did then and there take or drive away from out of the possession of the said Henry & James one pare of stears in yoke by presenting at the said Henry a cocked Pestal and threatning to shoot said Henry & James & thereby taking off said stears." A Jury of "twelve good & lawful men not of kin to said Pulliam nor Henry Clark" found the pioneer guilty and assessed $30.50 in damages and $7.815 in court costs against him. Just four months later, John Wallace accused Pulliam of "taking away and converting to his own use one hog," and Robert was saddled with another $10 in damages as well as $16.50 in court costs. The pioneer could not expect much good will from the justices when his creditors dragged him into court.

Despite the judgments against him, Pulliam was still unable to pay his debts, and his creditors presented their cases before the judge of the circuit court in Springfield, who issued a warrant for Pulliam's arrest when he failed to appear. Several weeks later the pioneer surrendered, offering an ingenious explanation for his absence:

> The Asiatic or Spasmodic Cholera was then prevailing in Springfield. Such was the panic occasioned thereby that he could not procure any person to go with him to Springfield to become his security so that he was unable to give any security until the time for appeal had elapsed. Indeed there was an almost total suspension of business in and about Springfield occasioned by the alarm, but for which circumstance your petitioner would undoubtedly have taken an appeal in the regular mode.

But appeals were fruitless. Creditors even tried, unsuccessfully, to attach the property of Pulliam's sons. In July 1833, the mortgage on the sugar grove was foreclosed, and it was sold to the agent of a Natchez land speculator. The sheriff auctioned off the adjacent land partially to repay the other creditors.

But other bill collectors continued to plague the Pulliams like the cholera itself, so Robert and Mary packed their personal belongings and fled the county, taking up an exiled residence in Macoupin County. Pulliam had never been a religious man, but, according to his sons, during these bitter years he came to regret his wild and wooly ways, and both he and Mary joined a revivalist congregation. A few years later, in July 1838, during a visit to his sons in Sugar Creek, sixty-two-year-old Pulliam fell sick, was carried to the house of a neighbor, Dr. Alexander Shields, but expired. Robert Pulliam died as landless as his father before him.

At least Pulliam had held the title to land against which he could secure loans; but because squatters had no property to mortgage, most of them could obtain no credit at all. Democratic politicians, President Andrew Jackson prominent among them, constantly talked of increasing the farmer's ability to purchase and hold the land he farmed but very little was actually done for the squatters. Indeed, when Jackson refused to recharter the Bank of the United States, instead depositing federal funds in state banks in 1834, he inadvertently provided capital for loans to land speculators, fueling with state-issued paper currency the greatest land boom yet seen in the United States. In 1837, belatedly awakened to these effects of his emotional war on the bank, Jackson declared his intention to "save the new States from a nonresident proprietorship," issuing his famous "Specie Circular," an executive order declaring gold or silver the only legal tender for the purchase of public land. The president's action indeed burst the speculative bubble, bringing on financial panic, deflation, and a decade of agricultural depression. During the ensuing hard times, almost no congress land sold in the West. Then, in the wake of the general business expansion that accompanied the California Gold Rush in 1849, speculators gobbled up the last available Sugar Creek sections.

During the first period of Sugar Creek land sales, from 1823 to 1833, most purchasers were resident settlers; non resident speculators bought only about two thousand acres, less than 15 percent of the total. But in the land boom of 1834–37, then again during 1849–51, speculators—several well-to-do Sugar Creek farmers among them—gained control of nearly seventy-five square miles of prairie land, 70 percent of all Sugar Creek lands sold. Joseph Poley and his brother-in-law, Jacob Rauch, for example, participated in both land booms, accumulating several sections of prairie holdings at The Sources of the creek; James Patton and his boys bought the equivalent of two sections of prairie southeast of their neighborhood; and Philip Wineman accumulated over twelve hundred acres of prairie south of Auburn village.

Despite these prairie sales, however, into the 1840s Sugar Creek farmers continued to use the grasslands for common grazing, and a number of families continued to reside on otherwise unused land, though it was now privately owned. During the 1830s and early 1840s, when this opportunity to squat continued to exist, the number of owner-operator farms along the creek increased only slightly. But with the upturn of the national economy in the late forties, the new owners of the prairies began to warn off squatters, mark off prairie farms, and sell them at three to five dollars an acre, using newly available steel plows to break the formidable sod. The number of owner-operators, which had held steady through the decades of the twenties and thirties, jumped from 66 in 1840 to 128 in 1850, and to 189 by 1860. But only a quarter of the 53 squatter households of 1840 succeeded in buying parcels and persisting through the decade, and most of those who did were descendants of original settler families with nearby kin to assist them. The best that most squatter families could manage was the sale of their "improvements" to emigrants known as "strong-handed farmers"—men who arrived with capital enough to buy them out. After 1840, as the opportunities for squatting disappeared, and as conditions for the poor grew harsher, ten-year rates of persistence fell to just one household head in five.

By the 1850s, Sugar Creek had become a society with considerable distinctions of wealth. But differences in residents' access to productive property emerged not because control of the land passed from "cultivators" to "nonresident speculators," as Democrats feared, but as a result of dynamics internal to the Sugar Creek community. Elsewhere in central Illinois, nonresident speculators did create magnificent estates for large-scale farming, stock-raising, or tenant farming, but in Sugar Creek by the late 1850s, nonresident speculators had sold off their holdings in the form of rather modest-sized farms. Although Pulliam's sugar-grove farm had been bought by a nonresident land speculator, for example, it was sold in the mid-forties to Kentucky emigrant James Scott. By 1858 outsiders held only 16 percent of the land along the creek, and fewer than ten nonresident landlords owned estates in excess of two hundred acres. Well-to-do Sugar Creek farmers who participated in the land booms, on the other hand, tended to hold on to the acres they accumulated. After nonresident speculators had come and gone, these owner-operators with large estates remained. The transfer of large portions of the prairie commons from the federal government to a small group of resident farmers accomplished the single most important economic change along Sugar Creek since Americans had dispossessed the Kickapoo.

In 1838, the wealthiest tenth of Sugar Creek heads of household held 25 percent of the privately owned acreage; twenty years later, their proportion had risen to 35 percent. At the other end of the ownership scale, the poorest fifth owned 10 percent of the acreage in 1838 but only 5 percent in 1858. The rapid disappearance of the public domain compounded the effects of this increasing concentration of wealth. By the 1850s, the 35 to 40 percent of households without title to land had found ways other than squatting to subsist. The coexistence of a small group of families with large landed resources, on the one hand, and a large group of landless farmers, on the other, created the conditions for a new set of rural social relationships.

Between 1840 and 1860, tenant farming replaced squatting as the most common alternative for landless families. In 1850 at least 10 percent of farm households rented the land they cultivated from resident or absentee landlords, paying for the use of the land with shares of their crops. In the standard arrangement, the tenant family that provided tools, stock, and seed, and built their own cabin, gave over one-third of their crop; the tenant family that borrowed everything from the landlord, including the cabin, gave over two-thirds or, without the cabin, one-half:

> An agreement entered into between Willis F. Berry of one part and William Ward of the other part—the sd Berry having rented to sd Ward sixteen acres of ground more or less in his field it being the ground South of where sd Berry has sowed oats—the sd Berry agrees to furnish teem to work the

ground & his plows & how [hoe] and horse free—and sd Ward agrees to
work the ground in good farming order in corn, and to deliver one half of
the corn in sd Berrys crib for the above consideration, and to gether sd
crop against the first day of January next, and sd Berry reserves the pasture
of the field and privelige of sowing wheet on the ground.

Illinois farmers tilled fields on shares as early as the 1820s, but the practice
was relatively rare until the 1840s, when the alienation of common land
forced increasing numbers of landless families into a landlord-tenant relationship. According to agricultural essayist James Caird, tenancy had become
"very common in Illinois" by the mid-fifties. It became increasingly important
in Sugar Creek as well, for by 1860, eighty-seven tenant families, a quarter
of all Sugar Creek households, farmed land on shares, their ranks four times
greater than a decade before.

By that year Joseph Poley owned over seventeen hundred acres in the
southeastern prairie sections of township 13/6, although his household of
eight farmed only the quarter section upon which they had built their dwelling
in 1828. His grown son Elisha Poley and family, and daughter Nancy, with
her husband, Thomas Parks, and their children, lived on nearby land donated
by their father. North of the Poleys lived James Patton, on what had grown
into a twelve-hundred-acre estate. By 1860, Patton, now a widower approaching his three score and ten, lived with his youngest son, David, and
daughter-in-law, Susan Organ. Nearby were the households of his oldest
son's widow, his son Matthew and family, his daughter Rebecca and son-
in-law, Elihu Stout, surrounding old man Patton with fourteen grandchildren.
In addition to the forty-eight members of their extended families, however,
associated with Poley and Patton on the run of the 1860 census were another
sixteen tenant households. Each tenant family raised corn on an average of
fifty acres and ran stock, presumably on Poley and Patton's unbroken prairie
meadows; together, their operations supported ninety-eight persons. No records of the transactions between these landlords and tenants survive, but
the transfer of produce that took place must have added measurably to the
accumulating wealth of the Patton and the Poley estates.

The 1860 census enumeration reveals a number of tenant households
associated with each of the largest landowners in Sugar Creek. At the western
end of Drennan's Prairie, near Harlan's Grove, for example, the Masons
and Lockridges owned over half of the arable land and rented to thirteen
tenant and laborer families. The Kennedys, whose boy robbed the stage in
1842, were early tenants in this area. North of the sugar grove, Jonathan
Peddicord owned an entire section where he farmed and rented land to five
other households. Of the ten largest property owners along the creek, only
Philip Wineman, second to Poley in the size of his real estate, seemed to
have no tenants; instead, Wineman used his prairie acres to lay out the new
railroad village named for himself.

An alternate subsistence strategy for the poor took landless men and
boys to work as farm laborers. During the 1850s the number of male farm
laborers in the community tripled; most were young single men who lived
with their employers. Prosperous farmers had always hired help, particularly

during the busy harvest season, but by the 1850s the practice of hiring wage labor became widespread and commonplace. The changing sex ratio for the segment of the community in its twenties and thirties suggests the magnitude of the change; the 1830 ratio of 107 men to every 100 women had grown to 159:100 by 1860. In that year, over half the owner-operator households of Sugar Creek included live-in hands. Nine hired men and one woman lived in the households of the Patton brothers; Noah Mason's household included two young neighborhood boys and an Irish couple; Jon Peddicord employed three Irish laborers and a young Tennessee girl who helped his wife, Minerva, in the kitchen; and Phil Wineman employed three single men and a young couple to work in his fields, stockyard, orchard, garden, and kitchen. As wealthy farmers, these men could afford this many hands; the average owner-operator hired two.

A new relationship thus characterized the Sugar Creek economy of the 1850s. The ten richest Sugar Creek heads of household in 1860, seven of whom were members of original settler families, owned an average of nearly $26,000 in real property; but only two-thirds of this capital was invested in their own farms. These men were now landlords as well as farmers, renting their excess acres to tenant families, collecting rents in the form of crop shares, and employing several hired hands. For well-off Sugar Creek farmers like these, production had advanced well beyond mere subsistence needs, presenting them with both the opportunity and the necessity to market agricultural surpluses. The increased capitalist orientation of Sangamon farmers in the 1840s and 1850s, in other words, was not simply the result of a growing inclination to participate in the marketplace, but the result of a changing rural social structure.

Changes in the communal landscape also mirrored these new social relationships. Road improvement was perhaps the most important. During the early 1820s, Sugar Creek householders circulated and presented to the commissioners eight separate petitions for the declaration or relocation of county roads through their neighborhoods, all of them arteries like the St. Louis Road that linked Sugar Creek with other communities to the north and south. When this basic structure was in place, the number of Sugar Creek road petitions declined; from 1828 to 1845 only four were laid before the commissioners. In the mid-1840s, however, the changing economic relationships of the country side made good roads more of a necessity. Improved transportation from farm to market, many believed, offered the best chance of marketing the increasing surplus of agricultural commodities at fair prices. From 1846 to 1860 Sugar Creek men filed sixty-one petitions for the relocation and improvement of old roads and for the laying out of new ones.

Reform of the transportation system utilized the traditions of citizen participation and local autonomy. Since the county levied road duty as a "poll-tax" on all males over eighteen, "all hands" in the neighborhoods improved or "threw up" roads together; and since there was no county planning authority, the initiative for location or improvement depended upon groups of local men deciding what they needed, soliciting the support of their neighbors, and petitioning the commissioners for approval. The enthusiasm for reform, however, came predominantly from the landed sector of the community. Before 1845 owners made up only half of the signers of petitions for relocation or declaration; but on petitions filed between 1846 and 1860, by contrast, the proportion of owners rose to four signators out of five, despite the relatively constant proportion of landed men in the Sugar Creek community. By and large, road improvement was the project of Sugar Creek owner-operators and landlords.

Owner-operator petitions brought about several changes in the landscape. Eight new east-west county roads in the Sugar Creek community linked newly created prairie farms with the main north-south highways. These new roads channeled traffic from both prairie and timber toward the village of Auburn. In 1846 a large group from the west side of the creek, "feeling the great necessity of a permanent county road" to the village, petitioned the commissioners to authorize a route on "the nearest and best route to Auburn, having due regard to private property & the right of way." The village, small as it was, nevertheless attracted open-country farmers to its tavern, shops, post office, and fellowship. A decade later, the same west-bank group wrote of the "high importance" of improving the road from Chatham to Auburn for "the convenience of the neighbourhood and the publick generally" and "begged" for an appropriation "for the purpose of building a Bridge over Panther Creek," which "would render the road more useful to the Public." When the railroad made it clear that Wineman, not old Auburn, would become the dominant central place, these citizens "prayed" the court "to grant a revew [sic] of the Road leading from Chatham . . . so as to run due South to the Town of Wyneman."

These petitions paid increasing attention to property lines. Citizens laid out their new roads precisely along the section lines, so as not to infringe on the land of adjacent owners. Owners similarly petitioned to change the routes of older north-south roadways. In the early 1850s, for example, a group of owners appealed to the commissioners to

> change so much of the Alton and Springfield state road as lies between Micajah Organs and the north-east corner of section sixteen . . . beginning at or near the aforesaid Organs Lane and running to the south-east corner of the north-east quarter of section twenty-one, making the road on the west side of said line until said road strikes the south-east corner of section sixteen, running on the east line of sixteen, and from thence to the northeast corner of said sixteenth section, and from thence to the original road, which will be about two hundred yards, we the under assigned petitioners being satisfied that the said change of road will add verry little to the distance of the aforesaid road as it will run over better ground by the aforesaid change.

Like all the original north-south highways, this stage road had struck a course across the prairie in a beeline from the bridge at Rauch's mill to the village. The galloping stage teams required these sweeping curves. But the railroad outmoded the stage and allowed farmers to modify the course of highways.

By the end of the 1850s, after a long series of petitions from owner-operators, most highways had been realigned to conform to section lines, or, where the original road had angled radically across the sections, to jog in ninety-degree twists and turns to protect the property lines and corners of owners. This reform made the roads impossible for the old stage to navigate without slowing almost to a stop, but it presented no problem for lumbering farmers' wagons carrying crops to village markets, or for the light buggies that came into fashion in the 1850s. The highways would no longer, in the words of another petition, "run angling across lands," cutting through fields and meadows now increasingly valuable for commodity production. The vestiges of old highways that clung to contours of land or timber might still be found in a few "angling" roads, or in those odd, perpendicular turns. But by 1860 a general reform of the landscape was well under way, bringing it into greater conformity with the rectilinear precision of the federal surveyor's original plat.

Accompanying the new arrow-straight section roads came other changes in the look of things. As the improvement of stock became more important with the new commercial outlook, farmers used pine lumber imported by the railroad to enclose their stockyards with post and board fencing. Farm implement dealers in Chatham and Auburn sold steel plows, and men broke the prairies to plant corn where big bluestem had flourished, breaking up as well the old rail fences that had once protected the crops from marauding stock thus eliminating the shelter provided for prairie critters by the interstices of the rails, overgrown with grass and vines. In the decades of the 1850s and 1860s, the most prosperous owner-operators built new dwellings, replacing log cabins with substantial two-story frame houses, usually simple "I" houses in the popular Greek Revival style—houses that were the very symbol of agrarian stability. Successful owners also first constructed small but solid barns in the 1840s.

Thus did a "common" landscape give way to a landscape of class. Most Sugar Creek residents, certainly the tenants and poor laboring heads of household, continued to live in log cabins until late in the century, giving architectural testimony to the difference between landlord and tenant. Stock, timber, and hunting laws, passed in the late 1850s, restricted tenants, laborers, and poor farmers from grazing their herds on prairie meadows or helping themselves to the fruits of the countryside. Farm owners initiated the creation of a new landscape, one that we now consider typical of the rural American Midwest; but that now familiar landscape was part of a profound social change that marked the departure of an old era.

✢ *F U R T H E R   R E A D I N G*

Jeremy Atack and Fred Bateman, *To Their Own Soil: Agriculture in the Antebellum North* (1987)
Ray A. Billington and Martin Ridge, *Westward Expansion: A History of the American Frontier* (1982)

John Boessenecker, *Badge and Buckshot: Lawlessness in Old California* (1988)

R. Carlyle Buley, *The Old Northwest: The Pioneer Period, 1815–1840* (1950)

Andrew R. L. Cayton, *The Frontier Republic: Ideology and Politics in the Ohio Country, 1780–1825* (1989)

———— and Peter Onuf, *The Midwest and the Nation: Rethinking the History of an American Region* (1990)

William Cronin, *Nature's Metropolis: Chicago and the Great West* (1991)

Clarence Danhof, *Change in Agriculture: The Northern United States, 1820–1870* (1969)

Angie Debo, *A History of the Indians of the United States* (1970)

Don H. Doyle, *The Social Order of a Frontier Community: Jacksonville, Illinois, 1825–1870* (1978)

John Mack Faragher, *Women and Men on the Overland Trail* (1979)

Vincente Filisola, *Memoirs from the History of the War in Texas* (1985–1987)

Paul W. Gates, *The Farmer's Age: Agriculture, 1815–1850* (1950)

William Goetzmann, *Expansion and Empire: The Explorer and the Scientist in the Winning of the American West* (1966)

Norman A. Graebner, *Empire on the Pacific: A Study in American Continental Expansion* (1955)

William T. Hagan, *The Sac and Fox Indians* (1958)

Neal Harlow, *California Conquered: War and Peace on the Pacific, 1846–1850* (1982)

John A. Hawgood, *America's Western Frontiers: The Exploration and Settlement of the Trans-Mississippi West* (1967)

Stewart H. Holbrook, *The Yankee Exodus: An Account of Migration from New England* (1950)

Julie Roy Jeffrey, *Frontier Women: The Trans-Mississippi West, 1840–1880* (1979)

David C. Klingaman and Richard K. Vedder, *Essays on the Economy of the Old Northwest* (1987)

Allan Kulikoff, "The Transition to Capitalism in Rural America," *William & Mary Quarterly*, 3rd series, 46 (1989), 120–144

Patricia N. Limerick, *The Legacy of Conquest: The Unbroken Past of the American West* (1987)

Seymour Martin Lipset and Richard Hofstadter, eds., *Turner and the Sociology of the Frontier* (1968)

Frederick Merk, *History of the Westward Movement* (1978)

Leonard M. Pitt, *The Decline of the Californios: A Social History of the Spanish-Speaking Californians, 1846–1890* (1966)

Andrews Reichstein, *Rise of the Lone Star: The Making of Texas* (1989)

David E. Schob, *Hired Hands and Ploughboys: Farm Labor and the Midwest, 1815–1860* (1975)

Richard Slotkin, *Regeneration Through Violence: The Mythology of the American Frontier, 1600–1860* (1973)

Henry Nash Smith, *Virgin Land: The American West as Symbol and Myth* (1950)

Frederick Jackson Turner, *The Frontier in American History* (1920)

John D. Unruh, *The Plains Across: The Overland Emigrants and the Trans-Mississippi West, 1840–1860* (1979)

Richard White, *"It's Your Misfortune and None of My Own": A New History of the American West* (1991)

William Appleman Williams, *The Contours of American History* (1961)

CHAPTER
10

The Era of Bad Feelings

How did the social and economic changes described in the preceding chapters affect American politics, and vice versa? The answers became clear beginning in
the decade after the War of 1812. Traditionally historians have referred to the
period as the Era of Good Feelings, a phrase borrowed from a contemporary
journalist. With the Federalist party in retreat and James Monroe's election to
the presidency in 1816, formal political conflict seemed on the wane. Nationalist
enthusiasm obscured persistent sectional divisions. A burst of political reform at
the state level—above all, the toppling of remaining property requirements for
voting, which seemingly enfranchised virtually all white male citizens—presaged
the fulfillment of democratic ideals that had originated during the Revolution
(although significantly, the reforms often curtailed black suffrage).

Yet if the war's end stoked good feelings, they did not last long, certainly
not long enough to constitute an era. A severe financial panic in 1819 left thousands of urban workers jobless and ruined many more laborers in the countryside. Class resentments, latent since Jefferson's day, resurfaced in angry attacks
on the Second Bank of the United States, land speculators, and established local
elites; by the late 1820s eastern workingmen had begun organizing new political
and trade-union movements. In the same year as the panic, Congress opened
debates over whether Missouri should be admitted to the Union as a slave state
or a free state, touching off bitter sectional wrangling. Although eventually settled by a delicate compromise barring slavery in Louisiana Purchase lands (except Missouri) north of 36° 30', the controversy showed that slavery's expansion
would remain a nettlesome question in both the nation's capital and the country
at large.

Still, nationalism hardly evaporated. The Supreme Court, under John Marshall, remained a bulwark of nationalist federal power. The Monroe Doctrine of
1823 enlarged nationalist claims to hemispheric dimensions. Monroe and his
friends also pursued a policy of political amalgamation, blurring old partisan
divisions and in effect creating a one-party system. The 1824 election of Monroe's successor, John Quincy Adams, brought to power an administration even
more favorable to vigorous internal improvements, national economic growth,
and political consensus. But the ascendency of the Adams Republicans—tainted
from the start by charges that their leader had gained the White House through
a shady political deal—only exacerbated the growing political tensions. Before
long, a coalition of forces alienated from the administration began to unify

behind Andrew Jackson. After 1828 that coalition would bring a dramatic change in the nation's political direction.

Was the slavery issue mainly responsible for the deepening disharmony, as some historians have suggested? Were broader economic and cultural issues at stake, turning as much on class and religious resentments as on sectional mistrust? How much does any genuine issue or social division explain the era of bad feelings? Might the politics of the 1820s be better understood in terms of personalities, political psychology, and demagogic appeals to an expanding white male electorate? Or did these seemingly empty appeals—the hoopla that marked the first stirrings of a new partisan political culture—convey some important social and political messages? Was the "mere" rhetoric of the time only that, or did it contain more substantive meanings?

⊞ D O C U M E N T S

The excerpts in the opening document from James Monroe's first inaugural address in 1817 convey the prevailing mood of political harmony and nationalist enthusiasm. In the second selection, two letters from the tycoon John Jacob Astor to Albert Gallatin, along with a letter from an English visitor in Indiana, show how quickly the Panic of 1819 sapped that mood. The debate over Missouri statehood, and its aftermath, are the focus of the three-part third selection. In 1819 Senator Rufus King of New York, the leading opponent of Missouri's admission as a slave state, explained his position in a widely circulated paper; Senator William Pinkney of Maryland replied to King in 1820. The reverberations of the Missouri debate lasted long after a final compromise was ironed out in Washington. In 1822 authorities in Charleston, South Carolina, discovered and narrowly thwarted a planned insurrection of slaves and freedmen, led by the ex-slave Denmark Vesey. The confessions extracted amid the trials of Vesey's alleged coconspirators provided some lessons about public discussion of slavery—lessons not entirely wasted on an increasingly touchy master class.

In the fourth document, the new president John Quincy Adams reformulates the themes of American nationalism, in a paean to improvement. But other political forces challenged Adams's vision of national accord. In 1827 journeymen mechanics in Philadelphia, buffeted by the market revolution, organized on their own and issued a manifesto (document five) to make their grievances known; a year later, they would run their own candidates for local offices. On a different political front, the New Yorker Martin Van Buren's personal letter (document six) to editor Thomas Ritchie of Richmond, Virginia, sketched out the basis for a renewed partisan alliance, repudiating the anti-party notion of amalgamation. Then, in South Carolina, the former nationalist and war hawk John C. Calhoun wrote out his own objections to the Adamsites' policies, with particular reference to the so-called Tariff of Abominations of 1828. Calhoun's remarks, excerpted in the seventh selection, were eventually incorporated, largely verbatim, by the South Carolina legislature in its famous "Exposition." The presidential election of 1828 brought matters to a head—but note, in the final, two-part selection, the tone of that contest.

President James Monroe on the "Harmony of Opinion," 1817

Some who might admit the competency of our Government to these beneficent duties might doubt it in trials which put to the test its strength and efficiency as a member of the great community of nations. Here too experience has afforded us the most satisfactory proof in its favor. Just as this Constitution was put into action several of the principal States of Europe had become much agitated and some of them seriously convulsed. Destructive wars ensued, which have of late only been terminated. In the course of these conflicts the United States received great injury from several of the parties. It was their interest to stand aloof from the contest, to demand justice from the party committing the injury, and to cultivate by a fair and honorable conduct the friendship of all. War became at length inevitable, and the result has shown that our Government is equal to that, the greatest of trials, under the most unfavorable circumstances. Of the virtue of the people and of the heroic exploits of the Army, the Navy, and the militia I need not speak.

Such, then, is the happy Government under which we live— a Government adequate to every purpose for which the social compact is formed; a Government elective in all its branches, under which every citizen may by his merit obtain the highest trust recognized by the Constitution; which contains within it no cause of discord, none to put at variance one portion of the community with another; a Government which protects every citizen in the full enjoyment of his rights, and is able to protect the nation against injustice from foreign powers.

Other considerations of the highest importance admonish us to cherish our Union and to cling to the Government which supports it. Fortunate as we are in our political institutions, we have not been less so in other circumstances on which our prosperity and happiness essentially depend. Situated within the temperate zone, and extending through many degrees of latitude along the Atlantic, the United States enjoy all the varieties of climate, and every production incident to that portion of the globe. Penetrating internally to the Great Lakes and beyond the sources of the great rivers which communicate through our whole interior, no country was ever happier with respect to its domain. Blessed, too, with a fertile soil, our produce has always been very abundant, leaving, even in years the least favorable, a surplus for the wants of our fellow-men in other countries. Such is our peculiar felicity that there is not a part of our Union that is not particularly interested in preserving it. The great agricultural interest of the nation prospers under its protection. Local interests are not less fostered by it. Our fellow-citizens of the North engaged in navigation find great encouragement in being made the favored carriers of the vast productions of the other portions of the United States, while the inhabitants of these are amply recompensed, in their turn, by the nursery for seamen and naval force thus formed and reared up for the support of our common rights. . . .

Other interests of high importance will claim attention, among which the improvement of our country by roads and canals, proceeding always with a constitutional sanction, holds a distinguished place. By thus facilitating the intercourse between the States we shall add much to the convenience and comfort of our fellow-citizens, much to the ornament of the country, and, what is of greater importance, we shall shorten distances, and, by making each part more accessible to and dependent on the other, we shall bind the Union more closely together. Nature has done so much for us by intersecting the country with so many great rivers, bays, and lakes, approaching from distant points so near to each other, that the inducement to complete the work seems to be peculiarly strong. A more interesting spectacle was perhaps never seen than is exhibited within the limits of the United States—a territory so vast and advantageously situated, containing objects so grand, so useful, so happily connected in all their parts!

Our manufactures will likewise require the systematic and fostering care of the Government. Possessing as we do all the raw materials, the fruit of our own soil and industry, we ought not to depend in the degree we have done on supplies from other countries. While we are thus dependent the sudden event of war, unsought and unexpected, can not fail to plunge us into the most serious difficulties. It is important, too, that the capital which nourishes our manufactures should be domestic, as its influence in that case instead of exhausting, as it may do in foreign hands, would be felt advantageously on agriculture and every other branch of industry. Equally important is it to provide at home a market for our raw materials, as by extending the competition it will enhance the price and protect the cultivator against the casualties incident to foreign markets. . .

It is particularly gratifying to me to enter on the discharge of these duties at a time when the United States are blessed with peace. It is a state most consistent with their prosperity and happiness. . . .

Equally gratifying is it to witness the increased harmony of opinion which pervades our Union. Discord does not belong to our system. Union is recommended as well by the free and benign principles of our Government, extending its blessings to every individual, as by the other eminent advantages attending it. The American people have encountered together great dangers and sustained severe trials with success. They constitute one great family with a common interest. Experience has enlightened us on some questions of essential importance to the country. The progress has been slow, dictated by a just reflection and a faithful regard to every interest connected with it. To promote this harmony in accord with the principles of our republican Government and in a manner to give them the most complete effect, and to advance in all other respects the best interests of our Union, will be the object of my constant and zealous exertions.

Observations on Banking and the Panic of 1819; 1817, 1818, 1820

John Jacob Astor to Albert Gallatin, 1817, 1818

New York   3 March 1817

Dear Sir

. . . It will have given you pleasure to have seen the effects of the operation of the Bank of united States. it was Like Magic at 10 oClock on the 20 Feby bills on Baltimore were 2 1/2 pct Discount and Specie at 2 1/2 pct Premium for our Banke notes. We oppened here our office and agreed to take Bills on Baltimore Virginia & Phila in half an hour all was at par. . . . our Branch here is Doing well . . . we have no pressure for money all good paper is Readily Discounted. . . . the U.S. Bank thus far may be calld a national Blessing & you have much Merit in haveing aided to get it passd through Congress . . .

New York   14 March 1818

Dear Sir

. . . the u.s. Bank is not doing so well as they might have done. there has been too much Speculation and too much assumption of Power on the Part of the Bank Directors which has causd the Institution to become unpopular & I may say genrally . . . Those who have Sold out at 50 pct Profit I think have Done best to make Large Dividends. To Raise the Price of the Stock they have Discounted too freely & made money so Cheap that everything else has becom Dear & the Result is that our merchants in Stead of Shiping Produce Ship Specie, so much so that I tell you In confidence that it is not without difficulty that Specie payments are maintained. the Different States are still going on making more Banks & I shall not be surprised if by & by there be a general Blow up among them—. . . .

James Flint on Hard Times, 1820

Jeffersonville, Indiana
May 4, 1820

Agriculture languishes—farmers cannot find profit in hiring labourers. . . . Labourers and mechanics are in want of employment. I think that I have seen upwards of 1500 men in quest of work within eleven months past, and many of these declared, that they had no money. Newspapers and private letters agree in stating, that wages are so low as eighteen and three-fourths cents (about ten-pence) per day, with board, at Philadelphia, and some other places. Great numbers of strangers lately camped in the open field near Baltimore, depending on the contributions of the charitable for subsistence.

Gallatin Papers, from Astor to Gallatin, New-York Historical Society.

You have no doubt heard of emigrants returning to Europe without finding the prospect of a livelihood in America. Some who have come out to this part of the country do not succeed well. Labourers' wages are at present a dollar and an eighth part per day. Board costs them two [and] three-fourths or three dollars per week; and washing three-fourths of a dollar for a dozen pieces. On these terms, it is plain that they cannot live two days by the labour of one, with the other deductions which are to be taken from their wages. Clothing, for example, will cost about three times its price in Britain: and the poor labourer is almost certain of being paid in depreciated money; perhaps from thirty to fifty per cent under par. I have seen several men turned out of boarding houses, where their money would not be taken. They had no other resource left but to lodge in the woods, without any covering except their clothes. They set fire to a decayed log, spread some boards alongside of it for a bed, laid a block of timber across for a pillow, and pursued their labour by day as usual. A still greater misfortune than being paid with bad money is to be guarded against, namely, that of not being paid at all.

Three Views of the Missouri Crisis, 1819, 1820, 1822

Rufus King Opposes the Admission of Missouri, 1819

The constitution declares "that congress shall have power to dispose of, and make all needful rules and regulations respecting the territory and other property of the United States."

The power to make all needful regulations, includes the power to determine what regulations are needful: and if a regulation prohibiting slavery within any territory of the United States be, as it has been, deemed needful, congress possess the power to make the same, and moreover to pass all laws necessary to carry this power into execution.

The territory of Missouri is a portion of Louisiana, which was purchased of France, . . . and is subject, like other territories of the United States, to the regulations and temporary government which has been, or shall be, prescribed by congress. The clause of the constitution, which grants this power to congress, is so comprehensive and unambiguous, and its purpose so manifest, that commentary will not render the power, or the object of its establishment, more explicit or plain.

The constitution further provides, that "new states may be admitted by congress into the union."—As this power is conferred without limitation, the time, terms, and circumstances of the admission of new states are referred to the discretion of congress—which may admit new states, but are not obliged to do so—of right no new state can demand admission into the union, unless such demand be founded upon some previous engagement with the United States. . . .

The motives for the admission of new states into the union, are the extension of the principles of our free government, the equalizing of the public burdens, and the consolidation of the power of the confederated nation. Unless these objects be promoted by the admission of new states, no such administration can be expedient or justified.

. . . If Missouri, and the other states that may be formed to the west of the river Mississippi, are permitted to introduce and establish slavery, the repose, if not the security of the union may be endangered; all the states south of the river Ohio and west of Pennsylvania and Delaware, will be peopled with slaves, and the establishment of new states west of the river Mississippi, will serve to extend slavery instead of freedom over that boundless region.

Such increase of the states, whatever other interests it may promote, will be sure to add nothing to the security of the public liberties; and can hardly fail hereafter to require and produce a change in our government. . . .

. . . if, instead of freedom, slavery is to prevail, and spread as we extend our dominion, can any reflecting man fail to see the necessity of giving to the general government greater powers; to enable it to afford the protection that will be demanded of it: powers that will be difficult to control, and which may prove fatal to the public liberties.

William Pinkney Replies to King, 1820

. . . the whole amount of the argument on the other side is, that you may refuse to admit a new State, and that therefore if you admit, you may prescribe the terms.

The answer to that argument is, that even if you can refuse, you can . . . prescribe no conditions which, if carried into effect, would make the new State less a sovereign State than, under the Union as it stands, it would be. You can prescribe no terms which will make the compact of Union between it and the original States essentially different from the compact among the original States. You may admit, or refuse to admit: but if you admit, you must admit a State in the sense of the Constitution—a State with all such sovereignty as belongs to the original parties; and it must be into *this Union* that you are to admit it, not into a Union of your own dictating, formed out of the existing Union by qualifications and new compacts, altering its character and effect. . . .

I may be told perhaps that the restriction, in this case, is the act of Missouri itself. . . .

A Territory cannot surrender to Congress by anticipation, the whole, or a part, of the sovereign power, which, by the Constitution of the Union will belong to it when it becomes a State and a member of the Union. . . . If it can barter away a part of its sovereignty, by anticipation, it can do so as to the whole; for where will you stop? . . .

The honorable gentleman on the other side (Mr. King) has told us, as a proof of his great position, that man cannot enslave his fellow man, in which is implied that all laws upholding slavery are absolute nullities; that the nations of antiquity, as well as of modern times, have concurred in laying down that position is incontrovertible.

He refers us, in the first place, to the Roman law, in which he finds it laid down as a maxim: *Jure naturali omnes homines ab initio liberi nasce-*

bantur. From the manner in which this maxim was pressed upon us, it would not readily have been conjectured that the honorable gentleman who used it had borrowed it from a slaveholding Empire, and still less from a book of the Institutes of Justinian, which treats of slavery, and justifies and regulates it. . . .

The honorable gentleman might also have gone to Greece for a similar maxim and similar commentary, speculative and practical.

He next refers us to Magna Charta. . . . The great charter was extorted from John, and his feeble son and successor, by haughty slaveholding barons, who thought only of themselves and the commons of England, (then inconsiderable,) whom they wished to enlist in their efforts against the Crown. There is not a single word which condemns slavery. . . .

The self-evident truths announced in the Declaration of Independence are not truths at all, if taken literally; and the practical conclusions contained in the same passage of that declaration prove that they were never designed to be so received. . . .

If it be true that all men in all republican Government must help to wield its power, and be equal in its rights, I beg leave to ask . . . and why not all *women?* They, too, are God's creatures; and not only very fair but very rational creatures. . . .

The Missouri Crisis and the Denmark Vesey Plot, 1822

The trial of Jack, a mulatto man, belonging to Mrs. Purcell—Mr. Thomas Smith, the brother of his owner, attending.

Evidence

MONDAY testified as follows: I have seen Jack and Vesey talking together before my door—he told me that he was one of those to rise against the whites, and Vesey told me so before. The message that Frank Ferguson gave to me to give to Vesey, I got Jack to carry to Vesey for me. The message was, that he had just come from the country, that he had there got four plantations of men to join—and to go to Vesey and ask him to be at home tonight, as he would call on him. I know he carried it, because Vesey told me so that night. He came to my shop afterwards and said to me he was looking for Vesey, and be sure that I called no name.

FRANK testified as follows: I know Jack Purcell, but don't know that he is concerned in this business. I did give to Monday Gell a message for Vesey.

CHARLES gave the following evidence: Jack told me he had been at his Mistress' Plantation and tried to get the people to join in this business—but could not go again. He said he had joined, and asked me where Lot Forrester lived, that he was the proper person to go into the country to bring the people down.

THE PRISONER asked permission to cross-examine Charles, which was granted; but his questions were such, that no one could well answer them but himself. In the course of this examination he admitted, that a large meeting had been called on Stono by Lot, and that considerable preparations were made to receive him, but that Lot did not attend, and he was requested to reprove him for not doing so.

THE COURT unanimously found Jack guilty, and passed upon him the sentence of death. A few moments preceding his execution, he made the following confession to the Intendant of Charleston:

If it had not been for the cunning of that old villain Vesey, I should not now be in my present situation. He employed every stratagem to induce me to join him. He was in the habit of reading to me all the passages in the newspapers that related to Santo Domingo, and apparently every pamphlet he could lay his hands on, that had any connection with slavery. He one day brought me a speech which he told me had been delivered in Congress by a Mr. King on the subject of slavery; he told me this Mr. King was the black man's friend, that Mr. King had declared he would continue to speak, write, and publish pamphlets against slavery as long as he lived, until the Southern States consented to emancipate their slaves, for that slavery was a disgrace to the country.

President John Quincy Adams on Liberty and Power, 1825

The spirit of improvement is abroad upon the earth. It stimulates the hearts and sharpens the faculties not of our fellow-citizens alone, but of the nations of Europe and of their rulers. While dwelling with pleasing satisfaction upon the superior excellence of our political institutions, let us not be unmindful that liberty is power; that the nation blessed with the largest portion of liberty must in proportion to its numbers be the most powerful nation upon earth, and that the tenure of power by man is, in the moral purposes of his Creator, upon condition that it shall be exercised to ends of beneficence, to improve the condition of himself and his fellowmen. While foreign nations less blessed with that freedom which is power than ourselves are advancing with gigantic strides in the career of public improvement, were we to slumber in indolence or fold up our arms and proclaim to the world that we are palsied by the will of our constituents, would it not be to cast away the bounties of Providence and doom ourselves to perpetual inferiority? In the course of the year now drawing to its close we have beheld, under the auspices and at the expense of one State of this Union, a new university unfolding its portals to the sons of science and holding up the torch of human improvement to eyes that seek the light. We have seen under the persevering and enlightened enterprise of another State the waters of our Western lakes mingle with those of the ocean. If undertakings like these have been accomplished in the compass of a few years by the authority of single members of our Confederation, can we, the representative authorities of the whole Union, fall behind our fellow-servants in the exercise of the trust committed to us for the benefit of our common sovereign by the accomplishment of works important to the whole and to which neither the authority nor the resources of any one State can be adequate?

A Craft Workers' Manifesto, 1827

We, the Journeymen Mechanics of the City and County of Philadelphia, conscious that our condition in society is lower than justice demands it should be, and feeling our inability, individually, to ward off from ourselves and families those numerous evils which result from an unequal and very excessive accumulation of wealth and power into the hands of a few, are desirous of forming an Association, which shall avert as much as possible those evils with which poverty and incessant toil have already inflicted, and which threaten ultimately to overwhelm and destroy us. . . .

As freemen and republicans, we feel it a duty incumbent on us to make known our sentiments fearlessly and faithfully on any subject connected with the general welfare; and we are prepared to maintain, that all who toil have a natural and unalienable right to reap the fruits of their own industry; and that they who by labour (the only source) are the authors of every comfort, convenience and luxury, are in justice entitled to an equal participation, not only in the meanest and the coarsest, but likewise the richest and the choicest of them all. . . .

With respect to the relation existing between employers and the employed, we are prepared, we think, to demonstrate, that it is only through an extremely limited view of their real interests, that the former can be induced to attempt to depreciate the value of human labour. The workman is not more dependent upon his wages for the support of his family than they are upon the demand for the various articles they fabricate or vend. If the mass of the people were enabled by their labour to procure for themselves and families a full and abundant supply of the comforts and conveniences of life, the consumption of articles, particularly of dwellings, furniture and clothing, would amount to at least twice the quantity it does at present, and of course the demand, by which alone employers are enabled either to subsist or accumulate, would likewise be increased in an equal proportion. Each would be enabled to effect twice the quantity of sales or loans which he can effect at present, and the whole industry of a people, consisting of their entire productive powers, whether manual or scientific, together with all their capital, might be put into a full, healthful, and profitable action. The workman need not languish for want of employment, the vender for sales, nor the capitalist complain for want of profitable modes of investment. . . .

No greater error exists in the world than the notion that society will be benefited by deprecating the value of human labour. Let this principle (as at this day in England) be carried towards its full extent, and it is in vain that scientific power shall pour fourth its inexhaustible treasures of wealth upon the world. Its products will all be amassed to glut the over-flowing storehouses, and useless hoards of its insatiable monopolizers; while the mechanic and productive classes, who constitute the great mass of the population, and who have wielded the power and laboured in the production of this immense abundance, having no other resource for subsistence than what they derive from the miserable pittance, which they are compelled by competition to receive in exchange for their inestimable labour, must first begin to pine, languish, and suffer under its destructive and withering influence. But the evil stops not here. The middling classes next, venders of the products of human industry, will begin to experience its deleterious effects. The demand for their articles must necessarily cease from the forced inability of the people to consume: trade must in consequence languish, and losses and failures become the order of the day. At last the contagion will reach the capitalist, throned as he is, in the midst of his ill gotten abundance, and his capital, from the most evident and certain causes, will become useless, unemployed and stagnant, himself the trembling victim of continual alarms from robberies, burnings, and murder, the unhappy and perhaps ill fated object of innumerable imprecations, insults and implacable hatred from the wronged, impoverished, and despairing multitude. The experience of the most commercial parts of the world sufficiently demonstrates that this is the natural, inevitable, and, shall we not say, righteous consequences of a principle, whose origin is injustice and an unrighteous depreciation of the value and abstraction of the products of human labour—a principle which in its ultimate effects, must be productive of universal ruin and misery, and destroy alike the happiness of every class and individual in society. . . .

Martin Van Buren Proposes a New Opposition Party, 1827

Washington, Jany 13th 1827

Dear Sir,

You will have observed an article in the Argus upon the subject of a national convention. That matter will soon be brought under discussion here & I sincerely wish you would bestow upon it some portion of your attention. It was first suggested to me by the Vice President. he and Mr. Ingham of Penn. are the only two persons with whom I have as yet conversed. They think it essential. It will be an important movement & should be fully and deeply considered. . . . The following may, I think, justly be ranked among its probable advantages. First, It is the best and probably the only practicable mode of concentrating the entire vote of the opposition and of effecting what is of still greater importance, the substantial reorganization of the Old Republican Party. 2nd Its first result cannot be doubtful. Mr. Adams occupying the seat and being determined not to surrender it except *in extremis* will not submit his pretensions to the convention. . . . I have long been satisfied that we can only get rid of the present, and restore a better state of things, by combining Genl. Jackson's personal popularity with the portion of old party feeling yet remaining. This sentiment is spreading, and would of itself be sufficient to nominate him at the Convention. 3rd The call of such a convention, its exclusive Republican character, and the refusal of Mr. Adams and his friends to become parties to it, would draw anew the old Party lines and the subsequent contest would reestablish them. State nominations alone would fall far short of that object. 4th It would greatly improve the condition of the Republicans of the North and Middle States by substituting *party principle* for *personal preference* as one of the leading points in the contest. The location of the candidates would in a great degree, be merged in its consideration. Instead of the question being between a northern and Southern man, it would be whether or not the ties which have heretofore bound together a great political party should be severed. The difference between the two questions would be found to be immense in the elective field. Altho' this is a mere party consideration, it is not on that account less likely to be effectual. Considerations of this character not infrequently operate as efficiently as those which bear upon the most important questions of constitutional doctrine. Indeed Genl. Jackson has been so little in public life, that it will be not a little difficult to contrast his opinions on great questions with those of Mr. Adams. . . . Hence the importance, if not necessity of collateral matter. . . . 5^{thly} It would place our Republican friends in New England on new and strong grounds. They would have to decide between an indulgence in sectional and personal feelings with an entire separation from their old political friends, on the one hand or acquiescence in the fairly expressed will of the party, on the other. In all the states the division between Republicans and Federalists is still kept up and cannot be laid aside whatever the leaders of the two parties may desire. Such a question would greatly divide the democracy of the east. In N. Hampshire I think it would give us the victory; in all New England it would give them trouble, keep them employ'd at home and check the hopes of their friends elsewhere. 6th Its effects would be highly salutary on your section of the union by the revival of old party distinctions. We must always have party distinctions and the old ones are the best of which the nature of the case admits. Political combinations between the inhabitants of the different states are unavoidable & the most natural and beneficial to the country is that between the planters of the South and the plain Republicans of the north. The country has once flourished under a party thus constituted & may again. It would take longer than our lives (even if it were practicable) to create new party feelings to keep those masses together. If the old ones are suppressed, Geographical divisions founded on local interests or, what is worse, prejudices between free and slave holding states will inevitably take their place. Party attachment in former times furnished a complete antidote for sectional prejudices by producing counteracting feelings. It was not until that defence had been broken down that the clamour agt. Southern Influence and African Slavery could be made effectual in the North. Those in the South who assisted in producing the change are, I am satisfied, now deeply sensible of their errour. Every honest Federalist of the South therefore (and would if he duly reflected upon the subject) prefer the revival of old party feelings to any other state of things he has a right to expect. Formerly, attacks upon Southern Republicans were regarded by those of the north as assaults upon their political brethren & resented accordingly. This all powerful sympathy has been much weakened, if not destroyed by the amalgamating policy of Mr. Monroe. It can & ought to be revived and the proposed convention would be eminently serviceable in effecting that object. . . . Lastly, the effect of such a nomination on Genl Jackson could not fail to be considerable. His election, as the result of his military services without reference to party & so far as he alone is concerned scarcely to principle would be one thing. His election as the result of a combined and concerted effort of a political party, holding in the main to certain tenets and opposed to certain prevailing principles, might be another and a far different thing. . . .

John C. Calhoun on States' Rights, 1828

The Committee do not propose to enter into an elaborate, or refined argument on the question of the Constitutionality of the Tariff System. The Gen[era]l Government is one of specifick powers, and it can rightfully exercise only the powers expressly granted, and those that may be necessary and proper to carry them into effect, all others being reserved expressly to the States, or the people. It results necessarily, that those who claim to exercise power under the Constitution, are bound to show, that it is expressly granted, or that it is necessary and proper as a means to some of the granted powers. The advocates of the Tariff have offered no such proof.

In the absence of argument drawn from the Constitution itself the advocates of the power have attempted to call in the aid of precedent. The Committee will not waste their time in examining the instances quoted. If they were strictly in point, they would be entitled to little weight. Ours is not a government of precedents, nor can they be admitted except to a very limited extent and with great caution in the interpretation of the Constitution, without changing in time the entire character of the instrument. . . .

So partial are the effects of the system, that its burdens are exclusively on one side, and the benefits on the other. It imposes on the agricultural interest of the south, including the South west, with that portion of our commerce and navigation engaged in foreign trade, the burden not only of sustaining the system itself, but that also of the Government. . . .

That the manufacturing States, even in their own opinion, bear no share of the burden of the Tariff in reality, we may infer with the greatest certainty from their conduct. The fact that they urgently demand an increase, and consider any addition as a blessing, and a failure to obtain one, a curse, is the strongest confession, that whatever burden it imposes in reality, falls, not on them but on others. Men ask not for burdens, but benefits. The tax paid by the duties on impost [sic] by which, with the exception of the receipts in the sale of publick land and a few incidental items, the Government is wholly supported, and which in its gross amount annually equals about $23,000,000 is then in truth no tax on them. Whatever portion of it they advance, as consumers of the articles on which it is imposed, returns to them . . . with usurious interest through an artfully contrived system. That such are the facts, the Committee will proceed to demonstrate by other arguments, besides the confession of the party interested through their acts, as conclusive as that ought to be considered.

Excerpts from *The Papers of John C. Calhoun* by Clyde N. Wilson and W. Edwin Hemphill, eds. (Columbia, S.C.: University of South Carolina Press, 1959), Vol. X, pp. 444–532. Reprinted by permission.

If the duties were imposed on the exports, instead of the imports, no one would doubt their partial operation, and that the duties in that case would fall on those engaged in ["rearing products" *canceled and* "producing articles" *interlined*] for the foreign market; and as rice, tobacco and cotton constitute the great mass of our exports, such duties would of necessity mainly fall on the Southern States, where they are exclusively cultivated. . . .

We cultivate certain great staples for the supply of the general market of the world; they manufacture almost exclusively for the home market. Their object in the Tariff is to keep down foreign competition, in order to obtain a monopoly of the domestick market. The effect on us is to compel us to purchase at a higher price, both what we purchase from them and from others, without receiving a correspondent increase in the price, of what we sell. The price at which we can afford to cultivate must depend on the price, at which we receive our supplies. The lower the latter, the lower we may dispose of our products with profit, and in the same degree our capacity of meeting competition is increased; and, on the contrary, the higher the price of our supplies, the less the profit and the less consequently the capacity for meeting competition. If for instance, cotton can be cultivated at 10 cents the pound under our increase[d] price of forty-five per cent for what we purchase in return, it is clear, if the prices of what we consume were reduced forty-five per cent, we could, under such reduced prices, afford to raise the article at 5½ cents per pound, with a profit, as great as what we now obtain, at 10 cents, and that our capacity of meeting the competition of foreigners in the general market of the world would be increased in the same proportion. If we can now with the increased price from the Tariff contend with success, under a reduction of 45 per cent in the prices of our supplies, we would drive out all competition, and thus add annually to the consumption of our cotton, three or four hundred thousand bales, with a corresponding increase of profit. The case then fairly stated between us and the manufacturing States is, that the Tariff gives them a protection against foreign competition in our own market, by diminishing in the same proportion our capacity to compete with our rivals in the General market of the world. They who say, that they cannot compete with foreigners at their own doors without an advantage of ["nearly fifty" *canceled and* "45" *interlined*] per cent, expect us to meet them abroad under disadvantage equal to their encouragement. . . .

We are told by those who pretend to understand our interest better than we do, that the excess of production, and not the Tariff, is the evil which afflicts us, and that our true remedy is a reduction of the quantity of cotton, rice and tobacco which we raise, and not a repeal of the Tariff. They assert that low prices are the necessary consequence of excess of supply, and that the only proper correction is in diminishing the quantity. We would feel more disposed to respect the spirit in which the advice is offered, if those from whom it comes, accompanied it with the ["benefit" *canceled and* "weight" *interlined*] of their example. They also occasionally complain of low prices, but instead of diminishing the supply as a remedy for the evil, demand an enlargement of the market, by the exclusion of all competition.

Our market is the world, and as we cannot imitate their example by enlarging it for our products through the exclusion of others, we must decline to their advice, which instead of alleviating would increase our embarrassment. We have no monopoly in the supply of our products. One half of the globe may produce them. Should we reduce our production, others stand ready by increasing theirs to take our place, and instead of raising prices, we would only diminish our share of the supply. We are thus compelled to produce on the penalty of loosing our hold on the general market. Once lost it may be lost forever; and lose it we must, if we continue to be compelled as we now are, on the one hand by general competition of the world to sell low, and on the other by the Tariff to buy high. We cannot withstand this double action. Our ruin must follow. In fact our only permanent and safe remedy is not the rise in the price of what we sell in which we can receive but little aid from our Government, but a reduction in that which we buy which is prevented by the interference of the Government. Give us a free and open competition in our own market, and we fear not to encounter like competition in the general market of the world. If under all of our discouragement by the acts of our Government, we are still able to contend there against the world, can it be doubted, if this impediment were removed, we would force out all competitors; and thus also enlarge our market, not by the oppression of our fellow citizens of other States, but by our industry, enterprize [*sic*] and natural advantages. . . .

The question, in what manner the loss and gain of the [tariff] system distribute themselves among the several classes of society is intimately connected with that of their distribution among the several sections. Few subjects present more important points for consideration, but as it is not possible for the Committee to enter fully into discussion of them, without swelling their report beyond all reasonable bounds, they will pass them over with a few brief and general remarks.

The system has not been sufficiently long in operation with us to display its real character in reference to the point now under discussion. To understand its ultimate tendency in distributing the wealth of society among the several classes, we must turn our eyes to Europe, where it has been in action for centuries, and has been among the efficient causes of that great inequality of property, which prevails in most European countries. No system can be more efficient to rear up a monied aristocracy. Its tendency is to make the poor, poorer, and the rich, richer. Heretofore in our country this tendency has displayed itself principally in its effects as regards[?] the different sections, but the time will come, when it will produce the same result between ["the several" *canceled*] classes in the manufacturing States. After we are exhausted, the contest will be between the Capitalists and operatives, for into these two classes it ultimately must divide society. The issue of the struggle here, ["between them" *canceled*] must be the same as it has been in Europe. Under operation of the system wages will sink much more rapidly than the prices of the necessaries of life, till the operatives will be reduced to the lowest point, where the portion of the products of their labour left to them, will be barely necessary to preserve existence. For the present, the pressure of the system is on our section. Its effects on the staple States produce almost universal suffering ["and the loss to each individual is nearly in proportion to his production and consumption" *canceled*]. In the mean time an opposite state of things exists in the manufacturing States. For the present every interest there, except foreign trade and navigation, flourishes. Such must be the effect of a monopoly of so rich and extensive a market as that of the Southern States, till it is impoverished, as ours rapidly must be, by the operation of the system, when its natural effects on the several classes of the community will unfold themselves. . . .

The Political Cultures of a Presidential Campaign, 1828

The Jackson Campaign: A Pamphlet

Were [Adams's] advocates to praise him for his steadiness of purpose, they could not conceal from the public, the notorious fact, that the present administration has been characterized by vacillation and inconsistency—that they have trimmed their sails to every appearance of a breeze, from whatever quarter it was expected; whilst, with their repeated veering, they have evidently been carried backward instead of forward, and are at the moment drifting, with frightful rapidity, upon a lee shore. These are all vulnerable points in Mr. Adams's character. His friends know it, and keep him in the shade. They talk, in swelling strains, of his *learning,* and *diplomatic* skill. That he possesses diplomatic *experience* we do not deny: but his diplomatic *skill* is subject of serious question. . . .

That Mr. Adams is possessed of *learning* too we are willing to admit. We are not ignorant that he has received a college education,—that he has been a professor of rhetoric—that he can round a period, dress out a figure, and exhibit in his writing many of the graces of classical composition. . . . That he is *learned* we are willing to admit: but his *wisdom* we take leave to question, and again call for proof. . . . We confess our attachment to the homely doctrine, thus happily expressed by the great English poet:—

> That not to know of things remote
> From use, obscure and subtle, but to know
> That which before us lies in daily life,
> Is the prime wisdom.

This wisdom we believe that Gen. Jackson possesses in an eminent degree. . . . Few men can exhibit more numerous and striking proofs of public confidence; especially when it is considered, that they were so many acts of homage paid to his merit, and all conferred without solicitation or request. *In the whole course of his service, in the various offices which he consented to accept, no man can adduce a single complaint of his want of integrity or ability, by the authority from which the appointment emanated: Whether it be his constituents in Tennessee, the legislature of that State, or the general government.* . . . Notwithstanding these facts, it has been lately discovered, if the friends of the present administration are to be believed, that he can neither write grammatically, nor spell: but that, both in syntax and orthography, he is decidedly inferior to an ordinary school boy of twelve years of age. This is too heavy a tax upon public credulity. The attempt at imposition is as senseless, as the charge is malicious, and the evidence is disgraceful. The preposterous accusation was endeavored to be sustained by the basest forgery; which, if it had not been obvious in itself, could not fail to be detected by means of the many public documents, and the thousand private letters, which have come from his pen in the course of a long and active life. . . .

The Adams Campaign: A Broadside

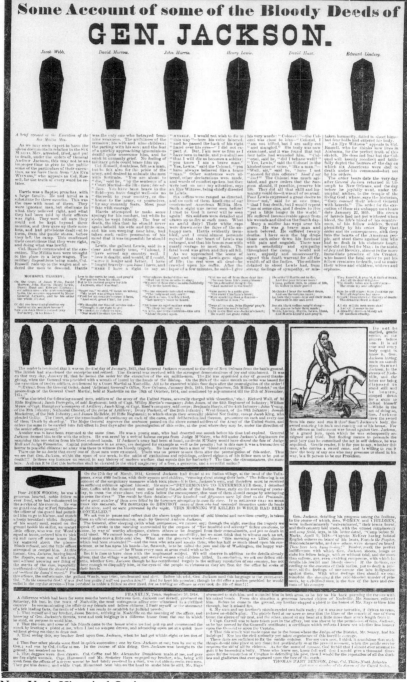

New-York Historical Society.

⊞ *E S S A Y S*

Why did the seemingly invincible sense of national unity and patriotism evident in 1815 disintegrate so quickly and create the conditions for an entirely new political alignment? The historian Richard H. Brown, now at the Newberry Library in Chicago, startled the conventional wisdom in the mid-1960s with his discussion of how the Missouri crisis and ensuing concerns over slavery lay at the heart of things—an argument that, though criticized since, still merits attention. In the second essay the historian Ronald P. Formisano of the University of Florida turns to intrasectional as well as intersectional tensions. This excerpt from his larger study of parties and political culture in Massachusetts suggests how mounting divisions between what Formisano calls the Core and Periphery spelled the doom of an older form of deferential politics and the birth of a new party regime. The author of the third essay, the late John William Ward, for many years the president of Amherst College, was a pioneering student of what is now called political culture. By taking a close look at the campaign literature from 1828, his essay uncovers some of the overarching emotional themes that came into direct conflict, thanks to the contenders' political managers. Is it possible to detect any links between these themes and the social and economic transformations of the era?

The Missouri Crisis, Slavery, and the Rise of the Jacksonians

RICHARD H. BROWN

From the inauguration of Washington until the Civil War the South was in the saddle of national politics. . . . [T]here are no exceptions [to this central fact], not even in that period when the "common man" stormed the ramparts of government under the banner of Andrew Jackson. In Jackson's day the chief agent of Southern power was a Northern man with Southern principles, Martin Van Buren of New York. It was he who put together the party coalition which Andrew Jackson led to power. That coalition had its wellsprings in the dramatic crisis over slavery in Missouri, the first great public airing of the slavery question in ante bellum America. . . .

. . . The insistence that slavery was uniquely a Southern concern, not to be touched by outsiders, had been from the outset a *sine qua non* for Southern participation in national politics. It underlay the Constitution and its creation of a government of limited powers, without which Southern participation would have been unthinkable. And when in the 1790's Jefferson and Madison perceived that a constitution was only the first step in guaranteeing Southern security, because a constitution meant what those who governed under it said it meant, it led to the creation of the first national political party to protect that Constitution against change by interpretation. The party which they constructed converted a Southern minority into a national majority through alliance with congenial interests outside the South. Organically, it

Richard H. Brown. "The Missouri Crisis, Slavery, and the Politics of Jacksonianism" *South Atlantic Quarterly,* vol. 65, pp. 55–70. Copyright 1966, Duke University Press, Durham, N.C. Reprinted by permission of the publisher.

represented an alliance between New York and Virginia, pulling between them Pennsylvania, and after them North Carolina, Georgia, and (at first) Kentucky and Tennessee, all states strongly subject to Virginia's influence. At bottom it rested on the support of people who lived on that rich belt of fertile farmland which stretched from the Great Lakes across upstate New York and Pennsylvania, southward through the Southern piedmont into Georgia, entirely oblivious of the Mason-Dixon line. North as well as South it was an area of prosperous, well-settled small farms. More farmers than capitalists, its residents wanted little from government but to be let alone. Resting his party on them, Jefferson had found a formula for national politics which at the same time was a formula for Southern pre-eminence. . . .

So long as the Federalists remained an effective opposition, Jefferson's party worked as a party should. It maintained its identity in relation to the opposition by a moderate and pragmatic advocacy of strict construction of the Constitution. Because it had competition, it could maintain discipline. It responded to its constituent elements because it depended on them for support. But eventually its very success was its undoing. After 1815, stirred by the nationalism of the postwar era, and with the Federalists in decline, the Republicans took up Federalist positions on a number of the great public issues of the day, sweeping all before them as they did. The Federalists gave up the ghost. In the Era of Good Feelings which followed, everybody began to call himself a Republican, and a new theory of party amalgamation preached the doctrine that party division was bad and that a one-party system best served the national interest. Only gradually did it become apparent that in victory the Republican party had lost its identity—and its usefulness. As the party of the whole nation it ceased to be responsive to any particular elements in its constituency. It ceased to be responsive to the South.

When it did, and because it did, it invited the Missouri crisis of 1819–1820, and that crisis in turn revealed the basis for a possible configuration of national parties which eventually would divide the nation free against slave. As John Quincy Adams put it, the crisis had revealed "the basis for a new organization of parties . . . here was a new party ready formed, . . . terrible to the whole Union, but portentously terrible to the South—threatening in its progress the emancipation of all their slaves, threatening in its immediate effect that Southern domination which has swayed the Union for the last twenty years." Because it did so, Jefferson, in equally famous phrase, "considered it at once as the knell of the Union."

. . . [T]he Missouri crisis gave rise not to prophecy alone, but to action. It led to an urgent and finally successful attempt to revive the old Jeffersonian party and with it the Jeffersonian formula for Southern pre-eminence. . . .

In Jefferson's day the tie between slavery, strict construction of the Constitution, and the Republican party was implicit, not explicit. After Missouri it was explicit, and commented upon time and again in both public and private discussion. Perceptive Southerners saw (1) that unless effective means were taken to quiet discussion of the question, slavery might be used at any time in the future to force the South into a permanent minority in the Union, endangering all its interests; and (2) that if the loose constitutional construction of the day were allowed to prevail, the time might come when the government would be held to have the power to deal with slavery. Vital to preventing both of these—to keeping the slavery question quiet and to gaining a reassertion of strict construction principles—was the re-establishment of conditions which would make the party in power responsive once again to the South.

[T]he Missouri crisis . . . shaped the conditions which would govern what followed. In the South it gave marked impetus to a reaction against the nationalism and amalgamationism of postwar Republicanism and handed the offensive to a hardy band of Old Republican politicians who had been crying in the wilderness since 1816. In the early 1820's the struggle between Old Republicans and New would be the stuff of Southern politics, and on the strength of the new imperatives to which the Missouri conflict gave rise the Old Republicans would carry off the victory in state after Southern state, providing thereby a base of power on which a new strict construction party could be reared.

For precisely the same reason that it gave the offensive to the Old Republicans of the South—because it portrayed the tie between slavery and party in starkest form—the Missouri crisis put Northern Old Republicans on the defense. Doing so, it handed the keys to national party success thereafter to whatever Northern leader could surmount charges of being pro-Southern and command the necessary Northern votes to bring the party to power. For that reason Thomas Jefferson's formula for national politics would become, when resurrected, Martin Van Buren's formula for national politics. . . .

Because they shaped the context of what was to come, the reactions to the Missouri crisis in the two citadels of Old Republican power, Richmond and Albany, were significant. Each cast its light ahead. As the donnybrook mounted in Congress in the winter of 1820, the Virginia capital was reported to be as "agitated as if affected by all the Volcanic Eruptions of Vesuvius." At the heart of the clamor were the Old Republicans of the Richmond Junto, particularly Thomas Ritchie's famous *Enquirer,* which spoke for the Junto and had been for years the most influential newspaper in the South. Associates of Jefferson, architects of Southern power, the Old Republicans were not long in perceiving the political implications of the crisis. Conviction grew in their minds that the point of Northern agitation was not Missouri at all but to use slavery as an anvil on which to forge a new party which would carry either Rufus King or DeWitt Clinton of New York to the presidency and force the South from power forever. But what excited them even more was the enormity of the price of peace which alone seemed likely to avert the disaster. This was the so-called Thomas Proviso, amending the Missouri bill to draw the ill-fated 36°30' line across the Louisiana Purchase, prohibiting slavery in the territory to the north, giving up the lion's share to freedom.

No sooner had the proviso been introduced in Congress than the temper of the Old Republicans boiled over, and with prescient glances to the future they leapt to the attack. Ritchie challenged the constitutionality of the proviso at once in the *Enquirer* . . . Nathaniel Macon agreed. "To compromise is to acknowledge the right of Congress to interfere and to legislate on the subject," he wrote; "this would be acknowledging too much." Equally important was the fact that, by prohibiting slavery in most of the West, the proviso forecast a course of national development ultimately intolerable to the South because, as Spencer Roane put it to Monroe, Southerners could not consent to be "dammed up in a land of Slaves." As the debates thundered to their climax, Ritchie in two separate editorials predicted that if the proviso passed, the South must in due time have Texas. "If we are cooped up on the north," he wrote with grim prophecy, "we must have elbow room to the west."

When finally the Southern Old Republicans tacitly consented to the Missouri Compromise, it was therefore not so much a measure of illusion about what the South had given up, as of how desperately necessary they felt peace to be. They had yielded not so much in the spirit of a bargain as in the spirit of a man caught in a holdup, who yields his fortune rather than risk his life in the hope that he may live to see a better day and perhaps even to get his fortune back. As Ritchie summed it up when news of the settlement reached Richmond, "Instead of joy, we scarcely ever recollect to have tasted of a bitterer cup." That they tasted it at all was because of the manipulative genius of Henry Clay, who managed to bring up the separate parts of the compromise separately in the House, enabling the Old Republicans to provide him his margin of victory on the closely contested Missouri bill while they saved their pride by voting to the end against the Thomas Proviso. They had not bound themselves by their votes to the proviso, as Ritchie warned they should not. If it was cold comfort for the moment, it was potent with significance for the future.

In fact, the vote on the proviso illuminated an important division in Southern sentiment. Thirty-seven slave state congressmen opposed it, while thirty-nine voted for it. On the surface the line of division ran along the Appalachian crest and the Potomac, pointing out seemingly a distinction in interest between the South Atlantic states on the one hand and those in the Southwest and mid-Atlantic regions on the other—between those states most characteristically Southern and those which in 1820 were essentially more Western or Northern in outlook. More fundamental, within each section it divided Southerners between those who were more sensitive to the relationship of slavery to politics and those who were less so; between those who thought the party formula for Southern pre-eminence and defense important and those who thought parties outmoded; between particularists and postwar Republican nationalists; between the proponents of an old Republican polity and the proponents of a new one as defined in the years of postwar exuberance; between those closest to Jefferson, such as the Richmond Junto and Macon, and those closest to Monroe, such as Calhoun. It was a division which prefigured Southern political struggles of the twenties. When two years later 70 per cent of those congressmen from the South Atlantic states who had opposed the Thomas Proviso returned to the next Congress, compared to 39 per cent of those who had supported it, it was a measure of the resurgence of Old Republicanism. Two years after that, in the chaotic presidential election of 1824, the Southerners who had opposed the proviso were the Southerners who sought to sustain the party caucus as a method of nominating in a vain attempt to restore old party discipline. Four years after that they marched back to power at last under the banner of Andrew Jackson, restoring to effectiveness in so doing a political system intended to make future Missouri crises impossible, and committed in due time to rectify the Thomas Proviso. . . .

In private, Van Buren left no doubt where he stood, or where he meant to go once the storm had passed. No sooner had the compromise been adopted in Washington than the Little Magician got off a letter to his friendly rival Rufus King, promising at "some future day" to give that veteran Federalist his own views on the expediency of making slavery a party question, and remarking meanwhile that notwithstanding the strong public interest in the Missouri question, "the excitement which exists in regard to it, or which is likely to arise from it, is not so great as you suppose." It was a singularly important assessment of Northern public opinion for a politician who had fallen heir to a tattered Southern alliance, and in it King apprehensively saw the panorama of forty years of national politics stretching before him:

> The inveteracy of party feelings in the Eastern States [he wrote a friend], the hopes of influence and distinction by taking part in favor of the slave States, which call themselves, and are spoken of by others as the truly republican States and the peculiar friends of liberty, will keep alive & sustain a body considerably numerous, and who will have sufficient influence, to preserve to the slave States their disproportionate, I might say exclusive, dominance over the Union.

Twenty months after that, in the late fall of 1821, Van Buren set off for Washington as a newly elected United States senator. . . . He carried with him into the lion's den of presidential politics effective command of the thirty-six uncommitted electoral votes of New York. If he would be the most disinterested statesman in all the land, he could not avoid for long the responsibility that went with that power. It was an opportunity to be used for large purposes or small, as a man might choose, and the Little Magician lost no time in indicating his intended course. Within weeks of his arrival he was pulling the strings of the New York delegation in the House to bring about return of the speakership to the slave states, from whom it had been wrested by a straight sectional vote upon Clay's retirement the year before. . . . Three months after that Van Buren was on his way to Richmond to plan the resurrection of the Old Republican Party.

That he should do so was partly for reasons of personal ambition, partly because the Bucktails after years of frustrating struggle with Clinton had their own clear reasons for wanting to redraw party lines. Beyond this there would appear to be the simple fact that Van Buren believed implicitly in the whole system of republican polity as Thomas Jefferson had staked it out. Committed to the principle of the least possible government, the Republican party was the defender of that republican liberty which was the sole political concern of the disinterested agrarian constituency for which, through life, Van Buren saw himself as a spokesman, and which constituted the majority of Americans. That majority was strongest where it was purest, least subject to the corrupting power of money. That was in the South. Slavery was a lesser issue than republicanism. Nor was it by any means clear in 1820 that agitation was the best way to deal with it. For while some who were nominally Old Republicans, such as Senator William Smith of South Carolina, were beginning to argue that slavery was a positive good, it was generally true that no men in America were more honestly committed to the notion that the institution was wrong than those men of Jeffersonian conscience who were the Old Republicans of the South. . . . Because he believed as he did, Van Buren's efforts to revive party distinctions and restore the Old Republican Party were to be more than a mere matter of machinations with politicians, looking toward the making of the Democratic party. He looked to Southern power, and he would quiet the slavery question if he could. He was dealing with the root principle of the whole structure of ante bellum politics.

In the long history of the American presidency no election appears quite so formless as that of 1824. With no competing party to force unity on the Republicans, candidates who could not command the party nomination were free to defy it. They did so, charging that "King Caucus" was undemocratic. Eventually no fewer than four candidates competed down to the wire, each a Republican, every man for himself. Because they divided the electoral votes between them, none came close to a majority, and the election went to the House of Representatives. There, with the help of Henry Clay, John Quincy Adams outpolled the popular Andrew Jackson and the caucus nominee, William H. Crawford of Georgia, and carried off the prize. . . .

Hidden in the currents and crosscurrents of [the 1824] campaign was the reiterated issue of party versus amalgamation. Behind it, in turn, were repeated pleas by Old Republican presses, North and South alike, that unless genuine Republicans agreed on a method of choosing a candidate the division must be along sectional lines, in which case a Federalist or proto-Federalist might sneak into the White House. Behind it too was the repeated warning that party organization alone would make democracy work. Without it, the Old Republicans correctly prophesied, the election would end up in the House of Representatives, subject to the worst kind of political intrigue, and with the votes of the smallest states the equals of those of populous Virginia and New York.

When the caucus failed it was because amalgamation had destroyed the levers which made party discipline possible. Exhortation could not restore them. Meantime the issue of democracy had been turned against the advocates of party, because in key states like New York and North Carolina they tried to use the power of the party organizations for Crawford, bucking more popular candidates such as Jackson and Adams. It was a bogus issue. The real issue was whether a party was necessary to make democracy work, and because they were more nearly right than their opponents about this, and the election in the House shortly proved it, the Old Republicans would recover quickly after 1824, after Crawford and the caucus issue were politically dead. Let circumstances limit the number of candidates, and tie up party and democracy on the same side, and the results would be different another time.

In the campaign of 1824 and the years immediately following, the slavery issue was never far below the surface. The Denmark Vesey conspiracy for an insurrection in Charleston . . . was to contemporaries a grim reminder of the Missouri debates, and it was attributed publicly to Rufus King's speeches on the Missouri question. In 1823–1824 some Southerners suspected that an attempt by Secretary of State Adams to conclude a slave trade convention with Great Britain was an attempt to reap the benefit of Northern anti-slavery sentiment; and some, notably Representative John Floyd of Virginia, sought to turn the tables on Adams by attacking him for allegedly ceding Texas to Spain in the Florida treaty, thus ceding what Floyd called "two slaveholding states" and costing "the Southern interest" four Senators.

Old Republicans made no bones about their concern over the issue, or their fear that it might be turned against them. . . . "Call it the Missouri question, the Illinois question, what you please; it was the *Slave question*," Ritchie shrilled. . . . "The more general question of the North and South," the [Van Burenite *Albany*] *Argus* warned, "will be urged to the uttermost, by those who can never triumph when they meet the democracy of the country, openly, and with the hostility they bear towards it." Over and over the debate rang out the argument that the attempt to revive party distinctions was an attempt to allay sectional prejudices, and by the time the debate was over only the most obtuse citizen could have missed the point.

Nor was the election of Adams destined to calm Southern fears on issues having to do with slavery. A series of incidents early in 1825 suggested that the New Englander's election had made antislavery advocates more bold, and Southern tempers grew shorter in the summer of 1825 than they had been at any time since Missouri. One of the incidents was a reported argument before the Supreme Court in the case of the South Carolina Negro Seaman's Act by Attorney General William Wirt, stating that slavery was "inconsistent with the laws of God and nature." A second was a resolution offered in the Senate a scant nine days after Adams' election by Rufus King, proposing to turn the proceeds from the sale of western lands to the emancipation and export of slaves, through the agency of the American Colonization Society. In the same week the New Jersey legislature proposed a system of foreign colonization which "would, in due time, effect the entire emancipation of the slaves in our country." John Floyd enclosed a copy of the New Jersey resolution to Claiborne Gooch, Ritchie's silent partner on the *Enquirer,* with salient warning:

> Long before this manifestation I have believed, connected with the Missouri question, would come up the general question of slavery, upon the principles avowed by Rufus King in the Senate. . . .
> If this indication is well received, who can tell, after the elevation of Mr. A. to the presidency—that he, of Missouri effort, or DeWitt C. or some such aspirant, may not, for the sake of that office, fan this flame—

to array the non-slaveholding States against the Slaveholding states, and finally quiet our clamor or opposition, by the application of the slaves knife to our throats. Think of this much, and often.

Meantime, the New York *Commercial Advertiser* expressed publicly the hope that Adams' administration would introduce "a new era, when the northern, eastern, and non-slaveholding states, will assume an attitude in the Union, proportionate to their moral and physical power." Ritchie responded hotly in an editorial asking what the designs of such a combination would be against the "southern and *slave-holding* states." Soon in Georgia the Old Republican Governor George M. Troup, at the instigation of Senator John M. Berrien, put before the legislature a request for resolutions stating slavery to be exclusively within the control of the states and asking that the federal government "abstain from intermeddling." . . .

With the slavery issue thus drawn taut, the Old Republicans recovered quickly from the setback of 1824. Calhoun's inveterate foe William Smith was returned to the Senate from South Carolina, completing for the moment an Old Republican sweep of the South Atlantic states begun in 1821, a sweep which put Calhoun's political career in jeopardy and forced the Carolinian, now vice president, to break with Adams. For the Old Republicans, moreover, Adams made an infinitely better target than Monroe. The high-toned nationalism of the New Englander, combined with popular revulsion to the alleged bargain which secured his election, put the kiss of death on amalgamation as a political theory. The stage was set, under more favorable circumstances, for the Old Republicans to try again. . . .

When finally it rode to power, the Jacksonian party was made up of two clearly discernible and distinct wings. One comprised the original Jacksonians, those who had supported him in 1824 when he ran on his own, bereft, like all the rest, of party, and nearly of allies. As measured in that election this strength was predominantly in the West. It spilled over into a few states east of the mountains, most notably Pennsylvania, where the chaos of the existing political structure enabled Jackson as military hero to ride roughshod over all the rest. But this was all. The Western vote, especially when shared with Clay, amounted in electoral terms to little. Even with the votes of the Carolinas, thrown to him gratuitously by Calhoun and counting one-quarter of his total, he was far short of an electoral majority. To get even this much he had been formally before the public for two years, and all his considerable natural appeal as a Westerner and a hero had gone into the bargain.

After 1824 Jackson found himself the candidate of a combined opposition. The concrete measure of difference between defeat in 1824 and victory in 1828 was the Old Republican strength of the South Atlantic states and New York, brought to the Jackson camp carefully tended and carefully drilled by Van Buren. Nearly equal in size to the original Jackson following, they constituted a political faction far older, far more permanent, far more purposeful, far better led, and in the long run far more important. Their purposes were set forth by Van Buren in a notable letter to Ritchie in January, 1827, proposing support of the old hero. Such support, as the New Yorker put it, would be "the best and probably the only practicable mode of concentrating the entire vote of the opposition & of effecting what is of still greater importance, the substantial reorganization of the Old Republican Party." It would "restore a better state of things, by combining Genl Jackson's personal popularity with the portion of old party feeling yet remaining." It would aid Republicans of the North and middle states "by substituting *party principle* for *personal preference* as one of the leading points in the contest. . . . Instead of the question being between a northern and Southern man, it would be whether or not the ties, which have hitherto bound together a great political party should be severed." Most important, its effects would be highly salutary for the South:

> We must always have party distinctions and the old ones are the best of which the nature of the case admits. Political combinations between the inhabitants of the different states are unavoidable & the most natural & beneficial to the country is that between the planters of the South and the plain Republicans of the north. The country has once flourished under a party thus constituted & may again. It would take longer than our lives (even if it were practicable) to create new party feelings to keep those masses together. If the old ones are suppressed, geographical divisions founded on local interests or, what is worse prejudices between free and slave holding states will inevitably take their place. Party attachment in former times furnished a complete antidote for sectional prejudices by producing counteracting feelings. It was not until that defence had been broken down that the clamour agt. [against] Southern Influence and African Slavery could be made effectual in the North. . . . Formerly, attacks upon Southern Republicans were regarded by those of the north as assaults upon their political brethren & resented accordingly. This all powerful sympathy has been much weakened, if not, destroyed by the amalgamating policy. . . . it can & ought to be revived.

Lastly, Van Buren noted, a Jackson administration brought to power by the "concerted effort of a political party, holding in the main, to certain tenets & opposed to certain prevailing principles" would be a far different thing from one brought to power by the popularity of a military hero alone. An administration brought to power by Old Republican votes would be governed by Old Republican principles. Van Buren would make himself the guarantor of that. . . .

Social Development and Political Parties from 1789 to 1828

RONALD P. FORMISANO

Four "critical lines of cleavage" have shaped the party systems of Western democracies, according to S. M. Lipset and S. Rokkan. The Industrial Rev-

Excerpts from *The Transformation of Political Culture: Massachusetts Parties, 1790–1840,* by Ronald P. Formisano (New York: Oxford University Press, 1983, pp. 3–17).

olution largely created two of these "cleavages," one involving the clash of social classes and another involving different propertied groups. Before industrialization, however, two earlier lines of division had sprung from the "National Revolution," and both of these seem roughly relevant to the United States, where parties had formed in a new nation and before the Industrial Revolution. The first American parties, indeed, emerged precisely during the era when "securing the Republic" and issues of early national development dominated politics. Lipset and Rokkan maintain that in many Western countries the "National Revolution" gave rise to a conflict between a *central,* dominating, nation-building culture and the *peripheral* subcultures of ethnically, linguistically, or religiously distinct provincial populations resistant to state centralization. The other division pitted the centralizing nation-state against the historical corporate privileges of the church or otherwise involved, as in the United States, the struggle of *core* religious groups to remain dominant, while religious minorities fought against discrimination or sought to defend their practices or to extend their values. . . .

Historians of early U.S. politics can agree, certainly, that the process of nation forming laid the bases for the development of parties. Though the U.S. had no national church, conflict between dominant and lesser religious groups was extremely important to politics in certain states, and particularly in New England, where Connecticut and Massachusetts possessed formally established churches until 1818 and 1833. Though Lipset and Rokkan's two lines of division cannot be applied directly to the U.S., they can be adapted to discern rough patterns of alignment between Center and Periphery in many states, and to a degree in the country at large. Michael Hechter defines the *"core"* as the "dominant cultural group which occupies territory extending from the political center of the society (e.g., the locus of the central government) outward to those territories largely occupied by the subordinate, or peripheral cultural group." In this study, Center and Core will be used less as geographic concepts—though they often had spatial relevance—and more as ideological ones. Center groups will be those economically and politically aggressive groups wishing to strengthen governmental power and to use the state to promote development; Core groups will be more or less the same as the Center groups considered as culturally or religiously dominant groups seeking to maintain or extend their values over out-groups or minorities which the paternalist Core usually regard as subordinate or inferior. Those outgroups resisting the political, economic, or cultural hegemony of the Center/Core will be regarded as peripheral. It is not claimed here that this is the only way of looking at early U.S. politics, only that it is one approach that permits some comparison with the process of party formation in other Western liberal regimes.

In the 1790s the centralizing, pro-English, and Anglicizing elites of New England and the Middle States controlled the national government and energetically pushed the new Union as far as it would go toward statism and alliance with England. To what extent the federal government would actually function as a central government was *the* issue of the 1790s. It fused with the question of relations with England, as Anglophiles and centralizers coalesced as "federalists" (the party of order), opposed by "republicans" (the party of liberty) who reacted against the government's taking form and acting as a central government. The individualist gentry of the slaveholding South joined with northern representatives of religious, cultural, and status minorities in the Middle and Eastern states under the leadership of the Virginians Madison and Jefferson. In 1800 Jefferson's victory in the presidential electoral college represented a successful "mobilization of the periphery." . . .

The Jeffersonian Republicans, in control of the government for more than a quarter century of peace and war, gradually adopted some of the centralizing policies of their opponents, especially as a result of trying to conduct a war. The Republicans soon advocated a national bank, tariffs, internal improvements, a stronger navy, and other federal measures. With the end of the war and of the long foreign-policy crisis, sectionalism and partisanship collapsed in an era of "good feelings." In some states partisan divisions persisted, but in the mid-1820s, with the election of a New England president, and a Republican who happened to be the son of John Adams and a former Federalist, the old partisan identities, such as they were, completely dissolved.

The first parties, in any case, had not become established as ends in themselves. While some members of the Federal-Republican generation were precocious partisans seeking to regularize political competition with permanent organizations, most early republicans regarded parties as means to ends. Opposition outside of the group of central officeholders was regarded not as healthy criticism of an incumbent administration but as opposition to "government" or "the government." The goals of Federalists and Republicans in power were the same—to eliminate and absorb their opponents. It was fitting that the era should be closed with the presidency of John Quincy Adams, a restless and introspective Puritan who always held parties lightly and who would not even use the appointive power of his office to aid his own re-election.

The lack of institutionalized parties had been particularly evident on the national scene. Of course, interstate planning among like-minded elites influenced national politics, but congressional voting blocs and voting in the electoral college possessed a pronounced sectional basis. National organizations and campaigns as such did not exist. Republicans used the congressional caucus to nominate presidents, while some Federal leaders from different states held two secret meetings, one of which had no nomination at all. Foreign-policy crises in the 1790s and again in the period 1807–1815 had done most to create ideological conflict and to articulate divergent views of domestic policy. When the pressure from outside abated, the differing views of the good society which fueled Federal-Republican competition did not suffice to sustain even the rudimentary level of partisanship attained within the federal arena.

In the states it was different. In Massachusetts, Delaware, Maryland, New Jersey, and Vermont, and in other states in the principal cities and towns, partisan consciousness had grown, and often at least one party and sometimes two had reached rather high levels of development: as parties-in-office, as organizations, and as parties-in-the-electorate. Yet even in the states, these experimental parties did not mature into the kind of political institutions that were to become widespread in the United States by the 1840s.

The period from the 1780s to the 1820s possessed almost a split personality: intensely passionate in partisan conviction but inhibited by powerful antipartisan assumptions about the nature of politics and society. While Federalism and Republicanism pulled the men of that early republican generation toward opposite poles, powerful moderating or centrist tendencies acted as a counterforce. Since party competition was dominant during the rest of the nineteenth century, historians have tended to minimize the significance of the centrist ethos which rivaled partisanship during the first quarter of the nineteenth century. Centrism and antipartyism were expressed especially in a mode which might be called the *Politics of the Revolutionary Center.*

This pattern of politics not only characterized the early republican era in the United States but has flourished in other new nations and has resulted from the quite natural popularity of the military and political leaders of anti-colonial wars for national independence. The warriors and "politicians," that is, the statesmen and public men of the Revolution (in an age when "politician" served as a synonym for "statesman"), provided much of the leadership of both the Federal and the Republican parties. Military heroes or men who were thoroughly identified with the Whig-patriot cause and active in the revolutionary state governments or Continental Congresses, and who possessed a modicum of political ability or ambition, enjoyed long careers in politics. Many of these men could in most states be found as popular consensus candidates enjoying bipartisan support, especially for the higher elective offices in the gift of the people. . . .

The appeal to the Revolutionary mainstream by Federalists and Republicans expressed in part the antipartisan tendencies of the political culture. At the same time many states were already heterogeneous in social composition, containing various and often antagonistic cultural, religious, status, economic, and geographic groups. And the alignment of these groups as between Federalists and Republicans tended to polarize, as in the nation, between Core (or Center) and Periphery.

In Massachusetts and Rhode Island, one readily sees a geographic pattern of political alignment, with the commercial centers and ancient cores tending toward Federalism. In New Hampshire, however, Republicans tended to be stronger in the coastal towns than in other regions. Indeed, Republicans did well elsewhere in many of the growing and rapidly changing ports, and especially in towns where small manufacturing had begun. Within the cities of Philadelphia and New York, Federalism remained strong the longest in the oldest and wealthiest wards. Baltimore, a boom town filled with outsiders and new wealth, turned to Republicanism early, but while supporting Jeffersonian policy in national affairs, Baltimore's Republicans fell into disarray on state and local issues. In such states as New Jersey, Delaware, Virginia, and North Carolina, Federal strength had a distinct regional cast. But the Core-Periphery conflict was not only geographic. It usually expressed several heavily overlapping lines of division: geographic, cultural, religious, status, or economic.

Cultural and religious division appeared to shape Core-Periphery alignments as frequently as did any other division. In New England the dominant Congregational churches were strongly Federal, while dissenting religious groups, especially the Baptists and Methodists, gave the Republicans their surest sources of support. In Pennsylvania the Scotch-Irish and Germans swelled Republican majorities, while English-stock Quakers there and in New Jersey were staunchly Federal. Cultural and religious groups which enjoyed the highest status and which tended to dominate more recently arrived or historically subordinate peoples tended, in short, to be Federal, whereas those groups "beyond the pale" of core culture, core religion, or core status were peripheral and tended to be Republican.

In Delaware the core English stock lived downstate on the richest agricultural land in Kent and Sussex counties. Originally Anglican, the growing population there turned increasingly to Methodism. Delaware remained one of the few states in which Federalism survived well into the nineteenth century, and it did so in Kent and Sussex, which Jefferson once characterized as virtually "counties of England." Meanwhile, Republican majorities came from upstate New Castle County, which the historian of early Delaware called "the Rhode Island of Delaware—the county that was otherwise." New Castle was heterogeneous in its social and cultural life, receiving a continuing in-migration of Scotch-Irish Presbyterians and other non-English groups, and possessing, as lower Delaware did not, rising ports and cities, water power, and manufacturing. Thus in Delaware, an English, agrarian, Methodist, and downstate Core regularly opposed a non-English, non-Methodist, upstate, manufacturing, and commercial Periphery.

By the 1820s, when the last remnants of Federal-Republican competition died away, national political life had long been dominated by the Republican establishment. At the same time that the men of the Revolution aged and left the political arena, the social environment began to change in ways that would make possible an institutional development of party organizations not possible in the Federal-Republican era. In addition, attitudes to political party competition changed as the growing class of professional politicians increasingly believed that the partisan rivalry of 1800 to 1815 had had beneficial results for the welfare of the Republic.

The 1820s were among those watershed decades in which several different eras seemed to die and to be born and during which a confluence of material and spiritual changes combined to launch society and politics in new directions. In the mid-1840s Ralph Waldo Emerson looked back and decided that the period from about 1820 to 1840 had been an age of "great activity of thought and experimenting," and one in which the world had changed greatly. Many of his contemporaries agreed, and many later observers have also concurred.

Amid many kinds of changes, those associated with what historians have called the transportation and communications "revolutions" probably did the most to create the technical potential for mass political organizations. The difficulty of travel in the United States of 1800 is well known. By 1840 great improvements had been made, even before the creation of an extensive railroad network. And the speed with which mail and news traveled increased greatly *before* the invention of the telegraph. The growth in the number of post offices was an indicator of many changes: better roads, more rapid systems of travel by land and sea, increased commerce, greater interdependence, and, of course, a greater volume of mail. From 1790 to 1828 the population of the country grew 3.3 times, but post offices multiplied 107 times, from 75 to almost 8,500. In 1790 there was one post office for every 52,389 persons—forty years later one for every 1,597 persons. And while the amount of correspondence also burgeoned, newspapers formed by far the heaviest component of the mails. In the same period the number of papers published went from 92 to 861—and in 1840 the figure was over 1,400. In Massachusetts over 90 newspapers were published in 1840, an average of one for every 2,000 voters, a ratio well below the national average.

Newspapers became essential to the organization of parties, as vehicles of intraparty communication, as proselytizing agents, as a kind of public-address system to supporters, and sometimes as forums for debating controversial issues. Editors and publishers rose in political power and status, and usually were part of or close to the inner circles of leaders who ran factions and parties.

Indeed, post offices and newspapers provided basic building blocs of political patronage. By the 1830s party politicians had gone far toward tying together these elements of the communications and patronage systems into political engines. This process, while gradual throughout the years from 1800 to 1830, accelerated after Andrew Jackson's inauguration in 1829 and especially during his second term as the Jacksonian, or Democratic, Republicans prepared to elect Martin Van Buren to the presidency. Of course, other branches of the federal government also became important patronage networks by which to reward loyal partisans and to put them into positions of influence to promote the party's cause. For example, the Customs Service, the Internal Revenue Service, Land Office, and the Indian Bureau, some of which had been politicized earlier, all became thoroughly exploited. The Jackson administration's support of Isaac Hill's Concord Regency in its attempt to politicize the Portsmouth branch of the Bank of the United States became one of the precipitating causes of the "Bank War." But the Post Office, extending as it did throughout the land, and constituting a nodal point for the transmission of information, best reflected the uses made of patronage and new communications capacities in the organization of parties.

In the 1820s the vast majority of citizens had lost interest in politics. They had never voted much in presidential elections anyway, and now they involved themselves only sporadically in state and local affairs. The presidential contests of 1828 and 1832 awakened some significant voter interest, however, and began a process, culminating in 1840, by which most citizens would place great importance on presidential elections. This attentiveness to national affairs initially resulted less from an expanded suffrage or improved communications than from the emergence of an opposition to Adams's administration (1825–1829) which used anticentralizing and antistatist appeals similar to those of the Jeffersonian Republicans in the 1790s. Portrayed as a man of the new West and as a hero of the people, the slaveholder Andrew Jackson occupied the presidency in 1829 as a result once again of the mobilization of the Periphery against a presumed threat from a hegemonic Center. While John Quincy Adams and his secretary of state Henry Clay were economic nationalists, the actions of the federal government were hardly aggressive under the second Adams. Although his inaugural raised the specter of a "consolidating" (that is, centralizing) state, his administration was pitfully weak in dealing with the onslaught of its opponents, and the threats against which the Periphery mobilized from 1825 to 1828 were in large part of politicians' manufacture. Once again a sectional division in the presidential electoral vote quite like that of 1800 occurred, and a triumphant antistatist Periphery took over the appointive power. Political parties, however, were not yet organized. . . .

The Political Cultures of 1828

JOHN WILLIAM WARD

. . . One of the many indices to the difference between Jeffersonian and Jacksonian democracy is to observe the shift in mental attitude that supported each. The shift may be one of emphasis, as all shifts in intellectual history are, but it is fair to say that where the Jeffersonians rested their case on the power of man's mind, the Jacksonians rested theirs on the prompting of man's heart. However, the Jacksonian rejection of the mind was not as simple as this statement might make it seem. The reason of the university was rejected in behalf of the higher reason of nature. . . .

When in the election of 1824 the selection of the President devolved upon the House of Representatives, an article in a western newspaper offered two reasons why Jackson should be the choice. The first reason was the simple one that he had received the most votes. The second was that he was the best qualified.

> In regard to the second point [wrote the editor] we conceive General Jackson to be the only man among the candidates, to whom it will apply, and for one simple, but all-powerful reason—he alone of the three is gifted with genius—with those great powers of mind that can generalize with as much ease as a common intellect can go through detail. Endowed with the faculties to see the whole, and grasp the most remote relations of vast and comprehensive designs, he is the most qualified to govern. We should blush, if we could say with truth, that he would make a good secretary of the

From *Andrew Jackson: Symbol for an Age* by John William Ward. Copyright © 1955, 1983 by John William Ward, pp. 49–52, 64–71. Reprinted by permission of Oxford University Press, Inc.

Treasury, of the Navy, of State, or of the Post Office. We hope and we believe that he would not; we hope that he is above such works, incompetent he cannot be. But for great designs he is fashioned by nature, and therefore would he advance the general interest and glory of this republic, beyond any other man.

One attribute of 'genius,' according to this account, is its superiority to detail, the area to which the understanding is restricted. Here . . . the Jacksonians anticipate the Transcendental scheme which opposed Genius to Talent, just as Reason is opposed to Understanding. In the next Presidential election of 1828, another publicist of the Jackson cause made the same point: 'As to the qualifications of Gen. Jackson . . . we shall say but little. His services . . . prove him. . . . He has unfortunately, perhaps for himself, (but fortunately for his country,) been called to act on some most trying occasions, when safety was to be found only in that bold and decided course which is ever pursued by Nature's great men, but which is far above the reach of the man of official detail.' In New Hampshire, it was suggested that the bold and decided course would necessarily be impeded by acquaintance with the forms of official detail. 'Nor have I much respect [said Nathan B. Felton] for the long unprofitable experience of a plodding politician, and diplomatist. . . . Jackson is one of the most distinguished statesmen in our country; for acuteness and penetration of mind. He is one of the few great men, who, untrammeled by forms, are qualified, by nature, to innovate, successfully upon the maxims of those who have gone before them.' The Jacksonians of New York concurred: 'Jackson is recommended . . . by his *capacity*. He possesses in an extraordinary degree, that native strength of mind, that practical common sense, that power and discrimination of judgement which, for all useful purposes, are more valuable than all the acquired learning of a sage.' The Jacksonians upstate agreed with the stress on Jackson's 'native' strength of mind: 'We do not claim for General Jackson the distinction of the academy . . . but we do claim for him those higher attributes which an active public life alone can teach, and which can never be acquired in the halls of the university—a knowledge of mankind. . . . We claim for him, above all other qualities, an integrity never known to yield to interest or ambition, and a judgement unclouded by the visionary speculations of the academician.' A Boston editor, also stressing Jackson's 'natural sense,' concluded that 'it can never be acquired by reading books—it can only be acquired, in perfection, by reading men.' . . . One of the factors in Jackson's success [in 1828] seems to have been that the people believed that their will had been thwarted in the election of 1824. Another was that, running against an ex-Harvard professor, Jackson embodied a rejection of the intellectual.

The followers of Adams never could bring themselves to believe that the American people in selecting a President could spurn a trained diplomatist and statesman like John Quincy Adams and embrace a man so eminently unqualified by background as Andrew Jackson. Their only solace finally had to be that of another Adams that the people, being coarse, preferred a coarse instrument. But before a coarse people had laid rude hands on John Quincy Adams, he and his supporters made their appeal on the grounds of the intricacy of government and the need of training for its proper administration. 'General Jackson is not qualified [went the address of the friends of Adams in New Hampshire] . . . he has had little experience . . . If elected, could he possibly, even with the best intentions, discharge the complicated and arduous duties of President.' To prove Jackson's lack of qualifications the friends of Adams were not above circulating forgeries which demonstrated Jackson's illiteracy. An Adams campaign pamphlet purporting to be an impartial and true history of Jackson asked with horror, 'What will the English malignants . . . the Edinburgh and Quarterly reviewers,—who have hitherto defamed even the best writings of our countrymen, say of a people who want a man to govern them who cannot spell *more than about one word in four?*' The answer should have been fairly obvious. The people didn't give much of a damn what the English malignants thought and, as has been the case until recently in American politics, were disposed to support the candidate who stood at the farthest pole from English opinion. Adams's campaign on the basis of learning and experience was, as a student of Ohio has said, 'not of the sort to arouse popular enthusiasm.'

In the election of 1828, the American people were presented with a choice between the plowman and the professor that was not limited to the area of morals, although morals figured prominently in the campaign. But the Jacksonians did not repudiate academic training, personified in the Harvard professor, simply to embrace ignorance in its stead. Pursuing the distinction between reason and understanding, they took the higher ground that the type of intelligence represented by Adams was the corruption of real intelligence.

> That Mr. Adams is possessed of *learning* [wrote the Republican General Committee of New York City] we are willing to admit. We are not ignorant that he has received a college education—that he has been a professor of rhetoric. . . . He may be a philosopher, a lawyer, an elegant scholar, and a poet, too, forsooth (we know he wrote doggerel verses upon Mr. Jefferson,) and yet the nation may be little better off for all these endowments and accomplishments. That he is *learned* we are willing to admit; but his *wisdom* we take leave to question. . . . We confess our attachment to the homely doctrine; thus happily expressed by the great Englis[h] poet:—
>> That not to know of things remote
>> From use, obscure and subtle, but to know
>> That which before us lies in daily life,
>> Is the prime wisdom.'
> That wisdom we believe Gen. Jackson possesses in an eminent degree.

The contrast between learning and wisdom was also implicit in the sarcasm of a Boston editor, probably Theodore Lyman:

> Plain simple common sense [marks Jackson's style. One] will encounter few brilliant metaphors, no Greek quotations, no toilsome and painful struggles after eloquence—. . . But Mr. Adams is a learned man; he reads Byron and Puffendorf, and Jean Jacques Rousseau; has studied chemistry and meteorology, and metaphysics, and will dispute with any man 'de omnibus rebus et quibusdam aliis' . . . were I am [*sic*] a member of the Corporation

at Harvard, I should certainly defer a selection of a president of that Institution till after the Ides of March.

An Ohio paper stressed that Jackson did not secure his knowledge 'from Voltaire, and Oriental legends,' but it introduced another element by expressing confidence in the old hero because he was 'not raised in the lap of luxury and wealth.' The corruption of wisdom by learning, of Reason by Understanding, is here linked to the material advance of society, the movement away from nature. In national terms the problem could then be phrased as the simple West *versus* the effete East; in a wider frame of reference, as the United States *versus* Europe. For the American mind Europe stood for tradition, training, and luxury. The repudiation of formal training was thus inextricably involved with the repudiation of Europe, and the two attitudes lent each other mutual support. This is part of the significance of the boast that Andrew Jackson had not spent his life in foreign courts. To account for the fall from grace of another westerner, the western press said of Henry Clay that 'once he was the open and frank servant of the people. . . . Since his return from Europe, he has been a changed man.' The reason education and culture, represented by Europe, could be dismissed is that they were conceived to be at best no more than adornments to the natural intellect. Thus Levi Woodbury, while asserting that Jackson was a great statesman, did not wish to claim for him 'what he himself was the last man to tolerate as deserved—any deep researches into the writings of political economists, or that wide range of historical reading which *sometimes* instructs, no less than it adorns. . . . He had been endowed, by nature, with a strong intellect.' Even the suggestion of qualification was repugnant to another eulogist: 'Regular and classical education has been thought by some distinguished men, to be unfavorable to great vigour and originality of the understanding; and that, like civilization, whilst it made society more interesting and agreeable, yet, at the same time, it levelled the distinctions of nature. That whilst it strengthened and assisted the feeble, it was calculated to deprive the strong of their triumph, and beat down the hopes of the aspiring. . . . Andrew Jackson escaped the training and dialects of the schools.'

Jackson's political friend, John Henry Eaton, played on these ideas in his famous *Letters of Wyoming*.

It is certainly necessary, remarked a gentleman the other day, [wrote Eaton] that the President of the United States should be acquainted with the particular etiquette and ceremonies which appertain to the intercourse of different courts. Of Jackson I entertain the most exalted opinion, but then he has been reared in the interior and having never been to any of the European courts it is impossible he should be informed on those rules of polite intercourse, which the head of a nation should be acquainted with. . . . To wiser heads [commented Eaton], and to those who may be conversant in the sublime science of dancing, is it left for discussion, if in the choice of a Chief Magistrate, if it be a material inquiry, whether he may bow with the right or left foot foremast [sic]. Upon this subject the constitution is silent.

I am indeed sorry to see my country manifest such fondness and partiality for exotics. In manners, dress, and language we are imitators, and borrowers from abroad; native genius sinks. . . . All that we have national, is our government, and even that, ere long, without much caution, will have introduced into it, many notions and idioms, other than the growth of this country; already have some appeared: witness for example those things called etiquette and courtly parade (and nonsense) so much in vogue at our metropolis. . . .

But 'tis folly I know to rail against fashion; she is a tyrant that has long ruled us and will bear sway. In Europe she has decreed that kings shall rule, and the people submit. In this wilderness, as if by magic, a new and different order of things has appeared; but vigilance apart and that order will soon be encroached upon. Well! be it so.

In Eaton's conversation with his imaginary gentleman, Jackson, simplicity, and native genius are counterpoised against the metropolis, exoticism, and the influence of Europe. The diplomat, here reduced to the level of the dancing master, has nothing to bring to the United States except the corruption of Europe. The founding fathers have embodied all necessary governmental wisdom in the Constitution, which needs no additions. More important is the stress upon the wilderness as the magical source of Republicanism, with the implication of a radical break with Europe and civilization and the further suggestion that the interior, the West, still in touch with the wilderness, maintains the promise of American life.

Francis Boylies of Massachusetts had made the same point when he said that '[Jackson] had not the privilege of visiting *the courts of Europe at public expense* and mingling with the kings and great men of the earth and glittering in the beams of royal splendor. He grew up in the wilds of the West, but he was the noblest tree in the forest. He was not dandled into consequence by lying in the cradle of state, but inured from infancy to the storms and tempests of life, his mind was strengthened to fortitude and fashioned to wisdom.' The West might not have the artificial brilliance of Europe, but it possessed substance which Europe lacked. Employing an image that has remained a favorite in American expression, a New York Jacksonian drew an analogy between the first Adams and George Washington and the second Adams and Andrew Jackson. 'The discernment of our fathers [he wrote], unseduced by artificial splendour, knew well how little the value of the diamond depends upon its polish. Undeceived by the sound of learning and diplomacy, they saw and prized . . . those intrinsic and substantial qualities, which their sons appreciate in the Hero of New Orleans.'

Perhaps the greatest irony of the campaign of 1828 was the success of the Jacksonians in casting upon John Quincy Adams the stigma of sensuality and profligacy. The imputation was achieved by connecting Adams, through his foreign service, to Europe. As one student of the period has observed, 'To accuse that forbidding Puritan in the executive mansion of carousing all night with wastrels and sharpers was a feat even for the Nineteenth Congress; but the accusation was, after all, no more than the *reductio ad absurdum* of the people's case against him.'

In an attempt to dispose of Jackson's claim to simplicity, the administration press made the facetious suggestion that should he be elected President he could effect a great saving in the executive department by living upon acorns. The allusion was to a widespread story about Jackson concerning an incident supposed to have occurred after the battle of Talledega in the Creek campaign. When the troops were without provisions, a soldier spied Jackson seated beneath a tree eating. Deciding that what was good enough for the officers was good enough for the men, he approached Jackson and reproached him for eating while his men were without bread. Jackson replied, 'I will most cheerfully divide with you such food as I have,' and offered the private a handful of acorns upon which he was dining. The story varied in the telling. Some versions had Jackson offer the meal to his junior officers to drive home to them their duty to the troops, but the moral remained the same. At first the story was used to stress Jackson's sacrifice in the field; later it was used to contrast the hard simplicity of Jackson's life with the soft degeneracy of Adams. As an Ohioan expressed it, 'Although General Jackson has not been educated at foreign courts and reared on sweetmeats from the tables of kings and princes, we think him nevertheless much better qualified to fill the dignified station of president of the United States than Mr. Adams.'

Underlying the rejection of education and training, which were personified in John Quincy Adams, was the assumption that, at best, training was unnecessary and, at worst, it corrupted reason, which is intrinsic and not acquired. The sentiment should have sounded familiar to an Adams whose Puritan forbears had argued in rejecting the embellishment of man-made ritual that 'God's Altar needs not our pollishings.' In similar fashion, as in the 'diamond in the rough' analogy, Adams's contemporary opponents argued that God's handiwork, Man, needed not the ornamental polish of human institutions. . . .

✠ *F U R T H E R   R E A D I N G*

Harry Ammon, *James Monroe: The Quest for National Identity* (1971)
Samuel Flagg Bemis, *John Quincy Adams and the Union* (1956)
———, *John Quincy Adams and the Foundations of American Foreign Policy* (1949)
George Dangerfield, *The Awakening of American Nationalism, 1815–1828* (1965)
———, *The Era of Good Feelings* (1952)
Donald E. Fehrenbacher, *The South and Three Sectional Crises* (1980)
Mary H. W. Hargreaves, *The Presidency of John Quincy Adams* (1985)
Shaw Livermore, *The Twilight of Federalism: The Disintegration of the Federalist Party, 1815–1830* (1962)
John Lofton, *Denmark Vesey's Revolt* (1983)
Ernest R. May, *The Making of the Monroe Doctrine* (1975)
Glover Moore, *The Missouri Controversy, 1819–1821* (1953)
Bradford Perkins, *Castlereagh and Adams: England and the United States, 1812–1823* (1964)
Dexter Perkins, *A History of the Monroe Doctrine* (1963)
Merrill D. Peterson, ed., *Democracy, Liberty, and Property: The State Constitutional Conventions of the 1820s* (1966)
Robert V. Remini, *The Election of Andrew Jackson* (1963)

Samuel Rezneck, "The Depression of 1819–1822, A Social History," *American Historical Review* 39 (1933), 28–47

Murray N. Rothbard, *The Panic of 1819: Reactions and Policies* (1962)

Charles Grier Sellers, Jr., "Jackson Men with Feet of Clay," *American Historical Review* 62 (1957), 537–551

P. J. Staudenraus, " 'Era of Good Feelings' Reconsidered," *Mid-America* 38 (1956), 180–194

Charles S. Sydnor, "The One-Party Period of American History," *American Historical Review* 51 (1946), 439–451

Michael Wallace, "Changing Concepts of Party in the United States: New York, 1815–1828," *American Historical Review* 74 (1968), 453–491

Jacksonians, Whigs, and the Politics of the 1830s

⊞

Whatever doubts Americans had about Andrew Jackson's political intentions evaporated during his first administration. Jackson's early pronouncements on Indian removal and internal improvements signaled new departures in executive policy. In the subsequent war on the Second Bank of the United States, and the nullification crisis, the president acted with disarming firmness while he and his aides fashioned a coherent egalitarian ideology. ''The majority is to govern,'' Jackson thundered—and with this basic refrain, the Jacksonians consolidated the first mass democratic party in modern history.

The Jacksonians' opponents, who after 1829 included growing numbers of offended ex-allies, were quick to condemn what was happening but slow to build a national alliance to rival the Democrats. Only in the mid-1830s did the Whig party supersede the tattered National Republican alliance and come into its own. Although the Whigs honored the virtues of Henry Clay's American System of protective tariffs and federally-funded internal improvements, they initially fell on the defensive, bemoaning the administration's alleged tyranny, spoilsmanship, and fiscal incompetence. Gradually, however, they adapted to the new political realities and learned to counterpunch with a democratic rhetoric of prosperity and moral rectitude. In 1840, helped by a brutal depression, the Whigs unseated Jackson's loyal successor, Martin Van Buren, and elected to the White House their own personal backwoods general, William Henry Harrison.

National politics had not been so fractious since the 1790s. But were the Jacksonians truly the champions of common workers and farmers, as they claimed—out to destroy all vestiges of favoritism and political inequality? Were their attacks on the vested interests really as radical as they sometimes sounded, or did they betray a conservative nostalgia for a mythic simpler past? Were the Jacksonian leaders, as some historians insist, actually political opportunists—or self-serving capitalists—masquerading as populists? Or were they what other historians call herrenvolk *(i.e., master race) democrats, sincerely vigilant in the defense of white men's rights but irrevocably tied to slavery and an ideology of racial subjugation? And how should we judge the Whigs? As unimaginative conservatives? Idealistic moralizers? Democratic capitalists? Antidemocratic capitalists? Might these very categories be misleading, given that both parties drew on diverse coalitions, each containing contending points of view?*

Behind these matters of political labeling lurk further questions. What was at stake in the bank war and the nullification crisis, apart from the critical constitutional issues? What did the theory and practice of Jacksonian Indian policy signify? Did the so-called second party system—Whigs versus Democrats—involve a revival of the old divisions between Jeffersonians and Federalists (as Van Buren claimed) or something different? What were the connections between the Democrats' and Whigs' respective coalitions and the continuing impact of the market revolution?

Clearly, something—or some things—shook American politics in the 1830s. Assessing what they were and what they produced is one of the major problems in all of U.S. history.

⧉ D O C U M E N T S

Years later, the Democrat James Hamilton recalled a startling incident in 1827, relayed in the first document, that he thought suggestive of Andrew Jackson's character. In Jackson's annual message of 1830, excerpted in the second document, the president explained his Indian removal plans; in the third selection, his veto of the Maysville Road improvement bill that same year earns a swift reply from his old Kentucky nemesis Henry Clay, the National Republican and future Whig leader. (Note where the road was supposed to run.) The South Carolina nullification crisis, the subject of the fourth, multipart selection, brought the long-simmering battle over the tariff, as well as the feud between Jackson and John C. Calhoun, to the brink of a military showdown. Intellectually and politically, the crisis described the limits of both southern sectionalism and Jacksonian states' rights localism in the 1830s. Jackson's bank veto message, excerpted in the first part of document five, proved the most electrifying Democratic political statement of the 1830s; Daniel Webster's reply elaborates the objections of the enraged opposition on constitutional and economic grounds. Shortly after Jackson's veto, a partisan cartoonist sketched the Jacksonians' view of the opposition (see document six). A contrasting, apocalyptic view of the Democratic party turns up in a diary excerpt (document seven) of the Whig Philip Hone, a leading conservative gentleman-politician.

In 1836 the Democratic ticket of Van Buren and Richard Mentor Johnson (the purported slayer of Tecumseh) defeated a divided field of challengers. But the Van Buren presidency quickly ran into difficulties. Abolitionist petitions swamped the Congress, demanding an end to slavery in the District of Columbia; an alliance of congressional Democrats and southern Whigs shut off debate by enforcing a gag rule (document eight) automatically tabling the petitions. Ex-President John Quincy Adams, now a Massachusetts Whig congressman, led an unyielding, often lonely fight against the gag. The forced westward march of the Cherokees along the notorious Trail of Tears was the subject of a Maine traveler's newspaper dispatch, reprinted as the ninth selection. (Van Buren later expressed satisfaction at the removal process.) Meanwhile, the Panic of 1837 triggered a prolonged depression, which the Whigs blamed on Jackson's banking policies and Van Buren's hard-money stance. Taking to the woods, the Whigs successfully promoted their own "log-cabin" nominee, William Henry Harrison, in 1840 (although the candidate had been reared in a Virginia mansion and was quite well off). A bit of campaign fluff in the form of an 1840 Whig songsheet shows what the party was up to. A somewhat more substantive and revealing summary of Whig political professions appeared four years later in Calvin Colton's *Junius Papers,* excerpted in the final documentary reading.

A Retrospective Glance at the Character of Andrew Jackson, 1827

The steamer Pocahontas was chartered by citizens of New Orleans to convey the General and his party from Nashville to that city. She was fitted out in the most sumptuous manner. The party was General and Mrs. Jackson, two gentlemen with their wives, a young lady, Miss B—, Governor Samuel Houston, Wm. B. Lewis, Robert Armstrong, and others, and the New York delegate. The only freight was the General's cotton-crop.

During the voyage we stopped at the different towns on the river, at the most of which the people were assembled; and at the principal ones, committees addressed the General, to whom he made appropriate replies. In the course of the voyage an event occurred, which I repeat, as it is suggestive of character. A steamer of greater speed than ours, going in the same direction, passed us, crossed our bow; then stopped and let us pass her; and then passed us again in triumph. This was repeated again and again, until the General, being excited by the offensive course, ordered a rifle to be brought to him; hailed the pilot of the other steamer, and swore that if he did the same thing again he would shoot him. As I believed the General was in earnest, and as such an outrage could not be of service to our cause, I went below and stated to Mrs. Jackson what had occurred; she said mildly, "Colonel, do me the favor to say to the General I wish to speak to him." I did so. He went to the cabin with me, and remained there in chat with her.

President Jackson on Indian Removal, 1830

The condition and ulterior destiny of the Indian tribes within the limits of some of our States have become objects of much interest and importance. It has long been the policy of Government to introduce among them the arts of civilization, in the hope of gradually reclaiming them from a wandering life. This policy has, however, been coupled with another wholly incompatible with its success. Professing a desire to civilize and settle them, we have at the same time lost no opportunity to purchase their lands and thrust them farther into the wilderness. By this means they have not only been kept in a wandering state, but been led to look upon us as unjust and indifferent to their fate. Thus, though lavish in its expenditures upon the subject, Government has constantly defeated its own policy, and the Indians in general, receding farther and farther to the west, have retained their savage habits. A portion, however, of the Southern tribes, having mingled much with the whites and made some progress in the arts of civilized life, have lately attempted to erect an independent government within the limits of Georgia and Alabama. These States, claiming to be the only sovereigns within their territories, extended their laws over the Indians, which induced the latter to call upon the United States for protection.

Under these circumstances the question presented was whether the General Government had a right to sustain those people in their pretensions. The Constitution declares that "no new State shall be formed or erected within the jurisdiction of any other State" without the consent of its legislature. If the General Government is not permitted to tolerate the erection of a confederate State within the territory of one of the members of this Union against her consent, much less could it allow a foreign and independent government to establish itself there. Georgia became a member of the Confederacy which eventuated in our Federal Union as a sovereign State, always asserting her claim to certain limits, which, having been originally defined in her colonial charter and subsequently recognized in the treaty of peace, she has ever since continued to enjoy, except as they have been circumscribed by her own voluntary transfer of a portion of her territory to the United States in the articles of cession of 1802. Alabama was admitted into the Union on the same footing with the original States, with boundaries which were prescribed by Congress. There is no constitutional, conventional, or legal provision which allows them less power over the Indians within their borders than is possessed by Maine or New York. Would the people of Maine permit the Penobscot tribe to erect an independent government within their State? And unless they did would it not be the duty of the General Government to support them in resisting such a measure? Would the people of New York permit each remnant of the Six Nations within her borders to declare itself an independent people under the protection of the United States? Could the Indians establish a separate republic on each of their reservations in Ohio? And if they were so disposed would it be the duty of this Government to protect them in the attempt? If the principle involved in the obvious answer to these questions be abandoned, it will follow that the objects of this Government are reversed, and that it has become a part of its duty to aid in destroying the States which it was established to protect.

Actuated by this view of the subject, I informed the Indians inhabiting parts of Georgia and Alabama that their attempt to establish an independent government would not be countenanced by the Executive of the United States, and advised them to emigrate beyond the Mississippi or submit to the laws of those States.

Our conduct toward these people is deeply interesting to our national character. Their present condition, contrasted with what they once were, makes a most powerful appeal to our sympathies. Our ancestors found them the uncontrolled possessors of these vast regions. By persuasion and force they have been made to retire from river to river and from mountain to mountain, until some of the tribes have become extinct and others have left but remnants to preserve for awhile their once terrible names. Surrounded by the whites with their arts of civilization, which by destroying the resources of the savage doom him to weakness and decay, the fate of the Mohegan, the Narragansett, and the Delaware is fast overtaking the Choctaw, the Cherokee, and the Creek. That this fate surely awaits them if they remain within the limits of the States does not admit of a doubt. Humanity and national honor demand that every effort should be made to avert so great a calamity. It is too late to inquire whether it was just in the United States to include them and their territory within the bounds of new States, whose limits they could control. That step can not be retraced. A State can not be dismembered by Congress or restricted in the exercise of her constitutional power. But the people of those States and of every State, actuated by feelings of justice and a regard for our national honor, submit to you the interesting question whether something can not be done, consistently with the rights of the States, to preserve this much-injured race.

As a means of effecting this end I suggest for your consideration the propriety of setting apart an ample district west of the Mississippi, and without the limits of any State or Territory now formed, to be guaranteed to the Indian tribes as long as they shall occupy it, each tribe having a distinct control over the portion designated for its use. There they may be secured in the enjoyment of governments of their own choice, subject to no other control from the United States than such as may be necessary to preserve peace on the frontier and between the several tribes. There the benevolent may endeavor to teach them the arts of civilization, and, by promoting union and harmony among them, to raise up an interesting commonwealth, destined to perpetuate the race and to attest the humanity and justice of this Government.

This emigration should be voluntary, for it would be as cruel as unjust to compel the aborigines to abandon the graves of their fathers and seek a home in a distant land. But they should be distinctly informed that if they remain within the limits of the States they must be subject to their laws. In return for their obedience as individuals they will without doubt be protected in the enjoyment of those possessions which they have improved by their industry. But it seems to me visionary to suppose that in this state of things claims can be allowed on tracts of country on which they have neither dwelt nor made improvements, merely because they have seen them from the mountain or passed them in the chase. Submitting to the laws of the States, and receiving, like other citizens, protection in their persons and property, they will ere long become merged in the mass of our population. . . .

Jackson and Internal Improvements:
The Maysville Road, 1830

Jackson's Veto Message, May 27, 1830

To the House of Representatives.

GENTLEMEN: I have maturely considered the bill proposing to authorize "a subscription of stock in the Maysville, Washington, Paris, and Lexington Turnpike Road Company," and now return the same to the House of Representatives, in which it originated, with my objections to its passage. . . .

The bill before me does not call for a more definite opinion upon the particular circumstances which will warrant appropriations of money by Congress to aid works of internal improvement, for although the extension of the power to apply money beyond that of carrying into effect the object for which it is appropriated has, as we have seen, been long claimed and exercised by the Federal Government, yet such grants have always been professedly under the control of the general principle that the works which might be thus aided should be "of a general, not local, national, not State," character. A disregard of this distinction would of necessity lead to the subversion of the federal system. That even this is an unsafe one, arbitrary in its nature, and liable, consequently, to great abuses, is too obvious to require the confirmation of experience. It is, however, sufficiently definite and imperative to my mind to forbid my approbation of any bill having the character of the one under consideration. I have given to its provisions all the reflection demanded by a just regard for the interests of those of our fellow-citizens who have desired its passage, and by the respect which is due to a coordinate branch of the Government, but I am not able to view it in any other light than as a measure of purely local character; or, if it can be considered national, that no further distinction between the appropriate duties of the General and State Governments need be attempted, for there can be no local interest that may not with equal propriety be denominated national. It has no connection with any established system of improvements; is exclusively within the limits of a State [Kentucky], starting at a point on the Ohio River and running out 60 miles to an interior town, and even as far as the State is interested conferring partial instead of general advantages. . . .

Although many of the States, with a laudable zeal and under the influence of an enlightened policy, are successfully applying their separate efforts to works of this character, the desire to enlist the aid of the General Government in the construction of such as from their nature ought to devolve upon it, and to which the means of the individual States are inadequate, is both rational and patriotic, and if that desire is not gratified now it does not follow that it never will be. The general intelligence and public spirit of the American people furnish a sure guaranty that at the proper time this policy will be made to prevail under circumstances more auspicious to its successful prosecution than those which now exist. But great as this object undoubtedly is, it is not the only one which demands the fostering care of the Government. The preservation and success of the republican principle rest with us. To elevate its character and extend its influence rank among our most important duties, and the best means to accomplish this desirable end are those which will rivet the attachment of our citizens to the Government of their choice by the comparative lightness of their public burthens and by the attraction which the superior success of its operations will present to the admiration and respect of the world. Through the favor of an overruling and indulgent Providence our country is blessed with general prosperity and our citizens exempted from the pressure of taxation, which other less favored portions of the human family are obliged to bear; yet it is true that many of the taxes collected from our citizens through the medium of imposts have for a considerable period been onerous. In many particulars these taxes have borne severely upon the laboring and less prosperous classes of the community, being imposed on the necessaries of life, and this, too, in cases where the burthen was not relieved by the consciousness that it would ultimately contribute to make us independent of foreign nations for articles of prime necessity by the encouragement of their growth and manufacture at home. They have been cheerfully borne because they were thought to be necessary to the support of Government and the payment of the debts unavoidably incurred in the acquisition and maintenance of our national rights and liberties. But have we a right to calculate on the same cheerful acquiescence when it is known that the necessity for their continuance would cease were it not for irregular, improvident, and unequal appropriations of the public funds? Will not the people demand, as they have a right to do, such a prudent system of expenditure as will pay the debts of the Union and authorize the reduction of every tax to as low a point as the wise observance of the necessity to protect that portion of our manufactures and labor whose prosperity is essential to our national safety and independence will allow? When the national debt is paid, the duties upon those articles which we do not raise may be repealed with safety, and still leave, I trust, without oppression to any section of the country, an accumulating surplus fund, which may be beneficially applied to some well-digested system of improvement. . . .

If it be the wish of the people that the construction of roads and canals should be conducted by the Federal Government, it is not only highly expedient, but indispensably necessary, that a previous amendment of the Constitution, delegating the necessary power and defining and restricting its exercise with reference to the sovereignty of the States, should be made. Without it nothing extensively useful can be effected. . . .

A supposed connection between appropriations for internal improvement and the system of protecting duties, growing out of the anxieties of those more immediately interested in their success, has given rise to suggestions which it is proper I should notice on this occasion. My opinions on these subjects have never been concealed from those who had a right to know them. . . .

As long as the encouragement of domestic manufactures is directed to national ends it shall receive from me a temperate but steady support. . . .

Henry Clay Responds, 1830

With respect to the American system . . . its great object is to secure the independence of our country, to augment its wealth, and to diffuse the comforts of civilization throughout society. . . . It has increased the wealth, and power, and population of the nation. It has diminished the price of articles of consumption, and has placed them within the reach of a far greater number of our people than could have found means to command them, if they had been manufactured abroad instead of at home. . . . Its opponents opened the campaign at the last session of Congress, and, with the most obliging frankness, have since publicly exposed their plan of operations. It is, to divide and conquer; to attack and subdue the system in detail. . . .

The strategem which has been adopted by the foes of the system, to destroy it, requires the exercise of constant vigilance and firmness, to prevent the accomplishment of the object. They have resolved to divide and conquer—the friends of the system should assume the revolutionary motto of our ancestors, "United we stand, divided we fall." . . . If any thing could be considered as settled, under the present Constitution of our government, I had supposed that it was its authority to construct such internal improvements as may be deemed by Congress necessary and proper to carry into effect the power granted to it. For nearly twenty-five years, the power has been asserted and exercised by the government. . . . This power, necessary to all parts of the Union, is indispensable to the West. Without it, this section can never enjoy any part of the benefit of a regular disbursement of the vast revenues of the United States. . . . Yet we are told that this power can no longer be exercised without an amendment of the Constitution. . . .

If I could believe that the executive message, which was communicated to Congress upon the application of the veto to the Maysville road, really expressed the opinion of the President of the United States . . . I would forbear to make any observation upon it. It has his name affixed to it; but it is not every paper which bears the name of a distinguished personage, that is his, or expresses his opinions. . . . The veto message proceeds to insist, that the Maysville and Lexington road is not a national but a local road, of sixty miles in length, and confined within the limits of a particular State. . . . The Maysville road was undoubtedly national. It connects the largest body perhaps, of fertile land in the Union, with the navigation of the Ohio and Mississippi rivers, and with the canals of the States of Ohio, Pennsylvania, and New York. It begins on the line which divides the States of Ohio and Kentucky, and, of course, quickens trade and intercourse between them. Tested by the character of other works, for which the president, as a senator, voted, or which were approved by him only about a month before he rejected the Maysville bill, the road was undoubtedly national. . . .

The same scheme which has been devised and practiced to defeat the tariff, has been adopted to undermine internal improvements. They are to be attacked in detail. . . . But is this fair? Ought each proposed road to be viewed separately and detached? Ought it not to be considered in connection with other great works which are in process of execution, or are projected? The policy of the foes indicates what ought to be the policy of the friends of the power. . . .

Perspectives on the Nullification Crisis, 1832, 1833

South Carolina's Ordinance of Nullification, November 24, 1832

Whereas the Congress of the United States, by various acts, purporting to be acts laying duties and imposts on foreign imports, but in reality intended for the protection of domestic manufacturers, and the giving of bounties to classes and individuals engaged in particular employments, at the expense and to the injury and oppression of other classes and individuals, and by wholly exempting from taxation certain foreign commodities, such as are not produced or manufactured in the United States, to afford a pretext for imposing higher and excessive duties on articles similar to those intended to be protected, hath exceeded its just powers under the Constitution, which confers on it no authority to afford such protection, and hath violated the true meaning and intent of the Constitution, which provides for equality in imposing the burthens of taxation upon the several States and portions of the Confederacy: *And whereas* the said Congress, exceeding its just power to impose taxes and collect revenue for the purpose of effecting and accomplishing the specific objects and purposes which the Constitution of the United States authorizes it to effect and accomplish, hath raised and collected unnecessary revenue for objects unauthorized by the Constitution:

We, therefore, the people of the State of South Carolina in Convention assembled, do declare and ordain . . . That the several acts and parts of acts of the Congress of the United States, purporting to be laws for the imposing of duties and imposts on the importation of foreign commodities . . . and, more especially . . . [the tariff acts of 1828 and 1832] . . . are unauthorized by the Constitution of the United States, and violate the true meaning and intent thereof, and are null, void, and no law, nor binding upon this State, its officers or citizens; and all promises, contracts, and obligations, made or entered into, or to be made or entered into, with purpose to secure the duties imposed by the said acts, and all judicial proceedings which shall be hereafter had in affirmance thereof, are and shall be held utterly null and void.

And it is further Ordained, That it shall not be lawful for any of the constituted authorities, whether of this State or of the United States, to enforce the payment of duties imposed by the said acts within the limits of this State; but it shall be the duty of the Legislature to adopt such measures and pass such acts as may be necessary to give full effect to this Ordinance, and to prevent the enforcement and arrest the operation of the said acts and parts of acts of the Congress of the United States within the limits of this State, from and after the 1st day of February next. . . .

And it is further Ordained, That in no case of law or equity, decided in the courts of this State, wherein shall be drawn in question the authority of this ordinance, or the validity of such act or acts of the Legislature as may be passed for the purpose of giving effect thereto, or the validity of the aforesaid acts of Congress, imposing duties, shall any appeal be taken or allowed to the Supreme Court of the United States, nor shall any copy of the record be printed or allowed for that purpose; and if any such appeal shall be attempted to be taken, the courts of this State shall proceed to execute and enforce their judgments, according to the laws and usages of the State, without reference to such attempted appeal, and the person or persons attempting to take such appeal may be dealt with as for a contempt of the court.

And it is further Ordained, That all persons now holding any office of honor, profit, or trust, civil or military, under this State (members of the Legislature excepted), shall, within such time, and in such manner as the

Legislature shall prescribe, take an oath well and truly to obey, execute, and enforce, this Ordinance, and such act or acts of the Legislature as may be passed in pursuance thereof, according to the true intent and meaning of the same; and on the neglect or omission of any such person or persons so to do, his or their office or offices, shall be forthwith vacated . . . and no person hereafter elected to any office of honor, profit, or trust, civil or military (members of the Legislature excepted), shall, until the Legislature shall otherwise provide and direct, enter on the execution of his office . . . until he shall, in like manner, have taken a similar oath; and no juror shall be empannelled in any of the courts of this State, in any cause in which shall be in question this Ordinance, or any act of the Legislature passed in pursuance thereof, unless he shall first, in addition to the usual oath, have taken an oath that he will well and truly obey, execute, and enforce this Ordinance, and such act or acts of the Legislature as may be passed to carry the same into operation and effect, according to the true intent and meaning thereof.

And we, the People of South Carolina, to the end that it may be fully understood by the Government of the United States, and the people of the co-States, that we are determined to maintain this, our Ordinance and Declaration, at every hazard, *Do further Declare* that we will not submit to the application of force, on the part of the Federal Government, to reduce this State to obedience; but that we will consider the passage, by Congress, of any act . . . to coerce the State, shut up her ports, destroy or harass her commerce, or to enforce the acts hereby declared to be null and void, otherwise than through the civil tribunals of the country, as inconsistent with the longer continuance of South Carolina in the Union: and that the people of this State will thenceforth hold themselves absolved from all further obligation to maintain or preserve their political connexion with the people of the other States, and will forthwith proceed to organize a separate Government, and do all other acts and things which sovereign and independent States may of right do. . . .

Jackson Addresses the People of South Carolina, December 10, 1832

PROCLAMATION.

By Andrew Jackson, President of the United States.

Whereas the said ordinance prescribes to the people of South Carolina a course of conduct in direct violation of their duty as citizens of the United States, contrary to the laws of their country, subversive of its Constitution, and having for its object the destruction of the Union—that Union which, coeval with our political existence, led our fathers, without any other ties to unite them than those of patriotism and a common cause, through a sanguinary struggle to a glorious independence; that sacred Union, hitherto inviolate, which, perfected by our happy Constitution, has brought us, by the favor of Heaven, to a state of prosperity at home and high consideration abroad rarely, if ever, equaled in the history of nations:

To preserve this bond of our political existence from destruction, to maintain inviolate this state of national honor and prosperity, and to justify the confidence my fellow-citizens have reposed in me, I, Andrew Jackson, President of the United States, have thought proper to issue this my proclamation, stating my views of the Constitution and laws applicable to the measures adopted by the convention of South Carolina and to the reasons they have put forth to sustain them, declaring the course which duty will require me to pursue, and, appealing to the understanding and patriotism of the people, warn them of the consequences that must inevitably result from an observance of the dictates of the convention.

The ordinance is founded, not on the indefeasible right of resisting acts which are plainly unconstitutional and too oppressive to be endured, but on the strange position that any one State may not only declare an act of Congress void, but prohibit its execution; that they may do this consistently with the Constitution; that the true construction of that instrument permits a State to retain its place in the Union and yet be bound by no other of its laws than those it may choose to consider as constitutional. It is true, they add, that to justify this abrogation of a law it must be palpably contrary to the Constitution; but it is evident that to give the right of resisting laws of that description, coupled with the uncontrolled right to decide what laws deserve that character, is to give the power of resisting all laws; for as by the theory there is no appeal, the reasons alleged by the State, good or bad, must prevail. . . .

If this doctrine had been established at an earlier day, the Union would have been dissolved in its infancy. The excise law in Pennsylvania, the embargo and nonintercourse law in the Eastern States, the carriage tax in Virginia, were all deemed unconstitutional, and were more unequal in their operation than any of the laws now complained of; but, fortunately, none of those States discovered that they had the right now claimed by South Carolina. The war into which we were forced to support the dignity of the nation and the rights of our citizens might have ended in defeat and disgrace, instead of victory and honor, if the States who supposed it a ruinous and unconstitutional measure had thought they possessed the right of nullifying the act by which it was declared and denying supplies for its prosecution. Hardly and unequally as those measures bore upon several members of the Union, to the legislatures of none did this efficient and peaceable remedy, as it is called, suggest itself. The discovery of this important feature in our Constitution was reserved to the present day. To the statesmen of South Carolina belongs the invention, and upon the citizens of that State will unfortunately fall the evils of reducing it to practice. . . .

This right to secede is deduced from the nature of the Constitution, which, they say, is a compact between sovereign States who have preserved their whole sovereignty and therefore are subject to no superior; that because they made the compact they can break it when in their opinion it has been departed from by the other States. Fallacious as this course of reasoning is, it enlists State pride and finds advocates in the honest prejudices of those who have not studied the nature of our Government sufficiently to see the radical error on which it rests.

The people of the United States formed the Constitution, acting through the State legislatures in making the compact, to meet and discuss its provisions, and acting in separate conventions when they ratified those provisions; but the terms used in its construction show it to be a Government in which the people of all the States, collectively, are represented. We are *one people* in the choice of President and Vice-President. Here the States have no other agency than to direct the mode in which the votes shall be given. The candidates having the majority of all the votes are chosen. The electors of a majority of States may have given their votes for one candidate, and yet another may be chosen. The people, then, and not the States, are represented in the executive branch.

In the House of Representatives there is this difference, that the people of one State do not, as in the case of President and Vice-President, all vote for the same officers. The people of all the States do not vote for all the members, each State electing only its own representatives. But this creates no material distinction. When chosen, they are all representatives of the United States, not representatives of the particular State from which they come. They are paid by the United States, not by the State; nor are they accountable to it for any act done in the performance of their legislative functions; and however they may in practice, as it is their duty to do, consult and prefer the interests of their particular constituents when they come in conflict with any other partial or local interest, yet it is their first and highest duty, as representatives of the United States, to promote the general good.

The Constitution of the United States, then, forms a *government,* not a league; and whether it be formed by compact between the States or in any other manner, its character is the same. It is a Government in which all the people are represented, which operates directly on the people individually, not upon the States; they retained all the power they did not grant. But each State, having expressly parted with so many powers as to constitute, jointly with the other States, a single nation, can not, from that period, possess any right to secede, because such secession does not break a league, but destroys the unity of a nation; and any injury to that unity is not only a breach which would result from the contravention of a compact, but it is an offense against the whole Union. To say that any State may at pleasure secede from the Union is to say that the United States are not a nation, because it would be a solecism to contend that any part of a nation might dissolve its connection with the other parts, to their injury or ruin, without committing any offense. Secession, like any other revolutionary act, may be morally justified by the extremity of oppression; but to call it a constitutional right is confounding the meaning of terms, and can only be done through gross error or to deceive those who are willing to assert a right, but would pause before they made a revolution or incur the penalties consequent on a failure.

Because the Union was formed by a compact, it is said the parties to that compact may, when they feel themselves aggrieved, depart from it; but it is precisely because it is a compact that they can not. A compact is an agreement or binding obligation. It may by its terms have a sanction or penalty for its breach, or it may not. If it contains no sanction, it may be broken with no other consequence than moral guilt; if it have a sanction, then the breach incurs the designated or implied penalty. . . .

Fellow-citizens of my native State, let me not only admonish you, as the First Magistrate of our common country, not to incur the penalty of its laws, but use the influence that a father would over his children whom he saw rushing to certain ruin. In that paternal language, with that paternal feeling, let me tell you, my countrymen, that you are deluded by men who are either deceived themselves or wish to deceive you. Mark under what pretenses you have been led on to the brink of insurrection and treason on which you stand. . . . Let those among your leaders who once approved and advocated the principle of protective duties answer the question; and let them choose whether they will be considered as incapable then of perceiving that which must have been apparent to every man of common understanding, or as imposing upon your confidence and endeavoring to mislead you now. In either case they are unsafe guides in the perilous path they urge you to tread. Ponder well on this circumstance, and you will know how to appreciate the exaggerated language they address to you. They are not champions of liberty, emulating the fame of our Revolutionary fathers, nor are you an oppressed people, contending, as they repeat to you, against worse than colonial vassalage. You are free members of a flourishing and happy Union. There is no settled design to oppress you. You have indeed felt the unequal operation of laws which may have been unwisely, not unconstitutionally, passed; but that inequality must necessarily be removed. At the very moment when you were madly urged on to the unfortunate course you have begun a change in public opinion had commenced. The nearly approaching payment of the public debt and the consequent necessity of a diminution of duties had already produced a considerable reduction, and that, too, on some articles of general consumption in your State. . . .

I adjure you, as you honor their memory, as you love the cause of freedom, to which they dedicated their lives, as you prize the peace of your country, the lives of its best citizens, and your own fair fame, to retrace your steps. Snatch from the archives of your State the disorganizing edict of its convention; bid its members to reassemble and promulgate the decided expressions of your will to remain in the path which alone can conduct you to safety, prosperity, and honor. Tell them that compared to disunion all other evils are light, because that brings with it an accumulation of all. Declare that you will never take the field unless the star-spangled banner of your country shall float over you; that you will not be stigmatized when dead, and dishonored and scorned while you live, as the authors of the first attack on the Constitution of your country. Its destroyers you can not be. . . .

Views on the Bank War, 1832

Jackson's Veto Message, July 10, 1832

Washington, *July 10, 1832*. A bank of the United States is in many respects convenient for the Government and useful to the people. Entertaining this opinion, and deeply impressed with the belief that some of the powers and privileges possessed by the existing bank are unauthorized by the Constitution, subversive of the rights of the States, and dangerous to the liberties of the people, I felt it my duty at an early period of my Administration to call the attention of Congress to the practicability of organizing an institution combining all its advantages and obviating these objections. I sincerely regret that in the act before me I can perceive none of those modifications of the bank charter which are necessary, in my opinion, to make it compatible with justice, with sound policy, or with the Constitution of our country.

The present corporate body, denominated the president, directors, and company of the Bank of the United States, will have existed at the time this act is intended to take effect twenty years. It enjoys an exclusive privilege of banking under the authority of the General Government, a monopoly of its favor and support, and, as a necessary consequence, almost a monopoly of the foreign and domestic exchange. The powers, privileges, and favors bestowed upon it in the original charter, by increasing the value of the stock far above its par value, operated as a gratuity of many millions to the stockholders. . . . More than eight millions of the stock of this bank are held by foreigners. By this act the American Republic proposes virtually to make them a present of some millions of dollars. For these gratuities to foreigners and to some of our own opulent citizens the act secures no equivalent whatever. They are the certain gains of the present stockholders under the operation of this act, after making full allowance for the payment of the bonus.

Every monopoly and all exclusive privileges are granted at the expense of the public, which ought to receive a fair equivalent. The many millions which this act proposes to bestow on the stockholders of the existing bank must come directly or indirectly out of the earnings of the American people. It is due to them, therefore, if their Government sell monopolies and exclusive privileges, that they should at least exact for them as much as they are worth in open market. . . .

It has been urged as an argument in favor of rechartering the present bank that the calling in its loans will produce great embarrassment and distress. The time allowed to close its concerns is ample, and if it has been well managed its pressure will be light, and heavy only in case its management has been bad. If, therefore, it shall produce distress, the fault will be its own, and it would furnish a reason against renewing a power which has been so obviously abused. . . .

. . . As little stock is held in the West, it is obvious that the debt of the people in that section to the bank is principally a debt to the Eastern and foreign stockholders; that the interest they pay upon it is carried into the

Eastern States and into Europe, and that it is a burden upon their industry and a drain of their currency, which no country can bear without inconvenience and occasional distress. . . . The tendency of the plan of taxation which this act proposes will be to place the whole United States in the same relation to foreign countries which the Western States now bear to the Eastern. When by a tax on resident stockholders the stock of this bank is made worth 10 or 15 per cent more to foreigners than to residents, most of it will inevitably leave the country.

Thus will this provision in its practical effect deprive the Eastern as well as the Southern and Western States of the means of raising a revenue from the extension of business and great profits of this institution. It will make the American people debtors to aliens in nearly the whole amount due to this bank, and send across the Atlantic from two to five millions of specie every year to pay the bank dividends.

In another of its bearings this provision is fraught with danger. Of the twenty-five directors of this bank five are chosen by the Government and twenty by the citizen stockholders. From all voice in these elections the foreign stockholders are excluded by the charter. In proportion, therefore, as the stock is transferred to foreign holders the extent of suffrage in the choice of directors is curtailed. Already is almost a third of the stock in foreign hands and not represented in elections. . . .

Is there no danger to our liberty and independence in a bank that in its nature has so little to bind it to our country? The president of the bank has told us that most of the State banks exist by its forbearance. Should its influence become concentered, as it may under the operation of such an act as this, in the hands of a self-elected directory whose interests are identified with those of the foreign stockholders, will there not be cause to tremble for the purity of our elections in peace and for the independence of our country in war? . . .

Should the stock of the bank principally pass into the hands of the subjects of a foreign country, and we should unfortunately become involved in a war with that country, what would be our condition? Of the course which would be pursued by a bank almost wholly owned by the subjects of a foreign power, and managed by those whose interests, if not affections, would run in the same direction there can be no doubt. All its operations within would be in aid of the hostile fleets and armies without. Controlling our currency, receiving our public moneys, and holding thousands of our citizens in dependence, it would be more formidable and dangerous than the naval and military power of the enemy.

If we must have a bank with private stockholders, every consideration of sound policy and every impulse of American feeling admonishes that it should be *purely American*. Its stockholders should be composed exclusively of our own citizens, who at least ought to be friendly to our Government and willing to support it in times of difficulty and danger. So abundant is domestic capital that competition in subscribing for the stock of local banks has recently led almost to riots. To a bank exclusively of American stockholders, possessing the powers and privileges granted by this act, subscriptions for $200,000,000 could be readily obtained. Instead of sending abroad the stock of the bank in which the Government must deposit its funds and on which it must rely to sustain its credit in times of emergency, it would rather seem to be expedient to prohibit its sale to aliens under penalty of absolute forfeiture.

It is maintained by the advocates of the bank that its constitutionality in all its features ought to be considered as settled by precedent and by the decision of the Supreme Court. To this conclusion I can not assent. . . .

If the opinion of the Supreme Court covered the whole ground of this act, it ought not to control the coordinate authorities of this Government. The Congress, the Executive, and the Court must each for itself be guided by its own opinion of the Constitution. Each public officer who takes an oath to support the Constitution swears that he will support it as he understands it, and not as it is understood by others. It is as much the duty of the House of Representatives, of the Senate, and of the President to decide upon the constitutionality of any bill or resolution which may be presented to them for passage or approval as it is of the supreme judges when it may be brought before them for judicial decision. The opinion of the judges has no more authority over Congress than the opinion of Congress has over the judges, and on that point the President is independent of both. The authority of the Supreme Court must not, therefore, be permitted to controll the Congress or the Executive when acting in their legislative capacities, but to have only such influence as the force of their reasoning may deserve. . . .

The principle here affirmed is that the "degree of its necessity," involving all the details of a banking institution, is a question exclusively for legislative consideration. A bank is constitutional, but it is the province of the Legislature to determine whether this or that particular power, privilege, or exemption is "necessary and proper" to enable the bank to discharge its duties to the Government, and from their decision there is no appeal to the courts of justice. Under the decision of the Supreme Court, therefore, it is the exclusive province of Congress and the President to decide whether the particular features of this act are *necessary* and *proper* in order to enable the bank to perform conveniently and efficiently the public duties assigned to it as a fiscal agent, and therefore constitutional, or *unnecessary* and *improper,* and therefore unconstitutional. . . .

The Government is the only *"proper"* judge where its agents should reside and keep their offices, because it best knows where their presence will be *"necessary."* It can not, therefore, be *"necessary"* or *"proper"* to authorize the bank to locate branches where it pleases to perform the public service, without consulting the Government, and contrary to its will. The principle laid down by the Supreme Court concedes that Congress can not establish a bank for purposes of private speculation and gain, but only as a means of executing the delegated powers of the General Government. By the same principle a branch bank can not constitutionally be established for other than public purposes. The power which this act gives to establish two branches in any State, without the injunction or request of the Government and for other than public purposes, is not *"necessary"* to the due *execution* of the powers delegated to Congress. . . .

The bank is professedly established as an agent of the executive branch of the Government, and its constitutionality is maintained on that ground. Neither upon the propriety of present action nor upon the provisions of this act was the Executive consulted. It has had no opportunity to say that it neither needs nor wants an agent clothed with such powers and favored by such exemptions. There is nothing in its legitimate functions which makes it necessary or proper. Whatever interest or influence, whether public or private, has given birth to this act, it can not be found either in the wishes or necessities of the executive department, by which present action is deemed premature, and the powers conferred upon its agent not only unnecessary, but dangerous to the Government and country.

It is to be regretted that the rich and powerful too often bend the acts of government to their selfish purposes. Distinctions in society will always exist under every just government. Equality of talents, of education, or of wealth can not be produced by human institutions. In the full enjoyment of the gifts of Heaven and the fruits of superior industry, economy, and virtue, every man is equally entitled to protection by law; but when the laws undertake to add to these natural and just advantages artificial distinctions, to grant titles, gratuities, and exclusive privileges, to make the rich richer and the potent more powerful, the humble members of society—the farmers, mechanics, and laborers—who have neither the time nor the means of securing like favors to themselves, have a right to complain of the injustice of their Government. There are no necessary evils in government. Its evils exist only in its abuses. If it would confine itself to equal protection, and, as Heaven does its rains, shower its favors alike on the high and the low, the rich and the poor, it would be an unqualified blessing. In the act before me there seems to be a wide and unnecessary departure from these just principles.

Nor is our Government to be maintained or our Union preserved by invasions of the rights and powers of the several States. In thus attempting to make our General Government strong we make it weak. Its true strength consists in leaving individuals and States as much as possible to themselves—in making itself felt, not in its power, but in its beneficence; not in its control, but in its protection; not in binding the States more closely to the center, but leaving each to move unobstructed in its proper orbit.

Experience should teach us wisdom. Most of the difficulties our Government now encounters and most of the dangers which impend over our Union have sprung from an abandonment of the legitimate objects of Government by our national legislation, and the adoption of such principles as are embodied in this act. Many of our rich men have not been content with equal protection and equal benefits, but have besought us to make them richer by act of Congress. By attempting to gratify their desires we have in the results of our legislation arrayed section against section, interest against interest, and man against man, in a fearful commotion which threatens to shake the foundations of our Union. It is time to pause in our career to review our principles, and if possible revive that devoted patriotism and spirit of compromise which distinguished the sages of the Revolution and the fathers of our Union. If we can not at once, in justice to interests vested under improvident legislation, make our Government what it ought to be, we can at least take a stand against all new grants of monopolies and exclusive privileges, against any prostitution of our Government to the advancement of the few at the expense of the many, and in favor of compromise and gradual reform in our code of laws and system of political economy.

I have now done my duty to my country. If sustained by my fellow-citizens, I shall be grateful and happy; if not, I shall find in the motives which impel me ample grounds for contentment and peace. In the difficulties which surround us and the dangers which threaten our institutions there is cause for neither dismay nor alarm. For relief and deliverance let us firmly rely on that kind Providence which I am sure watches with peculiar care over the destinies of our Republic, and on the intelligence and wisdom of our countrymen. Through *His* abundant goodness and *their* patriotic devotion our liberty and Union will be preserved.

Daniel Webster's Reply, July 11, 1832

. . . I will not conceal my opinion that the affairs of the country are approaching an important and dangerous crisis. At the very moment of almost unparalleled general prosperity, there appears an unaccountable disposition to destroy the most useful and most approved institutions of the government. Indeed, it seems to be in the midst of all this national happiness that some are found openly to question the advantages of the Constitution itself; and many more ready to embarrass the exercise of its just power, weaken its authority, and undermine its foundations. How far these notions may be carried, it is impossible yet to say. We have before us the practical result of one of them. The bank has fallen, or is to fall. . . .

The responsibility justly lies with [the President], and there it ought to remain. A great majority of the people are satisfied with the bank as it is, and desirous that it should be continued. They wished no change. The strength of this public sentiment has carried the bill through Congress, against all the influence of the administration, and all the power of organized party. But the President has undertaken, on his own responsibility, to arrest the measure, by refusing his assent to the bill. He is answerable for the consequences, therefore, which necessarily follow the change which the expiration of the bank charter may produce; and if these consequences shall prove disastrous, they can fairly be ascribed to his policy only, and the policy of his administration. . . .

The bill was not passed for the purpose of benefiting the present stockholders. Their benefit, if any, is incidental and collateral. Nor was it passed on any idea that they had a *right* to a renewed charter, although the message argues against such right, as if it had been somewhere set up and asserted. No such right has been asserted by any body. Congress passed the bill, not as a bounty or a favor to the present stockholders, nor to comply with any demand of right on their part; but to promote great public interests, for great public objects. Every bank must have some stockholders, unless it be such a bank as the President has recommended, and in regard to which he seems not likely to find much concurrence of other men's opinions; and if the stockholders, whoever they may be, conduct the affairs of the bank prudently, the expectation is always, of course, that they will make it profitable to themselves, as well as useful to the public. If a bank charter is not to be granted, because, to some extent, it may be profitable to the stockholders, no charter can be granted. The objection lies against all banks.

Sir, the object aimed at by such institutions is to connect the public safety and convenience with private interests. It has been found by experience, that banks are safest under private management, and that government banks are among the most dangerous of all inventions. Now, Sir, the whole drift of the message is to reverse the settled judgment of all the civilized world, and to set up government banks, independent of private interest or private control. For this purpose the message labors, even beyond the measure of all its other labors, to create jealousies and prejudices, on the ground of the alleged benefit which individuals will derive from the renewal of this charter. Much less effort is made to show that government, or the public, will be injured by the bill, than that individuals will profit by it. . . .

The President is as much bound by the law as any private citizen, and can no more contest its validity than any private citizen. He may refuse to obey the law, and so may a private citizen; but both do it at their own peril, and neither of them can settle the question of its validity. The President may *say* a law is unconstitutional, but he is not the judge. Who is to decide that question? The judiciary alone possesses this unquestionable and hitherto unquestioned right. The judiciary is the constitutional tribunal of appeal for the citizens, against both Congress and the executive, in regard to the constitutionality of laws. It has this jurisdiction expressly conferred upon it, and when it has decided the question, its judgment must, from the very nature of all judgments that are final, and from which there is no appeal, be conclusive. . . .

[W]e have arrived at a new epoch. We are entering on experiments, with the government and the Constitution of the country, hitherto untried, and of fearful and appalling aspect. This message calls us to the contemplation of a future which little resembles the past. . . . It appeals to every prejudice which may betray men into a mistaken view of their own interests, and to every passion which may lead them to disobey the impulses of their understanding. It urges all the specious topics of State rights and national encroachment against that which a great majority of the States have affirmed to be rightful, and in which all of them have acquiesced. It sows, in an unsparing manner, the seeds of jealousy and ill-will against that government of which its author is the official head. It raises a cry, that liberty is in danger, at the very moment when it puts forth claims to powers heretofore unknown and unheard of. It affects alarm for the public freedom, when nothing endangers that freedom so much as its own unparalleled pretences. This, even, is not all. It manifestly seeks to inflame the poor against the rich; it wantonly attacks whole classes of the people, for the purpose of turning against them the prejudices and the resentments of other classes. It is a state paper which finds no topic too exciting for its use, no passion too inflammable for its address and its solicitation.

Such is this message. It remains now for the people of the United States to choose between the principles here avowed and their government. These cannot subsist together. The one or the other must be rejected. If the sentiments of the message shall receive general approbation, the Constitution will have perished even earlier than the moment which its enemies originally allowed for the termination of its existence. It will not have survived to its fiftieth year.

A Jacksonian View of the Opposition, 1833

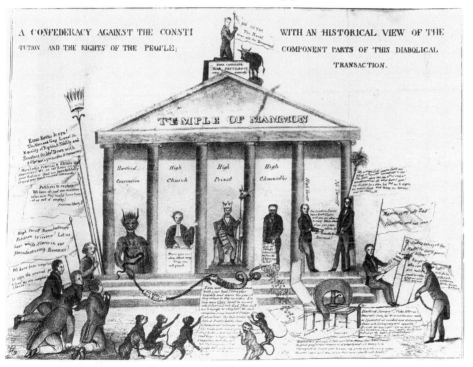

A Confederacy Against the Constitution and the Rights of the People, lithograph, 1833. Beneath the temple's pillars, "High Tariff," a Yankee capitalist, plots with "No Tariff," a South Carolinian resembling John C. Calhoun: "You Southern Barons have Black Slaves; will you not allow us to make White Slaves of our poor population in our Manufacturing Baronies?" Library Company of Philadelphia.

Philip Hone on the Democratic Party, 1834

Nov. 6 [1834]—The triumph was celebrated last night by the worshippers of Jackson with the refinement and forbearance which might have been expected. I had been taken in the morning with an attack of vertigo and headache, which confined me to the house nearly the whole day, but I made out to walk up in the evening to Masonic Hall, where the news I received was not calculated to make me feel better. I returned home much indisposed, and retired to bed at an early hour, where I was kept awake during the greater part of the night by the unmanly insults of the ruffian crew from Tammany Hall, who came over to my door every half-hour and saluted me with groans and hisses. This continued until past three o'clock, and for what? Because I have exercised the right which, in common with every American citizen, I enjoy (or have enjoyed until this time), of expressing my disapprobation of a course of measures which I conceive to be dangerous to the liberties of the people, and inimical to the free institutions of my native land. This I have done with truth, zeal, and firmness, but always, I trust, with decorum and propriety; and for this I have been insulted and annoyed. I have for many years sacrificed my comfort, exhausted my time, and abridged my enjoyments by a devotion to the service of my fellow-citizens. A member of all the public institutions, charitable, public-spirited, or patriotic, where time was to be lost, labour performed, and no pay to be had; my own affairs neglected, and my money frequently poured out like water; the friend and patron of the working-men, without regard to party;—and now my reward is found in the revilings of a mob of midnight ruffians, among whom, I have no doubt, were some of the very men whom I have assisted to support, to the exclusion of others who are proud to acknowledge themselves my personal and political friends. I believe I am rightly served. . . .

NOVEMBER 10.—I apprehend that Mr. Van Buren and his friends have no permanent cause of triumph in their victory. They have succeeded by the means of instruments which may work their own destruction; they have mounted a vicious horse, who, taking the bit in his mouth, will run away with him. The agrarian party, who have had things pretty much their own way, will not stop at Martin Van Buren,—they will dig deeper into the swamps of political depravity, and the good men of our community, the supporters of the Constitution, and the true friends of civil liberty may be soon called upon to unite in his favour, against a worse man and principles more dangerous than his. This battle had been fought upon the ground of the poor against the rich, and this unworthy prejudice, this dangerous delusion, has been encouraged by the leaders of the triumphant party, and fanned into a flame by the polluted breath of the hireling press in their employ. In the saturnalian orgies with which our streets have been disgraced, the unmannerly epithets which were so liberally bestowed upon myself and other peaceable citizens for having exercised the privilege of freemen in opposing a party whose political doctrines we thought unfavourable to the true interests of the nation, the cry of "Down with the aristocracy!" mingled with the shouts of victory, and must have grated on the ears of some of their own leaders like the croaking of the evil-boding raven. They have succeeded in raising this dangerous spirit, and have gladly availed themselves of its support to accomplish a temporary object; but can they allay it at pleasure? Will their voices be heard when they cry "Thus far shalt thou go and no farther"? Eighteen thousand men in New York have voted for the high-priest of the party whose professed design is to bring down the property, the talents, the industry, the steady habits of that class which constituted the real strength of the Commonwealth, to the common level of the idle, the worthless, and the unenlightened. Look to it, ye men of respectability in the Jackson party, are ye not afraid of the weapons ye have used in this warfare? . . .

The Gag Rule: Floor Debate
in the U.S. House of Representatives, 1837

Mr. PATTON then asked leave to submit the following resolution:

Resolved, That all petitions, memorials, and papers touching the abolition of slavery, or the buying, selling, or transferring of slaves, in any State, District, or Territory, of the United States, be laid on the table, without being debated, printed, read, or referred, and that no further motion whatever shall be had thereon.

Mr. ADAMS objected.

Mr. PATTON moved a suspension of the rule.

Mr. CUSHMAN asked for the yeas and nays, which were ordered, and were yeas 135, nays 60. . . .

So the rules were suspended.

Mr. PATTON said he had offered this resolution in the spirit of peace and harmony. It involves (said Mr. P) so far as I am concerned, and so far as concerns some portion of the representatives of the slave holding States, a concession; a concession which we make for the sake of peace, harmony, and union. We offer it in the hope that it may allay, not exasperate excitement; we desire to extinguish, not to kindle a flame in the country in that spirit, sir, . . . I shall do what I have never yet done since I have been a member of this House, and which I have very rarely sustained, when done by others: I move the previous question.

Mr. ADAMS rose and said: Mr. Speaker, the gentleman precedes his resolution—(Loud cries of "Order! order!" from all parts of the hall.) Mr. A. He preceded it with remarks—("Order! order!")

The CHAIR reminded the gentleman that it was out of order to address the House after the demand for the previous question.

Mr. ADAMS. I ask the House—(continued cries of "Order!" which completely drowned the honorable member's voice.)

Mr. ADAMS then demanded tellers on the second to the previous question, which were ordered; and Mr. CLAIBORNE of Mississippi, and Mr. BRIGGS of Massachusetts, having been appointed, the motion prevailed, 124 voting for it.

So the demand for the previous question was seconded by the House.

On the question; "Shall the main question be now put?" being propounded—

Mr. CALHOUN of Massachusetts asked for the yeas and nays, which were ordered, and were—yeas 129, nays 62. . . .

So the main question was ordered to be put.

The main question, being on agreeing to the resolution, was then propounded.

Mr. CALHOUN of Massachusetts asked for the yeas and nays, which were ordered, and were—yeas 122, nays 74. . . .

[When the name of Mr. ADAMS was called, that gentleman rose, and said: "I hold the resolution to be in violation of the Constitution of the United States." [Loud cries of "Order!" "order!" from every part of the Hall.]

The SPEAKER said, the gentleman from Massachusetts violates order, and must resume his seat.

"A Native of Maine" on the Emigrating Cherokees in Southern Kentucky, 1838

On Tuesday evening we fell in with a detachment of the poor Cherokee Indians. . . . That poor despised people are now on their long and tedious march to their place of destination beyond the Mississippi River. In the first detachment which we met, were about eleven hundred Indians—sixty wag- gons—six hundred horses, and perhaps forty pairs of oxen. We found them in the forest camped for the night by the road side, comfortable—if com- fortable they might be in a December night, and under a severe fall of rain accompanied with heavy wind. With their canvass for a shield from the inclemency of the weather, and the cold wet ground for a resting place, after the fatigue of the day, they spent the night with probably as little of the reality as the appearance of comfort. We learned from the officers and overseers of the detachment in the morning, that many of the aged Indians were suffering extremely from the fatigue of the journey, and the ill health consequent upon it.—Several were then quite ill, and one aged man we were informed was then in the last struggles of death.—There were about ten officers and overseers in each detachment whose business it was to provide supplies for the journey, and attend to the general wants of the company. The cost of the journey, is paid by the American Government as one of the conditions of the pretended treaty which many of the Indians still call fraudulent.

The officers informed us that the Indians were very unwilling to go— so much so that some two hundred had escaped, in collecting them together, and secreted themselves in the mountains in Georgia and the eastern part of Tennessee,—and those who were on the way were so unwilling to pursue their journey, that it was some days quite evening before they could get them under way—and even then they went reluctantly. I know it is said that "only a few were unwilling to go"—"the most go willingly and think the remove on the whole, an advantage to the nation." The testimony of the officers and observation have both tended to confirm the belief, however, in my mind that the great majority of the nation feel that they are wronged— grievously wronged, and nothing but arbitrary power compels them to remove. . . .

The last detachment which we passed on the 7th, embraced rising two thousand Indians with horses and mules in proportion. The forward part of the train we found just pitching their tents for the night, and notwithstanding some thirty or forty wagons were already stationed, we found the road literally filled with the procession for about three miles in length. The sick and feeble were carried in wagons—about as comfortable for travelling as a New England ox cart with a covering over it—a great many ride on horseback and multitudes go on foot—even aged females, apparently, nearly ready to drop into the grave—were travelling with heavy burdens attached to the back—on the sometimes frozen ground, and sometimes muddy streets, with no covering for the feet except what nature had given them. We were some hours making our way through the crowd, which brought us in close contact with the wagons and the multitude, so much that we felt fortunate to find ourselves freed from the crowd without leaving any part of our carriage. We learned from the inhabitants on the road where the Indians passed that they buried fourteen to fifteen at every stopping place—and they make a journey of ten miles per day only on an average. . . . One aged Indian, who was commander of the friendly Creeks and Seminoles in a very important engagement in company with General Jackson, was accosted on arriving in a little village in Kentucky by an aged man residing there, and who was one of Jackson's men in the engagement referred to, and asked if he (the Indian) recollected him? The aged Chieftain looked him in the face and recognised him, and with a down-cast look and heavy sigh, referring to the engagement, he said, "Ah! my life and the lives of my people were then at stake for you and your country. I then thought Jackson my best friend. But, ah! Jackson no serve me right. Your country no do me justice now."

The Whigs Take to the Woods, 1840

"General Harrison's Log-Cabin March. A Quick Step," songsheet, 1840: A bit of rousing paraphernalia from the Whigs' "Log Cabin and Hard Cider" campaign. The Granger Collection.

Calvin Colton on Whig Ideals, 1844

Number Six: Democracy

The Genius of Whig Democracy

. . . The Whig party of the Union is composed of men, who have been long out of power; who have been forced in the meantime to act on the conservative side, that is, as far as possible, to prevent mischief; who are of course, and necessarily, *lean men,* as regards the fattening effects of office; have none of the corruptions which are at least *supposed* to appertain to a protracted tenure of power; and if such men can anywhere be found, may fairly be regarded, as in a reasonable degree, disinterested patriots, from the fact of their choice to remain in the minority so long a period. *Principles* alone, not power, have bound them together. Their party organization has been sustained, not by the patronage of office, but by putting their hands in their own pockets. It was a glorious sight, in 1840, to see what sacrifices and efforts they could make, to rescue the country from bad hands. The obvious truth of their facts, and the force of their arguments, brought a great majority of the people over to their side, and they triumphed; but treachery has left them precisely in the situation they were in then. Still without power, still relying on *principles,* and the practical *results* of principles, "though betrayed, not dismayed," they still adhere, and press onward.

Every man in the Whig ranks, is a MAN—a man that thinks for himself, and acts for himself—an uncompromising *American Democrat.* It is perhaps an evil in the Whig party, that they are *all* leaders; but it is *not* an evil, that they are SERVILE to leaders. Nobody has ever dared to name in their ranks that wicked, corrupt, and corrupting maxim, that "to the victors belong the spoils." The great mass of them would never care who governs the country, if it were well governed. But when it is badly governed, they resolve, in the spirit of true patriots, to put the reins in better hands, that they may return to and prosper in their own private affairs, as independent American citizens—as *Democrats.*

Such, for the most part, is the genius of Whig Democracy. They recognise no authority of leaders, that binds them to obsequiousness; it is not party, but the *country* they go for; it is not MEN, but PRINCIPLES; and they adopt party organization, and sustain it, not as an *end,* but as *means* to an end. . . .

"Democrats" the Friends of the Laboring and Poorer Classes

This has not only been a standing text, but there has been much effective preaching from it, by the Locofoco "Democracy." But the laboring and poorer classes have made an important discovery in three particulars. 1. That they have been made *tools of,* . . . 2. That Whig policy and Whig measures are best for them. 3. They like that democracy which does them most good; which gives them food, clothing, and a comfortable home, instead of *promises.* They have at least *begun* to make this discovery, and are advancing in it rapidly. The tariff, a great Whig measure, is diffusing its blessings everywhere, and gladdening the hearts of the laboring and poorer classes. We have just noticed the remarkable fact, that a little girl, in a Cotton Bag Factory at Cincinnati, earns *six dollars* for five and a half days' labor every week, and that there are fifty-five females and forty-five males working in the same factory, with similar results. (See also our tract on the Tariff.)

Take away the *name,* by which the Locofocos have deceived the people, and their power is gone. . . .

The Morals of Locofocoism

It results from a moral necessity, growing out of the history of the thing, that it should be corrupt. Founded in untruth, erected and sustained by it, it is impossible it should be pure. The system of party tactics introduced by General Jackson, and carried out by Mr. Van Buren, is one of utter and revolting corruption. . . .

Number Seven: Labor and Capital

The Dignity of Labor

"The mandate of God to his creature man is, WORK!" "The GENIUS of work is the Conqueror, the supreme Lawgiver, the *born* King over affluent idleness." "The Leaders of Industry are the Captains of the world. If there be no nobleness in them, there will never be an aristocracy more."

This is higher-toned phrase than we are addicted to employ, as they who read us well know. Nevertheless, as there is such a vast body of comprehensive truth in it, we have borrowed it for the sake of brevity. It plants labor where God intended it should stand, in the loftiest, most influential position. The *plan* of Creation is visible in her works. Behold the constitution of man, contemplate the character of his mind, and judge, if he was not made for work, if idleness is not a disease, a fatal malady. Creation itself is called the WORK of God. "In the sweat of thy face shalt thou eat bread," which, though announced as part of the DOOM of the first transgression, is, by the remedial scheme of man's redemption, converted into a BLESSING AND A DIGNITY. Earth is a work-field, and heaven a rest. It is as bad, as vicious, not to work here, since God has so appointed, as to violate any other precept of Divine authority. The example of God in the WORK of Creation, and the example of Christ in the WORK of Redemption, aside from the force of command, impart the highest possible sanction and the highest possible DIGNITY to those labors of man which have become necessary in this life. Human labor will never have attained its true position, till it shall stand at the head of human affairs. "The Leaders of Industry are the Captains of the world." Such was the design—such is the *tendency*. They who work, *will govern*. We know it has not always been so, and that was a vicious state of society when and wherever it was not so. We know that labor has not, in all history, received due homage. But this fact does not affect, nor impair the validity of its claims. . . .

The Chief Cause

It is undoubtedly true, that the causes, more properly, perhaps, the *instruments,* have been several, and the system of injury complicated, by which the country has been so fearfully run down. But the *great aim* of that destructive policy, which has been practised upon us, was *to set labor to war against moneyed capital, by legislation and Government;* and the *mode* of this warfare was an endeavor to cripple and break down those institutions and enterprises, in which the moneyed capital of the country was chiefly vested.

The Destructive and Fatal Effects of This Warfare

Unless it were proposed to rob moneyed capitalists, and divide the spoils *directly,* any attempt to cripple them by legislation and Government, with the design of better securing the rights of the laboring classes, must necessarily cripple and destroy the latter. Whatever war the Government may wage against capitalists, short of robbing, it is always in their power to withdraw their funds from those uses which have heretofore, in our experience, so well served the convenience of the public and the wants of labor, and turn them into investments, which will over serve themselves. . . . If the great law of mutual dependence in society be overlooked or violated, in the policy and measures of Government, and an attempt be made to injure and cripple moneyed capitalists, for the benefit of laborers, the most fatal consequences must unavoidably ensue. . . . If the rich can do without the poor, by turning their capital into other investments, than those which give to the latter employment, food, raiment, and a comfortable home, with chances of rising in the world, and of becoming rich in their turn, the poor can not do without the rich, who, in these ways, minister to their necessities, and secure to them the means of bettering their condition. A war upon the rich, in legislation and government, is a war upon the poor, of the worst kind, and of the most disastrous effects. It is a war upon the most vital interests of society, and upon the relations of mankind in the social state, which, if carried out, the entire social fabric must bend and break.

The Chances of Life in This Country

Ours is a country, where men start from an humble origin, and from small beginnings rise gradually in the world, as the reward of merit and industry, and where they can attain to the most elevated positions, or acquire a large amount of wealth, according to the pursuits they elect for themselves. No exclusive privileges of birth, no entailment of estates, no civil or political disqualifications, stand in their path; but one has as good a chance as another, according to his talents, prudence, and personal exertions. This is a country

of *self-made men,* than which nothing better could be said of any state of
society.

✣ *E S S A Y S*

Contemporary scholarship on Jacksonian politics remains influenced by the controversies initiated by Arthur Schlesinger, Jr.'s, *The Age of Jackson* (1945).
Schlesinger contended that Jacksonianism involved a liberal uprising by the people
against conservative business interests, instigated by the growing class disturbances
of the 1820s and 1830s. Beginning in the 1950s, some scholars argued that ethnic
differences and cultural issues were far more important than class, and that the
Jacksonians represented not "the people" but a rising entrepreneurial elite. Then,
in the 1960s, a new generation of historians tried to tie the Jacksonian legacy to
Indian removal and the desire to keep slavery out of national political debates.
More recently, interest has revived in class interpretations of the period, although
greatly modified by the discoveries and disputes of the past five decades.

A full review of the arguments is impossible here; rather, these selections focus on the character of Jacksonian and Whig political thought. Robert V. Remini
of the University of Illinois-Chicago circle is Jackson's foremost modern biogra-
pher. In the opening essay, his summary of Jackson's beliefs updates some of
Schlesinger's formulations and adds a number of others. In his other writings,
Remini follows up on his passing observations in this selection on Indian removal,
describing the policy's devastation but also insisting on Jackson's genuinely benevolent motives in a difficult, ultimately tragic situation. Alexander Saxton, of the
University of California at Los Angeles, looks in the second essay at the broader
Jacksonian movement and its producer ideology. The Jacksonians succeeded, Saxton argues, because they managed to yoke together a disparate national coalition.
To hold this alliance together, Saxton contends, the Jacksonians skillfully de-
ployed racist appeals, making white supremacy a central feature of the Democrats' peculiar form of egalitarianism. In his study of the Whigs, Daniel Walker
Howe, also of the University of California at Los Angeles, accepts the idea that
the party was probusiness but transcends that view by examining the party's wider
moral outlook. A closer look at the southern Whigs—led, through the mid-1840s,
by the great planters—might prompt modifications in one or more of these essays. Consider, as well, a paradox provoked by Howe's contribution: that the
leading Whigs' seeming openness to the plight of nonwhite "outsiders" may have
stemmed from their deeply paternalistic, antidemocratic prejudices and their abiding suspicions of lower-class whites. What does this tell us about the major parties
in the 1830s and after? On a broader front, what really were the galvanizing
forces in U.S. politics, nationally and locally?

Andrew Jackson and Jacksonian Democracy

ROBERT V. REMINI

To Andrew Jackson and the American people at large it seemed obvious
and incontestable that the nation was indeed a democracy. Perhaps they

Excerpts from *Andrew Jackson and the Course of American Democracy 1832–1845* by Robert
V. Remini (New York: HarperCollins Publishers, Inc., 1984), pp. 337–345).

believed it had always been one. But under Jackson the concept of popular or majority rule really took hold. The Democrats trumpeted the rights of the people; they called the people wise and good and virtuous; and they insisted that the will of the people must in all instances be obeyed by their representatives. They denounced elitism and the pretensions of aristocracy. And although Jackson called this old-fashioned republicanism—or, to use his exact words, "jeffersonian Democratic republican principles"—it would later, and more properly, be called Jacksonian Democracy. The transformation of the United States from a republic to a democracy was a slow process that had begun long before Jackson came to office. But more than any other single individual he contributed to and symbolized the arrival and acceptance of that concept. His charisma, popularity, and accomplishments made it all possible.

Historians generally have tended to deny that Jackson held any firm philosophy of government that guided his actions. They choose to believe that he was principally motivated by private animosities and deep-seated prejudices, by passion and pride. They do him a grave injustice. Actually Jackson not only subscribed to a definite philosophy of government but he imposed that philosophy on his party and because of it markedly hurried the democratizing process.

To understand the thrust and direction of Jackson's political thinking it is necessary to remember the single, central event that shaped many of his ideas about government, to wit the "stolen election" of 1825 when John Quincy Adams and Henry Clay entered a "corrupt bargain" and elevated Adams to the presidency in defiance of the popular will. To Jackson this was the ultimate corruption in a general Era of Corruption. It produced what became "the first principle" of Jacksonian Democracy, namely *"the majority is to govern."* This doctrine Jackson announced in his first message to Congress and he repeated it at every opportunity. He brushed aside any and all intermediary agencies that stood between the people and their government—even those placed there by the Founding Fathers. To the people, he said, belonged the right "of electing their Chief Magistrate"; neither an electoral college nor the House of Representatives may alter their choice, nor was it ever meant that they should. Not to put too fine a point on it, Jackson was clearly on shaky historical ground in making this assertion— but make it he did. As far as he was concerned, absolutely nothing could block the execution of the popular will. For the experience of 1825 proved beyond all doubt, he insisted, that the more agencies are erected to execute the people's will the more it will be frustrated. And that must be prevented at all costs.

Jackson placed his entire confidence in the wisdom of a virtuous people "to arrive at right conclusions," conclusions binding on all their representatives. That was the message carried by his speeches and public pronouncements to the Democratic party and the electorate. In asserting this principle he was subverting (consciously or not) republicanism and the constitutional system as devised by the Founding Fathers. For the perceived wisdom at the time insisted that a government had been established by the

Constitution which distributed power among three branches of government and provided checks and balances to keep the branches equal and prevent any one of them from dominating the others. The language of the Constitution, according to this view, *is* the will of the people. Having spoken, the people are excluded from speaking again except through the difficult, if not impossible, process of amending the Constitution. The agency or branch of government that is given the final say on the meaning of the Constitution is the Supreme Court. And the Supreme Court is the most removed body from the people.

This view Jackson totally rejected. Not only did he deny that the people may speak no more except by amending the Constitution, but he denied that the Supreme Court was the final interpreter of the meaning of the Constitution. Jackson subscribed to another view. He maintained that the people remain active in the governing process. The people are *never* excluded from the power that is theirs by right. They never surrendered that right. And they exercise that right through the ballot box which all agencies of government (including the Supreme Court) must obey. A form of government, such as the one provided by the Constitution, does not divest the people of the right to self-government. It does not give the Supreme Court, for example, the right to tell them what is or is not allowed under that form. "Forms of government," wrote George Sidney Camp in *Democracy,* a work published in 1841 and obviously written under the influence of Jacksonianism, "have been, for the most part, only so many various modes of tyranny. Where the people are everything, and political forms . . . nothing, there and there only is liberty."

That was Jackson's philosophy precisely. The people govern. Their will must be obeyed. Majority rule constitutes the only true meaning of liberty. All of which subverts the earlier notion of republicanism which did indeed provide for intermediate agencies to refine and alter the popular will when it was deemed necessary, such as occurred in 1825.

The "constant celebration" of the people, therefore, is basic to Jacksonian Democracy. And it was this celebration throughout Jackson's administration—a celebration the people enjoyed and acknowledged—that steadily advanced the march toward greater democracy in the United States.

At one point Jackson himself made a stab at defining Jacksonian Democracy and listed many of its identifying marks. If the "virtuous yeomanry of Tennessee," he wrote as he struggled with the definition, would simply ask political candidates a few basic questions, they could distinguish true Democrats from "Whiggs, nullies and blue light federalists*" by the answers they received. The people, said Jackson, "ought to enquire of them, are you opposed to a national Bank—are you in favor of a strict construction of the federal and State constitution—are you in favor of rotation in office—do you subscribe to the republican rule that the people are the sovereign power, the officers their agents, and that upon all national or general subjects, as

---

* Blue light Federalists supposedly signaled to the British fleet off the New England coast with blue lights during the War of 1812 to indicate a safe haven.

well as local, they have a right to instruct their agents & representatives, and they are bound to obey or resign—in short are they true republicans agreeable to the true Jeffersonian creed."

Sovereign power resides with the people, declared Jackson, and that power applies to all national and local issues. Moreover, the people have a right to "instruct their agents & representatives" as to their will. It is not enough to say that once the people elect their representatives they have no further control of the governing process. For Jackson, they always retain control through the doctrine of instruction. He would take away from representatives the power or right to "correct" or alter the popular will.

Jackson would also deny the courts this power. But he made a distinction. He would allow the courts the right to review and interpret the *law* but he would not assign them ultimate authority in pronouncing "the true meaning of a doubtful clause of the Constitution" binding on all. The right to review and interpret the law may be "endured," he argued, "because it is subject to the control of the majority of the people." But pronouncing the true meaning of the Constitution was altogether objectionable because "it claims the right to bind" the states and the people with bonds that no one can loose except by amending the Constitution, a difficult process at best. To allow the Supreme Court the ultimate authority to interpret the Constitution perpetuates an aristocratic rather than a democratic system of government because four persons (five today) can dictate to a nation, with or without popular consent. And that was intolerable. As Jackson said in his Bank veto, "The Congress, the Executive, and the Court must each for itself be guided by its own opinion of the Constitution." In a truly democratic state, he argued, the people ultimately decide the question of constitutionality. And they do it through the ballot box. . . .

[W]hen Andrew Jackson talked about the "people" he knew precisely whom he meant. Over and over in his public and private statements the term "the people" was defined as "the farmers, mechanics, and laborers," or "the humble members of society," or "those who earn their living by the sweat of their brow." Certainly not businessmen, monopolists, emerging capitalists, or any other elitist group, as sometimes suggested by historians. He repeatedly referred to the "working classes" of America as constituting "the people" and, to a very large extent, he meant laborers in the urban areas. For example, when Amos Kendall wrote him about a labor problem at the Navy Yard in Philadelphia, Jackson responded sympathetically to labor's complaint. It seems that the Navy Yard had problems obtaining good mechanics because the government demanded more than twelve hours per day from each worker and the mechanics would not work that long. The rate of pay was $2 per day for shipwrights, and in order to overcome the excessively long workday the Navy Yard had advertised that the rate per day would be increased to $2.50. But not a single mechanic applied because they had agreed "to a resolution that for a day's work they would labor only from 6 to 6." Other agencies in the Philadelphia area had acquiesced to this demand. "The government of the United States only holds out against it," Kendall told Jackson. "The concession of the richer classes was considered a triumph of the Democracy, and the Democracy here complain that the only opposition which exists, comes from an administration which relies on them for its support."

Kendall made his point as forcibly as possible: The working classes look to Jackson as their representative. In turn, the administration "relies on them" for support. "I think the point ought to be conceded," Kendall continued. "The demand of the workingmen that twelve hours shall constitute the working day, is not unreasonable. At Washington the extension of service in the Public Offices to ten hours is considered a hardship." What is to be gained in exacting more than twelve hours from the workingmen in the public service at Philadelphia? asked Kendall. In the first place, it has brought public service to a dead halt. In the second, "the democratic friends of the administration are disgusted and discouraged." I hope, he added, that the secretary of the navy will direct the Navy Board to comply with the wishes of the workingmen. "Concession will do much good; obstinacy will produce nothing but mischief . . . to the republican cause in this quarter."

After Jackson read this letter he referred it to his secretary of the navy. But first he scribbled a note of instructions to the secretary: "If the Navy board have not been directed to order that the hours, from 6 oclock to 6 be agreed to as pr. my former, intimation that it may be forthwith adopted." Clearly, then, Jacksonianism was not a movement of small businessmen. Jacksonian Democracy was more concerned with workingmen in places like the Philadelphia Navy Yard. This was confirmed in a long conversation a newspaper reporter had with the President on the subject. Jackson invariably "left upon the minds of all who have conversed with him," said the reporter, "a deep impression of his solicitude to see the laboring class of the country" freed from the burdens imposed by a business aristocracy. "He has expressed no sentiment in regard to other classes of society. . . . His motto is, Let labor have security, prosperity will follow—all other interests rest upon it, and must flourish if it flourishes." Contrast that statement with the opinion of Whigs, gloated the *Globe*. During the last congressional session, Daniel Webster said: *"Take care of the rich, and the rich will take care of the poor."* Webster denied making the remark, said Blair, but, "as the Indians say, he speaks with a forked tongue."

The policy of the Jackson administration on labor was best defined in the *Globe,* taking its cue from a series of editorials in the Boston *Morning Post* and addressed directly "To All Democrats or Working Men." "If Democracy be the rule of your policy," the article read, "suffer no act to be passed . . . however it may promise local or personal advantage, if it tends in the smallest degree, to give *legal* advantages to *capital,* over *labor;* if it have that effect, it must necessarily increase the natural inequality in society; and finally, make two distinct classes: namely—masters and slaves." . . .

[I]n addition to preaching majoritarian rule, Old Hickory cited strict construction of the Constitution as an essential article of faith. However much he himself subverted that doctrine, Jackson believed fundamentally in limited government and the necessity of keeping government spending to an absolute minimum. He also included opposition to a national bank and rotation in office as part of his creed. Rotation in office was simply his way of stating that the operation of government must be open to all. No elitism. No official class. Again, he himself may have failed to recruit from every social and economic class, but he insisted that democratizing the government be regarded as a cardinal doctrine of Jacksonianism.

Indeed, the General's views on holding office became even more democratic as he grew older. He proceeded from the premise that all offices—whether appointed or elected—must ultimately fall under the absolute control of the people. Appointed offices should be rotated, preferably every four years. Elected offices must be filled *directly* by the people. In keeping with this principle, Jackson tried to abolish the College of Electors in the selection of the chief executive by proposing a constitutional amendment. In addition, he said, the President should serve no more than a single term of either four or six years. Jackson advocated a single term in order to place the President beyond the reach of improper—"corrupting"—influences. Moreover, he believed that United States senators should be directly elected by the people. Also, their term should be limited to four years and they should be subject to removal. In Jackson's mind, the Senate was an elitist body of men committed to the principles of aristocracy and totally unrepresentative of the American people. Considering his long and bitter struggle with the upper house it is not surprising that he should feel so vehement. . . .

Interestingly, Jackson would also require federal judges to stand for election, and presumably he would include the justices of the Supreme Court once the Constitution had been properly amended. And he would limit judicial terms to seven years but permit reelection. By this time Jackson was so totally devoted to the democratic principle of officeholding that he could conceive no better method of preserving freedom and ensuring justice for all. His remarkably advanced views were regarded by some as very radical—if not dangerous. The historian George Bancroft interviewed Jackson on the subject and recorded some of the President's opinions. "He thinks every officer should in his turn pass before the people, for their approval or rejection," wrote Bancroft. "In England the judges should have independence to protect the people against the crown," said Jackson. But not in America. "Here the judges should not be independent of the people, but be appointed for not more than seven years. The people would always re-elect the good judges."

Jacksonian Democracy, then, stretches the concept of democracy about as far as it can go and still remain workable. Obviously, Jackson himself was far ahead of his times—and maybe further than this country can ever achieve.

It should be noticed in reading Jackson's attempt at defining his brand of democracy that he said nothing about slavery, Indian removal, tariffs, or internal improvements—although his opposition to internal improvements might be implied by his strict constructionism. As to slavery, there has been much misunderstanding among modern historians about the position of Jacksonian Democrats on this issue. Contrary to wide belief, Democrats were not committed to the preservation of slavery—at least not as Jacksonians, however they may have felt about the issue individually and personally. True, they abhorred abolitionists. They regarded them as malcontents who, like aristocrats, feared the people and the kind of government that majoritarian rule produced. Abolitionists decried the demise of their Republic— just like all other elites—and blamed the demise on the rise of democracy. They therefore sought to create as much trouble as possible in order to discredit the democracy and bring about the restoration of their "elitist" rule. So the slavery question, as far as Jackson and his friends believed, was simply a blind to create trouble in order to prostrate the democracy.

Nullifiers aided and abetted the abolitionists, according to the Democrats, for the same reason and objective. These two groups of malcontents were linked together to produce havoc, and out of that havoc would ultimately rise to power "blue light federalists" in the north, consisting of monopolists, bankers, and wealthy businessmen, and nullifiers in the south, who would be their counterparts and agents. "The universal courtesy and kindness extended to the abolitionists in Congress," wrote Blair in the *Globe,* ". . . by all the *would be thought* Hotspurs of the South, while their fury and frenzy is directed against the Democrats . . . who are fighting the battles of the South, against the fanatics of the North, are all signs to prove the identity of political design between the nullifiers and abolitionists in every branch of federalism."

Jacksonian Democracy did not represent a defense of slavery. Jacksonian Democrats believed they were defending the notion of majority rule and that the abolitionists and nullifiers and Whigs abhorred the notion of democracy and entered any sort of political alliance to discredit the new political system. The abolition question, wrote Martin Van Buren, was a vicious device "of evil disposed persons to disturb the harmony of our happy Union through its agency." Besides, slavery was not a matter for the government to concern itself—not if it expected to preserve "the harmony of our happy Union." The right of an individual to his private property without interference by the federal government was basic to the whole concept of freedom. For the government to legislate abolition would strike at the very foundation of American principles and institutions. Everyone knew this. Why, then, would abolitionists continue their agitation against slavery except that they were "evil disposed persons" with evil designs upon "our happy Union"?

To a large extent, therefore, Jackson and his friends equated all things in terms of the emerging democracy. Wherever they saw a linkage or connection that might be interpreted as a conspiracy against majority rule they instantly raised their voices in protest and alarm. Another example was their reaction to the increasing incidence of urban violence during the Jacksonian age. Again, the enemies of democracy were accused of inciting the violence to restore elitist rule. "Aristocrats, ever ready to take every unfair advantage of our situation," reported the *Globe,* "seize on these occurrences [of urban violence] as so many proofs that man is not capable of self-government and that the theory of a Republic where men will be equal is founded in error and can never be reduced to successful practice." The Whigs constantly complained about the rising rate of crime and city violence and claimed it started when Jackson came to power. They said that the presence of this brawler and duelist in the White House, supported by the ignorant masses, served to sanction violence as a legitimate response in public discourse and argument. Violence can be terminated by putting down the democracy. Once the democracy goes, Jackson and his "reforms" go with it.

The leadership of the Democratic party not only believed this theory, they preached it. The Whigs blame every evil in the country on the rise of democracy, they said. Edwin Croswell, editor of the Albany *Argus,* the mouthpiece of Van Buren's political machine, the Albany Regency, explained their thinking to George Bancroft. "The Tory leaders labor to convey the impression that the modern tendency to violence & to the disregard of the law," he wrote, "arises from too great an infusion of the democratic spirit, & from the character & example of the Executive. . . . It is important . . . that the public mind . . . should be disabused on the subject; & that the excesses of the day sh'd be traced to their true source,—the revolutionary speeches, sundry harangues, threatened assassinations, and defiance & violation of law, by the Bank & its party leaders & agents, of the Tory school, in & out of Congress, during the memorable Panic season."

It is instructive that Croswell traced the true cause of every evil in society—at least as far as Democrats saw it—to "the Bank & its party leaders & agents." Jacksonians not only vilified the Bank at every opportunity, they also warned against the power of money to corrupt government, betray the people, and jeopardize liberty. "Money is power," Jackson had said, and when controlled by a business elite it will inevitably destroy the democracy. Even in his speech to Tennesseans at Columbia, the President swiped at the "moneyed aristocracy." Never "can we hope to see our domestic relations entirely tranquilized," he declared, as long as the bankers and industrialists can unite the "heterogeneous elements of discord into one common foe to the principles of republicanism." They would concentrate power in the federal government, he went on, to promote the interests of the wealthy and subvert the rights of the people.

Equally malignant in "undermining the purity and complicating the simplicity of our virtuous Government," according to Jackson, was "the *paper system.*" This wretched business, he said, "has introduced a thousand ways of robbing honest labour of its earnings to make knaves rich, powerful and dangerous." Also, "it seems to me that one of the greatest threatners of our admirable form of Government, is the gradual consuming corruption, which is spreading and carrying stockjobbing, Land jobbing and every species of speculation into our Legislature, state and national." In writing these words, Jackson almost seemed to have a sense of what would happen to the country after the Civil War. . . .

Equality, Racism, and Jacksonian Democracy

ALEXANDER SAXTON

Class components of the Democratic party included urban workers and small middle-class, yeoman farmers, aspirant entrepreneurs and southern planters. . . .

Urban workers in the 1830s were mostly artisans. Artisans might be masters of their own shops who employed others, or they might be wage earners. Some moved back and forth from one status to the other. Moreover, the circumstances of artisanry were changing as manufacturing increased in volume and scale. A few artisans would move up into the new class of industrial capitalists. Others would convert their skills to the specializations of machine designers, millwrights, industrial mechanics, foremen and superintendents; and some remained journeymen in lines like the printing, building and metal trades that survived as craft skills. Some also moved down to join the growing ranks of industrial workers. And there had of course always been the unskilled in the cities—porters, stevedores, seamen, day laborers.

After the War of 1812, most of the diverse groups collectively referred to as urban workers and the small middle class, if they participated in politics, must have been Jeffersonian, then National Republicans. Did they become Democrats? Not all, by any means. In cities of the central and eastern seaboard, a significant number joined workingmen's parties, from which they opposed both Adams men and Jacksonians. Essentially these parties spoke for independent artisans facing the onset of industrialization. Short-lived, since the logic of the party system tended to isolate them or force them into the major parties, the workingmen's parties nonetheless furnished a conduit of radical thought from the revolutionary era to the romantic egalitarianism of the nineteenth century. Their heroes were Thomas Jefferson and Ethan Allen, Tom Paine and Frances Wright, Irish rebels and English Chartists. Clearly the main transit of workingmen was into the so-called Locofoco wing of the Jacksonian Democracy, from which emanated the most radicalizing impulses of American politics, including proposals for land distribution that eventually found their way into the Homestead and Free Soil movements.

Other wage earners followed different routes. Free blacks in New England and New York, most of whom certainly worked for wages, solidly backed the Whigs. So also, though not so solidly, did native-born Protestant workers in cities where recent immigrants, especially if they were Irish or German Catholics, became prominent in Democratic politics. Despite these exceptions, however, it seems reasonable to conclude from secondary literature, based on vast amounts of primary evidence, that American workingmen during the Jacksonian era, skilled and unskilled, East and West, were more likely to be Democrats than Whigs. . . .

With respect to yeomen farmers, as to urban workers, the difficulty of

Excerpts from *The Rise and Fall of the White Republic: Class Politics and Mass Culture in Nineteenth Century America* by Alexander Saxton, 1990, pp. 131–136, 142–153. Reprinted by permission of Verso, London.

generalization is compounded by ambiguities of definition. Farmers often hired out for wages and in some areas moved between agrarian and industrial pursuits. . . . The problem is not so much one of terminology as of history. Farmers in nineteenth-century America comprised a vast matrix of class formation; the yeoman identity constantly played host to speculative, entrepreneurial and wage worker identities.

As to their politics, what can be said is that nationally they divided about equally between Whigs and Democrats in the early years of Democratic dominance and had become more favorable to the Democrats by the 1850s. Given the volatility of their class tendencies and the limited choice offered by the party system, it is hardly surprising that yeoman farmer status proved insufficient by itself to dictate a national commitment to one party or the other. Certainly there were marked regional preferences. Areas of upper New York and the Old Northwest into which New England population migrated were likely to be whiggish. South of the Yankee corridor, areas in transition from a frontier economy (characterized by dependence on current migration for agricultural markets and cash flow) to an 'Old West' economy (characterized by commercial agriculture, developing urban markets and beginnings of manufacturing) also were likely to show whiggish proclivities. On the other hand, the careers of agrarian radicals like Thomas Hart Benton and Andrew Johnson demonstrate how solidly the Democracy had established itself in the lower Mississippi Valley. . . .

A third element of the Democratic coalition was a group even more troublesome to define than the first two. Perhaps it is better identified as a state of mind than a class. According to the great tradition every white American boy . . . was supposed to cherish ambitions of becoming president. This tradition was Jacksonian; it had not existed before the advent of the first mass party. . . . 'To the dissatisfied, whether through distress or ambition', Bray Hammond wrote in his study of banks and Jacksonian politics,

> . . . Andrew Jackson offered a distinct and attractive change. . . . He became champion of the common man, even though the latter might be no longer either frontiersman or farmer but speculator, capitalist or entrepreneur of a new, democratic sort, who in every village and township was beginning to profit by the Industrial Revolution, the growth of population, and the expanding supply of bank credit. This new common man was manufacturer, banker, builder, carrier and promoter. He belonged to the 'active and enterprising', in the luminous contrast put by Churchill C. Cambreleng, as against the 'wealthier classes'.

. . . The fourth component of the Jacksonian coalition—southern planters—presents no difficulty of definition. Not all slaveowners, of course, were planters. . . . Allowing five members to a family, planter families would have numbered 125,000, about 1.5 percent of the white population of the South. During the 1840s and 1850s planters tended to shift from the Whigs to the Democracy. This shift contributed to the creation of a virtually solid South prior to the Civil War. . . .

Jacksonian Democrats asserted the political, civil and moral equality of white male citizens. This did not mean that they advocated equality by act of government, rather that they advocated the equal opportunity of all white male citizens to engage in the pursuit of happiness and to get ahead—not necessarily ahead of their fellow citizens, but ahead of where they had been last year and the year before. In America, presumably, people got ahead by diligence and skill at producing goods and services for which there was a market demand. Disciples of Adam Smith, devotees of the labor theory of value, and Jacksonians all proclaimed free competition among individual producers. This view was incompatible with slavery; yet so long as the immediate political needs of slaveholders, yeoman farmers, urban working-men and aspirant entrepreneurs ran parallel, the contradiction could be held off by rhetorical skills and selective concessions to other partners in the coalition. . . .

Jacksonian legitimation grouped these components under a single head. They were *producers*—'planters, farmers, mechanics (with a slight infusion from the commercial and professional classes)'—the 'productive and bur-then-bearing classes' of the nation. That Senator Thomas Hart Benton, the Missouri agrarian, used *class* in its plural form signals the polemical thrust of his thought. He was refuting class with *classes*. In a society composed of many classes, equally 'productive and burthen-bearing', class was reduced to mere category or division of labor. Producers might be poor and humble, or they might win fame and fortune through their own efforts applied to opportunity, as Benton himself and Andrew Jackson had done. Such achieve-ments, creating the abundance by which the nation lived and prospered, merited the acclaim of fellow-citizens. No matter how great or how modest their success, producers would never lose touch with the soil and the work-bench, with the shared life of productive labor from which they came. Far from being a class, they comprised the nation itself, the 'bone and sinew of our country', as President Jackson addressed them.

Even within the producers' nation, however, there resided an enemy that had to be defeated again and again. Not long after the overthrow of the Adams administration, Benton had identified this foe as a 'Federal' party that 'discouraged the settlement of the West by refusing . . . to vote for equitable prices for the public lands. . . .' In Democratic rhetoric the term did not so much refer to a native upper class as to an alien element rendered subservient to foreign influence through its own corrupt hankering after aristocratic pretensions. The real nation, the producers, Jackson warned in his farewell address, must stand ever vigilant against the selfish minority that enriched itself, not by producing, but by manipulating money and credit: bankers, monopolists, masters of 'great moneyed corporations'. . . .

Just as its economic policies and social theory flowed from the egalitarian premise, so did the Democracy's enthusiasm for territorial acquisition. In a predominantly agricultural society it would appear obvious that equal op-portunity for an increasing population must depend on opening new regions to settlement. Each component of the Jacksonian coalition anticipated gains from expansion. For southern planters, these included new cotton lands, perhaps sugar in Cuba and Tamaulipas as well; and the entry of additional slave states to enhance the political power of the South. For yeoman farmers the gains were more and cheaper land for themselves and their children.

For aspirant entrepreneurs new territory always seemed the realm of the big chance. Even to workingmen and the middle class of the eastern cities, territorial expansion appeared promising. It is unlikely that many urban artisans expected to stake out homesteads, yet it was not illogical to suppose that open land in the West would reduce competition for jobs in the east and might speed the growth of western industrial centers to which working people could (and did in fact) remove. . . .

Although territorial aggrandizement raised particular class aspirations, the practice of mass politics evoked larger visions of the producers' republic. Democrats successfully appropriated the emblems of nationalism. This crucial achievement resulted largely from the efforts of new professionals, distinct from the older and already abundant professional politicians in that their goal was not merely to win office (although they sometimes did) but to fashion marketable commodities from the raw materials of information and ideas. Outstanding among such intellectual artisans was the historian George Bancroft, himself a party leader in Massachusetts and chief theoretician of the Democracy. In his popular *History,* Bancroft celebrated the yeoman farmers' defiance of British tyranny at Lexington as the fulfillment of a beneficent preparation 'of providence and of time.' 'The light that led them on' had originated from 'Republican Greece and Rome', from Christianity 'as taught by Paul of Tarsus and Augustine, through Calvin and the divines of New England.'

> . . . All the centuries bowed themselves from the recesses of the past to cheer in their sacrifice the lowly men who proved themselves worthy of their forerunners, and whose children rise up and call them blessed.

Born too late to stand with the farmers at Lexington, Bancroft was nonetheless able to carry on what he considered their mission by serving simultaneously as secretary of war and of the navy under President Polk. In these offices he detailed arrangements for the seizure of California and the invasion of Mexico. . . .

[Ralph Waldo] Emerson, a Whig, observed that although the Whigs put up the more dependable candidates, Democrats offered the more generous and exciting program. Emerson referred explicitly to the egalitarian premise and opening of opportunities 'for the young and the poor to the sources of wealth and power.' The ideological construct that compelled Emerson's grudging admiration as well as the allegiance of so many of his talented contemporaries made use of white racism to legitimize slavery, territorial expansion at the expense of Mexico and the removal or the extermination of Indians. In the South, Democratic doctrine sustained the planter class in several interrelated ways. It reassured planters themselves that slavery, being neither their fault nor within their power to change, would, so long as it remained in their hands, function as a benignly Christian social system. It neutralized the potential opposition of non-slaveholders by offering equal partnership in the *herrenvolk* democracy, while simultaneously threatening them with the fate of the whites of Santo Domingo should they fail to sustain the hegemony of the planters. Finally, it encircled the slaves by making the ongoingness of their daily lives depend upon perceiving the master's imposed view of their circumstances as divinely ordained in nature. Slavery could hardly have existed in the American South without these three transactions.

Racism in the South, as throughout the nation, showed both hard and soft sides. At first these corresponded directly to class and party separation: planters soft, yeomen hard; Whigs soft, Democrats hard. Planters favored controlled nurture; . . . they were apt to practice diversified training, incentives and rewards. Yeomen (together with white workingmen in the South) were more likely to speak for segregation, denial of training, exclusion from labor markets, deportation; ultimately for extermination, if that could be brought about by natural means. . . . In the American South, these tendencies coexisted, one prevalent in the Black Belt, the other in the hills and hinterland.

Out of these paired characteristics arose one other crucial set. The soft side, appropriately to paternalism, envisioned the object of racism as a child. [The novelist] John Pendleton Kennedy's slave children at Swallow Barn precisely convey the image: little bright-eyed animals, comic, sometimes lovable, always troublesome; yet less than human because incapable of maturing beyond the mental and moral limits of childishness. For the hard side, by contrast, childishness was mere camouflage hypocritically connived at by slaveowners themselves. The real African was grimly adult: a sexual colossus, a Dominican ravisher, worse than savage because clothed in the false garb of civilization. The two images counseled opposite modes of treatment— good-natured manipulation, on the one hand, suppression and terror, on the other.

In the South the images of slaves and the modes of treating them tended to merge, because the plantation, as a labor system, required both. The planter could laugh at—or even with—and manipulate his slaves so long as the overseer (likely to be of yeoman origin) wielded the whip. More important, they merged because the paternalist and competitionist societies coexisted. Planters' sons rode out with yeoman farmers in the security patrols. When political parties divided on class lines, planters found themselves in an untenable position since they could not exclude yeomen from political activity. Planters, once they turned Democrats, adopted the hard side as part of their egalitarian rhetoric; but egalitarianism could be relevant only to the external relations of their class. In domestic affairs—in justifying class dominance to themselves, and at home with their families and slaves—the soft side remained indispensable. As the South moved from two-party competition to one-party solidarity [in the 1840s], the hard and soft sides of racism became optional styles of speech, each appropriate to certain situations or audiences. . . .

The hard and soft sides were mutually reinforcing. Together they presented themselves, ready for uses old and new, to successive generations of slaveowners and non-slaveowners, planters and yeomen, Whigs, Jacksonians—and Southern Democrats.

Moreover, in the arena of mass politics, racist doctrine acquired that pragmatic, anti-intellectual unity characteristic of the legal brief. Logically incompatible arguments offer alternate routes by which divided juries (or voters) may arrive at common verdicts. Whether believers in the curse of

Ham ought to reconcile their differences with environmentalists, or orthodox Christians share the Lord's Supper with separate creationists, were issues of relatively small concern, for example, to Virginia legislators confronting the aftermath of Nat Turner's rebellion. More immediate verdicts took precedence. In 1831 and 1832, non-slaveholding Virginians, mainly from western counties, argued publicly for the last time in the South for a plan of gradual emancipation. They lost. After the Virginia constitutional debates the South moved from its traditionally Jeffersonian apology for slavery as a burden imposed by history to an aggressive assertion that slavery not only worked to the advantage of the South, but was the best possible system man could devise. . . .

Tactical applications of racism . . . differed in the North and West from those of the South. Southern planters who might still need the paternalistic metaphor at home had shuffled off earlier linkages to the Whig party nationally and sought instead to cement their alliance with the Jacksonian coalition. Consequently the initial thrust was on the hard side of racism. At the cutting edge were northern and western party leaders whose political careers depended upon the southern connection. What they perceived as a main danger to their expectations came not from traditional Whig projects like internal improvements and protective tariffs, but from antislavery agitation emanating in part (but by no means entirely) from whiggish sources.

Their response was to identify all anti-slavery agitation with special interest, especially that of manufacturing capital; and to use racist invective to discredit the sincerity, patriotism, even sanity, of anti-slavery advocates. This was the hard side at its hardest. It reinforced the already widespread conviction that Whig softness on racial questions cloaked an intent to use Africans and Indians to undermine the status of white producers. In the countryside, especially in the West, this led to denunciations of sentimentally romantic pampering of Indians; in cities it intensified fears that Africans, freed from slavery, might undercut the wages and living conditions of white workingmen.

James K. Paulding provided what may be regarded as an official statement of the northern Democratic position on slavery and anti-slavery. A friend and collaborator of Washington Irving, Paulding figured prominently in New York literary circles from the War of 1812 to the war against Mexico. . . . He published *Slavery* to aid Martin Van Buren's 1836 presidential campaign, his reward being the secretaryship of the Navy, which he held till the end of Van Buren's administration. Paulding recapitulated the southern defense of slavery, adapting it to what he considered the sensibilities of northern readers. He separated himself from the extreme 'positive' defense by conceding that if slavery were to be established *de novo* he would not favor it; but as it presently existed in the United States he found it by no means 'of such surpassing enormity as to demand the sacrifice of the harmony and consequent union of the states.' On the contrary, so valuable was the Union in itself and to human progress 'that no beneficial consequences to any class of mankind or to the whole universe' could 'counterbalance' the evil that must result from its 'dissolution.'

'The government of the United States, its institutions and its privileges', Paulding wrote, 'belong of right wholly and exclusively to white men; for they were purchased, not by the blood of the negroes, but by that of our fathers.' Africans, like Indians, had showed themselves incapable either of participating in, or standing against, the white republic. Failure of the 'late insurrection in Lower Virginia', and its inevitable outcome in a 'most terrible retribution' demonstrated this truth. Even were they given their freedom they could never provide for themselves. 'The mind of the African, not only in his native country, but through every change, and in all circumstances, seems in a great degree divested of this divine attribute of improvement.' To educate and impart aspiration to those too dull to pursue it was like giving the curse of Tantalus. Yet, if simply left as they were they would remain happy and well cared for, 'never beset by the gnawing cares of the free white man, whose whole life is one continued effort to provide for himself and his children.' How could any right-minded person advocate uprooting these limited and dependent creatures by freeing them? The answer was that none could. Opponents of slavery then must be either enemies of the nation or mentally ill. For Paulding the bottom line of anti-slavery was miscegenation. 'The project for intermarrying with blacks is a project for debasing the whites by a mixture of that blood, which, wherever it flows, carries with it the seeds of deterioration . . . a scheme for lowering the standard of our nature by approximating the highest grade of human being to the lowest . . . . They are traitors to the white skin, influenced by mad-brained fanaticism, or the victims of licentious and ungovernable passions, perverted into an unnatural taste by their own indulgence.' . . .

Tapping the subtreasury of American racism, Paulding had put together formulations appropriate to a particular constituency. Other Democratic politicians did likewise. Thomas Hart Benton warned Missouri voters in 1829 against the machinations of those who opposed cheap lands in the West, charging that this 'Federal' party 'in every question between the white people and the negroes or Indians, regularly, officially, impertinently and wickedly takes part with the Indians and negroes against their white fellow citizens and fellow Christians . . .' All such actions tended 'to one point . . . the abolition of slavery, under the clause of the Declaration of Independence which asserts the natural equality of man.'

'What good man', President Jackson asked the Congress in 1830, 'would prefer a country covered with forests and ranged by a few thousand savages, to our extensive Republic, studded with towns and prosperous farms . . . and filled with all the blessings of liberty, civilization and religion?' Questions such as these with their liturgical responses could be expanded to meet new circumstances. 'Massive, yet most sweet and plain character!' Walt Whitman lamented on the first anniversary of President Jackson's death. '. . . Ah, there has lived among us but *one* purer!' Soon afterwards, in sharp contrast to the notion later expressed in 'Passage to India' of races marrying and being given in marriage, Whitman demanded of his Brooklyn *Eagle* readers: 'What has miserable, inefficient Mexico to do with the mission of peopling the New World with a noble race? . . . Be it ours to achieve that mission.'

In the two questions from Jackson and Whitman the racist component turns solely against Indians (or Indian-ness as embodied in Mexicans). This reflected the events of the 1830s and 1840s. Indian removal and westward expansion had proved spectacularly successful. Political opposition dwindled to spotty and opportunist criticisms. As John Quincy Adams had foreseen, there could be no effective resistance to the Democracy on the question of expansion because a majority of Americans, Whigs included, agreed with what was being done. The expansionist consensus merged the hard and soft sides of anti-Indian racism by incorporating expressions of regret over the fate of Indians into narratives that traced the inevitability of their extinction. Ideologically, the effect was to exonerate individuals, parties, nations, of any moral blame for what history had decreed. . . .

Fully as successful as Jacksonian Indian policy—at first—was the planter alliance with northern urban Democracy. More than any other factor, this alliance perpetuated Democratic dominance in the party system. . . .

The Party of Moral Discipline: Whig Values

DANIEL WALKER HOWE

When John Bell of Tennessee announced in 1835 that he was joining the Whig party, he declared: "We have, in truth, in the last eight or ten years, been in a continual state of moral war." With such moral pronouncements Whig leaders reached out to their followers. The party's economic program was quite clearly designed to appeal to "haves" rather than "have-nots." A protective tariff would most directly benefit northern factory owners and the large-scale planters of certain southern staples like hemp and sugar, while a national bank would be of greatest use to businessmen in all parts of the country. As for internal improvements, these "could vitally concern only those producers, of whatsoever, who produced more than they could use themselves or sell locally." It is scarcely surprising that most rich men in America were Whigs. What is more remarkable, and requires more explanation, is the party's broad support in the electorate. Many men voted Whig whose economic stake in Whig policies was no clearer than that of their Democratic neighbors. To persuade them, the party relied heavily on moral appeals.

Probably all political parties take moral stands at least occasionally, but for the Whigs these had particular importance. Moral appeals were the Whigs' substitute for party loyalty. Less well knit than the Democrats by patronage and organization, the Whigs emerged as a party only intermittently, at election time. This gave their campaigns something of the flavor of religious revivals. If the Whig party won over most rich men by its economic program and some poor men by its ethnic identity, its moral appeal was particularly effective for those in between, the large middle class. Most voters, of course, would not have sorted out economic, ethnic, and moral appeals into separate compartments but would have taken note of the overall persuasive effect. To borrow a term from psychology, their voting patterns would have been "overdetermined" by many factors.

In making their moral appeals, the leaders of the Whig party were addressing widely shared values; if they had not, they would not have remained leaders of a major party for long. . . . Of course, all Whig voters did not share all aspects of the Whig value system; many would not even have been fully aware of all of them. For ordinary Whig voters, the values must often have been implicit in their lives rather than the product of much self-conscious reflection. From the leaders we can derive the fullest, most detailed picture of this value system. Probably every culture known to mankind possesses such a system; the Whigs, however, asserted their values with unusual insistence. Indeed, the first aspect of Whig culture deserving attention is this: it was didactic.

This aggressive didacticism of theirs was something new. It was probably related to the rise of the missionary spirit in religion that accompanied the Second Great Awakening and sent Protestant emissaries all over the world in search of converts. There had been different "political cultures" even in the eighteenth-century American colonies, it would appear. The political culture of the coastal and urban areas was more elitist, commercial, and "cosmopolitan"; the remote areas were more democratic, agrarian, and "localist." To some extent the political culture of nineteenth-century Whiggery represented a continuation of this colonial "cosmopolitan" culture. A number of monographic studies have shown a tendency for more economically developed counties to vote Whig, except as concentrations of ethnic blocs distort the pattern. But no one (so far as I know) has claimed that the cosmopolitan culture of colonial times was allied to, or transmitted by, the First Great Awakening as nineteenth-century Whig culture was propagated by the Second Awakening. Indeed, a powerful argument has been made for the reverse proposition: that the evangelical and cosmopolitan cultures were hostile to each other in the eighteenth century.

The Whig party's electoral campaigns formed part of a cultural struggle to impose on the United States the standards of morality we usually term Victorian. They were standards of self-control and restraint, which dovetailed well with the economic program of the party, for they emphasized thrift, sobriety, and public responsibility. E. P. Thompson has called the evangelical reformers of early nineteenth-century England the "disciplinarians." It is a term that fits the American Whigs too. They looked upon the Democratic voters as undisciplined—men who had escaped the institutional controls of European society but had not yet learned to impose internal restraints on themselves. The Whigs wanted to teach these people that liberty has no real value without responsibility and order. The objective was well stated by the great English Victorian, John Stuart Mill: "The test of what is right in politics is not the *will* of the people, but the *good* of the people, and our object is not to compel but to persuade the people to impose, for the sake of their own good, some restraint on the immediate and unlimited exercise of their own will."

Running through Whig political appeals was the concept of consciously arranged order. This was characteristic of their reliance on government planning rather than the invisible forces of the marketplace. It was characteristic of their economic program, so carefully contrived to integrate tariff policy, land policy, internal improvements, and federal revenue-sharing. It was characteristic of the standards of personal morality that the evangelical reformers promoted. It was even characteristic of the formal, not to say pedantic, arrangement of ideas that constituted Whig rhetoric and moral philosophy. In the absence of order, the threat of a Hobbesian state of nature, where men behaved like "famished, infuriated animals, goaded by instinct and unrestrained by protective hopes and fears," seemed very real to the Whigs. . . .

Like John Stuart Mill, American Whigs typically assumed moral responsibility for others. They called this assumption "rectitude": the love of virtue, by whomever manifested. To them, it seemed proof of their sincerity. To many of the others involved, it seemed meddlesome at best, coercive at worst. The debate over whether Whig moral reform should be condemned as middle-class repressiveness—a debate that historians still carry on—was begun by contemporaries. When Lyman Beecher's church on Hanover Street burned down, the volunteer fire companies, who hated his temperance crusading, refused to fight the flames. Instead, it is reported, they watched and sang: "While Beecher's church holds out to burn / The vilest sinner may return"—a parody of a hymn.

There were many, like those firemen, who resisted the moral didacticism of the Whigs. A network of what sociologists call "negative reference groups" existed in America, and, since there were only two major parties to choose between, political alliances were often made according to the venerable principle that "the enemy of my enemy is my friend." So the Irish Catholic immigrants became the most loyal of Democrats in reaction against Whig Protestantism, and the blacks voted Whig in reaction against the Irish, who hated them. In Louisiana, where the French Catholics were prosperous and long-established sugar planters, they were the Whigs, while the Protestant small farmers who resented them were the Democrats. On the whole, however, the Whigs were the more homogeneous party because they drew upon the most powerful single culture in the society, evangelical Protestantism. There is much to be said for applying to cultural politics the interpretation that Arthur Schlesinger, Jr., has applied to the politics of economic interests: the Whigs sought to strengthen the hegemony of the dominant group, while the Democrats represented all those out-groups who resisted. As the more heterogeneous party, the Democrats were naturally more inclined to tolerate cultural differences. . . .

The object of Whig didacticism was redemption: to make people better. One of the greatest Whig reformers explained it this way: "I look for the harmonizing of Desire with Duty, not through the blotting out of the latter, but through the chastening, renovating, and purifying of the former." If people were made to want to be good, there would be nothing to fear from their freedom. The Democrats, by contrast, wanted liberation: to get rid of every vestige of oppression, at least as far as white men were concerned. The reactions of the two parties to the extinction of the national debt during Jackson's administration typify these orientations. The Democrats welcomed the chance to liberate people from the burden of taxation. The Whigs favored redeeming the people by retaining the taxes and spending the money on worthwhile improvements; a society that did not respond positively to such an opportunity for collective self-improvement would become "a community of self-degradation," warned John Quincy Adams. . . .

The Whigs assumed that human nature was malleable. It could and should be shaped by schools, benevolent societies, reformatories, asylums. But the wise person shaped his own nature. This promise is what gave Whig values their appeal for those who did not find them coercive or patronizing. Self-denial, self-help, self-control: these were all part of the process of self-culture. It was not an ideal peculiar to the American Whigs but one they shared with many middle-class European contemporaries. A European intellectual historian has described it well. "The really free man," in this system of values, "is not the man who can choose any line of conduct indifferently— this is being rather a frivolous and weak-willed man—but the man who has the energy to choose that which is most conformable to his moral destiny." Democrats rejected the ideal of self-culture, often implicitly, occasionally explicitly. What the Whigs called "culture" they thought "artificial." It was desirable to remove artificial impediments and assert the rights of the natural man and his freedom to act.

The reforms the Jacksonian Democrats fought for were the kind of reforms people undertake for themselves in pursuit of greater liberation and greater participation in decision-making. They included reapportionment of state legislatures, popular election of judges and presidential Electors, dismantling the national banking monopoly, and some early efforts at labor organization. Whig reforms, by contrast, were frequently altruistic efforts to redeem others rather than examples of self-help. Whigs supported Dorothea Dix's campaign for federal aid to mental hospitals; Democrats opposed. Whig prison reformers sought to make prison a place of redemption as well as retribution (from this hope comes our word "penitentiary"); Democratic prison reformers, on the other hand, were usually concerned with economy, efficiency, and deterrence.

Redemptive Whig reform was benevolent yet restrictive. The two aspects are well illustrated in the opposition to both flogging and the grog ration in the U.S. Navy. Ralph Waldo Emerson, a perceptive if uninvolved observer of the political scene, satirized Whig didacticism and anxiousness to redeem people by calling the archetypal Whig an overprotective physician, whose "social frame is a hospital." He dresses everyone in "slippers & flannels, with bib & pap-spoon," and prescribes "pills & herb tea, whig preaching, whig poetry, whig philosophy, [and] whig marriages."

If the Whigs could be officious, the Democrats could be callous. They were interested in the liberation of free white men but cared little for others. . . . Some Whig congressmen, like Adams and Giddings, persisted in bringing up questions related to slavery until northern Whig opinion swung round to supporting them. By contrast, the party of Jackson started out by being almost unanimous in its hostility to antislavery, even in the North, and was slower to feel the impact of the issue.

. . . Within limits, Whig legislators showed greater willingness to support measures like trade with Haiti and civil rights for free Negroes. The deferential concept of society that Whigs generally shared can plausibly explain this willingness: Whigs could help blacks without having to acknowledge their equality. On the other hand, the Democrats' egalitarianism seemed to force them to deny the very humanity of nonwhites lest they have to confront them as equals.

Even antislavery Whigs did not think so much in terms of liberating the blacks as of redeeming them. Lyman Beecher, a good example, was preaching temperance to black congregations before he preached emancipation to white ones. Of course, the black ministers invited him to come. A philosophy of "improvement" and "uplift" was supported by many black intellectuals in the prewar period—by more of them, in fact, than were actively involved in abolitionism. The black community's affiliation with the Whigs was not simply a negative reaction to the hatred they experienced from Democratic groups like the Irish-Americans or southern poor whites; it also expressed, quite accurately, the cultural program of these black leaders. . . .

. . . The Whigs were a political party with a large British-American constituency, both old Yankee and recent immigrant. Some of the party's appeal was based on ethnic identification. Not surprisingly, the Whigs' language included celebrations of this heritage. However, their ethnocentrism was more cultural or ideological than genetic. "I am no great believer in the natural excellencies of Anglo-Saxon blood, but I have great faith in the acquired excellencies of Anglo-Saxon institutions," declared one moral philosopher who was an especially outspoken Whig. Daniel Webster at Plymouth Rock praised the many achievements of the English-speaking peoples, but he affirmed that their highest glory was dedication to "the freedom of human thought and the respectability of individual character"—principles he maintained were applicable to all humanity, "I care not of what complexion, white or brown." Henry W. Bellows, writing in the *American Whig Review,* actually welcomed intermarriage on the ground that it would improve the genetic stock of the Anglo-Saxons while facilitating the extension of their culture. He also looked forward to the time when all South Americans would speak English and be converted to Protestantism and the common law. The converse of such hopes for cultural imperialism was the fear of cultural degeneracy. An eminent divine writing on behalf of the American Home Missionary Society warned that the Boers of South Africa illustrated just such a process. They had become nomads, practicing lynch law and torture, neglecting education, letting "their women do the work." As a result, "They are now a race of nominally christian barbarians—barbarians under the Synod of Dort, a standing proof that Protestants, and they too of Saxon blood, may drop out of civilization. . . . Let no American that loves his country refuse to heed the example."

The contrasting positions of the two major parties on race and culture are dramatically illustrated in the controversy over government policy toward the Indians. This issue was actually second only to banking in provoking the polarization of parties under Jackson. The controversy was provoked by the removal of the Cherokee Nation from Georgia to Oklahoma. The Cherokees had adopted sedentary agriculture, commerce, Christianity, constitutional government, and—thanks to Sequoia—literacy. Although they were by no means assimilated, they were showing great progress in becoming what the Whigs considered "redeemed" and were referred to as one of the "Five Civilized Tribes" of the Southeast. "They are civilized, not in the same degree that we are, but in the same way that we are," explained Edward Everett. The "truly benevolent" policy was to encourage this "improvement." As long as the Indians remained nomadic hunters and gatherers, they had no right to their land that could not be extinguished by compensation from settlers who represented a higher stage of cultural development, John Quincy Adams believed. When, however, they became settled agriculturalists, they acquired an absolute right of domain and could justly refuse to sell. This was what the Cherokee Nation had done, and its rights were guaranteed by a federal treaty of 1785.

When the state of Georgia determined to expel the Cherokees despite their treaty rights, it arrested Samuel Worcester and Elizur Butler, two white missionaries living with the Indians, who had defied the state's claim to authority. The evangelical united front swung into action to support the missionaries, organizing mass protests and condemning Indian removal as appalling and disgraceful. "He must be worse than savage who can view with cold indifference [such] an exterminating policy." A leading evangelical organ, examining the Cherokee case as one instance of a historical pattern, concluded that white Americans were all implicated in a gigantic crime. But the Georgia authorities were not without their supporters, too. Heading the list was President Jackson, renowned for his hatred of Indians and the contempt for international law he had displayed during the First Seminole War. White settlers throughout the Deep South coveted the rich lands of the Five Tribes, with their cotton-growing potential. The Democratic-party press encouraged them by popularizing theories of the ineradicable inferiority of the nonwhite races, which taught that hopes for civilizing the Indians were delusive. The debate continued for a generation. Despite opposition from a number of Whig writers, including the great anthropologist, Lewis Henry Morgan, the new "scientific racism" proved increasingly attractive as a rationale for dispossession.

Chief Justice Marshall delivered the judgment of the United States Supreme Court in *Worcester et al.* v. *Georgia* on March 3, 1832. He found Georgia's action unconstitutional: the state had no right to legislate for the Cherokee Nation, whose autonomy was guaranteed by federal treaty. But Georgia defied the Court's decision, kept the appellants in prison, and went ahead with its expulsion of the Indians. Jackson made it clear that he would never enforce the Court's mandate, and loopholes in federal appellate procedures enabled him to avoid doing so. Meanwhile, he used the Army to facilitate the dispossession of the Indians, not to protect them. Jackson's reelection later in the year sealed the doom of the Cherokee Nation in Georgia.

The opposition in Congress protested eloquently but vainly on behalf of morality and the supremacy of the Constitution. Then, during the winter of 1832–33, the Nullification Crisis forced a truce between Jackson and the National Republicans (who had not yet adopted the name Whig), since both wanted to sustain national authority against Calhoun's South Carolina. Vice-President Van Buren negotiated the release of Worcester and Butler from the hardships of their captivity. They requested a pardon from the governor of Georgia, which was granted, terminating their legal case. The Cherokees set forth along the grisly Trail of Tears that led the survivors to the West. Some escaped into the mountains of North Carolina.

The dispossession of the Cherokees did not mark the end of the "Indian Question" as a political issue; other tribes had their confrontations in the years to come. Calvin Colton, one of the most prominent spokesmen for Henry Clay, debated at length against Lewis Cass, spokesman for the administration, in defense of tribal rights in the Old Northwest. Colton vigorously asserted the innate equality of the red and white races and maintained that the Indians should be accorded equal protection of the laws in their existing location while they acquired Christianity and Western civilization. Of course, his arguments were futile. Later, the Second Seminole War in Florida brought the cause of red and black people together in resisting white aggression. Antislavery Whigs joined with abolitionists to denounce the conduct of the war. The Supreme Court, however, became less sympathetic to Indian rights after Jackson had replaced John Marshall with Roger B. Taney as chief justice.

The Whigs' sympathy for the Indians was congruent with their preference for restrictive land policies that would keep the white population relatively concentrated in the East and facilitate industrialization. However, a simplistic reduction of all their moral concern to hypocritical self-advantage will not do. Horace Greeley defended the rights of the Indians even though he was an early convert to the cause of western homesteads. Davy Crockett, Tennessee frontier Whig, put moral principle and party loyalty above the wishes of his constituents and opposed Cherokee dispossession; he lost his seat in Congress at the next election. People act out of many motives, and if some Whigs stood to benefit by curtailing the dispersion of white settlement, they or other Whigs stood to lose if the Deep South and the Northwest were irretrievably alienated from their party. In the end, prudential considerations dictated Whig acquiescence in the removal of the tribes.

To be sure, the contrast between Whig and Democratic attitudes toward the Indians was not absolute. There were some Whigs who favored removal, particularly among the Conservative Democrats who joined the Whig party in 1835–36. Nor did the Democratic party altogether disavow humanitarian objectives. Still, the Whig party never lost its reputation for being less hostile to the Indians than its rival. Though William Henry Harrison had originally become famous as an Indian-fighter, during his long preparation for the election of 1840 he published a sympathetic history of the northwestern

Indians, and in the campaign itself his supporters were careful to portray him as humane and just toward them. In 1844, when Henry Clay let the Whig convention freely ballot for the vice-presidential candidate, the delegates chose Theodore Frelinghuysen of New Jersey, an ardent evangelical well known for his spirited and unquestionably sincere defense of the Cherokees. As for the Democrats, they elected as vice-president in 1836 Richard Mentor Johnson, vaunted killer of Tecumseh, whose mounted riflemen cut razor strops out of the dead chief's skin. And in 1848 their presidential nominee was Lewis Cass, who, as secretary of war, had borne heavy responsibility for the atrocities committed on the Trail of Tears.

⊞ *F U R T H E R   R E A D I N G*

John Ashworth, *"Agrarians" and "Aristocrats": Party Political Ideology in the United States, 1837–1846* (1983)

Irving H. Bartlett, *Daniel Webster* (1978)

John M. Belohlavek, *Let the Eagle Soar!: The Foreign Policy of Andrew Jackson* (1985)

Lee Benson, *The Concept of Jacksonian Democracy: New York as a Test Case* (1961)

Thomas Brown, *Politics and Statesmanship: Essays on the American Whig Party* (1985)

Donald B. Cole, *Martin Van Buren and the American Political System* (1984)

William J. Cooper, *Liberty and Slavery: Southern Politics to 1860* (1983)

Richard E. Ellis, *The Union at Risk: Jacksonian Democracy, State's Rights, and the Nullification Crisis* (1987)

Herbert Ershkowitz and William G. Shade, "Consensus or Conflict?: Political Behavior in the State Legislatures During the Jacksonian Era," *Journal of American History* 58 (1971), 591 621

Daniel Feller, "Politics and Society: Toward a Jacksonian Synthesis," *Journal of the Early Republic* 10 (1990).

——, *The Public Lands in Jacksonian Politics* (1984)

Ronald P. Formisano, "Toward a Reconstruction of Jacksonian Politics: A Review of the Literature, 1959–1975," *Journal of American History* 63 (1976), 42–65

William W. Freehling, *The Road to Disunion: Secessionists at Bay, 1776–1854* (1990)

——, *Prelude to Civil War: The Nullification Movement in South Carolina, 1816–1836* (1966)

Frank Otto Gatell, "Sober Second Thoughts on Van Buren, the Albany Recency, and the Wall Street Conspiracy," *Mississippi Valley Historical Review* 53 (1966), 19–40

Bray Hammond, *Banks and Politics in America from the Revolution to the Civil War* (1957)

Oscar Handlin and Mary Flug Handlin, *Commonwealth: A Study of the Role of Government in the American Economy: Massachusetts, 1774–1861* (1947)

Richard Hofstadter, *The American Political Tradition and the Men Who Made It* (1948)

Lawrence Kohl, *The Politics of Individualism: Parties and the American Character in the Jacksonian Era* (1989)

Michael A. Lebowitz, "The Jacksonians: Paradox Lost?" in Barton J. Bernstein, ed., *Towards a New Past: Dissenting Essays in American History* (1968)

Richard P. McCormick, *The Second American Party System: Party Formation in the Jacksonian Era* (1966)

————, "New Perspectives in Jacksonian Politics," *American Historical Review* 65 (1960), 288–301

John M. McFaul, "Expedience vs. Morality: Jacksonian Politics and Slavery," *Journal of American History* 62 (1975), 24–39

————, *The Politics of Jacksonian Finance* (1972)

William G. McLoughlin, *Cherokee Renascence in the New Republic* (1985)

Lynn L. Marshall, "The Strange Stillbirth of the Whig Party," *American Historical Review* 72 (1967), 425–444

Marvin Meyers, *The Jacksonian Persuasion: Politics and Belief* (1957)

John Niven, *John C. Calhoun and the Price of Union* (1988)

Edward Pessen, *Jacksonian America: Society, Personality, and Politics* (1985)

————, *Riches, Class, and Power Before the Civil War* (1973)

Merrill D. Peterson, *The Great Triumvirate: Webster, Clay, and Calhoun* (1987)

Francis Paul Prucha, "Andrew Jackson's Indian Policy: A Reassessment," *Journal of American History* 56 (1969), 527–539

Robert V. Remini, *The Legacy of Andrew Jackson: Essays on Democracy, Indian Removal, and Slavery* (1988)

————, *Andrew Jackson,* 3 vols. (1977–1984)

Leonard L. Richards, *The Life and Times of Congressman John Quincy Adams* (1986)

————, "The Jacksonians and Slavery," in Lewis Perry and Michael Fellman, eds., *Antislavery Reconsidered: New Perspectives on the Abolitionists* (1979)

Michael P. Rogin, *Fathers and Children: Andrew Jackson and the Subjugation of the American Indian* (1975)

Ronald N. Satz, *American Indian Policy in the Jacksonian Era* (1975)

Arthur M. Schlesinger, Jr., *The Age of Jackson* (1945)

James Roger Sharp, *The Jacksonians Versus the Banks: Politics in the States After the Panic of 1837* (1970)

Joel H. Silbey, ed., *Political Ideology and Voting Behavior in the Age of Jackson* (1973)

Peter Temin, *The Jacksonian Economy* (1969)

J. Mills Thornton, *Politics and Power in a Slave Society: Alabama, 1800–1860* (1978)

Glyndon G. Van Deusen, *The Jacksonian Era, 1828–1845* (1959)

Harry L. Watson, *Liberty and Power: The Politics of Jacksonian America* (1990)

————, *Jacksonian Politics and Community Conflict: The Emergence of the Second Party System in Cumberland County, North Carolina* (1981)

Sean Wilentz, "On Class and Politics in Jacksonian America," *Reviews in American History* 10 (1982), 45–63

Major L. Wilson, *The Presidency of Martin Van Buren* (1984)

————, *Space, Time, and Freedom: The Quest for Nationality and the Irrepressible Conflict, 1815–1861* (1974)

Mary E. Young, *Redskins, Ruffleshirts, and Rednecks: Indian Allotments in Alabama and Mississippi, 1830–1860* (1961)

Reforms in Conflict

⊞

*The Democratic and Whig parties were not the only important vehicles for popu-
lar idealism after 1828. Far from the corridors of power, numerous short-lived
political organizations—the Anti-Masons, the Working Men's parties, and various nativist groups—pressed their own grievances, often to see them adopted by
the Whigs and Democrats. Other movements arose outside of politics, some of
which opposed the entire idea of institutionalized party competition. Many of
these reform efforts had roots in religious life, especially in the evangelical explosion known as the Second Great Awakening. (As suggested in the last chapter,
the Awakening's moral imperatives also had a decisive effect among the Whigs.)
Other movements drew on wholly different philosophical sources, ranging from
British freethought and German metaphysics to the homespun democratic ideals
of 1776. Collectively they spoke to the widespread anxieties of the era, as well as
to the exhilarating hope that, with human effort and institutional reform, the
world might be perfected.*

*It seems trite to ascribe this sudden pandemonium of reform to some vague
notion about a ferment of freedom or a breakthrough of American individualism. Many Americans at the time, and today, would seek a more purely divine
explanation. Current social and cultural historians have explored other possible
origins, touching on group psychology, class conflicts, changing gender relations,
and other developments. How satisfactory are these explanations? How else
might we interpret the cross-cutting currents of reform? Why did some Americans support one or another kind of reformism while others did not? The sectional differences are striking: although southerners, black and white, experienced their own versions of the Second Great Awakening and knew something of
benevolent reformism, many of the most popular northern movements made little
headway or assumed very different shapes in the South. By the 1850s leading
southern spokesmen would be likening the North, with its noisy reformers of
every kind, to a kennel of squealing pups. Why? And is it even possible to
speak, as some do, of an American reform impulse, considering that so many
movements of the time conflicted with each other, either implicitly or openly?*

✤ D O C U M E N T S

No single chapter can cover all the important reform movements of the late 1820s and after. These documents sample materials from a few of the most interesting of them, moving across a wide intellectual and social spectrum.

Charles Grandison Finney was the outstanding northern proponent of the evangelical new measures associated with the Second Great Awakening, and he was a superb revival preacher. A selection from one of his sermons (the first document) explains some of his key theological tenets—important in their own right, as well as clues to understanding the religiously inspired moral reform movements. Lyman Beecher, the father of Harriet Beecher Stowe, Catharine Beecher, and Henry Ward Beecher, was an influential New England minister who initially distrusted Finney, only to join forces with him in the 1830s. By then Beecher had gained considerable notice for his work in temperance reform (see the second document), which eventually became one of the most powerful and controversial of the new movements. In document three, a cartoon by an impious, self-styled "Fanny Wright Mechanic" illustrates the resentments such religious reformers could provoke, particularly among those people most drawn to the Democratic party.

The "Fanny Wright" who inspired the antievangelical cartoon was Frances Wright, a British emigrée freethinker and feminist and one of the most electrifying radical speakers in America. Along with Thomas Skidmore (see Chapter 7), Wright was active in the dissenting circles in and around the original New York Working Men's movement. Before that, she and her associate, Robert Dale Owen (son of the British socialist Robert Owen) had lived in Tennessee, where they established a notorious community, Nashoba, for ex-slaves and white sympathizers. Wright and Owen's antislavery views and communitarian experiments were not the only sources of public disapproval: their ideas on free love and absolute racial and sexual equality (as explained by Wright in her defense of Nashoba, the fourth selection) scandalized even liberal opinion. With Wright, we run into a current of moral reform that clashed fiercely with evangelicalism and the cult of domesticity described earlier. A rather different, though related sort of feminism emerged with the birth of the woman suffrage movement in the 1840s, also documented in the fourth selection, in the famous Declaration of Sentiments issued by the Seneca Falls women's rights convention in 1848.

Not every reform movement was so radical; some were conservative, even reactionary. Nativist reform, the subject of the fifth two-part selection, had links to evangelicalism, the cultural restrictiveness of the Whigs, and the militant popular republicanism of the Jacksonians. All these currents joined in an outburst of despair and intolerance at the growing presence of Catholic immigrants. Samuel F. B. Morse, the painter and inventor, was a leading nativist writer and activist in the 1830s. Morse opposed violence, but his polemic against Catholic immigrants greatly emboldened the nativist cause. Nativism's ugliest side was revealed in the mob uprising that burned a Charlestown, Massachusetts, convent to the ground in 1834. (The antinativist cartoon from Boston featured at the end of the fifth selection denounced and ridiculed the rioters.)

Alongside the various social movements, some reformers tried to use public or semipublic institutions to help ameliorate American life—designing new forms of public schooling, reforming prisons, improving the condition of the poor, building mental asylums, and so forth. These efforts raised powerful philosophical claims about humanity, social uplift, and the state that defined their urge to do good. The reports of the Massachusetts school reformer Horace Mann, an excerpt

from which is featured in the sixth selection, were among the strongest statements
of these reformist purposes.

Labor reform is the focus of the seventh selection. In the 1830s such reform
concentrated on trade-union efforts, which aimed at halting a steady deterioration
of conditions and real wages. A mounting strike wave at mid-decade met, in turn,
with stout resistance from employers, who used the courts to try and crush the
unions. In 1836 the successful prosecution of a group of New York journeymen
tailors for conspiracy led to an angry mass demonstration attended by upwards of
thirty thousand protesters. Philip Hone's diary notes captured elite apprehensions
at the impending unionist show of force; a transcript of the handbill that so
alarmed Hone announced the depth of the unionists' fury. In the end, the demonstration was peaceful and the union movement survived, only to be destroyed,
temporarily, by the calamitous impact of the financial panic in 1837.

The final document touches on benevolent reform in the South. Although increasingly alienated by the egalitarian enthusiasms of the North, many southerners
undertook their own uplifting efforts in the 1830s—tied, above all, to strengthening the slave regime. Frances Kemble briefly alluded to these in the excerpt offered in Chapter 8; here Charles Colcock Jones of Georgia explains the reasons
for spreading religious instruction among the slaves and free blacks. How do
Jones's remarks compare with those of the northern moral reformers?

Charles Grandison Finney on Sin and Redemption, 1835

*Ezek. xviii, 31: Make you a new heart and a new spirit, for why will
ye die?*

. . . A change of heart . . . consists in changing the controlling preference
of the mind in regard to the *end* of pursuit. The selfish heart is a preference
of self-interest to the glory of God and the interests of his kingdom. A new
heart consists in a preference of the glory of God and the interests of his
kingdom to one's own happiness. In other words, it is a change from selfishness to benevolence, from having a supreme regard to one's own interest
to an absorbing and controlling choice of the happiness and glory of God
and his kingdom.

It is a change in the choice of a *Supreme Ruler*. The conduct of impenitent
sinners demonstrates that they prefer Satan as the ruler of the world, they
obey his laws, electioneer for him, and are zealous for his interests, even
to martyrdom. They carry their attachment to him and his government so
far as to sacrifice both body and soul to promote his interest and establish
his dominion. A new heart is the choice of JEHOVAH as the supreme ruler;
a deep-seated and abiding preference of his laws, and government, and
character, and person, as the supreme Legislator and Governor of the
universe.

Thus the world is divided into two great political parties; the difference
between them is, that one party choose Satan as the god of this world, yield
obedience to his laws, and are devoted to his interest. Selfishness is the law
of Satan's empire, and all impenitent sinners yield it a willing obedience.
The other party choose Jehovah for their governor, and consecrate themselves, with all their interests, to his service and glory. Nor does this change
imply a constitutional alteration of the powers of body or mind, any more

than a change of mind in regard to the form or administration of a human government. . . .

God has established a government, and proposed by the exhibition of his own character, to produce the greatest practicable amount of happiness in the universe. He has enacted laws wisely calculated to promote this object, to which he conforms all his own conduct, and to which he requires all his subjects perfectly and undeviatingly to conform theirs. After a season of obedience, Adam changed his heart, and set up for himself. So with every sinner, although he *does not first obey, as Adam did;* yet his wicked heart consists in setting up his own interest in opposition to the interest and government of God. In aiming to promote his own private happiness, in a way that is opposed to the general good. Self-gratification becomes the law to which he conforms his conduct. It is that minding of the flesh, which is enmity against God. A change of heart, therefore, is to prefer a different *end.* To prefer supremely the glory of God and the public good, to the promotion of his own interest; and whenever this preference is changed, we see of course a corresponding change of conduct. If a man change sides in politics, you will see him meeting with those that entertain the same views and feelings with himself; devising plans and using his influence to elect the candidate which he has now chosen. He has new political friends on the one side, and new political enemies on the other. So with a sinner; if his heart is changed, you will see that Christians become his friends—Christ his candidate. He aims at honoring him and promoting his interest in all his ways. Before, the language of his conduct was, "Let Satan govern the world." Now, the language of his heart and of his life is, "Let Christ rule King of nations, as he is King of saints." Before, his conduct said, "O Satan, let thy kingdom come, and let thy will be done." Now, his heart, his life, his lips cry out, "O Jesus, let thy kingdom come, let thy will be done on earth as it is in heaven." . . .

As God requires men to make to themselves a new heart, on pain of eternal death, it is the strongest possible evidence that they are able to do it. To say that he has commanded them to do it, without telling them they are able, is consummate trifling. Their ability is implied as strongly as it can be, in the command itself. . . .

The strivings of the Spirit of God with men, is not a physical scuffling, but a debate; a strife not of body with body, but of mind with mind; and that in the action and reaction of vehement argumentation. From these remarks, it is easy to answer the question sometimes put by individuals who seem to be entirely in the dark upon this subject, whether in converting the soul the Spirit acts directly on the mind, or on the truth. This is the same nonsense as if you should ask, whether an earthly advocate who had gained his cause, did it by acting directly and physically on the jury, or on his argument. . . .

You see from this subject that a sinner, under the influence of the Spirit of God, is just as free as a jury under the arguments of an advocate.

Here also you may see the importance of right views on this point. Suppose a lawyer, in addressing a jury, should not expect to change their minds by any thing he could say, but should wait for an invisible, and physical agency, to be exerted by the Holy Ghost upon them. And suppose, on the other hand, that the jury thought that in making up their verdict, they must be passive, and wait for a direct physical agency to be exerted upon them. In vain might the lawyer plead, and in vain might the jury hear, for until he pressed his arguments as if he was determined to bow their hearts, and until they make up their minds, and decide the question, and thus act like rational beings, both his pleading, and their hearing is in vain. So if a minister goes into a desk to preach to sinners, believing that they have no power to obey the truth, and under the impression that a direct physical influence must be exerted upon them before they *can* believe, and if his audience be of the same opinion, in vain does he preach, and in vain do they hear, "for they are yet in their sins;" they sit and quietly wait for some invisible hand to be stretched down from heaven, and perform some surgical operation, infuse some new principle, or implant some constitutional taste; *after* which they suppose they shall be *able* to obey God. Ministers should labor with sinners, as a lawyer does with a jury, and upon the same principles of mental philosophy; and the sinner should weigh his arguments, and make up his mind as upon oath and for his life, and give a verdict upon the spot, according to law and evidence. . . .

Sinner! instead of waiting and praying for God to change your heart, you should at once summon up your powers, put forth the effort, and change the governing preference of your mind. . . .

Sinner! your obligation to love God is equal to the excellence of his character, and your guilt in not obeying him is of course equal to your obligation. You cannot therefore for an hour or a moment defer obedience to the commandment in the text, without deserving eternal damnation. . . .

And now, sinner, while the subject is before you, will you yield? To keep yourself away from under the motives of the gospel, by neglecting church, and neglecting your Bible, will prove fatal to your soul. And to be careless when you do attend, or to hear with attention and refuse to make up your mind and yield, will be equally fatal. And now, "I beseech you, by the mercies of God, that you at *this time* render your body and soul, a living sacrifice to God, which is your reasonable service." Let the truth take hold upon your conscience—throw down your rebellious weapons—give up your refuges of lies—fix your mind steadfastly upon the world of considerations that should instantly decide you to close in with the offer of reconciliation while it now lies before you. Another moment's delay, and it may be too late forever. The Spirit of God may depart from you—the offer of life may be made no more, and this one more slighted offer of mercy may close up your account, and seal you over to all the horrors of eternal death. Hear, then, O sinner, I beseech you, and obey the word of the Lord—"Make you a new heart and a new spirit, for why will ye die?"

Lyman Beecher on the Temperance Crusade, 1826

No sin has fewer apologies than intemperance. The suffrage of the world is against it; and yet there is no sin so naked in its character, and whose commencement and progress is indicated by so many signs, concerning which there is among mankind such profound ignorance. All reprobate drunkenness; and yet, not one of the thousands who fall into it, dreams of danger when he enters the way that leads to it.

The soldier, approaching the deadly breach, and seeing rank after rank of those who preceded him swept away, hesitates sometimes and recoils from certain death. But men behold the effects upon others . . . they see them begin, advance, and end, in confirmed intemperance, and unappalled rush heedlessly upon the same ruin.

A part of this heedlessness arises from the undefined nature of the crime in its early stages, and the ignorance of men, concerning what may be termed the experimental [empirical] indications of its approach. Theft and falsehood are definite actions. But intemperance is a state of internal sensation, and the indications may exist long, and multiply, and the subject of them not be aware that they are the signs of intemperance. It is not unfrequent, that men become irreclaimable in their habits, without suspicion of danger. . . .

Intemperance is the sin of our land, and, with our boundless prosperity, is coming in upon us like a flood; and if anything shall defeat the hopes of the world, which hang upon our experiment of civil liberty, it is that river of fire, which is rolling through the land, destroying the vital air, and extending around an atmosphere of death. . . .

Ardent spirits, given as a matter of hospitality, is not unfrequently the occasion of intemperance. In this case the temptation is a stated inmate of the family. The utensils are present, and the occasions for their use are not unfrequent. And when there is no guest, the sight of the liquor, the state of the health, or even lassitude of spirits, may indicate the propriety of the "prudent use," until the prudent use becomes, by repetition, habitual use— and habitual use becomes irreclaimable intemperance. In this manner, doubtless, has many a father, and mother, and son, and daughter, been ruined forever.

In the commencement of this evil habit, there are many who drink to excess only on particular days, such as days for military exhibition, the anniversary of our independence, the birth-day of Washington, Christmas, New Year's day, election, and others of the like nature. When any of these holidays arrive, and they come as often almost as saints' days in the calendar, they bring with them, to many, the insatiable desire of drinking, as well as a dispensation from the sin, as efficacious and quieting to the conscience, as papal indulgences. . . .

There are others who feel the desire of drinking stirred up within them by the associations of place. They could go from end to end of a day's journey without ardent spirits, were there no taverns on the road. But the very sight of these receptacles of pilgrims awakens the desire "just to step in and take something." And so powerful does this association become, that many will no more pass the tavern than they would pass a fortified place with all the engines of death directed against them. There are in every city, town, and village, places of resort, which in like manner, as soon as the eye falls upon them, create the thirst of drinking. . . .

There is no remedy for intemperance but the cessation of it. Nature must be released from the unnatural war which is made upon her, and be allowed to rest, and then nutrition, and sleep, and exercise, will perform the work of restoration. Gradually the spring of life will recover tone, appetite will return, digestion become efficient, sleep sweet, and the muscular system vigorous, until the elastic heart with every beat shall send health through the system, and joy through the soul. . . .

In every city and town the poor-tax, created chiefly by intemperance, is augmenting. . . . [T]he frequency of going upon the town [relying on public welfare] has taken away the reluctance of pride, and destroyed the motives to providence which the fear of poverty and suffering once supplied. The prospect of a destitute old age, or of a suffering family, no longer troubles the vicious portion of our community. They drink up their daily earnings, and bless God for the poor-house, and begin to look upon it as, of right, the drunkard's home, and contrive to arrive thither as early as idleness and excess will give them a passport to this sinecure of vice. Thus is the insatiable destroyer of industry marching through the land, rearing poor-houses, and augmenting taxation: night and day, with sleepless activity, squandering property, cutting the sinews of industry, undermining vigor, engendering disease. . . .

Add the loss sustained by the subtraction of labor, and the shortened date of life, to the expense of sustaining the poor, created by intemperance; and the nation is now taxed annually more than the expense which would be requisite for the maintenance of government, and for the support of all our schools and colleges, and all the religious instruction of the nation. Already a portion of the entire capital of the nation is mortgaged for the support of drunkards. . . .

Every intemperate and idle man, whom you behold tottering about the streets and steeping himself at the stores, regards your houses and lands as pledged to take care of him,—puts his hands deep, annually, into your pockets, and eats his bread in the sweat of your brows, instead of his own; and with marvellous good nature you bear it. If a robber should break loose on the highway, to levy taxation, an armed force would be raised to hunt him from society. But the tippler may do it fearlessly, in open day, and not a voice is raised, not a finger is lifted.

Intemperance in our land is not accidental; it is rolling in upon us by the violation of some great laws of human nature. In our views, and in our practice as a nation, there is something fundamentally wrong; and the remedy, like the evil, must be found in the correct application of general principles. It must be a universal and national remedy.

What then is this universal, natural, and national remedy for intemperance?

IT IS THE BANISHMENT OF ARDENT SPIRITS FROM THE LIST OF LAWFUL ARTICLES OF COMMERCE, BY A CORRECT AND EFFICIENT PUBLIC SENTIMENT; SUCH AS HAS TURNED SLAVERY OUT OF HALF OUR LAND, AND WILL YET EXPEL IT FROM THE WORLD. . . .

We are not therefore to come down in wrath upon the distillers, and importers, and venders of ardent spirits. None of us are enough without sin to cast the first stone. For who would have imported, or distilled, or vended, if all the nominally temperate in the land had refused to drink? It is the buyers who have created the demand for ardent spirits, and made distillation and importation a gainful traffic. And it is the custom of the temperate too, which inundates the land with the occasion of so much and such unmanageable temptation. Let the temperate cease to buy—and the demand for ardent spirits will fall in the market three fourths, and ultimately will fail wholly, as the generation of drunkards shall hasten out of time.

To insist that men, whose capital is embarked in the production, or vending of ardent spirits, shall manifest the entire magnanimity and self-denial, which is needful to save the land, though the example would be glorious to them, is more than we have a right to expect or demand. Let the consumer do his duty, and the capitalist, finding his employment unproductive, will quickly discover other channels of useful enterprise. . . .

A Counterattack on Religious Reform, 1831

ADVERTISEMENT.

WANTED, for the use of the Bible, Tract, and Missionary Society, a number of JACKASSES of the real Tappaan breed: they must be in first-rate order.—A number of JENNIES are also wanted, but they must be of pious breed, and warranted not to run after the Jacks.

The plate above, represents a Jackass, well fed, and in fine order, laying golden eggs, which a Priest receives in his hand, whilst with he other he lifts up his tail. He says to his colleague, who stands by the head of the ass, "We must administer a gentle dose of physic; he dont seem to give very freely." The ass, (who like Balaam's ass has the power of speech,) says, "I understand you, Mr. Parson; I know you are never satisfied until you have all; but I'll take care you dont reduce me to a skeleton, like my poor neighbour, whom your colleague is now kicking away.

An antievangelical cartoon by a self-styled "Fanny Wright Mechanic," from *The Magdalen Report Burlesqued,* 1831. New-York Historical Society.

Feminist Declarations, 1828, 1848

Free Love and Racial Equality: Frances Wright Defends Nashoba, 1827

One nation, and, as yet, one nation only, has declared all men "born free and equal," and conquered the political freedom and equality of its citizens— with the lamentable exception, indeed, of its citizens of color. But is there not a liberty yet more precious than what is termed *national,* and an equality more precious than what is termed *political?* Before we are citizens, are we not human beings, and ère we can exercise equal rights, must we not possess equal advantages, equal means of improvement and of enjoyment?

Political liberty may be said to exist in the United States of America, and (without adverting to the yet unsettled, though we may fondly trust secured republics of America's southern continent) *only there.* Moral liberty exists *no where.*

By political liberty we may understand the liberty of speech and of action without incurring the violence of authority or the penalties of law. By moral liberty may we not understand the *free exercise of the liberty of speech and of action,* without incurring the intolerance of popular prejudice and ignorant public opinion? To secure the latter where the former liberty exists, what is necessary "but to will it." Far truer is the assertion as here applied to moral liberty than as heretofore applied to political liberty. To free ourselves of thrones, aristocracies and hierarchies, of fleets and armies, and all the arrayed panoply of organized despotism, it is *not* sufficient to will it. We must fight for it, and fight for it too with all the odds of wealth, and power, and position against us. . . . It is much to have *declared* men free and equal, but it shall be more when they are rendered so; when means shall be sought and found, and employed to develope all the intellectual and physical powers of all human beings, without regard to sex or condition, class, race, nation or color; and when men shall learn to view each other as members of one great family, with equal claims to enjoyment and equal capacities for labor and instruction, admitting always the sole differences arising out of the varieties exhibited in individual organization.

It were superfluous to elucidate, by argument, the baleful effects arising out of the division of labor as now existing, and which condemns the large half of mankind to an existence purely physical, and the remaining portion to pernicious idleness, and occasionally to exertions painfully, because solely, intellectual. He who lives in the single exercise of his mental faculties, however usefully or curiously directed, is equally an imperfect animal with the man who knows only the exercise of his muscles.

Let us consider the actual condition of our species. Where shall we find even a single individual, male or female, whose mental and physical powers have been fairly cultivated and developed? How then is it with the great family of human kind? We have addressed our ingenuity to improve the nature and beautify the forms of all the tribe of animals domesticated by our care, but man has still neglected man; ourselves, our own species, our own nature are deemed unworthy, even unbecoming, objects of experiment. Why should we refuse to the human animal care at least equal to that bestowed on the horse or the dog? His forms are surely not less susceptible of beauty, and his faculties, more numerous and exalted, may challenge, at the least, equal development. . . .

In the moral, intellectual and physical cultivation of both sexes should we seek, as we can only find, the source and security of human happiness and human virtue. Prejudice and fear are weak barriers against passions, which, inherent in our nature and demanding only judicious training to form the ornament, and supply the best joys of our existence, are maddened into violence by pernicious example and pernicious restraint, varied with as pernicious indulgence. Let us correct our views of right and wrong, correct our moral lessons, and so correct the practice of rising generations! Let us not teach that virtue consists in the crucifying of the affections and appetites, but in their judicious government. Let us not attach ideas of purity to monastic chastity, impossible to man or woman without consequences fraught with evil, nor ideas of vice to connections formed under the auspices of kind feelings. Let us enquire, not if a mother be a wife, or a father a husband, but if parents can supply to the creatures they have brought into being, all things requisite to render existence a blessing! Let the force of public opinion be brought against the thoughtless ignorance, or cruel selfishness, which, either with or without the sanction of a legal or religious permit, so frequently multiplies offspring beyond the resources of the parents. Let us check the force of passions, as well as their precocity, not by the idle terror of imaginary crime in the desire itself, but by the just and benevolent apprehension of bringing into existence, unhappy or imperfect beings. Let us teach the young mind to reason, and the young heart to feel, and instead of shrouding our bodies, wants, desires, senses, affections and faculties in mystery, let us court enquiry, and show that acquaintance with our own nature can alone guide us to judicious practice, and that in the consequence of human actions, exists the only true test of their virtue or their vice. . . .

The tyranny usurped by the matrimonial law over the most sacred of the human affections, can perhaps only be equalled by that of the unjust public opinion, which so frequently stamps with infamy, or condemns to martyrdom the best-grounded and most generous attachments, which ever did honor to the human heart, simply because unlegalized by human ceremonies, equally idle and offensive in the form and mischievous in the tendency.

This tyranny, as now exercised over the strongest and at the same time, if refined by mental cultivation, the noblest of the human passions, had probably its source in religious prejudice, or priestly rapacity, while it has found its plausible and more philosophical apology in the apparent dependence of children on the union of the parents. To this plea it might, perhaps, be replied, that the end, how important soever, is not secured by the means. That the forcible union of unsuitable and unsuited parents can little promote the happiness of the offspring; and, supposing the protection of children to be the real source and object of our code of morals and of our matrimonial laws, what shall we say of the effects of these humane provisions on the fate and fortunes of one large family of helpless innocents, born into the world in spite of all prohibitions and persecutions, and whom a cruel law, and yet more cruel opinion, disown and stigmatize. But how wide a field does this topic embrace? How much cruelty—how much oppression of the weak and the helpless does it not involve! The children denominated illegitimate, or *natural,* (as if in contradiction of others who should be *out of nature,* because *under law*) may be multiplied to any number by an unprincipled father, easily exonerated by law and custom from the duties of paternity, while these duties, and their accompanying shame, are left to a mother but too often rendered desperate by misfortune! And should we follow out our review of the law of civilized countries, we shall find the offspring termed legitimate, with whom honor and power and possession are associated, adjudged, in case of matrimonial dissensions to the father, who by means of this legal claim, has, not unfrequently, bowed to servitude the spirit of a fond mother, and held ber, as a galley slave, to the oar. . . .

Let us look into our streets, our hospitals, our asylums; let us look into the secret thoughts of the anxious parent trembling for the minds and bodies of sons starting into life, or mourning over the dying health of daughters condemned to the unnatural repression of feelings and desires inherent in their very organization and necessary alike to their moral and physical well-being. Or let us look to the victims—not of pleasure, not of love, nor yet of their own depravity, but of those ignorant laws, ignorant prejudices, ignorant code of morals, which condemn one portion of the female sex to vicious excess, another to as vicious restraint, and all to defenceless help-lessness and slavery, and generally the whole of the male sex to debasing licentiousness, if not to loathsome brutality. . . .

The strength of the prejudice of color as existing in the United States and in the European colonies can in general be little conceived and less understood in the old continent. Yet however whimsical it may there appear, is it in fact more ridiculous than the European prejudice of birth? The superior excellence which the one supposes in a peculiar descent or merely in a peculiar name, the other imagines in a peculiar complexion or set of features. And perhaps it is only by considering man in many countries and observing all his varying and contradictory prejudices that we can discover the equal absurdity of all.

Those to whom the American institutions and American character are familiar, and who have considered the question of American negro slavery in all its bearings, will probably be disposed to pronounce with the writer of this address that the emancipation of the colored population cannot be *progressive thro' the laws*. It must and can only be *progressive through the feelings;* and, through that medium, be finally complete and entire, involving at once political equality and the amalgamation of the races.

And has nature (as slave apologists would tell us) drawn a Rubicon between the human varieties of physiognomy and complexion, or must we enter into details to prove that no natural antipathy blinds the white Louis-ianian to the charms of the graceful quadroon—however the force of prej-udice or the fear of public censure makes of her his mistress, and of the white-skinned, but often not more accomplished or more attractive female, his wife? Or must we point to the intercourse in its most degraded forms where the child is the marketable slave of its father? Idle indeed is the assertion that the mixture of the races is not in nature. If not in nature, it could not happen; and, being in nature, since it *does* happen, the only question is whether it shall take place in good taste and good feeling and be made at once the means of sealing the tranquillity, and perfecting the liberty of the country, and of peopling it with a race more suited to its southern climate than the pure European,—or whether it shall proceed, as it now does, viciously and degradingly, mingling hatred and fear with the ties of blood—denied indeed, but stamped by nature herself upon the skin.

The education of the race of color would doubtless make the amalgamation more rapid as well as more creditable; and so far from considering the physical amalgamation of the two colors, when accompanied by a moral approximation, as an evil, it must surely be viewed as a good equally desirable for both. In this belief the more especial object of the founder of Nashoba is to raise the man of color to the level of the white. Where fitted by habits of industry and suitable dispositions to receive him as a brother and equal, and, after due trial, as proprietor trustee of the property; to educate his children with white children, and thus approaching their minds, tastes and occupations, to leave the affections of future generations to the dictates of free choice.

The Seneca Falls Convention
on the Equality of Men and Women, 1848

When, in the course of human events, it becomes necessary for one portion of the family of man to assume among the people of the earth a position different from that which they have hitherto occupied, but one to which the laws of nature and of nature's God entitle them, a decent respect to the opinions of mankind requires that they should declare the causes that impel them to such a course.

We hold these truths to be self-evident: that all men and women are created equal; that they are endowed by their Creator with certain inalienable rights; that among these are life, liberty, and the pursuit of happiness; that to secure these rights governments are instituted, deriving their just powers from the consent of the governed. Whenever any form of government becomes destructive of these ends, it is the right of those who suffer from it to refuse allegiance to it, and to insist upon the institution of a new government, laying its foundation on such principles, and organizing its powers in such form, as to them shall seem most likely to effect their safety and happiness. Prudence, indeed, will dictate that governments long established should not be changed for light and transient causes; and accordingly all experience hath shown that mankind are more disposed to suffer, while evils are sufferable, than to right themselves by abolishing the forms to which they were accustomed. But when a long train of abuses and usurpations, pursuing invariably the same object, evinces a design to reduce them under absolute despotism, it is their duty to throw off such government, and to provide new guards for their future security. Such has been the patient sufferance of the women under this government, and such is now the necessity which constrains them to demand the equal station to which they are entitled.

The history of mankind is a history of repeated injuries and usurpations on the part of man toward woman, having in direct object the establishment of an absolute tyranny over her. To prove this, let facts be submitted to a candid world.

He has never permitted her to exercise her inalienable right to the elective franchise.

He has compelled her to submit to laws, in the formation of which she had no voice.

He has withheld from her rights which are given to the most ignorant and degraded men—both natives and foreigners.

Having deprived her of this first right of a citizen, the elective franchise, thereby leaving her without representation in the halls of legislation, he has oppressed her on all sides.

He has made her, if married, in the eye of the law, civilly dead.

He has taken from her all right in property, even to the wages she earns.

He has made her, morally, an irresponsible being, as she can commit many crimes with impunity, provided they be done in the presence of her husband. In the covenant of marriage, she is compelled to promise obedience to her husband, he becoming to all intents and purposes, her master—the law giving him power to deprive her of her liberty, and to administer chastisement.

He has so framed the laws of divorce, as to what shall be the proper causes, and in case of separation, to whom the guardianship of the children shall be given, as to be wholly regardless of the happiness of women—the law, in all cases, going upon a false supposition of the supremacy of man, and giving all power into his hands.

After depriving her of all rights as a married woman, if single, and the owner of property, he has taxed her to support a government which recognizes her only when her property can be made profitable to it.

He has monopolized nearly all the profitable employments, and from those she is permitted to follow, she receives but a scanty remuneration. He closes against her all the avenues to wealth and distinction which he considers most honorable to himself. As a teacher of theology, medicine, or law, she is not known.

He has denied her the facilities for obtaining a thorough education, all colleges being closed against her.

He allows her in Church, as well as State, but a subordinate position, claiming Apostolic authority for her exclusion from the ministry, and, with some exceptions, from any public participation in the affairs of the Church.

He has created a false public sentiment by giving to the world a different code of morals for men and women, by which moral delinquencies which exclude women from society, are not only tolerated, but deemed of little account in man.

He has usurped the prerogative of Jehovah himself, claiming it as his right to assign for her a sphere of action, when that belongs to her conscience and to her God.

He has endeavored, in every way that he could, to destroy her confidence in her own powers, to lessen her self-respect, and to make her willing to lead a dependent and abject life.

Now, in view of this entire disfranchisement of one-half the people of this country, their social and religious degradation—in view of the unjust laws above mentioned, and because women do feel themselves aggrieved, oppressed, and fraudulently deprived of their most sacred rights, we insist that they have immediate admission to all the rights and privileges which belong to them as citizens of the United States.

In entering upon the great work before us, we anticipate no small amount of misconception, misrepresentation, and ridicule; but we shall use every instrumentality within our power to effect our object. We shall employ agents, circulate tracts, petition the State and National legislatures, and endeavor to enlist the pulpit and the press in our behalf. We hope this Convention will be followed by a series of Conventions embracing every part of the country.

Resolutions

Whereas, The great precept of nature is conceded to be, that "man shall pursue his own true and substantial happiness." Blackstone in his Commentaries remarks, that this law of Nature being coeval with mankind, and dictated by God himself, is of course superior in obligation to any other. It is binding over all the globe, in all countries and at all times; no human laws are of any validity if contrary to this, and such of them as are valid, derive all their force, and all their validity, and all their authority, mediately and immediately, from this original; therefore,

Resolved, That such laws as conflict, in any way, with the true and substantial happiness of woman, are contrary to the great precept of nature and of no validity, for this is "superior in obligation to any other."

Resolved, That all laws which prevent woman from occupying such a station in society as her conscience shall dictate, or which place her in a position inferior to that of man, are contrary to the great precept of nature, and therefore of no force or authority.

Resolved, That woman is man's equal—was intended to be so by the Creator, and the highest good of the race demands that she should be recognized as such.

Resolved, That the women of this country ought to be enlightened in regard to the laws under which they live, that they may no longer publish their degradation by declaring themselves satisfied with their present position, nor their ignorance, by asserting that they have all the rights they want.

Resolved, That inasmuch as man, while claiming for himself intellectual superiority, does accord to woman moral superiority, it is pre-eminently his duty to encourage her to speak and teach, as she has an opportunity, in all religious assemblies.

Resolved, That the same amount of virtue, delicacy, and refinement of behavior that is required of woman in the social state, should also be required of man, and the same transgressions should be visited with equal severity on both man and woman.

Resolved, That the objection of indelicacy and impropriety, which is so often brought against woman when she addresses a public audience, comes with a very ill-grace from those who encourage, by their attendance, her appearance on the stage, in the concert, or in feats of the circus.

Resolved, That woman has too long rested satisfied in the circumscribed limits which corrupt customs and a perverted application of the Scriptures have marked out for her, and that it is time she should move in the enlarged sphere which her great Creator has assigned her.

Resolved, That it is the duty of the women of this country to secure to themselves their sacred right to the elective franchise.

Resolved, That the equality of human rights results necessarily from the fact of the identity of the race in capabilities and responsibilities.

Resolved, therefore, That, being invested by the Creator with the same capabilities, and the same consciousness of responsibility for their exercise, it is demonstrably the right and duty of woman, equally with man, to promote every righteous cause by every righteous means; and especially in regard to the great subjects of morals and religion, it is self-evidently her right to participate with her brother in teaching them, both in private and in public, by writing and by speaking, by any instrumentalities proper to be used, and in any assemblies proper to be held; and this being a self-evident truth growing out of the divinely implanted principles of human nature, any custom or authority adverse to it, whether modern or wearing the hoary sanction of antiquity, is to be regarded as a self-evident falsehood, and at war with mankind.

[At the last session Lucretia Mott offered the following resolution.]

Resolved, That the speedy success of our cause depends upon the zealous and untiring efforts of both men and women, for the overthrow of the monopoly of the pulpit, and for the securing to woman an equal participation with men in the various trades, professions, and commerce.

Contemporary Views of Nativism, 1834, 1835

Nativism Attacked, 1834

"Defenders of the True Faith," cartoon, Boston, 1834, published following a violent attack on a Catholic convent in Charlestown, Massachusetts. Boston Athenaeum.

Samuel F. B. Morse on the Popish Plot, 1835

. . . I deem it a duty to warn the Christian community against the temptation to which they were exposed, in guarding against the political dangers arising from Popery, of leaving their proper sphere of action, and degrading themselves to a common political interest. This is a snare into which they might easily fall, and into which, if Popery could invite or force them, it might keep a jubilee, for its triumph would be sure. The propensity to resist by unlawful means the encroachments of an enemy, because that enemy uses such means against us, belongs to human nature. We are very apt to think, in the irritation of being attacked, that we may lawfully hurl back the darts of a foe, whatever may be their character; that we may "fight the Devil with fire," instead of the milder, yet more effective weapon of "the Lord rebuke thee." The same spirit of Christianity which forbids us to return railing for railing, and persecution for persecution, forbids the use of unlawful or even of doubtful means of defence, merely because an enemy uses them to attack us. If Popery, (as is unblushingly the case,) organizes itself at our elections, if it interferes politically and sells itself to this or that political demagogue or party, it should be remembered, that this is notoriously the true character of Popery. It is its nature. It cannot act otherwise. Intrigue is its appropriate business. But all this is foreign to Christianity. Christianity must not enter the political arena with Popery, nor be mailed in Popish armor. The weapons and stratagems of Popery suit not with the simplicity and frankness of Christianity. . . .

But whilst deprecating a *union of religious sects* to act politically against Popery, I must not be misunderstood as recommending no political opposition to Popery by the American community. I have endeavored to rouse Protestants to a renewed and more vigorous use of their religious weapons in their *moral* war with Popery, but I am not unmindful of another duty, the *political* duty, which the double character of Popery makes it necessary to urge upon American citizens, with equal force,—the imperious duty of defending the distinctive principles of our civil government. It must be sufficiently manifest to every republican citizen that the civil polity of Popery is in direct opposition to all which he deems sacred in government. He must perceive that Popery cannot from its very nature tolerate any of those civil rights which are the peculiar boast of Americans. Should Popery increase but for a little time longer in this country with the alarming rapidity with which, as authentic statistics testify, it is advancing at the present time, (and it must not be forgotten that despotism in Europe, in its desperate struggles for existence, is lending its powerful aid to the enterprise,) we may even in this generation learn by sad experience what common sagacity and ordinary research might now teach, in time to arrest the evil, that Popery cannot tolerate our form of government in any of its essential principles.

Popery does not acknowledge *the right of the people to govern;* but claims for itself the supreme right to govern all people and all rulers by divine right.

It does not tolerate *the Liberty of the Press;* it takes advantage indeed of our liberty of the press to use its own press against our liberty; but it proclaims in the thunders of the Vatican, and with a voice which it pronounces *infallible and unchangeable,* that it is a liberty *"never sufficiently to be execrated and detested."*

It does not tolerate *liberty of conscience* nor *liberty of opinion.* The one is denounced by the Sovereign Pontiff as *"a most pestilential error,"* and the other, *"a pest of all others most to be dreaded in a state."*

It is not responsible to the people in its financial matters. *It taxes at will, and is accountable to none but itself.*

Now these are *political* tenets held by Papists in close union with their religious belief, yet these are not *religious* but *civil* tenets; they belong to despotic government. Conscience cannot be pleaded against our dealing politically with them. They are separable from religious belief; and if Papists will separate them, and repudiate these noxious principles, and teach and act accordingly, the political duty of exposing and opposing Papists, on the ground of the enmity of their political tenets to our republican government, will cease. But can they do it? If they can, it behoves them to do it without delay. If they cannot, or will not, let them not complain of *religious* persecution, or of *religious* intolerance, if this republican people, when it shall wake to a sense of the danger that threatens its blood-bought institutions, shall rally to their defence with some show of indignation. Let them not whine about *religious* oppression, if the democracy turns its searching eye upon this secret treason to the state, and shall in future scrutinize with something of suspicion, the professions of those *foreign friends,* who are so ready to rush to a fraternal embrace. Let them not raise the cry of *religious* proscription, if American republicans shall stamp an indelible brand upon the *liveried slaves of a foreign* despot, . . . who now sheltered behind the shield of our religious liberty, dream of security, while sapping the foundations of our civil government. . . . America may for a time, sleep soundly, as innocence is wont to sleep, unsuspicious of hostile attack; but if any foreign power, jealous of the increasing strength of the embryo giant, sends its serpents to lurk within his cradle, let such presumption be assured that the waking energies of the infant are not to be despised, that once having grasped his foes, he will neither be tempted from his hold by admiration of their painted and gilded covering, nor by fear of the fatal embrace of their treacherous folds.

Horace Mann on the Philosophy of Public Schooling, 1846

. . . In the district-school-meeting, in the town-meeting, in legislative halls, everywhere, the advocates for a more generous education could carry their respective audiences with them in behalf of increased privileges for our children, were it not instinctively foreseen that increased privileges must be followed by increased taxation. Against this obstacle, argument falls dead. The rich man who has no children declares that the exaction of a contribution from him to educate the children of his neighbor is an invasion of his rights of property. The man who has reared and educated a family of children denounces it as a double tax when he is called upon to assist in educating the children of others also; or, if he has reared his own children without educating them, he thinks it peculiarly oppressive to be obliged to do for others what he refrained from doing even for himself. Another, having children, but disdaining to educate them with the common mass, withdraws them from the public school, puts them under what he calls "selecter influences," and then thinks it a grievance to be obliged to support a school which he [regards with contempt]. . . .

It seems not irrelevant, therefore . . . to inquire into the nature of a man's right to the property he possesses; and to satisfy ourselves respecting the question, whether any man has such an indefeasible title to his estates, or such an absolute ownership of them, as renders it unjust in the government to assess upon him his share of the expenses of educating the children of the community up to such a point as the nature of the institutions under which he lives, and the well-being of society, require.

I believe in the existence of a great, immortal, immutable principle of

natural law, or natural ethics,—a principle antecedent to all human institutions, and incapable of being abrogated by any ordinance of man,—a
principle of divine origin, which proves the *absolute right* to an education
of every human being that comes into the world; and which, of course,
proves the correlative duty of every government to see that the means of
that education are provided for all.

In regard to the application of this principle of natural law,—that is, in
regard to the extent of the education to be provided for all at the public
expense,—some differences of opinion may fairly exist under different political organizations; but, under our republican government, it seems clear
that the minimum of this education can never be less than such as is sufficient
to qualify each citizen for the civil and social duties he will be called to
discharge. . . .

The claim of a child, then, to a portion of pre-existent property, begins
with the first breath he draws. The new-born infant must have sustenance
and shelter and care. If the natural parents are removed, or parental ability
fails; in a word, if parents either cannot or will not supply the infant's
wants,—then society at large—the government having assumed to itself the
ultimate control of all property—is bound to step in and fill the parent's
place. To deny this to any child would be equivalent to a sentence of death,
a capital execution of the innocent,—at which every soul shudders. It would
be a more cruel form of infanticide than any which is practised in China or
in Africa. . . .

The three following propositions, then, describe the broad and ever-
during [enduring] foundation on which the common-school system of Massachusetts reposes:—

The successive generations of men, taken collectively, constitute one
great commonwealth.

The property of this commonwealth is pledged for the education of all
its youth, up to such a point as will save them from poverty and vice, and
prepare them for the adequate performance of their social and civil duties.

The successive holders of this property are trustees, bound to the faithful
execution of their trust by the most sacred obligations; and embezzlement
and pillage from children and descendants have not less of criminality, and
have more of meanness, than the same offences when perpetrated against
contemporaries. . . .

Massachusetts is *parental* in her government. More and more, as year
after year rolls by, she seeks to substitute prevention for remedy, and rewards
for penalties. She strives to make industry the antidote to poverty, and to
counterwork the progress of vice and crime by the diffusion of knowledge
and the culture of virtuous principles. She seeks not only to mitigate those
great physical and mental calamities of which mankind are the sad inheritors,
but also to avert those infinitely greater moral calamities which form the
disastrous heritage of depraved passions. Hence it has long been her policy
to endow or to aid asylums for the cure of disease. She succors and maintains
all the poor within her borders, whatever may have been the land of their
nativity. She founds and supports hospitals for restoring reason to the insane;

and, even for those violators of the law whom she is obliged to sequestrate from society, she provides daily instruction and the ministrations of the gospel at the public charge. To those who, in the order of Nature and Providence, have been bereft of the noble faculties of hearing and of speech, she teaches a new language, and opens their imprisoned minds and hearts to conversation with men and to communion with God; and it hardly transcends the literal truth to say that she gives sight to the blind. . . . The public highway is not more open and free for every man in the community than is the public schoolhouse for every child; and each parent feels that a free education is as secure a part of the birthright of his offspring as Heaven's bounties of light and air. . . .

Labor Reform Considered, 1836

Philip Hone on the Labor Movement, 1836

June 6 [1836].—In corroboration of the remarks which I have occasionally made of late, on the spirit of faction and contempt of the laws which pervades the community at this time, is the conduct of the journeymen tailors, instigated by a set of vile foreigners (principally English), who, unable to endure the restraints of wholesome law, well administered in their own country, take refuge here, establish tradesunions, and vilify Yankee judges and juries. Twenty odd of these were convicted at the Oyer and Terminer of a conspiracy to raise their wages and to prevent any of the craft from working at prices less than those for which they struck. Judge Edwards gave notice that he would proceed to sentence them this day; but, in consequence of the continuance of Robinson's trial, the Court postponed the sentence until Friday.

This, however, being the day on which it was expected, crowds of people have been collected in the park, ready for any mischief to which they may have been instigated, and a most diabolical and inflammatory hand-bill was circulated yesterday, headed by a coffin. The Board of Aldermen held an informal meeting this evening, at which a resolution was adopted authorizing the Mayor to offer a reward for the discovery of the author, printer, publisher, or distributor of this incendiary publication. . . .

The Coffin Handbill, 1836

Journeymen tailors. A placard was seen in various parts of the city on Sunday, which contained within the representation of a coffin, the following words:

"The Rich against the Poor! Judge Edwards, the tool of the Aristocracy, against the People! Mechanics and workingmen! a deadly blow has been struck at your Liberty! The prize for which your fathers fought has been robbed from you! The Freemen of the North are now on a level with the slaves of the South! with no other privileges than laboring that drones may fatten on your life-blood! Twenty of your brethren have been found guilty for presuming to resist a reduction of their wages! and Judge Edwards has charged an American jury, and agreeably to that charge, they have established the precedent, that workingmen have no right to regulate the price of labor! or, in other words, the Rich are the only judges of the wants of the Poor Man! On Monday, June 6, 1836, these Freemen are to receive their sentence, to gratify the hellish appetites of the Aristocracy! On Monday, the Liberty of the Workingmen will be interred! Judge Edwards is to chant the Requiem! Go! Go! Go! every Freeman, every Workingman, and hear the hollow and the melancholy sound of the earth on the Coffin of Equality! Let the Court-room, the City-hall—yea, the whole Park, be filled with Mourners! But, remember, offer no violence to Judge Edwards! Bend meekly, and receive the chains wherewith you are to be bound! Keep the peace! Above all things keep the peace! . . ."

Reverend Charles Colcock Jones on Religious Instruction for Negroes, 1847

Were the negroes but an inconsiderable handful of people, they might be left to fall in with the mass, and be benefitted by the means of grace enjoyed by all, without any special efforts being made for them. But they make up *one sixth* of our *entire* population, and are steadily increasing, and seem destined to become an immense multitude! Will you let them alone? Shall we do nothing for them? Surely they do demand the attention of all men who love their country, and who seek the improvement and salvation of their species.

And what is *the moral and religious condition of this people?*

I do not deem it essential to my present purpose, in returning an answer to this question, to enter into minute details to show what that condition is. We, of the South, have been familiar with it from our youth, and none who will be at the pains of seeking information, need remain ignorant of it.

We are aware of the ignorance which prevails among them of the word of God, of the doctrines and duties of Christianity, and of the superstition which is necessarily connected with that ignorance. We know the extreme feebleness of their sense of obligation to improve the means of grace and of instruction, placed within their reach, and expressly designed for their good. We know how defective is their standard of character, and even of *Christian* character; and what constant care and trouble, and frequently what grief they are to the churches with which they are connected, and how gross are the crimes for which they are ordinarily disciplined. We are acquainted with their violations of the marriage contract; their general disregard of virtue, honesty, and truth; their want of kindness to each other, and fidelity in business: their tendency to drunkenness, and to idleness; and their profanation of the Sabbath day. These characteristics attach to them, *both in a state of slavery, and in a state of freedom,* and they are generally considered as degraded as any other class of people in the United States. . . .

Owners are remiss in the discharge of their duties to their people, in respect to their better and higher interests; and those who carry them through a course of religious instruction, and make permanent provision for it, are few. Plantations that now lie all abroad over the face of the country, wildernesses and moral wastes, through the judicious, Christian, and persevering efforts of owners, might be converted into fruitful fields and vineyards of the Lord; but the work is not done, neither indeed is it in progress.

Are our *ministers* supplying the spiritual wants of the negroes? Have they considered their destitution in respect to churches, and church accommodations? . . . Are ministers enlightening their churches, and moving them to a discharge of their duties to the negroes? How many of them consider *the servants as really a part of their charge, as masters,* and watch for their souls as they that must give account? Do they during the week and upon the Sabbath day hold religious meetings for their special benefit, and at stated times collect and catechize the children, and hold themselves in readiness to solemnize their marriages, and bury their dead? How many live in the midst of a large population of negroes, and never make an effort for their salvation; but content themselves with preaching sermons to the whites, which, for the most part, are of no advantage to the negroes, being quite above their comprehension! . . .

But have not the negroes *preachers, and watchmen, and class leaders of their own colour?* They have. But who supposes that they exist in sufficient numbers, and are possessed of sufficient ability to furnish the bread of life to the multitudes around them? They are *helpers,* and the Lord uses their instrumentality in the conversion of sinners: but the teachers need to be taught—and frequently they are blind leaders of the blind! . . .

Our provisions for the evangelization of the negroes, are not sufficient to supply the wants of the people! If nothing more is done, than is now doing; if we do not multiply men and means more rapidly than in years past, what multitudes of these poor people are destined to go down, annually, from the very bosom of a land denominated enlightened, and Christian, and benevolent, into everlasting ruin! What shall we say in that day when God shall make inquisition for the blood of these souls, slain in our hearing, and in the sight of our own eyes, and neither did we send, nor did we go to their deliverance? . . .

The conscientious minister will understand that churches and congregations in the South are made up of *households*—of parents and children, masters *and servants:* that the whole make but *one charge;* that he is settled as a pastor *over the whole,* and "must rightly divide the word," giving unto every man "a portion in due season." This is the view which reason and justice, and grace in the heart, and the Scriptures themselves oblige us to take. Read the epistles, and are not the churches composed of parents and children, masters and servants? Do not the households compose the charge committed to the shepherds of the flock?

Under this conviction, the minister will *inform himself* of the number, the character, and the spiritual condition and wants of the negroes, whether in town or country, in circuit or parish, with whom he stands *officially* connected. . . .

He should preach on the Sabbath, at least, *once* to the negroes of his charge, assembled in the church, or in some building erected and set apart for their accommodation. Great importance should be attached to this service, as there are, or may be, more negroes collected on the Sabbath at the church than on any other day, or at any other place.

The matter of preaching should, of course, be *the pure word of God;* thoroughly studied, clearly presented, forcibly illustrated, and practically applied. If a minister is of opinion that *any kind of preaching* will do for the negroes, let him try it, and he will presently be of another mind. They are good judges of a good sermon. They are human nature, and like to be treated with some consideration, and are as fond of an able ministry as are any other people. He who preaches to the negroes, should study just as profoundly, and as extensively, as he who preaches to the whites. . . .

For permanent impression and for the promotion of intelligence and piety, the public worship of God should be conducted *with reverence and stillness on the part of the congregation;* nor should the minister—whatever may have been the previous habits and training of the people—encourage demonstrations of approbation or disapprobation, or exclamations, or responses, or noises, or outcries of any kind during the progress of divine worship; nor boisterous singing immediately at its close. These practices prevail over large portions of the Southern country, and are not confined to one denomination, but appear to some extent in all. The extent to which they are carried, depends upon the encouragement given by ministers and denominations. I cannot think them beneficial. Ignorant people may be easily excited, and they soon fall into the error of confounding things that differ essentially. The appearance is put for the reality; the sound for the substance; feeling in religious worship, for religion itself. And so false and perverted may they become in their notions, that the absence of these outward signs and sounds, is in their view an evidence of the absence of all religion; and so accustomed to these things may they become, and so fond of the excitement connected with them, that they will choose such meetings where they are practiced, before all others! And this, as it is manifest to all who will judge righteous judgment, to their most serious injury! Let the minister in attempting a reformation, be forebearing, prudent, kind and patient.

Some owners forgetful of God and eternity, treat their people too much as creatures of profit. They locate them any and every where without, it would seem, the least reference to their eternal well-being. We know that men of no religion do this even with their own families; but Christian men should endeavour to do better. Some owners live in the enjoyment of every religious privilege; nay, more, remove from their plantations for the express purpose of enjoying those privileges, while their people are left in entire destitution from year to year! Many have large incomes and never expend one cent directly for the religious instruction of their people. He, who is in the providence of God, called to be a "master in the flesh," should acquaint himself with his duties and responsibilities, taking the word of God as his infallible guide to truth in his peculiar relation. His rights are founded upon a discharge of his duties; and one of his first duties is to remember that his servants are immortal beings, and to the best of his ability and opportunity *he should provide for their religious instruction.*

If we *preach,* to be influential we must *practise* also. If we require others to do their duty to us, we must endeavour to do our duty to them. And in vain will any owner look for improvement on the part of his people, notwithstanding all his efforts, unless his people see that he is himself under the control of correct principles, and conscientiously strives to do his duty to them.

Servants should be provided with *abundant food,* and that wholesome and good, and as diversified as it can conveniently be made. In like manner *their clothing* should be ample, and pains taken to make them careful of it. *Their houses* large enough for their families; each family dwelling in a separate house of its own; and the houses made tight and comfortable, with a good supply of cooking utensils, &c. *The houses, and the yards and grounds* about them, should be kept *clean. The sick, the infirm, and the aged* carefully nursed and attended to. *The labour of the plantation,* such as the people can successfully accomplish with due preservation of health and spirits, and the saving of time sufficient to attend to their own domestic affairs. They should have *opportunity to plant* something for themselves, and opportunity to attend to, and to harvest their crops, and to dispose of what they raise or make for sale. Special care should be taken by the master to secure to his servants the *full benefit of the entire Sabbath* for the purposes of rest and devotion; and while the master does not require them to do any work for him on that day, he should not allow them to do any for themselves: such as attending their crops, repairing houses and fences, washing, mending, hunting, fishing, grinding, &c. All these things should be done during the week. Their disposition to visit and go from place to place, as is common in some parts of the country, he must restrain and regulate in the most efficient and judicious manner he can. He should restrain his people from visiting Sunday-markets, or trading at shops and stores on God's holy day; and use all the influence in his power to promote *temperance* among them. The *retail-stores* and *tippling-shops,* set up at the corners of the streets and in obscure lanes and retreats in town, and cities and villages, and scattered throughout the country, purposely for the *"negro-trade,"* where stolen goods, and any and every kind of produce and articles are received without ticket or question, *exert a most ruinous and demoralizing influence over the coloured population of the South.* They are kept open secretly on the Sabbath-day, and at late hours in the night. Here are the negroes encouraged in dishonesty, made dissatisfied with their condition, confirmed in drunkenness, and enticed into debauchery, while they are imposed upon, and cheated, and defrauded to an amazing extent. Their suppression would be a blessing to the country. As a part of the privileges of the Sabbath-day, the owner should allow his people to attend the public worship of God, and he should urge them to do so; and also, have all the children sent to the Sabbath-school. This latter duty may require some attention on his part; but for the good of his young servants, and for the encouragement of those who are engaged in this labour of love, he ought not to omit it. Some owners know nothing of their people from Saturday evening to Monday morning. They put them under no restraints whatever; they may stay at home, or visit miles and miles away; go to church, or not, as they please; be with the whites, or go to a negro meeting, where scenes are enacted that are sufficient to draw out the police, and to require the suppression of such ridiculous and lawless assemblages. Other owners maintain stricter discipline; and because there are negroes who abuse the privileges allowed them on the Sabbath, especially that of going to public worship, and it may be their own people have been transgressors, they are inclined to forbid their going to Church at all on the Sabbath-day. Both parties are in extremes, and extremes are neither safe nor beneficial. The extremes before us tend to precisely the same results, immorality and reckless insubordination. Persons under authority should feel that they are so; they should feel the power of that authority, not for their injury, but for their benefit. They should be governed, not only for the good of those who are set over them, but for their own also. Hence we say, *maintain just discipline at all times, and in all particulars;* without it no plantation can prosper; and institute wholesome regulations; but permit your servants to go to church on the Sabbath, and see that the instructions which they receive are for their edification and salvation.

The owner should frown upon, and restrain, and punish *immorality*. He should encourage *marriages,* and *defend families* from the invasions of unprincipled men and women, and conscientiously *keep them together.* We know that it has been said, "The owner can do no good here;" i. e. in checking lewd immoralities. But we beg leave to say, that our experience and observation teach the opposite doctrine. *Quarrelling, and fighting, and profane swearing, lying and stealing* in every form, should meet with due correction. They should be taught to respect the persons, and families, and feelings, and property of each other, and of all men. *Punishments* should be in proportion to offences, and not cruel in kind, nor excessive in degree: and *rewards* be given not only to those who excel, and are most deserving, but also, to all, when they do well. Owners should pay special attention to *the character and conduct of their drivers or foremen*—whatever name they bear. As a class, they need watchfulness and care, lest they abuse their authority to purposes of interest, of lust, of pride, of partiality, or of revenge. They should also give attention to the *character and conduct of overseers or managers.* An overseer has it in his power to ruin a plantation as much in a *moral* as in a *pecuniary* point of view. And no skill in management, nor success in cropping, can compensate an owner for the corruption of the principles and morals of his people, on the part of either driver or overseer. To conclude, in the language of an experienced planter, and friend of the religious instruction of the negroes, "To make this system (of religious instruction on plantations,) truly and permanently beneficial, *the entire discipline and economy of the plantation must be established and regulated in harmony with it.* The master must not only provide that his people be religiously instructed, but he must manage them on those very principles he wishes them to govern themselves by. He must keep his own temper, and in all things be temperate. He must hold the truth sacred, and his word must be truth. He must respect the rights of property in the smallest matters, and cherish among his people a care of property honestly acquired. It will help them to become honest, and possibly teach him to control a passion— the love of accumulation—that may be too strong in his own bosom. A spirit of truth, kindness, and justice, manifested by the master, will pervade his people, and he will find that while he has been trying to do *his people* good, by teaching them fidelity and subordination, *he* has received a greater good, the mastery of himself."—*Thomas S. Clay, Bryan county, Georgia.* Owners who conscientiously, perseveringly, and prayerfully undertake the improvement of their people in the plan now suggested, will—if experience and observation are to be credited—be amply rewarded. Let them invest a little capital in *the minds and hearts* of their people, and it will prove to all concerned, a peace-giving and profitable investment for time and for eternity. . . .

⌗ *E S S A Y S*

No region of the country was hit harder by reform enthusiasms than the so-called Burned Over District of western New York State. Its canal towns and rural villages have long been testing grounds for social historians interested in reformism's origins and effects. Paul E. Johnson, a professor of history at the University of Utah, focuses in the first essay on the young city of Rochester, the site of Charles Finney's greatest early revival in 1831. Johnson finds that the frictions caused by the city's rapid growth in the 1820s bred a growing sense of impasse and despair among the city's businessmen—class concerns that ignited the city's early temperance movement and (later) the Finneyite explosion. In the second essay, the historian Mary P. Ryan of the University of California at Berkeley examines the nearby settlement of Utica. Like Johnson, she discovers a new, palpably middle-class morality emanating from the temperance movement and similar voluntary associations. But whereas Johnson stresses the conflicts between men of different classes, Ryan is struck by the extraordinary participation of women in the new movements. On a different but related front, the historian David Brion Davis of Yale University, in the third essay, surveys national trends in various strains of nativism and identifies common themes about social dislocation and a search for order. How might these contrasting interpretations inform each other?

Class, Liquor, and Reform in Rochester

PAUL E. JOHNSON

By 1830 the household economy had all but passed out of existence, and so had the social order that it sustained. Work, family life, the makeup of

Excerpts from *A Shopkeeper's Millennium* by Paul E. Johnson. Copyright © 1978 by Paul E. Johnson. Reprinted by permission of Hill and Wang, a division of Farrar, Straus & Giroux, Inc.

neighborhoods—the whole pattern of society—separated class from class: master and wage earner inhabited distinct social worlds. Workmen experienced new kinds of harassment on the job. But after work they entered a fraternal, neighborhood-based society in which they were free to do what they wanted. At the same time masters devised standards of work discipline, domestic privacy, and social peace that were directly antithetical to the spontaneous and noisy sociability of the workingmen. The two worlds stood within a few yards of each other, and they fought constantly. That battle took place on many fronts. But from the beginning it centered on alcohol.

The temperance question was nonexistent in 1825. Three years later it was a middle-class obsession. Sullen and disrespectful employees, runaway husbands, paupers, Sabbath breakers, brawlers, theatergoers: middle-class minds joined them in the image of a drink-crazed proletariat. In 1829 the county grand jury repeated what had become, in a remarkably short time, bourgeois knowledge: strong drink was "the cause of almost all of the crime and almost all of the misery that flesh is heir to."

These sentiments were new in the late 1820s. Whiskey was not, and we must ask how liquor became a problem, and particularly how it came to shape perceptions of every other social ill. That search will take us back into workshops, households, and neighborhoods. For working-class drinking and middle-class anxieties about it were bound up with the economic and social transformation of the 1820s. Liquor was indeed a fitting symbol of what had happened: nowhere was the making of distinct classes and the collapse of old social controls dramatized more neatly, more angrily, and in so many aspects of life.

Most temperance advocates had been drinking all their lives, for until the middle 1820s liquor was an absolutely normal accompaniment to whatever men did in groups. Nearly every family kept a bottle in the house to "treat" their guests and workmen, and such community gatherings as election days, militia musters, and Fourth of July celebrations invariably witnessed heavy drinking by men at all levels of society. Merchants who would become temperance spokesmen stocked huge supplies of whiskey, and rich men joined freely in groups where bottles were passed from hand to hand. The flour mills in particular were community gathering places, and farmers waiting to use the mills lounged with the millers and with other local citizens and drank. Among laborers and building tradesmen, the dram was an indispensable part of daily wages. And in the workshops, drinking was universal. Not only independent craftsmen and shoemakers hidden away in boardinghouses, but men who worked directly under churchgoing proprietors drank on the job and with their employers. A store clerk remembered that Edwin Scrantom ([an] editor who expressed concern for unprayed-for apprentices and clerks) "often came into our store for a pitcher of ale to cheer up the boys in the printing offices nearby." Only once in the early years is there record of drinking having caused trouble. In 1818 musicians in the town band—prominent professionals and master craftsmen among them—found themselves too drunk to play. Thereafter, they reduced consumption at rehearsals.

Liquor was embedded in the pattern of irregular work and easy sociability sustained by the household economy. It was a bond between men who lived, worked, and played together, a compliment to the unique kind of domination associated with that round of life. Workmen drank with their employers, in situations that employers controlled. The informal mixing of work and leisure and of master and wage earner softened and helped legitimate inequality. At the same time drunkenness remained within the bounds of what the master considered appropriate. For it was in his house that most routine drinking was done, and it was he who bought the drinks.

That changed abruptly in the 1820s. Masters increased the pace, scale, and regularity of production, and they hired young strangers with whom they shared no more than contractual obligations. The masters were becoming businessmen, concerned more with the purchase of labor and raw materials and the distribution of finished goods than with production itself. They began to absent themselves from the workshops. At the same time they demanded new standards of discipline and regularity within those rooms. [T]hose standards included abstinence from strong drink. Now workmen drank less often and less openly on the job. And when they drank, they shared the relaxation and conviviality only with each other, while masters sat in the front room or in another part of town dealing with customers and dreaming up new ways to make things cheaply and quickly.

After work, master and wage earner retreated further into worlds of their own. Masters walked down quiet side streets and entered households that had seceded from the marketplace. Separated from work and workingmen, they and their wives and children turned the middle-class family into a refuge from the amoral economy and disorderly society outside its doors. It was not only the need for clearheaded calculation at work but the new ethos of bourgeois family life that drove businessmen away from the bottle. For unlike the large and public households of 1820, these private little homes—increasingly under the governance of pious housewives—were inappropriate places in which to get drunk. By 1830 the doorway to a middle-class home separated radically different kinds of space: drunkenness and promiscuous sociability on the outside, privacy and icy sobriety indoors.

In the middle and late 1820s whiskey disappeared from settings that the middle class controlled. But in banishing liquor from their workshops and homes, proprietors reached the new limits of what they could in fact control. And it was at those limits that alcohol took on its symbolic force.

Workingmen were building an autonomous social life, and heavy drinking remained part of it. In 1827 Rochester contained nearly 100 establishments licensed to sell drinks. These were not great beer halls and saloons (they would arrive much later in the century) but houses and little businesses where workmen combined drinking with everyday social transactions. On the downtown streets a workman could get a glass of whiskey at groceries, at either of two candy stores, or at a barber shop a few steps from the central business intersection—all of them gathering places for men like himself. At night he could join the crowds at the theater, spending time before and after the show in the noisy and crowded barroom that occupied the basement. On the way home, he would pass the establishments of other licensed grogsellers, for they were everywhere in the workingman's Rochester. The men who operated bars in the poorer neighborhoods shared the sensibilities and many of the experiences of their patrons, for fully 43 percent of them were wage earners themselves. These part-time barkeepers included thirteen journeymen and eight laborers, two boatmen, two teamsters, three clerks, and a pair of schoolteachers. A five-dollar license permitted them to sell drinks, adding to their incomes and fitting their households into the emerging pattern of working-class neighborhood life.

Alongside these kitchen barrooms stood businesses licensed to sell whiskey: food shops and small variety stores, taverns, and the home workshops of a few of the smaller master craftsmen. These were social centers on a large scale, for many of them doubled as boardinghouses. Of shopkeepers and petty proprietors licensed to sell drinks in 1827 (N = 23), 52 percent took in lodgers. (Among the 51 who did not serve drinks, the comparable figure was 8 percent.) These ramshackle establishments—"disorderly," the newspaper called them—carried on traditions that had been abandoned in the workshops, maintaining an easy integration of economic, domestic, and leisure activities, and of life indoors with the life of the neighborhood. Perhaps typical was the bakery run by John C. Stevens on the canal towpath off Exchange Street. During the day Stevens and his family baked bread. But they stopped at odd times to serve drinks and talk with canal men and dock workers from the boat basin a few steps away. In the evenings they were joined by the journeyman carpenter and the schoolteacher who boarded in their home, and by whoever else decided to drop by, and the activities of the household merged imperceptibly with the flow of neighborhood life.

The Stevens bakery was a lively and crowded place, lively in a very old way. Merchants and masters might peer down the towpath and see that functions they once performed—the provision of food and a place to sleep, whiskey and the companionship and relaxation that went with it—were being taken up by workingmen themselves, or by such questionable proprietors as John C. Stevens. It gave the old family governors something to ponder as they disappeared into their own secluded homes.

The link between drinking and violence was, of course, more than a figment of middle-class imaginations. Alcohol was surrounded by new, perhaps looser cultural controls. At the same time, workingmen experienced punishing changes in what they could expect from life, and some social drinkers took a turn toward the pathological. The laborer who stabbed a friend in 1828, the boat carpenter who beat a workmate to death with a calking mallet in 1829, and the man who killed his wife in the middle of North St. Paul Street were all drunk and can all, I think, be put into that category. But we must also note that official intervention in working-class neighborhoods—and it came with increasing frequency—sometimes created violence where there had been none. In 1830 a Negro blacksmith turned on the constable who was arresting him for gambling and beat him unconscious. A few months later, neighbors rescued an offender before officials could get him off the block. And in 1833 a constable entered a grocery to quiet a disturbance and was kicked to death. The new neighborhoods were building an independent social life, and some workmen were demonstrating that they would meet outside meddling with force.

The drinking problem of the late 1820s stemmed directly from the new relationship between master and wage earner. Alcohol had been a builder of morale in household workshops, a subtle and pleasant bond between men. But in the 1820s proprietors turned their workshops into little factories, moved their families away from their places of business, and devised standards of discipline, self-control, and domesticity that banned liquor. By default, drinking became part of an autonomous working-class social life, and its meaning changed. When proprietors sent temperance messages into the new neighborhoods, they received replies such as this:

> Who are the most temperate men of modern times? Those who quaff the juice of the grape with their friends, with the greatest good nature, after the manner of the ancient patriarchs, without any malice in their hearts, or the cold-water, pale-faced, money-making men, who make the necessities of their neighbors their opportunity for grinding the face of the poor?

An ancient bond between classes had become, within a very short time, an angry badge of working-class status.

The liquor question dominated social and political conflict in Rochester from the late 1820s onward. At every step, it pitted a culturally independent working class against entrepreneurs who had dissolved the social relationships through which they had controlled others, but who continued to consider themselves the rightful protectors and governors of their city.

. . . In 1828, worried gentlemen formed the Rochester Society for the Promotion of Temperance, and affiliated with a national movement led by Lyman Beecher of Boston. These men proposed to end drunkenness through persuasion, example, and the weight of their names. Every old family and every church submerged their differences and contributed leaders to the society. Colonel Rochester himself, along with his son-in-law Jonothan Child, represented the Rochester clan and the Episcopal Church. They were joined by their old enemies Matthew Brown and Levi Ward, and by Ward's son-in-law Moses Chapin. The Presbyterian, Baptist, and Methodist ministers were among the founders. So, temporarily, was Father McNamara of the Catholic chapel. The *Observer* scanned the names and concluded that "when we see that they are the most respectable, wealthy, moral, and influential individuals in society, we feel confident that this reformation will not cease but with the extermination of intemperance from our land."

The temperance reformers were wealthy men, and they possessed enormous power. But they preferred to translate power into authority, and to reform lesser men by persuasion rather than by force. Lyman Beecher, whose *Six Sermons on Intemperance* guided the movement from its beginning, defined the goal as "THE BANISHMENT OF ARDENT SPIRITS FROM THE LIST OF LAWFUL ARTICLES OF COMMERCE BY A CORRECT AND EFFICIENT PUBLIC SENTIMENT . . ." by social pressure and an aroused public opinion. The society aimed its appeals at wealthy men, for these had always set standards for others. Members of the society gave up even the most moderate use of liquor. They would not buy it, drink it, sell it, manufacture it, or provide it for their guests or employees, and they would use all their influence to encourage others to do the same. The organization and its methods were based on the touching faith that poor men would drink only "so long as the traffic in liquor is regarded as lawful, and is patronized by men of reputation and moral worth . . ." Temperance men did not want to outlaw liquor or to run drunkards and grogsellers out of town. They wanted only to make men ashamed to drink. Reform would come quietly and voluntarily, and it would come from the top down.

Most temperance appeals were directed at businessmen and masters who hired wage labor and who were in daily contact with those elements of society with the strongest taste for alcohol. " 'I'LL LEAVE OFF WHEN THE BOSS DOES,' said a young mechanic to his companions. This shows the influence and responsibility of those who carry on an extensive business. If an employer refuses to abstain from strong drink, we need not wonder if many whom he employs refuse to abstain, encouraged by his example." Temperance-minded masters stopped providing the daily dram as part of a workman's wages, and set out to convince others that work, particularly strenuous outdoor work, was better and more profitably done without the stimulus of alcohol. Master carpenters reported putting up houses "without the use of ardent spirits—*without the least difficulty.* Indeed it is much the safest way to put up frames." A nearby farmer announced that he had grown tired of the "bobbling and idleness which ardent spirits uniformly produces" and that he no longer gave whiskey to his harvesters. The happy result was that "he had no difficulty in keeping them perfectly subject to his directions. They conducted and labored like sober, rational men, and not like intoxicated mutineers."

Temperance propaganda promised masters social peace, a disciplined and docile labor force, and an opportunity to assert moral authority over their men. The movement enjoyed widespread success among those merchants and masters who considered themselves respectable. After one year's agitation the *Observer* announced proudly that "public opinion has already, in a great degree, branded as disgraceful, the practice of dramdrinking, among the more respectable part of the community." Of course hundreds of less "respectable" men continued to drink. But temperance men stood firm in their belief that "regiments of drunkards can present but a feeble resistance compared with a few *respectable church members.*"

In workshop after workshop, masters gathered their men and announced that they would no longer provide drinks or allow drinking in the shop, and that the new rules derived from patriotism and religion. Sometimes employees took a hand. When a printer's apprentice completed his training in 1829, he refused to buy his shopmates the customary round of drinks. Instead, he gave them each a Bible, a glass of cold water, and a knowing look. If a workman continued to drink off the job, the master took him aside for a firm but friendly talk and tried "by persuasion and all other proper and suitable means" to bring him to his senses. These must have been odd conversations—earnest pomposity on one side, foot shuffling and hidden grins on the other. Masters finished talking with the assurance that they had done all that they properly could. It only remained for workingmen to take their advice.

Underneath these gentle methods lay the assumption that Rochester had legitimate opinion makers, and that attitudes could radiate from them into every corner of society. Indeed for many reformers the temperance crusade may have been a final test of that belief. But while masters asked wage earners to give up their evil ways, they turned workers out of their homes and into streets and neighborhoods where drinking remained a normal part of life. A journeyman who put up with strange new practices on the job experienced strong pressures to drink on his own block, where the grocery was the principal place to relax with workmates and friends. Temperance men talked loudest in 1828 and 1829, years in which the autonomy of working-class neighborhoods grew at a dizzying rate. In each of those years the village granted nearly 100 licenses to sell whiskey by the glass, suggesting that there was a legal drinking establishment for every twenty-eight adult men in Rochester. These neighborhood bars dispensed nearly 200,000 gallons of whiskey annually. Perhaps the workshops were dry. The neighborhoods certainly were not.

By 1830 the temperance crusade was, on its own terms, a success: society's leading men were encouraging abstinence. But even as they preached, they withdrew from the social relationships in which their ability to command obedience was embedded. Wage earners continued to drink. But now they drank only in their own neighborhoods and only with each other, and in direct defiance of their employers. It taught the masters a disheartening lesson: if authority collapsed whenever they turned their backs, then there was in fact no authority. It was a lesson that masters were learning in a wide variety of situations. But nowhere was it dramatized more starkly than in the social relations and cultural meaning that had come to surround a glass of whiskey.

Middle-Class Women and Moral Reform

MARY P. RYAN

An evangelical publication of the late 1820s introduced a "Dialogue between a Little Girl and Her Mother" with this childish query: "Mother there are so many societies! . . . I longed for you this afternoon when I came home from school, and they told me you were gone to the Maternal Society: You go very often. Mother what is a Maternal Society?" This fragment of fictional conversation is full of meaning for the history of family and society. . . . The first is the intimation that even a child would be impressed by the sheer volume of "societies." When this dialogue was written in the late 1820s the

Excerpts from *Cradle of the Middle Class: The Family in Oneida County, New York, 1790–1865* (New York: Cambridge University Press) 1981, pp. 105–108, 116–125, 132–136.

town of Utica and the surrounding villages were in fact overrun with societies, or associations, as they were alternatively called. . . . The associational fervor began to subside around the mid-1840s. Until then, however, much of community life seemed organized around these associations, which garnered far more space in the directory than did public institutions or offices.

Second, this piece of juvenile dialogue harbors a more qualitative and startling clue about American social history. From it, even out of the mouth of a babe, it would seem, comes quiet approval of the mothers who left home for this larger world of "societies." Mothers joined fathers, sons, and daughters in the heavy traffic streaming out from homes of Oneida County and into voluntary associations. . . .

The town [of Utica] was large enough to sustain a variety of secondary social institutions and yet small enough to foster the casual familiarity and intermingling on which they throve. This community ambience is illustrated in a lithograph dated 1838 that portrays an intersection in the heart of town between Washington and Genesee streets. In the artist's perception the city's associated activities were given equal play with its commerce. Merchants' Hall and the Presbyterian Church were featured just as prominently amid the shops and houses, and in between there was ample room for informal, neighborly interchanges. Men and women stopped beside a crude farm wagon to chat. Workers and businessmen paused in the street for leisurely conversation. Children used the same streets as their playground. Voluntary associations were nurtured by, and entangled with, this active street life of Utica in the age of commercial capitalism.

At the same time many of the occupants of these cozy social spaces felt a dearth of formal institutions to meet their everyday needs. Neither the public sector nor the church was equipped to serve a population that more than doubled in the 1820s and grew by more than 50 percent in the next decade. It was left to voluntary associations to provide such fundamental services as fire and police protection and the care of the poor. Much of the local population also felt the lack of the basic emotional sustenance usually found in families. The city was inundated by young men and women, mostly recent arrivals who had traveled to Utica without an entourage of relatives. In the 1830s more than one in four Uticans was between the ages of twenty and thirty and one in three adults males was listed in the directory as a boarder rather than as head of a household. Association was also called into play to provide psychological services and supportive everyday human contacts to this deracinated population. . . .

It seemed from the perspective of [some local] ministers that Utica and Whitestown had [in the middle 1830s] become open breeding ground for every sort of vice. To the imagination of Samuel Aiken, writing in 1834, the busy, crowded streets of the commercial town were playing host to "a whole tribe of libertines." A month later a visiting minister rose before the Bleecker Street congregation to warn against a "loathesome monster—licentiousness—[which] crawls, tracking the earth with his fetid slime and poisoning the atmosphere with his syphilitic breath." The sin might be intemperance, fornication, gambling, or Sabbath breaking, but the imagery of the sinners and seducers were always the same. In the imagination of the ministers, Utica was beset with reptiles (the frogs of Egypt being a favorite simile) lying in wait to ensnare and defile the sons and daughters of Christians. Certainly some new and stringent measures were necessary to preserve public morality in the face of this horrific attack. . . .

It was yet another form of association that would fill this social and cultural vacuum. The first example of this new species of association peculiar to the canal era went by the generic title "moral reform," was organized by females, and set as its goal the promulgation and enforcement of a stringent code of sexual ethics. The Female Moral Reform Society, like other associations concerned with the public advocacy of personal ethics, flourished throughout Oneida County. Like the Maternal Association, it too drew its membership from a broader population than had the benevolent societies of the earlier period. The Utica chapter, for example, did not confine itself to one class but enrolled the wives and daughters of merchants, artisans, and professionals, as well as an occasional seamstress. The married, single, and widowed of all ages joined the cause of sexual reform. . . .

The members of the Female Moral Reform Society began by adapting traditional family and social forms to their reform purposes. They often worked within the home economy and the private social circle. Mrs. Whittelsey, who endorsed female moral reform from the editor's desk of the *Mother's Magazine,* depicted one such tactic in 1833:

> Such has been my sympathy for my sex, I cheerily testify, that for many years, no young woman has come to my dwelling, seeking temporary employment, or a permanent situation, toward whom I have not endeavored to reach forth the hand of compassion. When I could, I have either written a note or sent with them a messenger, to such of my friends as might be able either to employ them themselves, or direct them to others. Were this course or some other equivalent oftener pursued, (I speak from experience) many of the unfortunate victims of vice and wretchedness, which at present claim the attentions and charity of enlightened benevolence, would be greatly diminished. Yes, it is for mothers in Israel to say how many of the unfortunate "Magdalenes," the present year, shall be found clothed with Savior's righteousness, washing his feet with their tears, and wiping them with the hairs of their head.

Mrs. Whittelsey had performed one favored function of female reform, the protection of young women from seduction and prostitution, without stepping outside the boundaries of woman's customary role. By placing vulnerable young women as servants within the households of her friends, she activated a women's network as a kind of informal employment agency and working girls' protective association.

The adaptability of the women's network for reform purposes was recognized by correspondents to *MacDowall's Journal.* A male representative of Utica's publishing industry, Charles Hastings, wrote to MacDowall in July 1833 to report that the work of promoting moral reform was already under way in Utica. Hastings pleaded preoccupation with other business but was pleased to report that "a female in my family says she will go around among the families and see if she can't get something for your support." Support for *MacDowall's Journal* and female moral reform in general was collected in this piecemeal process of female solicitation. Contributions came in small sums of cash or poignant donations like that from "a lady in Utica" dated February 1836—"two rings and a breast pin." This distinctive method of association was described in the language of the Female Missionary Society and the Maternal Association as a communication between "Dear Sisters," as a "labor of love." . . .

As time went on, and the magnitude of licentiousness loomed even larger in the imagination of its members, the Female Moral Reform Society resorted to increasingly radical tactics. At first the most belligerent method of the reformer was ostracism, a method described by the Clinton society as "discountenancing all men reputed to be licentious, in excluding them from our society and by every other laudable means in our power." These women were in effect using a strategy similar to the church elders' sanction of excommunication. The tactics of the Utica society were significantly escalated in 1838 after a meeting with the representatives of the parent society. Utica's reformers were reawakened to the "vital importance of the cause" and the growing magnitude of the evil. "Even our small children are infested by it. Who among us have not had our hearts pained by the obscenity of little children; who among us does not tremble lest some who are dear to us should be led away by the thousand snares of the destroyer. Who among us can tell that our sisters and daughters are safe while the seducer is unhesitatingly received into our society and treated with that attention which virtue alone can claim." The suppression of lewdness now bore the stamp of a woman's reform; it focused on the defense of females from the dishonorable intentions and inordinate lusts of men and aimed to relieve mothers of the heartache of a child's moral degeneration.

At this point the female reformers began to entertain the notion that a good offense was the best defense. Timidly, the Utica society began to tread out into the world of the seducer. A visiting committee was formed in 1841 and ventured out into the streets of Utica with something less than high hopes and bold spirits: "For should we meet opposition we felt that we should balk in our weakness and leave the ground for the enemy." The expectations of this anonymous little band were quickly raised by the warm response of the city's mothers. One widow tearfully accepted a tract (entitled "Mother Will You Read It?") saying, "I need assistance to train up my fatherless boys in purity." At another home the visiting committee heard the story of a son who had become a hopeless drunkard and of a daughter "lost to iniquity." The distraught mother's problems were compounded by the callousness of her husband, who "was not willing she should go anywhere [not even to church]; they kept boarders who on Sunday expect something extra for dinner." The Reverend John Frost had encountered similar examples of tyrannical and irreligious household heads in 1813, but now they reached a sympathetic female ear and received a supportive if impotent response: "Poor woman! She should have remembered the injunction of Paul, 'Be not unequally yoked together with unbelievers.' " . . .

There is no hard evidence to support the claim of moral reformers that sexual license was mushrooming in Utica after 1830. A survey conducted by the Female Moral Reform Society uncovered only two arrests for prostitution and nine cases of illegitimacy in the criminal files of 1841. Even given gross underreporting, this rate of misbehavior is hardly sufficient to indict a city of almost thirteen thousand persons as a modern-day Sodom. A more relevant statistic is found in the shifting age structure of Utica during these years. During the 1830s the centers of female moral reform were invaded by young, single men and women, marking a sudden and dramatic increase in the population of unprotected sons and daughters for whom female moral reformers expressed particular concern. In Utica it was young clerks, seamstresses, and domestic servants who swelled the ranks of potential victims and perpetrators of licentiousness. In Clinton it was the students at Hamilton College who caused particular worry. Societies grew up around the factories and boardinghouses of Whitestown, in Oriskany Falls and New York Mills. . . . Wherever the young and mobile congregated, their pious mothers had cause for anxiety. The old mechanisms of the patriarchal household order were no longer available to regulate and supervise the sexual habits of the young. Neither the church nor the patriarchal family was there to ensure a marriage, for example, should errant youngsters conceive a child out of wedlock. The Female Moral Reform Society had devised a means of preventing such sexual offenses and social problems. By propagating refined notions of chastity, they strove to plant the force of sexual repression within the individual character of a mobile youth.

Under the cover of privacy, without benefit of official encouragement, in association with one another, women exerted real social power and engineered major social change. This was especially true of the groups like the Female Moral Reform Society and the Maternal Association that arose during the 1830s in the wake of revivalism. . . .

[O]bservers of the Thanksgiving Day parade in the year 1840 would find that the ranks of association had been replenished once again in support of a widely popular reform. The marching units for that year included the Utica Total Abstinence Society, the Catholic Total Abstinence Society, the Youth Abstinence Society, and the Utica City Total Abstinence Association. When it came to the issue of temperance, and indeed even its most extreme doctrine, total abstinence, a wide spectrum of the community endorsed and participated in association. A collection of temperance songs, published in Utica and called the *Washingtonian Pocket Companion,* voiced the new wave of associationism in the following dulcet tones:

> Hark! hark the sweet music that sounds o'er the land,
> And thrills in the ears of us all;
> As louder and more loud does each cold water band
> Respond to the temperance call;
> While thousands spring up from each valley and hill,
> And seizing the spirited strain,
> Send back the glad challenge with hearty good will,
> From hilltop to valley again.

The Washingtonian movement, founded in 1840 by some apprentices in Baltimore, Maryland, was particularly popular in Utica and throughout the hills and valleys that the market town served. One chapter of Washingtonians met nearly every weekday evening in Utica in the 1840s, when it was estimated that eight thousand citizens had signed the Washingtonian pledge to abstain from the use of all intoxicating beverages. Another chapter in New York Mills enlisted more than 350 members at its first meeting in 1842.

Temperance men and women, assembled in their various divisions, perhaps marked off by occupational, neighborhood, ethnic, or religious affiliations, together constituted one large cold-water army. Cognizant of the pitfalls of association in the age of evangelism and Jacksonianism, the Washingtonian association pledged "carefully to avoid any course of conduct which shall give countenance to one particular religion or political sect of men in preference to another." The benign yet ennobling nature of the cause legitimized the participation of everyone regardless of age or sex. Children could, and did, form juvenile temperance associations without challenging adult authority. Sunday-school pupils joined the cold-water army, following in the age ranks that included the Sons, and the Cadets, of Temperance. Women were welcomed into the Daughters of Temperance and the Martha Washington Union. The potential for ethnic or class conflict was defused by the pluralism of temperance associations. Irishmen formed their Hibernian associations, and a group of self-conscious members of the producing class formed the Workingmen's Temperance Union. There was even a contingent of black women in Utica's cold-water army. The separate associations respected one another's boundaries and were tolerant of outsiders and even of inebriates. The Hibernian Total Abstinence Society, for example, patiently held a cold-water celebration every St. Patrick's Day in the shadow of the major celebration, which featured the convivial drunkenness produced by a score of toasts and was sanguinely tabulated the following morning by bleary-eyed newspaper editors.

The membership of the temperance associations of the 1840s was characteristically presented as a group of young men, as "sons of temperance," not as patriarchal heads of households. The commonest symbol of their solidarity was the metaphor of fraternity. . . .

Class and occupation could at the same time also take on a chameleonlike quality in the perspective of temperance advocates. Intemperance, on the one hand, was conceived of as the classic precipitant of downward mobility; abstinence, on the other, was the highway to wealth. One temperance newspaper supplied its readers with advice on "How to Rise in Business" and assured them that under the discipline of temperate habits "nothing can hinder you from accumulating." Temperance was advanced as a kind of class characteristic in its own right, a sure guarantee of respectability, reliability, and general moral and economic worth. . . . The good old days when business could be blended with the brew, and when adolescent drinking was a sign of manliness, had long passed. In the risky market conditions of the canal era, a shrewd businessman would not place his stock in the hands of an intemperate clerk or lawyer. In other words, temperance was advertised as a kind of solvent of whatever class differences were developing within the commercial city. All occupations would benefit from its practice and each rank might find it the avenue to upward mobility.

The hierarchy of sex and age seemed equally vulnerable to the leveling tendency of temperance association. It is quite likely that, contrary to all the rhetoric about brotherhood, women dominated the temperance ranks. In the New York Mills Washingtonian Society, for example (the only Oneida County temperance group to leave an extensive roster), 61 percent of all members were female. Furthermore, contrary to the sex segregation of most associations, this society enrolled males and females in one common organization. The leveling of age distinctions was also officially sanctioned by the temperance movement. In 1850 the *Utica Teetotaler* found it archaic to presume that "young men are fit neither for generals nor statesmen, and that they must be kept in the background until their physical strength is impaired by age, and their intellectual faculties become blunted by the weight of years." In the estimation of the editors, men in their twenties and thirties were fit to exercise civic power and responsibility. The status of youth seemed, like that of women, to rise wherever the forces of association gathered strength.

The last remnants of the old household order seemed to be dissolving in the fraternal draughts of Oneida County teetotalers. The very walls of the homes of Utica appeared to break open as all ages, both genders, and a range of occupations streamed out into the reformers halls. The temperance meeting was in itself a kind of ersatz and sentimental home. The *Utica Teetotaler* printed a poetic rendition of this theory of association in 1850.

> I was far from my home not a relative near
> To sooth all my sorrows or quell the deep sigh;
> Not a friend could I see, or a voice could I hear
> To cheer me in hope that could brighten my eye . . .
> Then she lifted her banner high o'er my head
> Whose folds are all cherished on land and on sea
> When the trumpet of wisdom awoke from the dead
> My soul when I found a mother to me.

The metaphor of a maternal embrace, like that of fraternity, affirmed affection as the primary bond between members of both associations and families. In the 1840s in Oneida County, however, this hallmark of the cult of domesticity found its most enthusiastic expression not in the family itself but in the temperance association. . . .

It was actually the reform association that best articulated the more affectionate and voluntaristic ambience of the family. The Washingtonians sang hymns to this new domesticity to the tune of "Home Sweet Home." The ideal of family life can be read between the lines of a typical maudlin tableau:

> Oh sad was the heart of his grief-stricken wife,
> Whom he vow'd at the altar to cherish for life.

His children once fondled, now trembled with fear,
As the sound of his footsteps fell sad in their ear.

This favorite image of the temperance writers assumed that the good and sober family had an affectionate infrastructure, where wives were "cherished" and children "fondled." At the same time, this temperance literature prescribed a distinctive division of roles and differentiation of personality within the ideal home. The refrain of the poem, quoted above put the responsibility for domestic disaster squarely on the shoulders of the husband and father. "He felt all the world, but himself was to Blame. Blame. Blame." Hymn number 26 in the *Washingtonian Pocket Companion* rendered the same message in an even more incisive manner. "The Song of the Drunkard's Child" began this way:

Oh, pity me lady, I am hungry and cold;
Should I all my sorrows to you unfold,
I'm sure your kind breast with compassion would flame,
My father's a drunkard—but I'm not to blame.

It was the temperance movement that most actively and emphatically enjoined men to practice the prudence and self-control incumbent upon them as husbands, fathers, and breadwinners. . . .

Simultaneously, the temperance movement projected revisions in the familial roles of women. The grieving wives and bountiful ladies honored in the Washingtonian hymnal seemed exempted from the economic burdens of husbands and fathers. Their specialty was pure, altruistic moral service to their families. One writer put women's role this way: "with gentle weapons of filial, maternal and conjugal persuasion [to] accomplish more than men even if clad in a panoply of steel." The details of this gentle ministry had been worked out not in the temperance movement but in the women's organizations that predated it, especially the maternal associations and female moral reform societies. These two associations devised methods of cultivating temperate habits and restraining sexual drives, as well as appetites for liquor, in their husbands and children. The remodeled female role of maternal socialization, as well as the image of the Victorian wife setting a pure standard for her more passionate husband, were first enunciated by associated women in the 1820s and 1830s and were put to the service of the temperance cause in the 1840s. . . .

Nativist Reform and the Fear of Subversive Conspiracies

DAVID BRION DAVIS

During the second quarter of the nineteenth century, when danger of foreign invasion appeared increasingly remote, Americans were told by various respected leaders that Freemasons had infiltrated the government and had

Davis, David Brion, "Some Themes of Counter-Subversion: An Analysis of Anti-Masonic, Anti-Catholic, and Anti-Mormon Literature," *Mississippi Valley Historical Review,* 47 (Sept. 1960), pp. 205–224. Reprinted by permission of the Organization of American Historians.

seized control of the courts, that Mormons were undermining political and economic freedom in the West, and that Roman Catholic priests, receiving instructions from Rome, had made frightening progress in a plot to subject the nation to popish despotism. This fear of internal subversion was channeled into a number of powerful counter movements which attracted wide public support. The literature produced by these movements evoked images of a great American enemy that closely resembled traditional European stereotypes of conspiracy and subversion. In Europe, however, the idea of subversion implied a threat to the established order—to the king, the church, or the ruling aristocracy—rather than to ideals or a way of life. If free Americans borrowed their images of subversion from frightened kings and uneasy aristocrats, these images had to be shaped and blended to fit American conditions. The movements would have to come from the people, and the themes of counter-subversion would be likely to reflect their fears, prejudices, hopes, and perhaps even unconscious desires.

There are obvious dangers in treating such reactions against imagined subversion as part of a single tendency or spirit of an age. Anti-Catholicism was nourished by ethnic conflict and uneasiness over immigration in the expanding cities of the Northeast; anti-Mormonism arose largely from a contest for economic and political power between western settlers and a group that voluntarily withdrew from society and claimed the undivided allegiance of its members. Anti-Masonry, on the other hand, was directed against a group thoroughly integrated in American society and did not reflect a clear division of economic, religious, or political interests. Moreover, anti-Masonry gained power in the late 1820's and soon spent its energies as it became absorbed in national politics; anti-Catholicism reached its maximum force in national politics a full generation later; anti-Mormonism, though increasing in intensity in the 1850's, became an important national issue only after the Civil War. These movements seem even more widely separated when we note that Freemasonry was traditionally associated with anti-Catholicism and that Mormonism itself absorbed considerable anti-Masonic and anti-Catholic sentiment.

Despite such obvious differences, there were certain similarities in these campaigns against subversion. All three gained widespread support in the northeastern states within the space of a generation; anti-Masonry and anti-Catholicism resulted in the sudden emergence of separate political parties; and in 1856 the new Republican party explicitly condemned the Mormons' most controversial institution. The movements of counter-subversion differed markedly in historical origin, but as the image of an un-American conspiracy took form in the nativist press, in sensational exposés, in the countless fantasies of treason and mysterious criminality, the lines separating Mason, Catholic, and Mormon became almost indistinguishable. . . .

If Masons, Catholics, and Mormons bore little resemblance to one another in actuality, as imagined enemies they merged into a nearly common stereotype. Behind specious professions of philanthropy or religious sentiment, nativists discerned a group of unscrupulous leaders plotting to subvert the American social order. Though rank-and-file members were not indi-

vidually evil, they were blinded and corrupted by a persuasive ideology that
justified treason and gross immorality in the interest of the subversive group.
Trapped in the meshes of a machine-like organization, deluded by a false
sense of loyalty and moral obligation, these dupes followed orders like
professional soldiers and labored unknowingly to abolish free society, to
enslave their fellow men, and to overthrow divine principles of law and
justice. Should an occasional member free himself from bondage to superstition and fraudulent authority, he could still be disciplined by the threat
of death or dreadful tortures. There were no limits to the ambitious designs
of leaders equipped with such organizations. According to nativist prophets,
they chose to subvert American society because control of America meant
control of the world's destiny. . . .

The subversive group was essentially an inverted image of Jacksonian
democracy and the cult of the common man; as such it not only challenged
the dominant values but stimulated those suppressed needs and yearnings
that are unfulfilled in a mobile, rootless, and individualistic society. It was
therefore both frightening and fascinating.

It is well known that expansion and material progress in the Jacksonian
era evoked a fervid optimism and that nationalists became intoxicated with
visions of America's millennial glory. The simultaneous growth of prosperity
and social democracy seemed to prove that Providence would bless a nation
that allowed her citizens maximum liberty. When each individual was left
free to pursue happiness in his own way, unhampered by the tyranny of
custom or special privilege, justice and well-being would inevitably emerge.
But if a doctrine of laissez-faire individualism seemed to promise material
expansion and prosperity, it also raised disturbing problems. As one early
anti-Mormon writer expressed it: What was to prevent liberty and popular
sovereignty from sweeping away "the old landmarks of Christendom, and
the glorious old common law of our fathers"? How was the individual to
preserve a sense of continuity with the past, or identify himself with a given
cause or tradition? What, indeed, was to ensure a common loyalty and a
fundamental unity among the people?

Such questions acquired a special urgency as economic growth intensified
mobility, destroyed old ways of life, and transformed traditional symbols of
status and prestige. Though most Americans took pride in their material
progress, they also expressed a yearning for reassurance and security, for
unity in some cause transcending individual self-interest. This need for meaningful group activity was filled in part by religious revivals, reform movements, and a proliferation of fraternal orders and associations. In politics
Americans tended to assume the posture of what Marvin Meyers has termed
"venturesome conservatives," mitigating their acquisitive impulses by an
appeal for unity against extraneous forces that allegedly threatened a noble
heritage of republican ideals. Without abandoning a belief in progress
through laissez-faire individualism, the Jacksonians achieved a sense of unity
and righteousness by styling themselves as restorers of tradition. Perhaps no
theme is so evident in the Jacksonian era as the strained attempt to provide
America with a glorious heritage and a noble destiny. With only a loose

and often ephemeral attachment to places and institutions, many Americans felt a compelling need to articulate their loyalties, to prove their faith, and to demonstrate their allegiance to certain ideals and institutions. By so doing they acquired a sense of self-identity and personal direction in an otherwise rootless and shifting environment.

But was abstract nationalism sufficient to reassure a nation strained by sectional conflict, divided by an increasing number of sects and associations, and perplexed by the unexpected consequences of rapid growth? One might desire to protect the Republic against her enemies, to preserve the glorious traditions of the Founders, and to help insure continued expansion and prosperity, but first it was necessary to discover an enemy by distinguishing subversion from simple diversity. . . .

Few men questioned traditional beliefs in freedom of conscience and the right of association. Yet what was to prevent "all the errors and worn out theories of the Old World, of schisms in the early Church, the monkish age and the rationalistic period," from flourishing in such salubrious air? Nativists often praised the work of benevolent societies, but they were disturbed by the thought that monstrous conspiracies might also "show kindness and patriotism, when it is necessary for their better concealment; and oftentimes do much good for the sole purpose of getting a better opportunity to do evil." When confronted by so many sects and associations, how was the patriot to distinguish the loyal from the disloyal? It was clear that mere disagreement over theology or economic policy was invalid as a test, since honest men disputed over the significance of baptism or the wisdom of protective tariffs. But neither could one rely on expression of allegiance to common democratic principles, since subversives would cunningly profess to believe in freedom and toleration of dissent as long as they remained a powerless minority.

As nativists studied this troubling question, they discovered that most groups and denominations claimed only a partial loyalty from their members, freely subordinating themselves to the higher and more abstract demands of the Constitution, Christianity, and American public opinion. Moreover, they openly exposed their objects and activities to public scrutiny and exercised little discrimination in enlisting members. Some groups, however, dominated a larger portion of their members' lives, demanded unlimited allegiance as a condition of membership, and excluded certain activities from the gaze of a curious public.

Of all governments, said Richard Rush, ours was the one with most to fear from secret societies, since popular sovereignty by its very nature required perfect freedom of public inquiry and judgment. In a virtuous republic why should anyone fear publicity or desire to conceal activities, unless those activities were somehow contrary to the public interest? When no one could be quite sure what the public interest was, and when no one could take for granted a secure and well-defined place in the social order, it was most difficult to acknowledge legitimate spheres of privacy. Most Americans of the Jacksonian era appeared willing to tolerate diversity and even eccentricity, but when they saw themselves excluded and even barred from witnessing certain proceedings, they imagined a "mystic power" conspiring to enslave them. . . .

The distinguishing mark of Masonic, Catholic, and Mormon conspiracies was a secrecy that cloaked the members' unconditional loyalty to an autonomous body. Since the organizations had corrupted the private moral judgment of their members, Americans could not rely on the ordinary forces of progress to spread truth and enlightenment among their ranks. Yet the affairs of such organizations were not outside the jurisdiction of democratic government, for no body politic could be asked to tolerate a power that was designed to destroy it. Once the true nature of subversive groups was thoroughly understood, the alternatives were as clear as life and death. . . .

When the images of different enemies conform to a similar pattern, it is highly probable that this pattern reflects important tensions within a given culture. The themes of nativist literature suggest that its authors simplified problems of personal insecurity and bewildering social change by trying to unite Americans of diverse political, religious, and economic interests against a common enemy. Just as revivalists sought to stimulate Christian fellowship by awakening men to the horrors of sin, so nativists used apocalyptic images to ignite human passions, destroy selfish indifference, and join patriots in a cohesive brotherhood. . . .

Without explicitly rejecting the philosophy of laissez-faire individualism, with its toleration of dissent and innovation, nativist literature conveyed a sense of common dedication to a noble cause and sacred tradition. Though the nation had begun with the blessings of God and with the noblest institutions known to man, the people had somehow become selfish and complacent, divided by petty disputes, and insensitive to signs of danger. In his sermons attacking such self-interest, such indifference to public concerns, and such a lack of devotion to common ideals and sentiments, the nativist revealed the true source of his anguish. Indeed, he seemed at times to recognize an almost beneficient side to subversive organizations, since they joined the nation in a glorious crusade and thus kept it from moral and social disintegration.

The exposure of subversion was a means of promoting unity, but it also served to clarify national values and provide the individual ego with a sense of high moral sanction and imputed righteousness. Nativists identified themselves repeatedly with a strangely incoherent tradition in which images of Pilgrims, Minute Men, Founding Fathers, and true Christians appeared in a confusing montage. Opposed to this heritage of stability and perfect integrity, to this society founded on the highest principles of divine and natural law, were organizations formed by the grossest frauds and impostures, and based on the wickedest impulses of human nature. Bitterly refuting Masonic claims to ancient tradition and Christian sanction, anti-Masons charged that the Order was of recent origin, that it was shaped by Jews, Jesuits, and French atheists as an engine for spreading infidelity, and that it was employed by kings and aristocrats to undermine republic institutions. If the illustrious Franklin and Washington had been duped by Masonry, this only proved how treacherous was its appeal and how subtly persuasive were its pretensions. Though the Catholic Church had an undeniable claim to tradition, nativists argued that it had originated in stupendous frauds and forgeries "in comparison with which the forgeries of Mormonism are completely thrown into the shade." Yet anti-Mormons saw an even more sinister conspiracy based on the "shrewd cunning" of Joseph Smith, who convinced gullible souls that he conversed with angels and received direct revelations from the Lord.

By emphasizing the fraudulent character of their opponents' claims, nativists sought to establish the legitimacy and just authority of American institutions. Masonic rituals, Roman Catholic sacraments, and Mormon revelations were preposterous hoaxes used to delude naive or superstitious minds; but public schools, a free press, and jury trials were eternally valid prerequisites for a free and virtuous society.

Moreover, the finest values of an enlightened nation stood out in bold relief when contrasted with the corrupting tendencies of subversive groups. Perversion of the sexual instinct seemed inevitably to accompany religious error. Deprived of the tender affections of normal married love, shut off from the elevating sentiments of fatherhood, Catholic priests looked on women only as insensitive objects for the gratification of their frustrated desires. In similar fashion polygamy struck at the heart of a morality based on the inspiring influence of woman's affections: "It renders man coarse, tyrannical, brutal, and heartless. It deals death to all sentiments of true manhood. It enslaves and ruins woman. It crucifies every God-given feeling of her nature." Some anti-Mormons concluded that plural marriage could only have been established among foreigners who had never learned to respect women. But the more common explanation was that the false ideology of Mormonism had deadened the moral sense and liberated man's wild sexual impulse from the normal restraints of civilization. Such degradation of women and corruption of man served to highlight the importance of democratic marriage, a respect for women, and careful cultivation of the finer sensibilities.

But if nativist literature was a medium for articulating common values and exhorting individuals to transcend self-interest and join in a dedicated union against evil, it also performed a more subtle function. Why, we may ask, did nativist literature dwell so persistently on themes of brutal sadism and sexual immorality? Why did its authors describe sin in such minute details, endowing even the worst offenses of their enemies with a certain fascinating appeal?

Such a projection of forbidden desires can be seen in the exaggeration of the stereotyped enemy's powers, which made him appear at times as a virtual superman. Catholics and Mormon leaders, never hindered by conscience or respect for traditional morality, were curiously superior to ordinary Americans in cunning, in exercising power over others, and especially in captivating gullible women. It was an ancient theme of anti-Catholic literature that friars and priests were somehow more potent and sexually attractive than married laymen, and were thus astonishingly successful at seducing supposedly virtuous wives. Americans were cautioned repeatedly that no priest recognized Protestant marriages as valid, and might consider any wife legitimate prey. Furthermore, priests had access to the pornographic teachings of Dens and Liguori, sinister names that aroused the curiosity of anti-Catholics, and hence learned subtle techniques of seduction perfected over the centuries. Speaking with the authority of an ex-priest, William Hogan described the shocking result: "I have seen husbands unsuspiciously and hospitably entertaining the very priest who seduced their wives in the confessional, and was the parent of some of the children who sat at the same table with them, each of the wives unconscious of the other's guilt, and the husbands of both, not even suspecting them." Such blatant immorality was horrifying, but everyone was apparently happy in this domestic scene, and we may suspect that the image was not entirely repugnant to husbands who, despite their respect for the Lord's Commandments, occasionally coveted their neighbors' wives.

The literature of counter-subversion could also embody the somewhat different projective fantasies of women. Ann Eliza Young dramatized her seduction by the Prophet Brigham, whose almost superhuman powers enchanted her and paralyzed her will. Though she submitted finally only because her parents were in danger of being ruined by the Church, she clearly indicated that it was an exciting privilege to be pursued by a Great Man. When Anti-Mormons claimed that Joseph Smith and other prominent Saints knew the mysteries of Animal Magnetism, or were endowed with the highest degree of "amativeness" in their phrenological makeup, this did not detract from their covert appeal. In a ridiculous fantasy written by Maria Ward, such alluring qualities were extended even to Mormon women. Many bold-hearted girls could doubtless identify themselves with Anna Bradish, a fearless Amazon of a creature, who rode like a man, killed without compunction, and had no pity for weak women who failed to look out for themselves. Tall, elegant, and "intellectual," Anna was attractive enough to arouse the insatiable desires of Brigham Young, though she ultimately rejected him and renounced Mormonism.

While nativists affirmed their faith in Protestant monogamy, they obviously took pleasure in imagining the variety of sexual experience supposedly available to their enemies. By picturing themselves exposed to similar temptations, they assumed they could know how priests and Mormons actually sinned. Imagine, said innumerable anti-Catholic writers, a beautiful young woman kneeling before an ardent young priest in a deserted room. As she confesses, he leans over, looking into her eyes, until their heads are nearly touching. Day after day she reveals to him her innermost secrets, secrets she would not think of unveiling to her parents, her dearest friends, or even her suitor. By skillful questioning the priest fills her mind with immodest and even sensual ideas, "until this wretch has worked up her passions to a tension almost snapping, and then becomes his easy prey." How could any man resist such provocative temptations, and how could any girl's virtue withstand such a test?

We should recall that this literature was written in a period of increasing anxiety and uncertainty over sexual values and the proper role of woman.

As ministers and journalists pointed with alarm at the spread of prostitution, the incidence of divorce, and the lax and hypocritical morality of the growing cities, a discussion of licentious subversives offered a convenient means for the projection of guilt as well as desire. The sins of individuals, or of the nation as a whole, could be pushed off upon the shoulders of the enemy and there punished in righteous anger. . . .

If the consciences of many Americans were troubled by the growth of red light districts in major cities, they could divert their attention to the "legalized brothels" called nunneries, for which no one was responsible but lecherous Catholic priests. If others were disturbed by the moral implications of divorce, they could point in horror at the Mormon elder who took his quota of wives all at once. The literature of counter-subversion could thus serve the double purpose of vicariously fulfilling repressed desires, and of releasing the tension and guilt arising from rapid social change and conflicting values.

Though the enemy's sexual freedom might at first seem enticing, it was always made repugnant in the end by associations with perversion or brutal cruelty. Both Catholics and Mormons were accused of practicing nearly every form of incest. The persistent emphasis on this theme might indicate deep-rooted feelings of fear and guilt, but it also helped demonstrate, on a more objective level, the loathsome consequences of unrestrained lust. Sheer brutality and a delight in human suffering were supposed to be the even more horrible results of sexual depravity. Masons disemboweled or slit the throats of their victims; Catholics cut unborn infants from their mothers' wombs and threw them to the dogs before their parents' eyes; Mormons raped and lashed recalcitrant women, or seared their mouths with red-hot irons. This obsession with details of sadism, which reached pathological proportions in much of the literature, showed a furious determination to purge the enemy of every admirable quality. The imagined enemy might serve at first as an outlet for forbidden desires, but nativist authors escaped from guilt by finally making him an agent of unmitigated aggression. In such a role the subversive seemed to deserve both righteous anger and the most terrible punishments.

The nativist escape from guilt was more clearly revealed in the themes of confession and conversion. For most American Protestants the crucial step in anyone's life was a profession of true faith resulting from a genuine religious experience. Only when a man became conscious of his inner guilt, when he struggled against the temptations of Satan, could he prepare his soul for the infusion of the regenerative spirit. Those most deeply involved in sin often made the most dramatic conversions. It is not surprising that conversion to nativism followed the same pattern, since nativists sought unity and moral certainty in the regenerative spirit of nationalism. Men who had been associated in some way with un-American conspiracies were not only capable of spectacular confessions of guilt, but were best equipped to expose the insidious work of supposedly harmless organizations. Even those who lacked such an exciting history of corruption usually made some confession of guilt, though it might involve only a previous indifference to subversive groups. Like ardent Christians, nativists searched in their own experiences for the meanings of sin, delusion, awakening to truth, and liberation from spiritual bondage. These personal confessions proved that one had recognized and conquered evil, and also served as ritual cleansings preparatory to full acceptance in a group of dedicated patriots. . . .

In his image of an evil group conspiring against the nation's welfare, and in his vision of a glorious millennium that was to dawn after the enemy's defeat, the nativist found satisfaction for many desires. His own interests became legitimate and dignified by fusion with the national interest, and various opponents became loosely associated with the un-American conspiracy. Thus Freemasonry in New York State was linked in the nativist mind with economic and political interests that were thought to discriminate against certain groups and regions; southerners imagined a union of abolitionists and Catholics to promote unrest and rebellion among slaves; gentile businessmen in Utah merged anti-Mormonism with plans for exploiting mines and lands.

Then too the nativist could style himself as a restorer of the past, as a defender of a stable order against disturbing changes, and at the same time proclaim his faith in future progress. By focusing his attention on the imaginary threat of a secret conspiracy, he found an outlet for many irrational impulses, yet professed his loyalty to the ideals of equal rights and government by law. He paid lip service to the doctrine of laissez-faire individualism, but preached selfless dedication to a transcendent cause. The imposing threat of subversion justified a group loyalty and subordination of the individual that would otherwise have been unacceptable. In a rootless environment shaken by bewildering social change the nativist found unity and meaning by conspiring against imaginary conspiracies.

⌗ *F U R T H E R   R E A D I N G*

Glenn C. Altschuler and Jan M. Saltzgaber, *Revivalism, Social Conscience, and Community in the Burned-Over District: The Trial of Rhoda Bement* (1983)

Lois W. Banner, "Religious Benevolence as Social Control: A Critique of an Interpretation," *Journal of American History* 60 (1973), 23–41

Michael Barkem, *Crucible of the Millennium: The Burned-Over District of New York in the 1840s* (1986)

Arthur E. Bestor, *Backwoods Utopias: The Sectarian and Owenite Phases of Communitarian Socialism in America: 1663–1829* (1950)

Ray Billington, *The Protestant Crusade, 1800–1860: A Study of the Origins of American Nativism* (1938)

Richard L. Bushman, *Joseph Smith and the Beginnings of Mormonism* (1984)

Whitney R. Cross, *The Burned-Over District: The Social and Intellectual History of Enthusiastic Religion in Western New York, 1800–1850* (1950)

David Brion Davis, ed., *Ante-Bellum Reform* (1967)

Ellen Carol DuBois, *Elizabeth Cady Stanton, Susan B. Anthony/ Correspondence, Writings, Speeches* (1981)

Celia Morris Eckhardt, *Fanny Wright: Rebel in America* (1984)

Michael Fellman, *The Unbounded Frame: Freedom and Community in Nineteenth-Century American Utopianism* (1973)

Eleanor Flexner, *Century of Struggle: The Woman's Rights Movement in the United States* (1959)

Lawrence Foster, *Religion and Sexuality: Three American Communal Experiments of the Nineteenth Century* (1981)

Edwin S. Gaustad, ed., *The Rise of Adventism: Religion and Society in Mid-Nineteenth Century America* (1974)

Clifford S. Griffen, *Their Brother's Keeper: Moral Stewardship in the United States, 1800–1865* (1960)

Gerald N. Grob, *Mental Institutions in America: Social Policy to 1875* (1973)

J. F. C. Harrison, *Quest for the New Moral World: Robert Owen and the Owenites in Britain and America* (1969)

Nancy A. Hewitt, *Women's Activism and Social Change: Rochester, New York, 1822–1872* (1984)

Carl F. Kaestle, *Pillars of the Republic: Common Schools and American Society, 1780–1860* (1983)

———and Maris Vinovskis, *Education and Social Change in Nineteenth-Century Massachusetts* (1980)

Michael B. Katz, *The Irony of Early School Reform: Educational Innovation in Mid-Nineteenth Century Massachusetts* (1968)

Lois J. Kern, *An Ordered Love: Sex Roles and Sexuality in Victorian Utopias: The Shakers, the Mormons, and the Oneida Community* (1981)

Dale T. Knobel, *Paddy and the Republic: Ethnicity and Nationality in Antebellum America* (1986)

Ira L. Mandeller, *Religion, Society, and Utopia in Nineteenth-Century America* (1984)

Donald Mathews, *Religion in the Old South* (1977)

Stephen Nissenbaum, *Sex, Diet, and Debility in Jacksonian America* (1980)

William J. Rorabaugh, *The Alcoholic Republic: An American Tradition* (1979)

Anne C. Rose, *Transcendentalism as a Social Movement, 1830–1850* (1981)

David J. Rothman, *The Discovery of the Asylum: Social Order and Disorder in the New Republic* (1971)

Timothy L. Smith, *Revivalism and Social Reform in Mid-Nineteenth Century America* (1957)

Carroll Smith Rosenberg, *Disorderly Conduct: Visions of Gender in Victorian America* (1985)

———, *Religion and the Rise of the American City: The New York City Mission Movement, 1812–1870* (1971)

Christine Stansell, *City of Women: Sex and Class in New York, 1789–1860* (1986)

Alice Felt Tyler, *Freedom's Ferment* (1944)

Ian Tyrrell, *Sobering Up: From Temperance to Prohibition in Antebellum America, 1800–1860* (1979)

Ronald G. Walters, *American Reformers, 1815–1860* (1978)

Sean Wilentz, *Chants Democratic: New York City and the Rise of the American Working Class* (1984)

Abolitionism,

Antiabolitionism,

and Proslavery

⊕

In 1830 no American reform movement seemed farther from its goals than antislavery. The movement's mainstream favored gradual emancipation, followed by colonization of the freed slaves—a plan that appeared to be heading nowhere. Meanwhile, radical freethinkers and artisans submerged their antislavery convictions in various antievangelical and labor insurgencies. Antislavery activities by free blacks had produced some forceful statements and would create an impressive movement but made little progress outside of the black community.

A fresh jolt came when the Bostonian William Lloyd Garrison broke with gradualism and in 1831 established The Liberator, *which advocated immediate abolition. Thereafter the immediatist cause enlisted tens of thousands of supporters, building partly on the passions and the organizational expertise of the northern evangelical reform empire. Never before in U.S. history had so many worked so hard toward forever ending American bondage—breaking the conspiracy of silence that had surrounded the issue for years. Still, only a tiny part of the white population acquired much sympathy for abolitionism. In the North as well as the South, abolitionists and their friends faced public scorn and mob violence. In politics, the managers of both major parties stayed determined to keep slavery discussions out of national affairs. And at the end of the 1830s, the abolitionists themselves divided sharply over strategy and tactics, between radical Garrisonians and more moderate, politically minded organizers.*

Under the circumstances, what is surprising is not that the abolitionists failed to gain greater success but that they succeeded as much as they did. What drove some Americans—but not others—to support them? How much did the emergence of immediatism reflect broader social and intellectual trends? What about the antiabolitionists? For obvious reasons, there has been a tendency to write these people off as hidebound conservatives who were flying in the face of history. Yet they certainly came closer than the abolitionists did to the majority American viewpoint in the 1830s. Just as much as their foes, they believed they were upholding Christian morality and the republic's well-being. Some claimed, with the utmost sincerity, that they were serving the best interests of black people. So, for that matter, did those Americans (mostly but not exclusively southerners) who replied to the abolitionists with increasingly vehement defenses of slavery as a way of life. Purely on the grounds of intellectual consistency—a matter distinct from the rights and wrongs of the issue—some proslavery conservatives more than held their own. What did all of these arguments say about the multiplying social and ideological divisions connected to slavery?

✣ D O C U M E N T S

David Walker, a free black born in North Carolina who later moved to Boston, became active in the Massachusetts Colored Association and in 1829 published his famous incendiary abolitionist appeal, directed to "the colored citizens of the world" (excerpted in the first document). Several radical abolitionists (including William Lloyd Garrison) later said that Walker's shocking pamphlet help goad them to greater militance despite their misgivings about its hints toward violent insurrection. Southern legislatures responded by outlawing the pamphlet's circulation and cracking down on blacks' education. (Recall the free black petition in Chapter 8.) Subsequent black abolitionists, foremost among them the ex-slave Frederick Douglass, would build upon Walker's themes.

David Walker died in mysterious circumstances in 1830. By then Garrison and others had begun to gravitate to the doctrine of immediatism. In the first issue of *The Liberator,* an excerpt of which is reprinted as the second document, Garrison proclaimed his uncompromising position and elaborated some of his other ideas about labor and justice. Two years later, the New-England Anti-Slavery Society offered a definition of immediatism (document three).

William Jay, the son of the Federalist leader John Jay, became one of the more acerbic abolitionist writers, and in 1836 he replied (see the fourth document) to Thomas Roderick Dew's defense of slavery, which was reprinted in Chapter 8 of this volume. Women played important roles in the abolitionist movement, to the consternation of the more conventional, single-minded antislavery men. Angelina Grimké and her sister Sarah, after moving from their native South Carolina to New England, were especially active and articulate; their work would eventually force a rift within abolitionism over the question of women's rights. Angelina Grimké's appeal to Christian women of the South is excerpted in the fifth document.

Antiabolitionism, the subject of the sixth, two-part selection, had many faces. The arguments of T. H. Sullivan of New Hampshire encompassed a wider conservative world view. More crudely racist were the popular cartoons that lampooned the abolitionists—to say nothing of the violent mobs that attacked abolitionist speakers and periodically invaded black neighborhoods. These riots, part of a string of crowd disorders that hit northern cities in the 1830s, convinced some observers that Yankee society was falling apart at the seams.

As the abolitionists grew bolder, southern replies increasingly depicted slavery as a positive good—moving well beyond Thomas Roderick Dew's more measured remarks of 1832. Taking their stand on solidly conservative moral and political ground, slavery's champions would begin to utterly repudiate the natural rights tradition and enunciate a more reactionary republicanism. In 1836 J. H. Hammond (whom we met in Chapter 8) delivered an especially interesting speech in the U.S. House of Representatives about slavery and aristocracy. Hammond's perspective emerges clearly in the seventh documentary selection. Some of slavery's most powerful defenders, however, were not politicians but clergymen, as confirmed in the final selection, a reply by the Reverend Richard Fuller of South Carolina to the correspondence of a Northern colleague.

African-American Abolitionism: David Walker Appeals to the Colored Citizens of the World, 1829

. . . [W]e, (coloured people of these United States of America) are the *most wretched, degraded* and *abject* set of beings that *ever lived* since the world began, and that the white Americans having reduced us to the wretched state of *slavery,* treat us in that condition *more cruel* (they being an enlighted and Christian people,) than any heathen nation did any people whom it had reduced to our condition. These affirmations are so well confirmed in the minds of all unprejudiced men, who have taken the trouble to read histories, that they need no elucidation from me. . . . [T]hose enemies who have for hundreds of years stolen our *rights,* and kept us ignorant of Him and His divine worship, he will remove. Millions of whom, are this day, so ignorant and avaricious, that they cannot conceive how God can have an attribute of justice, and show mercy to us because it pleased Him to make us black— which colour, Mr. Jefferson calls unfortunate!!!!!! As though we are not as thankful to our God, for having made us as it pleased himself, as they (the whites,) are for having made them white. They think because they hold us in their infernal chains of slavery, that we wish to be white, or of their color—but they are dreadfully deceived—we wish to be just as it pleased our Creator to have made us, and no avaricious and unmerciful wretches, have any business to make slaves of, or hold us in slavery. How would they like for us to make slaves of, and hold them in cruel slavery, and murder them as they do us?—But is Mr. Jefferson's assertions true? viz. "that it is unfortunate for us that our Creator has been pleased to make us *black.*" We will not take his say so, for the fact. The world will have an opportunity to see whether it is unfortunate for us, that our Creator *has made us* darker than the *whites.*

Fear not the number and education of our *enemies,* against whom we shall have to contend for our lawful right; guaranteed to us by our Maker; for why should we be afraid, when God is, and will continue, (if we continue humble) to be on our side?

The man who would not fight under our Lord and Master Jesus Christ, in the glorious and heavenly cause of freedom and of God—to be delivered from the most wretched, abject and servile slavery, that ever a people was afflicted with since the foundation of the world, to the present day—ought to be kept with all of his children or family, in slavery, or in chains, to be butchered by his *cruel enemies.* . . .

Here let me ask Mr. Jefferson, (but he is gone to answer at the bar of God, for the deeds done in his body while living,) I therefore ask the whole American people, had I not rather die, or be put to death, than to be a slave to any tyrant, who takes not only my own, but my wife and children's lives by the inches? Yea, would I meet death with avidity far! far!! in preference to such *servile submission* to the murderous hands of tyrants. Mr. Jefferson's very severe remarks on us have been so extensively argued upon by men whose attainments in literature, I shall never be able to reach, that I would not have meddled with it, were it not to solicit each of my brethren, who has the spirit of a man, to buy a copy of Mr. Jefferson's "Notes on Virginia," and put it in the hand of his son. For let no one of us suppose that the refutations which have been written by our white friends are enough—they are *whites*—we are *blacks*.

We, and the world wish to see the charges of Mr. Jefferson refuted by the blacks *themselves,* according to their chance; for we must remember that what the whites have written respecting this subject, is other men's labours, and did not emanate from the blacks. I know well, that there are some talents and learning among the coloured people of this country, which we have not a chance to develop, in consequence of oppression; but our oppression ought not to hinder us from acquiring all we can. For we will have a chance to develop them by and by. God will not suffer us, always to be oppressed. Our sufferings will come to an *end,* in spite of all the Americans this side of *eternity.* Then we will want all the learning and talents among ourselves, and perhaps more, to govern ourselves.—"Every dog must have its day," the American's is coming to an end. . . .

[A]t the close of the first Revolution in this country, with Great Britain, there were but thirteen States in the Union, now there are twenty-four, most of which are slave-holding States, and the whites are dragging us around in chains and in handcuffs, to their new States and Territories to work their mines and farms, to enrich them and their children—and millions of them believing firmly that we being a little darker than they, were made by our Creator to be an inheritance to them and their children for ever—the same as a parcel of *brutes.*

Are we MEN!!—I ask you, O my brethren! are we MEN? Did our Creator make us to be slaves to dust and ashes like ourselves? Are they not dying worms as well as we? Have they not to make their appearance before the tribunal of Heaven, to answer for the deeds done in the body, as well as we? Have we any other Master but Jesus Christ alone? Is he not their Master as well as ours?—What right then, have we to obey and call any other Master, but Himself? How we could be so *submissive* to a gang of men, whom we cannot tell whether they are *as good* as ourselves or not, I never could conceive. However, this is shut up with the Lord, and we cannot precisely tell—but I declare, we judge men by their works. . . .

Americans! notwithstanding you have and do continue to treat us more cruel than any heathen nation ever did a people it had subjected to the same condition that you have us. Now let us reason—I mean you of the United States, whom I believe God designs to save from destruction, if you will hear. For I declare to you, whether you believe it or not, that there are some on the continent of America, who will never be able to repent. God will surely destroy them, to show you his disapprobation of the murders they and you have inflicted on us. I say, let us reason; had you not better take our body, while you have it in your power, and while we are yet ignorant and wretched, not knowing but a little, give us education, and teach us the pure religion of our Lord and Master, which is calculated to make the lion lay down in peace with the lamb, and which millions of you have beaten us nearly to death for trying to obtain since we have been among you, and thus at once, gain our affection while we are ignorant? Remember Americans, that we must and shall be free and enlightened as you are, will you wait until we shall, under God, obtain our liberty by the crushing arm of power? Will it not be dreadful for you? I speak Americans for your good. We must and shall be free I say, in spite of you. You may do your best to keep us in wretchedness and misery, to enrich you and your children, but God will deliver us from under you. And wo, wo, will be to you if we have to obtain our freedom by fighting. Throw away your fears and prejudices then, and enlighten us and treat us like men, and we will like you more than we do now hate you, and tell us now no more about colonization, for America is as much our country, as it is yours. —

Treat us like men, and there is no danger but we will all live in peace and happiness together. For we are not like you, hard hearted, unmerciful, and unforgiving. What a happy country this will be, if the whites will listen. What nation under heaven, will be able to do any thing with us, unless God gives us up into its hand? But Americans, I declare to you, while you keep us and our children in bondage, and treat us like brutes, to make us support you and your families, we cannot be your friends. You do not look for it, do you? Treat us then like men, and we will be your friends. And there is not a doubt in my mind, but that the whole of the past will be sunk into oblivion, and we yet, under God, will become a united and happy people. The whites may say it is impossible, but remember that nothing is impossible with God. . . .

If any are anxious to ascertain who I am, know the world, that I am one of the oppressed, degraded and wretched sons of Africa, rendered so by the avaricious and unmerciful, among the whites. —If any wish to plunge me into the wretched incapacity of a slave, or murder me for the truth, know ye, that I am in the hand of God, and at your disposal. I count my life not dear unto me, but I am ready to be offered at any moment. For what is the use of living, when in fact I am dead. But remember, Americans, that as miserable, wretched, degraded and abject as you have made us in preceding, and in this generation, to support you and your families, that some of you, (whites) on the continent of America, will yet curse the day that you ever were born. You want slaves, and want us for your slaves!!! My colour will yet, root some of you out of the very face of the earth!!!!!! . . .

See your Declaration Americans!!! Do you understand your own language? Hear your language, proclaimed to the world, July 4th, 1776—

We hold these truths to be self evident—that ALL men are created EQUAL!! that they *are endowed by their creator with certain unalienable rights;* that among these are life, *liberty,* and the pursuit of happiness!!

Compare your own language above, extracted from your Declaration of Independence, with your cruelties and murders inflicted by your cruel and unmerciful fathers and yourselves on our fathers and on us—men who have never given your fathers or you the least provocation!!!!!!
Hear your language further!

> But when a long train of abuses and usurpation, pursuing invariably the same object, evinces a design to reduce them under absolute despotism, it is their *right,* it is their *duty,* to throw off such government, and to provide new guards for their future security.

Now, Americans! I ask you candidly, was your sufferings under Great Britain, one hundredth part as cruel and tyrannical as you have rendered ours under you? Some of you, no doubt, believe that we will never throw off your murderous government and "provide new guards for our future security." If Satan has made you believe it, will he not deceive you?* Do the whites say, I being a black man, ought to be humble, which I readily admit? I ask them, ought they not to be as humble as I? or do they think that they can measure arms with Jehovah? Will not the Lord yet humble them? or will not these very coloured people whom they now treat worse than brutes, yet under God, humble them low down enough? Some of the whites are ignorant enough to tell us, that we ought to be submissive to them that they may keep their feet on our throats. And if we do not submit to be beaten to death by them, we are bad creatures and of course must be damned, &c.

If any man wishes to hear this doctrine openly preached to us by the American preachers, let him go into the Southern and Western sections of this country—I do not speak from hear say—what I have written, is what I have seen and heard myself. No man may think that my book is made up of conjecture—I have travelled and observed nearly the whole of those things myself, and what little I did not get by my own observation, I received from those among the whites and blacks, in whom the greatest confidence may be placed.

The Americans may be as vigilant as they please, but they cannot be vigilant enough for the Lord, neither can they hide themselves, where he will not find and bring them out. . . .

William Lloyd Garrison Urges Immediate Abolition, 1831

To the Public

During my recent tour for the purpose of exciting the minds of the people by a series of discourses on the subject of slavery, every place that I visited gave fresh evidence of the fact, that a greater revolution in public sentiment

---

* The Lord has not taught the Americans that we will not some day or other throw off their chains and hand-cuffs from our hands and feet, and their devilish lashes (which some of them shall have enough of yet) from off our backs.

was to be effected in the free States—*and particularly in New-England*—than at the South. I found contempt more bitter, opposition more active, detraction more relentless, prejudice more stubborn, and apathy more frozen, than among slave-owners themselves. Of course, there were individual exceptions to the contrary. This state of things afflicted, but did not dishearten me. I determined, at every hazard, to lift up the standard of emancipation in the eyes of the nation, *within sight of Bunker Hill and in the birthplace of liberty.* That standard is now unfurled; and long may it float, unhurt by the spoliations of time or the missiles of a desperate foe—yea, till every chain be broken, and every bondman set free! Let Southern oppressors tremble—let their secret abettors tremble—let their Northern apologists tremble—let all the enemies of the persecuted blacks tremble. . . .

In defending the great cause of human rights, I wish to derive the assistance of all religions and of all parties.

Assenting to the "self-evident truth" maintained in the American Declaration of Independence, "that all men are created equal, and endowed by their Creator with certain inalienable rights—among which are life, liberty and the pursuit of happiness," I shall strenuously contend for the immediate enfranchisement of our slave population. In Park-Street Church, on the Fourth of July, 1829, in an address on slavery, I unreflectingly assented to the popular but pernicious doctrine of *gradual* abolition. I seize this opportunity to make a full and unequivocal recantation, and thus publicly to ask pardon of my God, of my country, and of my brethren the poor slaves, for having uttered a sentiment so full of timidity, injustice, and absurdity. A similar recantation, from my pen, was published in the *Genius of Universal Emancipation* at Baltimore, in September, 1829. My conscience is now satisfied.

I am aware that many object to the severity of my language; but is there not cause for severity? I *will be* as harsh as truth, and as uncompromising as justice. On this subject, I do not wish to think, or speak, or write, with moderation. No! no! Tell a man whose house is on fire to give a moderate alarm; tell him to moderately rescue his wife from the hands of the ravisher; tell the mother to gradually extricate her babe from the fire into which it has fallen;—but urge me not to use moderation in a cause like the present. I am in earnest—I will not equivocate—I will not excuse—I will not retreat a single inch—AND I WILL BE HEARD. The apathy of the people is enough to make every statue leap from its pedestal, and to hasten the resurrection of the dead.

It is pretended, that I am retarding the cause of emancipation by the coarseness of my invective and the precipitancy of my measures. *The charge is not true.* On this question my influence,—humble as it is,—is felt at this moment to a considerable extent, and shall be felt in coming years—not perniciously, but beneficially—not as a curse, but as a blessing; and posterity will bear testimony that I was right. I desire to thank God, that he enables me to disregard "the fear of man which bringeth a snare," and to speak his truth in its simplicity and power. . . .

Working Men

An attempt has been made—it is still making—we regret to say, with considerable success—to inflame the minds of our working classes against the more opulent, and to persuade men that they are contemned and oppressed by a wealthy aristocracy. That public grievances exist, is unquestionably true; but they are not confined to any one class of society. Every profession is interested in their removal—the rich as well as the poor. It is in the highest degree criminal, therefore, to exasperate our mechanics to deeds of violence, or to array them under a party banner; for it is not true, that, at any time, they have been the objects of reproach. Labor is not dishonorable. The industrious artisan, in a government like ours, will always be held in better estimation than the wealthy idler.

Our limits will not allow us to enlarge on this subject: we may return to it another time. We are the friends of reform; but that is not reform, which, in curing one evil, threatens to inflict a thousand others. . . .

Walker's Pamphlet

The Legislature of North Carolina has lately been sitting with closed doors, in consequence of a message from the Governor relative to the above pamphlet. The south may reasonably be alarmed at the circulation of Mr Walker's Appeal; for a better promoter of insurrection was never sent forth to an oppressed people. In a future number, we propose to examine it, as also various editorial comments thereon—it being one of the most remarkable productions of the age. We have already publicly deprecated its spirit.

The New-England Anti-Slavery Society on Immediatism, 1833

The New-England Anti-Slavery Society maintains that the slaves ought instantly to be emancipated from their fetters. It acknowledges no claims upon their persons by their masters. It regards the holders of slaves as guilty of a heinous sin. . . . It says to every individual—"Let the principle be clearly and firmly established in your mind that there is, and can be, no such thing as *property in man,* and you cannot, as a patriot, a philanthropist, or a disciple of Christ, oppose the immediate liberation of the slaves—you cannot but demand that liberation—you cannot be satisfied with any thing short of an immediate liberation." It is not for men of Christian integrity to calculate how far it is expedient to do wrong. . . .

The Board of Managers are satisfied that the doctrine of immediate abolition is opposed by many, not because they really mean to justify crime, but simply through ignorance or a misapprehension of its nature. It is associated in their minds with something undefinable, yet dreadful—they see, in imagination, cities and villages in flames, and blood flowing in torrents, and hear the roll of drums, the shouts of blood-thirsty savages, and the shrieks of the dying—and thus bringing upon themselves a strong delusion, they naturally stand aghast at the proposition. All this ruffling of mind is indeed ridiculous; but as it originates unwittingly in error, it merits a charitable allowance rather than satire.

What, then, is meant by IMMEDIATE ABOLITION?

It means, in the first place, that all title of property in the slaves shall instantly cease, because their Creator has never relinquished his claim of ownership, and because none have a right to sell their own bodies or buy those of their own species as cattle. Is there any thing terrific in this arrangement?

It means, secondly, that every husband shall have his own wife, and every wife her own husband, both being united in wedlock according to its proper forms, and placed under the protection of law. Is this unreasonable?

It means, thirdly, that parents shall have the control and government of their own children, and that the children shall belong to their parents. What is there sanguinary in this concession?

It means, fourthly, that all trade in human beings shall be regarded as felony, and entitled to the highest punishment. Can this be productive of evil?

It means, fifthly, that the tremendous power which is now vested in every slaveholder to punish his slaves without trial, and to a savage extent, shall be at once taken away. Is this undesirable?

It means, sixthly, that all those laws which not probit the instruction of the slaves, shall instantly be repealed, and others enacted, providing schools and instruction for their intellectual illumination. Would this prove a calamity?

It means, seventhly, that the planters shall employ their slaves as free laborers, and pay them just wages. Would this recompense infuriate them?

It means, eighthly, that the slaves, instead of being forced to labor for the exclusive benefit of others by cruel drivers, and the application of the lash upon their bodies, shall be encouraged to toil for the mutual profit of themselves and their employers, by the infusion of new motives into their hearts, growing out of their recognition and reward as men. Is this diabolical?

It means, finally, that right shall take the supremacy over wrong, principle over brute force, humanity over cruelty, honesty over theft, purity over lust, honor over baseness, love over hatred, and religion over heathenism. Is this wrong?

This is our meaning of Immediate Abolition. . . .

It will remove the cause of bloodshed and insurrection. No patrols at night, no standing army, will be longer needed to keep the slaves in awe. The planters may dismiss their fears, and sleep soundly; for, by one act, they will have transformed their enemies into grateful friends and servants.

William Jay Mocks and Dismisses the Proslavery Argument, 1836

The massacre at Southampton in 1831 naturally directed public attention in Virginia, to the danger and consequences of servile insurrections. In the succeeding legislature, a portion of the members were led by the recent tragedy, to suggest the expediency of extinguishing slavery in the State at some distant period, and to propose plans for effecting this object. . . .

. . . The debates were published, and they disclosed the alarming fact, that there were native Virginians, men of character and influence, who believed slavery to be a moral and political evil which ought to be removed at some future day. It was important to the permanency of the institution, that this dangerous heresy should be at once assailed and vanquished, and Mr. Thomas R. Dew, Professor of History, Metaphysics, and Political Law, in William and Mary College, immediately buckled on his armor, and sallied forth a champion for the true faith. And never did a knight-errant exhibit a more gallant bearing; nor did even the hero of La Mancha, rush upon the windmills with more reckless intrepidity, than does our chivalric Professor battle with history and experience, and reason, and the moral sense of mankind. . . .

Our author now enters upon the defence of slavery, and satisfactorily proves that it is not a modern institution. Indeed he traces it to very high antiquity, and shows that it has prevailed over a large portion of the globe. In these respects, however, it must yield the palm to murder, since the latter crime dates its commencement in the family of Adam, and has been more or less perpetrated among every people from the time of Cain to the present hour. . . .

[I]n the catalogue of blessings conferred by slavery, the most extraordinary, and we venture to say, the one least anticipated by our readers, is its influence "ON THE CONDITION OF THE FEMALE SEX"! That we may not do injustice to the Professor, we will permit him to speak for himself. "Slavery changes the hunting into the shepherd and agricultural states— gives rise to augmented productions, and consequently furnishes more abundant supplies for man: the labor of the slave thus becomes a substitute for that of the woman: man no longer wanders through the forest in quest of gain; and woman, consequently, is relieved from following on his track, under the enervating and harrassing burthen of her children: she is now surrounded by her domestics, and the abundance of their labor, lightens the toil and hardships of the whole family; she ceases to be a mere beast of burthen." p. 36.

It seems to have escaped Mr. Dew's recollection while penning this argument, that there were such beings in the world as *female* slaves. Where slavery prevails, we are told that woman ceases to be "a mere beast of burthen," and yet it so happens that in the slave states, there are more than ONE MILLION OF WOMEN, who in consequence of slavery, are mere beasts of burthen, exposed and sold like cattle in the public market, deprived of the rights and endearments belonging to the relations of daughter, wife and mother, unprotected from violence, and kept in ignorance and degradation.

Such is the influence of slavery on the "female sex." But our author refers to its influence on the LADY, and not on the *"domestics,"* by whom she is "surrounded." She, we are assured, "becomes the charming and animating centre of the family circle—time is afforded for reflection, and the cultivation of all those mild and fascinating virtues which throw a charm and delight around our homes and firesides, and calm and tranquilize the harsher tempers and more restless propensities of the male." p. 36. Far be it from us to question the charms and virtues of the southern ladies, to whatever cause Mr. Dew may ascribe them; but surely no one acquainted with northern society, will dare to assert, that it is necessary to brutalize one portion of the sex, in order to elevate the other to the highest degree of purity and loveliness, of which the female character is susceptible. . . .

Having explained the principle which is to determine the continuance or abolition of slavery, he proceeds to apply it, by asserting that the free blacks taken as a whole, "must be considered the most worthless and indolent of the citizens of the United States—the very drones and pests of society"; and we are assured, that this character does *not* arise "from the disabilities and disfranchisements by which the law attempts to guard against them." p. 88. After dwelling much on their idleness and profligacy, he proposes the important question, "Why are our colored freemen so generally indolent and worthless, among the industrious and enterprising citizens of even our northern and New England states?" p. 92. Now to this question *we* would reply, because they are deprived by unjust laws, and cruel prejudices, of almost every incentive to vigorous and honorable exertion, and are *kept* in ignorance, depravity and idleness. We conscientiously believe that had Mr. Dew been reared and treated from infancy, just as most of the southern free blacks are usually reared and treated, great as his natural endowments unquestionably are, he would himself have been a drone and a pest. But let us attend to the answer he gives to the question. "It is because there is an *inherent* and *intrinsic* cause at work which will produce its effect under *all circumstances*. In the free blacks, the *principle of idleness and dissipation* triumphs over that of accumulation, and the desire to better our condition: the animal part of man gains the victory over the moral." p. 92. Such is the solution of this moral phenomenon, given by our Professor of Metaphysics; and what does it amount to? Why, that God has implanted in the constitution of the black man, "a principle of idleness and dissipation," which is "inherent and intrinsic," and which of course does not belong to the white man. Unfortunately for this inherent and intrinsic principle, the Professor cites the example of the liberated serfs of Poland, Livonia, and Hungary, to prove that emancipated slaves will not work. These serfs who were in fact *white* slaves, he describes as being in the lowest state of degration [*sic*] and wretchedness. . . .

Mr. Dew proceeds at great length to vindicate the *moral influence* of slavery on the character and condition of both master and slave. We will not contest the matter with him. His own book, were other testimony wanting, would settle the question with us. Such heartlessness, such balancings of dollars and cents against the social and intellectual enjoyments and everlasting happiness of millions of his countrymen; such complacency in the contemplation of perpetual bondage, ignorance and degradation; such strange estimates of duty, cannot, we are persuaded, be the natural outpourings of his heart, but are the baneful fruits of the institution in which he has been nurtured. . . .

Angelina Grimké Appeals to the Christian Women of the South, 1836

. . . There is no difference in *principle,* in *Christian ethics,* between the despised slavedealer and the *Christian* who buys slaves from, or sells slaves to him; indeed, if slaves were not wanted by the respectable, the wealthy, and the religious in a community, there would be no slaves in that community, and of course no *slavedealers.* It is then the *Christians* and the *honorable men* and *women* of the South, who are the *main pillars* of this grand temple built to Mammon and to Moloch. It is the *most enlightened* in every country who are *most* to blame when any public sin is supported by public opinion. . . .

But it may be asked, why are *they* most culpable? I will tell you, my friends. It is because sin is imputed to us just in proportion to the spiritual light we receive. . . .

But perhaps you will be ready to query, why appeal to *women* on this subject? *We* do not make the laws which perpetuate slavery. *No* legislative power is vested in *us; we* can do nothing to overthrow the system, even if we wished to do so. To this I reply, I know you do not make the laws, but I also know that *you are the wives and mothers, the sisters and daughters of those who do;* and if you really suppose *you* can do nothing to overthrow slavery, you are greatly mistaken. You can do much in every way: four things I will name. 1st. You can read on this subject. 2d. You can pray over this subject. 3d. You can speak on this subject. 4th. You can *act* on this subject. I have not placed reading before praying because I regard it more important, but because, in order to pray aright, we must understand what we are praying for; it is only then we can "pray with the understanding and the spirit also." . . .

But you may say we are *women,* how can *our* hearts endure persecution? And why not? Have not *women* arisen in all the dignity and strength of moral courage to be the leaders of the people, and to bear a faithful testimony for the truth whenever the providence of God has called them to do so? Are there no *women* in that noble army of martyrs who are now singing the song of Moses and the Lamb? Who led out the women of Israel from the house of bondage, striking the timbrel, and singing the song of deliverance on the banks of that sea whose waters stood up like walls of crystal to open a passage for their escape? It was a *woman;* Miriam, the prophetess, the sister of Moses and Aaron. Who went up with Barak to Kadesh to fight against Jabin, King of Canaan, into whose hand Israel had been sold because of their iniquities? It was a *woman!* Deborah the wife of Lapidoth, the judge, as well as the prophetess of that backsliding people; Judges iv, 9. . . . What human voice first proclaimed to Mary that she should be the mother of our Lord? It was a *woman!* Elizabeth, the wife of Zacharias; Luke i, 42, 43. . . .

And what, I would ask in conclusion, have *women* done for the great and glorious cause of Emancipation? Who wrote that pamphlet which moved the heart of Wilberforce to pray over the wrongs, and his tongue to plead the cause of the oppressed African? It was a *woman,* Elizabeth Heyrick. Who labored assiduously to keep the sufferings of the slave continually before the British public? They were *women*. And how did they do it? By their needles, paint brushes and pens, by speaking the truth, and petitioning Parliament for the abolition of slavery. And what was the effect of their labors? Read it in the Emancipation bill of Great Britain. Read it, in the present state of her West India Colonies. Read it, in the impulse which has been given to the cause of freedom, in the United States of America. Have English women then done so much for the negro, and shall American women do nothing? Oh no! Already are there sixty female Anti-Slavery Societies in operation. These are doing just what the English women did, telling the story of the colored man's wrongs, praying for his deliverance, and presenting his kneeling image constantly before the public eye on bags and needle-books, card-racks, pen-wipers, pin-cushions, &c. Even the children of the north are inscribing on their handy work, "May the points of our needles prick the slaveholder's conscience." Some of the reports of these Societies exhibit not only considerable talent, but a deep sense of religious duty, and a determination to persevere through evil as well as good report, until every scourge, and every shackle, is buried under the feet of the manumitted slave.

The Ladies' Anti-Slavery Society of Boston was called last fall, to a severe trial of their faith and constancy. They were mobbed by "the gentlemen of property and standing," in that city at their anniversary meeting, and their lives were jeoparded by an infuriated crowd; but their conduct on that occasion did credit to our sex, and affords a full assurance that they will *never* abandon the cause of the slave. The pamphlet, Right and Wrong in Boston, issued by them in which a particular account is given of that "mob of broad cloth in broad day," does equal credit to the head and the heart of her who wrote it. I wish my Southern sisters could read it; they would then understand that the women of the North have engaged in this work from a sense of *religious duty,* and that nothing will ever induce them to take their hands from it until it is fully accomplished. They feel no hostility to you, no bitterness or wrath; they rather sympathize in your trials and difficulties; but they well know that the first thing to be done to help you, is to pour in the light of truth on your minds, to urge you to reflect on, and pray over the subject. This is all *they* can do for you, *you* must work out your own deliverance with fear and trembling, and with the direction and blessing of God, *you can do it*. Northern women may labor to produce a correct public opinion at the North, but if Southern women sit down in listless indifference and criminal idleness, public opinion cannot be rectified and purified at the South. It is manifest to every reflecting mind, that slavery must be abolished; the era in which we live, and the light which is over-spreading the whole world on this subject, clearly show that the time cannot be distant when it will be done. Now there are only two ways in which it can be effected, by moral power or physical force, and it is for *you* to choose which of these you prefer. Slavery always has, and always will produce insurrections wherever it exists, because it is a violation of the natural order of things, and no human power can much longer perpetuate it. The opposers of abolitionists fully believe this; one of them remarked to me not long since, there is no doubt there will be a most terrible overturning at the South in a few years, such cruelty and wrong, must be visited with Divine vengeance soon. Abolitionists believe, too, that this must inevitably be the case if you do not repent, and they are not willing to leave you to perish without entreating you, to save yourselves from destruction; well may they say with the apostle, "am I then your enemy because I tell you the truth," and warn you to flee from impending judgments. . . .

The *women of the South can overthrow* this horrible system of oppression and cruelty, licentiousness and wrong. Such appeals to your legislatures would be irresistible, for there is something in the heart of man which *will bend under moral suasion.* There is a swift witness for truth in his bosom, which *will respond to truth* when it is uttered with calmness and dignity. If you could obtain but six signatures to such a petition in only one state, I would say, send up that petition, and be not in the least discouraged by the scoffs and jeers of the heartless, or the resolution of the house to lay it on the table. It will be a great thing if the subject can be introduced into your legislatures in any way, even by *women,* and *they* will be the most likely to introduce it there in the best possible manner, as a matter of *morals* and *religion,* not of expediency or politics. You may petition, too, the different ecclesiastical bodies of the slave states. Slavery must be attacked with the whole power of truth and the sword of the spirit. You must take it up on *Christian* ground, and fight against it with Christian weapons, whilst your feet are shod with the preparation of the gospel of peace. And *you are now* loudly called upon by the cries of the widow and the orphan, to arise and gird yourselves for this great moral conflict, "with the whole armour of righteousness on the right hand and on the left."

The Antiabolitionist Outlook, 1833, 1835

T. H. Sullivan's Letters Against Immediate Abolition; Addressed to The Free Blacks of the Non-Slave-Holding States, *1835*

The design of these Letters is to convince you that those gentlemen at the North, who are opposed to Immediate Abolition, are not hostile to the welfare of yourselves and your brethren in bonds; and that, accordingly, you can by no means be certain that you are promoting the elevation of your race and the removal of Slavery, when you give your sympathy and influence to the system and measures of the Immediate Abolitionists. They come from one who is a friend to the children of Africa, and who desires, in humble imitation of your Master and his, to be the servant of you all. He addresses you as the free *Blacks,* not reproachfully, but because he does not feel, and thinks you should not, that you have cause to be ashamed of being designated by the color with which your Creator has tinged your skin. He addresses himself to the free blacks of the *non-slave-holding states,* because he would think it dishonorable to interfere with the legal property or political rights of a slave owner at a distance, as he would not dare to do before his face; and he confesses that he should not venture, were he at the South, to call together and address, on any subject connected with Slavery, the free black population of a slave-holding state, without the general consent of the slave owners. He calls himself your friend because he is writing in opposition to men whom he regards as your false friends, without questioning that they are sincere in deeming themselves your best friends.

The African negro *may* not be able to compete with the leading European races in commerce and the arts, in education and literature, in legislation, politics, and government, (though this has not been proved by a sufficiently long and fair experiment;) he *may* not be naturally equal to the white man in intellectual capacities, (for, as I said, it has not been proved,) but he is his equal in natural *moral characteristics,* and perhaps excels him in a predisposition to some virtues of a high order. The negro, by native disposition, is good-natured, obliging, and affectionate, grateful for favors, forgetful of injuries, susceptible to kindness, and ready in deference to superiority in character and station. He is, accordingly, material for peaceable neighbors and quiet citizens. . . .

[T]he Immediate Abolitionist has mistaken the interest of the cause which he advocates, and that of the country he would serve, your interest and his own. . . .

The system which I thus designate, consists in *commencing the agitation of a legal, constitutional, or political reform* (for whatever name beside be given to Immediate Abolition, it is this also,) *by measures adapted to inflame the passions of the multitude,* including the women and children, the boarding-school misses and factory girls, in short, "man, woman, and child," upon the avowed plan of turning the current of popular opinion at the North so strongly in favor of the principles of northern anti-slavery, that the "man-stealers" and man-owners at the South shall feel the necessity of voluntarily abrogating the "laws" by which slavery is allowed and fortified in the slave states. . . .

I am not unjust to the American Anti-Slavery Society, and its active friends, when I illustrate their system of influence . . . at the large and promiscuous assemblies by them called together. There I have seen woman's tears testifying to the portion of the audience, in an appeal to which the anti-slavery agitator best loves to indulge; and I have seen that appeal enforced by allusions to points on which woman is the most sensitive, (in relation, that is, to the illicit intercourse to which the relation of master and slave is said to give opportunity) at which the face of modest woman was turned from the speaker, and covered from the [spectator's] eye. Who does not know that *popular art* is never more triumphant than when it can enlist the *peculiar* feelings (whether of party, denomination, or sex) on the side of what is called public justice, or sound policy, or righteous indignation? . . .

Suppose all New England one great Anti-Slavery Society, on the principles of Immediate Abolition, "man, woman, and child"? What would be the effect at the South? What but to double lock the fetters of slavery? what but to fix the slave statutes even as the laws of the Medes and Persians? what but to render them, still more than now of necessity they are, like the laws of Draco, which were said to be written in blood? Can any reflecting man think that such are the means to abolish slavery in this country; to pierce, (according to the style of the northern enthusiast) the "criminal," "man-stealer," man-owner, and man-seller of the South with the pang of repentance, till he shall restore to his brother the stolen birthright of freedom, and substitute for the code of oppression, laws consistent with the principles of eternal justice, and the stifled calls of humanity? We know our spirited southern brethren better. We know ourselves better. We know human nature better. Is it by such means, my respected friends of African descent, that your brethren in bonds are to be released from their thraldom? . . .

Every community, from a nation down to a village, contains a class of ardent and restless men, standing ever ready to agitate, heat, and control the multitude, who, as a multitude, are always like the sea, passive, fluctuating, and easy to be raised into tumult, and while harmless, when undisturbed, as each particular drop that contributes to form it, becoming, when agitated, like the sea swelled into violence and moving in mass, the most terrible of the agents which the Almighty holds in the hollow of his hand. When persons of this description start an excitement, the wise and moderate stand aloof, waiting a favorable crisis for interposing to smooth the waves and direct the storm, while the cooler and more calculating among the unprincipled keep still, watching how they may turn to their private advantage the commotion that its less wary authors have stirred up for their own. Not all among the calm are indifferent; not all among the sanguine are visionary; not all among the enthusiastic are wild. But when the passionate sway the crowd, the sagacious begin to be doubtful, the benevolent to grow cold, and the virtuous to feel timid, in relation to the end proposed, how excellent soever and desirable in itself. . . .

This use of popular excitement, aided by combination, is the more objectionable and alarming, on account of the extent of the field on which its power has been tried; especially regarded as including the intermixture of female influence in legal and political concerns. Woman, moving regularly and calmly in her own sphere, is as lovely as the evening star, and at once serviceable and delightful, like the planet of night. It is as unbecoming to her to appear in the world *dis-orbed,* as unattired. But something more than the violation of decorum is here involved. When woman leaves her place, and with combined voice and action, mingles with men in the struggles of ambition and power, nothing that poet ever dreamed of the disastrous shock of comets, striking our trembling globe, out-measures the evil that might follow from her political interference in times which try men's souls, when fear of change perplexes the wise, and the hearts of the boldest fail at that which may come upon the earth. . . .

No man can attain true mental independence who permits domestic entreaty or dictation to deter him from forming his mind, or exerting his influence in the manner that unbiased examination and a deliberate conscience would prescribe. And it is wrong and reprehensible, accordingly, to make use of combined female influence to work upon the feelings of men, when legal and political changes are proposed. Women, from their natural excitability and domestic training, are as unfit to take part in the stern and stormy scenes of legislation and politics, as, from their physical delicacy, to wield the axe in the woods, or the hammer at the forge. . . .

Southern slavery, the subject wherefrom the General Excitement, in this violent and systematic manner attempted, grew, is one in regard to which the citizens of the non-slave-holding States have no right to *originate action,* but which it belongs *exclusively* to the slave States, severally, to manage; and that accordingly for citizens at the North to act in it at all, except by cooperation in measures begun at the South, is justly regarded there as MEDDLING with the rights and customs of the Southern States in an injurious and AGGRESSIVE manner. . . .

The guilt of slavery in this country does not lie at the door of the slave-holders. They should not be expected to work their own temporal ruin to expiate an error having its origin in another country and in other times. The evil of slavery was entailed upon the United States by the mother country during the period of our colonial dependence. The colonies made repeated efforts to prevent the importation of the slaves into this country, but could not obtain the consent of the English government. Mr. Jefferson alludes distinctly to this fact in his *draft* of the Declaration of Independence. Though the United States were unable at the adoption of the Constitution to relieve themselves from the burden of slavery, they were the first to prohibit the prosecution of the slave trade. . . .

It is obvious that if this institution could not be abolished in 1789, the difficulties in the way of it must have multiplied since, especially considering the commotion and exasperation, to which it has given rise of late. A deep-rooted and long-growing evil is not to be removed by sudden and violent means. . . . It is not our duty to aggravate, by false zeal and political aggression, the natural retribution that slavery—regarded as "an institution founded on violence"—carries with it. . . .

If the Immediate Abolitionists go on till the passions of the North and South are brought into collision, the non-slave-holding States, so far as they concur with the northern agitators, *put themselves in the wrong,* and just to the degree that they might have effectually counteracted the instruments of that collision, they will be *responsible for the consequences.* . . . Anti-slavery, prosecuted in this manner any further, or publicly advocated in any manner, (for it is now too late for gradual abolition societies, composed of men of wisdom and moderation,) will keep sharpening the irritability of the passionate, and chafing the temper of the fiery, and, which is more formidable, will rouse the just indignation of the rational, the good, and the patriotic, till our national government totters to its fall. . . .

In such a conflict, New England would have the disadvantage and the odium of being the aggressive party, and of seeing her standard waving on the unrighteous side. For the excitement which now threatens our sectional concord and national union with destruction, will burden us with the guilt of SEDITION and AGGRESSION, unless *timely* and *effectual* measures are adopted by us, to restrain the public agitators of a subject, with which the non-slave-holding States have *no right to interfere,* but which it belongs "*exclusively*" to the slave States to control; and in which the former cannot interfere without violating the national compact, and invading the right of property and the tenure of personal security and human life at the South, in an injurious and exasperating manner, and to a possible extent, at the thought of which humanity shudders, and patriotism and public justice stand aghast!

An Antiabolitionist Cartoon

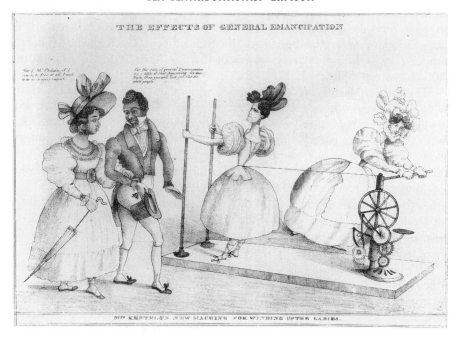

This cartoon captures the underlying fears about color, class, and gender norms that often accompanied the anti-abolitionist argument. Mr. Philader, the gentlemanly black, advises his "dear Niobe" to "try a little of that squeezing" for the sake of general emancipation, since it would make her look "just like the white people." Niobe refuses, asserting that if she is to be free at all, she wishes to be so in every respect. New-York Historical Society.

J. H. Hammond Defends Slavery, 1836

Allow me now, sir, to examine more closely the real designs of those abolitionists, the means by which they will attempt to effect them, and the probable result. Their designs are very succinctly stated in the volume which I hold in my hand. It is a treatise on this subject, entitled "Jay's Inquiry," written by William Jay, a judge, I believe, of the State of New York, and a son—a most degenerate son—of the distinguished John Jay. More than five thousand copies of this work, I am told, have been sold. He says, "the society aimed at effecting the following objects, viz:

"1st. The immediate abolition of slavery throughout the United States.

"2d. As a necessary consequence, the suppression of the American slave trade.

"3d. The ultimate elevation of the black population to an equality with the white, in civil and religious privileges."—P. 141.

Sir, the abolition of slavery can be expected to be effected in but three ways: through the medium of the slaveholder—or the Government—or the slaves themselves. I think I may say that any appeal to the slaveholders will be in vain. In the whole history of the question of emancipation, in Europe or America, I do not remember a dozen instances of masters freeing their slaves, at least during their own lifetime, from any qualms of conscience. If they are seized with these qualms, they usually sell their slaves first, and then give in their adhesion to the cause, as has been the case with some whom I could mention.

The abolitionist can appeal only to the hopes or fears or interest of the slaveholder, to induce him to emancipate his slaves. So far as our hopes are concerned, I believe I can say we are perfectly satisfied. We have been born and bred in a slave country. Our habits are accommodated to them, and so far as we have been able to observe other states of society abroad, we see nothing to invite us to exchange our own; but, on the contrary, every thing to induce us to prefer it above all others.

As to our fears, I know it has been said by a distinguished Virginian, and quoted on this floor, "that the fire bell in Richmond never rings at night, but the mother presses her infant more closely to her breast, in dread of servile insurrection." Sir, it is all a flourish. There may be nervous men and timid women, whose imaginations are haunted with unwonted fears, among us, as there are in all communities on earth; but in no part of the world have men of ordinary firmness less fear of danger from their operatives than we have. The fires which in a few years have desolated Normandy and Anjou, the great machine burning in the heart of England, the bloody and eternal struggles of the Irish Catholics, and the mobs which for some years past have figured in the northern States, burning convents, tearing down houses, spreading dismay and ruin through their cities, and even taking life, are appropriate illustrations of the peace and security of a community whose laborers are all free. On the other hand, during the two hundred years that slavery has existed in this country, there has, I believe, been but one serious insurrection, and that one very limited in its extent. . . .

If you will look over the world, you will find that in all those countries where slavery has been found unprofitable, it has been abolished. In northern latitudes, where no great agricultural staple is produced, and where care, skill, and a close economy, enter largely into the elements of production, free labor has been found more valuable than that of slaves. You will there find labor usually exercised in small combinations, under the immediate eye of a watchful and frugal master. I speak more particularly of those who cultivate the soil; but the large masses of mechanical operatives who are brought together form no exception to the principle. They are classified. There is an accurate division of their labor; each branch of it requires peculiar art, and, in the higher departments, a degree of skill must be attained, to produce which, stronger stimulants are necessary than can be ordinarily applied to slaves.

In such countries the dominant classes have also found it to their advantage to permit each individual to accumulate for himself, and to deprive him of a portion of his earnings, sufficient for their purposes, through the operations of the Government. Hence the partial emancipation of the serfs of the continent of Europe; hence the abandonment of villeinage in England;

and hence the emancipation of slaves in the free States of this Union. But in southern latitudes, where great agricultural staples are produced, and where not only a large combination of labor under the direction of one head is required, but it is also necessary that the connexion between the operatives and that head should be absolute and indissoluble, domestic slavery is indispensable. To such a country it is as natural as the clime itself—as the birds and beasts to which that climate is congenial. The camel loves the desert; the reindeer seeks everlasting snows; the wild fowl gather to the waters; and the eagle wings his flight above the mountains. It is equally the order of Providence that slavery should exist among a planting people, beneath a southern sun. There the laborer must become a fixture of the soil. His task is not from day to day, nor from month to month; but from season to season, and from year to year. He must be there to clear, to break, to plant, to till, to gather, to fallow, and to clear again; and he must be kept there by a never-ceasing, unavoidable, and irresistible force. The system of "strikes" so universally practiced in all other kinds of labor, would desolate a planting country in five years. If, in the heat of the crop, when the loss of one or two days even may irreparably ruin it, the laborers were to abandon the fields and demand higher wages, the owner would have no other alternative than to say to them, "work, and take enough to satisfy yourselves"—which would, of course, be all. Sir, it is not the interest of the planters of the South to emancipate their slaves, and it never can be shown to be so.

Slavery is said to be an evil; that it impoverishes the people, and destroys their morale. If it be an evil, it is one to us alone, and we are contented with it—why should others interfere? But it is no evil. On the contrary, I believe it to be the greatest of all the great blessings which a kind Providence has bestowed upon our glorious region. For without it, our fertile soil and our fructifying climate would have been given to us in vain. And as to its impoverishing and demoralizing influence, the simple and irresistible answer to that is, that the history of the short period during which we have enjoyed it has rendered our southern country proverbial for its wealth, its genius, and its manners. . . .

The only remaining chance for the abolitionists to succeed in their nefarious schemes will be by appealing to the slaves themselves' and, say what they will, this is the great object at which they aim. For this are all their meetings, publications, lectures, and missions; to excite a servile insurrection. . . . This will be no easy task. Sir, it is a proverb, that no human being is perfectly contented with his lot, and it may be true that some strolling emissary may extract, occasionally, complaints from southern slaves, and spread them before the world. But such instances are rare. As a class, I say it boldly, there is not a happier, more contented race upon the face of the earth. I have been born and brought up in the midst of them, and, so far as my knowledge and experience extend, I should say they have every reason to be happy. Lightly tasked, well clothed, well fed—far better than the free laborers of any country in the world, our own and those perhaps of the other States of this confederacy alone excepted—their lives and persons protected by the law, all their suffering alleviated by the kindest and most interested care, and their domestic affections cherished and maintained, at least so far as I have known, with conscientious delicacy. . . .

The doom of Ham has been branded on the form and features of his African descendants. The hand of fate has united his color and his destiny. Man cannot separate what God hath joined. . . .

Permit me now, sir, for a moment to look into the causes of this vast and dangerous excitement; for it is intimately connected with the true merits of this important question. I am not disposed to attribute it to any peculiar feelings of hostility entertained by the North against the South, arising from position merely. It is indeed natural that a people not owning slaves should entertain a strong aversion to domestic servitude. It is natural that the descendants of the Puritans, without any deep investigation of the subject, should have an instinctive hostility to slavery in every shape. . . .

But other causes are at work. This excitement belongs to the spirit of the age. Every close observer must perceive that we are approaching, if we have not already reached, a new era in civilization. The man of the nineteenth century is not the man of the seventeenth, and widely different from him of the eighteenth. Within the last sixty years there have been greater changes—not on the face of the earth, but in the history of civilized man— than has taken place before perhaps since the reign of Charlemagne. . . .

During the period of this mighty change, the great struggle between the rulers and the ruled has been carried on with corresponding vigor: through the thousand channels which genius has opened, wealth has flown in to aid it in its contest with the strong arm of power. The two combined, finding themselves still unable to cope with the time-hardened strength of hereditary government, and eager, impatient, almost frenzied, to achieve its conquest, have called in to their assistance another ally—the people: not the "people," as we have hitherto been accustomed in this country to define that term, but the mob—the *sans-culottes*. Proclaiming as their watchword that immortal but now prostituted sentiment, "that all men are both free and equal," they have rallied to their standard the ignorant, uneducated, semi-barbarous mass which swarms and starves upon the face of Europe! Unnatural and debasing union! Hereditary institutions are gone. Already have the nobility of France been overthrown. Their days are numbered in the British empire. Let them go. I am not their advocate. What next? Confiscation has begun! The result is as obvious as if it were written on the wall. The hounds of Acteon turned upon their master. Genius and wealth, stimulated by "an ambition that o'erleaps itself," have called these spirits from the vasty deep; they will down no more. The spoils of victory are theirs, and they will gorge and batten on them.

In this country we have no hereditary institutions to attract the first fury of this tempest, which is also brewing here, for the electric fluid has crossed the ocean, and the elements denote that it is expanding over the northern arch of our horizon. The question of emancipation, which in Europe is only a collateral issue, a mere ramification of the great controversy between hereditary power and ultimate agrarianism, has become with us the first and most important question; partly because the levellers here have not yet felt the heavy pressure of political oppression, and partly because they have regarded our institutions of slavery as most assimilated to an aristocracy. In this they are right. I accept the term. It is a government of the best. Combining all the advantages, and possessing but few of the disadvantages, of the aristocracy of the old world, without fostering to an unwarrantable extent the pride, the exclusiveness, the selfishness, the thirst for sway, the contempt for the rights of others, which distinguish the nobility of Europe, it gives us their education, their polish, their munificence, their high honor, their undaunted spirit. Slavery does indeed create an aristocracy—an aristocracy of talents, of virtue, of generosity and courage. In a slave country every freeman is an aristocrat. Be he rich or poor, if he does not possess a single slave, he has been born to all the natural advantages of the society in which he is placed, and all its honors lie open before him, inviting his genius and industry. Sir, I do firmly believe that domestic slavery, regulated as ours is, produces the highest toned, the purest, best organization of society that has ever existed on the face of the earth. . . .

A Christian Defense of Slavery, 1845

The issue now before us regards the essential moral character of slavery; and on such a question I am strongly disposed to pass by all ethical and metaphysical dissertation, and appeal at once to the only standard of right and wrong which can prove decisive. For my own part, I am heartily sick and weary of the controversies and debates waged and waging on every side, in which each party is contending, not for truth, but victory, and which have effected just nothing, for the want of some arbiter recognised by all, and whose decree shall be final and infallible. Now such an umpire we have. Whatever importance others may attach to the deductions of human reasoning, and thus impiously array against the Scriptures those "oppositions of science falsely so called," which the Apostle terms "profane and vain babblings," you and I have long since put on our shields one motto—"Let God be true and every man a liar." . . .

Now, in order to clear away rubbish, and arrive at once at the point, let me remind you that it is simply the essential character of slavery which we are discussing; and that slavery is a term whose meaning can be easily and accurately defined. Slavery is bondage. It is (to give Paley's idea in other language) the condition of one to whose service another has a right, without the consent or contract of the servant. . . .

Is it necessarily a crime in the sight of God to control or curtail the natural personal liberty of a human being? A question admitting no debate at all.

It will not be disputed that government is the ordinance of God. But government is restraint; the very idea of government includes an abridgment of that personal freedom which a savage has in the forest, and a modification of it into political freedom, or civil rights and privileges.

Is it, then, necessarily a crime for a government to discriminate between those whom it controls, in the distribution of civil privileges and political liberty? It would surely be preposterous to affirm this. Every government has necessarily a right to pass laws indispensable to its existence; and it has a right, also, to establish those regulations which shall best promote the good of the whole population. Whether any particular enactments be necessary, and whether they do secure the greatest good, are points as to which error may be committed, but as to which each government is the judge; and if it acts uprightly, with all the lights possessed, there is no crime. We boast of our liberties, and are forever quoting the words of the Declaration of Independence; yet in this country it has been deemed most for the good of the whole, that one half of the citizens (and I believe by far the noblest, purest, and best half) should be disfranchised of a great many civil rights. This is true, also, of all citizens until they reach an age wholly conventional, — viz. twenty-one. Is this a sin? Will it be urged that all are born free and equal, and that it is wicked to violate the indefeasible rights of women and minors? The day is coming, I venture to predict, when our regenerators will utter such frantic arguments; for they drive on, unrecking and unheeding alike the plainest dictates of reason and experience, and the stern lessons of the French Revolution, and the warning voice which spoke in such fearful accents amid the havoc and butchery and desolation of St. Domingo. But no good citizen considers the inequalities existing in these States criminal. . . .

As soon as slavery is mentioned at the North, there is conjured up, in the minds of many persons, I know not what confused, revolting combination, and heart-rending spectacle, of chains, and whips, and cruelty, and crime, and wretchedness. But, I repeat it, even at the peril of tediousness, that necessarily and essentially—(and in a multitude of instances, practically and actually)—slavery is nothing more than the condition of one who is deprived of political power, and does service,—without his contract and consent, it is true, but yet it may be, cheerfully and happily, and for a compensation reasonable and certain, paid in modes of return best for the slave himself. With what is strictly physical liberty, the master interferes no more, in such cases, than you do with a hired servant. The work assigned is confessedly very light—scarcely one half of that performed by a white laborer with you. When that is performed, the slaves (to use an expression common with them) are "their own masters." And if you ever allow us the pleasure of seeing you at the South, you will find slaves tilling land for themselves; working as mechanics for themselves, and selling various articles of merchandise for themselves; and when you inquire of them some explanation, they will speak of their rights, and their property, with as clear a sense of what is due to them, and as much confidence, as they could if free; and tell you (to use another of their phrases) that they do all this "in their own time." . . .

Having described the condition of a slave, I ought now to advert to the obligations of the master; but I have not space, nor is it requisite. Let me only say, (and with the most solemn earnestness, for God forbid I should ever utter a word which may perpetuate cruelty and sin,) that the right of the master not only does not give him any such license of wholesale oppression and wrong as you suppose, but really places him under the deepest corresponding obligations to promote the interest, temporal and eternal, of his slaves. And though we have all been "verily guilty concerning our brethren" who are dependent on us, yet I trust the South is becoming every day more alive to its responsibility. Already much has been effected; and, as a class, I believe our slaves to be now better compensated, and, in moral, intellectual, and religious condition, superior to most operatives in Europe. From parliamentary reports, it appears that in Ireland three millions and a half of people live in mud hovels, having one room, and without chimney or window. In England and Wales there are three millions of people without any pastoral provision. In London itself the statistics of misery and vice are appalling. On one occasion, said a speaker in Exeter Hall, four families occupied one small room, each hiring a corner; and in one of these corners there was a corpse lately dead, and four men using it as a table to play cards upon. And if this be so in Great Britain, need I speak of Spain and Russia, or attest what I myself have seen of ignorance and superstition and degradation in Italy? We are far, however, from having acquitted ourselves of our duty; and I do not wish to palliate, much less defend by recrimination, the unfaithfulness of the South to the sacred trust imposed upon us. . . .

The natural descendants of Abraham were holders of slaves, and God took them into special relation to himself. "He made known his ways unto Moses, his acts unto the children of Israel;" and he instituted regulations for their government, into which he expressly incorporated a permission to buy and hold slaves. These institutes not only recognise slavery as lawful, but contain very minute directions. It is not necessary for me to argue this point, as it is conceded by you. Slaves were held by the priests. "A sojourner of a priest, or an hired servant, shall not eat of the holy thing. But if the priest buy any soul with his money, he shall eat of it, and he that is born in his house, they shall eat of it." (Lev. xxii. 10, 11.) They might be bought of the Canaanites around, or of strangers living among the Hebrews. "Both thy bondmen, and thy bondmaids, which thou shalt have, shall be of the heathen that are round about you; of them shall ye buy bondmen and bondmaids. Moreover, of the children of the strangers that do sojourn among you, of them shall ye buy, and of their families that are with you, which they begat in your land; and they shall be your possession." (Lev. xxv.) They were regarded as property, and were called "money," "possession:" "If a man smite his servant or his maid, with a rod, and he die under his hand; he shall be surely punished. Notwithstanding, if he continue a day or two, he shall not be punished: for he is his money." (Exod. xxi. 20, 21.) They might be sold. This is implied in the term "money;" but it is plainly taken for granted: "Thou shalt not make merchandise of her, because thou hast humbled her." (Deut. xxi. 14.) See also Exod. xxi. 7, 8. "And if a man sell his daughter to be a maid-servant, she shall not go out as the menservants do. If she please not her master, who hath betrothed her to himself, then shall he let her be redeemed: to sell her to a strange nation he shall have no power, seeing he hath dealt deceitfully with her." The slavery thus expressly sanctioned was hereditary and perpetual: "Ye shall take them as an inheritance for your children after you, to inherit them for a possession. They shall be your bondmen forever." (Lev. xxv.) Lastly, Hebrews, if bought, were to be treated, not as slaves, but as hired servants, and to go free at the year of jubilee. "If thy brother that dwelleth by thee be waxen poor, and be sold unto thee, thous shalt not compel him to serve as a bondservant; but as an hired servant and as a sojourner shall he be with thee, and shall serve thee unto the year of jubilee: and then shall he depart from thee, both he and his children with him, and shall return unto his own family, and unto the possession of his father shall he return." (Lev. xxv. 29.) If during the Hebrew's time of service he married a slave, and had children, the wife and children were not set at liberty with him. If he consented, he might become a slave for life: "If thou buy a Hebrew servant, six years shall he serve: and in the seventh he shall go out free for nothing. If he came in by himself, he shall go out by himself: if he were married, then his wife shall go out with him. If his master have given him a wife, and she have borne him sons or daughters, the wife and her children shall be her master's, and he shall go out by himself. And if the servant shall plainly say, I love my master, my wife, and my children; I will not go out free: Then his master shall bring him unto the judges: he shall also bring him to the door, or unto the door-post; and his master shall bore his ear through with an awl; and he shall serve him forever." (Exod. xxi. 2–6.)

Such are some parts of the Mosaic institution. Let me add, also, that the decalogue twice recognises slavery, and forbids one Israelite to covet the man-servant or maid-servant of another. And, now, how does all this appear if your assumption be for a moment tenable, that slavery is as great a crime as can be committed? Suppose these regulations had thus sanctioned piracy, or idolatry, would they ever have commanded the faith of the world as divine? How conclusive this that slavery is not among crimes in the estimation of mankind, and according to the immutable and eternal principles of morality! . . .

The New Testament is not silent as to slavery; it recognises the relation, and commands slaves to obey their masters; and what I now affirm is this, that, when we consider the previous permission by the Old Testament, such commands to slaves are not only a *suppressio veri,* but a *suggestio falsi*—not only a suppression of the truth, but a suggestion of what is false—if slavery be a sin of appalling magnitude. Let it be borne in mind that the previous sanction had been both by God's conduct and express precept, and demanded, therefore, a countervailing revelation of no equivocal sort. Yet, not only is no condemnation uttered, but slaves are addressed as such, and required to obey. . . .

You affirm . . . that although the apostles did not condemn slavery by express precept, they did so by the inculcation of truths that must abolish slavery. As to which allegation, occupying the ground I now do, it would be quite enough for me to reply, that no matter what truths the apostles taught, if they received slaveholders into the churches, and pronounced them *"faithful and beloved,"* they put to silence the charge that slaveholding is always and everywhere a sin.

If you had said that the gospel, wherever received, at once eradicated the Roman system of slavery, and made the relation "a very different thing;" and if you had added, that everywhere the gospel requires of a master the moral and intellectual improvement of his slaves; I at least should have had no controversy with you. Then, too, while Christians at the South are enjoined to perform their solemn duty, the good and the wise through the Union might consult in the spirit of a prospective and far-seeing philanthropy, as to the designs of God for the African race. But the proposition defended by you has no connection with all this. Slavery is averred by you to be always, and every moment, a sin of appalling magnitude. . . .

Slavery may be a sin; and may be rendered so by the manner in which the present master obtained his power, or by the abuse of that power, or by the means employed to perpetuate that power. But supposing there is no sin (as there is manifestly none) in being the heir or legatee of this power, then the use of it may be most virtuous; as in the bequests mentioned in my third letter; and in all cases where slaves are unprepared for liberty, and the master's authority is exercised for their truest benefit, temporal and eternal.

⌗ *E S S A Y S*

Collectively the abolitionists' appeals amounted to one of the most scathing social indictments in all of U.S. history. And in attacking slavery, the abolitionists also inevitably described what they hoped the nation would become. Several scholars have detected a basic compatibility between American abolitionist ideals and the underlying assumptions of an emerging commercial society. Yet the antislavery vanguard was hardly a collection of complacent bourgeois. David Brion Davis of Yale University, the greatest modern authority on the movement, has shown that abolitionism contained diverse currents, criss-crossing the Atlantic and bearing some of the most revolutionary ideas of a revolutionary age. Nor was the movement's leadership or constituency monolithic, including (as it did) pious evangelicals, anticlerical radicals, politically minded moderates, and free black activists of various persuasions.

As the following essays make clear, antislavery and abolitionism very quickly raised enormous questions about labor, autonomy, God, and equality that had no simple answers in the 1830s—or even today. In the first essay, the historian Eric Foner of Columbia University examines the strained relations between abolitionism and the labor movement and challenges some old scholarly stereotypes about both. Ellen Carol Dubois, of the University of California at Los Angeles, in the second selection assesses the ties between Garrisonian abolitionism and early feminism, stressing the primacy of politics. In the third essay, Vincent Harding of the Iliffe School of Theology, University of Denver, charges that the white abolitionist leadership, although well intentioned, could not fully overcome its own racial and political preconceptions. Harding makes no pretense about his belief in the centrality of race and his sympathies for an embryonic black separatism, although he goes on to note that the mainstream of what he calls the Great Tradition of black protest led elsewhere. His analysis emphasizes the underlying tensions among black abolitionists as well as between them and the larger abolitionist movement.

With their different viewpoints, Foner, Dubois, and Harding complicate our appreciation of abolitionism's meaning. In the final essay, the discussion of proslavery thought by professor of history Drew Gilpin Faust of the University of Pennsylvania complicates matters even further, by showing what the abolitionists were up against. Far from some new, exotic southern aberration, proslavery arguments had a long pedigree in America in 1830, on both sides of the Mason-Dixon line. After 1830 slavery's advocates produced an increasingly coherent secular and religious defense of an entire way of life. Historians and students fool themselves, Faust argues, if they approach proslavery as a backward, guilt-ridden mania, running against the American grain. Other scholars have asserted that, judging the contest strictly on intellectual grounds, the proslavery spokesmen actually defeated their abolitionist enemies. Do you agree?

Abolitionism and the Labor Movement

ERIC FONER

. . . It is well known that relations between abolitionists and the radical labor leaders of the North were by no means cordial during the 1830s and 1840s. But the reasons remain elusive. Nonetheless, the not-too-close encounter between abolitionism and the labor movement not only raises important questions about the constituencies and ideological assumptions underpinning each movement, but also illuminates in a new way that historical perennial, the relationship between capitalism and slavery.

The emergence of the nation's first labor movement in the late 1820s and 1830s was, of course, a response to fundamental changes taking place in the work patterns and authority relationships within traditional artisan production. Labor historians have made the elements of this transformation familiar: the emergence of the factory system, the dilution of craft skill, the imposition of a new labor discipline in traditional craft production, the growing gap between masters and journeymen, and the increasing stratification of the social order, especially in the large eastern cities. Workingmen responded to these developments within the context of an ideology dating back to the Paineite republicanism of the American Revolution. The central ingredients in this ideology were a passionate attachment to equality (defined not as a leveling of all distinctions, but as the absence of large inequalities of wealth and influence), belief that independence—the ability to resist personal or economic coercion—was an essential attribute of the republican citizenry, and a commitment to the labor theory of value, along with its corollary, that labor should receive the full value of its product. The economic changes of the early nineteenth century posed a direct challenge to these traditional ideals. . . .

Originally published in *Anti-Slavery, Religion, and Reform* edited by Christine Bolt and Seymour Drescher (Folkestone, 1980).

The phrase which entered the language of politics in the 1830s to describe the plight and grievances of the labor movement was "wage slavery." A comparison between the status of the northern worker and the southern slave—usually to the detriment of the former—became a standard component of labor rhetoric in these years. In language remarkably similar to the southern critique of northern labor conditions, Seth Luther declared that northern mill workers labored longer each day than southern slaves, and in worse conditions. A New Hampshire labor newspaper asked, "A great cry is raised in the northern states against southern slavery. The sin of slavery may be abominable there, but is it not equally so here? If they have black slaves, have we not white ones? Or how much better is the condition of some of our laborers here at the North, than the slaves of the South?" The famous Coffin handbill distributed in New York City after striking journeymen tailors were convicted of conspiracy declared, "The Freemen of the North are now on a level with the slaves of the South." And the militant female textile workers of Lowell, Massachusetts, referred to themselves during one strike as the "white slaves" of New England, and their newspaper, the *Voice of Industry,* claimed the women operatives were "in fact nothing more nor less than slaves in every sense of the word."

Sometimes, "wage slavery" was used more or less as an equivalent for long working hours or for poverty. But the meaning of the metaphor was far broader than this. The phrase evoked the fears so prevalent in the labor movement of the 1830s and 1840s of the erosion of respect for labor, the loss of independence by the craftsman, and the emergence of "European" social conditions and class stratification in republican America. Most importantly, working for wages itself was often perceived as a form of "slavery," an affront to the traditional artisanal ideal of economic and personal independence. . . .

What was the attitude of those who raised the cry of "wage slavery" toward slavery in the South? It has often been argued that northern workingmen were indifferent or hostile to the anti-slavery crusade, or even pro-slavery. White laborers, it is argued, feared emancipation would unleash a flood of freedmen to compete for northern jobs and further degrade the dignity of labor. Yet it is important to distinguish the labor movement's response to abolitionism, and, indeed, to black competition, from its attitude toward slavery. After all, inherent in the notion of "wage slavery," in the comparison of the status of the northern laborer with the southern slave, was a critique of the peculiar institution as an extreme form of oppression. . . . The entire ideology of the labor movement was implicitly hostile to slavery: slavery contradicted the central ideas and values of artisan radicalism—liberty, democracy, equality, independence. The ideological fathers of the movement, Thomas Paine and Robert Owen, were both strongly anti-slavery.

Recent research, moreover . . . has underscored the central role played by artisans in the urban abolitionist constituency (although not the leadership of the movement). In Lynn, Massachusetts, according to Alan Dawley, shoemakers equated slaveowners with the city's factory magnates as "a set of lordly tyrants." In Utica and Cincinnati, writes Leonard Richards, artisans were represented far more heavily among the abolitionist constituency than in the mobs which broke up abolitionist meetings. And the careful analysis of New York City anti-slavery petitions between 1829 and 1837 by John Jentz reveals that in most cases, artisans were the largest occupational group among the signers. In New York, the only newspaper publicly to defend Nat Turner's rebellion was not an anti-slavery journal, but the *Daily Sentinel,* edited for the Workingman's party by the immigrant English radical George Henry Evans. The radical artisans who met each year in New York to celebrate Tom Paine's birthday often included a toast to the liberators of Haiti in their celebrations, and Evans's *Workingman's Advocate* went so far as to claim, rather implausibly, that "the Government of Haiti approaches nearer to pure Republicanism than any other now in use or on record." Evans did acknowledge in 1831 that the labor movement sometimes neglected the cause of the slave because of its preoccupation with the grievances of northern workers. But he added that he remained committed to the total eradication of slavery in the South.

The year 1831, of course, was also the one in which William Lloyd Garrison commenced publication of *The Liberator,* the point from which historians usually date the emergence of a new, militant, immediatist abolitionist crusade. As is well known, Garrison addressed the condition of northern labor, and the activities of the labor movement, in his very first issue:

> An attempt has been made—it is still making—we regret to say, with considerable success—to inflame the minds of our working classes against the more opulent, and to persuade men that they are contemned and oppressed by a wealthy aristocracy. . . . It is in the highest degree criminal . . . to exasperate our mechanics to deeds of violence, or to array them under a party banner, for it is not true that, at any time, they have been the objects of reproach. Labour is not dishonourable. The industrious artisan, in a government like ours, will always be held in better estimation than the wealthy idler. . . . We are the friends of reform; but this is not reform, which in curing one evil, threatens to inflict a thousand others.

Of course, Garrison's point about the high regard in which labor was held was precisely what the labor movement contended was no longer true. Four weeks after the editorial appeared, Garrison published a response by the labor reformer William West, arguing that there was, in fact, a "very intimate connexion" between abolition and the labor movement, since each was striving to secure "the fruits of their toil" to a class of workingmen. To which Garrison responded with another denunciation, phrased in the extreme language so characteristic of all his writing:

> In a republican government . . . where hereditary distinctions are obsolete . . . where the avenues of wealth, distinction and supremacy are open to all; [society] must, in the nature of things, be full of inequalities. But these can exist without an assumption of rights—without even a semblance of oppression. There is a prevalent opinion, that wealth and aristocracy are indissolubly allied; and the poor and vulgar are taught to consider the

opulent as their natural enemies. Those who inculcate this pernicious doctrine are the worst enemies of the people, and, in the grain, the real nobility. . . . It is a miserable characteristic of human nature to look with an envious eye upon those who are more fortunate in their pursuits, or more exalted in their station.

Thus, from the very outset, a failure of communication characterized relations between the two movements. . . . It is not precisely that the abolitionists were complacently "middle class" in outlook, a characterization found quite frequently in the recent historical literature. Abolitionists—both Garrisonians and their opponents within the movement—threw themselves with enthusiasm into all sorts of other movements to reform American society, from the abolition of capital punishment to women's rights, temperance, peace, etc. They often criticized the spirit of competition, individualism, and greed so visible in northern life, as the antithesis of Christian brotherhood and love. It will not do to defang the abolitionist crusade: it was indeed a radical impulse, challenging fundamental aspects of American life (and none so deeply embedded as racism). But in its view of economic relations it did speak the language of northern society. . . .

In contrast to the labor movement, most abolitionists—as Garrison's early editorials made clear—accepted social inequality as a natural reflection of individual differences in talent, ambition, and diligence, and perceived the interests of capital and labor as existing in harmony rather than conflict. As a result, they were unable to understand, much less sympathize with, the aims of the labor movement or the concept of "wage slavery." Their attitude toward labor was graphicly revealed in a pamphlet published by the New York abolitionist William Jay in the mid-1830s. In the course of a discussion of the benefits of immediate emancipation, Jay sought to answer the perennial question, what would happen to the slave when free:

> He is free, and his own master, and can ask for no more. Yet he is, in fact, for a time, absolutely dependent on his late owner. He can look to no other person for food to eat, clothes to put on, or house to shelter him. . . . [He is required to work], but labor is no longer the badge of his servitude and the consummation of his misery, for it is *voluntary*. For the first time in his life, he is a party to a contract. . . . In the course of time, the value of negro labor, like all other vendible commodities, will be regulated by the supply and demand.

What is particularly noteworthy in this extraordinary argument is, first, Jay's ready acceptance of the condition which caused so much complaint among the labor movement—the treatment of human labor as a "vendible commodity," and second, the rather loose use of the word "voluntary" to describe the labor of an individual who owns nothing and is "absolutely dependent" on his employer. To the labor movement, Jay's description of emancipation would qualify as a classic instance of "wage slavery"; to Jay, it was an economic definition of freedom.

The labor movement, . . . equated freedom with ownership of productive property. To the abolitionists, expressing a newer, liberal definition, freedom meant self-ownership—that is, simply not being a slave. It is one of the more tragic ironies of this complex debate that, in the process of attempting to liberate the slave, the abolitionists did so much to promote a new and severely truncated definition of freedom for both blacks and whites. As many historians have observed, the abolitionist conception of both slavery and freedom was profoundly individualistic. Abolitionism understood slavery not as a class relationship, but as a system of arbitrary and illegitimate power exercised by one individual over another. The slaves and, to some extent, northern workers, were not downtrodden classes but suffering individuals, and it was this liberal, individualist definition of personal freedom which not only cut abolitionists off from the labor movement, but, as Gilbert Osofsky argued, prevented them from making a meaningful response to the economic condition of the Irish, despite a principled effort to overcome nativism and reach out for Irish-American support in the 1840s.

The intense individualism of the abolitionists, historians are agreed, derived from the great revivals of the Second Great Awakening, which identified moral progress with each individual's capacity to act as an instrument of God and opened the possibility of conversion for all as the prelude to eliminating sin from society and paving the way for the Second Coming. Religious benevolence was, it seems clear, the primary root of ante-bellum reform. But it was not the only root, and historians' single-minded emphasis on revivalist Protestantism as the origin of immediate abolitionism has tended to obscure the equally sincere anti-slavery convictions of the radical artisans, so many of whom were influenced by Enlightenment deism. Indeed, the tensions between the labor movement and evangelical abolitionism were part of a larger confrontation during the 1830s between evangelicalism and the powerful opposition it generated within northern society. As Jentz has shown, the New York Workingman's leaders were intensely hostile to the evangelical campaign, viewing it as an attempt to unite church and state in a campaign for special privileges incompatible with the principles of republicanism. The campaign against the Sunday mails, led by Lewis and Arthur Tappan shortly before their involvement in abolitionism, aroused considerable opposition among free-thinking artisans, and these same radical artisans were estranged from the anti-slavery movement because of the presence of evangelicals like the Tappans in leadership positions. Nonetheless, when New York's anti-abolitionist riot occurred in 1834, George Henry Evans defended the right of the Tappan brothers to freedom of speech. Later, he again praised abolition as a "just and good cause," although he could not resist the opportunity to add, "many of the Abolitionists are actuated by a species of fanaticism, and are desirous of freeing the slaves, more for the purpose of adding them to a religious sect, than for a love of liberty and justice."

In the eyes of Evans and the radical workingmen for whom he spoke, moreover, Tappan the intolerant Sabbatarian was not unrelated to Tappan the wealthy merchant who was one of the very men helping to transform labor relations at the expense of the laborer. Certainly, the Tappan brothers were not averse to using their economic power to coerce artisans into supporting their various causes. In January 1830, a tailor complained that Lewis Tappan approached him with a petition against the Sunday mails and, when refused, threatened that the tailor would get no more of the trade of his brother Arthur's mercantile firm. To the tailor, Tappan was a "redoubtable champion of Calvinism, illiberalism, etc." To the Tappans, the "infidelity" of men like Robert Owen and George Henry Evans was as offensive as their economic views. Indeed, before leaders of the benevolent empire like the Tappans took control of New York City's abolition movement, anti-slavery had a reputation for being "largely composed of irreligious men, some of infidel sentiments." The great revival of the 1830s changed that, identifying abolitionism with evangelicalism and, one presumes, alienating anti-slavery men like Evans from organized abolitionism. But, given the large number of artisans who signed abolitionist petitions, we should not let the evangelicalism of the abolitionist leaders obscure that portion of the anti-slavery constituency whose roots lay in Enlightenment rationalism and republican notions of equality and liberty, rather than in Christian benevolence.

For most of the 1830s and 1840s, relations between the abolitionist and labor movements remained strained. Open attacks on labor organizations, such as that in the first issue of *The Liberator,* were not, however, typical of abolitionist literature. By the end of the 1830s, abolitionists were making an attempt to appeal to workingmen for support. But, whereas labor leaders tended to see abolition as a diversion from the grievances of northern labor and slavery as simply one example of more pervasive problems in American life, abolitionists considered the labor issue as artificial or secondary. Whatever problems northern labor might have, whatever legitimate grievances it might articulate, were all rooted in the peculiar institution. Slavery, said abolitionist literature, made all labor disreputable and was the cause of the degradation of labor in the North. "American slavery," as one abolitionist resolution put it, "is an evil of such gigantic magnitude, that it must be uprooted and overthrown, before the elevation sought by the laboring classes can be effected." Both abolitionists and labor leaders spoke of the alliance between the Lords of the Loom and Lords of the Lash—the textile manufacturers of New England and slaveowners of the South—but each drew from it a different conclusion. To the labor movement, factory owner and slaveowner were both nonproducers who fattened on the fruits of the labor of others; to the abolitionists what was objectionable in the factory owners was precisely their pro-slavery political stance, not their treatment of their employees. . . .

Perhaps the differences in perception which characterized relations between abolitionists and labor leaders down to the late 1840s are symbolized by the fact that when *The Liberator* in 1847 reprinted an article identifying the condition of northern workers as "white slavery," it did so in its column, "Refuge of Oppression"—a portion of the newspaper reserved for items from the pro-slavery press. Garrison could not free himself from the conviction that, by diverting attention from slavery in the South, the labor movement was, in effect, playing into the hands of the defenders of slavery. Yet at this very moment, changes were taking place within both movements which would transform the relations between labor leaders and anti-slavery. One set of changes involved the emergence of opposition to the expansion of slavery as the central political question of the late 1840s, and the vehicle by which anti-slavery became, for the first time, a truly mass movement in the North. Increasingly, the abolitionists were pushed to the side, while free-soilism took center stage as the most available mode of anti-slavery and anti-southern protest. Evangelical abolitionism, it may be suggested, had done its main work in the 1830s. It had succeeded in shattering the conspiracy of silence surrounding the question of slavery. But because it also generated a powerful opposition within northern society—not only from pro-slavery forces, but from those who could not accept the impulse toward "moral stewardship" which was so integral a part of benevolent reform—evangelicalism could not make of abolition a majority sentiment. The more secular, rational, and moderate free-soil position could succeed in a way abolitionism could not.

At the same time, the labor movement, devastated by the depression of 1837–42, was turning toward more individualist and self-help-oriented solutions to the problems of northern workingmen. Evans's own emphasis on the land question, which linked social justice so closely to individual ownership of private property, while seemingly abandoning the cooperative thrust of the labor movement of the 1830s, reflected the change. Evans, as we have seen, still insisted that true freedom required economic independence, but he appeared to be abandoning his critique of the wage system itself. Land reform, not a change in the system of production and labor relations, would solve the problem of urban poverty and offer every workingman the opportunity to achieve economic independence, in the form of a homestead.

Free-soilism was not only the means by which anti-slavery rose to political dominance in the 1850s, but the meeting ground for the two strands of anti-slavery thought which had remained estranged in the 1830s and 1840s. . . .

Women's Rights and Abolition

ELLEN CAROL DUBOIS

It is a common error among historians of American feminism to attribute American women's consciousness about the oppression of their sex to the impact of the antislavery movement, particularly to its ultraist Garrisonian element. This argument suggests that, reasoning by analogy, female abolitionists perceived the similarities between their status before the law and that of the chattel slave. Certainly the rhetoric of the prewar women's rights movement abounded in the use of the slave metaphor to describe women's oppression. "Slaves are we, politically and legally," wrote J. Elizabeth Jones

Excerpts from "Women's Rights and Abolition: The Nature of the Connection" by Ellen DuBois. Reprinted by permission of Louisiana State University Press from *Antislavery Reconsidered: New Perspectives on the Abolitionists,* Lewis Perry and Michael Fellman ed., pp. 238–247. Copyright © 1979 by Louisiana State University Press.

in an 1848 address to the women of Ohio. Yet other historical studies have contradicted this hypothesis of a direct connection between antislavery partisanship and awareness of women's oppression by demonstrating the incipient feminism in a wide range of other early nineteenth-century female activities. Since it is undeniably true that antislavery women provided the political leadership for the prewar women's rights movement, we must therefore look for other explanations for the connection between their abolitionism and their historic contribution to American feminism.

Starting in the 1820s and 1830s, American women began to express what might be called caste consciousness in a wide range of contexts. They evidenced a critical awareness of the importance of their femaleness in determining their experiences, began to think of themselves as united by the fact of their sex, and most important, exhibited considerable discontent with their womanly lot. Scholars have discovered such "prepolitical" elements in church-affiliated benevolent societies, the domestic novels written and read by women, pioneers of women's education, and the prewar popular health movement. Caste consciousness and a sense of discontent among women, what we might call protofeminism, seems to have been a phenomenon carried widely through the social fabric and culture of early nineteenth-century America. Many antislavery women experienced it prior to or independent of their abolitionist activity. Lucretia Mott, the matriarch of female abolitionists, was an active member of a female moral reform society in Philadelphia, and Paulina Wright Davis began her public career as an itinerant lecturer on women's physiology. Elizabeth Stanton was a student of Emma Willard, Angelina Grimké considered becoming a pupil of Catherine Beecher, and Lucy Stone, for a short period, studied with Mary Lyon. Willard, Beecher, and Lyon were the early nineteenth-century triumvirate of women's education. As a self-supporting woman, Susan B. Anthony had defended women's right to speak publicly in New York state teacher's conventions well before her first contact with abolitionists.

In some of these contexts, women were beginning to move from a generalized caste consciousness and sense of discontent to a specific program for altering woman's situation, that is, to activism. A more detailed examination of one such attempt, the moral reform societies of the 1830s and 1840s, can suggest the problems women were meeting in translating their protofeminist consciousness into a genuine feminist movement. Contrasting moral reformers with women abolitionists suggests why the latter were able to execute this transformation successfully and therefore to build the women's rights movement.

In her analysis of the feminism of the New York Female Moral Reform Society, Carroll Smith Rosenberg portrays the society as one manifestation of "a growing self-awareness among middle class American women . . . [and] an ordinarily repressed desire for an expansion of their role." In turn she attributes this widespread female restlessness to the contradiction between the passive, constricted, and static role prescribed for women and a general belief in the possibilities for and desirability of social change in Jacksonian

America. Smith Rosenberg finds many aspects of the society's pursuit of moral purity that seem to have gone beyond contemporary notions of female propriety. On the grounds of their traditionally pietistic prerogatives, female moral reformers developed a militant stance on issues explicitly prohibited to women, such as prostitution, the double standard, and male sexual behavior. They resisted male efforts to supersede their work and, in Smith Rosenberg's phrase, claimed moral reform as a "self consciously female" endeavor. They projected a nationwide union of women dedicated to purifying American sexual morals. The activities they undertook in pursuit of their goals went well beyond those permitted in woman's sphere to include visiting brothels, managing the society's finances, editing their own journal, and even lobbying for ten years in the New York legislature in behalf of an antiseduction statute.

Yet the Female Moral Reform Society did not continue to develop a feminist program, and evolved instead in the direction of a charity organization. Most of the protofeminist militance which so impresses Smith Rosenberg had disappeared by 1840. The reasons for this are complex, but an episode early in the society's history permits the identification of two of the major obstacles to the development of feminism within the reform society. In 1838, the society's journal printed an article by Sarah Grimké, then at the height of her notoriety as the first woman in the abolitionist movement to become a public lecturer and agitator. While Smith Rosenberg interprets this episode as evidence of the moral reform society's sympathy with women's rights, it also indicates important differences between the protofeminism of moral reformers and that of female abolitionists. The journal's readership found Grimké far too radical for their tastes. They seem to have objected, first to her disregard for woman's proper sphere, and second to her anticlericalism. Moral reformers castigated men for usurping women's power, but limited their attack to "male tyranny in the HOME department." Grimké's call for women to reject the limitations of home and family and pursue their rights and duties outside the domestic sphere greatly disturbed them. Moreover, they objected to her explicit attack on "priestcraft." Like her, their sense of religious vocation had carried them out of passivity and into new realms of thought and action, but unlike her, they could not distinguish between religion and religious institutions, between their own vocation and the authority of ministers and the church. Grimké's identification of the priesthood as a source of moral corruption and her charge to women to reinterpret the Bible for themselves was her most specific affront to moral reformers' sensibilities.

By contrast with the moral reform movement, Garrisonian abolitionism provided women with a political framework that assisted the development of a feminist movement. As Garrisonians, women learned a way to view the world and a theory and practice of social change that they found most useful in elaborating their protofeminist insights. In addition, the antislavery movement provided them with a constituency and a political alliance on which they were able to rely until the Civil War. Thus, American feminism developed within the context of abolitionism less because abolitionists taught women that they were oppressed than because abolitionists taught women what to do with that perception, how to develop it into a social movement.

Two aspects of the way that Garrisonians approached social reality were particularly important to the development of nineteenth-century American feminism: the ability to perceive and analyze entire institutions; and the assumption of absolute human equality as a first principle of morality and politics. Both habits of mind, though seemingly abstract, were derived from the concrete task facing abolitionists, to make slavery a burning issue for northern whites. The women who built the women's rights movement borrowed these approaches and found them eminently useful in overcoming obstacles that had stopped other protofeminists. The habit of institutional analysis permitted Garrisonian women to escape the control of the clergy and move beyond pietistic activism. The principle of absolute human equality freed them from the necessity of justifying all their duties in terms of woman's sphere.

Stanley Elkins has argued that the "anti-institutionalism" of Garrisonians was their basic political weakness. While it is true that Garrisonians refused to act through institutions, it is certainly not true that they were blind to them. On the contrary, Garrisonians broke new ground for the antislavery movement by analyzing and moving to attack at least two basic institutions— organized religion and the institution of slavery itself. Unlike many other antislavery people, Garrisonians' indictment of slavery did not rest on specific incidents of cruel treatment, and therefore could not be refuted by evidence that many masters were kind and generous to their slaves. Instead, Garrisonians located evil in the institutional arrangements of chattel slavery, which permitted even one case of brutality. Garrisonians criticized the institution of slavery, not the behavior of individuals within it. Similarly, Garrisonians grasped the fact that the churches were human institutions, therefore subject to human criticism. Their ability to comprehend religious institutions and to distinguish them from their own profoundly religious impulses was an impressive achievement for evangelicals in an evangelical age.

The abolitionist women who built the women's rights movement profited from this ability to criticize entire institutions, most specifically from the militant anticlericalism of Garrisonians. This can best be seen in the 1837 conflict between the Grimké sisters and the Congregational clergy of Massachusetts. Like women in moral reform and other pious activisms, the Grimkés had been led by their religious vocation to step outside woman's sphere. At that point, like other benevolent women, they were confronted by clerical authority and ordered to return to more womanly pursuits. Yet the fact that they were Garrisonians enabled them to hold fast to their religious convictions, ignore clerical criticism, and instead indict the churches themselves for being institutional bulwarks of slavery and women's oppression. In the face of the clerical authority that had long restrained women's impulses for a larger life, the Grimkés continued to pursue their feminist inclinations and to lay the groundwork for the women's rights movement a decade later. The Grimkés' successors also relied on the anticlericalism that they had learned as abolitionists. Elizabeth Stanton had wrestled with religious dogma throughout her adolescence and early adulthood, but credited Garrison with her ultimate spiritual liberation.

> In the darkness and gloom of a false theology, I was slowly sawing off the chains of my spiritual bondage, when, for the first time, I met Garrison in London. A few bold strokes from the hammer of his truth, I was free! Only those who have lived all their lives under the dark clouds of vague, undefined fears can appreciate the joy of a doubting soul suddenly born into the kingdom of reason and free thought. Is the bondage of the priest-ridden less galling than that of the slave, because we do not see the chains, the indelible scars, the festering wounds, the deep degradation of all the powers of the God-like mind?

Almost until the Civil War, conflict with clerical authority was the most important issue in the women's rights movement. The 1854 National Women's Rights Convention resolved: "We feel it a duty to declare in regard to the sacred cause which has brought us together, that the most determined opposition it encounters is from the clergy generally, whose teachings of the Bible are intensely inimical to the equality of woman with man." With increasing defensiveness, representatives of the clergy pursued their fleeting authority onto the very platform of the women's rights movement. However, Garrisonian women had learned the techniques of biblical exegesis and absolute faith in their own interpretations in numerous debates over the biblical basis of slavery. They met the clergy on their own ground, skillfully refuting them quote for quote. "[T]he pulpit has been prostituted, the Bible has been ill-used," Lucretia Mott said during an argument with the Reverend Henry Grew at the 1854 National Women's Rights Convention. "It has been turned over and over in every reform. The temperance people have had to feel its supposed denunciations. Then the anti-slavery, and now this reform has met, and still continues to meet, passage after passage of the Bible, never intended to be so used." When ministers with national reputations started to offer their support to the women's rights movement in the late 1850s, the issue of clerical authority began to recede in importance. It was not a major aspect of postwar feminism, both because of changes in the movement and changes in the clergy.

The principle of absolute human equality was the other basic philosophical premise that American feminism borrowed from Garrisonian abolitionism. Because the abolitionists' target was northern racial prejudice and their goal the development of white empathy for the suffering of the slave, the core of their argument was the essential unity of whites with blacks. Although many Garrisonians believed in biological differences between the races, their politics ignored physical, cultural, and historical characteristics that might distinguish blacks from whites. They stressed instead the common humanity and the moral identity of the races. They expressed this approach as a moral abstraction, a first principle, but its basis was the very concrete demands of the agitational task they faced.

Garrisonian feminists appropriated this belief and applied it to women.

The philosophical tenet that women were essentially human and only incidentally female liberated them from the sexual ideology that had constrained their predecessors in other reform movements, who had felt it necessary to justify their actions as appropriate to woman's sphere. Abolitionist women did not. Although they continued to believe in the existence of such a sphere, its demands were secondary to those of the common humanity that united women and men, blacks and whites.

As with the issue of clerical authority, this lack of concern for woman's sphere characterized the first episode in abolitionist feminism, the Grimkés' 1837 answer to the pastoral letter. In response to the Congregational clergy's demand that she return to "the appropriate duties and influence of women," Sarah Grimké wrote:

> The Lord Jesus defines the duties of his followers in his Sermon on the Mount. He lays down grand principles by which they should be governed, without any reference to sex or condition. . . . I follow him through all his precepts and find him giving the same direction to women as to man, never even referring to the distinction now so strenuously insisted upon between masculine and feminine virtues. . . . Men and women are CREATED EQUAL! They are both moral and accountable beings, and whatever is *right* for man to do, is *right* for woman.

The prewar women's rights movement continued to be distinguished from other movements for the improvement of women's status by its refusal to be sidetracked into the consideration of what was appropriate to woman's sphere. At the fifth national convention, Lucy Stone rejected the notion that the women's rights movement was a matter "of sphere." "Too much has already been said and written about woman's sphere," she contended. "Trace all the doctrines to their source and they will be found to have no basis except in the usages and prejudices of the age. . . . Leave woman, then, to find her own sphere." Similarly, the 1851 convention resolved that "we deny the right of any portion of the species to define for another portion . . . what is and what is not their 'proper sphere'; that the proper sphere for all human beings is the largest and highest to which they are able to attain." The approach of Garrisonian women to the ideology of sexual spheres appears all the more remarkable in light of the facts that the three decades before the Civil War were precisely the years in which that ideology was being elaborated, and that benevolent women played an important part in its elaboration.

As Aileen Kraditor has demonstrated, the Garrisonians' focus on "empathy" had important political limitations, both tactical and analytical. By stressing the moral identity and human equality of blacks and whites, Garrisonians were unable to explain why blacks were regarded and treated so differently from whites. Similarly, the women's rights belief in the moral irrelevance of sexual spheres ignored the reality of women's domestic confinement, which distinguished them from men, structured their relative powerlessness, and gave credence to the doctrine of spheres. Indeed, Garrisonian women ignored the question of woman's sphere while simultaneously believing in its existence. They accepted the particular suitability of women to domestic activities and did not project a reorganization of the division of labor within the home. Like women outside the antislavery movement, they believed that domestic activities were as "naturally" female as childbearing, and as little subject to deliberate social manipulation. This contradiction between the belief in woman's sphere and in its moral irrelevance remained unexamined in the prewar women's rights movement. A convention in Ohio in 1852 simultaneously resolved that "since every human being has an individual sphere, and that is the largest he or she can fill, no one has the right to determine the proper sphere of another," and that "in demanding for women equality of rights with their fathers, husbands, brothers and sons, we neither deny that distinctive character, nor wish them to avoid any duty, or to lay aside that feminine delicacy which legitimately belongs to them as mothers, wives, sisters and daughters." During this early period in the development of an American feminism, the Garrisonian emphasis on the ultimate moral identity of women with men helped the women's rights movement to establish sexual equality as the definition of women's emancipation. The work of examining sexual *in*equality, its origins and the mechanisms that preserved it, remained for the future. . . .

Racial Tensions Within Northern Abolitionism

VINCENT HARDING

. . . Canaan was a strange land. In many crucial ways, it had been easier to understand black struggle in the South. At the most personal levels, the objective there was to break with slavery and move to a land where the institution was no longer legal, defying the dominance of the slaveholders over black lives. In the Southern setting all white people often seemed to be the institution's defenders; therefore, in the ultimate sense, all could be considered the enemy. That was the meaning of Nat Turner, of Vesey, of the depredations of many of the outlyers. Below the Mason-Dixon line, then, the nature of the white system appeared in sharper relief. . . .

Matters appeared more complex in the North. Black people were free, yet not free. They were their own men and women, and yet they were not. They were protected by laws, yet many statutes left the black community open to its enemies. And who precisely were the enemies? David Walker had pointed to the slaveholders, their advocates and supporters. But advocacy took many forms. Andrew Jackson was an advocate. There were advocates in the halls of Congress, and silent, consenting supporters in every Northern community. The advocate enemies were also the many persons and institutions, including the federal government, who were creating and condoning the complex system of Jim Crow, with all its debilitating effects. This network would seem to include most white people. Scattered as blacks were, comprising not more than a small minority in the population of almost

Excerpts from *There Is a River: The Black Struggle for Freedom in America* by Vincent Harding (New York: Harcourt Brace Jovanovich, Inc. 1981), pp. 119–134.

any Northern state, how should they struggle against such complex, elusive, pervasive enemies? What were the goals? What did "freedom" mean in the free North? What did any freedom mean there, when the vast majority of the black community was enslaved elsewhere?

Undeniably, it was a perplexing, often exasperating set of questions, through which the total pattern of struggle was not easy to discern. Nevertheless, for those black persons in the North who determined to take up the fight for freedom and justice in whatever forms it came, there were certain rather unambiguous tasks immediately available. Then, as they directly confronted these more obvious responsibilities, they discovered that they were inevitably drawn into other struggles at once more difficult and more radical.

In the two decades following David Walker's death (1830–50), at least five clear responsibilities confronted participants in the freedom struggle of the North. First, the black community had to face the stark, immediate needs of their kinsmen who were repeatedly coming under physical attack from white mobs in the Northern cities, and who needed food, shelter, clothing, and public advocacy, as well as comrades in defensive warfare. Second, the black North had to protest and struggle against the less physical but equally destructive and more widespread systems of segregation and discrimination arrayed against them in every area of Northern life. Third, it was absolutely necessary to build black institutions wherever they could in the North, partly as a base for the ongoing fights against white injustice, but largely as repositories for the visions and hopes of the future. Fourth, black voices in the North had to be raised incessantly against the institution of American slavery, on behalf of their fellow Africans in Southern chains. Like David Walker, they recognized that their situation was indivisible from that of the enslaved community. Fifth and last, they must also identify, protect, and otherwise actively assist the black fugitives who daily found their way to the North.

. . . As they attempted to grapple with each of the obvious, specific tasks, they were often unwittingly building the basis for their own new community of struggle, defining its shape, scope, and directions. Thus when, in 1829 and 1830, savage white mob action forced more than a thousand blacks to leave Cincinnati—most of whom headed for Canada in desperation and great need—the determination of their Northern brothers and sisters to develop organized assistance for the exiles led to the creation of the National Black Convention movement of the 1830s. In turn, the conventions provided a crucial platform for the development of new leadership in the Northern freedom struggle, and made available a sounding board for much of the mainstream black protest of the time. . . .

As long as there had been runaway slaves in the North and the South, there had been black civil disobedience on their behalf. By the 1830s, as the fugitive movement out of slavery grew in significance, so too did the black response. Every Northern city participated, but Detroit, standing as it did on the edge of Canada's relative freedom, was especially noted for such action. There, for instance, in the summer of 1833, the black populace's determination to rescue a fugitive was so powerful and organized that members of the apprehensive white community took up arms against them. Indeed, the situation was so volatile that the mayor eventually requested federal troops to assist the whites in putting down the defiant black action.

Then, in the National Black Convention of 1835, one of the first and most important organizational statements of this civil disobedience was put forth. Meeting in Philadelphia, a city with one of the strongest black communities in the North, the delegates resolved: "That our duty to God, and to the principles of human rights, so far exceeds our allegiance to those laws that return the slave again to his master . . . that we recommend our people to peaceably bear the punishment those [laws] inflict, rather than aid in returning their brethren again to slavery." The language was not abrasive or militant, but appropriate to the uncompromising resolve. Quietly, black folk were moving toward radical action.

. . . Throughout the cities and towns of the North, black men and women had formed vigilance committees to organize their assistance to the fugitives from the South. These committees provided initial hiding places and often armed protection against the federally approved slave catchers. They made food and lodging available for the hungry and weary travelers, and provided comfort and understanding to those overcome with distrust and fear. For the ones who would not stop . . . they provided means of transportation to Canada, and sought jobs for the majority who decided to stay. All this assistance came out of a seriously embattled and widely persecuted Northern black community. All this placed that community in direct opposition to many of the statutes of the federal and state governments. . . .

Among these vigilance leaders . . . was David Ruggles. Born in 1810, Ruggles had made his way to New York City when he was seventeen. Although he drifted into many modes of earning a living, from selling butter to selling books, he resembled David Walker in making the struggle for liberty the center of his life. By 1835 the young and vigorous advocate had become the leading force in a biracial New York vigilance committee. In that year he paid a double price for his role: his bookstore was burned and he was almost kidnaped by slave catchers.

Over a period of some five years, displaying an evangelistic tenacity which led to his being jailed several times before he was thirty, and which finally broke his health and took away most of his sight, David Ruggles helped more than a thousand fugitives to escape. So it was not surprising that in 1838, when Frederick Augustus Bailey—using an assumed name and borrowed identification—finally broke loose from Maryland and, lonely and afraid, ventured into New York City, it was Ruggles who took him in. It was Ruggles again who brought to his home his brilliant friend, the black clergyman J. W. C. Pennington, secretly to marry Bailey and Anna Muray, the woman whom Frederick later called "the wife of my youth." Finally, Ruggles quietly sent the couple off to New Bedford, Massachusetts, where the young fugitive could practice his trade of caulker in the shipyards. Later Frederick Douglass would say of this patron, "He was a whole-souled man, fully imbued with a love of his afflicted and haunted people." . . .

When he met Ruggles, Douglass was on his way to add his own talents and his own complex soul to the Northern-based struggle. In a sense the two lives provided the necessary confluence of the Southern and Northern branches of the river. Once more, through the integrity of the Northern black response to the flight of the Southern fugitives, the two movements had been joined. . . .

By the time Douglass arrived in New York, abolitionism was a crucial part of the black struggle in the North, perhaps its mainstream movement. By that time, too, white abolitionist organizations, springing from different roots, had established themselves as significant dissident elements in the life of America. Most often these white antislavery groups built on the base that the independent black struggle for freedom had prepared, for blacks had provided the first abolitionists, the first martyrs in the long battle, starting in the slave castles, on the ships of the middle passage, continuing on the soil of the new land. At the beginning of the 1830s there were some fifty local and national predominantly white abolitionist groups, and these often depended upon black churches for meeting places. In Afro-Americans like Charles Remond and his sister, Sarah Remond, of Boston, J. W. C. Pennington of New York, Robert Purvis of Philadelphia, Sojourner Truth of everywhere, and soon Douglass himself, the organized antislavery movement found many of its most effective speakers, organizers, and exemplars. Thus by the 1830s black people had provided much of the base and the heart for the abolitionist movement.

Nevertheless, by the time Douglass arrived in the North, there were many troubling questions among black leaders concerning their proper relationship to the white abolitionists. The problems stemmed from harsh organizational and personal realities alike. For instance, although three black men were on the board of the all-important American Anti-Slavery Society when it was organized in 1833, this was a white Protestant middle-class organization with its essential internal machinery in white hands. From the outset men like Theodore Dwight Weld, Arthur and Lewis Tappan, Elizur Wright, and James G. Birney molded and directed the organization and, through it, the organized abolitionist movement. Chief spokesman, curmudgeon, and embattled leader among them all was William Lloyd Garrison, the prophet, publicist, and courageous moral reformer. It was this combative practitioner of nonresistance whose weekly, Boston-based *Liberator* newspaper and whose presidency of the AASS set the tone and established the agenda of struggle—both internal and external—for much of American abolitionism in the three decades prior to the Civil War.

No one could deny the personal courage and self-sacrifice of such men as these, and the women who worked by their side. Relentlessly, often at the cost of fortunes, families, and friends, they crisscrossed the nation lecturing, preaching, and agitating in the antislavery cause, facing white mobs that were sometimes murderous. But by the same token, no one among them would have doubted that their movement and its national and state organizations were meant to be white, under essential white control, and for the healing of a white-defined nation. In theory their dual purpose was "the entire abolition of slavery in the United States" and the "elevation" of black people to "share an equity with the whites, of civil and religious privileges." In practice, the second part often proved very difficult for the white abolitionists, which created a thorny set of problems in their dealings with black coworkers.

On certain levels, of course, agreement among black and white abolitionists could and did exist. Many members of the two groups were inspired by the same Protestant revivalist religion and democratic rhetoric of the age. They could agree that slavery was an evil system which went counter to the justice and goodness of God, and contradicted the best insights of natural law. They also agreed on the cruelty and exploitation inherent in the system, and gave unrelenting broadside publicity to the many available examples of this ruthlessness. Together, black and white, they were at least rhetorically opposed to any talk of gradualism, urging slavery's immediate overthrow. To be sure, as time went on they found it increasingly difficult to agree on whether or not the American Constitution actually condoned and protected slavery, but that was not simply a black-white disagreement, and both groups were fully in accord that no constitution of a democratic republic *ought* to give such aid and comfort. But then, sometimes subtly, at precisely this point emphases tended to shift, and differences were more starkly revealed.

To a large degree, most white abolitionists saw slavery as a dishonor to their vision of the real America—the democratic, divinely led, essentially just America. For almost all of them, slavery was a sin against God, an obstacle in the way of His Kingdom's establishment in an otherwise generally fair land. (Of course some of the strongly evangelical Protestant abolitionists did indicate that slavery was only one of the many sins to be fought, in order to clear the way for the coming Kingdom. Among other evils, for instance, were intemperance, Sabbath-breaking, profanity, prostitution, and Roman Catholicism—especially that variety of Catholicism which accompanied the rising tide of non-Anglo-Saxon immigrants from Europe.)

From this white vantage point, the fight against slavery was, on the one hand, a negative battle against an evil which was undeniably immense, but in most cases not very close to them; and on the other hand, a positive struggle for the honor of America, in which they felt great personal involvement, not only to right the wrongs of the present, but also to vindicate their divinely inspired forefathers—sometimes Puritans and Pilgrims, sometimes the Revolutionary leaders, often all of them. Among white abolitionists, then, the positive aspects of the fight against slavery emerged primarily out of their commitment to a special vision of America, its righteous origins, and its no less righteous destiny.

The struggle in which the black abolitionists were involved was at once more personal and more profound. They were fighting against slavery but also, and more importantly, *for* the enslaved people. These were not simply "the slaves"; they were fathers and mothers, sisters and brothers, uncles and cousins immediate or several times removed. They were "our people," toward whom objectivity was neither possible nor desirable. Firm in the minds of black abolitionists was the conviction that the end of slavery would be the beginning of freedom for their people. Often they were far more sanguine in this conviction than they might have been, but the conviction was fully evident and operative. Black abolitionists fought for the chance to join unshackled hands with their kinsmen in the South. At their best, like David Walker, they wanted the body of black people to be one in freedom and self-determination. Even on the most selfish levels of the struggle, they knew that their own ultimate freedom depended upon freeing the black people in the South.

Although black abolitionists often used the rhetoric of the times, for tactical purposes as much as any other, the vindication of America was at best a secondary cause on their agenda. Instead the freedom, dignity, and self-determination of black people were central to the struggle. . . .

The significance of the differences between the black and white antislavery workers became most apparent when members of the two groups faced each other in common tasks in the North. Many of the black abolitionists had been captives in the South, had made the courageous inner break with the system of white domination, and now presented something other than the popular image of the humble, grateful slave. Because many of the white abolitionists usually had no desire to know—in the best sense of the word—a truly free black man or woman, tensions and conflicts inevitably developed between them. Since many white abolitionists assumed that they were to be the saviors of the American society and its black underclass, they often treated their black coworkers with patronizing disdain at worst (or was awestruck idolatry the worst?), or at best as almost equal but clearly subservient allies of their white-defined cause.

Martin Delany, an occasional black participant in the early biracial abolitionist partnership, was one of its most perceptive critics. He not only saw the dangers of black dependence on whites for freedom work which only blacks could do, but also, in those areas where whites could make legitimate contributions in the North, found whites a source of constant disappointment. As he reviewed his own involvement in this black-white movement, Delany pointed especially to two shattered hopes: that of equality with whites in the abolitionist organizations that these whites controlled; and that of equitable treatment and hiring in the businesses owned and managed by many of these same white allies. In both situations, said Delany, "we find ourselves occupying the very same position in relation to our Anti-Slavery friends, as we do in relation to the pro-slavery part of the community—a mere secondary, underling position, in all our relations to them, and anything more than this, is not a matter of course affair—it comes not by established anti-slavery custom or right, but . . . by mere suffrance."

This was typical of the black experience with the Northern white abolitionist forces. It was a reminder not only of the complex ideological roots of a Martin Delany, but of white abolitionism's inability to deal with many black problems in the North. An abolitionism that was unclear about its own relationship to electoral politics found it hard to fight against the black disfranchisement which was sweeping the North at the time. An abolitionism deeply entrenched in the burgeoning capitalism of white America did not force the issue of economic exploitation and discrimination against blacks in the North. A middle-class, largely professional and mercantile white move-ment had little access to the white working class, and almost no leverage against its antiblack attitudes and actions. Men and women who were not prepared to examine closely the nature of their own deep fears and conflicts concerning black people could not easily deal with the irrational elements which surfaced in the responses of their fellow whites. A movement affirming the white-dominated origins and destiny of America was not easily stirred to consider the meaning of full black participation in the present. Moreover, those who believed in white-defined Canaans and white-controlled Kingdoms of God often backed away from the implications of an independent, self-affirming black presence in either. So the making of slaves went on in the most unexpected places in the North.

Of course, even with the best intentions and attitudes—and white anti-slavery leaders like William Lloyd Garrison, Theodore Dwight Weld, and James G. Birney often possessed both—no one in the late 1830s could forget two central realities in the struggle: not only were the white abolitionists developing deep divisions among themselves, but within white society they constituted a small and routinely despised minority. Unlike their black co-workers, they were not part of the mainstream aspirations of their own community. On many levels, then, these white allies could be considered a burden, adding to the problems of black people in the North; even in their most helpful manifestations, they were themselves a beleaguered justice-seeking minority whose real influence is still questionable. In a sense, their most important role was as a signal of the problems black struggle would continue to face when it was allied with white men and women whose first, overarching commitment was not to black freedom, but to the past and future of white America. By the end of the 1830s, black men and women in the abolitionist movement felt these vibrations deeply even as they preached, lectured, organized, wrote, and engaged in civil disobedience at the side of their white allies. . . .

The Proslavery Argument

DREW GILPIN FAUST

. . . In the century that has followed Appomattox, historians have debated the sources and meaning of the slavery agitation nearly as vigorously as early nineteenth-century Americans argued about human bondage itself. But a disproportionate amount of this scholarly attention has been devoted to antislavery movements and ideologies. Whereas studies of abolitionism have established it as both a product and an index of fundamental aspects of nineteenth-century culture, historical treatment of proslavery has emphasized its aberrant qualities, identifying it as the evanescent product of the unique

Reprinted by permission of Louisiana State University Press from *The Ideology of Slavery: Proslavery Thought in the Old South, 1830–1860* edited by Drew Gilpin Faust, pp. 1–14. Copyright © 1981 by Louisiana State University Press.

civilization that flourished in the South during the last three decades before
the Civil War. . . .

In recent years, however, interpretations of proslavery thought have
shifted. Perhaps more accustomed to the notion of a timeless and geographically extensive American racism, scholars have began to place proslavery
within a wider context, to regard it as more than simply a distasteful manifestation of a collective paranoia gripping the South in the years before the
Civil War. Historians have come to view the proslavery argument less as
evidence of moral failure and more as a key to wider patterns of beliefs and
values. The defense of human bondage, they recognize, was perhaps more
important as an effort to construct a coherent southern social philosophy
than as a political weapon of short-lived usefulness during the height of
sectional conflict. In defending what they repeatedly referred to as the "cornerstone" of their social order, slavery's apologists were offering posterity
an unusual opportunity to examine the world view of articulate southerners,
their sources of social legitimation, and their self-conscious definition of
themselves. Slavery became a vehicle for the discussion of fundamental social
issues—the meaning of natural law, the conflicting desires for freedom and
order, the relationship between tradition and progress, the respective roles
of liberty and equality, dependence and autonomy. "The question of negro
slavery," one apologist recognized in 1856, "is implicated with all the great
social problems of the current age." Addressing topics of deepest import to
Americans North and South, the proslavery argument embodied the South's
particular perspective on those philosophical, moral, and social dilemmas
confronting the nation as a whole. "Proslavery thought," as one recent
scholar has remarked, "was nothing more or less than thought about
society." . . .

Although proslavery thought demonstrated remarkable consistency from
the seventeenth century on, it became in the South of the 1830s, forties,
and fifties more systematic and self-conscious; it took on the characteristics
of a formal ideology with its resulting social movement. The intensification
of proslavery argumentation produced an increase in conceptual organization
and coherence within the treatises themselves, which sought methodically
to enumerate all possible foundations for human bondage—"a *discussion
on Slavery in all its bearings,*" as one southern apologist explained, "in the
lights of History, Political Economy, Moral Philosophy, Political Science,
Theology, Social Life, Ethnology and International Law." At the same time,
more structured arrangements developed among the apologists and their
publishers for the production and distribution of these tracts. Southerners
united to call upon the region's finest minds for defenses of slavery, to
discuss with one another the appropriate contents and goals for their writings,
and to arrange their wide dissemination in newspapers, pamphlets, and even
book-sized collections of previously printed favorites. One publisher explained his intention of producing an anthology of arguments on fine paper
"fit to take its place in the Library or Drawing Room, and to serve as a
Text Book on the subject, so that every one in our community may have
at hand good strong arguments . . . coming in a respectable shape and in

good style it will attract much more attention than if simply sent in pamphlet form." The need for a vigorous southern publishing industry became particularly obvious as a result of these efforts to diffuse proslavery views, and the defense of the peculiar institution had an important impact upon southern letters. "We shall be indebted," one southern intellectual and proslavery essayist proclaimed, "to the continuance and asperity of this controversy for the creation of a genuine Southern literature. . . . For out of this slavery agitation has sprung not merely essays on slavery, valuable and suggestive as these have been, but also the literary activity, and the literary movement which have lately characterized the intellect of the South."

Whereas earlier proslavery writers had attracted little attention, the South now rewarded her defenders with acclaim. Francis Lieber, a German emigré with little sympathy for the peculiar institution of his adopted South, remarked bitterly that "nothing would give me greater renown than a pamphlet written . . . in favor of slavery." After a long and unrewarding career as an agricultural essayist, Edmund Ruffin found that "I have had more notice taken of my late pamphlet [on slavery] than of anything I ever wrote before."

Current scholarship regards the change in southern writings about slavery in the 1830s as more one of style and tone than of substance. Southerners did not move from an anti- to a proslavery position. Slaveholders were less troubled about *whether* slavery was right than precisely *why* it was right and how its justice could best be demonstrated. Unsympathetic to the Perfectionism embraced by many of their abolitionist counterparts, proslavery advocates always saw evils in slavery, as they were sure they would in any terrestrial system of society and government. All earthly arrangements, they believed, necessarily required men to cope as best they could with sin; it was the relative merits of social systems, their comparative success in dealing with inherent evil, that should be discussed. As William Harper explained in his *Memoir on Slavery*, "the condition of our whole existence is but to struggle with evils—to compare them—to choose between them, and so far as we can, to mitigate them. To say that there is evil in any institution, is only to say that it is human." With the intensification of the slavery controversy, however, apologists began to acknowledge the institution's shortcomings less openly and to consider only the positive aspects of the system. "I see great evils in slavery," George Fitzhugh confessed to a friend, "but I think in a controversial work I ought not to admit them."

Antebellum southerners themselves recognized and justified their heightened involvement in slavery's defense in the years after 1830. In spite of "speculative doubts by which the slave-owners were troubled," a Virginian observed in 1856, "the general sentiment among them . . . had always tenaciously maintained the sanctity and inviolability of slavery, but they have not arrived at a clear comprehension of the reasons by which slavery is justified and proved to be right and expedient, without the aid of the . . . treatises which the controversy still raging has called forth." Southerners, Mississippian Henry Hughes agreed, could successfully defend slavery only when they learned "to give the reasons for it." "Few of our own people," a South Carolinian advocate similarly complained, "understand it in its philosophical and economical bearing." These explanations suggest, as historian Ralph Morrow argued in 1961, that proslavery writings were directed primarily at other southerners. "We think it hardly to be expected," one apologist candidly admitted in 1843, "that anything which can be said at this late date will at all diminish the wrongheaded fanaticism and perverse intolerance of the Northern abolitionists." Northern antislavery had progressed "past the cure of argument."

Many scholars have long acknowledged Thomas Roderick Dew's *Review of the Debate in the Virginia Legislature* as a herald of this new post-1830 era in proslavery ideology. Prompted by legislative discussion of emancipation in the winter of 1831–32, Dew's essay sought to establish the impracticality of the antislavery sentiments that had swept the state after Nat Turner's slave uprising left more than sixty whites dead in Virginia's Southside. Dew himself proclaimed his argument to be a new departure in proslavery writing, and his pragmatic tone was to serve as the inspiration for the inductive mode of almost all proslavery tracts henceforth. Rejecting the deductive principles of the Lockean contractual social theory that had influenced the Founding Fathers, Dew embraced the conservative organic view of social order that had been implicit in proslavery thought from its earliest beginnings. Social institutions and arrangements evolved slowly over time, he believed, and could not be beneficially altered by abrupt human intervention. Like the proslavery advocates that followed him, Dew called upon his audience to study society as it had existed through the ages and to derive social principles and bases for action from these empirical observations. Theoretical notions of equality could not controvert the striking differences in men's capacities evident to any impartial observer. Idealized conceptions of justice—such as those of the abolitionists—could never serve as reliable bases for social organization. It was all very well, Dew counseled his fellow Virginians, to admit the abstract evils of slavery, but the relative dangers of the alternatives—abolition with or without colonization—were far greater.

Dew called upon southerners to recognize the implications of their own social order and to assume responsibility for it. "One generation," as historian Eugene Genovese has remarked about the South in the years after the Revolution, "might be able to oppose slavery and favor everything it made possible, but the next had to choose sides." Dew was important because he demonstrated the implausibility of straddling the issue any longer, of maintaining the stance of relativism that many southerners had found so comfortable during the Revolutionary era and its aftermath. As antislavery sentiment began to strengthen in the years after the Missouri debates of 1818–20, it was impossible any longer to endeavor to reconcile the North to the existence of the peculiar institution by conceding slavery's shortcomings. Once the issue was joined, Dew proclaimed, the South must acknowledge her commitment to her way of life and come out firmly on the proslavery side; the South must recognize that her superficial flirtation with the Revolutionary ideology of liberty and equality could be no more than just that.

Although Dew inaugurated a new era in proslavery, a flood of defenses did not appear at once. Only when northern abolitionists in 1835 inundated the South with antislavery propaganda sent through the federal mails did southerners respond in force, exhibiting a new vehemence in their defenses of their way of life. The attack from the North made southern mobilization an immediate necessity, and latent proslavery feeling was quickly translated into action.

In the course of the next decade, slavery's apologists would, in their collective oeuvre, develop a comprehensive defense of the peculiar institution that invoked the most important sources of authority in their intellectual culture and associated slavery with the fundamental values of their civilization. Their specific arguments showed striking continuity with earlier proslavery positions, elaborating rather than contradicting existing writing. The defenses of slavery of this period were, in addition, remarkably consistent with one another. While one advocate might specialize in religious arguments and another in the details of political economy, most acknowledged, accepted, and sometimes repeated the conclusions of their fellow apologists. The high level of conformity within proslavery thought was not accidental. Consistency was seen as the mark of strength and the emblem of truth. "Earlier and later writers," the editor of a collection of proslavery classics remarked proudly in 1860, "stood on substantially the same ground, and take the same general views of the institution."

To ensure this uniformity, slavery's apologists articulated a series of what we might regard as rules guiding the post-1835 proslavery movement. Endeavoring to avoid the "domain of sectional controversy and political warfare," the defenders of slavery sought broader arguments and wider appeal. Basing their essays in "sober and cautious reflection" upon "purely scientific principles" with "no appeal to passion or to sordid interest," the South's proslavery theorists hoped to attract those who "wished for argument instead of abuse." Many of the South's apologists communicated with one another about their essays and ideas, so that the mature proslavery argument might well be seen as a community product.

As a result of this group criticism and evaluation, there emerged what could be considered a proslavery mainstream. The Bible served as the core of this defense. In the face of abolitionist claims that slavery violated the principles of Christianity, southerners demonstrated with ever more elaborate detail that both Old and New Testaments sanctioned human bondage. God's Chosen People had been slaveholders; Christ had made no attack on the institution; his disciple Paul had demonstrated a commitment to maintaining it.

But for an age increasingly enamored of the vocabulary and methods of natural science, biblical guidance was not enough. The accepted foundations for truth were changing in European and American thought, as intellectuals sought to apply the rigor of science to the study of society and morality, as well as the natural world. The proslavery argument accordingly called not only upon divine revelation, the traditional source and arbiter of truth, but sought at the same time to embrace the positivistic standards increasingly accepted for the assessment of all social problems. Man could and must, these authors contended, determine his social and moral duties scientifically, through the examination of God's will revealed in nature and in history. A subspecies of general social thought, the defense of slavery assumed the methods and arguments of broader social theories and reflected an intellectual perspective that in these years first began to regard "social science" as a discrete and legitimate domain of human learning. Reverend Thornton Stringfellow would devise a proslavery theory designed to be at once "Scriptural and Statistical"; George Fitzhugh would write a *Sociology for the South;* Henry Hughes's proslavery tract would appear in the guise of *A Treatise on Sociology* in which the author's striving for relevance and legitimacy beyond the confines of the Old South even led him to replace the term *slavery* with that of *warranteeism.*

But most advocates did not go so far. Sociology was not yet the academic discipline it has since become; moral science—from which sociology would later emerge—still remained the central framework for social analysis in colleges and among the educated both North and South. Thus the mainstream of proslavery argument sought to imbed the peculiar institution within the legitimating context of nineteenth-century moral philosophy, with its emphasis on man's duties and responsibilities and its invocation of historical precedent as guide for future action.

Turning to the past as a catalog of social experiments, slavery's defenders discovered that from the time of Greece and Rome, human bondage had produced the world's greatest civilizations. The peculiar institution, they argued, was not so very peculiar, but had provided the social foundation for man's greatest achievements. Moreover, the experience of the ages showed the fundamental principles of the American Revolution to be sadly misguided. Social law as revealed in history demonstrated that men had not in reality been created equal and free, as Jefferson had asserted; this was a mistaken view arising from erroneous modes of abstract and deductive thought. Nature produced individuals strikingly unequal in both qualities and circumstances. "Scientific" truths demonstrated through empirical study prescribed a hierarchically structured society reproducing nature's orderly differentiations. The Revolutionary concepts of natural law were thus replaced by the tenets of social organicism; the prestige of modern science served to legitimate tradition and conservatism in a manner that held implications far wider than the boundaries of the slavery controversy.

Such an approach to social order stressed the importance of man's duties rather than his rights. And for rhetorical purposes, it was often the duties of masters, rather than those of slaves, that apologists chose to emphasize. Within the organic community of a slave society, they argued, the master could not ignore the human obligation to care for his bondsman. "Fed, clothed, protected," the slave was far better off, William J. Grayson proclaimed, than the northern factory worker whose employer had no interest in his health or even his survival. "Free but in name," northern laborers had liberty only to starve. As William Harper argued, there existed "some form of slavery in all ages and countries." It was always necessary, Abel

Upshur explained, "that one portion of mankind shall live upon the labor of another portion." Every civilization needed what James Henry Hammond dubbed a "mud-sill" class to do the menial labor of society. The southern system of human bondage, they argued, simply organized this interdependence and inequality in accordance with principles of morality and Christianity.

The humanitarian arrangements of slavery, the southerners proclaimed, contrasted favorably with the avaricious materialism of the "miscalled" free society of the North. Whereas the Yankees cared only about the wealth that their operatives might produce, southerners accepted costly responsibility for the human beings whom God had "entrusted" to them. A number of defenders even maintained, like Harper, that "slave labor can never be so cheap as what is called free labor." Nevertheless, Hammond piously advised, slavery's moral purposes dictated that "we must . . . content ourselves with . . . the consoling reflection that what is lost to us is gained to humanity." The proslavery argument asserted its opposition to the growing materialism of the age and offered the model of evangelical stewardship as the best representation of its labor system. The master was God's surrogate on earth; the southern system institutionalized the Christian duties of charity in the master and humility in the slave. "You have been chosen," Nathaniel Beverley Tucker declared to his fellow slaveholders, "as the instrument, in the hand of God, for accomplishing the great purpose of his benevolence." The nineteenth-century concern with philanthropy, defenders of slavery argued, was most successfully realized in the South's system of human bondage. Reflecting the lessons of human experience through the ages, as well as the prescriptions of both divine and natural order, slavery seemed unassailable. The truths of science, religion, and history united to offer proslavery southerners ready support for their position. . . .

⊞ F U R T H E R   R E A D I N G

Gebert H. Barnes, *The Antislavery Impulse, 1830–1844* (1933)
R. J. M. Blackett, *Building an Antislavery Wall: Black Americans in the Atlantic Antislavery Movement* (1983)
Robert M. Cover, *Justice Accused: Antislavery and the Judicial Process* (1975)
David Brion Davis, *From Homicide to Slavery: Studies in American Culture* (1986)
———, *Slavery and Human Freedom* (1984)
———, *The Problem of Slavery in the Age of Revolution, 1770–1823* (1975)
Carl N. Degler, *The Other South: Southern Dissenters in the Nineteenth Century* (1974)
Mertin L. Dillon, *The Abolitionists: The Growth of a Dissenting Minority* (1974)
David H. Donald, "The Proslavery Argument Reconsidered," *Journal of Southern History* 37 (1971), 3–18
Martin Duberman, ed., *The Antislavery Vanguard: New Essays on the Abolitionists* (1965)
Dwight L. Dumond, *Antislavery: The Crusade for Freedom* (1961)
Clement Eaton, *The Freedom-of-Thought Struggle in the Old South* (1940)
Drew Gilpin Faust, *A Sacred Circle: The Dilemma of the Intellectual in the Old South, 1840–1860* (1977)

Michael Feldberg, *The Turbulent Era: Riot and Disorder in Jacksonian America* (1980)

Louis Filler, *The Crusade Against Slavery, 1830–1860* (1960)

Lawrence J. Friedman, *Gregarious Saints: Self and Community in American Abolitionism, 1830–1870* (1982)

Eugene D. Genovese, *The World the Slaveholders Made* (1969)

Louis S. Gerteis, *Morality and Utility in American Antislavery Reform* (1987)

Aileen Kraditor, *Means and Ends in American Abolitionism: Garrison and His Critics on Strategy and Tactics, 1834–1850* (1969)

Gerda Lerner, *The Grimké Sisters from South Carolina: Rebels Against Slavery* (1967)

William S. McFeely, *Frederick Douglass* (1991)

John R. McKivigan, *The War Against Pro-Slavery Religion: Abolitionism and the Northern Churches, 1830–1865* (1984)

Edward Magdol, *The Antislavery Rank and File: A Social Profile of the Abolitionist Constituency* (1986)

Jane H. Pease and William H. Pease, *They Who Would Be Free: Blacks' Search for Freedom, 1830–1861* (1974)

Lewis Perry, *Radical Abolitionism: Anarchy and Government of God in Antislavery Thought* (1973)

Benjamin Quarles, *Black Abolitionists* (1969)

Lorman P. Ratner, *Powder Keg: Northern Opposition to the Antislavery Movement, 1831–1840* (1968)

Leonard L. Richards, *"Gentlemen of Property and Standing": Anti-Abolition Mobs in Jacksonian America* (1970)

P. J. Staudenraus, *The African Colonization Movement, 1816–1865* (1961)

James Brewer Stewart, *Holy Warriors: The Abolitionists and American Slavery* (1976)

John L. Thomas, *The Liberator: William Lloyd Garrison, A Biography* (1964)

Larry E. Tise, *Pro-Slavery: A History of the Defense of Slavery in America, 1701–1840* (1987)

Ronald G. Walters, *The Antislavery Appeal: American Abolitionism After 1830* (1977)

Bertram Wyatt-Brown, *Lewis Tappan and the Evangelical War Against Slavery* (1969)

Jean F. Yellin, *Women and Sisters: The Antislavery Feminists in American Culture* (1989)

The Bitter Fruits
of Manifest Destiny

⊞

In 1840 American politics seemed to have reached a rough equilibrium. The Whigs, having elected William Henry Harrison to the presidency, appeared capable of matching the Democrats nationwide. A balanced two-party system now, in principle, could debate the overlapping economic, cultural, and ethnic issues generated by the market revolution, without upsetting the political system as a whole. The only threat to that balance—the tiny antislavery Liberty party, formed after the political split within abolitionism—polled too few votes to be taken seriously by anyone who knew anything about American politics.

So much for the smart money. Over the next eight years, sectional strains cracked open, and the national parties began to splinter. Van Burenites accused southern Democrats of treachery; southern Whigs wondered what they were doing in the same party with some of their northern colleagues. Why all this bitterness? Fortune played its part in the drama—in the sudden death of President Harrison and the elevation of the crypto-Democrat John Tyler to the White House; in some chance events around the 1844 election that helped defeat Henry Clay and enhance southern control of the Democracy. But the deeper causes had to do with land and slavery.

In 1845 a Democratic journalist enthused over the march of U.S. westward settlement as proof of the nation's "Manifest Destiny" to occupy and improve the furthest reaches of the continent. Pursuit of that supposed destiny had sparked a diplomatic crisis with Britain over the Oregon border and would soon bring the annexation of Texas to the union. The latter would lead to a divisive war with Mexico and a widened conflict over the spread of slavery into the territories. The expansive impulses that assured so many Americans of the country's lasting greatness imploded with terrific force. Sectional realignments in politics took a fresh turn in 1848, with the rise of a more formidable antislavery alliance, the sectional Free Soil party, which joined the Conscience Whigs and Barnburner Democrats to the old Liberty party base. Elsewhere—in their churches, secular voluntary associations, and literary salons—Americans tasted the bitter fruits of Manifest Destiny and reconsidered the republic's future.

The battles of the 1840s brought to a head virtually all of the contradictory

*developments of the previous half-century. Even today they touch a raw nerve.
Did Manifest Destiny contain some larger, noble aims, as many historians contend? Was it primarily directed at achieving more concrete, material goals, perceived by those who counted as being in the national interest? Was it merely a
gloss on racist anxieties and imperial ambitions? What did the struggles of the
1840s say about American democracy sixty years after the ratification of the federal Constitution? What did the nation's stresses and strains presage?*

✣ D O C U M E N T S

The Democrat John L. O'Sullivan edited *The United States Magazine and Democratic Review,* easily the most distinguished periodical ever published on behalf of
a major U.S. political party. (O'Sullivan's contributors included Nathaniel Hawthorne, Henry David Thoreau, Walt Whitman, Edgar Allen Poe, and many other
notables.) In many ways the *Review* stood at the more radical end of the Democracy—and beginning in the late 1830s, it was also a loud proponent for territorial
expansion. The first documentary selection, originally published at the climax of
the Texas annexation debate, contains O'Sullivan's coining of the immortal slogan
"Manifest Destiny" and spells out something of its meaning. A year later, President James K. Polk issued his war message (document two), signaling the start of
hostilities with Mexico.

The war with Mexico was the country's first to be fought wholly outside its
own borders. It was also the first to get reported and celebrated by a burgeoning
commercial culture of cheap paperbound books, penny newspapers, and nationally
known entertainers. George Washington Dixon was one of the country's most
popular blackface minstrels, famous chiefly for his character Zip Coon. He first
performed "On Our Way to Rio Grande" (selection three) at a mass prowar rally
in New York; the original ran to about one hundred verses. *Incidents and Sufferings in the Mexican War,* whose cover is reprinted in the third selection, exemplified a genre that would later culminate, commercially and artistically, in the dime
novel.

Not everyone joined in the enthusiasm. The liberal Mexican intellectual Carlos María de Bustamente had greatly admired the American democracy, only to
turn sour—a change of heart shared by many Mexicans. The original Bernal Díaz
del Castillo was a chronicler of the Spanish conquest of the Aztecs; the reference
to him in the fourth selection is ironic. Meanwhile, many northerners grew anxious at the war's course. In 1846 David Wilmot, a Pennsylvania Democrat, introduced his famous proviso (document five) to an appropriations bill and turned the
war debate into a sectional fracas. Northern abolitionists, among them Frederick
Douglass and James Russell Lowell, never doubted that the war was a slaveholder's aggression, as the two-part sixth selection reveals. A Brooklyn Democratic
newspaper editor, then known as Walter Whitman, followed a different progress;
enthusiastic about the war when it began, he grew more concerned as the debates
over Wilmot's Proviso continued, as the seventh, two-part selection reveals. By
1847 all these sectional voices had joined those of northern Whigs such as Senator
Charles Sumner of Massachusetts (document eight), who, like the abolitionists,
had opposed the war from the start.

Actually, the northern antiwar writings left serious misimpressions. Although
many southerners (especially in the Southwest) were enthusiastic hawks—some of
whom wanted to conquer all Mexico—others (especially in the Southeast) were

dubious, on political as well as economic grounds. Among the skeptical was Senator John C. Calhoun, who after fighting for Texas annexation did his best to restrain the Polk administration. Only after Wilmot introduced his proviso did Calhoun and his allies change their emphasis, responding to what they saw as an unprovoked political assault by Yankee sectionalists. Calhoun's speech in February 1847, excerpted in the ninth document, spelled out the southern case. The party platforms from the following year's presidential campaign, reprinted in the final, three-part selection, left little doubt about the state of American politics. The Whig document, tellingly, was really no platform at all but a vague, evasive declaration of principles, drawn up after the party convention had completed its main business—nominating the ultimately successful Zachary Taylor.

John L. O'Sullivan on Texas Annexation and Manifest Destiny, 1845

Texas is now ours. Already, before these words are written, her Convention has undoubtedly ratified the acceptance, by her Congress, of our proffered invitation into the Union; and made the requisite changes in her already republican form of constitution to adapt it to its future federal relations. Her star and her stripe may already be said to have taken their place in the glorious blazon of our common nationality; and the sweep of our eagle's wing already includes within its circuit the wide extent of her fair and fertile land. . . .

Why, were other reasoning wanting, in favor of now elevating this question of the reception of Texas into the Union, out of the lower region of our past party dissensions, up to its proper level of a high and broad nationality, it surely is to be found, found abundantly, in the manner in which other nations have undertaken to intrude themselves into it, between us and the proper parties to the case, in a spirit of hostile interference against us, for the avowed object of thwarting our policy and hampering our power, limiting our greatness and checking the fulfilment of our manifest destiny to overspread the continent allotted by Providence for the free development of our yearly multiplying millions. This we have seen done by England, our old rival and enemy; and by France, strangely coupled with her against us, under the influence of the Anglicism strongly tinging the policy of her present prime minister, Guizot. The zealous activity with which this effort to defeat us was pushed by the representatives of those governments, together with the character of intrigue accompanying it, fully constituted that case of foreign interference, which Mr. Clay himself declared should, and would unite us all in maintaining the common cause of our country against the foreigner and the foe. . . .

It is wholly untrue, and unjust to ourselves, the pretence that the Annexation has been a measure of spoliation, unrightful and unrighteous—of military conquest under forms of peace and law—of territorial aggrandizement at the expense of justice, and justice due by a double sanctity to the weak. . . . The independence of Texas was complete and absolute. It was an independence, not only in fact, but of right. No obligation of duty towards

Mexico tended in the least degree to restrain our right to effect the desired recovery of the fair province once our own—whatever motives of policy might have prompted a more deferential consideration of her feelings and her pride, as involved in the question. If Texas became peopled with an American population, it was by no contrivance of our government, but on the express invitation of that of Mexico herself; accompanied with such guaranties of State independence, and the maintenance of a federal system analogous to our own, as constituted a compact fully justifying the strongest measures of redress on the part of those afterwards deceived in this guaranty, and sought to be enslaved under the yoke imposed by its violation. She was released, rightfully and absolutely released, from all Mexican allegiance, or duty of cohesion to the Mexican political body, by the acts and fault of Mexico herself, and Mexico alone. There never was a clearer case. It was not revolution; it was resistance to revolution: and resistance under such circumstances as left independence the necessary resulting state, caused by the abandonment of those with whom her former federal association had existed. What then can be more preposterous than all this clamor by Mexico and the Mexican interest, against Annexation, as a violation of any rights of hers, any duties of ours? . . .

Nor is there any just foundation for the charge that Annexation is a great pro-slavery measure—calculated to increase and perpetuate that institution. Slavery had nothing to do with it. Opinions were and are greatly divided, both at the North and South, as to the influence to be exerted by it on Slavery and the Slave States. That it will tend to facilitate and hasten the disappearance of Slavery from all the northern tier of the present Slave States, cannot surely admit of serious question. The greater value in Texas of the slave labor now employed in those States, must soon produce the effect of draining off that labor southwardly, by the same unvarying law that bids water descend the slope that invites it. Every new Slave State in Texas will make at least one Free State from among those in which that institution now exists—to say nothing of those portions of Texas on which slavery cannot spring and grow—to say nothing of the far more rapid growth of new States in the free West and North-west, as these fine regions are overspread by the emigration fast flowing over them from Europe, as well as from the Northern and Eastern States of the Union as it exists. On the other hand, it is undeniably much gained for the cause of the eventual voluntary abolition of slavery; that it should have been thus drained off towards the only outlet which appeared to furnish much probability of the ultimate disappearance of the negro race from our borders. The Spanish-Indian-American populations of Mexico, Central America and South America, afford the only receptacle capable of absorbing that race whenever we shall be prepared to slough it off—to emancipate it from slavery, and (simultaneously necessary) to remove it from the midst of our own. Themselves already of mixed and confused blood, and free from the "prejudices" which among us so insuperably forbid the social amalgamation which can alone elevate the Negro race out of a virtually servile degradation, even though legally free, the regions occupied by those populations must strongly attract the black race in that direction; and as soon as the destined hour of emancipation shall arrive, will relieve the question of one of its worst difficulties, if not absolutely the greatest. . . .

In respect to the institution of slavery itself, we have not designed, in what has been said above, to express any judgment of its merits or demerits, *pro* or *con*. National in its character and aims, this Review abstains from the discussion of a topic pregnant with embarrassment and danger—intricate and double-sided—exciting and embittering—and necessarily excluded from a work circulating equally in the South as in the North. It is unquestionably one of the most difficult of the various social problems which at the present day so deeply agitate the thoughts of the civilized world. Is the negro race, or is it not, of equal attributes and capacities with our own? Can they, on a large scale, co-exist side by side in the same country on a footing of civil and social equality with the white race? In a free competition of labor with the latter, will they or will they not be ground down to a degradation and misery worse than slavery? When we view the condition of the operative masses of the population in England and other European countries, and feel all the difficulties of the great problem, of the distribution of the fruits of production between capital, skill, and labor, can our confidence be undoubting that in the present condition of society, the conferring of sudden freedom upon our negro race would be a boon to be grateful for? Is it certain that competitive wages are very much better, for a race so situated, than guarantied support and protection? Until a still deeper problem shall have been solved than that of slavery, the slavery of an inferior to a superior race—a relation reciprocal in certain important duties and obligations—is it certain that the cause of true wisdom and philanthropy is not rather, for the present, to aim to meliorate that institution as it exists, to guard against its abuses, to mitigate its evils, to modify it when it may contravene sacred principles and rights of humanity, by prohibiting the separation of families, excessive severities, subjection to the licentiousness of mastership, &c.? Great as may be its present evils, is it certain that we would not plunge the unhappy Helot race which has been entailed upon us, into still greater ones, by surrendering their fate into the rash hands of those fanatic zealots of a single idea, who claim to be their special friends and champions? . . .

To all these, and the similar questions which spring out of any intelligent reflection on the subject, we attempt no answer. Strong as are our sympathies in behalf of liberty, universal liberty, in all applications of the principle not forbidden by great and manifest evils, we confess ourselves not prepared with any satisfactory solution to the great problem of which these questions present various aspects. Far from us to say that either of the antagonist fanaticisms to be found on either side of the Potomac is right. . . . With no friendship for slavery, though unprepared to excommunicate to eternal damnation, with bell, book, and candle, those who are, we see nothing in the bearing of the Annexation of Texas on that institution to awaken a doubt of the wisdom of that measure, or a compunction for the humble part contributed by us towards its consummation.

California will, probably, next fall away from the loose adhesion which, in such a country as Mexico, holds a remote province in a slight equivocal kind of dependence on the metropolis. Imbecile and distracted, Mexico never can exert any real governmental authority over such a country. The impotence of the one and the distance of the other, must make the relation one of virtual independence; unless, by stunting the province of all natural growth, and forbidding that immigration which can alone develope its capabilities and fulfil the purposes of its creation, tyranny may retain a military dominion, which is no government in the legitimate sense of the term. In the case of California this is now impossible. The Anglo-Saxon foot is already on its borders. Already the advance guard of the irresistible army of Anglo-Saxon emigration has begun to pour down upon it, armed with the plough and the rifle, and marking its trail with schools and colleges, courts and representative halls, mills and meeting-houses. A population will soon be in actual occupation of California, over which it will be idle for Mexico to dream of dominion. They will necessarily become independent. All this without agency of our government, without responsibility of our people— in the natural flow of events, the spontaneous working of principles, and the adaptation of the tendencies and wants of the human race to the elemental circumstances in the midst of which they find themselves placed. And they will have a right to independence—to self-government—to the possession of the homes conquered from the wilderness by their own labors and dangers, sufferings and sacrifices—a better and a truer right than the artificial title of sovereignty in Mexico, a thousand miles distant, inheriting from Spain a title good only against those who have none better. Their right to independence will be the natural right of self-government belonging to any community strong enough to maintain it—distinct in position, origin and character, and free from any mutual obligations of membership of a common political body, binding it to others by the duty of loyalty and compact of public faith. . . .

President James K. Polk's War Message, 1846

The existing state of the relations between the United States and Mexico renders it proper that I should bring the subject to the consideration of Congress. . . .

The strong desire to establish peace with Mexico on liberal and honorable terms, and the readiness of this Government to regulate and adjust our boundary and other causes of difference with that power on such fair and equitable principles as would lead to permanent relations of the most friendly nature, induced me in September last to seek the reopening of diplomatic relations between the two countries. . . . An envoy of the United States repaired to Mexico with full powers to adjust every existing difference. But though present on the Mexican soil by agreement between the two Governments, invested with full powers, and bearing evidence of the most friendly dispositions, his mission has been unavailing. The Mexican Government not only refused to receive him or listen to his propositions, but after a long-continued series of menaces have at last invaded our territory and shed the blood of our fellow-citizens on our own soil.

It now becomes my duty to state more in detail the origin, progress, and failure of that mission. In pursuance of the instructions given in September last, an inquiry was made on the 13th of October, 1845, in the most friendly terms, through our consul in Mexico, of the minister for foreign affairs, whether the Mexican Government "would receive an envoy from the United States intrusted with full powers to adjust all the questions in dispute between the two Governments," with the assurance that "should the answer be in the affirmative such an envoy would be immediately dispatched to Mexico." The Mexican minister on the 15th of October gave an affirmative answer to this inquiry. . . . On the 10th of November, 1845, Mr. John Slidell, of Louisiana, was commissioned by me as envoy extraordinary and minister plenipotentiary of the United States to Mexico, and was intrusted with full powers to adjust both the questions of the Texas boundary and of indemnification to our citizens. The redress of the wrongs of our citizens naturally and inseparably blended itself with the question of boundary. The settlement of the one question in any correct view of the subject involves that of the other. I could not for a moment entertain the idea that the claims of our much-injured and long-suffering citizens, many of which had existed for more than twenty years, should be postponed or separated from the settlement of the boundary question.

Mr. Slidell arrived at Vera Cruz on the 30th of November, and was courteously received by the authorities of that city. But the Government of General Herrera was then tottering to its fall. The revolutionary party had seized upon the Texas question to effect or hasten its overthrow. Its determination to restore friendly relations with the United States, and to receive our minister to negotiate for the settlement of this question, was violently assailed, and was made the great theme of denunciation against it. The Government of General Herrera, there is good reason to believe, was sincerely desirous to receive our minister; but it yielded to the storm raised by its enemies, and on the 21st of December refused to accredit Mr. Slidell upon the most frivolous pretexts. These are so fully and ably exposed in the note of Mr. Slidell of the 24th of December last to the Mexican minister of foreign relations, herewith transmitted, that I deem it unnecessary to enter into further detail on this portion of the subject.

Five days after the date of Mr. Slidell's note General Herrera yielded the Government to General Paredes without a struggle, and on the 30th of December resigned the Presidency. This revolution was accomplished solely by the army, the people having taken little part in the contest; and thus the supreme power in Mexico passed into the hands of a military leader.

Determined to leave no effort untried to effect an amicable adjustment with Mexico, I directed Mr. Slidell to present his credentials to the Government of General Paredes and ask to be officially received by him. There would have been less ground for taking this step had General Paredes come into power by a regular constitutional succession. In that event his administration would have been considered but a mere constitutional continuance of the Government of General Herrera, and the refusal of the latter to receive our minister would have been deemed conclusive unless an intimation had been given by General Paredes of his desire to reverse the decision of his predecessor. But the Government of General Paredes owes its existence to a military revolution, by which the subsisting constitutional authorities had been subverted. The form of government was entirely changed, as well as all the high functionaries by whom it was administered.

Under these circumstances Mr. Slidell, in obedience to my direction, addressed a note to the Mexican minister of foreign relations, under date of the 1st of March last, asking to be received by that Government in the diplomatic character to which he had been appointed. This minister in his reply, under date of the 12th of March, reiterated the arguments of his predecessor, and in terms that may be considered as giving just grounds of offense to the Government and people of the United States denied the application of Mr. Slidell. Nothing therefore remained for our envoy but to demand his passports and return to his own country.

Thus the Government of Mexico, though solemnly pledged by official acts in October last to receive and accredit an American envoy, violated their plighted faith and refused the offer of a peaceful adjustment of our difficulties. Not only was the offer rejected, but the indignity of its rejection was enhanced by the manifest breach of faith in refusing to admit the envoy who came because they had bound themselves to receive him. Nor can it be said that the offer was fruitless from the want of opportunity of discussing it; our envoy was present on their own soil. Nor can it be ascribed to a want of sufficient powers; our envoy had full powers to adjust every question of difference. Nor was there room for complaint that our propositions for settlement were unreasonable; permission was not even given our envoy to make any proposition whatever. Nor can it be objected that we, on our part, would not listen to any reasonable terms of their suggestion; the Mexican Government refused all negotiation, and have made no proposition of any kind.

In my message at the commencement of the present session I informed you that upon the earnest appeal both of the Congress and convention of Texas I had ordered an efficient military force to take a position "between the Nueces and the Del Norte." This had become necessary to meet a threatened invasion of Texas by the Mexican forces, for which extensive military preparations had been made. The invasion was threatened solely because Texas had determined, in accordance with a solemn resolution of the Congress of the United States, to annex herself to our Union, and under these circumstances it was plainly our duty to extend our protection over her citizens and soil.

This force was concentrated at Corpus Christi, and remained there until after I had received such information from Mexico as rendered it probable, if not certain, that the Mexican Government would refuse to receive our envoy.

Meantime Texas, by the final action of our Congress, had become an integral part of our Union. The Congress of Texas, by its act of December

19, 1836, had declared the Rio del Norte to be the boundary of that Republic. Its jurisdiction had been extended and exercised beyond the Nueces. The country between that river and the Del Norte had been represented in the Congress and in the convention of Texas, had thus taken part in the act of annexation itself, and is now included within one of our Congressional districts. Our own Congress had, moreover, with great unanimity, by the act approved December 31, 1845, recognized the country beyond the Nueces as a part of our territory by including it within our own revenue system, and a revenue officer to reside within that district has been appointed by and with the advice and consent of the Senate. It became, therefore, of urgent necessity to provide for the defense of that portion of our country. Accordingly, on the 13th of January last instructions were issued to the general in command of these troops to occupy the left bank of the Del Norte. This river, which is the southwestern boundary of the State of Texas, is an exposed frontier. From this quarter invasion was threatened; upon it and in its immediate vicinity, in the judgment of high military experience, are the proper stations for the protecting forces of the Government. In addition to this important consideration, several others occurred to induce this movement. Among these are the facilities afforded by the ports at Brazos Santiago and the mouth of the Del Norte for the reception of supplies by sea, the stronger and more healthful military positions, the convenience for obtaining a ready and a more abundant supply of provisions, water, fuel, and forage, and the advantages which are afforded by the Del Norte in forwarding supplies to such posts as may be established in the interior and upon the Indian frontier.

The movement of the troops to the Del Norte was made by the commanding general under positive instructions to abstain from all aggressive acts toward Mexico or Mexican citizens and to regard the relations between that Republic and the United States as peaceful unless she should declare war or commit acts of hostility indicative of a state of war. He was specially directed to protect private property and respect personal rights.

The Army moved from Corpus Christi on the 11th of March, and on the 28th of that month arrived on the left bank of the Del Norte opposite to Matamoras, where it encamped on a commanding position, which has since been strengthened by the erection of fieldworks. A depot has also been established at Point Isabel, near the Brazos Santiago, 30 miles in the rear of the encampment. The selection of his position was necessarily confided to the judgment of the general in command.

The Mexican forces at Matamoras assumed a belligerent attitude, and on the 12th of April General Ampudia, then in command, notified General Taylor to break up his camp within twenty-four hours and to retire beyond the Nueces River, and in the event of his failure to comply with these demands announced that arms, and arms alone, must decide the question. But no open act of hostility was committed until the 24th of April. On that day General Arista, who had succeeded to the command of the Mexican forces, communicated to General Taylor that "he considered hostilities commenced and should prosecute them." A party of dragoons of 63 men and officers were on the same day dispatched from the American camp up the Rio del Norte, on its left bank, to ascertain whether the Mexican troops had crossed or were preparing to cross the river, "became engaged with a large body of these troops, and after a short affair, in which some 16 were killed and wounded, appear to have been surrounded and compelled to surrender."

The grievous wrongs perpetrated by Mexico upon our citizens throughout a long period of years remain unredressed, and solemn treaties pledging her public faith for this redress have been disregarded. A government either unable or unwilling to enforce the execution of such treaties fails to perform one of its plainest duties.

Our commerce with Mexico has been almost annihilated. It was formerly highly beneficial to both nations, but our merchants have been deterred from prosecuting it by the system of outrage and extortion which the Mexican authorities have pursued against them, whilst their appeals through their own Government for indemnity have been made in vain. Our forbearance has gone to such an extreme as to be mistaken in its character. Had we acted with vigor in repelling the insults and redressing the injuries inflicted by Mexico at the commencement, we should doubtless have escaped all the difficulties in which we are now involved.

Instead of this, however, we have been exerting our best efforts to propitiate her good will. Upon the pretext that Texas, a nation as independent as herself, thought proper to unite its destinies with our own she has affected to believe that we have severed her rightful territory, and in official proclamations and manifestoes has repeatedly threatened to make war upon us for the purpose of reconquering Texas. In the meantime we have tried every effort at reconciliation. The cup of forbearance had been exhausted even before the recent information from the frontier of the Del Norte. But now, after reiterated menaces, Mexico has passed the boundary of the United States, has invaded our territory and shed American blood upon the American soil. She has proclaimed that hostilities have commenced, and that the two nations are now at war.

As war exists, and, notwithstanding all our efforts to avoid it, exists by the act of Mexico herself, we are called upon by every consideration of duty and patriotism to vindicate with decision the honor, the rights, and the interests of our country.

Expressions of War Fever, 1846, 1847

War Minstrelsy, 1846

"On Our Way to Rio Grande"
by George Washington Dixon
To the tune: "Old Dan Tucker"

The Mexicans are on our soil
In war they wish us to embroil

They've tried their best and worst to vex us
By murdering our brave men in Texas
Chorus—We're on our way to Rio Grande
On our way to Rio Grande
On our way to Rio Grande
And with arms they'll find us handy

We are the boys who fear no noise
We'll leave behind us all our joys
To punish them half savage scamps
Who've slain our brethren in their camps
The God of War, the mighty Mars
Has smiled upon our stripes and stars
And spite of any ugly rumors
We'll vanquish all the Montezumas
We're on our way to Matamoros
On our way to Matamoros
On our way to Matamoros
And we'll conquer all before us!

War Stories, 1847

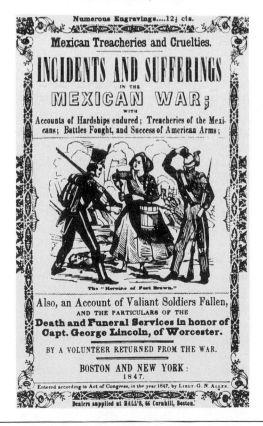

Cover of *Incidents and Sufferings in the Mexican War,* one of numerous inexpensive paperbound accounts of the fighting for the readers back home.

A Mexican View of the War, 1848

The New Bernal Díaz del Castillo

It is difficult to write with sincerity and impartiality about the great events that have been happening here when, aside from the factions which convulse the citizenry and disturb the inner peace of families, these same families find themselves infiltrated by an espionage that aims its fire from within private society, covering itself with a hypocritical mask, which, when it falls, has already produced the ruin of a family. Such is the position in which Mexicans find themselves today. Their natural enemies are the officers and soldiers of the North American army which dominates them through martial law, but also their enemies are the ungrateful foreigners of other nations whose only desire is the gold from our mines. Enemies too are the horde of citizens who have acted as guides to the American army. As legitimate descendants of the ancient Tlaxcalans, they glory in their immorality and maintain the same hatred as did those who aided in the taking of Mexico City while in the service of Hernan Cortés. . . . Such is the position in which he, who now aspires to write this history, finds himself. *Nevertheless,* he will do it, because truth prevails over terrorism and imposture. Truth is for all times; it is from God, and not even the Lord himself can make what really happened cease from having happened. . . .

The complaints of Mexico against the United States before the annexation of Texas are the following:

The introduction of troops from the United States army in the course of Mexico's campaign in Texas. A considerable number of cavalry under General Gaines crossed the Sabine. This was protested by our minister in Washington. The public enlistment and military equipping of troops, which has been done on various occasions in the port city of New Orleans, in order to invade Mexico through Texas and other points, despite the fact that the United States maintained diplomatic relations with Mexico and the guarantees of treaties of peace and commerce remained in force. This also has been the subject of altercations between the two governments. Mexico has never had the forthrightness to ask of the United States that it lend its assistance against Texas, but Mexico certainly has had the right to demand of the United States that it maintain absolute neutrality. The above mentioned palpable actions demonstrate that the United States has not done so.

As for the recognition of the independence of Texas by other nations, there is nothing unusual in that. The various powers recognize de facto governments, but that in no way takes away from Mexico the right to recover, if it were possible, the territory which it had lost. The independence of Mexico was equally recognized by the European powers and by the United States itself, but nevertheless Spain did not recognize Mexico until a great deal of time had passed, and it made an attempt in the year 1829 to invade Mexico without opposition from any nation.

Excerpts from *The View from Chapultepec: Mexican Writers on the Mexican-American War* ed. by Cecil Robinson (Tucson: University of Arizona Press) 1989, pp. 58–59, 64–73.

Now, if Texas were to be considered strong and capable of backing up its declaration of independence, why did it attach itself to the United States? Why did it seek this method to get the United States to come to its support in Mexico? This is just one more proof that Texas cannot be compared to other nations, including the United States, that have declared their independence and by deed have been able to sustain it and triumph.

As for the annexation, the person who is writing this piece was in the United States when these events were happening and was a witness to the fact that the greater part of the press in the northern states clamored strongly against this step, calling those who belonged to the annexation party thieves and usurpers, and setting forth strong and well-founded reasons, which at this point I will not repeat in order to prevent this exposition from becoming too lengthy. If the wise and honorable Henry Clay had attained the seat of the presidency, would the annexation of Texas have come to pass? Certainly not. The bringing in of Texas was the result of the intrigues and machinations of the Loco Foco party, and that which is done by such a farcical group cannot be considered rational or just.

The question of annexation was much debated in the Senate, and only by one vote (I believe that of Mr. Benton) was the measure passed.

In the Texas Convention [which voted for annexation] the majority present consisted of persons from the Southern states, notably partisan, and the newspapers [presumably of the United States] published their names and inveighed against this intrigue.

Thus matters have arrived at the state in which they are now, because evil parties and evil men, of which there are as many in this country as in the United States, have operated according to their partisan tendencies and have not attended to the well-being and justice of both republics. Can you deny this, American citizens, if you are not blind? Will you not confess that Mexico has suffered more than any other nation? The act of annexation was the equivalent of taking away from Mexico a considerable part of its territory, which had, rightly or wrongly, carried on a dispute with Mexico, but in no way can a nation be construed as friendly which has mixed itself in this affair to the point that Mexico has been deprived of its rights. Did not our minister in Washington protest against the annexation? Did he not declare that it would be a hostile act which would merit a declaration of war? Who, then, provoked the war—Mexico which only defended itself and protested, or the United States which became aggressors and scorned Mexico, taking advantage of its weakness and of its internecine agitations.

The administration of General Herrera, which was in fact one of the best that the country has had and that history will in time do justice to, had arranged the affair in a satisfactory manner to the considerable advantage of both Mexico and the United States, because the administration, composed of illustrious people, looked forward to the future, considering questions not only in terms of politics but from the vantage point of humanity as a whole and in particular of this generation of Mexicans whose fate has been to suffer throughout the last thirty years the lashes and calamities of war. The dignity of the government demanded, in effect, that the [American] naval forces withdraw, which in fact they did. Was it the administration of General Herrera that broke its word? Surely not, and the U.S. commissioner [John Slidell] was not received because the administration had changed. In effect, a cowardly general without honor or patriotism [Mariano Paredes] turned his back to the enemy while at the same time proclaiming a war that he had no intention of waging. Thus, like the villain he was, he destroyed the most legitimate and most popular government that Mexico has had. But I ask: Was this a failure on the part of the nation? Can it be blamed for some of this? And I must answer: Did not the nation manifest in all possible ways its displeasure, to the point of overthrowing this intrusive and evil government? Does not that general pine away in exile, one which he imposed upon himself in order to escape the vengeance of the nation?

Up to this point things could still have been arranged through diplomatic channels, and the rights of Mexico could have been guaranteed by a treaty, but the Loco Foco party was absolutely determined that Mexico should not only suffer the loss of its territory but it should bear the shame and humiliation of having its territory torn from it by force of arms. The sending of troops into Mexican territory doomed all moderation, and Mexico was left with no other recourse but to engage in battle. The territory between the Nueces and Rio Grande rivers neither by fact nor by law could have belonged to Texas. Not by fact because it was not populated by Texans. For ten years there existed only one little ranch in Corpus Christi, inhabited by Mr. Kyney and Mr. Aubry [sic], who had served as double agents, having had dealings with the Texans and with various Mexican generals, using them for the purpose of carrying on contraband trade. Nor did this territory belong to Texas by law because all this coast, through a territorial division recognized by all the nation and by the Texas colonists themselves, has belonged to the state of Tamaulipas. Thus, from the point of view of the Mexican government, the occupying of Corpus Christi by troops of the United States amounted to the same thing as if they had occupied the port of Tampico. In every way it was a violation of all treaties, of friendly relations, and of good faith. I wish now that you would judge these events with a Mexican heart and would ask yourself: Which has been the aggressor country? What would your government have done in the controversy with England over the Maine border if that nation had brought in troops, large or small in number? Without any doubt your government would have declared war and would not have entertained any propositions put forth until the armed force had evacuated the territory.

The war began because there was no other course, and Mexico will always be able to present a serene front before the world and maintain its innocence despite whatever misfortunes might befall it. . . .

The events and future prospects of the present war are prejudicial for Mexico, but nonetheless so are they for the United States. Can there be a comparison between the domestic joys of illuminating the streets of the United States on the one hand and on the other of the immense waste of sacrificing peaceful Germans, Irishmen, and native-born Americans who might otherwise be tranquilly at home, enjoying the harvests of the fertile fields of the North? What peace of mind can the United States enjoy while invading and destroying a nation that far from having offended it has clasped it to its bosom as a brother? Could not the Americans have availed themselves, through peaceful means, of the gold and silver of Mexico? Do you believe that the American nation will not lose, even though it triumphs over us completely, in the poor repute that it will have deserved among the nations of Europe?

Mexico finds itself in this contest absolutely alone. Spain was helped by England, and the Duke of Wellington with a powerful army routed the hosts of Napoleon. The United States had General Lafayette and the fleets and armies of France. The most powerful nations of Europe gathered together to defeat Napoleon. Mexico is alone, but that does not matter, nor do the reverses which it has suffered as long as it maintains its constancy. That is what made the United States triumph in its war of independence, and that is what will make us triumph. I imagine that the American army will triumph over Mexico, but what will happen if it cannot find anybody to make peace with?

It is necessary that you keep these considerations in mind and that you be persuaded that Mexico will prefer ruin before treating for peace while enemy forces still remain on Mexican soil.

The lower classes of Mexico generally believe that you are heretics, barbarians, and bloody-minded types. That is an error like the one that persists in the United States where we are judged as being the same as barbarians. The educated people of the Mexican Republic that know your history and have traveled and lived in the North judge the country with a proper impartiality, respect your human and democratic institutions, appreciate the industrious character of the people, and rightfully admire a nation that in a short time has become powerful, but at the same time these Mexicans have become seriously alarmed about the future fate of Mexico as they remember certain tendencies which are proved by events in that nation's history.

Before the Americans began to advance, the French held Louisiana, Canada, and parts of the banks of the Mississippi. The French population, one might say, formed a strip that encircled the coastal area where the American colonies had established themselves.

What has happened to the French race? It has almost totally disappeared and has been supplanted by the English race, invaders by character and ambitious of possessing more territory than they need.

History records that in addition to the sword, gunfire, and the dagger, which they used against the Indians, they practiced the infernal device of introducing smallpox among them.

Did they not send police dogs against the Seminole Indians to destroy them? And finally uproot them from their Florida lands to transplant them on the remote banks of the Missouri?

As a strange anomaly in the freest country in the world, slaves are sold, and the most beautiful women in the world, some of them well educated and amiable, are looked down upon because they are quadroons and are therefore irremediably condemned to dishonor and prostitution.

Does the United States need Texas? Is it not true that fifteen or twenty million more inhabitants could fit into the territory of the Union? Once they have Texas, does not that seem enough? And they still want three more provinces and California? Does not the press of the United States daily vociferate that the country should acquire those territories? They talk to us of peace, and they take California. They talk to us of peace, and they send expeditions to New Mexico and Chihuahua. They talk to us of peace, and the troops of General Taylor, according to his own admission, commit atrocities in the provinces of the north.

Thinking men do not believe the same things as do the lower classes, but they entertain more serious and well-grounded fears and consider the possibility of an interminable and profound war between the races, a war in which Mexico cannot yield without evident danger to its independence. These considerations pose still more obstacles to the peace. . . .

The Wilmot Proviso, 1846

Provided, That, as an express and fundamental condition to the acquisition of any territory from the Republic of Mexico by the United States, by virtue of any treaty which may be negotiated between them, and to the use by the Executive of the moneys herein appropriated, neither slavery nor involuntary servitude shall ever exist in any part of said territory, except for crime, whereof the party shall first be duly convicted.

Abolitionist Views of the Mexican War, 1846, 1848

Frederick Douglass to the Lynn [Mass.] Anti-Slavery Sewing Circle, 1846

London, August 18, 1846

My Dear Friends:

. . . I confess I feel sad, and sick at heart, by the present posture of political affairs in the United States. The spirit of slavery reigns triumphant throughout all the land. Every step in the onward march of political events is marked with blood—innocent blood; shed, too, in the cause of slavery. The war with Mexico rages; the green earth is drenched with warm blood, oozing out from human hearts; the air is darkened with smoke; the heavens are shaken by the terrible roar of the cannon; the groans and cries of the wounded and dying disturb the ear of God. Yet how few in that land care one farthing for it, or will move one inch to arrest and remove the cause of this horrible state of things? I am sad; I am sick; the whole land is cursed, if not given over to destruction. Massachusetts, the brightest of every other state, is now but the tool of Texas.

Texas may be said to give laws to the whole Union. She leads the way in plunder and murder; and Massachusetts, with all New England, follow in the crusade like hungry sharks in the bloody wake of a Brazilian slaveship. What a spectacle for men and angels!—Gov. Briggs [of Massachusetts] issuing his order to send the sons of those who fell in the cause of freedom on Bunker Hill, to fight the battle of Slavery in Mexico! Gov. Briggs, the teetotaller! Gov. Briggs, the Baptist! issuing his order to raise troops in Massachusetts, to establish with fire and sword the man-blasting and soul-damning system of slavery! Who would have thought it? And yet it was to be expected. The deed was done long ago. The foundation of this frowning monument of infamy was laid when the States were first declared the *United States*. This is but another link around your necks of the galling chain which your fathers placed about the heels of my race. It is the legitimate fruit of compromise—of attempting a union of freedom with slavery. . . .

James Russell Lowell Satirizes the Mexican War, 1848

A letter from Mr. Ezekiel Bigelow of Jaalem . . . inclosing a poem of his son, Mr. Hosea Bigelow

Thrash away, you'll *hev* to rattle
  On them kittle drums o' yourn,—
'Taint a knowin' kind o' cattle
  Thet is ketched with mouldy corn;
Put in stiff, you fifer feller,
  Let folks see how spry you be,—
Guess you'll toot till you are yeller
  'Fore you git ahold o' me!

'T would n't suit them Southern fellers,
  They're a dreffle graspin' set,
We must ollers blow the bellers
  Wen they want their irons het;
May be it 's all right ez preachin',
  But *my* narves it kind o' grates,
Wen I see the overreachin'
  O' them nigger-drivin' States.

Them thet rule us, them slave-traders,
  Haint they cut a thunderin' swarth,
(Helped by Yankee renegaders,)
  Thru the vartu o' the North!
We begin to think it 's nater
  To take sarse an' not be riled;—
Who'd expect to see a tater
  All on eend at bein' biled?

Ez fer war, I call it murder,—
  There you hev it plain an' flat;
I don't want to go no furder
  Than my Testyment fer that;
God hez sed so plump an' fairly,
  It 's ez long ez it is broad,

An' you 've gut to git up airly
  Ef you want to take in God.

'Taint your eppyletts an' feathers
  Make the thing a grain more right;
'Taint afollerin' your bell-wethers
  Will excuse ye in His sight;
Ef you take a sword an' dror it,
  An' go stick a feller thru,
Guv'ment aint to answer for it,
  God 'll send the bill to you. . . .

They may talk o' Freedom's airy
  Tell they 're pupple in the face,—
It 's a grand gret cemetary
  Fer the barthrights of our race;
They jest want this Californy
  So 's to lug new slave-states in
To abuse ye, an' to scorn ye,
  An' to plunder ye like sin.

Aint it cute to see a Yankee
  Take sech everlastin' pains
All to git the Devil's thankee,
  Helpin' on 'em weld their chains?
Wy, it 's jest ez clear ez figgers,
  Clear ez one an' one make two,
Chaps thet make black slaves o' niggers
  Want to make wite slaves o' you.

A Free Soil Democrat's View of the War:
Two Editorials by Walt Whitman, 1846, 1847

The Mexican War Justified

May 11, 1846

YES: Mexico must be thoroughly chastised!—We have reached a point in
our intercourse with that country, when prompt and effectual demonstrations
of force are enjoined upon us by every dictate of right and policy. The news
of yesterday has added the last argument wanted to prove the necessity of
an immediate Declaration of War by our government toward its southern
neighbor.

We are justified in the face of the world, in having treated Mexico with
more forbearance than we have ever yet treated an enemy—for Mexico,
though contemptible in many respects, is an enemy deserving a vigorous
"lesson." We have coaxed, excused, listened with deaf ears to the insolent
gasconnade of her government, submitted thus far to a most offensive rejection of an Ambassador personifying the American nation, and waited for
years without payment of the claims of our injured merchants. We have
sought peace through every avenue, and shut our eyes to many things, which

had they come from England or France, the President would not have dared to pass over without stern and speedy resentment. . . . Who has read the sickening story of those brutal wholesale murders [of some years ago] so useless for any purpose except gratifying the cowardly appetite of a nation of bravos, willing to shoot down men by the hundred in cold blood—without panting for the day when the prayer of that blood should be listened to—when the vengeance of a retributive God should be meted out to those who so ruthlessly and needlessly slaughtered His image?

That day has arrived. . . . Let our arms now be carried with a spirit which shall teach the world that, while we are not forward for a quarrel, America knows how to crush, as well as how to expand!

American Workingmen, versus Slavery

September 1, 1847

THE question whether or no there shall be slavery in the new territories which it seems conceded on all hands we are largely to get through this Mexican war, is a question between *the grand body of white workingmen, the millions of mechanics, farmers, and operatives of our country,* with their interests on the one side—and the interests of the few thousand rich, "polished," and aristocratic owners of slaves at the South, on the other side. Experience has proved, (and the evidence is to be seen now by any one who will look at it) that a stalwart mass of respectable workingmen, cannot exist, much less flourish, in a thorough slave State. Let any one think for a moment what a different appearance New York, Pennsylvania, or Ohio, would present—how much less sturdy independence and family happiness there would be—were slaves the workmen there, instead of each man as a general thing being his own workman. We wish not at all to sneer at the South; but leaving out of view the educated and refined gentry, and coming to the "common people" of the whites, everybody knows what a miserable, ignorant, and shiftless set of beings they are. Slavery is a good thing enough, (viewed partially,) to the rich—the one out of thousands; but it is destructive to the dignity and independence of all who work, and to labor itself. An honest poor mechanic, in a slave State, is put on a par with the negro slave mechanic—there being many of the latter, who are hired out by their owners. It is of no use to reason abstractly on this fact—farther than to say that the pride of a Northern American freeman, poor though he be, will not comfortably stand such degradation.

The influence of the slavery institution is to bring the dignity of labor down to the level of slavery, which, God knows! is low enough. And this it is which must induce *the workingmen of the North, East, and West, to come up, to a man, in defence of their rights, their honor, and that heritage of getting bread by the sweat of the brow, which we must leave to our children.* . . . We call upon every mechanic of the North, East, and West—upon the carpenter, in his rolled up sleeves, the mason with his trowel, the stonecutter with his brawny chest, the blacksmith with his sooty face, the brown fisted shipbuilder, whose clinking strokes rattle so merrily in our dock yards—

upon shoemakers, and cartmen, and drivers, and paviers, and porters, and millwrights, and furriers, and ropemakers, and butchers, and machinists, and tinmen, and tailors, and hatters, and coach and cabinet makers—upon the honest sawyer and mortarmixer too, whose sinews are their own—and every hard-working man—to speak in a voice whose great reverberations shall tell to all quarters that the *workingmen* of the free United States, and their business, are not willing to be put on the level of negro slaves, in territory which, if got at all, must be got by taxes sifted eventually through upon them, and by their hard work and blood. But most of all we call upon *the farmers,* the workers of the land—that prolific brood of brown faced fathers and sons who swarm over the free States, and form the bulwark of our Republic, mightier than walls or armies—upon them we call to say whether *they* too will exist "free and independent" not only in name but also by those social customs and laws which are greater than constitutions—or only so by statute, while in reality they are put down to an equality with slaves!

There can be no half way work in the matter of slavery in new territory: we must either have it there, or have it not. Now if either the slaves themselves, or their owners, had fought or paid for or gained this new territory, there would be some reason in the pro-slavery claims. But every body knows that the cost and work come, forty-nine fiftieths of it, upon the free men, the middling classes and workingmen, who do their own work and own no slaves. Shall *these* give up all to the aristocratic owners of the South? Will even the poor white freemen of the South be willing to do this? It is monstrous to ask such a thing!

. . . [A]ll practice and theory—the real interest of the planters themselves—and the potential weight of the opinions of all our great statesmen, Southern as well as Northern, from Washington to Silas Wright—are strongly arrayed in favor of limiting slavery to where it already exists. For this the clear eye of Washington looked longingly; for this the great voice of Jefferson plead, and his sacred fingers wrote; for this were uttered the prayers of Franklin and Madison and Monroe. But now, in the South, stands a little band, strong in chivalry, refinement and genius—headed by a sort of intellectual Saladin—assuming to speak in behalf of sovereign States, while in reality they utter their own idle theories; and disdainfully crying out against the rest of the Republic, for whom their contempt is but illy concealed. . . . Already the roar of the waters is heard; and if a few short-sighted ones seek to withstand it, the surge, terrible in its fury, will sweep them too in the ruin.

Senator Charles Sumner Gives a Northern Whig View of the War, 1846

Charles Sumner to Robert Winthrop, October 25, 1846

. . . By virtue of an unconstitutional Act of Congress, in conjunction with the *de facto* government of Texas, the latter was annexed to the United States some time in the month of December, 1845. If we regard Texas as a province of Mexico, its boundaries must be sought in the geography of that republic. If we regard it as an independent State, they must be determined by the extent of jurisdiction which the State was able to maintain. Now it seems clear that the river Nueces was always recognized by Mexico as the western boundary; and it is undisputed that the State of Texas, since its Declaration of Independence, never exercised any jurisdiction beyond the Nueces. The Act of Annexation could not, therefore, transfer to the United States any title to the region between the Nueces and the Rio Grande. That region belonged to Mexico. *Certainly* it did not belong to the United States.

In the month of January, 1846, the President of the United States directed the troops under General Taylor, called the Army of Occupation, to take possession of this region. Here was an act of aggression. As might have been expected, it produced collision. The Mexicans, aroused in self-defence, sought to repel the invaders from their hearths and churches. Unexpected tidings reached Washington that the American forces were in danger. The President, in a message to Congress, called for succors.

Here the question occurs, What was the duty of Congress in this emergency? Clearly to withhold all sanction to unjust war,—to aggression upon a neighboring Republic,—to spoliation of fellow-men. Our troops were in danger only because upon foreign soil, forcibly displacing the jurisdiction and laws of the rightful government. In this condition of things, the way of safety, just and honorable, was by instant withdrawal from the Rio Grande to the Nueces. Congress should have spoken like Washington, when General Braddock, staggered by the peril of the moment, asked the youthful soldier, "What shall I do, Colonel Washington?" "RETREAT, Sir! RETREAT, Sir!" was the earnest reply. The American forces should have been directed to *retreat*,—not from any human force, but from *wrongdoing;* and this would have been a true victory.

Alas! this was not the mood of Congress. With wicked speed a bill was introduced, furnishing large and unusual supplies of men and money. In any just sense, such provision was wasteful and unnecessary; but it would hardly be worthy of criticism, if confined in its object to the safety of the troops. When made, it must have been known that the fate of the troops was already decided, while the magnitude of the appropriations and the number of volunteers called for showed that measures were contemplated *beyond self-defence.* Self-defence is easy and cheap. Aggression and injustice are difficult and costly.

. . . This was adopted by a vote of 123 to 67; and the bill then leaped forth, fully armed, as a measure of open and active hostility against Mexico. . . .

This Act cannot be regarded merely as provision for the safety of General Taylor; nor, indeed can this be considered the principal end proposed. It has other and ulterior objects, broader and more general, in view of which his safety, important as it might be, is of comparative insignificance; as it would be less mournful to lose a whole army than lend the solemn sanction of legislation to an unjust war.

This Act may be considered in six different aspects. It is six times wrong.

Six different and unanswerable reasons should have urged its rejection. Six different appeals should have touched every heart. I shall consider them separately.

First. It is practically a DECLARATION OF WAR against a sister Republic. By the Constitution of the United States, the power of declaring war is vested in Congress. Before this Act was passed, the Mexican War had no legislative sanction. Without this Act it could have no legislative sanction. *By virtue of this Act* the present war is waged. *By virtue of this Act,* an American fleet, at immense cost of money, and without any gain of character, is now disturbing the commerce of Mexico, and of the civilized world, by the blockade of Vera Cruz. *By virtue of this Act,* a distant expedition, with pilfering rapacity, has seized the defenceless province of California. . . .

Secondly. This Act gives the sanction of Congress to an *unjust* war. War is barbarous and brutal; but this is unjust. It grows out of aggression on our part, and is continued by aggression. The statement of facts already made is sufficient on this head.

Thirdly. It declares that war exists *"by the act of the Republic of Mexico."* This statement of brazen falsehood is inserted in the front of the Act. But it is now admitted by most, if not all, of the Whigs who unhappily voted for it, that it is not founded in fact. It is a national lie.

> "Whose tongue soe'er speaks false
> Not truly speaks; *who speaks not truly* LIES."

Fourthly. It provides for the prosecution of the war *"to a speedy and successful termination,"*—that is, for the speedy and successful prosecution of *unjust* war. Surely no rule can be better founded in morals than that we should seek the establishment of *right.* How, then, can we strive to hasten the triumph of wrong?

Fifthly. The war has its origin in a series of measures to extend and perpetuate slavery. A wise and humane legislator should have discerned its source, and found fresh impulses to oppose it.

Sixthly. The war is dishonorable and cowardly, as the attack of a rich, powerful, numerous, and united republic upon a weak and defenceless neighbor, distracted by civil feud. Every consideration of honor, manliness, and Christian duty prompted gentleness and forbearance towards our unfortunate sister.

Such, Sir, is the Act of Congress which received your sanction. . . .

Senator John C. Calhoun Offers a Southern Perspective on the War's Outcome, 1847

. . . Mr. President, it was solemnly asserted on this floor, some time ago, that all parties in the non-slaveholding States had come to a fixed and solemn determination upon two propositions. One was, that there should be no further admission of any States into this Union which permitted by their constitution the existence of slavery; and the other was, that slavery shall not hereafter exist in any of the Territories of the United States; the effect of which would be to give to the non-slaveholding States the monopoly of the public domain, to the entire exclusion of the slaveholding States. Since that declaration was made, Mr. President, we have abundant proof that there was a satisfactory foundation for it. We have received already solemn resolutions passed by seven of the non-slaveholding States—one half of the number already in the Union, Iowa not being counted—using the strongest possible language to that effect; and no doubt in a short space of time similar resolutions will be received from all of the non-slaveholding States. But we need not go beyond the walls of Congress. The subject has been agitated in the other House, and they have sent you up a bill "prohibiting the extension of slavery" (using their own language) "to any territory which may be acquired by the United States hereafter." At the same time, two resolutions which have been moved to extend the compromise line from the Rocky Mountains to the Pacific, during the present session, have been rejected by a decided majority.

Sir, there is no mistaking the signs of the times; and it is high time that the southern States, the slaveholding States, should inquire what is now their relative strength in this Union, and what it will be if this determination should be carried into effect hereafter. Sir, already we are in a minority— I use the word "we," for brevity sake—already we are in a minority in the other House, in the electoral college, and, I may say, in every department of this Government, except at present in the Senate of the United States: there, for the present, we have an equality. Of the twenty-eight States, fourteen are non-slaveholding and fourteen are slaveholding, counting Delaware, which is doubtful, as one of the non-slaveholding States. But this equality of strength exists only in the Senate. . . .

Sir, what is the entire amount of this policy? I will not say that it is so designed. I will not say from what cause it originated. I will not say whether blind fanaticism on one side, whether a hostile feeling to slavery entertained by many not fanatical on the other, has produced it; or whether it has been the work of men, who, looking to political power, have considered the agitation of this question as the most effectual mode of obtaining the spoils of this Government. I look to the fact itself. It is a policy now openly avowed as one to be persisted in. It is a scheme, Mr. President, which aims to monopolize the powers of this Government and to obtain sole possession of its territories.

Now, I ask, is there any remedy? Does the Constitution afford any remedy? And if not, is there any hope? These, Mr. President, are solemn questions—not only to us, but, let me say to gentlemen from the non-slaveholding States: to them. Sir, the day that the balance between the two sections of the country—the slaveholding States and the non-slaveholding States—is destroyed, is a day that will not be far removed from political revolution, anarchy, civil war, and widespread disaster. The balance of this system is in the slaveholding States. They are the conservative portion— always have been the conservative portion—always will be the conservative portion; and with a due balance on their part may, for generations to come, uphold this glorious Union of ours. But if this scheme should be carried out—if we are to be reduced to a handful—if we are to become a mere ball to play the presidential game with—to count something in the Baltimore caucus—if this is to be the result—wo, wo, I say, to this Union!

Now, sir, I put again the solemn question—does the Constitution afford any remedy? Is there any provision in it by which this aggressive policy—boldly avowed, as if perfectly consistent with our institutions and the safety and prosperity of the United States!—may be confronted? Is this a policy consistent with the Constitution? No, Mr. President, no! It is, in all its features, daringly opposed to the Constitution. What is it? Ours is a Federal Constitution. The States are its constituents, and not the people. The twenty-eight States—the twenty-nine States (including Iowa)—stand under this Government as twenty-nine individuals, or as twenty-nine millions of individuals would stand to a consolidated power. It did not look to the prosperity of individuals, as such. No, sir; it was made for higher ends; it was formed that every State as a constituent member of this great Union of ours should enjoy all its advantages, natural and acquired, with greater security, and enjoy them more perfectly. The whole system is based on justice and equality—perfect equality between the members of this republic. Now can that be consistent with equality, which will make this public domain a monopoly on one side—which, in its consequences, would place the whole power in one section of the Union, to be wielded against the other sections of the Union? Is that equality?

How, then, do we stand in reference to this territorial question—this public domain of ours? Why, sir, what is it? It is the common property of the States of this Union. They are called "the territories of the United States." And what are the "United States" but the States united? Sir, these territories are the property of the States united; held jointly for their common use. And is it consistent with justice, is it consistent with equality, that any portion of the partners, outnumbering another portion, shall oust them of this common property of theirs—shall pass any law which shall proscribe the citizens of other portions of the Union from emigrating with their property to the Territories of the United States? Would that be consistent, can it be consistent with the idea of a common property, held jointly for the common benefit of all? Would it be so considered in private life? Would it not be considered the most flagrant outrage in the world, one which any court of equity would restrain by injunction—which any court of law in the world would overrule?

Mr. President, not only is that proposition grossly inconsistent with the Constitution, but the other, which undertakes to say that no State shall be admitted into this Union which shall not prohibit by its constitution the existence of slaves, is equally a great outrage against the Constitution of the United States. Sir, I hold it to be a fundamental principle of our political system that the people have a right to establish what government they may think proper for themselves; that every State about to become a member of this Union has a right to form its own Government as it pleases; and that, in order to be admitted, there is but one qualification, and that is, that the government shall be republican. There is no express provision to that effect, but it results from that important section which guarantees to every State in this Union a republican form of government. Now, sir, what is proposed? It is proposed, from a vague, indefinite, erroneous, and most dangerous conception of private individual liberty, to overrule this great common liberty which the people have of framing their own constitution! . . .

The Political System Fractures: Party Platforms, 1848

Democratic Party Platform

Resolved, That the American Democracy place their trust in the intelligence, the patriotism, and the discriminating justice of the American people.

Resolved, That we regard this as a distinctive feature of our political creed, which we are proud to maintain before the world as the great moral element in a form of government springing from and upheld by the popular will; and we contrast it with the creed and practice of Federalism, under whatever name or form, which seeks to palsy the will of the constituent, and which conceives no imposture too monstrous for the popular credulity.

Resolved, therefore, That, entertaining these views, the Democratic party of this Union, through their Delegates assembled in general convention of the States, coming together in a spirit of concord, of devotion to the doctrines and faith of a free representative government, and appealing to their fellow-citizens for the rectitude of their intentions, renew and reassert before the American people the declaration of principles avowed by them when, on a former occasion, in general convention, they presented their candidates for the popular suffrage. . . .

That Congress has no power under the Constitution to interfere with or control the domestic institutions of the several States, and that such States are the sole and proper judges of everything appertaining to their own affairs, not prohibited by the Constitution; that all efforts of the Abolitionists or others made to induce Congress to interfere with questions of slavery, or to take incipient steps in relation thereto, are calculated to lead to the most alarming and dangerous consequences; and that all such efforts have an inevitable tendency to diminish the happiness of the people, and endanger the stability and permanence of the Union, and ought not to be countenanced by any friend to our political institutions. . . .

Resolved, That the war with Mexico, provoked on her part by years of insult and injury, was commenced by her army crossing the Rio Grande, attacking the American troops, and invading our sister State of Texas; and that, upon all the principles of patriotism and laws of nations, it is a just and necessary war on our part, in which every American citizen should have shown himself on the side of his country, and neither morally nor physically, by word or by deed, have given "aid and comfort to the enemy."

Resolved, That we would be rejoiced at the assurance of peace with Mexico founded on the just principles of indemnity for the past and security for the future; but that, while the ratification of the liberal treaty offered to Mexico remains in doubt, it is the duty of the country to sustain the administration in every measure necessary to provide for the vigorous prosecution of the war, should that treated be rejected.

Resolved, That the officers and soldiers who have carried the arms of their country into Mexico, have crowned it with imperishable glory. Their unconquerable courage, their daring enterprise, their unfaltering perseverance and fortitude when assailed on all sides by innumerable foes, and that more formidable enemy, the diseases of the climate, exalt their devoted patriotism into the highest heroism, and give them a right to the profound gratitude of their country, and the admiration of the world.

Whig Party Platform

1. *Resolved,* That the Whigs of the United States, here assembled by their Representatives, heartily ratify the nominations of General Zachary Taylor as President and Millard Fillmore as Vice-President of the United States, and pledge themselves to their support.

2. *Resolved,* That the choice of General Taylor as the Whig candidate for President we are glad to discover sympathy with a great popular sentiment throughout the nation—a sentiment which, having its origin in admiration of great military success, has been strengthened by the development, in every action and every word, of sound conservative opinions, and of true fidelity to the great example of former days, and to the principles of the Constitution as administered by its founders.

3. *Resolved,* That General Taylor, in saying that, had he voted in 1844, he would have voted the Whig ticket, gives us the assurance—and no better is needed from a consistent and truthspeaking man—that his heart was with us at the crisis of our political destiny, when Henry Clay was our candidate and when not only Whig principles were well defined and clearly asserted, but Whig measures depended on success. The heart that was with us then is with us now, and we have a soldier's word of honor, and a life of public and private virtue, as the security.

4. *Resolved,* That we look on General Taylor's administration of the Government as one conducive of Peace, Prosperity, and Union. Of Peace—because no one better knows, or has greater reason to deplore, what he has seen sadly on the field of victory, the horrors of war, and especially of a foreign and aggressive war. Of Prosperity—now more than ever needed to relieve the nation from a burden of debt, and restore industry—agricultural, manufacturing and commercial—to its accustomed and peaceful functions and influences. Of Union—because we have a candidate whose very position as a Southwestern man, reared on the banks of the great stream whose tributaries, natural and artificial, embrace the whole Union, renders the protection of the interests of the whole country his first trust, and whose various duties in past life have been rendered, not on the soil or under the flag of any State or section, but over the wide frontier, and under the broad banner of the Nation. . . .

Free Soil Party Platform

Whereas, We have assembled in Convention, as a union of *Freemen,* for the sake of Freedom, forgetting all past political differences in a common resolve to maintain the rights of Free Labor against the aggressions of the Slave Power, and to secure Free Soil for a Free People:

And whereas, The political Conventions recently assembled at Baltimore and Philadelphia, the one stifling the voice of a great constituency entitled to be heard in its deliberations, and the other abandoning its distinctive principles for mere availability, have dissolved the national party organizations heretofore existing, by nominating for the Chief Magistracy of the United States, under Slaveholding dictation, candidates, *neither of whom* can be supported by the opponents of Slavery-extension, without a *sacrifice of consistency, duty,* and *self-respect.*

And whereas, These nominations, so made, furnish the occasion and demonstrate the necessity of the union of the People under the banners of Free Democracy, in a solemn and formal *declaration* of their *independence* of the *Slave Power,* and of their fixed determination to rescue the Federal Government from its control:

Resolved, therefore, that we, the people here assembled, remembering the example of our *fathers* in the days of the first Declaration of Independence, putting our trust in God for the triumph of our cause, and invoking his guidance in our endeavors to advance it, do now plant ourselves upon the NATIONAL PLATFORM OF FREEDOM, in opposition to the Sectional Platform of Slavery.

Resolved, That Slavery in the several States of this Union which recognize its existence, depends upon the State laws alone, which cannot be repealed or modified by the Federal Government, and for which laws that Government is not responsible. We therefore propose no interference by Congress with Slavery within the limits of any State.

Resolved, That the PROVISO of Jefferson, to prohibit the existence of Slavery, after 1800 in all the Territories of the United States, Southern and Northern; the votes of six States, and sixteen delegates, in the Congress of 1784, for the Proviso, to three States and seven delegates against it; the actual exclusion of Slavery from the Northwestern Territory by the ORDINANCE OF 1787, *unanimously* adopted by the States in Congress, and the entire history of that period, clearly show that it was the settled policy of the nation, *not* to *extend, nationalize,* or *encourage,* but to limit, localize, and discourage, Slavery; and to *this policy* which should never have been departed from, the Government ought to *return.*

Resolved, That our fathers ordained the Constitution of the United States, in order, among other great national objects, to establish justice, promote the general welfare, and secure the blessings of Liberty; but expressly *denied* to the Federal Government, which they created, all constitutional power to *deprive any person* of life, *liberty,* or property, without due legal process.

Resolved, That in the judgment of this Convention, Congress has no more power to make a SLAVE than to make a KING; no more power to institute or establish SLAVERY, than to institute or establish a MONARCHY. No such power can be found among those specifically conferred by the Constitution, or derived by just implication from them.

Resolved, THAT IT IS THE DUTY OF THE FEDERAL GOVERNMENT TO RELIEVE ITSELF FROM ALL RESPONSIBILITY FOR THE EXISTENCE OR CONTINUANCE OF SLAVERY WHEREVER THAT GOVERNMENT POSSESS CONSTITUTIONAL POWER TO LEGISLATE ON THAT SUBJECT, AND IS THUS RESPONSIBLE FOR ITS EXISTENCE.

Resolved, That the true, and, in the judgment of this Convention, the *only* safe means of preventing the extension of Slavery into territory now free, is to prohibit its existence in all such territory by *an act of Congress.*

Resolved, That we accept the issue which the Slave Power has forced upon us, and to their demand for more Slave States and more Slave Territory, our calm but final answer is: No more Slave States and no more Slave Territory. Let the soil of our extensive domains be kept free, for the hardy pioneers of our own land, and the oppressed and banished of other lands seeking homes of comfort and fields of enterprise in the New World.

Resolved, That the bill lately reported by the Committee of Eight in the Senate of the United States, was no compromise, but an absolute surrender of the rights of the non-slaveholders of the States; and while we rejoice to know that a measure which, while opening the door for the introduction of Slavery into Territories now free, would also have opened the door to litigation and strife among the future inhabitants thereof, to the ruin of their peace and prosperity, was defeated in the House of Representatives,—its passage, in hot haste, by a majority, embracing several Senators who voted in open violation of the known will of their constituents, should warn the People to see to it, that their representatives be not suffered to betray them. There must be no more compromises with Slavery: if made, they must be repealed.

Resolved, That we demand Freedom and established institutions for our brethren in Oregon, now exposed to hardships, peril, and massacre, by the reckless hostility of the Slave Power to the establishment of Free Government for Free Territories—and not only for them, but for our new brethren in California and New Mexico.

And whereas, It is due not only to this occasion, but to the whole people of the United States, that we should also declare ourselves on certain other questions of national policy, therefore,

Resolved, That we demand CHEAP POSTAGE for the people; a retrenchment of the expenses and patronage of the Federal Government; the *abolition* of all *unnecessary* offices and salaries; and the election by the People of all civil officers in the service of the Government, so far as the same may be practicable.

Resolved, That *river* and *harbor improvements,* when demanded by the safety and convenience of commerce with foreign nations, or among the several States, are objects of *national concern;* and that it is the duty of Congress, in the exercise of its constitutional powers, to provide therefor.

Resolved, That the FREE GRANT TO ACTUAL SETTLERS, in consideration of the expenses they incur in making settlements in the wilderness, which are usually fully equal to their actual cost, and of the public benefits resulting therefrom, of reasonable portions of the public lands, under suitable limitations, is a wise and just measure of public policy, which will promote, in various ways, the interest of all the States of this Union; and we therefore recommend it to the favorable consideration of the American People.

Resolved, That the obligations of honor and patriotism require the earliest practical payment of the national debt, and we are therefore in favor of such a tariff of duties as will raise revenue adequate to defray the necessary expenses of the Federal Government, and to pay annual instalments of our debt and the interest thereon.

Resolved, That we inscribe on our banner, "FREE SOIL, FREE SPEECH, FREE LABOR, and FREE MEN," and under it we will fight on, and fight ever, until a triumphant victory shall reward our exertions.

⌗ E S S A Y S

Manifest Destiny and the Mexican War were sources of both intense patriotic fervor and emotional dissent. Is it possible to see beyond these passions? Many historians would caution against doing so, for they interpret Manifest Destiny primarily as a national mood. Particularly in the eastern cities and the Old Northwest, it seems that expansionism had links to genuinely idealistic notions about spreading democracy and ridding the New World once and for all of meddlesome, aristocratic, European influences. Other scholars have preferred to concentrate on Polk and his immediate circle. Some have cast the president as a naturally indecisive man who tried to compensate by taking a hard line with Mexico.

The following essays take different approaches. For the historian Norman A. Graebner of the University of Virginia, Manifest Destiny had more to do with concrete interests than with emotions. To the extent that it expressed a national outlook, it was one of confidence. The historian Thomas Hietala of Grinnell College disagrees. Although he acknowledges the importance of material forces, Hietala finds flaws in the expansionists' stated premises. And at the core of America's involvement, he finds not confidence but a cultural and political anxiety, deeply rooted in the Jeffersonian tradition and in the nation's abiding racial antagonisms.

Manifest Destiny and National Interests

NORMAN A. GRAEBNER

Manifest destiny, a phrase used by contemporaries and historians to describe and explain the continental expansion of the United States in the 1840's, expressed merely a national mood. The belief in a national destiny was neither new nor strange; no nation or empire in history has ever been totally without it. But for its proponents of the 1840's the meaning conveyed by the phrase was clearly understood and peculiarly American. It implied that

Excerpts from *Manifest Destiny,* Norman Graebner ed. (Indianapolis: Bobbs-Merrill, 1968), pp. xv–xvi, xxii–xxiv, xxvi–xxvii, xlvi–xlii, liv, lvi–lx, lxviii–lxx, Macmillan Publishing Co., Inc.

the United States was destined by the will of Heaven to become a country of political and territorial eminence. It attributed the probability and even the necessity of this growth to a homogeneous process created by certain unique qualities in American civilization—the energy and vigor of its people, their idealism and faith in their democratic institutions, and their sense of mission now endowed with a new vitality. It assigned to the American people the obligation to extend the area of freedom to their less fortunate neighbors, but only to those trained for self-government and genuinely desirous of entering the American Union. Expansionists of the forties saw this self-imposed limitation on forceful annexation as no serious barrier to the Republic's growth. It was inconceivable to them that any neighboring population would decline an invitation to enter the realm of the United States. Eventually editors and politicians transformed the idea of manifest destiny into a significant expression of American nationalism.

Such convictions of destiny came easily to the American people in the mid-forties, for they logically emerged from the sheer size and dramatic achievements of the young Republic. From New England and Pennsylvania, reaching on into the Ohio Valley and the Great Lakes region, an industrial revolution was multiplying the productive resources of the United States. New forms of transportation, made possible by the efficient application of steam, rendered the national economy greater than the sum of its parts. Steamboats transformed the Mississippi and Ohio rivers—with their many tributaries—into a mighty inland system of commercial and human traffic. Railroads had long since left the Atlantic seaboard and were, by the forties, creeping toward the burgeoning cities of the Middle West. Asa Whitney had already projected a railroad line from Lake Michigan to the Pacific Northwest. Samuel F. B. Morse's successful demonstration of the magnetic telegraph in 1844 assured almost instantaneous communication across the entire continent. "What mighty distances have been overcome by railroads," exclaimed the *Southern Quarterly Review* (October, 1844), "and, stranger than all, is the transmission of intelligence with the speed and with the aid of lightning!" . . .

Never in history could a people more readily accept and proclaim a sense of destiny, for never were a people more perfectly situated to transform their whims into realities. Expansion was rationalized so effectively at each point of conflict that it seemed to many Americans an unchallengeable franchise. Confronted by problems neither of conscience nor of extensive countering force, the American people could claim as a natural right boundaries that seemed to satisfy the requirements of security and commerce. Expanding as they did into a vacuum—vast regions almost devoid of population—they could conclude that they were simply fulfilling the dictates of manifest destiny. For them the distinctions between sentiment and action, between individual purpose and national achievement, appeared inconsequential.

Historians, emphasizing the expansive mood of the forties, have tended to identify the westward extension of the United States to the Pacific with the concept of destiny itself. Such identifications are misleading, for they ignore all the genuine elements of successful policy. Those regions into which the nation threatened to expand were under the legal jurisdiction of other governments. Their acquisition required the formulation of policies which encompassed both the precise definition of ends and the creation of adequate means. Manifest destiny doctrines—a body of sentiment and nothing else— avoided completely the essential question of *means,* and it was only the absence of powerful opposition on the North American continent that permitted the fallacy that power and its employment were of little consequence. Occupying a wilderness created the illusion that power was less important than moral progress, and that expansion was indeed a civilizing, not a conquering, process.

Jeremy Bentham once termed the concept of natural right pure nonsense, for the claims of nations were natural only when supported by superior force. The natural right of the United States to a continental empire lay in its power of conquest, not in the uniqueness of its political institutions. American expansionism could triumph only when the nation could bring its diplomatic and military influence to bear on specific points of national concern. What created the easy victory of American expansion was not a sense of destiny, however widely and dramatically it was proclaimed, but the absence of powerful competitors which might have either prevented the expansion entirely or forced the country to pay an exorbitant price for its territorial gains. The advantages of geography and the political and military inefficiency of the Indian tribes or even of Mexican arms tended to obscure the elements of force which were no less real, only less obtrusive, than that employed by other nations in their efforts at empire building. It was no wonder that British and French cities concluded that the American conquest of the continent was by pick and shovel.

Concepts of manifest destiny were as totally negligent of *ends* as they were of means. Expansionists agreed that the nation was destined to reach its natural boundaries. But what were these natural frontiers? For Benjamin Franklin and John Adams they comprised the Mississippi River. But when the United States, through the purchase of Louisiana, crossed the Mississippi, there was no end in sight. Expansionists now regarded Florida as a natural appendage—belonging as naturally to the United States, declared one Kentucky newspaper, as Cornwall did to England. John Quincy Adams observed in his diary that the acquisition of Florida in 1819 "rendered it still more unavoidable that the remainder of the continent should ultimately be ours." Eventually Europe would discover, he predicted, that the United States and North America were identical. But President James Monroe revealed no more interest in building a state on the Pacific than had Jefferson. Equally convinced that the distances to Oregon were too great to be bridged by one empire, Thomas Hart Benton of Missouri in 1825 defined the natural boundary of the United States as "the ridge of the Rocky Mountains. . . . Along the back of this ridge, the Western limit of this republic should be drawn, and the statue of the fabled god, Terminus, should be raised upon its highest peak, never to be thrown down." President John Tyler, in his message of December, 1843, perpetuated this limited view of the nation's future. And as late as 1845 Daniel Webster continued to refer to an independent republic along the distant Pacific coast. Meanwhile expansionists could never agree on the natural boundaries of Texas. Representative C. J. Ingersoll of Pennsylvania found them in vast deserts between the Rio Grande and the Nueces. For others they comprised the Rio Grande itself, but James Gadsden discovered in the Sierra Madre mountains "a natural territorial boundary, imposing in its Mountain and Desert outlines." . . .

If the ultimate vision of American destiny in the forties comprised a vast federal republic that boasted continental dimensions and a government based on the principle of states rights, the future boundaries of the United States, as determined by the standards of geographical predestination, never seemed to possess any ultimate logic. Boundaries that appeared natural to one generation were rejected as utterly inadequate by the next. It was left for Robert Winthrop, the conservative Massachusetts Whig, in January, 1846, to reduce the doctrine of geographical predestination to an absurdity:

> It is not a little amusing to observe what different views are taken as to the indication of "the hand of nature" and the pointings of "the finger of God," by the same gentlemen, under different circumstances and upon different subjects. In one quarter of the compass they can descry the hand of nature in a level desert and a second-rate river, beckoning us impatiently to march up to them. But when they turn their eyes to another part of the horizon the loftiest mountains in the universe are quite lost upon their gaze. There is no hand of nature there. The configuration of the earth has no longer any significance. The Rocky Mountains are mere molehills. Our destiny is onward.

Democratic idealism was even less precise as a guide to national action than the doctrine of geographical predestination. By 1845 such goals of reaching the waters of the Pacific were far too limited for the more enthusiastic exponents of the new expansionism. As they interpreted the expression of democratic idealism, the dogma represented an ever-expanding force. Indeed, for some it had no visible limit at all. It looked beyond the North American continent to South America, to the islands of the Pacific, and to the Old World itself. One editorial in the New York *Herald* (September 15, 1845), declared, "American patriotism takes a wider and loftier range than heretofore. Its horizon is widening every day. No longer bounded by the limits of the confederacy, it looks abroad upon the whole earth, and into the mind of the republic daily sinks deeper and deeper the conviction that the civilization of the earth—the reform of the governments of the ancient world—the emancipation of the whole race, are dependent, in a great degree, on the United States." This was a magnificent vision for a democratic purpose, but it hardly explains the sweep of the United States across the continent. It bears no relationship whatever to the actual goals which the Tyler and Polk administrations pursued in their diplomacy with Texas, Mexico, and England.

Texas provided the necessary catalyst which fused all the elements of manifest destiny into a single national movement. When, in 1844, the annexation issue suddenly exploded on the national scene, the expansionist front had been quiescent for a full generation. The twenties and thirties had been years of introspection. The changing structure of American political and economic life had absorbed the people's energies and directed their thoughts inward. Yet the same inner-directed concerns which rendered the country generally oblivious to external affairs promoted both the sense of power and the democratic idealism which, under the impetus of expansionist oratory, could easily transform the nation's mood and forge a spirit of national destiny. . . .

California no less than Oregon demanded its own peculiar expansionist rationale, for its acquisition confronted the United States with a series of problems not present in either the Texas or Oregon issues. If the government in Mexico City lacked the energy to control, much less develop, this remote province, its title was still as clear as its hold was ephemeral. The annexation of this outpost required bargaining with its owner. Even that possibility seemed remote in 1845, for the Mexican government had carried out its threat to break diplomatic relations with the United States rather than condone the American annexation of Texas. For a decade American citizens had drifted into the inland valleys and coastal villages of California, but in 1845 they still comprised an infinitesimal number, even when compared to the small Mexican and Indian population.

Obviously the United States could not achieve its continental destiny without embracing California. Yet this Mexican province had never been an issue in American politics; its positive contribution to American civilization had scarcely been established. California, moreover, because of its alien population, was by the established principles of American expansion less than acceptable as a territorial objective. American acquisitiveness toward Texas and Oregon had been ethnocentric; it rejected the notion of annexing allegedly inferior peoples. "There seems to be something in our laws and institutions," Alexander Duncan of Ohio reminded the House of Representatives early in 1845, "peculiarly adapted to our Anglo-Saxon-American race, under which they will thrive and prosper, but under which all others wilt and die." He pointed to the decline of the French and Spanish on the North American continent when American laws had been extended to them. It was their unfitness for "liberal and equal laws, and equal institutions," he assumed, that accounted for this inability to prosper under the United States.

Such inhibitions toward the annexing of Mexican peoples gradually disintegrated under the pressure of events. The decision to annex Texas itself encouraged the process by weakening the respect which many Americans held for Mexico's territorial integrity, and thus pointed the way to further acquisitions in the Southwest. Having, through the annexation of Texas, passed its arm "down to the waist of the continent," observed the *Dublin Freeman,* the nation would certainly "not hesitate to pass it round." That the United States was destined to annex additional portions of Mexican territory seemed apparent enough, but only when its population had been absorbed by the Anglo-Saxons now overspreading the continent. As early as 1845 the rapid migration of pioneers into California promised to render the province fit for eventual annexation. In July, 1845, the *Democratic Review* noted that Mexican influence in California was nearing extinction, for the Anglo-Saxon foot was on its border.

American acquisitiveness toward California, like that displayed toward Texas and Oregon, progressed at two levels—that of abstract rationalization and that of concrete national interest. Polk alone carried the responsibility for United States diplomacy with Mexico, and interpreted American objectives in the Southwest—like those in Oregon—as precise and determined by the sea. Travelers and sea captains of the early forties agreed that two inlets gave special significance to the California coast—the bays of San Francisco and San Diego. These men viewed San Francisco harbor with wonderment. Charles Wilkes assured the readers of his *Narrative* . . . that California could boast "one of the finest, if not the very best harbor in the world." It was sufficiently extensive, he added, to shelter the combined navies of Europe. Thomas J. Farnham, the American traveler and writer, called it simply "the glory of the Western world." All who had visited the bay observed that it was the unqualified answer to American hopes for commercial greatness in the Pacific. To the south lay San Diego Bay—the rendezvous of the California hide trade. Here, all Boston firms maintained their coastal depots for cleaning, drying, and storing the hides until a full cargo of thirty to forty thousand had been collected for the long journey to Boston. The processing and storing of hides required a warm port, free from rain, fog, and heavy surf. San Diego alone met all these requirements. This beautiful bay, so deep and placid that ships could lie a cable's length from the smooth, hard-packed, sandy beach, became the chief point of New England's interest on the California coast. The bay was exposed to neither wind nor surf, for it was protected for its entire fifteen-mile length and possessed a narrow, deep entrance. Richard Henry Dana observed in *Two Years Before the Mast* (1840) that San Diego harbor was comparable in value and importance to San Francisco Bay. The noted sea captain, Benjamin Morrell, once termed San Diego "as fine a bay for vessels under three hundred tons as was ever formed by Nature in her most friendly mood to mariners."

During the autumn of 1845, even before his administration had disposed of the Oregon question, Polk embarked on a dual course to acquire at least a portion of California. English activity in that distant province convinced him that, in Great Britain, the United States faced a strong and determined competitor for possession, in particular, of San Francisco Bay. Thomas O. Larkin, an American merchant at Monterey, reported that the French and British governments maintained consuls in California although neither nation had any commercial interests along the Pacific coast. "Why they are in Service their Government best know and Uncle Sam will know to his cost," Larkin warned in July, 1845. Larkin's reports produced a wave of excitement in the administration. "The appearance of a British Vice Consul and French Consul in California at this present crisis without any apparent commercial business," Secretary of State James Buchanan answered Larkin, "is well calculated to produce the impression that their respective governments entertained designs on that country. . . ." On October 17, 1845, Buchanan drafted special instructions to Larkin:

> The future destiny of that country is a subject of anxious solicitude for the government and people of the United States. The interests of our commerce and our whale fisheries on the Pacific Ocean demand that you should exert the greatest vigilance in discovering and defeating any attempts which may be made by foreign governments to acquire a control over that country. . . . On all proper occasions, you should not fail prudently to warn the government and people of California of the danger of such an interference to their peace and prosperity; to inspire them with a jealousy of European domination, and to arouse in their bosoms that love of liberty and independence so natural to the American continent.

Polk appointed Larkin as his confidential agent in California to encourage the Californians, should they separate from Mexico, to cast their lot with the United States. "While the President will make no effort and use no influence to induce California to become one of the free and independent states of the Union, yet," continued Buchanan's instructions, "if the people should desire to unite their destiny with ours, they would be received as brethren, whenever this can be done without affording Mexico just cause of complaint." Larkin was told to let events take their course unless Britain or France should attempt to take California against the will of its residents.

During November, 1845, Polk initiated the second phase of his California policy—an immediate effort to purchase the province from Mexico. On November 9, William S. Parrott, a long-time resident of Mexico now serving as Polk's special agent at the Mexican capital, returned to Washington with confirming information that the officials in Mexico City would receive an American envoy. As early as September Polk and his cabinet had agreed to tender such a mission to John Slidell of Louisiana. In his instructions to Slidell, dated November 10, Buchanan clarified the administration's objectives in California. In a variety of boundary proposals Polk was adamant only on one—the Rio Grande. Those that applied to California were defined solely in terms of Pacific ports. They started with San Francisco and Monterey, the capital of the province, but they included also a suggested boundary line which would reach westward from El Paso along the 32nd parallel to the Pacific, this extended as far as the harbor of San Diego. Unfortunately Slidell was not received by the Mexican government. The administration's program of acquiring at least one of the important harbors along the California coast by purchase from Mexico had failed.

From the defeat of their diplomacy to achieve a boundary settlement with Mexico Polk and his cabinet moved early in May, 1846, toward a recommendation of war, employing as the immediate pretext the refusal of the Mexican government to pay the claims of American citizens against it for their losses in Mexico. Before the cabinet could agree on such a drastic course of action, Polk received word that a detachment of General Zachary Taylor's forces stationed along the disputed Rio Grande boundary of Texas had been fired upon by Mexican forces. Armed with such intelligence, the President now phrased his message to obtain an immediate and overwhelming endorsement for a policy of force. Mexico, he charged, "has passed the boundary of the United States, has invaded our territory and shed American blood upon American soil." War existed, in short, by act of Mexico. Polk explained that his action of stationing Taylor on the Rio Grande was not an act of aggression, but merely the attempt to occupy a disputed territory. Yet the possibility that the President had sought to provoke a clash of arms left sufficient doubt in the minds of his Whig opponents to permit them to make the Mexican War the most bitterly criticized in American history.

During the summer of 1846 the rapid American conquest of California quickly crystallized the expansionist arguments for the retention of the province. Indeed, California suddenly appeared totally satisfactory as a territorial addition. Amalgamation of the Mexican population no longer caused anxiety, for, as Andrew J. Donelson predicted, within five years the Anglo-American people would be dominant in the province. Lewis Cass in February, 1847, still believed any amalgamation between Americans and Mexicans quite deplorable. "We do not want the people of Mexico either as citizens or subjects," he warned, but then he added reassuringly with special reference to California, "all we want is a portion of territory which they nominally hold, generally uninhabited, or, where inhabited at all, sparsely so, and with a population which would soon recede or identify itself with ours." Buchanan, opposing the extension of the United States to the Sierra Madre Mountains, asked: "How should we govern the mongrel race which inhabit it?" Like Donelson and Cass, he harbored no fear of annexing California, for, he added, "The Californias are comparatively uninhabited and will therefore be almost exclusively colonised by our own people."

There was little sentimentality in the *Democratic Review*'s prediction in March, 1847, that American pioneers in California would dispossess the inhabitants as they had the American Indians. It declared that evidently "the process which has been gone through at the North of driving back the Indians, or annihilating them as a race, has yet to be gone through at the south." Similarly the *American Review* that same month saw Mexicans giving way to "a superior population, insensibly oozing into her territories, changing her customs, and out-living, out-trading, exterminating her weaker blood. . . ."

California's immense potential as the seat of a rich empire, contrasted to its backwardness under Mexican rule, added a new dimension to the doctrine of manifest destiny—the regeneration of California's soil. . . .

Polk, adequately supported by the Democratic expansionists in Congress, rationalized the American retention of California, not with references to the doctrine of regeneration, but with the principle of indemnity. "No terms can . . . be contemplated," O'Sullivan argued in July, 1846, "which will not require from [Mexico] indemnity . . . for the many wrongs which we have suffered at her hands. And if, in agreeing upon those terms, she finds it more for her interest to give us California than to satisfy our just demands in any other way, what objection can there be to the arrangement . . . ?"

Unfortunately for the President, indemnity, clearly recognized as a legitimate fruit of victory by the law of nations, was acceptable to only those Americans who placed responsibility of the war on Mexico. To those Whigs who attacked the war California constituted conquest, not indemnity, and therefore was scarcely an acceptable objective to be pursued through the agency of war. . . .

During December and January, with Congress in session, Democratic orators seized control of the all-of-Mexico movement and carried this new burst of expansionism to greater heights of grandeur and extravagance. Their speeches rang with appeals to the nationalism of war and the cause of liberty. Cass observed that annexation would sweep away the abuses of generations. Senator Ambrose Sevier of Arkansas pointed to the progress that awaited the most degenerate Mexican population from the application of American law and education. In January, 1848, the Democratic Party of New York, in convention, adopted resolutions favoring annexation. The new mission of regeneration was proclaimed everywhere in the banquet toasts to returning officers. At one Washington dinner in January Senator Daniel Dickinson of New York offered a toast to "A more perfect Union: embracing the entire North American continent." In Congress that month Senator R. M. T. Hunter of Virginia commented on the fever annexationism had stirred up. "Schemes of ambition, vast enough to have tasked even a Roman imagination to conceive," he cried, "present themselves suddenly as practical questions." Both Buchanan and Walker of the cabinet, as well as Vice President George M. Dallas, openly embraced the all-of-Mexico movement.

That conservative coalition which had upheld the Oregon compromise combined again early in 1848 to oppose and condemn this new crusade. This powerful and well-led group feared that the United States, unless it sought greater moderation in its external policies, would drift into a perilous career of conquest which would tax the nation's energies without bringing any commensurate advantages. Its spokesmen doubted that the annexation of Mexico would serve the cause of humanity or present a new world of opportunity for American immigrants. Waddy Thompson, the South Carolina Whig who had spent many years in Mexico, warned in October against annexation: "We shall get no land, but will add a large population, aliens to us in feeling, education, race, and religion—a people unaccustomed to work, and accustomed to insubordination and resistance to law, the expense of governing whom will be ten times as great as the revenues derived from them." Thompson, joined by Calhoun and other Southern antiannexationists, warned the South that no portion of Mexico was suitable for slavery. Mexico's annexation would merely endanger the South's interests with a new cordon of free states. In Congress Calhoun acknowledged the dilemma created by the thoughtless decision to invade Mexico and recommended that the United States withdraw all its military forces to a defensive line across northern Mexico and maintain that line until Mexico chose to negotiate a permanent and satisfactory boundary arrangement with the United States.

Neither the mission of regeneration nor its rejection by conservatives determined the American course of empire. The great debate between those who anticipated nothing less than the achievement of a continental destiny and those who, in the interest of morality or from fear of a bitter controversy over slavery expansion, opposed the further acquisition of national territory, was largely irrelevant. Polk and his advisers pursued a precise vision, shared by those expansionists who searched the Mexican borderlands for the American interest. In the mid-forties, when the nation's agricultural frontier was still pushing across Iowa and Missouri, the concern of those who knew California lay less in land than in the configuration of the coastline and its possible relationship to America's future in the entire world of the Pacific. If American continentalism during the war years provided a substantially favorable climate for the acquisition of Mexican lands, it contributed nothing to the actual formulation of the administration's expansionist program.

During the early weeks of the Mexican War the President noted repeatedly in his diary that he would accept no treaty which did not transfer New Mexico and Upper California to the United States. It was left only to hammer out his precise war aims. Initially, Polk and his cabinet were attracted to San Francisco and Monterey. Several days after the outbreak of war George Bancroft, Secretary of the Navy, assured the Marblehead merchant, Samuel Hooper, that by mid-June the United States flag would be floating over these two northern California ports. "I hope California is now in our possession, never to be given up," he added. "We were driven reluctantly to war; we must make a solid peace. . . ."

But Hooper did not rest at Bancroft's promise. He prodded the administration to look southward along the California coast. Settlement at the thirty-second parallel, Hooper informed Bancroft, would secure both Los Angeles and the bay of San Diego. Such a boundary, moreover, would encompass all the Anglo-American population in the province and remove future annoyance by leaving a barren wilderness between Upper California and the larger Mexican cities to the south. Should the United States acquire San Diego as well as Monterey and San Francisco, continued Hooper, "it would insure a peaceful state of things through the whole country and enable [the Americans] to continued their trade as before along the whole coast. . . ." Thereafter the administration looked to San Diego. Bancroft assured Hooper in June, 1846, that the administration would accede to New England's wishes. "If Mexico makes peace this month," he wrote, "the Rio del Norte and the Parallel of 35° may do as a boundary; after that 32° which will include San Diego." This harbor remained the ultimate and unshakable territorial objective of Polk's wartime diplomacy.

Eventually the President achieved this goal through the efforts of Nicholas P. Trist. Unable after almost a year of successful fighting in Mexico to force the Mexican government to sue for terms, Polk, in April, 1847, dispatched Trist as a secret diplomatic agent to join General Winfield Scott's army in Mexico and await any sudden shift in Mexican politics. Trist's official baggage contained detailed instructions and the *projet* for a treaty which aimed pointedly at the acquisition of the entire coast of California to San Diego Bay. Trist's subsequent negotiations secured not only a treaty of peace with Mexico which terminated the war but also the administration's precise territorial objectives. Manifest destiny fully revealed itself in the Mexican War only when it clamored for the whole of Mexico, but even that final burst of agrarian nationalism was killed effectively by the Treaty of Guadalupe Hidalgo. American victories along the road to Mexico City were important only in that they created the force which permitted the President to secure through war what he had once hoped to achieve through diplomacy alone. It was Trist, working alone and unobserved, who in the final analysis defined the southern boundary of California. . . .

Manifest destiny, in its evolution as a body of American thought, expressed a spirit of confidence and a sense of power. It set forth in extravagant language a vision of national greatness in territorial, political, or diplomatic concerns. It proclaimed a national mission to the downtrodden and oppressed, designed to rationalize in terms of a higher good the nation's right, and even its duty, to dispossess neighboring countries of portions of their landed possessions. But whatever its form and strength, manifest destiny was purely the creation of editors and politicians, expounded to churn the public's nationalistic emotions for the purpose of reaping larger political harvests. Those who preached the crusade created fanciful dreams of the Republic's future; they ignored specifics and were unmindful of means. They were ideologues, not statesmen.

Even their success in converting the nation to the wisdom or feasibility of their views was doubtful. It was the consideration of national interest alone that carried the annexations of the forties through Congress. In the case of Texas, where the final decision conformed to the will of the expansionists, the victory came hard. The Senate overwhelmingly rejected the Texas treaty of 1844, and only after months of intense party and sectional maneuvering—during which time the Texas issue became nationalized—was the joint resolution of annexation adopted by the narrow vote of 27 to 25. Where the nation would expand after Texas was the business of the national executive as the wielder of the nation's diplomacy, and the territory which the United States opened up across the continent to the Pacific satisfied a series of traditional and limited national interests. National growth itself had little or no connection with the continentalism which dominated the language of manifest destiny in the forties and which cloaked American expansionism with universal goals—abstract rather than precise. Manifest destiny created the sentiment that would underwrite governmental policies of expansion; it could not and did not create the policies themselves.

The Senate approved the Oregon Treaty of 1846 with an ample margin, but it was the minority of fourteen senators—the die-hard proponents of the whole-of-Oregon movement—who represented the cause of manifest destiny. The Oregon Treaty was a triumph for the moderates. Again, in 1848, the Senate agreed to the nation's expansion by accepting the Treaty of Guadalupe Hidalgo. But the Senate resolution which demanded more than California and New Mexico from the defeated enemy represented a futile effort to convert the all-of-Mexico sentiment into policy. It lost by eleven votes. The persistent failure of Democratic orators to achieve their declared political and diplomatic goals with appeals to both the emotions of patriotism and the actual record of American expansion culminated in their inability to elect their leading expansionist, Lewis Cass, to the White House in 1848.

Except for the Gadsden Purchase in 1853, a quiet transaction that responded to the needs of railroad building, the nation failed to expand between 1848 and 1860. However, manifest destiny suffered one last and glorious revival when, as late as 1859, James Buchanan sparked another burst of expansionism toward Cuba. But whatever the appeal of such sentiment in Washington, it had no influence in Madrid. Without the physical coercion of Spain there could be no expansion, and even those Americans who would accept the doctrine that the ends justified the means could not discover the "occasion"—at least one acceptable to the majority of United States citizens—for bringing the overwhelming power of the United States to bear on the weakening Spanish rule in Cuba.

American expansion before the Civil War, like all successful national action abroad, required specific and limited objectives, totally achievable within the context of diplomacy or force, whether that force be displayed or merely assumed. After national interest and diplomatic advantage combined, during the forties, to carry the United States to the Pacific, the necessary elements of policy and policy formulation never reoccurred to extend boundaries further. Perhaps it mattered little. The decade of the fifties—for the United States a decade of unprecedented internal development—amply proved the contention of the antiexpansionists that the country's material growth was not dependent upon its further territorial advancement.

The Anxieties of Manifest Destiny

THOMAS HIETALA

When John O'Sullivan coined the felicitous phrase "manifest destiny" in mid-1845, he provided Americans then and since with an invaluable legitimizing myth of empire. During the final phase of the Texas annexation crisis, he accused the European nations of "hostile interference" in American affairs, "for the avowed object of thwarting our policy and hampering our power, limiting our greatness and checking the fulfillment of our manifest destiny to overspread the continent allotted by Providence for the free development of our yearly multiplying millions." In his justification for American expansion, O'Sullivan reconciled democracy with empire while he implicitly sanctioned the dispossession of all non-Anglo peoples on the continent. During the mid-1840s, he repeatedly stressed that the United States must acquire abundant land for "the free development" of its "yearly multiplying millions"; without territorial expansion the novel experiment in free government and free enterprise might collapse.

The recurring emphasis on material factors in the Democrats' specula-

Excerpts from *Manifest Design: Anxious Aggrandizement in Late Jacksonian America* by Thomas Hietala (Ithaca, NY: Cornell University Press 1985), pp. 255–258, 261–264, 267–270).

tions about the need for expansion raises some important questions about the purported idealism of both "Jacksonian Democracy" and manifest destiny. To O'Sullivan and other Democrats, previous territorial acquisitions had been indispensable to the success of the American political and economic system. And though the Jacksonians were convinced of the superiority of popular government, they were much less certain about its viability. Their ambitions for a continental empire represented much more than simple romantic nationalism: they demanded land because they regarded it as the primary prerequisite for republican government and for an economy and society based upon individual acquisitiveness, geographical and social mobility, and a fluid class structure. These beliefs—best expressed by O'Sullivan but articulated by other Democrats as well—were crucial to most Jacksonian policies, especially those promoting territorial and commercial expansion. To consider manifest destiny in the context of such principles of political economy is a way of making more comprehensible the sustained drive for empire in the 1840s.

Misconceptions about manifest destiny still influence Americans' impressions about their nation's history. . . . Prevailing ideas about westward expansion are inextricably linked to the values associated with American exceptionalism and mission, fundamental components of the Jacksonian creed. . . .

Jacksonians exalted the pioneer as the epitome of the common man, and they celebrated American expansion as an integral part of their mission to obtain a better nation and a better world based on individual freedom, liberalized international trade, and peaceful coexistence. The Democrats equated American progress with global progress and repeatedly argued that European oligarchs were actually opposing the interests of their own people by trying to discourage the expansion of the United States. Geographically and ideologically separated from Europe, the United States, under Jacksonian direction, tried to improve its democratic institutions, utilize the land's rich resources, and demonstrate to the world the superiority of a system allowing free men to compete in a dynamic society. Consequently, the impact of the pioneering process transcended the concerns of the frontiersmen. In forming "a more perfect union" on a continually expanding frontier, Americans thought that they were actually serving the cause of all mankind.

Such a melding of exceptionalism and empire permitted the Jacksonians the luxury of righteous denunciation of their critics at home and abroad. Their domestic foes could be paired with European monarchs as spokesmen for an old order of aristocracy, privilege, and proscription; American expansionism and the Jacksonian domestic program, on the other hand, represented the antithesis of traditional systems. Since territorial acquisitions and Democratic policies fostered opportunity and democracy, they liberated men from oppressive social and economic relationships. The Jacksonians' program promised so much for so little; no wonder messianic imagery appeared so frequently in their rhetoric.

Skeptical Whigs often challenged the Democrats' sincerity, however, sensing that the Jacksonians' motives for aggrandizement were more selfish than they usually admitted. The Democrats' rhetoric proved more resilient than the Whigs' trenchant criticisms of "manifest destiny," however, and so subsequent generations of Americans have underestimated the extent and the intensity of opposition to the policies behind expansionism in the 1840s, especially the Mexican War. . . .

The expansionism of the 1840s acquires a new significance, however, when it is considered within the context of the cultural, social, and political factors that motivated the Jacksonians to pursue a continental empire. In promoting the acquisition of new lands and new markets, the Democrats greatly exaggerated the extent of European hostility to the United States and refused to admit the duplicity and brutality behind their own efforts to expand their nation's territory and trade. By joining their concepts of exceptionalism and empire, the expansionists found a rationale for denying to all other nations and peoples, whether strong or weak, any right to any portion of the entire North American continent. If a rival was strong, it posed a threat to American security and had to be removed; if a rival was weak, it proved its inferiority and lent sanction to whatever actions were taken by pioneers or policy makers to make the territory a part of the United States.

The confusion surrounding expansion results in part from the ambivalence of the Jacksonians themselves, who demonstrated both compassion and contempt in their policies, depending on the racial and ethnic identities of the peoples to be affected by Democratic measures. Generous and humane toward impoverished Americans and poor immigrants from Europe, the Democrats showed far less concern for nonwhites whom they dispossessed or exploited in the process of westward expansion and national development. Removal, eclipse, or extermination—not acculturation and assimilation—awaited the Indians, blacks, and mixed-blood Mexicans on the continent. Despite occasional statements to the contrary, the expansionists regarded the incorporation of nonwhite peoples into the country as both unlikely and undesirable. Without hint of hypocrisy the Jacksonians sought lenient naturalization laws and opportunities for newcomers while strenuously defending policies to separate Indians and Mexicans from their lands and programs to relocate blacks to Africa and Central America.

When expansionists did express concern for nonwhites, they did not question the basic assumptions behind racial proscription and dispossession. They trusted masters to treat their slaves humanely; they urged that the federal government compensate Indians adequately for their territorial cessions. Few expansionists, however, could see any alternative to the removal or extermination of Indians or the enslavement or proscription of blacks. Indians had no legitimate claim to land; blacks no legitimate claim to freedom. Even Free-Soilers who opposed the extension of slavery had little sympathy for the slave, arguing, in essence, that black freedom was detrimental to white status. The racism in Washington was matched by racism on the frontier: pioneers in both Oregon and California adopted restrictive measures in the late 1840s to discourage or prohibit the migration of free blacks to the far West.

The expansion to the Pacific was not primarily an expression of American confidence. Anxiety, not optimism, generally lay behind the quest for land, ports, and markets. A powerful combination of fears led the neo-Jeffersonians of the 1840s to embrace territorial and commercial expansionism as the best means of warding off both domestic and foreign threats to the United States. The Jacksonians were proponents of laissez-faire only in a limited sense, and their sustained efforts to acquire land and markets were their equivalents for what they saw as the Whigs' dangerous propensity to meddle in the domestic economy. Rather than give an "artificial" stimulus to the economy through protective duties or privileged charters, the Democrats preferred to assist American producers by means of territorial acquisitions, reciprocity treaties, improvements in the navy, and a liberal land policy. Frightened by rapid modernization in the United States, the Democrats warned that both European monarchs and the Whig opposition were threatening the Republic—the Europeans by their attempts to contain American expansion, the Whigs by their resistance to Jacksonian foreign policy and their support of legislation that would hasten industrialization, urbanization, and class polarization in the United States.

Jeffersonian ideology, especially its romantic agrarianism, its fear of industrialization, and its conviction that the United States had a natural right to free trade, contributed significantly to the ideology of manifest destiny. To the Jeffersonians and Jacksonians, American farms raised good republican citizens as well as corn, cotton, and wheat: cultivated fields produced virtuous, cultivated people. Whatever the realities of the late Jacksonian period, the expansionists insisted that agricultural societies fostered opportunity and political equality, the essential features of American uniqueness. Moreover, the neo-Jeffersonians contended that only industrial nations became international predators; agricultural countries were self-contained and did not need colonies or privileged markets. These misconceptions cloak some of the more unflattering aspects of antebellum economy and society: slavemasters, not sturdy yeomen, dominated the social and political life of the South; the country's most important export crops, cotton and tobacco, were produced by forced labor; Indians were cruelly dispossessed of their lands and often their culture to make room for American producers; "go-ahead" Americans frequently seemed more interested in land speculation schemes than in patient tilling of the soil; and the United States, like other empires, did prey upon other peoples and nations to augment its wealth, power, and security.

The fact that the United States acquired contiguous rather than non-contiguous territory makes American aggrandizement no less imperial than that of other empires of the mid-nineteenth century. The United States enjoyed several advantages that facilitated its enlargement and made it more antiseptic. Mexico's weakness, the inability of Indian tribes to unite and resist dispossession, the decline of France and Spain as colonizing powers in the New World, and geographical isolation from Europe all served the interests of the United States as it spread across the continent. In addition, the preference for an anticolonial empire embodied in the concept of a confederated Union also contributed to American success. But many Democrats wanted to venture beyond the continent, and had the party not become so divided during and after the Mexican War, the Polk administration probably would have taken steps to add Yucatán and Cuba to the United States, thereby extending the empire into the Caribbean.

The urge to expand beyond the continent was diminished by the fact that the continent itself was incredibly rich in resources. Those abundant resources provided the basis for unparalleled economic growth at home and power in relations with countries abroad. The expansionists regarded the nation's productivity as an irresistible weapon that could counterbalance the military strength of Europe. Here, again, an old Jeffersonian perception dating back to the 1790s came into play: the world desperately needed American commerce and would sacrifice a great deal to obtain it. Although the expansionists never had cause to drive the masses of Europe to starvation and revolution through an embargo on grain and cotton, their speculations on the subject showed them to be far more imperial than philanthropic in their attitudes toward their nation's wealth.

Distressed by many trends in American life, the Democrats formulated their domestic and foreign policies to safeguard themselves and their progeny from a potentially dismal future. They hoped to prevent domestic disturbances by acquiring additional territory and markets. Other measures were also devised to protect the country from various perils: the Democrats discouraged the growth of manufacturing and monopolistic banking, attempted to minimize the conflict over slavery, encouraged the sale and settlement of the national domain, and tried to discredit the efforts of dissidents to form third parties that might jeopardize the two-party system. . . .

The expansionists' far-fetched notions about nonwhites precluded their thinking constructively about racial questions. By denying the likelihood of a permanent black and Indian population on the continent, antebellum Americans had difficulty preparing themselves and their descendants for racial heterogeneity in the United States. The acceptance of racial diversity as a reality of national life came largely through necessity, not choice. As most European visitors realized, racial prejudice permeated the country and transcended the sectional dispute over slavery. Americans, however, hardly seemed to question the intense racial animus across the nation; it was such a commonplace of life that it drew only isolated comment or criticism. There were many gradations of racial feeling among Americans, of course, and a small corps of radical abolitionists indicted the North for its failure to practice racial egalitarianism in the free states. But there is no denying that racial prejudice was a basic determinant of American domestic and foreign policy during the Jacksonian period.

The expansionists' ethnocentrism also sowed the seeds of future discord between the United States and the peoples of Latin America. The annexation of Texas and the Mexican War created a legacy of suspicion and anger toward the United States among peoples south of the Rio Grande. However much the United States professed to be a "good neighbor" to other countries in the hemisphere, those countries often held more ambivalent views. . . .

In many respects the expansionists' outlook turned out to be strikingly unrealistic. The United States was hardly overcrowded in the early 1840s: millions of acres within the existing national domain remained to be occupied and cultivated. Racial fears were also exaggerated. When southern slaves attained their freedom in 1865, no war between blacks and whites ensued. After the Civil War, scores of large cities and hundreds of factories and corporations spread across the country, yet democratic institutions and capitalism survived the transformation. Despite the undeniable hardships and radical adjustments precipitated by rapid industrialization, few Americans would argue that manufacturing weakened rather than strengthened the United States. The Democrats also overestimated the hostility of Britain. The British ministry acquiesced in the annexation of Texas; it did not incite Mexico to make war upon the United States; and it did not try to acquire California before the United States seized it in 1846. Several major premises behind the expansion of the late Jacksonian period proved erroneous.

The decade of the 1840s should be placed in a different historical context: United States policy in this crucial decade prepared the way for both late-nineteenth-century and twentieth-century imperialism. . . .

⽥ *F U R T H E R   R E A D I N G*

K. Jack Bauer, *Zachary Taylor: Soldier, Planter, Statesman of the Old Southwest* (1985)

Paul Bergeron, *The Presidency of James K. Polk* (1987)

Gene Brack, *Mexico Views Manifest Destiny, 1821–1846* (1975)

Charles H. Brown, *Agents of Manifest Destiny: The Lives and Times of the Filibusters* (1980)

John S. D. Eisenhower, *So Far From God: The U.S. War with Mexico, 1846–1848* (1989)

Eric Foner, *Politics and Ideology in the Age of the Civil War* (1980)

William H. Goetzmann, *When the Eagle Screamed: The Romantic Horizon in American Diplomacy, 1800–1860* (1966)

Norman A. Graebner, "Lessons of the Mexican War," *Pacific Historical Review* 57 (1978): 325–342

———, "The Mexican War: A Study in Causation," *Pacific Historical Review* 59 (1980): 405–426

Reginald Horsman, *Race and Manifest Destiny: The Origins of American Anglo-Saxonism* (1981)

Robert W. Johannsen, *To the Halls of the Montezumas: The Mexican War in the American Imagination* (1985)

Ernest M. Lander, Jr., *Reluctant Imperialists: Calhoun, the South Carolinians, and the Mexican War* (1980)

Frederick Merk, *Manifest Destiny and Mission in American History* (1963)

———, *The Monroe Doctrine and American Expansionism, 1843–1849* (1966)

———, *The Oregon Question* (1967)

Allan Nevins, *Ordeal of the Union.* Volume I: *Fruits of Manifest Destiny, 1847–1852* (1947)

Norma Lois Peterson, *The Presidencies of William Henry Harrison and John Tyler* (1989)

David M. Pletcher, *The Diplomacy of Annexation: Texas, Oregon, and the Mexican War* (1973)

Joseph G. Rayback, *Free Soil: The Election of 1848* (1970)

John H. Schroeder, *Mr. Polk's War* (1973)

Charles G. Sellers, Jr., *James K. Polk: Continentalist, 1843–1846* (1966)

Richard H. Sewall, *Ballots for Freedom: Antislavery Politics in the United States, 1837–1860* (1976)

Justin H. Smith, *The War with Mexico* (1919)

Norman E. Tutorow, *Texas Annexation and the Mexican War: A Political Study of the Old Northwest* (1981)

Vernon L. Volpe, *Forlorn Hope of Freedom: The Liberty Party in the Old Northwest, 1838–1848* (1990)

Albert K. Weinberg, *Manifest Destiny* (1935)

Epilogue

⊕

Despite deep fractures, the political system held together after 1848. Renegade Free Soilers returned to their respective parties. Party leaders soothed the sectional passions of the rank and file. Ensuing debates over the fate of the newly-won territories did occasion a momentous struggle in Washington, in which the sectional recalcitrants held firm—none firmer than old John C. Calhoun, a spectral, admonishing presence in his final political performance. But for one last time, the familiar mainstays of both major parties patched together a deal that papered over the question of slavery and its expansion.

As the Compromise of 1850 took shape, Herman Melville sat in Pittsfield, Massachusetts, churning over the manuscript of Moby-Dick (1851). Melville came from a family with Democratic party connections, and like his idol, Nathaniel Hawthorne, he was not above putting those connections to use. Yet Melville was no simple party man. Moby-Dick would prove that, transcending mere political allegory but conjuring up those destructive historical forces that were overtaking the American republic. It would be a tale of the whaling ship, Pequod, evoking the Connecticut tribe massacred two centuries earlier. The crew members would be drawn from all over the globe; to them, Melville could ascribe "high qualities, though dark" and discern "thou just Spirit of Equality, which has spread one royal mantle of humanity over all my kind." Yet they were bound not on an ordinary voyage but on a diabolical quest, ruled by a monomaniac who drew power from his black, red, and brown harpooners and secured loyalty with rewards of virgin gold. "I came here to hunt whales, not my commander's vengeance," the Quaker Starbuck protests to Captain Ahab. But Ahab is master and he presses on, smashing his quadrant, plowing into the Pacific. There the Pequod would be smashed to bits and swallowed up by its own vortex.

The following passage from Moby-Dick begins as a discussion of maritime laws and customs but quickly moves to a higher philosophical plane. What do you make of fast fish and loose fish? And what do you make of Moby-Dick's prophecy?

Fast-Fish and Loose-Fish from Herman Melville's Moby-Dick, 1851

. . . It frequently happens that when several ships are cruising in company, a whale may be struck by one vessel, then escape, and be finally killed and captured by another vessel; and herein are indirectly comprised many minor contingencies, all partaking of this one grand feature. For example,—after a weary and perilous chase and capture of a whale, the body may get loose from the ship by reason of a violent storm; and drifting far away to leeward, be retaken by a second whaler, who, in a calm, snugly tows it alongside, without risk of life or line. Thus the most vexatious and violent disputes would often arise between the fishermen, were there not some written or unwritten, universal, undisputed law applicable to all cases.

Perhaps the only formal whaling code authorized by legislative enactment, was that of Holland. It was decreed by the States-General in A.D. 1695. But though no other nation has ever had any written whaling law, yet the American fishermen have been their own legislators and lawyers in this matter. They have provided a system which for terse comprehensiveness surpasses Justinian's Pandects and the By-laws of the Chinese Society for the Suppression of Meddling with other People's Business. Yes; these laws might be engraven on a Queen Anne's farthing, or the barb of a harpoon, and worn round the neck, so small are they.

I. A Fast-Fish belongs to the party fast to it.

II. A Loose-Fish is fair game for anybody who can soonest catch it.

But what plays the mischief with this masterly code is the admirable brevity of it, which necessitates a vast volume of commentaries to expound it.

First: What is a Fast-Fish? Alive or dead a fish is technically fast, when it is connected with an occupied ship or boat, by any medium at all controllable by the occupant or occupants,—a mast, an oar, a nine-inch cable, a telegraph wire, or a strand of cobweb, it is all the same. Likewise a fish is technically fast when it bears a waif, or any other recognised symbol of possession; so long as the party waifing it plainly evince their ability at any time to take it alongside, as well as their intention so to do.

These are scientific commentaries; but the commentaries of the whalemen themselves sometimes consist in hard words and harder knocks—the Coke-upon-Littleton of the fist. True, among the more upright and honorable whalemen allowances are always made for peculiar cases, where it would be an outrageous moral injustice for one party to claim possession of a whale previously chased or killed by another party. But others are by no means so scrupulous. . . .

Is it not a saying in every one's mouth, Possession is half of the law: that is, regardless of how the thing came into possession? But often possession is the whole of the law. What are the sinews and souls of Russian serfs and Republican slaves but Fast-Fish, whereof possession is the whole of the law? What to the rapacious landlord is the widow's last mite but a Fast-Fish? What is yonder undetected villain's marble mansion with a door-plate for a waif; what is that but a Fast-Fish? What is the ruinous discount which Mordecai, the broker, gets from poor Woebegone, the bankruption a loan to keep Woebegone's family from starvation; what is that ruinous discount but a Fast-Fish? What is the Archbishop of Savesoul's income of £100,000 seized from the scant bread and cheese of hundreds of thousands of broken-backed laborers (all sure of heaven without any of Savesoul's help) what is that globular 100,000 but a Fast-Fish? What are the Duke of Dunder's hereditary towns and hamlets but Fast-Fish? What to that redoubted harpooneer, John Bull, is poor Ireland, but a Fast-Fish? What to that apostolic lancer, Brother Jonathan, is Texas but a Fast-Fish? And concerning all these, is not Possession the whole of the law?

But if the doctrine of Fast-Fish be pretty generally applicable, the kindred doctrine of Loose-Fish is still more widely so. That is internationally and universally applicable.

What was America in 1492 but a Loose-Fish, in which Columbus struck the Spanish standard by way of waifing it for his royal master and mistress? What was Poland to the Czar? What Greece to the Turk? What India to England? What at last will Mexico be to the United States? All Loose-Fish.

What are the Rights of Man and the Liberties of the World but Loose-Fish? What all men's minds and opinions but Loose-Fish? What is the principle of religious belief in them but a Loose-Fish? What to the ostentatious smuggling verbalists are the thoughts of thinkers but Loose-Fish? What is the great globe itself but a Loose Fish? And what are you, reader, but a Loose-Fish and a Fast-Fish, too?

The Constitution of the United States of America and Amendments I–XII

We the People of the United States, in Order to form a more perfect Union, establish Justice, insure domestic Tranquility, provide for the common defence, promote the general Welfare, and secure the Blessings of Liberty to ourselves and our Posterity, do ordain and establish this CONSTITUTION for the United States of America.

Article 1

Section 1.   All legislative Powers herein granted shall be vested in a Congress of the United States, which shall consist of a Senate and House of Representatives.

Section 2.   The House of Representatives shall be composed of Members chosen every second Year by the People of the several States, and the Electors in each State shall have the Qualifications requisite for Electors of the most numerous Branch of the State Legislature.

No Person shall be a Representative who shall not have attained to the Age of twenty-five Years, and been seven Years a Citizen of the United States, and who shall not, when elected, be an inhabitant of that State in which he shall be chosen.

[Representatives and direct Taxes shall be apportioned among the several States which may be included within this Union, according to their respective Numbers, which shall be determined by adding to the whole Number of free Persons, including those bound to Service for a Term of Years, and excluding Indians not taxed, three fifths of all other Persons.] The actual Enumeration shall be made within three Years after the first Meeting of the Congress of the United States, and within every subsequent Term of ten Years, in such Manner as they shall by Law direct. The Number of Representatives shall not exceed one for every thirty Thousand, but each State shall have at Least one Representative; and until such enumeration shall be made, the State of New Hampshire shall be entitled to chuse three, Massachusetts eight, Rhode-Island and Providence Plantations one, Connecticut five, New York six, New Jersey four, Pennsylvania eight, Delaware one, Maryland six, Virginia ten, North Carolina five, South Carolina five, and Georgia three.

When vacancies happen in the Representation from any State, the Executive Authority thereof shall issue Writs of Election to fill such Vacancies.

The House of Representatives shall chuse their Speaker and other Officers; and shall have the sole Power of Impeachment.

Section 3. The Senate of the United States shall be composed of two Senators from each State, chosen by the Legislature thereof, for six Years; and each Senator shall have one Vote.

Immediately after they shall be assembled in Consequence of the first Election, they shall be divided as equally as may be into three Classes. The Seats of the Senators of the first Class shall be vacated at the Expiration of the second Year, of the second Class at the Expiration of the fourth Year, and of the third Class at the Expiration of the sixth Year, so that one-third may be chosen every second Year; and if Vacancies happen by Resignation, or otherwise, during the Recess of the Legislature of any State, the Executive thereof may make temporary Appointments until the next Meeting of the Legislature, which shall then fill such Vacancies.

No Person shall be a Senator who shall not have attained to the Age of thirty Years, and been nine Years a Citizen of the United States, and who shall not, when elected, be an Inhabitant of that State for which he shall be chosen.

The Vice President of the United States shall be President of the Senate, but shall have no vote, unless they be equally divided.

The Senate shall chuse their other Officers, and also a President pro tempore, in the absence of the Vice President, or when he shall exercise the Office of President of the United States.

The Senate shall have the sole Power to try all Impeachments. When sitting for that purpose they shall be on Oath or Affirmation. When the President of the United States is tried, the Chief Justice shall preside: And no person shall be convicted without the Concurrence of two thirds of the Members present.

Judgment in Cases of Impeachment shall not extend further than to removal from Office, and disqualification to hold and enjoy any Office of honor, Trust, or Profit under the United States: but the Party convicted shall nevertheless be liable and subject to Indictment, Trial, Judgment, and Punishment, according to Law.

Section 4. The Times, Places and Manner of holding Elections for Senators and Representatives, shall be prescribed in each State by the Legislature thereof; but the Congress may at any time by Law make or alter such Regulations, except as to the Places of Chusing Senators.

The Congress shall assemble at least once in every Year, and such Meeting shall be on the first Monday in December, unless they shall by Law appoint a different Day.

Section 5. Each House shall be the Judge of the Elections, Returns and Qualifications of its own Members, and a Majority of each shall constitute a Quorum to do Business; but a smaller number may adjourn from day to day, and may be authorized to compel the Attendance of absent Members, in such Manner, and under such Penalties, as each House may provide.

Each House may determine the Rules of its Proceedings, punish its

Members for disorderly Behaviour, and, with the Concurrence of two thirds, expel a Member.

Each House shall keep a Journal of its Proceedings, and from time to time publish the same, excepting such Parts as may in their Judgment require Secrecy; and the Yeas and Nays of the Members of either House on any question shall, at the Desire of one fifth of those Present, be entered on the Journal.

Neither House, during the Session of Congress, shall, without the Consent of the other, adjourn for more than three days, nor to any other Place than that in which the two Houses shall be sitting.

Section 6.   The Senators and Representatives shall receive a Compensation for their Services, to be ascertained by Law, and paid out of the Treasury of the United States. They shall in all Cases, except Treason, Felony, and Breach of the Peace, be privileged from Arrest during their Attendance at the Session of their respective Houses, and in going to and returning from the same; and for any Speech or Debate in either House, they shall not be questioned in any other Place.

No Senator or Representative shall, during the Time for which he was elected, be appointed to any civil Office under the Authority of the United States, which shall have been created, or the Emoluments whereof shall have been increased, during such time; and no Person holding any Office under the United States shall be a Member of either House during his continuance in Office.

Section 7.   All Bills for raising Revenue shall originate in the House of Representatives; but the Senate may propose or concur with Amendments as on other bills.

Every Bill which shall have passed the House of Representatives and the Senate, shall, before it become a Law, be presented to the President of the United States; If he approve he shall sign it, but if not he shall return it, with his Objections, to that House in which it shall have originated, who shall enter the Objections at large on their Journal, and proceed to reconsider it. If after such Reconsideration two thirds of that House shall agree to pass the bill, it shall be sent, together with the objections, to the other House, by which it shall likewise be reconsidered, and if approved by two thirds of that House, it shall become a Law. But in all such Cases the Votes of both Houses shall be determined by Yeas and Nays, and the Names of the Persons voting for and against the Bill shall be entered on the Journal of each House respectively. If any Bill shall not be returned by the President within ten Days (Sundays excepted) after it shall have been presented to him, the Same shall be a Law, in like Manner as if he had signed it, unless the Congress by their Adjournment prevent its Return, in which Case it shall not be a Law.

Every Order, Resolution, or Vote to which the Concurrence of the Senate and House of Representatives may be necessary (except on a question of Adjournment) shall be presented to the President of the United States;

and before the Same shall take Effect, shall be approved by him, or being disapproved by him, shall be repassed by two thirds of the Senate and House of Representatives, according to the Rules and Limitations prescribed in the Case of a Bill.

Section 8. The Congress shall have Power To lay and collect Taxes, Duties, Imposts and Excises, to pay the Debts and provide for the common Defence and general Welfare of the United States; but all Duties, Imposts and Excises shall be uniform throughout the United States;

To borrow money on the credit of the United States;

To regulate Commerce with foreign Nations, and among the several States, and with the Indian Tribes;

To establish an uniform rule of Naturalization, and uniform Laws on the subject of Bankruptcies throughout the United States;

To coin Money, regulate the Value thereof, and of foreign Coin, and fix the Standard of Weights and Measures;

To provide for the Punishment of counterfeiting the Securities and current Coin of the United States;

To establish Post Offices and post Roads;

To promote the Progress of Science and useful Arts, by securing for limited Times to Authors and Inventors the exclusive Right to their respective Writings and Discoveries;

To constitute Tribunals inferior to the Supreme Court;

To define and punish Piracies and Felonies committed on the high Seas, and Offenses against the Law of Nations;

To declare War, grant Letters of Marque and Reprisal, and make Rules concerning Captures on Land and Water;

To raise and support Armies, but no Appropriation of Money to that Use shall be for a longer Term than two Years;

To provide and maintain a Navy;

To make Rules for the Government and Regulation of the land and naval forces;

To provide for calling forth the Militia to execute the Laws of the Union, suppress Insurrections and repel Invasions;

To provide for organizing, arming, and disciplining the Militia, and for governing such Part of them as may be employed in the Service of the United States, reserving to the States respectively, the Appointment of the Officers, and the Authority of training the Militia according to the discipline prescribed by Congress;

To exercise exclusive Legislation in all Cases whatsoever, over such District (not exceeding ten Miles square) as may, by Cession of particular States, and the acceptance of Congress, become the Seat of the Government of the United States, and to exercise like Authority over all Places purchased by the Consent of the Legislature of the State in which the Same shall be, for the Erection of Forts, Magazines, Arsenals, Dock-yards, and other needful Buildings;—And

To make all Laws which shall be necessary and proper for carrying into

Execution the foregoing Powers, and all other Powers vested by this Constitution in the Government of the United States, or in any Department or Officer thereof.

Section 9.   The Migration or Importation of such Persons as any of the States now existing shall think proper to admit, shall not be prohibited by the Congress prior to the Year one thousand eight hundred and eight, but a tax or duty may be imposed on such Importation, not exceeding ten dollars for each Person.

The privilege of the Writ of Habeas Corpus shall not be suspended, unless when in Cases of Rebellion or Invasion the public Safety may require it.

No bill of Attainder or ex post facto Law shall be passed.

No capitation, or other direct, Tax shall be laid unless in Proportion to the Census or Enumeration herein before directed to be taken.

No Tax or Duty shall be laid on Articles exported from any State.

No Preference shall be given by any Regulation of Commerce or Revenue to the Ports of one State over those of another; nor shall Vessels bound to, or from, one State, be obliged to enter, clear, or pay Duties in another.

No Money shall be drawn from the Treasury, but in Consequence of Appropriations made by Law; and a regular Statement and Account of the Receipts and Expenditures of all public Money shall be published from time to time.

No Title of Nobility shall be granted by the United States: And no Person holding any Office of Profit or Trust under them, shall, without the Consent of the Congress, accept of any present, Emolument, Office, or Title, of any kind whatever, from any King, Prince, or foreign State.

Section 10.   No State shall enter into any Treaty, Alliance, or Confederation; grant Letters of Marque and Reprisal; coin Money; emit Bills of Credit; make any Thing but gold and silver Coin a Tender in Payment of Debts; pass any Bill of Attainder, ex post facto Law, or Law impairing the Obligation of Contracts, or grant any Title of Nobility.

No State shall, without the Consent of the Congress, lay any Imposts or Duties on Imports or Exports, except what may be absolutely necessary for executing its inspection Laws; and the net Produce of all Duties and Imposts, laid by any State on Imports or Exports, shall be for the use of the Treasury of the United States; and all such Laws shall be subject to the Revision and Control of the Congress.

No state shall, without the Consent of Congress, lay any duty of Tonnage, keep Troops, or Ships of War in time of Peace, enter into any Agreement or Compact with another State, or with a foreign Power, or engage in War, unless actually invaded, or in such imminent Danger as will not admit of delay.

Article II

Section 1. The executive Power shall be vested in a President of the United States of America. He shall hold his Office during the Term of four years, and, together with the Vice President, chosen for the same Term, be elected, as follows:

Each State shall appoint, in such Manner as the Legislature thereof may direct, a Number of Electors, equal to the whole Number of Senators and Representatives to which the State may be entitled in the Congress: but no Senator or Representative, or Person holding an Office of Trust or Profit under the United States, shall be appointed an Elector.

[The Electors shall meet in their respective States, and vote by Ballot for two persons, of whom one at least shall not be an Inhabitant of the same State with themselves. And they shall make a List of all the Persons voted for, and of the Number of Votes for each; which List they shall sign and certify, and transmit sealed to the Seat of the Government of the United States, directed to the President of the Senate. The President of the Senate shall, in the Presence of the Senate and House of Representatives, open all the Certificates, and the Votes shall then be counted. The Person having the greatest Number of Votes shall be the President, if such Number be a Majority of the whole Number of Electors appointed; and if there be more than one who have such Majority, and have an equal Number of Votes, then the House of Representatives shall immediately chuse by Ballot one of them for President; and if no Person have a Majority, then from the five highest on the List the said House shall in like Manner chuse the President. But in chusing the President, the Votes shall be taken by States, the Representation from each State having one Vote; a quorum for this Purpose shall consist of a Member or Members from two-thirds of the States, and a Majority of all the States shall be necessary to a Choice. In every Case, after the Choice of the President, the Person having the greatest Number of Votes of the Electors shall be the Vice President. But if there should remain two or more who have equal votes, the Senate shall chuse from them by Ballot the Vice President.]

The Congress may determine the Time of chusing the Electors, and the Day on which they shall give their Votes; which Day shall be the same throughout the United States.

No person except a natural-born Citizen, or a Citizen of the United States, at the time of the Adoption of this Constitution, shall be eligible to the Office of President; neither shall any Person be eligible to that Office who shall not have attained to the Age of thirty-five years, and been fourteen Years a Resident within the United States.

In Case of the Removal of the President from Office, or of his Death, Resignation, or Inability to discharge the Powers and Duties of the said Office, the same shall devolve on the Vice President, and the Congress may by Law provide for the Case of Removal, Death, Resignation, or Inability, both of the President and Vice President, declaring what Officer shall then act as President, and such Officer shall act accordingly, until the disability be removed, or a President shall be elected.

The President shall, at stated Times, receive for his Services a Compensation, which shall neither be increased nor diminished during the Period for which he shall have been elected, and he shall not receive within that Period any other Emolument from the United States, or any of them.

Before he enter on the execution of his Office, he shall take the following Oath or Affirmation:—"I do solemnly swear (or affirm) that I will faithfully execute the Office of President of the United States, and will, to the best of my Ability, preserve, protect, and defend the Constitution of the United States."

Section 2. The President shall be Commander in Chief of the Army and Navy of the United States, and of the Militia of the several States, when called into the actual Service of the United States; he may require the Opinion, in writing, of the principal Officer in each of the executive Departments, upon any subject relating to the Duties of their respective Offices, and he shall have power to Grant Reprieves and Pardons for Offenses against the United States, except in Cases of Impeachment.

He shall have Power, by and with the Advice and Consent of the Senate, to make Treaties, provided two-thirds of the Senators present concur; and he shall nominate, and by and with the Advice and Consent of the Senate, shall appoint Ambassadors, other public Ministers and Consuls, Judges of the supreme Court, and all other Officers of the United States, whose Appointments are not herein otherwise provided for, and which shall be established by Law: but the Congress may by Law vest the Appointment of such inferior Officers, as they think proper, in the President alone, in the Courts of Law, or in the Heads of Departments.

The President shall have Power to fill up all Vacancies that may happen during the Recess of the Senate, by granting Commissions which shall expire at the End of their next Session.

Section 3. He shall from time to time give to the Congress Information of the State of the Union, and recommend to their Consideration such Measures as he shall judge necessary and expedient; he may, on extraordinary occasions, convene both Houses, or either of them, and in Case of Disagreement between them, with respect to the Time of Adjournment, he may adjourn them to such Time as he shall think proper; he shall receive Ambassadors and other public Ministers; he shall take care that the Laws be faithfully executed, and shall Commission all the Officers of the United States.

Section 4. The President, Vice President and all civil Officers of the United States, shall be removed from Office on Impeachment for, and Conviction of, Treason, Bribery, or other high Crimes and Misdemeanors.

Article III

Section 1.   The judicial Power of the United States, shall be vested in one supreme Court, and in such inferior Courts as the Congress may from time to time ordain and establish. The Judges, both of the supreme and inferior Courts, shall hold their Offices during good Behaviour, and shall, at stated Times, receive for their Services, a Compensation, which shall not be diminished during their Continuance in Office.

Section 2.   The judicial Power shall extend to all Cases, in Law and Equity, arising under this Constitution, the Laws of the United States, and Treaties made, or which shall be made, under their Authority;—to all Cases affecting ambassadors, other public ministers and consuls;—to all cases of admiralty and maritime Jurisdiction;—to Controversies to which the United States shall be a Party;—to Controversies between two or more States;—between a State and Citizens of another State;—between Citizens of different States;—between Citizens of the same State claiming Lands under Grants of different States, and between a State, or the Citizens thereof, and foreign States, Citizens, or Subjects.

In all Cases affecting Ambassadors, other public Ministers and Consuls, and those in which a State shall be Party, the supreme Court shall have original Jurisdiction. In all the other Cases before mentioned, the supreme Court shall have appellate Jurisdiction, both as to Law and Fact, with such Exceptions, and under such Regulations as the Congress shall make.

The trial of all Crimes, except in Cases of Impeachment, shall be by Jury; and such Trial shall be held in the State where the said Crimes shall have been committed; but when not committed within any State, the Trial shall be at such Place or Places as the Congress may by Law have directed.

Section 3.   Treason against the United States, shall consist only in levying War against them, or in adhering to their Enemies, giving them Aid and Comfort. No Person shall be convicted of Treason unless on the Testimony of two Witnesses to the same overt Act, or on Confession in open Court.

The Congress shall have power to declare the Punishment of Treason, but no Attainder of Treason shall work Corruption of Blood, or Forfeiture except during the Life of the Person attainted.

Article IV

Section 1.   Full Faith and Credit shall be given in each State to the public Acts, Records, and judicial Proceedings of every other State. And the Congress may by general Laws prescribe the Manner in which such Acts, Records and Proceedings shall be proved, and the Effect thereof.

Section 2.   The Citizens of each State shall be entitled to all Privileges and Immunities of Citizens in the several States.

A Person charged in any State with Treason, Felony, or other Crime, who shall flee from Justice, and be found in another State, shall on demand of the executive Authority of the State from which he fled, be delivered up, to be removed to the State having Jurisdiction of the crime.

No Person held to Service or Labour in one State, under the Laws thereof, escaping into another, shall, in Consequence of any Law or Regulation therein, be discharged from such Service or Labour, but shall be delivered up on Claim of the Party to whom such Service or Labour may be due.

Section 3.   New States may be admitted by the Congress into this Union; but no new State shall be formed or erected within the Jurisdiction of any other State; nor any State be formed by the Junction of two or more States, or parts of States, without the Consent of the Legislatures of the States concerned as well as of the Congress.

The Congress shall have Power to dispose of and make all needful Rules and Regulations respecting the Territory or other Property belonging to the United States; and nothing in this Constitution shall be so construed as to Prejudice any Claims of the United States, or of any particular State.

Section 4.   The United States shall guarantee to every State in this Union a Republican Form of Government, and shall protect each of them against Invasion; and on Application of the Legislature, or of the Executive (when the Legislature cannot be convened) against domestic Violence.

Article V

The Congress, whenever two-thirds of both Houses shall deem it necessary, shall propose Amendments to this Constitution, or, on the Application of the Legislatures of two-thirds of the several States, shall call a Convention for proposing Amendments, which, in either Case, shall be valid to all Intents and Purposes, as part of this Constitution, when ratified by the Legislatures of three-fourths of the several States, or by Conventions in three-fourths thereof, as the one or the other Mode of Ratification may be proposed by the Congress; Provided that no Amendment which may be made prior to the Year One thousand eight hundred and eight shall in any Manner affect the first and fourth Clauses in the Ninth Section of the first Article; and that no State, without its Consent, shall be deprived of its equal Suffrage in the Senate.

Article VI

All Debts contracted and Engagements entered into, before the Adoption of this Constitution, shall be as valid against the United States under this Constitution, as under the Confederation.

This Constitution, and the Laws of the United States which shall be made in Pursuance thereof; and all Treaties made, or which shall be made, under the Authority of the United States, shall be the supreme Law of the Land; and the Judges in every State shall be bound thereby, any Thing in the Constitution or Laws of any State to the Contrary notwithstanding.

The Senators and Representatives before mentioned, and the Members of the several State Legislatures, and all executive and judicial Officers, both of the United States and of the several States, shall be bound by Oath or Affirmation to support this Constitution; but no religious Tests shall ever be required as a qualification to any Office or public Trust under the United States.

Article VII

The Ratification of the Conventions of nine States shall be sufficient for the Establishment of this Constitution between the States so ratifying the same.

Done in Convention by the Unanimous Consent of the States present the Seventeenth Day of September in the Year of our Lord one thousand seven hundred and Eighty seven, and of the Independence of the United States of America the Twelfth. . . .

Articles in Addition to, and Amendment of, the Constitution of the United States of America, Proposed by Congress, and Ratified by the Legislatures of the Several States, Pursuant to the Fifth Article of the Original Constitution

[Article I]

Congress shall make no law respecting an establishment of religion, or prohibiting the free exercise thereof; or abridging the freedom of speech, or of the press; or the right of the people peaceably to assemble, and to petition the Government for a redress of grievances.

[Article II]

A well regulated Militia, being necessary to the security of a free State, the right of the people to keep and bear Arms shall not be infringed.

[Article III]

No Soldier shall, in time of peace, be quartered in any house, without the consent of the Owner, nor in time of war, but in a manner to be prescribed by law.

[Article IV]

The right of the people to be secure in their persons, houses, papers, and effects, against unreasonable searches and seizures, shall not be violated, and no Warrants shall issue, but upon probable cause, supported by Oath or affirmation, and particularly describing the place to be searched, and the persons or things to be seized.

[Article V]

No person shall be held to answer for a capital or otherwise infamous crime, unless on a presentment or indictment of a Grand Jury, except in cases arising in the land or naval forces, or in the Militia, when in actual service in time of War or public danger; nor shall any person be subject for the same offence to be twice put in jeopardy of life or limb; nor shall be compelled in any criminal case to be a witness against himself, nor be deprived of life, liberty, or property, without due process of law; nor shall private property be taken for public use, without just compensation.

[Article VI]

In all criminal prosecutions, the accused shall enjoy the right to a speedy and public trial, by an impartial jury of the State and district wherein the crime shall have been committed, which district shall have been previously ascertained by law, and to be informed of the nature and cause of the accusation; to be confronted with the witnesses against him; to have compulsory process for obtaining witnesses in his favour, and to have the Assistance of Counsel for his defence.

[Article VII]

In suits at common law, where the value in controversy shall exceed twenty dollars, the right of trial by jury shall be preserved, and no fact tried by a jury, shall be otherwise reexamined in any Court of the United States, than according to the rules of the common law.

[Article VIII]

Excessive bail shall not be required, not excessive fines imposed, nor cruel and unusual punishments inflicted.

[Article IX]

The enumeration of the Constitution, of certain rights, shall not be construed to deny or disparage others retained by the people.

[Article X]

The powers not delegated to the United States by the Constitution, nor prohibited by it to the States, are reserved to the States respectively, or to the people.
    [Amendments I–X, in force 1791.]

[Article XI][1]

The Judicial power of the United States shall not be construed to extend to any suit in law or equity, commenced or prosecuted against one of the United States by Citizens of another State, or by Citizens or Subjects of any Foreign State.

[Article XII][2]

The Electors shall meet in their respective States and vote by ballot for President and Vice-President, one of whom, at least, shall not be an inhabitant of the same State with themselves; they shall name in their ballots the person voted for as President, and in distinct ballots the person voted for as Vice-President, and they shall make distinct lists of all persons voted for as President, and of all persons voted for as Vice-President, and of the number of votes for each, which lists they shall sign and certify, and transmit sealed to the seat of the government of the United States, directed to the President of the Senate;—The President of the Senate shall, in the presence of the Senate and House of Representatives, open all the certificates and the votes shall then be counted;—The person having the greatest number of votes for President, shall be the President, if such number be a majority of the whole number of Electors appointed; and if no person have such majority, then from the persons having the highest numbers not exceeding three on the list of those voted for as President, the House of Representatives shall choose immediately, by ballot, the President. But in choosing the President, the votes shall be taken by states, the representation from each state having one vote; a quorum for this purpose shall consist of a member or members from two-thirds of the states, and a majority of all the states shall be necessary to a choice. And if the House of Representatives shall not choose a President whenever the right of choice shall devolve upon them, before the fourth day of March next following, then the Vice-President shall act as President, as in the case of the death or other constitutional disability of the President.—The person having the greatest number of votes as Vice-President, shall be the Vice-President, if such number be a majority of the whole number of Electors appointed, and if no person have a majority, then from the two highest numbers on the list, the Senate shall choose the Vice-President; a quorum for the purpose shall consist of two-thirds of the whole number of Senators, and a majority of the whole number shall be necessary to a choice. But no person constitutionally ineligible to the office of President shall be eligible to that of Vice-President of the United States.

---

[1] Adopted in 1798.
[2] Adopted in 1804.